American Indian
Nonfiction
An Anthology of Writings,
1760s–1930s

Edited by Bernd C. Peyer

UNIVERSITY OF OKLAHOMA PRESS
Norman

To David Risling, Jr. (Hoopa, 1921–2005).
A soft voice that carried far.

Library of Congress Cataloging-in-Publication Data

American Indian nonfiction : an anthology of writings, 1760s–1930s / edited by Bernd C. Peyer.
 p. cm.
 ISBN 978-0-8061-3708-7 (pbk. : alk. paper) 1. American prose literature—Indian authors—History and criticism. 2. Indians of North America—Intellectual life. 3. Indians of North America—Historiography. 4. Indians in literature. I. Peyer, Bernd.
 PS153.I52A44 2007
 810.8′0897073—dc22   2006026610

The paper in this book meets the guidelines for permanence and durability of the Committee on Production Guidelines for Book Longevity of the Council on Library Resources, Inc. ∞

1 2 3 4 5 6 7 8 9 10

CONTENTS

PREFACE

The list of American Indian authors included here is by no means all-encompassing. Many more could have been added, but the limited space allotted compelled me to select those for whom writing was a major occupation and who produced a substantial body of writings that found its way into print in their own day or posthumously. I have focused on writings that reflect in some way upon the development of Indian-white relations in the United States, or what was once popularly referred to as "the Indian Problem." Canadian First Nations authors have also been included if they published in the United States and their topic bears some relation to American Indian issues.

The first half of the anthology is subdivided according to the regional or tribal networks in which the authors operated. The second half is dedicated to authors who wrote on national issues, most of whom were members of the Society of American Indians, the first national Indian intellectual network. The individual pieces within each subdivision are presented chronologically in the order in which they were written or published. The origin of each text is disclosed in an unnumbered endnote preceding numbered notes, along with due credits and a brief comment on its importance. All texts have been left unedited and are presented as they appeared originally except for obvious typographical errors or where individual spellings might be mistaken for such, in which case I have marked them with [*sic*]. The biographical sketches and bibliographical information following each author's contributions are intended as basic guidelines for further research. As far as the list of primary sources is concerned, I have tried to be as inclusive as possible with authors who have fewer known publications and more selective in the case of writers who produced more than could be included in the space allowed. Secondary sources follow the same principle. I have opted for a variety of critical interpretations in the case of the better known authors rather than presuming to make any qualitative judgments concerning their "scholarly value."

This project was made possible in part by a Deutsche Forschungs-Gemeinschaft Research Grant in 1997–99 and a Mellon Fellowship to the Newberry Library, Chicago, in 2000–2001. I also owe great thanks to the following individuals, listed in alphabetical order because kindness is not measurable: Colin Calloway, Jay Dew, Jack Forbes, Steven K. Gragert, Frederick Hoxie, Alessandra Jacobi, Karen Wieder, James Parins, Ross Hassig, A. La Vonne Brown Ruoff, Donald Smith, and Rüdiger Wersich. I am especially grateful to the good people at the Center for North American Studies (ZENAF) in Frankfurt for their support these many years.

AMERICAN INDIAN NONFICTION

INTRODUCTION

Grandfather, Now I exhort you to consider this seriously, and have compassion on your young men, women and children, and let them learn this, what our white brothers call A. B. C. which is the foundation of learning. . . . Grandfather, Be assured that by following this path I and my nation have found many advantages. Among other things, our white brothers cannot so easily cheat us now with regard to our land affairs as they have done our forefathers.
    A New England Christian Indian's Speech to the Delaware Nation, 1803

American Indian literature is generally thought to have emerged during the 1960s and to be primarily composed of poetry and fiction. Nonfiction prose, however, has been the dominant genre of American Indian letters since at least the second half of the eighteenth century.[1] It has received relatively little critical attention so far because "the keeping of written records" is still regarded as the essential distinction between "civilization" and "primal oral societies."[2] Most scholars agree that the Indian speech communities of North America lacked a true system of writing before the advent of Europeans. Whereas American Indian "orature" has found an appreciative audience since Thomas Jefferson's rendition of John Logan's famous lament in 1785, the early attempts by American Indian authors to bridge the hypothetical "impassable gulf" between expository writing and orally transmitted knowledge have only recently attracted critical attention. We are obviously much more familiar today with the melancholy "Indian monologues" that have been attributed to Logan, Chief Seattle, Chief Joseph, and other victims of American expansionism, which, as Roy Harvey Pearce points out, reinforce "the image of the Indian as a man out of society and out of history."[3] Less well known are the countless letters, sermons, petitions, and tracts penned and published by educated Indian intellectuals who sought to secure Native rights to a prosperous future in the United States through what might be characterized as a strategy of selective adaptation.

From its beginnings in the second half of the eighteenth century to the close of the nineteenth century, American Indian nonfiction prose is predominantly, but not exclusively, regional or tribally-specific in terms of subject matter. Although authors of this period also made free use of broad categories such as "Indians" or "Red Men" in their works and addressed overarching topics like the development of federal Indian policy, they were still primarily concerned with more specific political, historical, and cultural issues that immediately affected their own Native communities and the geographic locations in which they resided. Even in Indian Territory, with its highly sophisticated intertribal communications network, the thematic focus of the writers was almost entirely on local matters. "Our interests and sympathies are bound up in home affairs and home people," Creek poet laureate and journalist **Alexander L. Posey** (1873–1908) declared bluntly. "The rest of the world can go to grass."[4] The regional writers did interact with each other within these geographical limits, thus forming regional intellectual networks, but they did not coalesce into a national political body or formulate plans for a national Indian leadership as their successors would do in the early twentieth century. Nor did they consider their own work as constituting a distinct subgenre of American literature. This marked regional and/or tribal loyalty has continued to characterize the works of most American Indian authors to the present. As Jace Weaver has maintained, the single thing that most defines Indian literatures today is a sense of commitment to the community and the environment, or what he designates as "communitism."[5]

Early American Indian literature was dominated by mission-trained authors until the 1860s, after which the federal government gradually took over the responsibility of educating Indians. Regional American Indian literature (not to be confused with Regionalism) first emerged in three principal geographical areas: the Northeast, represented by the so-called New England Indians and New York Indians; the Southeast, represented primarily by Cherokee writers who continued their literary tradition along with other members of the "Five Civilized Tribes" in Indian Territory after their removal in the early decades of the nineteenth century; and the Great Lakes, represented by Central Algonquian (primarily Ojibwe) authors from both sides of the American-Canadian border. These regional literary enclaves obviously reflected the chronological progress of American expansionism on the one hand and standard ethnographic "culture areas" on the other.

American Indian nonfiction prose took on a more global thematic dimension with the arrival of an urban, middle-class, and professional Indian intellectual elite at the turn of the century, most of whom were educated at off-reservation boarding schools in the East and generally lived and worked in an Anglo-American social environment. This "new" generation of writers, directly influenced by the post-Civil War Indian reform movement that culminated with the passage of the General Allotment Act in 1887, turned increasingly to transregional issues affecting Indians in general and formed an official political network to promote the idea of an all-embracing American Indian nationalism—albeit without giving up or supplanting their regional/tribal loyalty.

The history of American Indian literature is, by virtue of the technical requirements of the skill of writing, inextricably tied to developments in the field of Indian education. American Indian nonfiction prose has its antecedents in seventeenth-century New England, where Protestant missionaries first sought to compose and disseminate religious texts in Algonquian languages. John Eliot's famous "Indian library," the first major publishing venture in colonial North America, would never have materialized without the indispensable assistance of bilingual Indian translators such as Cockenoe-de-Long Island (Montaukett), Job Nesuton (Massachusett), and James Printer (Nipmuck). Whatever information is now available in print about their personal experiences was recorded and transcribed into English by missionaries. The Algonquian-speaking "Praying Indians" of New England, however, who were taught to write in their own languages by missionaries for the express purpose of propagating the Gospel, quickly incorporated their vernacular literacy for purely domestic purposes, such as maintaining official community records.[6] Some of Eliot's translators did leave behind a few scattered contracts and letters commonly written in broken English. Cockenoe-de-Long Island, for instance, whose bilingual literacy earned him a prestigious position in the Massachusett community, drafted several deeds in English in the course of his dealings as mediator in a number of land settlement cases involving Indians and colonists. James Printer, who served as King Philip's personal scribe during the armed conflict with Massachusetts in 1675–76, probably formulated the conditions for the release of America's most famous captive, Mary Rowlandson, in a letter addressed to the governor and council of Boston in 1676. Furthermore, some of the Indian scholars who attended Harvard's short-lived "Indian College" in the 1660s–70s produced a number of religious writings in English, Latin, and Greek that have also been preserved. Likewise, hundreds of students attended special programs for Indians at the College of William and Mary, Dartmouth College, and the College of New Jersey (later Princeton) prior to the American Revolution, so perhaps substantial pieces of this nature are slumbering undetected in private and public archives.[7]

As far as is known today, authentic publications in English by North American Indians did not appear until the second half of the eighteenth century, primarily as a result of the Great Awakening, a massive religious revival that began in Europe around 1720 and then spread along the entire English-speaking Atlantic seaboard during the 1730s and 1740s. The foremost exponents of the Great Awakening, George Whitefield and Jonathan Edwards, introduced a number of fundamental innovations that greatly popularized religious life in the colonies, including the promotion of itinerant preachers with no credentials other than devotion and a sincere "calling" to spread the word of God, as well as a new kind of impromptu preaching that painted a grim picture of sin and eternal damnation but also promised salvation through a personal conversion experience. This populist approach to religion obviously attracted the masses of lesser-privileged members of colonial society, including African Americans and Indians, who otherwise found themselves excluded from regular church services.[8]

The Great Awakening also gave a renewed impulse to missionary efforts. In accordance with Enlightenment ideas on progress and universal human advancement from savagery to barbarism and civilization, it brought about a new kind of educational institution for Indians: the manual labor boarding school.[9] One of the earliest advocates of such an institution was John Sargeant, Sr., missionary to the Housatonic Valley Indians and founder of a Christian Indian community at Stockbridge, Massachusetts. Sargeant's plan, published in 1743, differed from the rigorous religious program that John Eliot had implemented a century earlier with his Praying Indian villages by stressing the importance of teaching Indians the English language along with menial skills.[10] His ideas were not realized until 1754, when Eleazar Wheelock, another major representative of the Great Awakening, founded Moor's Indian Charity School in

Lebanon, Connecticut. This institution remained in operation there for sixteen years before being transferred to Hanover, New Hampshire, where it eventually germinated into Dartmouth College.[11] Contrary to Sargeant, who wanted to set up his school within the Indian community, Wheelock felt that Indian children should be removed from the influence of their fellow tribesmen to be taught some useful "industry" in a special coeducational boarding school in which Indian boys and girls would have the advantage of associating directly with English youths. He thereby foreshadowed by more than a century the educational policies made famous by Richard Henry Pratt and the Carlisle Indian Industrial School. Wheelock's students were primarily recruited from the so-called remnant tribes of New England (Coastal Algonquian) and, at least temporarily, the Iroquois of New York.

The three principal Indian authors of the eighteenth century, **Samson Occom** (Mohegan, 1723–92), **Joseph Johnson** (Mohegan, 1751–76), and **Hendrick Aupaumut** (Mohican, 1757–1830), were intimately acquainted with the pedagogical philosophy of Sargeant and Wheelock. Other than similar educational and religious backgrounds, however, what tied these individuals together was that they collectively developed an effective strategy of selective adaptation based on adopted Christian ideals and time-honored Native traditions.

Sometime in the early 1770s, after becoming totally disillusioned with their situation in the Protestant missionary field, Samson Occom and Joseph Johnson conceived a plan to found an independent community of Christian Indians in Oneida territory in New York, where each had been active as missionaries earlier. They soon enlisted supporters among the Mohegans, Pequots, Tunxis, Niantics, Narragansets, and Montauketts, who referred to themselves collectively as the "New England Indians." In so doing, they were following an age-old Coastal Algonquian practice whereby conflicts within a village generally ended when a dissenting party either moved to another existing village, preferably one with close relatives, or founded a new one. The community Occom and Johnson envisioned was similar to Eliot's Praying Indian villages but with one important difference—it was, from inception to realization, an all-Indian affair. In New York they hoped to retain a permanent land base where they could keep the hybrid community together and live out their notions of a Christian Indian existence. Johnson, who had attended Moor's Indian Charity School from 1758 to 1765, conducted the official negotiations for a tract of land with the Oneidas in January of 1774. The Oneidas in turn adopted the Christianized New England Indians as "younger brothers," expecting to profit from their acquired expertise in their own dealings with encroaching European-American settlers. The project was postponed temporarily because of the outbreak of the American Revolution, when the first Oneida emigrants sought refuge among the Christian Indians at Stockbridge. On November 7, 1785, Occom made the following historical entry in his journal: "In the Evening we met on our Temporal and Religious concerns—we met once before but we did not come to proceed any business. But now we proceeded to form into a Body Politick—we Named our Town by the Name of Brotherton, in Indian Eeyamquittoowauconuck. . . . Concluded to live in Peace, and in Friendship and to go in all their Public Concerns in Harmony both in their Religious and Temporal concerns, and every one to bear his part of Public Charges in the Town."[12]

Occom and his followers completed their migration to Brothertown by the spring of 1789. Under the leadership of Hendrick Aupaumut, a Mohican sachem who had been educated at Sargeant's mission school and become a faithful supporter of Occom, the Stockbridge Indians of Massachusetts also decided to remove to New York between 1783 and 1786, where they set up their own Christian Indian community, named New Stockbridge, within six miles of Brothertown.

Conflicts with white neighbors and followers of the Handsome Lake religion among the Oneidas prompted the Christian Indians of Brothertown and New Stockbridge, now known collectively along with the Iroquois as the "New York Indians," to migrate once again. Younger educated leaders such as John W. Quinney (Mohican, 1797–1855), born in New Stockbridge, negotiated a land grant from the Menominee in the Green Bay area in 1822.[13] Separate parties from New Stockbridge and Brothertown then resettled permanently in present-day Wisconsin during the 1820s and 1830s. Christian Oneida also immigrated to Green Bay at this time, encouraged by the eccentric Mohawk Presbyterian minister Eleazer Williams (1788–1858), who had attended Moor's Indian Charity School for one week in 1807.[14] The Stockbridge Indians, joined by Delaware Munsees in the 1830s, managed to withstand the continuing incursions into their territory in Green Bay. In 1856 they concluded a new agreement with the Menominees allowing them to establish a separate reservation where they were eventually joined as well by some of their former neighbors from Brothertown. In 1938 the Bureau of Indian Affairs approved the tribal constitution of the Stockbridge-Munsee community and recognized its title to lands in Bartelme Township, Wisconsin. The Stockbridge-Munsees of today are regarded as an acculturated Indian community with a distinctly Indian value system, a relatively stable economic level, and a viable community organization headed by an effective leadership—one in which Hendrick Aupaumut's and John W. Quinney's direct descendants continue to play a prominent role.[15] The Brothertown Indian Nation, who honor Samson Occom as their founding father, are currently striving for federal recognition.[16] The Oneida Nation of Wisconsin, whose earliest Christian emigrants were undoubtedly influenced by the "New England Indians" of Brothertown and New Stockbridge, currently run a successful bingo and casino operation and hold close to seventeen thousand acres in both Brown and Outagamie counties.[17]

Missionary activities in the Northeast during the first half of the nineteenth century were dominated by a series of religious revivals that occurred in New England and elsewhere between the 1790s and 1830s known as the Second Great Awakening, which introduced several additional changes to Protestant ideology.[18] Along with the separation of church and state in the new republic there was also a marked tendency within religious bodies toward disestablishment in spiritual matters. Volunteer laymen began to take the initiative in areas that had hitherto been the sole responsibility of clergy or civil administrators. Established denominational bodies gradually atomized into countless interrelated but independent religious-humanitarian organizations. African Americans and Indians joined the clergy in greater numbers than ever before, particularly among Methodists and Baptists, who rose to prominence at this time. The Second Great Awakening brought about fundamental changes in theological doctrine. The Calvinist focus on depravity and original sin gave way to a belief in the human ability to do right according to God's will. This resulted in a general shift of moral concern from individual vices to broader social issues in American life, which in turn led to the creation of a myriad of so-called benevolent societies whose purpose was to prevent the moral decay of the nation. Beginning around the 1820s, the problem of slavery became the primary concern of this religiously based social reform movement. Tied closely to the expanding abolitionist movement was a widespread protest against the federal policy of forcefully moving Indians west of the Mississippi, which became official with the passage of the Indian Removal Act in 1830.[19]

The most remarkable author to emerge in the Northeast at this time was **William Apess** (Pequot, 1798–1839), who managed to rise from the ignominious status of an indentured servant to that of a licensed preacher of the dissenting Protestant Methodist Episcopal Church. Apess figured prominently in the so-called Woodland Revolt of 1834, in which the Christian Indian community of Mashpee in Cape Cod managed to secure a degree of autonomy from the Massachusetts legislature in 1834. This was an extraordinary feat because it stood as one of the very few substantial victories for Indian rights during the removal era when many other eastern Indian tribes were ruthlessly pushed out of their territory. The Mashpees, who now identify themselves as Wampanoag and have tried unsuccessfully to attain federal recognition since 1978, still acknowledge Apess's key role in a pivotal period of their tribal history.[20] The five monographs Apess produced between 1829 and 1836 constitute the most caustic Indian assessment of Indian-white relations to be published prior to the 1960s.

A successful Indian campaign against removal took place among the Senecas in New York, who were confronted with the fraudulent Treaty of Buffalo Creek, signed in 1838, that would have cost them their reservations in exchange for lands in Kansas. The ensuing ten-year controversy over this treaty, which also pitted Christian Senecas against each other, ushered in a thorough reformation of the Seneca government and the genesis of Seneca literature in English. **Maris Bryant Pierce** (1811–74), a Dartmouth graduate who received a stipend from funds originally collected by Occom for Moor's Indian Charity School, was one of the primary speakers and agitators against the treaty. Pierce maintained that the Senecas were absolutely capable of adopting civilized ways and that this could best be accomplished if they remained in New York. Opposing him was **Nathaniel Thayer Strong** (1810–72), a U.S. interpreter and "Young Chief" like Pierce, who argued that removal from the corrupting influences of the white population was a benevolent policy. In contrast to less fortunate tribes elsewhere, the concerted efforts of the Seneca anti-removal faction and the Society of Friends (Quakers) finally resulted in the signing of a supplemental treaty in 1842. According to this treaty the Senecas retained title to the Allegany and Cattaraugus reservations but had to give up Buffalo Creek and Tonawanda. Fortunately, however, with the able diplomatic assistance of **Ely Samuel Parker** (1828–95), a young engineer and sachem of the Iroquois Nation who would eventually serve as commissioner of Indian affairs under Ulysses S. Grant, the Tonawanda Senecas also managed to save their reservation by 1857.[21]

In the early decades of the nineteenth century missionaries affiliated with the Second Great Awakening, who organized themselves into interdenominational societies such as the American Board of Commissioners for Foreign Missions (ABCFM), concentrated their efforts on the more populous Indian nations of the Southeast, especially the Cherokee. The first mission school in the Cherokee Nation opened in 1804, but the most enduring educational institution before removal was established in 1817 by representatives of the ABCFM at the Brainerd Mission near Chattanooga, Tennessee. **Catherine Brown** (ca. 1800–23) and **John Ridge** (1803–39) were among the numerous Cherokee scholars who attended this celebrated institution.[22] That same year the ABCFM founded the Foreign Mission School at Cornwall, Connecticut, providing instruction for many Cherokee, Choctaw, and Chickasaw students between 1817 and 1827. At the request of influential part-Choctaw leaders such as David Folsom (1791–1847), the ABCFM set up similar mission schools in the Choctaw Nation in 1818 and 1820.[23] Following the passage of an act by Congress in 1819 "making provision for the civilization of the Indian tribes adjoining the frontier settlements," the number of mission schools increased accordingly. The type of institution favored by Presbyterians and Congregationalists of the ABCFM corresponded to the boarding school model introduced in the previous century by Wheelock, with instruction in mechanical arts and agriculture as an integral part of the curriculum. Baptists and Methodists also began to establish missions among the southeastern Indians in 1819 and 1823 respectively. Even though they were latecomers, their egalitarian approach and willingness to train Native preachers soon enabled them to outstrip the other denominations in terms of membership. In 1825 Methodists established the famed Choctaw Academy in Kentucky, which continued the policy promoted earlier by the Foreign Mission School of educating Indian students far away from their Native communities until it closed in 1842. Mission schools among the Cherokees and Choctaws, partially funded by tribal governments, flourished in the Southeast until the removal of these Indian nations in the 1830s.[24]

The reformist ideas propagated by the Protestant missionaries and their schools were readily adopted by a small but highly influential group of Indians with European-American ancestry, particularly the Cherokees, who in less than three decades managed to transform a relatively loosely organized coalition of villages into a centralized constitutional government closely patterned after the

United States. The extent of Christian influence among the Cherokee leadership at this time is made evident by a National Council resolution passed on October 13, 1826, which excluded from office anyone "who disbelieves in the existence of the Creator, and of rewards and punishments after death." The resolution was later qualified as Article VI, sec. 2, of the Cherokee Constitution of 1827 to the effect that "no person who denies the being of a God, or a future state of rewards and punishment, shall hold any office in the civil department of this Nation."[25]

The ultimate end that Christian Cherokee intellectuals such as John Ridge, **John Ross** (1790–1866), **Elias Boudinot** (1804–39), **John Rollin Ridge** (1827–67), and others envisioned was the annexation of the Cherokee Nation as an independent state of the Union. It was a goal that also seemed plausible to early American administrators. The first official pact between the Continental Congress and an Indian nation, the Fort Pitt Treaty of 1778 with the Delawares, invited them to join the confederation as a separate state with the prerogative of sending a representative to Congress. Article twelve of the 1785 Treaty of Hopewell foresaw the sending of a Cherokee "deputy" to Congress.[26]

The missionary societies reconstituted their school programs in Indian Territory, but now the tribal administrators also increasingly took educational matters into their own hands. In 1833 the Choctaws established a tribal school system that expanded to ten tribal schools by 1837 and included several higher-education seminaries for boys and girls by the 1850s. The Cherokee National Council also set up eleven tribal district schools in 1841. Ten years later more than a thousand Cherokee students were attending twenty-one tribal schools and two college-level academies, the Cherokee Female Seminary and Cherokee Male Seminary. The Chickasaw legislature appropriated funds for six schools in 1849. It also funded the Chickasaw Academy (later Chickasaw Manual Labor Academy), opened by the Methodist Episcopal Church South in 1851, as well as the Waupauneka Female Institute established under the auspices of the Presbyterians in 1852. The Creeks (Muskogees), generally more antagonistic toward missionary activities both before and immediately after their removal in 1826, agreed to provide funds for manual labor schools in 1847. By 1853 they had two manual labor schools and twelve neighborhood schools offering instruction for about six hundred students. By the close of the century the Creeks were funding about seventy neighborhood schools and six boarding schools along with several separate institutions for the Creek freedmen. The more conservative Seminoles established their first tribal school in 1844 and enlarged their educational program with four others by the 1860s. This independent tribal school system was reincorporated after the chaos of the Civil War, continued to function until terminated by the Curtis Act of 1898, and was finally taken over by the Bureau of Indian Affairs with the passage of the Five Tribes Act of March 4, 1906. The Cherokees, Creeks, Choctaws, Chickasaws, and Seminoles were so successful in their selective adaptation to European-American ways (for example, by adopting constitutions, printed law codes, and judicial systems) that they became known collectively as the "Five Civilized Tribes."[27]

Administrators of the Five Tribes attempted to resist the policy of removal with a strategy of non-violent resistance. The Cherokees tried to curb Georgia's illegal incursions into their territory and sovereignty by appealing to the Supreme Court on the one hand and by lobbying Congress with the support of the ABCFM and anti-Jackson politicians on the other. The resulting "Cherokee Nation Cases" (*Cherokee Nation v. Georgia,* 1831, and *Worcester v. Georgia,* 1832), though failing to prevent removal, did introduce the fundamental legal conception of Indians as "distinct, independent communities." After Sequoyah completed his famous 86-symbol Cherokee syllabary in 1821 and it was incorporated by the Cherokee government in 1824, a substantial portion of the Cherokee population became literate.[28] As a means of promoting their own progressive politics and initiating an effective propagandistic front against the looming threat of removal, Cherokee administrators established an independent bilingual press at Tahlequah and launched the *Cherokee Phoenix (Tsa-la-ge-Tsi-le-hi-sa-ni-hi)* on February 21, 1828.[29] This tribally owned newspaper initiated a rich journalistic tradition that was carried on by the Cherokee government west of the Mississippi with the establishment of the *Cherokee Advocate* in 1844. During the second half of the nineteenth century Indian journalism blossomed in Indian Territory, where several tribal and nontribal newspapers existed alongside a much larger number of periodicals that were neither owned nor edited by Indians but dealt intensively with local Indian issues.[30] This flourishing newspaper business, coupled with a sophisticated tribal school system set up by the Five Tribes before and after the Civil War, transformed Indian Territory into a literary center that brought forth numerous notable Indian writers, including **De Witt Clinton Duncan** (Cherokee, 1829–1909), **Elias Cornelius Boudinot** (Cherokee, 1839–90), **Charles Gibson** (Creek, 1846–1923), and the previously cited Alexander Lawrence Posey. Two professional Cherokee journalists from this period, John Rollin Ridge and Edward W. Bushyhead (1832–1907), also played prominent roles as pioneer newspapermen in California after the gold rush.[31] The principal driving force behind this journalistic renaissance in Indian Territory was partisan politics rather than religion. With the abolishment of the Indian governments in 1906, however, and the incorporation of Indian Territory into the state of Oklahoma in 1907, this productive regional journalistic tradition began to ebb rapidly.

Apart from newspaper editorials, the Indian writers of the Southeast and Indian Territory also produced countless politically oriented memorials, petitions, tracts, and pamphlets. These focused primarily on crucial issues such as removal, local elections, illegal white squatters, the legal status of citizen freedmen, the right-of-way for railroad corporations, territorial status for Indian Territory (not officially a territory in spite of the name). They also covered the allotment of lands after the Curtis Act of 1898 extended the policies of the 1887 General Allotment Act to Indian Territory, citizenship, and separate or single statehood for Indian Territory and Oklahoma Territory. A large number of these publications appeared in Washington, D.C., where delegations from the Five Tribes regularly vied with each other for Congressional support.

A distinctive regional school of American Indian literary humor also developed in direct association with the newspaper boom in Indian Territory during the second half of the nineteenth century. From the 1870s on, writers who were predominantly citizens of the Cherokee and Creek nations—often using pseudonyms such as Unakah, Skiatook, Choo-noo-lusky, Ah-sto-la-ta, Woochee Ochee, Choonstootee, Oo-law-nah-stee-sky, Chun-chustie, Too-stoo, King-fisher, Jeem Featherhead, or Pewter Dick—produced a large number of Indian-English dialect letters to the editor with sardonic comments on a great variety of local events. Charles Gibson and Alexander Lawrence Posey rank among the more prominent and talented practitioners of Indian Territory humor. Gibson is best remembered for his witty "horse sense" commentaries on Indian Territory affairs, particularly a regular feature column for the *Indian Journal* titled "Gibson's Rifle Shots." Posey, also widely recognized as a poet, produced just over seventy "Fus Fixico Letters" between 1902 and 1908. These brief humorous sketches in Creek-English dialect with a partly imaginary and partly historical set of conservative and seemingly naive Creek characters who regularly discuss contemporary issues were read far beyond Indian Territory. Nevertheless, Indian Territory humor is almost strictly regional in scope, which makes it as difficult for the modern-day audience to comprehend as Old Southwest humor.

National and world politics, however, dominate the work of the most illustrious practitioner of Indian Territory humor, **William Penn Adair Rogers** (Cherokee, 1879–1935). This is undoubtedly why "Will" Rogers is seldom studied within the context of American Indian literature. Nevertheless, America's famous "cowboy philosopher," who once jokingly referred to himself as a part-Cherokee with "enough white in me to make my honesty questionable," occasionally addressed Indian issues as well. Although his Indian-related sketches are few and far between, Rogers's overall philosophy—racial tolerance, anti-denominationalism, self-determination of nations—fits seamlessly with the ideas propagated by his Indian predecessors. In addition, his regular use of hyperbole, puns, deliberate misspellings, and an irregular application of the past tense tie him firmly to the literary conventions of Indian Territory humor. Will Rogers's famous opening line—"All I know is what I read in the papers"—is thus a befitting tribute to the fruitful union between a rich southeastern Indian sense of humor and the blossoming of Indian Territory journalism.

The area surrounding the upper and lower Great Lakes was also a dynamic contact environment for well over three hundred years. Various Indian and European peoples were forced to accommodate to each other's presence. Ojibwes, Odawas, and Potawatomis, who refer to themselves collectively as the Anishinabeg (various spellings exist), formed the most populous nations residing in this region during the postcontact era, when it was successively dominated by the French, British, Americans, and Canadians. Catholic and Protestant missionaries of different nationalities vied with each other for centuries to draw Native inhabitants into their fold.[32] The upper and lower Great Lakes region was thus an ideal space for cross-cultural exchange or, as Richard White describes it, a strategic "middle ground" situated "in between cultures, peoples, and in between empires and the nonstate world of villages" in which "diverse peoples adjust their differences through what amounts to a process of creative, and often expedient, misunderstandings."[33] The environmental conditions of the Great Lakes area and the exigencies of the fur trade actually made it more expedient for European and American traders and trappers to adapt to certain Indian lifestyles well into the nineteenth century. Ojibwe and Odawa languages served as the lingua franca for all interaction in the area, and intermarriage between whites and Indians was so common that it eventually led to the formation of a "new peoples" now known as Métis.[34]

Among other things, the cross-cultural dynamics of the upper and lower Great Lakes, particularly intermarriage and Catholic and Protestant proselytizing activities, gave rise to a number of bilingual writers (predominantly Ojibwe) during the second half of the nineteenth century. Jesuit missionaries had visited the Great Lakes region sporadically from 1690 to 1763, but regular missionary activity did not begin in the area until the early decades of the nineteenth century, when increasing numbers of white settlers and depleting game gradually displaced the reciprocally profitable fur trade. Quakers, Moravians, Presbyterians, Baptists, Episcopalians, and Anglicans scattered missions throughout the region. Of all the Christian denominations competing to fill the growing spiritual vacuum among the increasingly pressured Indians in the Great Lakes region at the turn of the century, however, the most successful by far was the American-based Methodist Episcopal Church, whose missionaries began arriving during the 1790s and then branched off into an independent Canadian Methodist Conference in 1828.[35] A key to Methodism's widespread popularity among Indians of the Great Lakes was its willingness to train Native preachers and to entrust them with important missionary duties, a liberal policy already successfully implemented among Indians elsewhere in the United States. In Upper Canada the activities of the Canadian Methodist Conference led to the emergence of a group of bilingual Ojibwe Methodist missionaries who produced a substantial body of English and Algonquian literature.[36]

The driving force behind this Christian Indian revival in Upper Canada was the Reverend Peter Jones (Mississauga Ojibwe, 1802–56), the son of a Mississauga Ojibwe chief's daughter and a Welsh-Canadian trader. In 1826 Jones was instrumental in establishing the Credit Mission, a model village for all Christian Indians of Upper Canada, located on the northern shore of Lake Ontario and moved to the Grand River Reserve in 1847. With this project Jones successfully put into place his notions of selective adaptation, namely the security of Indian property ownership, sufficient arable land to establish farming communities, access to a solid education, and acquisition of the basic civil rights enjoyed by British citizens. Jones, elected as one of the three chiefs of the

Credit band of Mississauga Ojibwes in 1829, also received widespread respect from other Indian communities in Upper Canada. He was entrusted with the duties of an agent by the Ojibwes of Munceytown, the Delawares of Moraviantown, and the Iroquois of the Grand River Reserve. His exemplary life as a missionary in many ways paralleled Occom's leadership role among the New England Christian Indians, inspiring a number of younger Great Lakes Indians to follow in his footsteps.[37] Included among these were three who published significant works in the United States: **John Johnson** (1808?–1902), **George Copway** (1818–69), and **George Henry** (ca. 1811–88).

The careers of John Johnson and George Copway, both markedly influenced by Peter Jones, actually took shape south of the border. Johnson transferred his allegiance from the Methodists to the Episcopalians, who were increasingly active in the Upper Mississippi area after 1850, and spent the rest of his life as a dedicated missionary to the resident Ojibwes. Like his missionary predecessors in New England and Upper Canada, Johnson believed that the establishment of farming Christian Indian communities was the most practicable survival strategy to pursue, especially after President Zachary Taylor authorized the immediate and complete removal of Ojibwes living in Michigan and Wisconsin to "unoccupied" territory in central Minnesota in 1850. Johnson was also actively involved in the execution of President Ulysses S. Grant's Peace Policy, which sought to enlist the services of churchmen as official Indian agents.

George Copway, whose preaching license was revoked by the Canadian Methodists for illicit doings, developed a more ambitious strategy when he migrated to the United States. He conceived a bold plan for the creation of a "Northwestern Indian Territory," first outlined in an 1848 article and then presented to the Thirty-first Congress in 1850. According to this plan, Indians from various tribes of the Old Northwest were to be gathered in an "unsettled" region between the territories of Nebraska and Minnesota, where they would find permanent homes and be introduced gradually to civilization with the ultimate goal of sending an official representative to Congress. Although not a novel idea, Copway's scheme nevertheless found the support of numerous eastern philanthropists and literati. In fact, the vision of a semi-sovereign Indian state continues to occupy the thoughts of contemporary Indian intellectuals.[38]

George Henry, half-brother of Peter Jones, abandoned a promising career as a Methodist missionary to form a professional dance troupe with which he toured throughout Europe, the United States, and Canada. His memoirs, published in England and the United States, represent a unique Indian contribution to nineteenth-century American-Canadian travel literature.[39]

Roman Catholics resumed their missionary activities in the Great Lakes region during the 1830s and found that some of the local Indian communities were still receptive to the teachings of the "Black Robes." Their educational institutions in the United States brought forth a second generation of notable Central Algonquian writers such as **Simon Pokagon** (Potawatomi, 1830–99) and **Andrew J. Blackbird** (Odawa, 1810–1900). Simon Pokagon pursued a partly successful strategy of initiating legal actions against the federal government in the Court of Claims for the reimbursement of back annuities. The publicity he generated with his at times selfishly motivated promotional tactics undoubtedly helped the Pokagons to obtain a substantial remuneration from the United States in 1896. On September 21, 1994, President Clinton signed a bill officially recognizing the Pokagon Band of Potawatomi Indians, which derived its general name from Simon's family.[40] Andrew Jackson Blackbird, a school acquaintance of Simon Pokagon, devoted himself to the promotion of public school education and citizenship for his community at L'Arbre Croche (now Harbor Springs) in Michigan, where a small museum now bears his name.[41]

The first three decades of the second half of the nineteenth century were not conducive to the production of American Indian nonfiction prose in the United States. As Robert Berkhofer, Jr., and others have determined, the romantic-evangelical preoccupation with Indians began to wane markedly in the United States after the 1850s as Americans became increasingly concerned with other domestic issues such as the expanding abolitionist movement. Indian themes were subsequently either burlesqued on stage or trivialized in American popular culture. The carnage of the Civil War, the subsequent antagonism of southern Reconstruction, and the consequences of a severe economic depression were now foremost on the public's mind. A few writers of the Far West, such as Joaquin Miller and Helen Hunt Jackson, continued to romanticize Indians in some of their works, but more significant authors such as Mark Twain or Bret Harte tended to reflect the racialist views of frontier whites. Not until the 1890s, when the propagandist machinery of a new reform movement brought Indian issues back to the attention of the reading public, did Indian authors again find a viable outlet for their works.[42]

Federal Indian policy actually changed more in scope than in principle during the second half of the nineteenth century. Philanthropists continued to voice familiar Christian and Enlightenment ideals, but now they bolstered their views with knowledge derived from recent advances in the social sciences. The idea of unlimited human progress was reinforced by social evolutionist theories that still traced the hierarchical development of society from savagery, through barbarism to civilization. Lewis H. Morgan, regarded as the father of American ethnology, maintained that Indians were situated somewhere between upper savagery and middle barbarism, and would first have to be led to a pastoral stage before they could reach the desirable agricultural-property phase of economy characterizing Western society. As historian Brian Dippie has documented, Morgan, John Wesley Powell, Alice Cunningham Fletcher, and other like-minded representatives of the budding "American School" of ethnology made a substantial impact on the goals and execution of Indian policy after the Civil War. The works of Charles Darwin and Herbert Spencer also influenced less patient promoters of Indian advancement, who readily adhered to the maxim that individualism and competition produced the best possible results and consequently favored the total immersion of Indians in American society on a sink-or-swim basis.[43]

After 1848, when the American domain extended to the Pacific, administrators increasingly favored the policy of segregating Indian nations on reservations. Although the reservation system can be traced back to seventeenth-century New England, it was not regarded as an all-encompassing political solution to what came to be designated as the "Indian Problem" (or "Indian Question") as long as there was still sufficient "unsettled" land available somewhere to the west. The original plan behind the creation of reservations was to settle Indians on tracts large enough to allow them to supplement their annual rations by hunting and gathering. At the same time, adults were to be introduced to farming and stock-raising while children were instructed in mission schools. In the not too distant future, according to this plan, Indians would need less land to sustain themselves—land that could then be opened for white settlement.[44]

The high cost of reservation maintenance and rampant corruption in the Indian Service soon led to calls for additional reforms, however. Following the inauguration of Ulysses S. Grant as president in 1869, the United States embarked upon a new program that has come to be known as Grant's Peace Policy, sometimes called the Quaker Policy. While Grant's administration continued to adhere to the usual tactics of segregating Indians on reservations, it did introduce a few radical innovations: It arranged for various church groups to appoint reservation agents and provide for Indian education with federal aid; it created a special monitoring institution, the Board of Indian Commissioners of Indian Affairs, that remained active until 1933; and it nominated an Indian, Ely S. Parker, as commissioner of Indian affairs.[45]

Although Parker's tenure as commissioner was brief (1869–71), his role in the development of Grant's Peace Policy should not be underestimated. Parker proposed to transfer the Office of Indian Affairs back to the War Department, to abolish private trade with Indians, to consolidate tribes in a number of districts under a territorial government, and to create a permanent Indian commission to oversee the situation on reservations. In his first annual report as commissioner in 1869 he recommended that the treaty making process be terminated at once. He also spoke strongly in favor of promoting citizenship and allotments. Considering that Grant had very little experience in Indian matters prior to the Civil War, it stands to reason that Parker, his personal friend, field secretary in the army, and acting commissioner of Indian affairs, exerted substantial influence on the policy that now bears the president's name.[46]

Despite an optimistic beginning, Grant's Peace Policy soon ran into insurmountable obstacles. Although cooperation between missionary societies and the government in the matter of educating Indians had been occurring since the colonial era, this officially sponsored fusion of state and church was an unusual administrative approach that eventually led to questions concerning its constitutionality. Rising costs on reservations, unchecked corruption in the

Indian Service, continuous squabbles between competing denominations, and the obvious failure to convert a substantial number of Indians into self-sufficient farmers made the policy increasingly unpopular. By the time Rutherford B. Hayes was sworn in as president in 1877, the policy of appointing churchmen as Indian agents was falling into widespread disfavor. Another issue that undermined Grant's Peace Policy was the drive from 1867 to 1879 to move the Indian Office back into the War Department. Grant's experiment was gradually abandoned after he left the presidency in 1876 and officially terminated in the summer of 1882.

The decade of the 1880s is generally regarded as a major turning point in the history of Indian-white relations. America's rise as a world power was accompanied by increasing social upheaval and racial intolerance. Vicious anti-Chinese riots throughout the country resulted in the passage of the Chinese Exclusion Act of 1882. Radical Reconstruction in the South was replaced by repressive "Jim Crow" legislation following the Civil Rights cases of 1883, initiating a new wave of discrimination against African Americans that culminated in the separate-but-equal decision by the Supreme Court in *Plessy v. Ferguson* in 1896. As "new immigration" brought in millions of central, southern, and eastern Europeans, an anti-foreigner sentiment coalesced in 1887 into the American Protective Association. American capitalists also eschewed any responsibility for the negative sides of industrial and urban growth or those who could not get ahead on their own initiative. The "great upheaval" of 1886 heightened anxieties about the labor movement, calling forth comparisons between working-class activists and "savages." According to Richard Slotkin, this "reversible analogy between workers and savages is the most significant new term in the language of American mythology after the war, and it informs the battery of responses that postwar American culture brought to bear on urban problems, southern problems, and on the Indian question." In view of such pronounced exclusionist sentiment, it is all the more astonishing that American reformers of the late nineteenth century, such as Commissioner of Indian Affairs Thomas J. Morgan, wanted to integrate Indians "peaceably if they will, forcibly if they must."[47]

One of the most tragic and widely publicized events occurring at the end of the 1870s that disclosed the shortcomings of the reservation system was the Ponca case of 1879, which became the cause célèbre around which the neo-reformists rallied. Because of a bureaucratic mistake, the Ponca reservation of 1865 was included within the reservation granted to the Lakota Sioux under the 1868 Treaty of Fort Laramie. Rather than antagonizing the warlike Sioux, the government decided instead to remove the peaceable Poncas to Indian Territory in 1877, where they suffered in the unaccustomed climate. In January 1879, Standing Bear and his band of Poncas made their way back north to Nebraska without official permission, where they were eventually arrested by the army and detained at Fort Omaha with the expectation of being returned to Indian Territory. Journalist Henry Tibbles took up the Poncas' cause and organized a promotional campaign that included a six-month speaking tour for

Standing Bear in the Midwest and East. Tibbles was assisted by **Susette La Flesche** (Omaha, 1854–1903) and her half-brother **Francis La Flesche** (Omaha, 1857–1932). The emotional lectures delivered by Susette in Indian costume, widely known by the English rendition of her Omaha name "Bright Eyes," kindled a concern for Indian affairs among influential New Englanders such as Senator Henry L. Dawes, author Helen Hunt Jackson, and archaeologist Alice Fletcher. They joined with other concerned Easterners to found the Boston Indian Citizenship Committee in 1879. Due to their concerted efforts, the Poncas were eventually given the choice of remaining in Indian Territory under improved conditions or returning to their homelands in Nebraska.[48]

Sarah Winnemucca (Northern Paiute, ca. 1845–91)*, who was addressing the plight of her own people in Washington, D.C. at about the same time that Susette testified before the Senate committee concerning the Ponca removal, managed to have her 1870 letter recommending the privatization of Paiute lands in Nevada reprinted in Helen Hunt Jackson's highly influential *A Century of Dishonor* in 1881. Ely S. Parker, Susette La Flesche, and Sarah Winnemucca had already formulated some of the principles of selective adaptation that would shape the political platform of the Society of American Indians. Their writings and activities had a direct influence on leading figures of the Indian reform movement after the Civil War and thus also played a role in the formation of a collective federal Indian policy.

Indian rights advocates, working independently or in loose associations until the 1870s, now began to pool their efforts in national reform organizations. The Indian Treaty Keeping and Protective Association (later the Women's National Indian Association) was founded in Philadelphia in 1879, followed by the Indian Rights Association in the same city in 1882, and the National Indian Defense Association in New York in 1885. These reform organizations promoted public and administrative concern for Indian affairs through an extensive network of publications, public talks, meetings, and lobbying activities. Beginning in 1883 and lasting until 1917, self-styled "Friends of the Indian" met every fall at a private resort on Lake Mohonk, New York, to discuss the future course of Indian policy. The annual Lake Mohonk conferences of the Friends of the Indian were attended by some of the nation's leading administrators, educators, agents, journalists, writers, scholars, churchpeople, and philanthropists. Conference debates and recommendations were regularly published in the press and read before Congress. Their influence on the development of Indian policy after the 1880s was substantial.

The Friends of the Indian also subscribed to the Enlightenment-based rationale of the earlier civilization, reservation, and peace programs, believing that Indians could be fully integrated into American society given the right "environment." Now, however, the reformers placed an increased emphasis on secularized activities. As Francis Paul Prucha has pointed out, their ideology reflected a complete identification of Protestantism with American nationalism. Central themes included the privatization of Indian lands in allotments, the dissolution of reservations, the promotion of farming and stock raising as a means to achieve Indian self-sufficiency, the normalization of Indian legal status through citizenship, and the education of Indian youths in government-supported schools with a focus on practical training. Even though it had become quite apparent by the 1880s that the expectations behind allotment could hardly be met because of railroad grants, speculators, the advent of cash-crop farming, and adverse environmental factors, the reformers still held on to the Jeffersonian creed that small farms would make Indians self-sufficient and automatically inculcate them with middle-class American ideals. With the notable exception of the National Indian Defense Association, all agreed that every aspect of Indian tribalism only retarded this desirable process. The close of the nineteenth century thus actually marked the beginning of what lawyer-philosopher Vine Deloria, Jr., has aptly characterized as a "period of cultural oppression in its most severe form."[49]

With these goals in mind, the reformers and their organizations set about determining the necessary means for carrying them out. The end result of a long debate in Congress was the passage in 1887 of the Dawes Severalty Act, better known as the General Allotment Act, lauded by Theodore Roosevelt in his first annual message to Congress in 1901 as "a mighty pulverizing engine to break up the tribal mass."[50] In 1898 the Curtis Act extended allotment to the Five Tribes and several other Indian communities initially exempted from the Dawes Act. Other than alienating about two-thirds of Indian land holdings, the Dawes Act failed to meet almost all of the reformers' expectations. Rather than producing self-sufficient, property-conscious farmers, it reduced the greater part of the Indian population to pauperism by destroying their former means of sustenance and making them entirely dependent upon government subsidies. The successive amendments to the act only resulted in a steady increase of administrative authority over Indians, which openly contradicted the reformist philosophy of rugged individualism and self-reliance. And yet, in spite its devastating effects on Indian communities, the Dawes Act never managed to root out Indian "tribalism" as had been predicted. Social and religious activities on reservations simply moved underground.[51]

One of the most enduring effects of the Indian reform movement was in the field of education. In the 1870s the government began to assume direct responsibility for the instruction of Indian children and to sponsor non-sectarian schools. In 1870 Congress authorized an annual appropriation of $100,000 to be spent exclusively on Indian education. Congress increased the amount to three million dollars by the end of the century. Mandatory Indian attendance was institutionalized in 1893, when Congress authorized the secretary of the interior to withhold rations from parents who were not willing to send their children to school, even though it was also specified the following year that Indian children could only be sent to off-reservation schools with parental consent. It has been estimated that the total number of Indian students rose from approximately 3,500 in 1870 to 21,000 in 1900. The number of government supported schools doubled from 150 to more than 300 during the same period. Although only about 20 percent of Indian children were being provided with an education during the early 1880s, this figure increased to about 70 percent by the 1920s. In order to keep up with the rapid expansion of Indian education, the government sought to systemize and improve the Indian Service by adopting the merit system in the appointment of teachers in 1892 and by incorporating Indian school personnel into the civil service in 1896.[52]

The Indian Service initially favored day schools and boarding schools on reservations but turned increasingly to off-reservation manual labor boarding schools. The model for manual labor boarding schools in the allotment era was Hampton Normal and Industrial Institute, a special institution for African American freedmen established under the direction of Samuel C. Armstrong in 1868, which then opened its doors to Indian students in 1878. Armstrong, a former abolitionist, thought that education should combine cultural improvement with moral and manual training. The Hampton curriculum consequently included various industrial arts, military drills, and physical labor programs. Hampton continued to function as a highly respected off-reservation school under federal contract until 1912, when reformers began calling for the separation of Indians and African Americans in schools and the government ceased to fund its Indian program. By then, however, Hampton had graduated a fairly large number of Indians, not a few of whom would go on to establish themselves professionally and assume influential positions in Indian communities as well as the national reform movement.[53]

The foremost off-reservation boarding school exclusively for Indians was Carlisle Indian Industrial School, founded in Pennsylvania by Richard Henry Pratt in 1879. Its famous motto was: "To civilize the Indian, get him into civilization. To keep him civilized, let him stay." Carlisle served close to five thousand students until Pratt's superintendency was terminated in 1905, and many more studied there before the army transformed the school into a hospital in 1918. Pratt, a firm believer in the environmentalist approach to human advancement, developed what he called the "outing system," where students were placed with local white families during the summer months to learn farm work and domestic skills.[54] Carlisle was followed in rapid succession by the Salem Indian Training School in Forest Grove, Oregon (1880), later moved to Chemawa; Chilocco School in Newkirk, Indian Territory (1884); Genoa Industrial School for Indian Youth in Nebraska (1884), and Haskell Institute in Lawrence, Kansas (1884). Off-reservation boarding schools were also established in New Mexico, Arizona, Nevada, South Dakota, Colorado, Montana, Minnesota, Michigan, Wisconsin, and California during the 1890s.

Most government-sponsored boarding schools developed a "half-and-half" curriculum that included ordinary public school courses, standardized after 1890, along with instruction in gender-specific manual labor. Boys were taught skills that related primarily to agricultural activities and girls learned domestic handiwork. There was also a strong emphasis on military drill, marching bands, and team sports. Indian students were expected to dress and act like their teachers at all times. English was strictly enforced as the sole language of instruction, even in most of the sectarian schools still receiving government funds. The main difference in the long established sectarian approach to education was that religious activities, though still an integral part of the daily school program, no longer dominated the overall pedagogical concept. The curriculum was greatly expanded in nonsectarian schools to include regular public-school courses such as modern sciences, English and American literature, general history, algebra, geometry, elementary physics, rhetoric, psychology, and pedagogy, as well as commercially related instruction in stenography, typewriting, parliamentary rules, bookkeeping, business correspondence, and banking.

As Frederick Hoxie has documented, the lofty ideals of the Friends of the Indian underwent a negative transformation at the end of the nineteenth century. The Indian's capacity to learn was not only limited by environmental and cultural factors, the majority view by this time, but also by racial considerations. The concept of coercive assimilation no longer comprised the promise of equal opportunity. Now it projected a permanent lower-class existence on the periphery of American society as the only alternative to extinction.[55] As Alan Trachtenberg observes, by the 1890s "the Indian had been incorporated into America no longer simply as 'savage,' a fantasy object of ambivalent romantic identification or racial hatred, but as 'lowest order,' outcast and pariah who represented the fate of all those who do not work, do not own, do not prefer the benefits of legal status within the hierarchies of modern institutions to the prerogatives of freedom and cultural autonomy."[56] Indian children were to be prepared for their future place in the American working class by concentrating on vocational training in school rather than on academics. "To train the average Indian as a lawyer or a doctor," Theodore Roosevelt had already concluded in 1893, "is in most cases simply to spoil him."[57]

By this time, however, several thousand educated Indians had somehow managed to come to terms with the repressive policy of coercive assimilation, and some of them had begun to formulate and actively promote their own views on the "Indian Problem." The pronounced focus on agricultural and commercial skills in government-sponsored schools, particularly during the more optimistic reform phase between the 1870s and 1890s, greatly expanded professional possibilities for Indians. A number of exceptionally motivated Indian students were even able to obtain higher education at regular American universities and then establish themselves as physicians, lawyers, journalists, or engineers. Indian preachers, once so prominent in Indian scholarship, politics, and literature, obviously did not vanish at this point. The careers of **Sherman Coolidge** (Arapaho, 1863–1932), **Henry Roe Cloud** (Winnebago, 1886?–1950), and Philip B. Gordon (Ojibwe, 1887–1948), for example, attest that the ministry remained a promising field in which educated Indians could advance professionally and that Indian clergy were still actively involved in contemporary Indian affairs.[58] Nevertheless, missionary work was no longer the only professional venue for Indian scholars. Consequently, evangelical concerns were increasingly pushed into the background by the more worldly ambitions of the rapidly growing urban middle-class American Indian intellectual elite.

Many of the children who attended Hampton and Carlisle were the sons and daughters of influential tribal leaders. Frequently, they were born into "progressive" families with marital connections to non-Indians, as in the case of Bright Eyes's sisters, Susan La Flesche (Omaha, 1865–1915) and Marguerite La Flesche (Omaha, 1862–1945), two particularly successful Hampton graduates.[59] Parents usually had a pragmatic interest in sending their offspring to some distant school where they could learn skills that might serve the community in its future dealings with white society. In his analysis of autobiographical accounts by former Indian students from the period between 1850 and 1930, Michael Coleman has tabulated that about half of them were sent to school by close kin or other influential tribal members, while only one-fourth were actually coerced by the authorities.[60]

"Progressive" Indian intellectuals, who referred to themselves as such because they shared the contemporary reformist belief in social improvement through governmental action, did not coordinate their activities on a national level until after the close of the nineteenth century, precisely at the time when reformers began to lose interest in the "Indian Problem." At the beginning of the second decade of the twentieth century, a small group of highly educated urban Indian professionals with various tribal backgrounds began to communicate regularly with each other, developing a distinctly national, or trans-regional, ideology. Six prototypes of the allotment-era Indian success story met in Columbus, Ohio, on April 3–4, 1911, and founded the American Indian Association. This group included **Dr. Charles Alexander Eastman** (Mdewakanton-Wahpeton Sioux, 1858–1939), a graduate from Dartmouth College and the Boston School of Medicine; **Dr. Carlos Montezuma** (Yavapai, ca. 1866–1923), a graduate from the Chicago Medical College; Thomas L. Sloan (Omaha, 1863–1932), Hampton graduate and lawyer; **Laura M. Cornelius** (Oneida, 1880–1947), a widely traveled activist with modern corporate ideals who had studied sporadically at Stanford, Barnard College, Columbia, Cornell, and the University of Wisconsin; Henry Standing Bear (Sicangu Sioux, 1874–1953), a Carlisle graduate; and Charles E. Dagenett (Peoria, ca. 1872–?), another Carlisle alumnus, graduate of Eastman College, and supervisor of employment with the Indian Office. The Temporary Executive Committee of the organization adopted a six-point platform listing among its objectives the promotion of Indian citizenship and "all efforts looking to the advancement of the Indian in enlightenment which makes him free, as a man, to develop according to the natural laws of social evolution."[61]

At its second gathering on June 20–21, the committee proposed once again "to bring together all progressive Indians and friends of Indian progress for the purpose of promoting the highest interests of the Indian as a race and as an individual."[62] At a convention held on the campus of the Ohio State University in Columbus from October 12 (Columbus Day) to October 16, 1911, forty-three active members changed the name of the organization to the Society of American Indians (SAI), elected officers, defined membership, and outlined objectives. Membership was opened to U.S. Indians (actives), Indians from other parts of the Americas (Indian associates), and interested persons of "non-Indian blood" (associates). Only actives and Indian associates were given the right to hold office and to vote.

A direct result of the convention talks and discussions on legal problems was a bill drafted for presentation to Congress that recommended the creation of an Indian Code Commission to codify the laws relating to Indians. This bill was introduced on January 19, 1912 as House Bill 18334 by Congressman Charles D. Carter (Chickasaw, 1869–1929), an active member of the SAI from Oklahoma, and was continually supported by the organization thereafter.[63] One year later, the SAI would also strongly advocate a bill calling for the admission of tribes to the U.S. Court of Claims. On December 10, 1914, representatives of the SAI presented a petition to President Woodrow Wilson urging him to sign legislation to this effect. Furthermore, it was decided to establish the SAI's headquarters in Washington, D.C.

The platform of the SAI, which regularly endorsed improvements in Indian education, closely reflected the views of contemporary reformers. There can be little doubt that the three major American reform organizations also served as models. Nevertheless, SAI members viewed their organization as a "revival of the old face-to-face discussion around the 'Old Council Fire' composed of Indian men and women not of one tribe only but of all tribes in the United States," and they related its goals to Tecumseh's vision of a great Indian confederacy. Another obvious source of influence came from contemporary American fraternal orders, for almost every male Indian involved in the organization was also a member of a Masonic lodge.[64]

By the time the SAI published the proceedings of its first meeting in April of 1912, its membership had increased to 101 actives, about one-third of whom were women, and approximately the same number of associates. Prominent among the female actives were Marie L. B. Baldwin (Chippewa, born ca. 1864), a graduate of the Washington School of Law, and **Angel DeCora Dietz** (Winnebago, 1871–1919), an artist who studied at the Smith College Art Department and Boston Museum of Fine Arts School. More so than their male colleagues, these Indian women stressed the need to maintain unique Indian cultural traits, especially in the field of art.[65] Strongly represented were tribes from New York, the Great Lakes, Oklahoma, and the Great Plains. At the second annual meeting, a provisional constitution was drafted, reserving active membership for Indians who had more than one-sixteenth Indian blood or those with less if they were listed on tribal rolls. The active members, whose numbers grew to nearly 230 individuals representing almost thirty tribes by the high point of the SAI in 1913, aspired to have more direct voice in the formulation of future Indian policy by means of promotional and educational campaigns and lobbying activities in the nation's capital. In the long run, however, the SAI lacked the financial means, political clout, community support, and intellectual cohesiveness necessary to fulfil its envisioned role of "race leadership."[66]

A major factor contributing to the SAI's difficulties as of 1914 was a constant altercation between the "moderates" headed by **Arthur C. Parker** (Seneca, 1881–1955) and the "radicals" led by Carlos Montezuma over key issues such as the abolition of the Office of Indian Affairs and reservations, SAI membership for Indians employed by the Indian Service, and the prohibition of the use of peyote in certain Indian ceremonies. Another source of conflict within the SAI was the permanent tension between Protestants, who formed the great majority of the active membership, and Catholics. Obviously these differences were dictated by regional loyalty (for example, Catholicism was prevalent among members from the Great Lakes and Peyote religion among those from Oklahoma). That reformers began to lose interest in Indian affairs after 1911, and that America would soon become involved in a global war, undoubtedly helped to curtail the organization's effectiveness. A rather inauspicious thirteenth convention (in reality the twelfth, as the seventh never took place) was held in Chicago in late September of 1923, but the SAI disbanded with little fanfare after the passage of the Indian Citizenship Act of 1924.

The catastrophic results of the General Allotment Act obviously forced many of the "progressive" Indians to reconsider their own positions long before the federal government officially terminated its commitment to coercive assimilation. In 1923 several active and retired members of the SAI, including Henry Roe Cloud, Sherman Coolidge, Charles Eastman, Arthur C. Parker, Thomas Sloan, and **J. N. B. Hewitt** (Tuscarora, 1859–1937), joined respected scholars such as Clark Wissler, Frederick W. Hodge, and Karl Kroeber to form the Advisory Council on Indian Affairs, which came to be known as the "Committee of One Hundred." The memorandum drafted by this body is said to have served as a stimulus for the so-called Meriam Report, prepared by the Brookings Institution from 1926–28 under the direction of Lewis M. Meriam. This report, formulated with the assistance of Henry Roe Cloud, painted a grim picture of the contemporary Indian Service, particularly in the field of education, and initiated a marked ideological shift in American Indian policy that has been referred to by optimists as the "Indian New Deal."[67] **Luther Standing Bear** (Sicangu Sioux, 1868?–1939), former Carlisle student and president of the California-based American Indian Progressive Association, gave an accurate synopsis of the era of coercive assimilation in 1933, one year prior to the passage of the Indian Reorganization Act (Wheeler-Howard Act), which officially terminated allotment:

The attempted transformation of the Indian by the white man and the chaos that has resulted are but the fruits of the white man's disobedience of a fundamental and spiritual law. The pressure that has been brought to bear upon the Native people, since the cessation of armed conflict, in the attempt to force conformity of custom and habit has caused a reaction more destructive than war, and the injury has not only affected the Indian, but has extended to the white population as well. Tyranny, stupidity, and lack of vision have brought about the situation now alluded to as the "Indian Problem."[68]

Although itself a relatively short-lived experiment, the SAI still stands as a major development in Indian-white relations because it marked the beginning of a new form of nation-wide Indian political and intellectual networking that would be carried on more effectively by more enduring organizations such as the National Congress of American Indians (NCAI). Indeed, two key members of the SAI, Arthur Parker and Henry Standing Bear, attended the constitutional convention of the NCAI in 1944. The preamble to the NCAI constitution drafted on November 16 proposed, among other things, "to enlighten the public toward a better understanding of the Indian race; to preserve cultural values; to seek equitable adjustment to tribal affairs; to secure and to preserve rights under Indian treaties with the United States; and to otherwise promote the common welfare of the American Indians."[69]

One of the more effective efforts of the reform movement, apart from the field of education, was the dissemination of literature about the "Indian Problem." Publications such as Helen Hunt Jackson's *A Century of Dishonor* probably did more to arouse public interest in Indian affairs than most other propaganda campaigns of the Friends of the Indian combined. Because many of America's foremost Indian writers were also active members of the SAI—other than those already mentioned the list includes **Gertrude Simmons Bonnin** (Yankton Sioux, 1876–1938) and **John Milton Oskison** (Cherokee, 1874–1947)—the organization's administrative body was not slow to take advantage of this formidable literary potential. On June 25, 1911 the Temporary Executive Committee of the Association of American Indians sent out a statement of intent to approximately four thousand Indians throughout the nation pointing out the vital necessity for an "organization that shall voice the best judgment of the Indian people, and that shall command the attention of the United States."[70] Accordingly, the SAI began publishing its own periodical in Washington, D.C., beginning in January 1913: *The Quarterly Journal of the Society of American Indians,* 1913–15, later renamed *The American Indian Magazine,* 1915–20). The SAI journal covered a wide array of topics, from editorial comments on current national political issues to personal communications about local reservation problems. As such it was not only an effective organ for the dissemination of the philosophy of the SAI but also one of the organization's most lasting testimonials. Partly in response to the prevailing "moderate" stand of the SAI journal, Carlos Montezuma established an independent forum for the "radical" reformist viewpoint, namely his own monthly newsletter entitled *Wassaja* (1916–22).[71]

Professional Indian writers of the early twentieth century also became increasingly aware of each other's work and, consequently, of the emergence of a distinctively Indian brand of literature in America. In a letter addressed to Fayette McKenzie in 1912, for instance, Arthur Parker pondered whether a properly staffed Indian school might not help to further develop "new" Indian literature so that the "poems of [Emily] Pauline Johnson, Alex Posey, the writings of Eastman, Simon Pokagon, Zitkalasa and others might be rescued from oblivion or popularized still further."[72] As Robert Allen Warrior has indicated more recently, "the establishment of the SAI and the interaction of the writers who emerged during the period represent the first coming together of Native intellectuals in a specific political project [and] their various writings are connected in content and context through their associations with one another."[73]

The propaganda campaign initiated by the reform movement in the 1880s also greatly expanded the press forum for American Indian literature. Eastern secular publications such as the Women's National Indian Association's *The Indian's Friend* (1888–1951) and the Indian Rights Association's *Indian Truth* (1924–86), or religious periodicals like the Roman Catholic *The Indian Sentinel: The Magazine of the Indian Missions* (1916–62), all of which focused on national as well as regional issues, frequently included material written by Indians. Also important were the newsletters, newspapers, and magazines published by Indian boarding schools, especially Hampton and Carlisle.[74] Each of these educational institutions promoted the skill of printing as part of their vocational training programs and encouraged contributions by Indians as an example of the successful implementation of reformist educational policies. Various boarding school papers frequently shared news items, constituting an efficient intercollegiate forum for the alumni as well. Together with Indian-launched independent publications such as the SAI's *Quarterly Journal* (*American Indian Magazine*) and Montezuma's *Wassaja,* these periodicals constitute a major source for Indian nonfiction prose from the last quarter of the nineteenth century to the 1920s.

Of course, the boom in Indian literature was also directly linked to more general cultural-historical trends in the United States, such as the rise of the mass publishing industry during the second half of the nineteenth century and its tremendous boost to the production of national newspapers and magazines. Modern mass-circulation periodicals such as *Atlantic Monthly, Century,* and *Harper's Monthly* temporarily showed a marked interest in content by and about Indians, particularly in connection with the local-color movement (ca. 1865–90) with its realistic focus on regional settings and customs. The back-to-nature movement, which began after the Civil War and culminated in a veritable national mania by the close of the century, proved to be highly receptive to expositions on the Indian's "healthy" relationship with the environment. Likewise, the scouting movement and its specialized publications such as *Boy's Life* obviously fuelled the demand for more information about expert Indian "woodcraft."[75] *The Craftsman,* a forum of the turn-of-the-century American Arts and Crafts Movement, also dedicated space to articles about "authentic" Indian material culture. The advent of the "golden age" of American anthropology with the founding of the Bureau of Ethnology in 1879 (known as the Bureau of American Ethnology after 1893), and also the American Anthropological Association in 1902, furthered interest in "vanishing" Indian traditions and observations thereof by knowledgeable Indian "informants." Finally, the rise of secret fraternal brotherhoods such as the Improved Order of Red Men and Ancient Order of the Foresters in the United States after the 1830s and their inherent fascination with "primitive" rituals generated strong interest in Indian customs as well.[76]

However much these different impulses may have encouraged Indian literary production quantitatively, the cultural intolerance of non-Indian editors, publishers, and readers also imposed certain limitations on what Robert Warrior and others refer to as Indian "intellectual sovereignty."[77] This social constraint is partially reflected in many of the works written by "progressive" Indian authors of this period who, with few exceptions, were well aware that they were primarily (though not exclusively) addressing Eurocentric readers. And yet, many Indian authors still made effective use of Western literary conventions as a medium to transmit their own cultural experiences and traditions. They sought to *relate*—a common English term that denotes narration, restoration, and association—their *personal* views on Indian-white relations to a misinformed European-American audience. To do so they had to operate within the extremely narrow margin of racial tolerance that characterized the cross-cultural dialogue in postbellum America. Although shaped by tribal memory, theirs is still an individualistic voice because, as Elizabeth Cook-Lynn cautions, they mostly functioned as self-appointed spokespeople for their respective Native communities.[78]

The "thinking Indian," as the Executive Council of the SAI came to designate its typical active member, was thus directly involved in directing the course of Indian-white relations in a political as well as literary sense. "All through North America, from the Arctic to the Florida peninsula," D'Arcy McNickle observes in *Native American Tribalism,* "the long submerged Indian minority has been discovering the value of the published word, and this may prove to be the decisive force in bringing into being an enduring policy of self-determined cultural pluralism."[79] The "Native American Renaissance," which literary critics usually situate in the latter part of the 1960s, thus really began with the nonfiction prose produced by the New England Christian Indians in the second half of the eighteenth century, blossomed in Indian Territory and the Great Lakes in the second half of the nineteenth century, and reached its first zenith with the formation of a national Indian intellectual network in the early decades of the twentieth century.

Contemporary "thinking Indians," many of whom prefer the designation "indigenous" because it denotes a special relationship to the land, are in the process of developing a tribally oriented methodology for the analysis of Indian-related topics, especially in the field of literary criticism, which they believe are excessively dominated by non-Indians. Consequently, Indian intellectuals have recently published a number of books as well as many articles in specialized scholarly journals such as the *American Indian Quarterly, American Indian Culture and Research Journal,* or *Wicazo Sa Review* in which they discuss and re-evaluate their own roles as authors and mediators in the twenty-first century. As might be expected, in this context they have also voiced ambivalent feelings about the bequest of their "progressive" predecessors. Did they successfully appropriate the English language to create what Simon Ortiz designated earlier as a "National Indian Literature," or do their works represent what Jack D. Forbes once referred to skeptically as a "colonized and submerged literature"?[80] Philip Deloria, for instance, suspects that several of the Indian writers of the Progressive Era trod on shaky intellectual ground when they sought to educate dominant society by "playing" along with seemingly complimentary stereotypes. Craig S. Womack, on the other hand, acknowledges that these "ancestral voices" actually paved the way for what Native authors can accomplish today.[81]

The authors included in this anthology were deeply committed to the welfare of their communities, thus meeting Weaver's criterion of "communitism." In their works there is little indication of an identity problem or floundering in the void between two purportedly incompatible cultures. On the contrary, most of them regarded themselves as being especially privileged members of their communities by virtue of their education, and many opined that traditional Indian ways already encompassed the basic Christian virtues that European-Americans professed to represent. Most of them spoke their native languages, either lived in or maintained regular contact with their communities, and were intimately familiar with tribal matters. Their main personal concern was to make an adequate living in the "white man's world," a basic existential problem that was often aggravated by racialist discrimination.

Indian intellectuals such as the late Vine Deloria, Jr., and Anna Lee Walters insist that tribal peoples have an inherent right to interpret their experiences in accordance with their own value system and that their views must be recognized as a valid component of American history even if they do not conform to mainstream historiography. This is precisely what many of their predecessors attempted to realize, albeit under much more restrictive publishing conditions than their successors have to deal with today. "To present in a just light the true history of the race, to preserve its records and emulate its distinguishing virtues," reads the third clause in the declaration of purpose drafted by the original founders of the SAI (then the American Indian Association).[82] They thus tried to set "the keeping of written records" straight at a time in which American historiography was dominated by the "anti-Indianism" propagated since the days of Increase Mather and inflated to mythical proportions by the likes of Frederick Jackson Turner and Theodore Roosevelt. With few exceptions, the voices in this anthology do not submit to "victimry," to borrow one of Gerald Vizenor's coinages, because the strategies of selective adaptation they advocate represent an alternative and in most cases more enduring response to the historical currents shaping the American frontier experience than the perennial stereotype of the heroic but ill-fated Indian warrior resisting the relentless march of "civilization" to his dying breath.[83] On the contrary, these authors were convinced that Indians still had much to contribute to American society.

Notes

Epigraph: John Sargeant, Jr., "Extracts from the Journal of Rev. John Sargeant," *The Panoplist* 1, no. 6 (November 1805): 270–72. Sargeant's original title was "Extract from the Journals of the Indians, being the Sixth Speech delivered the Delaware nation, residing at Waupekunmekuhk, or White river [Indiana], on the 15th of April, 1803." According to Sargeant, the speeches recorded in his journal were originally written down by the Christian Indians. This speech is generally attributed to Hendrick Aupaumut. For the reply by Tatepuhqsch, Sachem of the Delaware Nation, delivered on August 16, see *The Panoplist* 1, no. 7 (1805): 316–17.

1. See Daniel F. Littlefield, Jr., and James W. Parins, *A Biobibliography of Native American Writers, 1772–1924* (Metuchen, N.J.: Scarecrow Press, 1981), and Littlefield and Parins, *A Biobibliography of Native American Writers, 1772–1924: A Supplement* (Metuchen, N.J.: Scarecrow Press, 1985). Deserving of mention in this context is the American Native Press Archives, University of Arkansas at Little Rock, with its invaluable collection of early writings, some of which can be accessed through its digital library at http://www.anpa.ualr.edu. For critical texts dealing with early American Indian nonfiction prose, see Joanna Brooks, *American Lazarus: Religion and the Rise of African-American and Native American Literatures* (New York: Oxford University Press, 2003); Helen Jaskoski, ed., *Early Native American Writing: New Critical Essays* (New York: Cambridge University Press, 1996); Lucy Maddox, *Citizen Indians: Native American Intellectuals, Race and Reform* (Ithaca, N.Y.: Cornell University Press, 2005); Maureen Konkle, *Writing Indian Nations: Native Intellectuals and the Politics of Historiography, 1827–1863* (Chapel Hill: University of North Carolina Press, 2004); Bernd C. Peyer, *The Tutor'd Mind: Indian Missionary-Writers in Antebellum America* (Amherst: University of Massachusetts Press, 1997); Cheryl Walker, *Indian Nation: Native American Literature and Nineteenth-Century Nationalisms* (Durban: Duke University Press, 1997); Hilary E. Wyss, *Writing Indians: Literacy, Christianity and Native Community in Early America* (Amherst: University of Massachusetts Press, 2000); and Robert A. Warrior, *The People and the Word: Reading Native Nonfiction* (Minneapolis: University of Minnesota Press, 2005).

2. "The keeping of written records" is part of the definition for *civilization*. See *Merriam-Webster's Collegiate Dictionary*, 11th ed., s.v. "Civilization." See also Walter J. Ong, *Orality and Literacy: The Technologizing of the Word* (London: Methuen, 1982).

3. Roy Harvey Pearce, *Savagism and Civilization: A Study of the Indian and the American Mind* (Baltimore: Johns Hopkins University Press, 1965), 135.

4. *Indian Journal* 27, no. 24 (June 13, 1902): 4, columns 1–2, quoted in Leona G. Barnett, "Este Cate Emunkv: Red Man Always," *Chronicles of Oklahoma* 46, no. 1 (Spring 1968): 20–38, citation on p. 30; Daniel F. Littlefield, Jr., *Alex Posey: Creek Poet, Journalist, and Humorist* (Lincoln: University of Nebraska Press, 1992), 138.

5. Jace Weaver, *That the People Might Live: Native American Literatures and Native American Community* (New York: Oxford University Press, 1997), xii–xiii, 43.

6. Ives Goddard and Kathleen Bragdon, eds., *Native Writings in Massachusett,*

2 vols. (Philadelphia: The American Philosophical Society, 1988), esp. 1: 1–23; James C. Pilling, *Bibliography of Algonquin Languages*, Bureau of American Ethnology Bulletin 13 (Washington, D.C.: Government Printing Office, 1891).

7. Wolfgang Hochbruck and Beatrix Dudensing-Reichel, "'Honoratissimi Benefactores': Native American Students and Two Seventeenth-Century Texts in the University Tradition," *Studies in American Indian Literatures* 4, nos. 2–3, (Summer–Fall 1992): 35–47; Jaskoski, ed., *Early Native American Writing*, 1–14; Walter T. Meserve, "English Works of Seventeenth-Century Indians," *American Quarterly* 8 (Fall 1976): 264–76; Peyer, *The Tutor'd Mind*, 33–53; William W. Tooker, *John Eliot's First Indian Teacher and Interpreter, Cockenoe-De-Long Island and the Story of His Career from the Early Records* (New York: Francis P. Harper, 1896); and Wyss, *Writing Indians*, 17–80.

8. Joanna Brooks, *American Lazarus;* John F. Freeman, "The Indian Convert: Theme and Variation," *Ethnohistory* 12, no. 2 (Spring 1965): 113–28; William S. Simmons, "The Great Awakening and Indian Conversion in Southern New England," *Papers of the Tenth Algonquian Conference,* ed. William Cowan, (Ottawa: Carleton University, 1979), 25–36.

9. Henry W. Bowden, *American Indians and Christian Missions: Studies in Cultural Conflict* (Chicago: University of Chicago Press, 1981), 134–63; and Margaret C. Szasz, *Indian Education in the American Colonies, 1607–1783* (Albuquerque: University of New Mexico Press, 1988), 191–217.

10. John Sargeant, *A Letter from the Revd Mr. Sargeant of Stockbridge to Dr. Colman of Boston; Containing Mr. Sargeant's Proposal of a more effectual Method for the Education of Indian Children; to raise 'em if possible into a civil and industrious People; by introducing the English Language among them, and thereby instilling into their Minds and Hearts, with a more lasting Impression, the Principles of Virtue and Piety* (Boston: Printed by Rogers and Fowle for D. Henchman in Cornhill, 1743).

11. Wheelock outlined the history of his school in nine promotional pamphlets published between 1763 and 1775. The first and most important is *A Plain and Faithful Narrative of the Original Design, Rise, Progress and Present State of the Indian Charity School in Lebanon* (Boston: Richard and Samuel Draper, 1763). The subsequent publications were titled *A Continuation of the Narrative of the State, &c, of the Indian Charity-School, at Lebanon, In Connecticut . . .* (Boston, 1765; London, 1766; London, 1767; London, 1769; Hartford, 1771; Portsmouth, 1773; Hartford, 1773; Hartford, 1775). Wheelock also maintained a fairly regular correspondence with some of his former pupils, whose letters he carefully preserved and thus left to posterity an invaluable source of eighteenth-century Christian Indian epistolary writings in English. This correspondence is contained among the Wheelock Papers, Baker Library, Dartmouth College. Some are reproduced in J. D. McCallum, ed., *Letters of Eleazar Wheelock's Indians* (Hanover, N.H.: Dartmouth College Publications, 1932). See also Laura Murray, "'Pray Sir, Consider a Little': Rituals of Subordination and Strategies of Resistance in the Letters of Hezekiah Calvin and David Fowler to Eleazar Wheelock, 1764–1768," *Studies in American Indian Literatures* 4, nos. 2–3 (Summer–Fall 1992): 48–74.

12. Occom Journal, October 4, 1785 through December 4, 1785, Wheelock Papers, Baker Library, Dartmouth College. The name "Brothertown" was probably borrowed from the Delaware Christian Indian community founded by John Brainerd near Trenton, New Jersey (1758–1801). See Susanne Banta Hayes, "John

Brainerd and the First Indian Reservation," *The Indian Historian* 12, no. 4 (Winter 1979): 20–21.

13. John Wannuaucon Quinney was related to Hendrick Aupaumut by virtue of the latter's marriage to Lydia Quinney. See "Speech of John W. Quinney," *Albany Free-Holder* (July 12, 1854); repr. in *Wisconsin Historical Society Report and Collections* 4 (1859): 314–20; "Memorial of John W. Quinney," *Wisconsin Historical Society Report and Collections* 4 (1859): 321–33; "Death of John W. Quinney," *Wisconsin Historical Society Report and Collections 1857–58* 4 (1859): 309–11; Frederick Dockstader, *Great North American Indians: Profiles in Life and Leadership* (New York: Van Nostrand Reinhold Co., 1977), 227–28; Levi Konkapot, Jr., "The Last of the Mohicans," *Wisconsin Historical Society Report and Collections 1857–58* 4 (1859): 303–11.

14. Geoffrey E. Buerger, "Eleazar Williams: Elitism and Multiple Identity on Two Frontiers," in James A. Clifton, ed., *Being and Becoming Indian: Biographical Studies of North American Frontiers* (Chicago: The Dorsey Press, 1989), 112–36.

15. See Marion J. Mochon, "History of the Wisconsin Stockbridge Indians," *Wisconsin Archaeologist* n.s., 49 (1968): 81–95; and Quinney, "Memorial of John W. Quinney," 321–33.

16. Jack Campisi, *The Brothertown Indian Nation of Wisconsin: A Brief History* (Woodruff, Wis.: The Brothertown Indian Nation, 1991); Thomas Commuck, "Sketch of the Brothertown Indians," *Wisconsin Historical Society Report and Collections 1857–58* 4 (1859): 291–98; Will Ottery and Rudi Ottery, *A Man Called Samson* (Camden, Maine: Penobscot Press, 1989), 43–53. See also the Brothertown Indian Nation homepage at http://www.brothertownindians.org.

17. See the Oneida Nation Homepage at http://www.oneidanation.org.

18. Mary K. Cayton, "Social Reform from the Colonial Period through the Civil War," in Charles H. Lippy and Peter W. Williams, eds., *Encyclopedia of the American Religious Experience: Studies in Traditions and Movements* (New York: Scribner, 1988), 3: 1429–40.

19. Linda K. Kerber, "The Abolitionist Perception of the Indian," *Journal of American History* 62, no. 2 (September 1975): 271–95; Robert W. Mardock, "The Anti-slavery Humanitarians and the Indian Policy Reform," *Western Humanities Review* 7 (Spring 1958): 131–46.

20. Kim McQuaid, "William Apes, Pequot: An Indian Reformer in the Jackson Era," *New England Quarterly* 50, no. 4 (December 1977): 605–26; Donald M. Nielsen, "The Mashpee Indian Revolt of 1833," *New England Quarterly* 58, no. 3 (September 1985): 400–20; Russell M. Peters, *The Wampanoags of Mashpee: An Indian Perspective on American History* (Boston: Nimrod Press, 1987).

21. Daniel Littlefield, Jr., "'They Ought to Enjoy the Home of their Fathers': The Treaty of 1838, Seneca Intellectuals, and Literary Genesis," in Jaskoski, *Early Native American Writing*, 83–103; Anthony F. C. Wallace, *The Death and Rebirth of the Seneca* (New York: Vintage Books, 1972).

22. Joyce B. Phillips and Paul Gary Phillips, eds., *The Brainerd Journal: A Mission to the Cherokees, 1817–1823* (Lincoln: University of Nebraska Press, 1998); Robert S. Walker, *Torchlights to the Cherokees: The Brainerd Mission* (New York: Macmillan, 1931).

23. Czarina C. Conlan, "David Folsom," *Chronicles of Oklahoma* 4, no. 4 (December 1926): 340–55; Mary A. Higginbotham, "The Creek Path Mission," *Journal of Cherokee Studies* 1, no. 2 (Fall 1976): 72–86; Clara Sue Kidwell,

Choctaws and Missionaries in Mississippi, 1818–1918 (Norman: University of Oklahoma Press, 1995); W. B. Morrison, "The Choctaw Mission of the American Board of Commissioners for Foreign Missions," *Chronicles of Oklahoma* 4, no. 2 (June 1926): 166–82.

24. Robert Berkhofer, Jr., "Model Zions for the American Indian," *American Quarterly* 15, no. 2 (1963): 178–81; Carolyn Thomas Foreman, "The Choctaw Academy," *Chronicles of Oklahoma* 6, no. 4 (December 1928): 453–80; Carolyn Thomas Foreman, "The Choctaw Academy," *Chronicles of Oklahoma* 9, no. 4 (December 1931): 382–411; Carolyn Thomas Foreman, "The Choctaw Academy," *Chronicles of Oklahoma* 10, no. 1 (March 1932): 77–114. See also Walker, *Torchlights to the Cherokees.*

25. Robert Berkhofer, Jr., *Salvation and the Savage: An Analysis of Protestant Missions and American Indian Response, 1787–1862* (Lexington: University of Kentucky Press, 1965); Clara Sue Kidwell, *Choctaws and Missionaries in Mississippi;* William McLoughlin, *Cherokees and Missionaries, 1789–1839* (New Haven: Yale University Press, 1984); William McLoughlin, *Cherokee Renascence in the New Republic* (Princeton, N.J.: Princeton University Press, 1986); Theda Perdue, "The Conflict Within: Cherokees and Removal," in William L. Anderson, ed., *Cherokee Removal: Before and After* (Athens: University of Georgia Press, 1991), 55–74. See also *Laws of the Cherokee Nation: Adopted by the Council at Various Periods, Printed for the Benefit of the Nation* (Tahlequah, Cherokee Nation: Office of the Advocate, 1852).

26. Annie H. Abel, "Proposals for an Indian State, 1778–1878," *Annual Report of the American Historical Association for the Year 1907* (Washington, D.C.: Government Printing Office, 1908) 1: 87–104.

27. William G. McLoughlin, *After the Trail of Tears: The Cherokees' Struggle for Sovereignty, 1839–1880* (Chapel Hill: University of North Carolina Press, 1993), 86–96. See also Grant Foreman, *The Five Civilized Tribes* (Norman: University of Oklahoma Press, 1934).

28. Theda Perdue points out that, according to the Cherokee census of 1835, only 18 percent of the households had members who read English, while 43 percent contained Cherokee readers, and 39 percent were illiterate. See Theda Perdue, "Rising from the Ashes: The *Cherokee Phoenix* as an Ethnohistorical Source," *Enthnohistory* 24, no. 3 (Summer 1977): 207–17, esp. 213.

29. George E. Foster, "Journalism among the Cherokee Indians," *Magazine of American History* 18, nos. 1–5 (July 1887): 65–70; Henry T. Malone, "The Cherokee Phoenix: Supreme Expression of Cherokee Nationalism," *Georgia Historical Quarterly* 34, no. 3 (September 1950): 163–88; Robert G. Martin, "The *Cherokee Phoenix:* Pioneer of Indian Journalism," *Chronicles of Oklahoma* 25, no. 2 (Summer 1947): 102–18.

30. Daniel Littlefield, Jr., and James Parins, *American Indian and Alaska Native Newspapers and Periodicals, 1826–1924* (Westport, Conn: Greenwood Press, 1984), xi–xxxi. See also James P. Danky, ed., and Maureen E. Hady, comp., *Native American Periodicals and Newspapers 1828–1982: Bibliography, Publishing Record, and Holdings* (Westport, Conn.: Greenwood Press, 1984); Daniel F. Littlefield, Jr., and James W. Parins, eds., *Native American Writing In the Southeast: An Anthology, 1875–1935* (Jackson: University Press of Mississippi, 1995); James E. Murphy and Sharon M. Murphy, *Let My People Go: American Indian Journalism, 1828–1978* (Norman: University of Oklahoma Press, 1981).

31. Carolyn T. Foreman, "Edward W. Bushyhead and John Rollin Ridge, Cherokee Editors in California," *Chronicles of Oklahoma* 14, no. 3 (September 1936): 295–311. Mention should also be made of Creek historian George Washington Grayson (1843–1920), who was intimately acquainted with both Posey and Gibson. See Mary Jane Warde, *George Washington Grayson and the Creek Nation, 1843–1920* (Norman: University of Oklahoma Press, 1999).

32. Helen H. Tanner, ed., *Atlas of Great Lakes Indian History* (Norman: University of Oklahoma Press, 1987), 2–3.

33. Richard White, *The Middle Ground: Indians, Empires, and Republics in the Great Lakes Region, 1650–1815* (Cambridge: Cambridge University Press, 1991), x.

34. Julia D. Harrison, *Métis: People Between Two Worlds* (Vancouver: The Glenbow-Alberta Institute, 1985); and Jaqueline Peterson and Jennifer Brown, *The New Peoples: Being and Becoming Métis in North America* (Lincoln: University of Nebraska Press, 1984).

35. Elizabeth Graham, *Medicine Man to Missionary: Missionaries as Agents of Change among the Indians of Southern Ontario* (Toronto: Peter Martin Associates, 1975); and John W. Grant, *Moon of Wintertime: Missionaries and the Indians of Canada in Encounter since 1534* (Toronto: University of Toronto Press, 1984).

36. For samples of their works, see Penny Petrone, ed., *First People, First Voices*, 2nd ed. (Toronto: University of Toronto Press, 1988).

37. Peter Jones, *Life and Journals of Ka-ke-wa-quo-na-by (Rev. Peter Jones), Wesleyan Missionary* (Toronto: Anson Green, 1860); Donald B. Smith, *Sacred Feathers: The Reverend Peter Jones (Kahkewaquonaby) and the Mississauga Indians* (Lincoln: University of Nebraska Press, 1987).

38. See Vine Deloria, Jr., *Behind the Trail of Broken Treaties* (New York: Dell Publishing Co., 1974), 161–86.

39. See also George Copway, *Running Sketches of Men and Places, in England, France, Germany, Belgium, and Scotland* (New York: J. C. Riker, 1851).

40. James A. Clifton, *The Pokagons, 1683–1983: Catholic Potawatomi Indians of the St. Joseph River Valley* (Lenham, Md.: University Press of America, 1984); Harold Henderson, "This Land Is Their Land," *Reader* 30, no. 11 (December 8, 2000): 1, 44, 46–51.

41. Two other important Central Algonquian authors are Jane Johnston Schoolcraft (Ojibwe, 1800–41) and William Whipple Warren (Ojibwe, 1825–53). Johnston, wife and collaborator of Henry Roe Schoolcraft, produced a number of poems and renditions of Ojibwe oral traditions in *The Literary Voyager; or, Muzzeniegum* in 1826–27. See *The Literary Voyager; or, Muzzeniegum*, ed. with an introduction and notes by Phillip B. Mason (Westport, Conn.: Greenwood Press, 1974). For background information see Maureen Konkle, *Writing Indian Nations: Native Intellectuals and the Politics of Historiography, 1827–1863* (Chapel Hill: University of North Carolina Press, 2004), 166–81; A. La Vonne Brown Ruoff, "Early Native American Women Authors: Jane Johnson Schoolcraft, Sarah Winnemucca, S. Alice Callahan, E. Pauline Johnson, and Zitkala-Sa," in Karen L. Kilcup, ed., *Nineteenth-Century American Women Writers: A Critical Reader* (London: Blackwell, 1998), 80–111. Warren's history of the Ojibway Nation is still widely used by historians today. See Wiliam Whipple Warren, *History of the Ojibways, Based Upon Traditions and Oral Statements, Collections of the Minnesota Historical Society*, vol. 5 (1885): 21–394; repr. *History of the Ojibway Nation* (Minneapolis: Ross and Haines, Inc., 1970; St. Paul: Minnesota Historical Society, 1984). For

background information see W. Roger Buffalohead, "Introduction," in Warren, *History of the Ojibway Nation* (1984), ix–xvii; Konkle, *Writing Indian Nations,* 197–205; Theresa Schenck, "William W. Warren's *History of the Ojibway People:* Tradition, History, and Context," in Jennifer S. H. Brown and Elizabeth Vilbert, eds., *Reading Beyond Words: Contexts for Native History* (Peterborough, Ontario: Broadview Press, 1996), 242–60.

42. Robert Berkhofer, *The White Man's Indian: Images of the American Indian from Columbus to the Present* (New York: Alfred A. Knopf, 1978), 71–111; Werner Sollors, *Beyond Ethnicity: Consent and Descent in American Culture* (New York: Oxford University Press, 1986), 102–48.

43. Brian Dippie, *The Vanishing American: White Attitudes and U.S. Indian Policy* (Middleton, Conn.: Wesleyan University Press, 1982), 102–106, 166–69. See also Robert E. Bieder, *Science Encounters the Indian, 1820–1880: The Early Years of American Anthropology* (Norman: University of Oklahoma Press, 1986); Wilcomb E. Washburn, *The Assault on Indian Tribalism: The General Allotment Law (Dawes Act) of 1887* (Philadelphia: J. B. Lippincott Company, 1975), 10–12.

44. George Harwood Phillips, *Indians and Indian Agents: The Origins of the Reservation System in California, 1849–1852* (Norman: University of Oklahoma Press, 1997); Robert A. Trennert, Jr., *Alternative to Extinction: Federal Policy and the Beginnings of the Reservation System, 1846–1851* (Philadelphia: Temple University Press, 1975).

45. Henry E. Fritz, *The Movement for Indian Assimilation, 1860–1890* (Philadelphia: University of Pennsylvania Press, 1963; repr. Westport, Conn.: Greenwood Press, 1981); Robert H. Keller, Jr., *American Protestantism and United States Indian Policy, 1869–1882* (Lincoln: University of Nebraska Press, 1983); Loring B. Priest, *Uncle Sam's Stepchildren: The Reformation of the United States Indian Policy, 1865–1887* (New Brunswick, N.J.: Rutgers University Press, 1942; repr. New York: Octagon Books, 1969); Francis P. Prucha, *American Indian Policy in Crisis: Christian Reformers and the Indian, 1865–1900* (Norman: University of Oklahoma Press, 1976), 30–71.

46. Keller, *American Protestantism and United States Indian Policy,* 61; Prucha, *American Indian Policy in Crisis,* 50, 53. See also R. Pierce Beaver, *Church, State, and the American Indians: Two and a Half Centuries of Partnership in Missions Between Protestant Churches and Government* (St. Louis: Concordia Publishing House, 1966).

47. Richard Slotkin, *The Fatal Environment: The Myth of the Frontier in the Age of Industrialization, 1800–1890* (New York: Atheneum, 1985), 311. Citation from Thomas J. Morgan's report of October 1, 1890, in Francis P. Prucha, ed., *Americanizing the American Indian: Writings by the "Friends of the Indian," 1880–1900* (Cambridge: Harvard University Press, 1973), 75.

48. Prucha, *American Indian Policy in Crisis,* 113–23.

49. Vine Deloria, Jr., *God Is Red* (New York: Dell Publishing Company, Inc., 1973), 261. See Alexandra Harmon, "When Is an Indian Not an Indian? The 'Friends of the Indian' and the Problems of Indian Identity," *Journal of Ethnic Studies* 18, no. 2 (Summer 1990): 95–123; Prucha, *American Indian Policy in Crisis,* 132–68. See also William T. Hagan, *The Indian Rights Association: The Herbert Welsh Years, 1882–1904* (Tucson: University of Arizona Press, 1985).

50. Cited in Alan Trachtenberg, *The Incorporation of America: Culture and Society in the Gilded Age* (New York: Hill and Wang, 1982), 34.

51. Leonard A. Carlson, *Indians, Bureaucrats, and Land: The Dawes Act and the Decline of Indian Farming* (Westport, Conn.: Greenwood Press, 1981); Janet A. McDonnell, *The Dispossession of the American Indian, 1887–1934* (Bloomington: Indiana University Press, 1991). For a case study of cultural persistence during the allotment era see Donald J. Berthrong, *The Cheyenne and Arapaho Ordeal: Reservation and Agency Life in the Indian Territory, 1875–1907* (Norman: University of Oklahoma Press, 1976).

52. David Wallace Adams, *Education for Extinction: American Indians and the Boarding School Experience, 1875–1918* (Lawrence: University Press of Kansas, 1995), 26–7, 58. On educational programs during the allotment era see also Evelyn C. Adams, *American Indian Education: Government Schools and Economic Progress* (Morningside Heights, N.Y.: King's Crown Press, 1946), 47–65; Alice C. Fletcher, *Indian Education and Civilization* (1888; repr. Millwood, N.Y.: Kraus Reprint, 1973), 161–97; William N. Hailmann, *Education of the Indian*, ed. Nicholas M. Butler, Monographs on Education in the United States, 19 (Albany, N.Y.: J. B. Lyon, 1900), 8–25; Frederick E. Hoxie, *A Final Promise: The Campaign to Assimilate the Indians, 1880–1920* (1984; repr. New York: Cambridge University Press, 1989), 189–210; Margaret Connell Szasz, *Education and the American Indian: The Road to Self-Determination Since 1928*, 2nd ed. (Albuquerque: University of New Mexico Press, 1977), 8–15; Margaret Connell Szasz and Carmelita Ryan, "American Indian Education," in Wilcomb E. Washburn, ed., *Handbook of North American Indians: History of Indian-White Relations* (Washington, D.C.: Smithsonian Institution, 1988), 4: 290–94.

53. On Indians at Hampton see David Wallace Adams, "Education in Hues: Red and Black at Hampton Institute, 1878–1893," *South Atlantic Quarterly* 76 (Spring 1977): 159–76; Wilbert H. Ahern, "'The Returned Indian': Hampton Institute and Its Indian Alumni, 1879–1893," *Journal of Ethnic Studies* 10, no. 4 (Winter 1983): 101–24; Mary Lou Hultgren and Paulette Fairbanks Molin, eds., *To Lead and to Serve: American Indian Education at Hampton Institute, 1878–1923* (Virginia Beach: Virginia Foundation for the Humanities and Public Council in Cooperation with Hampton University, 1989); Donald F. Lindsey, *Indians at Hampton Institute, 1877–1923* (Urbana: University of Illinois Press, 1995); Abraham Makofsky, "Experience of Native Americans at a Black College: Indian Students at Hampton Institute, 1878–1923," *Journal of Ethnic Studies* 17, no. 3 (Fall 1989): 31–46.

54. Richard Henry Pratt, *Battlefield and Classroom: Four Decades with the American Indian, 1867–1904*, ed. Robert M. Utley (New Haven: Yale University Press, 1964), 282–93, 311–15.

55. On the "proletarianization" of Indian education see Hoxie, *A Final Promise*, chs. 6 and 7; Alice Littlefield, "Learning to Labor: Native American Education in the United States, 1880–1930," in John H. Moore, ed., *The Political Economy of North American Indians* (Norman: University of Oklahoma Press, 1993), 43–59; Alice Littlefield and Martha C. Knack, eds., *Native Americans and Wage Labor: Ethnohistorical Perspectives* (Norman: University of Oklahoma Press, 1996). For an opposing view see Francis Paul Prucha, *The Great Father: The United States Government and the American Indian*, 2 vols. (Lincoln: University of Nebraska Press, 1984), 2: 826–35.

56. Trachtenberg, *Incorporation of America*, 34.

57. Theodore Roosevelt, *Report of Hon. Theodore Roosevelt Made to the U.S.*

Civil Service Commission, upon a Visit to Certain Indian Reservations and Indian Schools in South Dakota, Nebraska and Kansas (Philadelphia: Indian Rights Association, 1893), 12. See also Tom Holm, *The Great Confusion in Indian Affairs: Native Americans and Whites in the Progressive Era* (Austin: University of Texas Press, 2005).

58. Philip Gordon (Ti-bish-ko-gi-jik), who attended universities in Rome and Innsbruck, was the first American Indian Catholic priest and last president of the SAI. He edited two newspapers: the *War Whoop* (Lawrence, Kansas) in 1916 and the *A-ni-shi-na-bwe E-na-mi-ad* (Reserve, Wisconsin) in 1918. On the continuing importance of Indian preachers in Indian communities see Ruth Muskrat Bronson, *Indians Are People, Too* (New York: Friendship Press, 1944), 127–56.

59. Susan La Flesche graduated from Hampton in 1886 with honors and went on to study at The Woman's Medical College in Philadelphia to become the first formally trained female Indian physician in 1889. Marguerite La Flesche graduated from Hampton in 1887 and became a teacher at the Omaha Agency. See Jerry E. Clark and Martha Ellen Webb, "Susette and Susan La Flesche: Reformer and Missionary," in James A. Clifton, ed., *Being and Becoming Indian: Biographical Studies of North American Frontiers* (Chicago: Dorsey Press, 1989), 137–59; Norma Kidd Green, *Iron Eye's Family: The Children of Joseph La Flesche* (Lincoln: Johnsen Publishing, 1969); Norma Kidd Green, "Four Sisters: Daughters of Joseph La Flesche," *Nebraska History* 45 (1964): 165–76; Kenny A. Franks, "La Flesche Family," in Frederick E. Hoxie, ed., *Encyclopedia of North American Indians* (Boston: Houghton Mifflin Company, 1996), 324–27; Valerie Sherer Mathes, "Dr. Susan La Flesche Picotte: The Reformed and the Reformer," in L. G. Moses and Raymond Wilson, eds., *Indian Lives: Essays on Nineteenth- and Twentieth-Century Native Americans* (Albuquerque: University of New Mexico Press, 1985), 61–90; Valerie Sherer Mathes, "Susan La Flesche Picotte: Nebraska's Indian Physician, 1865–1915," *Nebraska History* 63 (1982): 502–30; James W. Parins, "LaFlesche Farley, Rosalie," "LaFlesche Picotte, Susan," and "LaFlesche Picotte Diddock, Marguerite," in Gretchen M. Bataille, ed., *Native American Women: A Biographical Dictionary* (New York: Garland Publishing Co., 1993), 146–50; Benson Tong, *Susan La Flesche Picotte, M.D.: Omaha Indian Leader and Reformer* (Norman: University of Oklahoma Press, 1999).

60. Adams, *Education for Extinction*, 48, 244–55; Michael C. Coleman, *American Indian Children at School, 1850–1930* (Jackson: University Press of Mississippi, 1993), 60.

61. "American Indian Association: Purpose," April 4, 1911, in the microfilm edition of *The Papers of the Society of American Indians*, 10 Reels, John W. Larner, Jr., Editor, (Wilmington, Del.: Scholarly Sources Inc., 1987), Reel 2, Frame 02 0593. See also Hazel Hertzberg, *The Search for an American Indian Identity: Modern Pan-Indian Movements* (Syracuse: Syracuse University Press, 1971), 31–209; and Wilcomb E. Washburn, "The Society of American Indians," *The Indian Historian* 3, no. 7 (Winter 1970): 21–23.

62. *Report of the Executive Council on the Proceedings of the First Annual Conference of the Society of American Indians* (Washington, D.C.: 1912), 7–10.

63. Charles David Carter, member of the Democratic Party, served as a U.S. representative from Oklahoma from 1907 to 1927.

64. Hertzberg, *Search for an American Indian Identity*, 55, 101–102, 213–36,

312. See also Arthur C. Parker, "The Indian as a Mason," *The American Indian Magazine* 5, no. 1 (January–March 1917): 81; Arthur C. Parker, *American Indian Freemasonry* (Albany, N.Y.: Buffalo Consistory, 1919). A critical interpretation of Indians and Freemasons is found in Philip J. Deloria, "White Sacheme and Indian Masons: American Indian Otherness and Nineteenth Century Fraternalism," *Democratic Vistas* 1 , no. 2 (Autumn 1993): 27–43; Philip J. Deloria, *Playing Indian* (New Haven: Yale University Press, 1998), 38–70.

65. Carol Batker, "'Overcoming all Obstacles': The Assimilation Debate in Native American Women's Journalism of the Dawes Era," in Jaskoski, *Early Native American Writing*, 190–203. See also *Report of the Executive Council*, 43–55, 58–67, 82–7.

66. The Proceedings of the Second Annual Conference of the SAI are reproduced in the *Quarterly Journal of the Society of American Indians* 1, no. 2 (April–June 1913): 115–255, the constitution is found on 223–29. The "Constitution and Laws of the Society of American Indians" is also found in the *Quarterly Journal of the Society of American Indians* 2, no. 4 (October–December 1914): 324–28.

67. Hertzberg, *Search for an American Indian Identity*, 202–204. See also Institute for Governmental Research, *The Problem of Indian Administration* (Baltimore: Johns Hopkins Press, 1928; repr. New York: Johnson Reprint, 1971), 346–429; "Minutes of the Meeting of the Advisory Council on Indian Affairs Held in the Auditorium of the Interior Department, Washington, D.C., December 12–13, 1923," found in the Arthur C. Parker Papers, 1915–53, Box 2, Folder 51, New York State Library, Albany (Microfilm Reel 2); Hubert Work, *Indian Policies: Comments on the Resolutions of the Advisory Council on Indian Affairs, June 1924* (Washington, D.C.: Government Printing Office, 1924). More recently, the Committee of One Hundred has served as a model and namesake for a special council held regularly at the American Indian Graduate Center in Albuquerque for the purpose of bringing students and reservation elders together to discuss pressing community issues.

68. Luther Standing Bear, *Land of the Spotted Eagle* (Boston: Houghton-Mifflin, 1933; reprt. Lincoln: University of Nebraska Press, 1978), 248–49.

69. Thomas W. Cowger, *The National Congress of American Indians: The Founding Years* (Lincoln: University of Nebraska Press, 1999), 41, 42, 44; Lois E. Harlin, "The National Congress of American Indians," *Indians at Work* (November–December 1944): 18–22.

70. *Report of the Executive Council*, 15–17.

71. Copies of *Wassaja* 1, no. 3 (June 1916) to 8, no. 21 (November 1922) are found in the Montezuma Papers, State Historical Society of Wisconsin, Reel 5, Frames 0741–0845. On the history of the *American Indian Magazine* and *Wassaja*, see Littlefield and Parins, *American Indian and Alaska Native Newspapers and Periodicals*, 10–19, 382–85.

72. Arthur C. Parker to Dr. F. A. McKenzie, January 14, 1912, *Papers of the SAI*, cited in Joy Porter, *To Be Indian: The Life of Iroquois-Seneca Arthur Caswell Parker* (Norman: University of Oklahoma Press, 2001), 103. Emily Pauline Johnson (Mohawk, 1861–1913) was Canada's most acclaimed early First Nations author and elocutionist. Many of her short stories were also published in the United States. See Betty Keller, *Pauline: A Biography of Pauline Johnson* (Vancouver,

British Columbia: Douglas and McIntyre, 1981); Veronica Strong-Boag and Carole Gerson, *Paddling Her Own Canoe: The Times and Texts of E. Pauline Johnson* (Toronto, Ontario: University of Toronto Press, 2000).

73. Robert Allen Warrior, *Tribal Secrets: Recovering American Indian Intellectual Traditions* (Minneapolis: University of Minnesota Press, 1995), 10.

74. See Santee Normal Training School's *The Word Carrier of Santee Normal Training School* (formerly *The Word Carrier,* 1884–1937); Hampton's *Talks and Thoughts of the Hampton Indian Students* (1886–1907) and *The Southern Workman* (1872–1939); Carlisle's *The Indian Helper* (1885–1900), *The Red Man and Helper* (formerly *Eadle Keahtah Toh, The Morning Star, The Red Man,* 1880–1904), *The Carlisle Arrow and Red Man* (formerly *The Arrow, The Carlisle Arrow,* 1904–18), and *The Red Man* (formerly *The Indian Craftsman,* 1909–17, a monthly magazine not to be confused with the earlier school paper); Haskell's *The Indian Leader* (1897–1964); Genoa Indian School's *The Indian News* (1897?–1920); Chilocco's *The Indian School Journal* (formerly *Chilocco Beacon, The Chilocco Farmer and Stock Grower,* 1900–80); Salem Indian School's *The Chemawa American* (formerly *Weekly Chemawa American,* 1897–present); Phoenix Indian School's *The Native American* (later *The Phoenix Redskin, The Redskin, The Redskin News,* 1903–present); and Carson Indian School's *The Nevada American* (1913–16).

75. Elizabeth Ammons, *Conflicting Stories: American Women Writers at the Turn into the Twentieth Century* (New York: Oxford University Press, 1992), 3–19; Richard H. Brodhead, *Cultures of Letters: Scenes of Reading and Writing in Nineteenth-Century America* (Chicago: University of Chicago Press, 1993), 177; Deloria, *Playing Indian,* 95–127; Roderick Nash, *Wilderness and the American Mind* (rev. ed., New Haven: Yale University Press, 1974), 141–60; Don Scheese, *Nature Writing: The Pastoral Impulse in America* (New York: Twayne Publishers, 1996), 28–29.

76. Deloria, *Playing Indian,* 71–94.

77. Warrior, *Tribal Secrets,* xix, 111–15. See also Vine Deloria, Jr., "Intellectual Self-Determination and Sovereignty: Looking at the Windmills In Our Minds," *Wicazo Sa Review* 13, no. 1 (Spring 1998): 25–31; Jack D. Forbes, "Intellectual Self-Determination and Sovereignty: Implications for Native Studies and for Native Intellectuals," *Wicazo Sa Review* 13, no. 1 (Spring 1998): 11–24.

78. Elizabeth Cook-Lynn, "You May Consider Speaking About Your Art . . . ," in Brian Swann and Arnold Krupat, eds., *I Tell You Now: Autobiographical Essays by Native Americans* (Lincoln: University of Nebraska Press, 1987), 58.

79. D'Arcy McNickle, *Native American Tribalism: Indian Survivals and Renewals* (New York: Oxford University Press 1973), 169.

80. Jack D. Forbes, "Colonialism and Native American Literature," *Wicazo Sa Review* 3, no. 2 (1987): 17–23; Simon Ortiz, "Towards a National Indian Literature: Cultural Authenticity in Nationalism," *MELUS* 8, no. 2 (Summer 1981): 7–12.

81. Elizabeth Cook-Lynn, *Anti-Indianism in Modern America: A Voice from Tatekeya's Earth* (Urbana: University of Illinois Press, 2001); Deloria, *Playing Indian;* Donald L. Fixico, *The American Indian Mind in a Linear World: American Indian Studies and Traditional Knowledge* (New York: Routledge, 2003); Devon Abbott Mihesuah, ed., *Natives and Academics: Reading and Writing about American Indians* (Lincoln: University of Nebraska Press, 1998); Devon Abbott Mihesuah and Angela Cavender Wilson, eds., *Indigenizing the Academy: Transforming Scholarship and Empowering Communities* (Lincoln: University of Nebraska Press,

2004); MariJo Moore, *Genocide of the Mind: New Native American Writing* (New York: Thunder's Mouth Press/Nation Books, 2003); William S. Penn, *Feathering Custer* (Lincoln: University of Nebraska Press, 2001); Anna Lee Walters, *Talking Indian: Reflections on Survival and Writing* (Ithaca, N.Y.: Firebrand Books, 1992); Weaver, *That the People May Live;* Jace Weaver, *Other Words: American Indian Literature, Law, and Culture* (Norman: University of Oklahoma Press, 2001); Craig S. Womack, *Red on Red: Native Literary Separatism* (Minneapolis: University of Minnesota Press, 1999).

82. "American Indian Association: Purpose," April 4, 1911, in the microfilm edition of *Papers of the SAI*, 10 Reels, John W. Larner, Jr., ed. (Wilmington, Del.: Scholarly Sources Inc., 1987), Reel 2, Frame 02 0593; *Constitution and Laws of the Society of American Indians* (Washington, D.C.: SAI, 1912), Reel 9, Frames 09 1382 to 09 1391. See also Louis Owens, *Mixedblood Messages: Literature, Film, Family, Place* (Norman: University of Oklahoma Press, 1998).

83. Gerald Vizenor, *Fugitive Poses: Native American Indian Scenes of Absence and Presence* (Lincoln: University of Nebraska Press, 1998); Gerald Vizenor and A. Robert Lee, *Postindian Conversations* (Lincoln: University of Nebraska Press, 1999).

NORTHEAST

THE NEW ENGLAND INDIANS

A SHORT NARRATIVE OF MY LIFE

Samson Occom (1768)

From my Birth till I received the Christian Religion

I was Born a Heathen and Brought up In Heathenism, till I was between 16 & 17 years of age, at a Place Calld Mohegan, in New London, Connecticut, in New England. My Parents Livd a wandering life, for did all the Indians at Mohegan, they Chiefly Depended upon Hunting, Fishing, & Fowling for their Living and had no Connection with the English, excepting to Traffic with them in their small Trifles; and they Strictly maintained and followed their Heathenish Ways, Customs & Religion, though there was Some Preaching among them. Once a Fortnight, in ye Summer Season, a Minister from New London used to come up, and the Indians to attend; not that they regarded the Christian Religion, but they had Blankets given to them every Fall of the Year and for these things they would attend and there was a Sort of School kept, when I was quite, young, but I believe there never was one that ever Learnt to read any thing,—and when I was about 10 Years of age there was a man who went about among the Indian Wigwams, and wherever he Could find the Indian Children, would make them read; but the Children Used to take Care to keep out of his way;—and he used to Catch me Some times and make me Say over my Letters; and I believe I learnt Some of them.[1] But this was Soon over too; and all this Time there was not one amongst us, that made a Profession of Christianity—Neither did we Cultivate our Land, nor kept any Sort of Creatures except Dogs, which we used in Hunting; and we Dwelt in Wigwams. These are a Sort of Tents, Covered with Matts, made of Flags. And to this Time we were unaquainted with the English Tongue in general though there were a few, who understood a little of it.

From the Time of our Reformation till I left Mr. Wheelocks

When I was 16 years of age, we heard a Strange Rumor among the English, that there were Extraordinary Ministers Preaching from Place to Place and a Strange Concern among the White People.[2] This was in the Spring of the Year. But we Saw nothing of these things, till Some Time in the Summer, when Some Ministers began to visit us and Preach the Word of God; and the Common People all Came frequently and exhorted us to the things of God, which it pleased the Lord, as I humbly hope, to Bless and accompany with Divine Influence to the Conviction and Saving Conversion of a Number of us; amongst whom I was one that was Imprest with the things we had heard. These Preachers did not only come to us, but we frequently went to their meetings and Churches.[3] After I was awakened & converted, I went to all the meetings, I could come at; & Continued under Trouble of Mind about 6 months; at which time I began to Learn the English Letters; got me a Primer, and used to go to my English Neighbours frequently for Assistance in Reading, but went to no

School. And when I was 17 years of age, I had, as I trust, a Discovery of the way of Salvation through Jesus Christ, and was enabl'd to put my trust in him alone for Life & Salvation. From this Time the Distress and Burden of my mind was removed, and I found Serenity and Pleasure of Soul, in Serving God.[4] By this time I just began to Read in the New Testament without Spelling,—and I had a Stronger Desire Still to Learn to read the Word of God, and at the Same Time had an uncommon Pity and Compassion to my Poor Brethren According to the Flesh. I used to wish I was capable of Instructing my poor Kindred. I used to think, if I Could once Learn to Read I would Instruct the poor Children in Reading,—and used frequently to talk with our Indians Concerning Religion. This continued till I was in my 19th year: by this Time I Could Read a little in the Bible. At this Time my Poor Mother was going to Lebanon, and having had Some Knowledge of Mr. Wheelock and hearing he had a Number of English youth under his Tuition, I had a great Inclination to go to him and be with him a week or a Fortnight, and Desired my Mother to Ask Mr. Wheelock whether he would take me a little while to Instruct me in Reading. Mother did so; and when She Came Back, She Said Mr. Wheelock wanted to See me as Soon as possible. So I went up, thinking I Should be back again in a few Days; when I got up there, he received me With kindness and Compassion and in Stead of Staying a Forthnight or 3 Weeks, I Spent 4 Years with him.[5]— After I had been with him Some Time, he began to acquaint his Friends of my being with him, and of his Intentions of Educating me, and my Circumstances. And the good People began to give Some Assistance to Mr. Wheelock, and gave me Some old and Some New Clothes. Then he represented the Case to the Honorable Commissioners at Boston, who were Commission'd by the Honorable Society in London for Propagating the gospel among the Indians in New England and parts adjacent, and they allowed him 60 £ in old Tender, which was about 6 £ Sterling, and they Continu'd it 2 or 3 years, I cant't tell exactly.[6]— While I was at Mr. Wheelock's, I was very weakly and my Health much impaired, and at the End of 4 Years, I over Strained my Eyes to such a Degree, I Could not persue my Studies any Longer; and out of these 4 years I Lost Just about one year;—And was obliged to quit my Studies.

From the Time I left Mr. Wheelock till I went to Europe
As soon as I left Mr. Wheelock, I endeavored to find Some Employ among the Indians; went to Nahantuck, thinking they may want a School Master, but they had one; then went to Narraganset, and they were Indifferent about a School, and went back to Mohegan, and heard a number of our Indians were going to Montauk, on Long Island, and I went with them, and the Indians there were very desirous to have me keep a School amongst them, and I Consented, and went back a while to Mohegan and Some time in November I went on the Island, I think it is 17 years ago last November.[7] I agreed to keep School with them Half a Year, and left it with them to give me what they Pleased; and they took turns to Provide Food for me. I had near 30 Scholars this winter; I had an evening School too for those that could not attend the Day School—and began

to Carry on their meetings, they had a Minister, one Mr. Horton, the Scotch
Society's Missionary; but he Spent, I think two thirds of his Time at Sheenecock,
30 Miles from Montauk.[8] We met together 3 times for Divine Worship every
Sabbath and once on every Wednesday evening. I [used] to read the Scriptures to them and used to expound upon Some particular Passages in my own
Tongue. Visited the Sick and attended their Burials.—When the half year
expired, they Desired me to Continue with them, which I complied with, for
another half year, when I had fulfilled that, they were urgent to have me Stay
Longer, So I continued amongst them till I was Married, which was about
2 years after I went there.[9] And Continued to Instruct them in the Same manner as I did before. After I was married a while, I found there was need of a
Support more than I needed while I was Single,—and made my Case Known
to Mr. Buell and to Mr. Wheelock, and also the Needy Circumstances and the
Desires of these Indians of my Continuing amongst them, and the Commissioners were so good as to grant £15 a year Sterling—[10] And I kept on in my
Service as usual, yea I had additional Service; I kept School as I did before
and Carried on the Religious Meetings as often as ever, and attended the Sick
and their Funerals, and did what Writings they wanted, and often Sat as a Judge
to reconcile and Decide their Matters Between them, and had visitors of Indians from all Quarters; and, as our Custom is, we freely Entertain all Visitors.
And was fetched often from my Tribe and from others to see into their Affairs
Both Religious, Temporal,—Besides my Domestic Concerns. And it Pleased the
Lord to Increase my Family fast—and Soon after I was Married, Mr. Horton
left these Indians and the Shenecock & after this I was [alone] and then I had
the whole care of these Indians at Montauk, and visited the Shenecock Indians
often. Used to set out Saturdays towards Night and come back again Mondays.
I have been obliged to Set out from Home after Sun Set, and Ride 30 Miles in
the Night, to Preach to these Indians. And Some Indians at Shenecock Sent
their Children to my School at Montauk, I kept one of them Some Time, and
had a Young Man a half year from Mohegan, a Lad from Nahantuck. who was
with me almost a year; and had little or nothing for keeping them.

My Method in the School was, as Soon as the Children got together, and
took their proper Seats, I Prayed with them, then began to hear them. I generally began (after some of them Could Spell and Read,) With those that were
yet in their Alphabets, So around, as they were properly Seated till I got through
and I obliged them to Study their Books, and to help one another. When they
could not make out a hard word they Brought it to me—and I usually heard
them, in the Summer Season 8 Times a Day 4 in the morning, and in ye after
Noon.—In the Winter Season 6 Times a Day, As Soon as they could Spell, they
were obliged to Spell when ever they wanted to go out. I concluded with
Prayer; I generally heard my Evening Scholars 3 Times Round, And as they go
out the School, every one, that Can Spell, is obliged to Spell a Word, and to
go out Leisurely one after another. I Catechised 3 or 4 Times a Week according to the Assembly's Shout or Catechism, and many Times Proposed Questions
of my own, and in my own Tongue. I found Difficulty with Some Children, who

were Some what Dull, most of these can soon learn to Say over their Letters, they Distinguish the Sounds by the Ear, but their Eyes can't Distinguish the Letters, and the way I took to cure them was by making an Alphabet on Small bits of paper, and glued them on Small Chips of Cedar after this manner A B & C. I put these on Letters in order on a Bench then point to one Letter and bid a Child to take notice of it, and then I order the Child to fetch me the Letter from the Bench; if he Brings the Letter, it is well, if not he must go again and again till he brings ye right Letter. When they can bring any Letters this way, then I just Jumble them together, and bid them to set them in Alphabetical order, and it is a Pleasure to them; and they soon Learn their Letters this way.—[11] I frequently Discussed or Exhorted my Scholars, in Religious matters.—My Method in our Religious Meetings was this; Sabbath Morning we Assemble together about 10 o'C and begin with Singing; we generally Sung Dr. Watt's Psalms or Hymns.[12] I distinctly read the Psalm or Hymn first, and then gave the meaning of it to them, after that Sing, then Pray, and Sing again after Prayer. Then proceed to Read from Suitable portion of Scripture, and so Just give the plain Sense of it in Familiar Discourse and apply it to them. So continued with Prayer and Singing. In the after Noon and Evening we Proceed in the Same Manner, and so in Wednesday Evening. Some Time after Mr. Horton left these Indians, there was a remarkable revival of religion among these Indians and many were hopefully converted to the Saving knowledge of God in Jesus. It is to be observed before Mr. Horton left these Indians they had Some Prejudices infused in their minds, by Some Enthusiastical Exhorters from New England, against Mr. Horton, and many of them had left him; by this means he was Discouraged, and was disposed from these Indians.[13] And being acquainted with the Enthusiasts in New England & the make and the Disposition of the Indians I took a mild way to reclaim them. I opposed them not openly but let them go on in their way, and whenever I had an opportunity, I would read Such pages of the Scriptures, and I thought would confound their Notions, and I would come to them with all Authority, Saying "these Saith the Lord"; and by this means, the Lord was pleased to Bless my poor Endeavours, and they were reclaimed, and Brought to hear almost any of the ministers.—I am now to give an Account of my Circumstances and manner of Living. I Dwelt in a Wigwam, a Small Hut with Small Poles and Covered with Matts made of Flags, and I was obligd to remove twice a Year, about 2 miles Distance, by reason of the Scarcity of wood, for in one Neck of Land they Planted their Corn, and in another, they had their wood, and I was obligd to have my Corn carted and my Hay also,—and I got my Ground Plow'd every year, which Cost me about 12 shillings an acre; and I kept a Cow and a Horse, for which I paid 21 shillings every year York currency, and went 18 miles to Mill for every Dust of meal we used in my family. I Hired or Joined with my Neighbours to go to Mill, with a Horse or ox Cart, or on Horse Back, and Some time went myself. My Family Increasing fast, and my Visitors also. I was obligd to contrive every way to Support my Family; I took all opportunities, to get Some thing to feed my Family Daily. I Planted my own Corn, Potatoes, and Beans; I used to be out hoeing my Corn Some times before Sun Rise and after my School is Dismist, and by this means I was able to raise my own Pork, for I was allowed to keep 5 Swine. Some mornings & Evenings I would be out with my Hook and Line to Catch fish, and in the Fall of Year and in the Spring, I used my gun, and fed my Family with Fowls. I Could more than pay for my Powder & Shot with Feathers. At other Times I Bound old Books for Easthampton People, made wooden Spoons and Ladles, Stocked Guns, & worked on Cedar to make Pails, [Piggins], and Churns & C. Besides all these Difficulties I met with advers Providence, I bought a Mare, had it but a little while, and she fell into the Quick Sand and Died, After a while Bought another, I kept her about half year, and she was gone, and I never have heard of nor Seen her from that Day to this; it was Supposed Some Rogue Stole her. I got another and Died with a Distemper, and last of all I Bought a Young Mare, and kept her till She had one Colt, and She broke her Leg and Died, and Presently after the Cold Died also. In the whole I Lost 5 Horse Kind; all these Losses helped to pull me down; and by this Time I got greatly in Debt, and acquainted my Circumstances to Some of my Friends, and they Represented my Case to the Commissioners of Boston, and Interceded with them for me, and they were pleased to vote 15 £ for my Help, and Soon after Sent a Letter to my good Friend at New London, acquainting him that they had Superseded their Vote; and my Friends were so good as to represent my Needy Circumstances Still to them, and they were so good at Last, as to Vote £ 15 and Sent it, for which I am very thankful; and the Revd Mr. Buell was so kind as to write in my behalf to the gentlemen of Boston; and he told me they were much Displeased with him, and heard also once again that they blamed me for being Extravagant; I Can't Conceive how these gentlemen would have me Live. I am ready to [forgive] their Ignorance, and I would wish they had Changed Circumstances with me but one month, that they may know, by experience what my Case really was; but I am now fully convinced, that it was not Ignorance, For I believe it can be proved to the world that these Same Gentlemen gave a young Missionary a Single man, *one Hundred Pounds* for one year, and fifty Pounds for an Interpreter, and thirty Pounds for an Introducer; so it Cost them one Hundred & Eighty Pounds in one Single Year, and they Sent too where there was no Need of a Missionary.

Now you See what difference they made between me and other missionaries; they gave me 180 Pounds for 12 years Service, which they gave for one years Services in another Mission.—In my Service (I speak like a fool, but I am Constrained) I was my own Interpreter. I was both a School master and Minister to the Indians, yea I was their Ear, Eye & Hand, as Well as Mouth. I leave it with the World, as wicked as it is, to Judge, whether I ought not to have had half as much, they gave a young man Just mentioned which would have been but £ 50 a year; and if they ought to have given me that, I am not under obligations to them, I owe them nothing at all; what can be the Reason that they used me after this manner? I can't think of any thing, but this as a Poor Indian Boy Said, Who was Bound out to an English Family, and he used to Drive Plow for a young man, and he whipt and Beat him allmost every Day, and the young man found fault with him, and Complained of him to his master and the poor Boy was Called to answer for himself before his master, and he was asked, what it was he did, that he was So Complained of and beat almost every Day. He Said, he did not know, but he Supposed it was because he could not drive any better; but says he, I Drive as well as I know how; and at other Times he Beats me, because he is of a mind to beat me; but says he believes he Beats me for the most of the Time "because I am an Indian".

So I am *ready* to Say, they have used me thus, because I Can't Influence the Indians so well as other missionaries; but I can assure them I have endeavoured to teach them as well as I know how;—but I *must Say,* "I believe it is because I am a poor Indian". I Can't help that God has made me So; I did not make my self so.

Notes

The original, dated September 17, 1768, is a separate twenty-six page notebook found among Occom's journals in the Wheelock Papers, Special Collections, Baker Library, Dartmouth College, Hanover, New Hampshire. Courtesy of Dartmouth College Library. Reproduced earlier in Bernd C. Peyer, ed., *The Elders Wrote: An Anthology of Early Prose by North American Indians, 1768–1931* (Berlin: Dietrich Reimer Verlag, 1982), 12–18. That the text has been carefully corrected, changed in several places, and subdivided into sections (chapters?) with underlined headings indicate that it was intended for publication. Occom also wrote a shorter, one-page account of his life dated November 28, 1765 (Wheelock Papers, 765628.1). Occom uses the standard format of the spiritual autobiography to denounce the discriminatory treatment he experienced in the missionary service.

1. Rev. Eliphalet Adams (1677–1753), Harvard graduate and Congregationalist minister, occasionally preached to the Mohegans in 1729. Rev. Jonathan Barber (ca. 1712–61), Yale graduate and Presbyterian minister, instructed the Mohegans from 1733 to 1738.

2. Occom is referring to the "Great Awakening," a massive religious revival which began in Europe around 1720 and then spread along the entire English-speaking Atlantic seaboard during the 1730s and 1740s.

3. Rev. David Jewett (1714–83), Harvard graduate and pastor of North Church in New London, was appointed as minister to the Mohegans by the Boston Commissioners for the Society for the Propagation of the Gospel in New England in 1739; and Rev. Gilbert Tennent (1703–65), Yale graduate and Presbyterian minister, preached to the Mohegans in 1741. Occom's later involvement in internal disputes among the Mohegans over the Colony of Connecticut's questionable appropriation of their lands (the so-called Mason Controversy) and over the legitimate successor to the Mohegan sachemship brought him into direct conflict with Rev. Jewett in 1764–5. Jewett felt that Occom was subverting his authority and brought serious charges of misconduct against him before the Boston Commissioners. Although finally acquitted by the Board on March 12, 1765, Occom nevertheless had to write a humiliating letter regretting his "imprudent, rash, and offensive Conduct." See Harold Blodgett, *Samson Occom* (Hanover, N.H.: Dartmouth College Publications, 1935), 69–83; William De Loss Love, *Samson Occom and*

the Christian Indians of New England (Boston: Pilgrim Press, 1899), 119–29. On the "Mason Controversy" see Francis M. Caulkins, *History of Norwich, Connecticut: From Its Possession by the Indians, to the Year 1866* (1866; repr. Chester, Conn.: The Pequot Press, 1976): 261–70; John W. De Forest, *History of the Indians of Connecticut: From the Earliest Known Period to 1850* (Hartford, Conn.: Hamersley, 1851; repr. Hamden, Conn.: Shoestring Press, 1964), 303–46, 447–89.

4. Occom was converted by Rev. James Davenport (1716–57), a Yale graduate and Congregationalist minister who initiated a religious revival in East Hampton along with Rev. Barber.

5. Rev. Eleazar Wheelock (1711–79), Yale graduate and pastor of the Second Congregational Church of Lebanon, Connecticut, kept a private school at his home for English youths preparing for college. It is likely that Occom's mother, Sarah Samson, was employed there as a household servant.

6. The corporation that funded Occom's education in part was originally founded in England in 1649 as The President and Society for Propagation of the Gospel in New England. It was disbanded during the Restoration in 1660, then reincorporated in 1661–62 as The Company for the Propagation of the Gospel in New England and the Parts Adjacent in America. In 1685 it appointed a Board of Commissioners at Boston, which administered funds for missionary work in New England until 1779.

7. Nahantucket was a Western Niantic village in Connecticut. The Narragansets shared a reservation with the Eastern Niantics in Charlestown, Rhode Island. There was also a Narraganset village in Massachusetts. The Montaukett community, which Occom first visited in the summer of 1749, was located on the eastern tip of Long Island.

8. Rev. Azeriah Horton (1715–77) was a Yale graduate and Presbyterian minister. Between 1741 and 1751 he worked primarily among the Shinnecocks of Rhode Island under the patronage of the New York Correspondents for the Society in Scotland for Propagating Christian Knowledge.

9. In 1751 Occom married Mary Fowler (b. 1730), a member of a prominent Montaukett family. They had eleven children.

10. Rev. Samuel Buell (1716–98), Yale graduate and Presbyterian minister, preached at Occom's ordination ceremony at the Suffolk Presbytery, East Hampton, on August 30, 1759. Buell's sermon was published as *The Excellence and Importance of the Saving Knowledge of the Lord Jesus Christ . . . . A Sermon . . . . at the Ordination of Mr. Samson Occum* (New York: James Parker and Company, 1761).

11. A depiction of Occom's alphabet cards made of cedar chips is found in the original version. He also encouraged the older children to assist their younger schoolmates, long before this measure would become regular practice in American schools with the introduction of the British Lancastrian system in 1806.

12. Isaac Watts (1674–1748), Congregationalist pastor and the "Father of English Hymnody," wrote over spiritual 600 hymns. First published in 1707, his hymns were widely used for religious instruction and readily adopted by the Christian Indian communities.

13. "Enthusiastical Exhorters" were fanatical lay preachers claiming divine inspiration, thereby subverting Church hierarchy.

BELOVED BRETHREN

Samson Occom (ca. 1776)

Beloved Brethren

I Rejoice to hear, that you keep to your Promise, that you will not meddle with the Family Contentions of the English, but will be at peace and quietness. Peace never does any hurt. Peace is from the God of Peace and Love, and therefore be at Peace among yourselves, and with all men, and the God of Peace Dwell with you. Jesus Christ is the Prince of Peace, he is the Peace Maker, if all Mankind in the World Believed in Jesus Christ with all their Hearts, there would be no more Wars, they would live as one Family in Peace. Jesus Christ said to his Disciples just before he left them, Peace I leave with you, my Peace I give unto you, not as the World giveth give I unto you, and again, a New Command I give unto you that ye Love one another.[1] Now Consider, my Beloved Brethren who is the Author of these Bloody wars. Will God Set his People to kill one another? You will certainly say No. Well, who then makes all this Mischief? Methinks I hear you all say, the Devil, the Devil,—so he is, he makes all the Contentions as he sows the Seeds of Discord among the Children of men and makes all the Mischief in the World. Yet it is right for the Peaceable to Defend themselves when wicked People fall upon them without Reason or Cause, then they can look up to Heaven to their God and he will help them.

I will now give you a little insight into the Nature of the English Quarrils over the great Waters. They got to be rich, I mean the Nobles and the great, and they are very Proud and they keep the rest of their Brethren under their Feet, they make Slaves of them. The great ones have got all the Land and the rest are poor Tenants and the People in this Country live more upon a leavel and they live happy, and the former Kings of England use to let the People in this Country have their Freedom and Liberty; but the present King of England wants to make them Slaves to himself, and the People in this Country don't want to be Slaves,—and so they are come over to kill them, and the People here are oblig'd to Defend themselves, they dont go over the great Lake to kill them.[2] And now I think you must see who is the oppresser and who are the oppressed and now I think, if you must join on one way or other you cant join the oppresser, but will help the oppressed. But let me conclude with one word of Advice, use all your Influence to your Brethren, so far as you have any Connections to keep them in Peace and quietness, and not to intermeddle in these Quarrils among the White People. The Lord Jesus Christ says, Blessed are the Peacemakers, for they shall be called the Children of God.[3]

This with great Love is from
Your True Brother SAMSON OCCOM

Notes

The undated letter is in the Samson Occom Papers, at the Connecticut Historical Society, Hartford, Connecticut, Microfilm (0274-0275); it can also be found in Love, *Samson Occom,* 228–29; and in *Journal of Presbyterian History* 52, no. 4, (Winter 1974): 414–15. Reprinted with permission of the Connecticut Historical Society. It was probably addressed to the first emigrating party under Joseph Johnson and David Fowler, which had to find refuge among the Mahicans of Stockbridge. The Christian New England Indians were instrumental in keeping the Oneidas and Tuscaroras peaceful and may very well have been the authors of the celebrated Oneida "Declaration of Neutrality," dated June 19, 1775.

1. John 14:27.
2. George III.
3. Matthew 5:9.

BIOGRAPHY

Samson Occom (Mohegan, 1723–92) was born in a Mohegan village near New London, Connecticut, the son of Joshua Ockham and Sarah Samson. At seventeen he was converted to Christianity by Rev. James Davenport, an apostle of the Great Awakening. The "Pious Mohegan," as Occom came to be known, believed that the Christian ideals he embraced also provided a practical strategy for Indian survival. He was appointed to the Mohegan council by sachem Ben Uncas II on July 1, 1742. On December 6, 1743, Occom enrolled in Rev. Eleazar Wheelock's preparatory school in Lebanon, Connecticut, with a stipend from the Boston Commissioners for the Society for the Propagation of the Gospel in New England (SPGNE). In the course of five years he obtained a thorough education in English and theology. Poor health prevented Occom from transferring to Yale as planned, but his remarkable progress as a scholar motivated Wheelock to establish Moor's Indian Charity School in 1754, a special institution to train Indian missionaries.

Late in 1749 Occom was employed as schoolmaster by the Montauketts of Long Island, also serving as minister, scribe, and legal adviser until 1761. In recognition of his accomplishments as a missionary, Occom was ordained by the Suffolk Presbytery at East Hampton on August 30, 1759. Between 1761 and 1763 Occom journeyed three times to the Oneidas in New York, but his missionary endeavors there were upset by the outbreak of Pontiac's Rebellion in 1763. At the close of 1764, the SPGNE hired him to be a minister to the Mohegans, Niantics, and other Christian Indian communities in Connecticut. He was also taken into service by the newly established Connecticut Board of Correspondents of the Society in Scotland for Propagating Christian Knowledge (SSPCK), headed by Rev. Wheelock.

Following his return to the Mohegans in 1764, Occom became embroiled in a long-standing land dispute known as the Mason Controversy. In sympathizing with the Mohegan faction that demanded restitution, Occom incurred the disapproval of his superiors, who threatened to revoke his license. His relationship with the Boston Commissioners was strained thereafter.

Late in 1765 Occom accompanied Rev. Nathaniel Whitaker on a fund-raising tour to Great Britain. Occom delivered over three hundred sermons throughout England and Scotland, and collected nearly twelve thousand pounds for Wheelock's school by the time he departed in 1768.

Occom's occupational prospects dimmed after his return to New England. The Boston Commissioners refused to reemploy him. His relationship with Wheelock also deteriorated after it became evident that his former mentor was misappropriating the funds he had raised for the express purpose of educating Indians. Dartmouth College, established by Wheelock in 1769 with money collected by Occom, soon evolved into an elitist institution for whites. Although Occom received some financial support from the SSPCK, his subsequent activities were beset with privation.

Sometime in 1773 Occom developed a plan to found Brothertown, an independent community of Christian Indians in Oneida territory in New York. With the assistance of two relatives, **Joseph Johnson** (Mohegan, 1752–76) and David Fowler (Montauk, 1735–1807), Occom enlisted participants from among the Mohegan, Pequot, Tunxis, Niantic, Narraganset, and Montaukett communities in New England. The project was postponed temporarily because of the outbreak of the American Revolution. Occom and his family finally emigrated to Brothertown in the spring of 1789. He taught and ministered at Brothertown and the neighboring Christian Indian community of New Stockbridge until his death on July 14, 1792.

Occom's major work is *A Sermon Preached at the Execution of Moses Paul* (1772), a religious tract that went through at least nineteen editions by the turn of the century. It is thus the most successful example of a unique New England literary genre known as the execution sermon. Beginning in 1675, sermons delivered at public executions were made available in published form and soon became as popular as captivity narratives. They were widely read until the early nineteenth century, when public executions were prohibited. Several hymns contained in Occom's *Choice Collection of Hymns and Spiritual Songs* (1774) are believed to be original and still find their way into contemporary American hymnals. Occom also produced a brief ethnography of the Montauketts, published posthumously in 1809.

The descendants of the New England Christian Indians still honor Occom as an elder who helped them survive through difficult times. On the recommendation of the Montauk Historical Society, a "Samson Occom Day" was celebrated in June of 1970. Members of the Brothertown Indian Nation, now seeking federal recognition in Wisconsin, regard him as their founding father.

Selected Publications of Samson Occom

"An Account of the Montauk Indians, on Long Island." *Massachusetts Historical Society Collections* ser. 1, 10 (1809): 105–11.

A Choice Collection of Hymns and Spiritual Songs; Intended for the Edification of Sincere Christians, of All Denominations. By Samson Occom. New London, Conn.: printed and sold by Timothy Green, 1774.

Sermon Preached at the Execution of Moses Paul, an Indian who was executed at New Haven on the 2nd of September 1772 for the Murder of Mr. Moses Cook, late of Waterbury, on the 7th of December 1771/Preached at the Desire of Said Paul by Samson Occom, minister of the gospel and missionary to the Indians, New Haven, 1772. New Haven: Press of Thomas and Samuel Green, 1772; repr. in *Studies in American Indian Literature* 4, nos. 2–3 (Summer–Fall 1992): 82–105.

Ten Indian Remedies: From Manuscript Notes on Herbs and Roots, by Rev. Samson Occom as Compiled in the Year 1754. N.p.: printed by Edward C. Lathem, 1954.

Unpublished Writings

The bulk of Occom's voluminous writings, including letters, sermons, and a diary from December 6, 1743, to March 6, 1790, are in the Wheelock Papers, Baker

Library, Dartmouth College. Other writings, including a diary from July 5 to September 6, 1787, are in the Samson Occom Papers, 1727–1808, Connecticut Historical Society.

Selected Secondary Sources

Blodgett, Harold. *Samson Occom.* Hanover, N.H.: Dartmouth College Publications, 1935.

Brooks, Joanna. "Samson Occom and the Poetics of Native Revival," in Brooks, *American Lazarus: Religion and the Rise of African-American and Native American Literatures.* New York: Oxford University Press, 2003: 51–86.

Love, William De Loss. *Samson Occom and the Christian Indians of New England.* (oston: Pilgrim Press, 1899. Reprint, Syracuse, N.Y.: Syracuse University Press, 2000.

Nelson, Dana D. "'(I speak like a fool but I am constrained)': Samson Occom's *Short Narrative* and Economies of the Racial Self," in Helen Jaskoski, ed., *Early Native American Writing: New Critical Essays.* New York: Cambridge University Press, 1996: 42–65.

Peyer, Bernd. "Samson Occom and the Vision of a New England Christian Indian Polity," in Peyer, *The Tutor'd Mind: Indian Missionary-Writers in Antebellum America.* Amherst: University of Massachusetts Press, 1997: 54–116.

_____. "The Betrayal of Samson Occom." *Dartmouth Alumni Magazine* 91, no. 2 (November 1998): 32–37.

Richardson, Leon B., ed. *An Indian Preacher in England.* Hanover, N.H.: Dartmouth College Publications, 1933.

Szasz, Margaret C. "Samson Occom: Mohegan as Spiritual Intermediary," in Szasz, ed., *Between Indian and White Worlds: The Cultural Broker.* Norman: University of Oklahoma Press, 1994: 61–78.

Weaver, Jace. *That the People May Live: Native American Literatures and the Native American Community.* New York: Oxford University Press, 1997: 49–53.

Wheelock, Eleazar. *A Plain and Faithful Narrative of the Original Design, Rise, Progress and Present State of the Indian Charity School in Lebanon.* Boston: Richard and Samuel Draper, 1763.

Wyss, Hilary E. "'One Head, One Heart, and One Blood': Christian Community and Native Identity at Brotherton," in Wyss, *Writing Indians: Literacy, Christianity and Native Community in Early America.* Amherst: University of Massachusetts Press, 2000: 123–53.

SPEECHES TO THE ONEIDAS

Joseph Johnson (1774)

Kanoarohare January the 20th AD 1774
A Speech to the Onoida Indians, By Joseph Johnson an Indian of the Mohegan
Tribe, chosen to act on the Behalf of the New England Indians.

Our dear and well beloved Brethren it is with much pleasure that we see so many of you assembled together at this time upon this Occasion. We give you our great respects, and sincere love. We look upon you at present as upon an elder Brother as a Nation, and beloved Brethren, we pray you to consider of us, and harken to us, as to a younger Brother, not only consider of us as two Persons, but view us to be speaking, or acting for all our Brethren in New England, or at least for seven Towns.[1] We pray you to consider seriously of our Words, ye old men who are wise, also ye warriors, and stout hearted young men. Listen unto us, yea let Children harken, that what we say may not soon be forgotten. Brethren in the first place we will acquaint you of the State and Circumstances of our New England Brethren, and also we will inform you of our proceedings hitherto. Brethren we in New England, or at least many of us are very poor, by reason of the Ignorance of our forefathers who are now dead. Brethren ye know that the English are a very wise people, and can see great ways. But some says, that the Indians can see but little ways, and we believe that our forefathers could not see but very little ways. Brethren, ye also know that some of the English loves to take the advantage of poor, Ignorant, and blind Indians. Well so it was in the days of our forefathers in New England. But not to expose the unjust acts of our English Brethren I shall not say much more about them, least I cast a prejudice in your Hearts against the English Brethren. Notwithstanding there are so many wicked, or unjust men, among the English, yet there are great many good, and Just men amongst the English, who loves the poor Indians, from the bottom of their hearts, and wishes us all, a well being in this World, and in the World to come Lifeeverlasting. But all I have to say about the English at present is this Whilst our forefathers were blind, and ignorant, yea drowned in Spirituous Liquors; the English striped them, yea they as it were cut off their Right hands; and now we their Children just opening our Eyes, and having knowledge grafted, and growing in our hearts, and just reviving, or coming to our Senses, like one that has been drunk—I say that now we begin to look around, and Consider and we percieve that we are striped indeed, having nothing to help ourselves, and thus our English Brethren leaves us and laugh. So now Brethren, we leave the English those who have acted unjustly towards us in New England, I say we leave them all in the hands of that God who knoweth all things, and will reward every one according to their deeds whether good or Evil.

Brethren, we seeing ourselves in such Circumstances, began last spring to talk, and to consider together. A meeting was appointed at Mohegan that being nigh the Center, and was attended the 13th day of last March AD 1773, and there was a Vast number of People Men, Women, and Children. There we Met, and then we consulted together. There was present at this Meeting Indians of seven Towns, and it was proposed that certain men out of every town should go out and seek a Place somewhere, for us seven towns to settle down together in Peace. Some were of a Mind to go southward as far as to Ohio, and some not so far that way. Some said we could purchase land nigher and it would not do to live so far from the English. At last it Came into our minds to try to purchase some land from some of the Six Nations. So a time was appointed by our great men, Councilors and teachers, that those Chosen men should go forth one out of every town to seek a Place for us to settle on, and as our spring work was coming on our headmen thought proper that those chosen men should not go till the hurrying work was over, that is after mowing, and reaping, and as it pleased the Tribes to chuse me for one that should come into these Parts to try to get some land upon some terms. I thought proper to send to his Honour Sir William Johnson for advice, in this affair; and I wrote a Letter to his Honor Sir William and acquainted him of all our Circumstances, desires, and purposes, and it pleased his Honor in his great Condescention to take Notice of us, and sent back a word of Encouragement which made many of our hearts glad. And about the time that we was to come up, his Honor Sir William Johnson was down in that part of the Country, which hindered us from coming up then, and there we had an Opportunity to speak with his Honor Sir William. Nine of our Country men went to see Sir William from different Towns and he used us very kindly and still gave us Encouragement. Thus we have been Encouraged from time to time. His Honor Sir William appointed a time for some of our Country men to come up in these Parts, and that was last fall. It pleased Sir William to tell us that would help us as much as he could and advise us in the Affair. And according to the advice of his Honor some of us came to his house last fall, and to our joy He recieved us gladly, and shewed us great respects. Only two of us came up.[2] The reason it is supposed that no more came up to his Honors house is this, a bad News was heard in our Country. We heard that it was dangerous times, we heard that there was a considerable talk of war among the Indians in these Parts, which News discouraged many of our Brethren. But when we came to Sir Williams, He enformed us otherwise, also Sir William acquainted us, with your proceedings at which good News, we were very glad. And our minds was disposed to come even to this town, to converse with you more particularly—but according to your desire and the advice of his Honor Sir William we returned from his House; after he had fully acquainted us of your good will towards us in New England. At that time Sir William delivered to me few lines, so as I might shew them to my Brethren in New England. In them few lines was contained the answer which you gave to Sir Williams Message sent to you by Saghuagarat one of your Chiefs, concerning the Intentions of our New England Brethren, of removing to this part of the World if consistent with the minds of you our Elder Brothers. Not only consistent with your Minds, but also with the mind, or approbation of his Honor Sir William. Yea here is, in my hand the Writting drawn from the Records of his Honor Sir William, which if you please ye may hear, so as things past may be fresh in your Memory again. This Paper or Writting I carried myself thro' Six Towns of Indians in New England. And at every town I called the People together both small, and great, male, and female, and they recieved the good news with great joy. I did not go to the seventh town, by reason of the inconvenience of going by water; and also my Business called me to be at home: so I made as much hast as possible. However they have heard of your good will: and purposed to send one from that Tribe at this time, but perhaps wind was contrary so as he could not get over to the Main. From the Town where I live at present, we sent a Young man, down to Our Brethren few days before we sat away, to stir them up, or awoke them; and to tell them that the time is drawing nigh when we should go, to vizit our western Brethren: and to discourse with them more perticularly; So as we might be fully satisfied what do in the next place, or how we should take the next Step. But our Brethren thought it not Necessary to send great many at this time the reason is this, because there is a great body of snow the face of the Earth, which would hinder us from seeing ground. If there was no Snow, doubtless some of our elder Brethren would now be present at this Meeting to converse with you. But my friends we hope that ye will not be angry with us, because there is no more of us come to this place. There was four of us that sat off together, from four diffirent Towns. But two of our Companions gave out—the one his hip failed him, the other his Back, and they returned, we know not how it is with them. But God who is good—and doeth good continually, gave us health, and Strength, and prospered us by the way, and now in his own due time hath brought us safe to this place, and is allowing us an Oppertunity to [see] your faces in Comfort, and to converse with you in Peace at this time. So to God we give sincere thanks at time, in the presence of you all, for all his goodness towards us. We rejoice that God gave us favour in the Eyes of his Honor Sir William Johnson. And we rejoice that God gave us favour in your Eyes, and we were glad to hear that ye found it in your hearts pity us, or our Brethren in New England when ye heard of our Circumstances and not only we thank you, but all our Brethren in New England gave you their hearty thanks. Yea we have abundant reason to rejoice, we thought to try to purchase Land of you,—But we are exceeding glad that it is in your heart to give us land, yea we thank you that ye have given us so much already.

Brethren this Silver Pipe was sent to me, and this tobacco pouch with it, to dispose of them according to the advice of his Honor Sir William Johnson. Brethren with pleasure I would tell that Sir William recieved us gladly at this time also, and he advised me to deliver this pipe to the Chiefs at the Meeting, and let the Pipe be kept in the Council house Continually, so at your assemblings ye might look on it; and smoke out of it, and remember us your Brothers in New England. His Honor Sir William aid also, perhaps ye would think it very odd if there was no Tobacco in the Pouch, so his Honor was pleased to fill the Pouch, and sent it by me, to your chiefs, that this day ye might smoak out of this Silver Pipe. So now I deliver this Pipe unto you, as a Sure token from our Several Tribes in New England that we are one and sincere in what we say and do. And now our Elder Brothers, I have told you of the State, and Circumstances of our Brethren in New England, and we have enformed you of our proceedings hitherto. And all we desire at present is to know whether ye are of the same mind as ever. Whether your loves, and Pity is the Same towards your Brethren in New England. So our dear friends, and brethren, we leave these few words which I have spoken for you to consider of at present. And hereafter I shall speak few words more for you to consider of. &c&c.

The foregoing speech was delivered by Joseph Johnson, by the assistance of Mr Edward Johnson who acted in the Room of an Interpreter, after a short answer from the Indians, the assembly was dismissed, and could not give a fully answer as they had not time to consider, it being on Fryday towards sun set.

On Saturday towards Evening they gave us an Answer, to our Satisfaction, but were not ready to receive more for Consideration, because several were retired home being now almost night. The meeting was appointed again early on Monday Morning.

January 24th. Kanoaraohare. Brethren we ought all to adore god for his goodness to us from day to day and we ought to bless him, that he is allowing us this opportunity to assemble ourselves together this once more, in this house, to consult together a little about the affairs of this World. Brethren, what we have further for your consideration is this, our purposes, or designs if God willing. This I know my elder Brothers, we may consult together, and agree to do so, and so, yet if it is not the will of God all our Councils, and purposes will come to nought, or all will be in vain. But if it please God, and He open your hearts to pity us, and to recieve us as a younger Brother, and help us in very deed: then will we come up, and settle together in Peace, when you shall think fit, and where it will be most agreeable for us. All we desire is to live in peace, and to have things convenient. [if we cant have land enough we cant have things Convenient. We all have little land in New England, but it is very poor the greatest part, So there we cant have things convenient, that is many of us, and Some are obliged to turn their hands this way & that way to get a Livelihood. The town to which I belong is good Land, and we have Sufficient at present, We could live there this Hundred years yet, if we increased, But we are willing at least Some of us to come up, and Settle down together with our Brethren in peace. True the great drinkers, & Lazy Persons are back ward in coming in these parts, but we are quite willing to leave them there.][3]

Brethren, I am very glad that my Ears have heard, those things which I have heard from you, in your Consultations since we have been in your Town. And as perhaps this is the last Opertunity that I shall speak unto you my elder Brothers at this time, be so kind as to harken to the words of your younger Brother, who would speak this once more in the Name of seven Towns in New England. First, I return you my hearty thanks my elder Brothers, that ye have considered of me; or my Brethren in New England. And I rejoice that ye find in your hearts love, still remaining there, and pity towards your younger Brothers in

New England. I thank you that ye have so deliberately considered of those few words which I desired you to consider, and we thank you for your kind answer which ye gave to us to our Brethren in New England, we thank you that ye have taken us to be your younger Brothers; we thank you that ye look upon us to be of the same Blood as yourselves, and we thank you that ye have recieved us into your Body, so that now we may say we have one head, one heart, and one Blood, and may God keep us united together in very deed untill we both grow white headed, and may God grant, that we may set down together, in his own due time, in peace. And now Brethren we thank you, that according to our desire, ye have been pleased to assemble yourselves together this once more, and my elder Brothers, I have but few words more to communicate unto you which I beg ye would take under your deliberate Consideration. Brothers, ye was pleased last fall to give us an Encouragement of ten miles square, of Land, for which we all was very glad, but in our consultations we thought that it was not quite sufficient. Perhaps we should soon clear so much, or settle so much if prospered, or blessed. Then we should have somewhere else to look, to put our Children on, so as they may live. But our elder Brothers, ye know that it is a very hard thing for Parents, and Children to seperate, and we desire to live together in peace, if it be the pleasure of God our Creator, and Preserver. And Brethren, if it please you to give us Land Sufficient for us, and our Children after us, then will we be glad in deed, and Come and set down in peace Side of you our Elder Brothers. If ye be pleased to give us more land it will gladen the hearts of many poor Indians in New England. We are glad Brethren that ye have so much at your disposal. But thus much I have to say for your present Consideration.

Delivered Jan 24th
Wrote by Joseph Johnson, at Johnson-Hall. 1774.

Notes

The original speeches delivered January 20 and 24, along with the Oneidas' three answers on January 21, 22, and 24, are in the Wheelock Papers, Special Collections, Baker Library, Dartmouth College, Hanover, New Hampshire (774120, 774121). Courtesy of Dartmouth College Library. In the Dartmouth manuscript Johnson's two speeches are recorded concurrently. Copies in Johnson's handwriting are also in the Samson Occom Papers, Connecticut Historical Society. Reproduced in James D. McCallum, ed., *Letters of Eleazar Wheelock's Indians* (Hanover, N.H.: Dartmouth College Publications, 1932), 160–67; Laura J. Murray, ed., *"To Do Good to My Indian Brethren": The Writings of Joseph Johnson, 1751–1776* (Amherst: University of Massachusetts Press, 2001), 206–10, 220–21. English was obviously the lingua franca used at the meeting. Johnson's speeches adhere closely to the oratorical conventions of northeastern Indian diplomacy and thus represent a unique Indian contribution to what has been referred to as "treaty literature." See A. M. Drummond and Richard Woody, "Indians Treaties: The First American Drama," *Quarterly Journal of Speech* 39, no. 1 (February 1953): 15–24; Lawrence C. Wroth, "The Indian Treaty as Literature," *Yale Review* (July 1928): 749–66.

1. Seven towns: Charleston, Groton, Stonington, Niantic, Farmington, Montauk, and Mohegan.

2. Joseph Johnson and Elijah Wampy (Tunxis, 1734–ca. 1802) met with William Johnson at his residence in New York, Johnson Hall, on October 27, 1773. At this time William Johnson handed them a letter indicating that five representatives of the Oneidas had arrived there on October 15 and attesting that their people were willing to comply with the New England Christian Indians' request. The letter also suggested a council meeting be held to settle the matter after the hunting season. A copy of this document, written by Joseph Johnson on August 23, 1774, is in the Wheelock Papers.

3. The additional lines in brackets are in the copy found in the Samson Occom Papers, at the Connecticut Historical Society, Hartford, Connecticut. In this version the speeches are recorded separately. Cited in Murray, ed., *"To Do Good to My Indian Brethren,"* 221.

BIOGRAPHY

Joseph Johnson (Mohegan, 1751–76) was born in the Mohegan village near New London, Connecticut, the son of Elizabeth Garrett and Joseph Johnson, Sr. He was enrolled at Wheelock's Indian Charity School on December 7, 1758, where he studied for about seven years. In the winter of 1766, Wheelock sent him to New York to serve as schoolmaster to the Oneidas. Following a drinking spree in the spring of 1769, Johnson left Oneida in disgrace and made his way to Providence, Rhode Island, where he briefly taught school and then shipped out on a whaler.

After returning to Mohegan on October 9, 1771, he experienced a spiritual rebirth under the tutelage of Samson Occom. In November of 1772 Johnson obtained a commission from the Boston Commissioners to teach a group of Tunxis Indians at Farmington. In December of the following year he married Occom's daughter, Tabitha, who bore him a son. Finally, on August 25, 1774, Johnson was licensed as a minister at Dartmouth College.

Joseph Johnson began concentrating his efforts on the voluntary removal of the New England Christian Indians to Oneida territory almost immediately after his redemption. Being much younger than Occom, he soon became the driving force behind its realization. In the years between 1773 and the outbreak of the American Revolution he traveled repeatedly between Connecticut and New York in order to negotiate with the Oneidas for an appropriate tract of land, initiated several fund-raising ventures, and wrote numerous letters of solicitation to prominent citizens and colonial administrative bodies requesting their aid for the "grand Design" of teaching the Western Indians.

The New England Christian Indians elected him as their principal speaker for the project. The American Revolution temporarily interrupted the migration shortly after Johnson, David Fowler (Mohegan, 1735–1807) and Elijah Wampy (Tunxis, 1734–ca.1802) had led the first group of immigrants to Oneida in March 1775. During the early stages of the war, when the first group of emigrants was forced to leave its new settlement in Oneida facing the advance of British troops, Johnson acted as the Americans' peace emissary to the Six Nations. The Provincial Congress of New York presented commissions to him on June 22, 1775, as did the New Hampshire House of Representatives on January 16, 1776. George Washington, with whom he had conferred personally before embarking upon his delicate mission, wrote him a letter of recommendation on February 20, 1776. The diplomatic efforts by Johnson and other New England Christian Indians acting as couriers are thought to have been a decisive factor in the Oneidas' and Tuscaroras' final decision to remain neutral in spite of Tory anti-American propaganda and British political pressure.

Johnson died only five years after his reformation, at the tender age of twenty-six. The exact date and cause of his death remain unknown. During his short life Johnson had at least one manuscript published, namely a letter of exhortation titled "Letter from *J——h J——n,* one of the Mohegan Tribe of

Indians, to his Countryman, *Moses Paul,* under Sentence of Death, in New-Haven Goal" (1772). His numerous manuscripts, only recently published, show that Joseph Johnson was one of the most talented and verbose authors to emerge from Wheelock's Indian Charity School.

Selected Publications of Joseph Johnson

"Letter from J——h J——n, one of the Mohegan Tribe of Indians, to his Country-man, *Moses Paul,* under Sentence of Death, in New-Haven Goal." New London, Conn.: Press of Timothy Greene?, 1772.

McCallum, James D., ed. *Letters of Eleazar Wheelock's Indians.* Hanover, N.H.: Dartmouth College Publications, 1932: 123–99. Contains letters and speeches by Johnson.

Murray, Laura J., ed., *"To Do Good to My Indian Brethren": The Writings of Joseph Johnson, 1751–1776.* Amherst: University of Massachusetts Press, 2001.

Selected Secondary Sources

Murray, Laura J. "Introduction," in Murray, ed., *"To Do Good to My Indian Brethren": The Writings of Joseph Johnson, 1751–1776.* Amherst: University of Massachusetts Press, 2001: 1–49.

Murray, Laura J. "What Did Christianity Do for Joseph Johnson? A Mohegan Preacher and His Community," in *Possible Pasts: Becoming Colonial in Early America,* edited by Robert St. George. Ithaca: Cornell University Press, 2000: 160–80.

Wyss, Hilary E. "'One Head, One Heart, and One Blood': Christian Community and Native Identity at Brotherton," in Hilary E. Wyss, *Writing Indians: Literacy, Christianity and Native Community in Early America.* Amherst: University of Massachusetts Press, 2000: 123–53.

HISTORY OF THE MUH-HE-CON-NUK INDIANS

Hendrick Aupaumut (ca. 1790)

[The country formerly owned and possessed by Muh-heakunnuk nation, now called by white people Stockbridge Indians, is situated partly in the State of New York, partly in Massachusetts and Vermont.

The face of this country is in many places mountainous, supplied with excellent rivers, creeks and ponds; the side of these rivers, &c. was only known by natives capable of producing skommonun, or Indian corn, and tupohquaun or beans, and uhnunnekuthkoatkun or Indian squashes, until it fell into the hands of white people, who convert even many swamps and rocky hills into fruitful fields.

This extensive country abounded with almost every kind of wild game, such as moose, deer, bears, tigers, wolves, beavers, otters, minks, muskrats, martins, wild cats, fishes, ground hogs, back hogs. Of the feathered kind, turkies, wild geese, ducks, partridges, pigeons, quails, owls, &c. and the rivers, &c. abounded with variety of fish and turtles.

The inhabitants chiefly dwelt in little towns and villages. Their chief seat was on Hudson's river, now it is called Albany, which was called Pempotowwuthut, Muhhecanneuw, or the fire place of the Muhheakunnuk nation, where their allies used to come on any business whether relative of the covenants of their friendship, or other matters.

The etymology of the word Muhheakunnuk, according to original signifying, is great waters or sea, which are constantly in motion, either flowing or ebbing.

Our forefathers asserted, that their ancestors were emigrated from west by north of another country; they passed over the great waters, where this and the other country is nearly connected, called Ukhkokpeck; it signifies snake water, or water where snakes abounded; and that they lived by side of great water or sea, from whence they derive the name of Muhheakunnuk nation. Muhheakunneuw signifies a man of Muhheakunnuk tribe. Muhhekunneyuk is a plural number.

We understand that they were more civilized than what Indians are now in the wilderness; it was said that they lived in towns, and were very numerous, until there arose a mighty famine which obliged them to disperse throughout the regions of the wilderness after sustenance, and at length lost their ways of former living, and apostatized.][1] As they were coming from the West, they found many great waters, but none of them flowing and ebbing like Muh-he ku-nuk, until they came to Hudson River. Then they said one to another—this is like Muh-he-con-nuk, our nativity. And when they saw that game was very plenty in that country, they agreed to kindle fire there, and hang a kettle whereof they and their children after them may dip out their daily refreshment. (The name of the Hudson was Mahecanittuck). As our fathers had no

63

art of manufacturing any sort of metal, they had no implements of husbandry, therefore were not able to cultivate their lands but little—that of planting shammonon, or Indian corn, beans, and little squashes, which was chiefly left under the management of women, and old men who are incapable of hunting, and little boys. They made use of bone, either moose, bear's, deer's shoulder plate instead of hoe, to hoe their corn with tie it fast to one end of a stick or helve made for that purpose.

Their way of Clearing lands was not so difficult as we should imagine, and that without using an axe. When they find that their fields will fall, they are to prepare another piece of land. In the first place they do make fire around the foot of every tree, as many trees standing on the ground which they intended to clear, until the barks of trees burnt through; or trees are killed very easy in this manner. They planted while trees are standing, after they are killed. And as soon as trees is fell, they burnt it off such length that they might roll the logs together, and burnt them up to ashes. Thus they do till they get it quite clear. An industrious woman, when great many dry trees are fallen, could burnt off as many logs in one day as a smart man could chop in two or three days time with an axe. They make use of only a Hthon-ne tmuh-hecon, or a stone axe, something like the shape of an axe—helve to it, as of the hoe already mentioned, with which they rub the coals of the burning logs. But the employment of men was consisted in hunting and fishing. They used bow and arrows to kill game, with which they were very expert. They also used to catch deer by insnaring them with strings. By hunting they supplied themselves with both clothing and diet. They seldom feel much want, and they were very well contented in their condition; having food and raiment was their only aim. They were not to kill more than necessary, for there was none to barter with them that would have tempted them to waste their animals, as they did after the Chuh-ko-thuk came on this Island; consequently, game was never diminished.

They hunted occasionally whole year; but hunting seasons are properly divided into two parts of a year. In fall they hunt for deer, bear, beaver, otter, raccoon, fisher, martin, for their clothing, and drying meat for the ensuing season; and in the beginning of March they used to go out to hunt for moose on the Green Mountains, where these animals keep for winter quarters. From thence they go again for beaver hunting soon as the rivers, ponds, and creeks are opened, but they used to take good care not to stay over two months.

And as our ancestors were not subject to so many disorders, or sicknesses, as they were after Chuh-ko-thuk, or white people settled amongst them, they flourished in some measure—that before they began to decay. Our fathers informed us that Muh-he-con-nuk Nation could then raised about one thousand warriors who could turn out at any emergency. Their weapons of war, besides bow and arrows, already described, Puh-wy, made of wooden knot, helve to it, and Quen-neh-tuh he-con, or long cut, and Thut-te-con, or spear, made of bone or horn, and some of flinty stone, with long helve to it. They also wear quiver, commonly made of otter skin, which contain forty or fifty arrows; and in battle they use shields made of green hide, doubled two or three times;

and when it's dry so hard that sharpest arrow cannot penetrated. They also wear Hpe-thoon, made of green hide, or breastplate.

Muh-he-con-nuk Nation formerly deemed to be the best warriors in the field, truly formidable to any nation, which still acknowledged by the western tribes; for number of our nation have lived among almost every nation in westward to this day, and they used to go with these nations in all their wars; and they ever proved the characteristicalness of their ancestors—Muh-he-con-ne-yuk.

And our forefathers also distinguished in peaceableness, whereby they had allies, even the remotest nations; and according to the ancient custom many of these nations made renewal of the covenants with us which their forefathers and ours had made, with belts and strings of wampum. Some of the belts and strings are now in our possession. The friendships which our forefathers had between different nations were denominated after the manner of common relations.

And according to the ancient covenant of our ancestors, the Delaware nation are our Grandfathers. And the Shawanoe nation, when they were ready to be devoured by their enemies, the different nations, they sent runners to Muh-hu-con-nuk for help. Then our forefathers went to stand between the Shawanoe and the different tribes, to act as mediators, and to defend them. They rescued them from under the jaws of their enemies. The Shawanoe nation then called the Muh-hu-con-nuk nation to be their Elder Brothers, and promise obedience to them, which they still acknowledged to this day; and they are our Younger Brothers, or Nkheeth-mon nauk. There they left them under the care of the Delaware nation, their Grandfather.

Wmau-weew, or Miami nation, formerly had war with our nation, and when they were conquered they obliged to sue peace; and when peace was established, they enter into covenant of friendship with our nation, and kindle fire for them at Kekioke, near the head of the Miami River, which empties into Lake Erie, and voluntarily given them a large tract of land, wherein they desired them to live, and to be their head; they offered obedience to them as grandchildren ordinarily obey their grandfathers. But as our forefathers loved not superiority over their fellow Indians, or using authority as tyrants over any nation, they only accepted the present given to them out of friendship, remembering that it may in time to come, our children some occasion or other would come and live there. From that time the tract of land has been reserved for our nation to this day, and that covenant had been renewed at different times, and a number of our nation live on that land these several years past to this day. Therefore the Miami nation are our Grandchildren to this day; and also their allies, to wit, Wtuw-waw, or Uttawa Nation, Wchip-pow-waw, or Chipiwa Nation, Mi-si-sau-ky, Pot-au-waut-om-meew, Wnau-to-wuh-theh, Wthau-keew, Ke-kep-poow, Pa-sa-ke-yah, Wauw-yuh-ton-noow, and Mk-huth-ko-tau-weew.— All these nations ever acknowledge this friendship; and whenever they met any of our people they call them Muh-so-mis, or Grandfathers. These nations inhabit northwest of Ohio.

Kut-tooh-waw, or Cherokees, are our younger brothers, who has invited us to move our fire-place and kindled by the side of their fire-place; they offered to give us a large tract of land by belt of beads which we had in our bag to this day.

Mush-oow, or Creek Nation, the head of their confederacy also manifested their friendship with us with belt of wampum, and gave us invitation in like manner as Cherokees did.

Wmin-theew, Wnuh-thoow, Kuh-nau-wau-thuw—these three nations are our brothers according to the ancient covenant of our forefathers.

And the Seven Nations of Canada are our brothers also, who has renewed that covenant with us last Summer.[2] And part of the Six Nations are our Uncles, to wit, Mohawks, Onondagas, Cayogas, and Senecas. But the Oneidas, and Tuscaroras are our brothers. (The Oneidas were younger brethren).

Our ancestors, before they ever enjoyed Gospel revelation acknowledged one Supreme Being who dwells above, whom they styled Waun-theet Monnit-toow, or the Great, Good Spirit, the author of all things in heaven and on earth, and also believed that there is an evil one, called Mton-toow or Wicked Spirit that loves altogether to do mischief; that he excites person or persons to tell a lie—angry, fight, hate, steal, to commit murder, and to be envious, malicious, and evil-talking; also excites nations to war with one another, to violated their friendship which the Great, Good Spirit given them to maintain for their mutual good, and their children after them.

In Order to please the Great, Good Spirit which they acknowledged to be their dependence, and on the other hand to withstand the evil one—therefore, the following custom was observed, which handed down to them by their forefathers, and considered as communicated to them by Good Spirit.

The Head of each family—man or woman—would began with all tenderness, as soon as daylight, to waken up their children and teach them, as follows:

"My Children—you must remember that it is by the goodness of the Great, Good Spirit we are preserved through the night. My Children you must listen to my words. If you wish to see many good days and evenings you must love to all men, and be kind to all people.

"If you see any that are in distress, you must try to help them. Remember you must give him something to eat; though you should have but little cake, give him half of it, for you also liable to hunger. If you see one naked, you must cover him with your own raiment. For you must consider that some future time you will also stand in need of such help; but if you will not assist, or have compassion for the poor, you will displease the Good Spirit; you will be called Uhwu-theet, or hard-hearted, and nobody will pity on you the time of your distress, but will mock at you.

"My little Children, if you see aged man or woman on your way doing something, you must pity on them, and help them instantly. In so doing, you will make their hearts glad, and they will speak well of you. And further, if you see your neighbors quarreling, you must try to make them to be good friends again. And you must always listen to the instruction of old folks: thereby you will be wise. And you must not be hasty to speak, when you hear people talking, nor allow yourself too much laughing. And if you find any that will speak evil against you, you must not speak evil words back, but shut your ears and mouth as though you hear nothing, and shun such people. And you must never quarrel to any person for quarreling is belongs to evil spirit, and beast. But live in peace with all people: thereby you will please the Great, Good Spirit, and you will be happy.

"My little Children—you must be very kind to strangers. If you see stranger or strangers come by the side of your fire-place, you must salute them, and take them by the hand, and be friendly to them; because you will be a stranger some time or other. You must never speak any harsh word to strangers, but use them well as you can; thereby they will love you and will speak well of you wherever they be; and if you ever come into a strange country you will meet with such kindness. But if you will not be friendly to such, you will be in danger wherever you go.

"My Children—again listen. You must be honest in all your ways. You must always speak nothing but the truth wherever you are. But if you should love to tell lie, everybody will take notice of it; thereby you will bring a bad name to yourself. For instance—whenever people shall see you walking, they will say one to another with scorn, and point at you 'look at that liar!' and even when you should bring tidings of importance with the truth, they shall not regard what you say.

"My Children—you must never steal anything from your fellow men, for remember this—you will not be pleased if some of your neighbors should take away your things by way of stealing; and you must also remember that the Great, Good Spirit see you. But if you will allow yourself to steal, you will hurt your name, and disgrace your parents and all relations; and you will be despised by all good people.

"My Children—you must always avoid bad Company. And above all, *you* must never commit murder, because you wish to see long life. But if *you* commit murder, the Great, Good Spirit will be angry with you, and your life will be in great danger; also the life of your dear relations.

"My Children—you must be very industrious. You must always get up early morning to put on your clothes, muk-sens, and tie your belt about you, that you may be ready to do something; by so doing you will always have something to eat and to put on. But if you will be lazy, you will be always poor. Your eyes shall be on those who are industrious, and perhaps you will be shamefully beg or steal; and none will give you anything to eat without grudging.

"And further, my Children—when you grown up, you must not take wife or husband without the consent of your parents and all relations. But if you will do contrary to this, perhaps you will be joined to one who will bring great darkness to you, and thereby you will be very unhappy.

"My Children—at all times you must obey your Sachem and Chiefs, in all good counsels they give; never to speak evil against them, for they have taken much pains in promoting your happiness. And if you do not observe this, you will be looked upon worse than the beasts are."

Thus they inculcate instruction to their children day after day until they are grown up; and after they are grown, yet they would teach them occasionally. And when young people have children they also teach theirs in like manner.— This custom is handed down from generation to another; at the same time it may be observed that there were some that did not take no pains to instruct their children, but would set bad examples before them, as well as there are such among civilized nations. But such men were roving about, and could not be contented to stay at one place.

Our ancestors' Government was a Democratical. They had Wi-gow-wauw, or Chief Sachem, successively, as well as other nations had, chosen by the nation, whom they looked upon as conductor and promoter of their general welfare, and rendered him obedience as long as he behaved himself agreeably to the office of a Sachem. And this office was hereditary by the lineage of a female's offspring, but not on man's line, but on woman's part. That is when Wi-gow-wauw is fallen by death, one of his Nephews, (if he has any) will be appointed to succeed his Uncle as Sachem, and not any of his sons.

The Sachem always have Woh-weet-quan-pe-chee, or Counselors, and one Mo-quau-pauw, or Hero, and one Mkhooh-que-thoth, or Owl, and one Un-nuh-kau-kun, or Messenger, or Runner; and the rest of the men are called young men. (But the Six Nations call young men Warriors.) The Sachem is looked upon as a great tree under whose shade the whole nation is sit. His business is to contemplate the welfare of his people day and night—how to promote their peace and happiness. He also ever take pains to maintain and brighten the belt of friendship with all their allies. When he find any business of public nature, he is to call his counselors together to consult with them; and then they will determine what is good for the Nation. The Sachem must be a peaceable man—has nothing to do with wars—but he is at times go from house to house to exhort his people to live in unity and peace.

zzproach any man to ask reward for any of his public Services; but whatever he does for his nation must be done out of friendship and good will. But it was the custom to help their Sachem voluntarily in building a long We-ko-wohm, or wigwam, all complete; and the hunters, when they returned from hunting each man give him a skin. The women also at times, some give him Mkith-non, or Muk-sens, some belts for the body, others garters, and some other Orna-ments—as wampum to be for his own use. They are also to bring victuals to Sachem's to enable him to feed strangers; for whenever strangers arrived at their fireplace they are directed to go to Sachem's house. There they stay until their business is completed.

The Sachem is allowed to keep Mno-ti, or peaceable bag, or bag of peace, containing about one bushel, some less.—This bag is made of Weeth-kuhn-pauk, or bitter sort of hemp: grows on intervals, about three or four feet long; and sometimes made of Wau-pon-nep-pauk, or white hemp, which grows by the side of rivers, or edge of marshes.—amazing strong and lasting—of which they make strings, and die part of the strings different colors; then worked and made into bag of different marks. In this bag they keep all belts and strings which they received of their allies of different nations. The bag is, as it were, unmoveable; but it is always remain at Sachem's house, as hereditary with the office of a Sachem; and he is to keep the Pipe of Peace, made of red hard stone—a long stem to it. Besides this bag, they keep other smaller bags which they call Ne-mau-won-neh Mno-ti, or Scrip, which contains nourishment on journey, which they carry with them when they go out to hold treaties with other fire-places. In such scrips they occasionally put belts and strings for transacting business abroad. When they find the wampum will be fall short, besides what is kept in the bag, the Sachem and his counselors would sent their runner to gather or collect wampum from their women, which business they called mauw-peen, or sitting into one place.

The office of Counselors was not gotten by hereditary, but it was elective; therefore, the wise men were only entitled to the office of Counselors. They are called Chiefs. Their business is to consult with their Sachems in promoting peace and happiness for their people. They will also at all times exhort young people to every good work.

The title of Mo-quau-pauw, or Hero, is gotten only by merit; by remarkable conduct in the wars, by great courage and prudence. The business of Heroes in time of peace is to sit with their Sachem and Counselors in all their councils, and to confirm their agreements, but never to contradict them; for which they are beloved by their Sachem and Counselors, and by all their people. But when any warfare is sounded in their ears, then they will all meet together to hold a general Council: and when they find themselves under necessity of joining to such war, then the Sachem and Counselors will put the business in the hands of Heroes, exhorting them to be courageous and prudent, to take good care of their young men. But when the offers of peace is proposed, then the Hero will put the business in the hands of the Sachem and Counselors, who will cut or break the string of the bow, and bury the Puh-wi, and by certain ceremony or emblem wipe off all tears and blood, and cleanse their beds, scattered all dark clouds, that they may enjoy pleasant days again.

The office of Owl is come by merit also; who must have strong memory, and must be good Speaker, and have strong voice. He is to sit by the side of his Sachem; his business is to proclaim the orders of his Sachem to the people with loud voice. And he is also to get up every morning as soon as daylight. In the first place he is to make noise like an Owl, then shouted to wake the people, and then ordered them to their respective lawful duties for the day.

And the business of the Runner is to carry messages, or carry tidings; and he is always ready to run. He is to give notice to the people to attend. And when they go out another town to hold council, he is to run to inform the Chiefs that live in that town that his Chiefs will arrive—such a time. And when they hold treaty with any nation he is to light his Sachem's Pipe. And he must be a man of veracity: for if he tell a falsehood, his feathers will be pulled off.

Our Nation was divided into three clans or tribes, as Bear Tribe, Wolf Tribe, and Turtle Tribe. Our ancestors had particular opinion for each tribe to which they belonged. The Bear Tribe formerly considered as the head of the other tribes, and claims the title of hereditary office of Sachem. Yet they ever united as one family.

And at the death of Sachem they considered as though their light is put out, and sitting under dark clouds, and in the situation of mourning until another is appointed to succeed in the office; which must be done by the consent and approbation of the whole nation. Yet no other person has right to succeed but one of the nephews of the deceased Sachem, either the eldest, or the likeliest.

One of the wisest of their Counselors is employed on such occasions. In the first place, when all things are ready, He will address the whole Nation as follows,—

"My friends—grand-fathers, Uncles, Brothers, Cousins, attend. You also, my women—grand-mothers, Mothers, and Sisters, listen. You, the Children—you must also hear me attentively. It is the will of the Great, Wise, Good Spirit— our great tree has been fallen to the ground, and great darkness has been spread over our fire-places these many days, whereby we become as fatherless children. According to the custom of our good ancestors, and by the help of the Great, Good Spirit I now remove all dark clouds which hangs over our fire-place. (Strings of Wampum delivered.)

"Again listen: I now raise your heads which has been hang downwards, and wipe off all your tears from your face, so that you may see clear, and open ears that you may hear, and set your hearts right again, that you may understand distinctly." (Strings of Wampum again delivered.)

[It was also the custom of our Ancestors, when any murder was committed in the nation, to have the murderers executed by a relation of the murdered person. If the murderer repented his crime, had been useful to his friends and relations, and was beloved by them, in such a case they collected a quantity of wampum and gave it as a ransom for his life. Or, if this was not done, the murderer, to save his life, might go a great way, till he should find some enemy of his tribe, from whom, if he could bring a prisoner, to die for him, or a scalp, with wampum, either was received as Nanptanteon, or a ransom instead of his own death. But such murders were seldom committed before white people brought many evil spirits across the great waters, to this island.][3]

Notes

The main text is taken from the version in Electa Jones, *Stockbridge, Past and Present; or Records of an Old Mission Station* (Springfield, Mass.: Samuel Bowles and Co., 1854), 15–23. Reproduced earlier in Bernd C. Peyer, ed., *The Elders Wrote: An Anthology of Early Prose by North American Indians, 1768–1931* (Berlin: Dietrich Reimer Verlag, 1982), 25–33. One of the earliest tribal histories written by an Indian, it outlines the intricate kinship network of northeastern Indian nations and asserts that the Mohicans already possessed all of the tenets of Christian civilization prior to the arrival of Europeans.

1. Beginning lines in brackets taken from the abridged version titled "Extract from an Indian History," *Massachusetts Historical Society Collections* ser. 1, vol. 9 (1804): 99–102.

2. Seven Nations of Canada, or "Seven Fires," was an alliance of Iroquoian villages along the St. Lawrence River in Canada. It included Iroquois, Algonquin, Huron, Abenaki, and Nippissing members.

3. Closing lines in brackets taken from the edited version in *The First Annual Report of the American Society for Promoting the Civilization and General Improvement of the Indian Tribes in the United States,* ed. Jedidah Morse (New Haven, Conn.: Printed for the Society, by S. Converse, 1824), 41–45.

BIOGRAPHY

Hendrick Aupaumut (Mohican, 1757–1830) was born and raised in Stock-bridge, Rev. John Sargeant's Christian Indian settlement in Massachusetts. He attended Sargeant's school for an unknown number of years during which he became literate in both English and Mohican. In the summer of 1775, he enlisted in the Continental Army along with numerous other Indians from Stockbridge and was promoted to captain of his company in 1778 by George Washington. He is, therefore, frequently referred to as "Captain Hendrick" in historical documents. One year earlier he had also taken on the hereditary position of a Hudson River Mohican sachem.

After the Revolution, Aupaumut played a significant diplomatic role in the United States government's efforts to pacify the remaining "hostile" tribes of the Ohio Valley. In the summer and fall of 1791 and in February of 1792 he acted as the U.S. emissary of peace at councils with the Six Nations at Newton, New York, and Grand River, Upper Canada (now Ontario). In 1792 and 1793 Aupaumut attended meetings with several leaders of different Ohio Valley tribes along the Maumee River, attempting to convince them to cease hostilities.

After the Battle of Fallen Timbers in 1794, in which Aupaumut took an active role, he continued to render diplomatic service to the U.S. government in further dealings with northeastern Indians. He functioned as mediator for the Treaty of Greenville in 1795. He assisted the federal government in concluding the 1803 and 1809 Treaties of Fort Wayne, under which the Indian land base in the Old Northwest was reduced even further. In the period between 1805 and the outbreak of the War of 1812, Aupaumut was one of the most outspoken Indian adversaries of Tecumseh and his brother Tenskwatawa, the latter of whom he designated as "the emissary of Satan." Aupaumut voluntarily joined General William Harrison's successful campaign against them.

Aupaumut's belief in the necessity of Indian selective accommodation to the sociopolitical realities of his day was undoubtedly as sincere as that of his Mohegan contemporaries. After all, he had personally experienced the positive sides of such a symbiotic relationship in the community where he had grown up as a third-generation Christian Indian. The fate of the New Stockbridge community after the War of 1812, however, must have dampened Aupaumut's optimism considerably. Strained relations with the Oneidas, who were becoming more and more immersed in Handsome Lake's syncretic religion, had already led Aupaumut to consider another removal as early as 1791. In 1808 he secured a grant of land from the Miami in Indiana. The realization of the exodus itself was postponed by the events leading up to the War of 1812, so that the first emigrants did not actually begin their trek until 1817. In spite of the substantial record of Stockbridge Indian services to the United States and a written confirmation signed by Thomas Jefferson, the federal government had by this time forced the Miami to sell the land they had planned to settle. Aupaumut sent his son Solomon Hendrick to Washington to protest the issue, but this proved to be of little avail with a new administration keen on land speculation and preparing for another war with England. In 1821 Solomon managed to purchase 6,000 acres from the Menominee in Wisconsin, and the White River emigrants moved to the alternative site the year after. In 1828 John W. Quinney (1797–1855) led most of the remaining New Stockbridge residents to the new community on the Fox River, where he was joined by the aging Aupaumut in 1829.

Around 1793 Aupaumut wrote "A Narrative of an Embassy to the Western Indians . . . ," a fairly detailed account of his activities as a peace emissary, published posthumously in 1827. This historical document is another rare example of eighteenth-century Indian "treaty literature." Aupaumut also penned "History of the Muh-he-con-nuk Indians," written around 1790 but not published until 1854.

Selected Publications of Hendrick Aupaumut

"Extract from the Journals of the Indians, being the Sixth Speech delivered the Delaware nation, residing at Waupekunmekuhk, or White river [Indiana], on the 15th of April, 1803," *The Panoplist* 1, no. 6 (November 1805): 270–72.

"History of the Muh-he-con-nuk Indians," in Electa Jones, *Stockbridge, Past and Present; or Records of an Old Mission Station* (Springfield, Mass.: Samuel Bowles and Co., 1854): 15–23. A heavily edited version was published earlier in *The First Annual Report of the American Society for Promoting the Civilization and General Improvement of the Indian Tribes in the United States*, ed. Jedidiah Morse (New Haven, Conn.: Printed for the Society, by S. Converse, 1824): 41–45. An abridged version titled "Extract from an Indian History" is in *Massachusetts Historical Society Collections* ser. 1, vol. 9 (1804): 99–102.

"A Narrative of an Embassy to the Western Indians from the Original Manuscript of Hendrick Aupaumut, with Prefatory Remarks by Dr. B.H. Coates." *Historical Society of Pennsylvania Memoirs* vol. 2, pt. 1 (1827): 61–131. The original is found in the Pickering Papers, Reel 59, Massachusetts Historical Society.

Unpublished Writings

Several speeches and letters by Aupaumut are found in the Thomas Pickering Papers, Massachusetts Historical Society.

Selected Secondary Sources

Ronda, Jeanne, and James P. Ronda, "'As They Were Faithful': Chief Hendrick Aupaumut and the Struggle for Stockbridge Survival, 1757–1830." *American Indian Culture and Research Journal* 3, no. 3 (1979): 43–55.

Taylor, Alan. "Captain Hendrick Aupaumut: The Dilemmas of an Intercultural Broker." *Ethnohistory* 43, no. 3 (Summer 1996): 431–57.

Turner, Katherine C. *Red Men Calling on the Great White Father* Norman: University of Oklahoma Press, 1951: 3–27.

Wheeler, Rachel. "Hendrick Aupaumut: Christian-Mahican Prophet." *Journal of the Early Republic* 25, no. 2 (2005): 187–220.

Wyss, Hilary E. "Captivity and Christianity: Stockbridge, New Stockbridge, and the Place of History." in Wyss, *Writing Indians: Literacy, Christianity and Native Community in Early America.* Amherst: University of Massachusetts Press, 2000: 105–21.

AN INDIAN'S LOOKING-GLASS FOR THE WHITE MAN

William Apess (1833)

Having a desire to place a few things before my fellow creatures who are travelling with me to the grave, and to that God who is the maker and preserver both of the white man and the Indian, whose abilities are the same, and who are to be judged by one God, who will show no favor to outward appearances, but will judge righteousness. Now I ask if degradation has not been heaped long enough upon the Indians? And if so, can there not be a compromise; is it right to hold and promote prejudices? If not, why not put them all away? I mean here amongst those who are civilized. It may be that many are ignorant of the situation of many of my brethren within the limits of New England. Let me for a few moments turn your attention to the reservations in the different states of New England, and, with but few exceptions, we shall find them as follows: The most mean, abject, miserable race of beings in the world—a complete place of prodigality and prostitution.

Let a gentleman and lady, of integrity and respectability visit these places, and they would be surprised; as they wandered from one hut to the other they would view with the females who are left alone, children half starved, and some almost as naked as they came into the world. And it is a fact that I have seen them as much so—while the females are left without protection, and are seduced by white men, and are finally left to be common prostitutes for them, and to be destroyed by that burning, fiery curse, that has swept millions, both of red and white men, into the grave with sorrow and disgrace—Rum. One reason why they are left so is, because their most sensible and active men are absent at sea. Another reason is, because they are made to believe they are minors and have not the abilities given them from God, to take care of themselves, without it is to see to a few little articles, such as baskets and brooms. Their land is in common stock, and they have nothing to make them enterprising.

Another reason is because those men who are Agents, many of them are unfaithful, and care not whether the Indians live or die; they are much imposed upon by their neighbors who have no principle. They would think it no crime to go upon Indian lands and cut and carry off their most valuable timber, or any thing else they chose; and I doubt not but they think it clear gain. Another reason is because they have no education to take care of themselves; if they had, I would risk them to take care of their own property.

Now I will ask, if the Indians are not called the most ingenious people amongst us? And are they not said to be men of talents? And I would ask, could there be a more efficient way to distress and murder them by inches than the way they have taken? And there is no people in the world but who may be destroyed in the same way. Now if these people are what they are held up in our view to be, I would take the liberty to ask why they are not brought forward and pains taken to educate them? to give them all a common education,

and those of the brightest and firstrate talents put forward and held up to office. Perhaps some unholy, unprincipled men would cry out, the skin was not
good enough; but stop friends—I am not talking about the skin, but about principles. I would ask if there cannot be as good feelings and principles under a
red skin as there can be under a white? And let me ask, is it not on the account
of a bad principle, that we who are red children have had to suffer so much as
we have? And let me ask, did not this bad principle proceed from the whites
or their forefathers? And I would ask, is it worth while to nourish it any longer?
If not, then let us have a change; although some men no doubt will spout their
corrupt principles against it, that are in the halls of legislation and elsewhere.
But I presume this kind of talk will seem surprising and horrible. I do not see
why it should so long as they (the whites) say that they think as much of us as
they do of themselves.

This I have heard repeatedly, from the most respectable gentlemen and
ladies—and having heard so much precept, I should now wish to see the example. And I would ask who has a better right to look for these things than the
naturalist himself—the candid man would say none.

I know that many say that they are willing, perhaps the majority of the
people, that we should enjoy our rights and privileges as they do. If so, I would
ask why are not we protected in our persons and property throughout the
Union? Is it not because there reigns in the breast of many who are leaders, a
most unrighteous, unbecoming and impure black principle, and as corrupt and
unholy as it can be—while these very same unfeeling, self-esteemed characters pretend to take the skin as a pretext to keep us from our unalienable and
lawful rights? I would ask you if you would like to be disfranchised from all
your rights, merely because your skin is white, and for no other crime? I'll venture to say, these very characters who hold the skin to be such a barrier in the
way, would be the first to cry out, injustice! awful injustice!

But, reader, I acknowledge that this is a confused world, and I am not seeking for office; but merely placing before you the black inconsistency that you
place before me—which is ten times blacker than any skin that you will find in
the Universe. And now let me exhort you to do away that principle, as it appears ten times worse in the sight of God and candid men, than skins of color—
more disgraceful than all the skins that Jehovah ever made. If black or red skins,
or any other skin of color is disgraceful to God, it appears that he has disgraced
himself a great deal—for he has made fifteen colored people to one white, and
placed them here upon this earth.

Now let me ask you, white man, if it is a disgrace for to eat, drink and sleep
with the image of God, or sit, or walk and talk with them? Or have you the folly
to think that the white man, being one in fifteen or sixteen, are the only beloved
images of God? Assemble all nations together in your imagination, and then
let the whites be seated amongst them, and then let us look for the whites, and
I doubt not it would be hard finding them; for to the rest of the nations, they
are still but a handful. Now suppose these skins were put together, and each
skin had its national crimes written upon it—which skin do you think would

have the greatest? I will ask one question more. Can you charge the Indians with robbing a nation almost of their whole Continent, and murdering their women and children, and then depriving the remainder of their lawful rights, that nature and God require them to have? And to cap the climax, rob another nation to till their grounds, and welter out their days under the lash with hunger and fatigue under the scorching rays of a burning sun? I should look at all the skins, and I know that when I cast my eye upon that white skin, and if I saw those crimes written upon it, I should enter my protest against it immediately, and cleave to that which is more honorable. And I can tell you that I am satisfied with the manner of my creation, fully—whether others are or not.

But we will strive to penetrate more fully into the conduct of those who profess to have pure principles, and who tell us to follow Jesus Christ and imitate him and have his Spirit. Let us see if they come any where near him and his ancient disciples. The first thing we are to look at, are his precepts, of which we will mention a few. "Thou shalt love the Lord thy God with all thy heart, with all thy soul, with all thy mind, and with all thy strength." The second is like unto it. "Thou shalt love thy neighbor as thyself." On these two precepts hang all the law and the prophets.—Matt. xxii. 37, 38, 39, 40. "By this shall all men know that they are my disciples, if ye have love one to another."—John xiii. 35. Our Lord left this special command with his followers, that they should love one another.

Again, John in his Epistles says, "He who loveth God, loveth his brother also."—iv. 21. "Let us not love in word but in deed."—iii. 18. "Let your love be without dissimulation. See that ye love one another with a pure heart fervently."—1. Peter, vii. 22. "If any man say, I love God, and hateth his brother, he is a liar."—John iv. 20. "Whosoever hateth his brother is a murderer, and no murderer hath eternal life abiding in him."[1] The first thing that takes our attention, is the saying of Jesus, "Thou shalt love," &c. The first question I would ask my brethren in the ministry, as well as that of the membership, What is love, or its effects? Now if they who teach are not essentially affected with pure love, the love of God, how can they teach as they ought? Again, the holy teachers of old said, "Now if any man have not the spirit of Christ, he is none of his."—Rom. viii. 9. Now my brethren in the ministry, let me ask you a few sincere questions. Did you ever hear or read of Christ teaching his disciples that they ought to despise one because his skin was different from theirs? Jesus Christ being a Jew, and those of his Apostles certainly were not whites, and did not he who completed the plan of salvation complete it for the whites as well as for the Jews, and others? And were not the whites the most degraded people on the earth at that time, and none were more so; for they sacrificed their children to dumb idols! And did not St. Paul labor more abundantly for building up a Christian nation amongst you than any of the Apostles. And you know as well as I that you are not indebted to a principle beneath a white skin for your religious services, but to a colored one.

What then is the matter now; is not religion the same now under a colored skin as it ever was? If so I would ask why is not a man of color respected; you may say as many say, we have white men enough. But was this the spirit of Christ and his Apostles? If it had been, there would not have been one white preacher in the world—for Jesus Christ never would have imparted his grace or word to them, for he could forever have withheld it from them. But we find that Jesus Christ and his Apostles never looked at the outward appearances. Jesus in particular looked at the hearts, and his Apostles through him being discerners of the spirit, looked at their fruit without any regard to the skin, color or nation; as St. Paul himself speaks, "Where there is neither Greek nor Jew, circumcision nor uncircumcision, Barbarian nor Scythian, bond nor free—but Christ is all and in all."[2] If you can find a spirit like Jesus Christ and his Apostles prevailing now in any of the white congregations, I should like to know it. I ask, is it not the case that every body that is not white is treated with contempt and counted as barbarians? And I ask if the word of God justifies the white man in so doing? When the prophets prophesied, of whom did they speak? When they spoke of heathens, was it not the whites and others who were counted Gentiles? And I ask if all nations with the exception of the Jews were not counted heathens? and according to the writings of some, it could not mean the Indians, for they are counted Jews. And now I would ask, why is all this distinction made among these Christian societies? I would ask what is all this ado about Missionary Societies, if it be not to christianize those who are not Christians? And what is it for? To degrade them worse, to bring them into society where they must welter out their days in disgrace merely because their skin is of a different complexion. What folly it is to try to make the state of human society worse than it is. How astonished some may be at this—but let me ask, is it not so? Let me refer you to the churches only. And my brethren, is there any agreement? Do brethren and sisters love one another?—Do they not rather hate one another. Outward forms and ceremonies, the lusts of the flesh, the lusts of the eye and pride of life is of more value to many professors, than the love of God shed abroad in their hearts, or an attachment to his altar, to his ordinances or to his children. But you may ask who are the children of God? perhaps you may say none but white. If so, the word of the Lord is not true.

I will refer you to St. Peter's precepts—Acts 10. "God is no respecter of persons"—&c. Now if this is the case, my white brother, what better are you than God? And if no better, why do you who profess his gospel and to have his spirit, act so contrary to it? Let me ask why the men of a different skin are so despised, why are not they educated and placed in your pulpits? I ask if his services well performed are not as good as if a white man performed them? I ask if a marriage or a funeral ceremony, or the ordinance of the Lord's house would not be as acceptable in the sight of God as though he was white? And if so, why is it not to you? I ask again, why is it not as acceptable to have men to exercise their office in one place as well as in another? Perhaps you will say that if we admit you to all of these privileges you will want more. I expect that I can guess what that is—Why, say you, there would be intermarriages. How that would be I am not able to say—and if it should be, it would be nothing strange or new to me; for I can assure you that I know a great many that have intermarried, both of the whites and the Indians—and many are their sons and daughters—and people too of the first respectability. And I could point to some in the famous city of Boston and elsewhere. You may now look at the disgraceful act in the statute law passed by the Legislature of Massachusetts, and behold the fifty pound fine levied upon any Clergyman or Justice of the Peace that dare to encourage the laws of God and nature by a legitimate union in holy wedlock between the Indians and whites. I would ask how this looks to your law makers. I would ask if this corresponds with your sayings—that you think as much of the Indians as you do of the whites. I do not wonder that you blush many of you while you read; for many have broken the ill-fated laws made by man to hedge up the laws of God and nature. I would ask if they who have made the law have not broken it—but there is no other state in New England that has this law but Massachusetts; and I think as many of you do not, that you have done yourselves no credit.[3]

But as I am not looking for a wife, having one of the finest cast, as you no doubt would understand while you read her experience and travail of soul in the way to heaven, you will see that it is not my object.[4] And if I had none, I should not want any one to take my right from me and choose a wife for me; for I think that I or any of my brethren have a right to choose a wife for themselves as well as the whites—and as the whites have taken the liberty to choose my brethren, the Indians, hundreds and thousands of them as partners in life, I believe the Indians have as much right to choose their partners amongst the whites if they wish. I would ask you if you can see any thing inconsistent in your conduct and talk about the Indians? And if you do, I hope you will try to become more consistent. Now if the Lord Jesus Christ, who is counted by all to be a Jew, and it is well known that the Jews are a colored people, especially those living in the East, where Christ was born—and if he should appear amongst us, would he not be shut out of doors by many, very quickly? and by those too, who profess religion?

By what you read, you may learn how deep your principles are. I should say they were skin deep. I should not wonder if some of the most selfish and ignorant would spout a charge of their principles now and then at me. But I would ask, how are you to love your neighbors as yourself? Is it to cheat them? is it to wrong them in any thing? Now to cheat them out of any of their rights is robbery. And I ask, can you deny that you are not robbing the Indians daily, and many others? But at last you may think I am what is called a hard and uncharitable man. But not so. I believe there are many who would not hesitate to advocate our cause; and those too who are men of fame and respectability—as well as ladies of honor and virtue. There is a Webster, an Everett, and a Wirt, and many others who are distinguished characters besides an host of my fellow citizens, who advocate our cause daily.[5] And how I congratulate such noble spirits—how they are to be prized and valued; for they are well calculated to promote the happiness of mankind. They well know that man was made for society, and not for hissing stocks and outcasts. And when such a principle as this lies within the hearts of men, how much it is like its God—and how it honors its Maker—and how it imitates the feelings of the good Samaritan, that had his wounds bound up, who had been among thieves and robbers.

Do not get tired, ye noble-hearted—only think how many poor Indians want their wounds done up daily; the Lord will reward you, and pray you stop not till this tree of distinction shall be levelled to the earth, and the mantle of prejudice torn from every American heart—then shall peace pervade the Union.

Notes

From the original appended to Apess's *The Experiences of Five Christian Indians of the Pequot Tribe; or, An Indian's Looking-Glass for the White Man* (Boston: By the author; James B. Dow, Printer, 1833), 53–60. Reproduced earlier in Bernd C. Peyer, ed., *The Elders Wrote: An Anthology of Early Prose by North American Indians, 1768–1931* (Berlin: Dietrich Reimer Verlag, 1982), 44–50. Together with *Eulogy on King Philip*, this is one of Apess's most brilliant and often reproduced invectives. In his second edition of *The Experiences*, Apess replaced this critical essay with a much shorter and milder sketch titled "An Indian's Thought."

1. John 3:15
2. Colossians 3:11
3. Antimiscegenation laws had been in effect in Massachusetts since 1705 and were reinstated in 1786 with the so-called Solemnization of Marriage Act, which voided all unions between whites and African Americans. These restriction held sway in Massachusetts until 1839, long after they were banned in New York (1785) and Rhode Island (1798).
4. Apess married Mary Wood of Salem, Connecticut, on December 21, 1821. She was of Spanish Caribbean ancestry. Apess included her autobiography in *The Experiences of Five Christian Indians* under the title "The Experience of the Missionary's Consort (Written By Herself)."
5. Daniel Webster (1782–1852), senator and noted orator, disputed Georgia's claims to Cherokee lands in the House of Representatives in 1827; Edward Everett (1794–1865), Unitarian clergyman and gifted orator, spoke in favor of the Cherokees in the House of Representatives in 1831; William Wirt (1772–1834), Attorney General of the United States from 1817 to 1829 and presidential candidate under the Anti-Masonic ticket in 1832, served as counsel to the Cherokees in their unsuccessful appeal to the Supreme Court in 1831. All three were highly critical of Jackson's Indian policy.

BIOGRAPHY

William Apess (Pequot, 1798–1839) was born on January 31 in Colrain, Massachusetts, the son of William and Candace Apes. In 1801 his parents separated and left their five children under the care of their maternal grandparents in Colchester, Connecticut. As a consequence of a severe beating by his intoxicated grandmother in 1802, the town selectmen of Colchester bound Apess out to a white Baptist family in the vicinity. Apess's indenture was sold to another white man in New London in 1809, who in turn soon resold him to a neighbor because the eleven-year-old had run away repeatedly. Finally, in 1813 Apess escaped to New York City, where he enlisted in the American militia as a drummer boy and witnessed several abortive expeditions against Montreal. In the spring of 1815 he mustered out of the army and traveled through Canada working at odd jobs. Sometime in the fall or winter of 1816 he made his way back to Connecticut on foot.

Whatever knowledge Apess managed to absorb about Pequot traditions in the four years before his indenture was soon undermined by the racist attitudes of his proprietors. By the age of six or seven his alienation had progressed so far that a chance encounter in the woods with a group of sunburned white women whom he mistook for "wild Indians" caused him to flee in terror. Around 1809 Apess sought solace in a burgeoning Protestant revival movement known as the Second Great Awakening and began attending Methodist meetings on a regular basis. On March 15, 1813, Apess had a pivotal conversion experience which he described as a "great peace of mind." During his service in the army, however, Apess succumbed temporarily to the usual vicissitudes of a life of soldiering, particularly alcohol abuse. Following his return to Connecticut, Apess experienced another spiritual revival under the influence of his aunt Sally George, who personalized a successful blend of Christian piety and Pequot shamanism. Apess was subsequently baptized by immersion during a Methodist camp meeting in December of 1818.

On December 21, 1821, Apess married Mary Wood of Salem, Connecticut. In 1825 Apess moved with his wife and two children to Rhode Island, where he became a class leader in a local Methodist society and decided to become a missionary. After years of extensive traveling along the northeastern seaboard as an itinerant preacher and jack-of-all-trades, he applied for a preacher's license at the quarterly conference of the Methodist Episcopal Church in April 1829. When the application was denied, Apess joined the dissenting Protestant Methodist Church which ordained him that same year. In 1831 the New York Annual Conference of the Protestant Methodists appointed Apess to preach among the Pequots.

Early in 1833 Apess visited the Mashpees of Cape Cod and soon became actively engaged in their long-standing dispute with Massachusetts over political and religious sovereignty. Apess and his family were adopted by the community on May 21. In cooperation with several educated Mashpee leaders he then formed The Free and United Church, defying the officially appointed Congregationalist preacher as well as a temperance society. With his assistance, primarily as spokesperson and scribe, the Mashpees ultimately managed to secure a certain degree of autonomy in 1834. Apess is still venerated among the Mashpees today for his key role in what has been referred to as the "Woodland Revolt," the only successful (albeit temporarily) Indian insurrection during the height of the removal era.

Little is known about Apess's life or whereabouts after leaving Mashpee. His final years were beset with financial problems, especially as his estate was attached by the Barnstable Court of Common Pleas for debt in 1838. He died in New York City in April of 1839 as a result of apoplexy.

Apess is credited as the author of five books: *A Son of the Forest* (1829), a spiritual autobiography culminating with his ordination; *The Increase of the Kingdom of Christ* (1831), a sermon revolving around the theory that Indians were descendants of the "Ten Lost Tribes of Israel"; *The Experiences of Five Christian Indians of the Pequot Tribe* (1833), the conversion narratives of three Pequot women recorded by Apess and two autobiographical sketches written by Apess and his wife, appended with a diatribe against white racism; *Indian Nullification of the Unconstitutional Laws of Massachusetts Relative to the Marshpee Tribe* (1835), an account of his involvement in the "Woodland Revolt," written in cooperation with William G. Snelling; and *Eulogy on King Philip* (1836), an oration delivered in Boston on January 8, 1836, in which Apess celebrates King Philip (Metacom) and censures Puritan treatment of Indians. Apess's personal confrontation with deracination, poverty, bondage, and racism made him particularly receptive to the humanistic currents of thought in his day, especially the style of radical abolitionism propagated by David Walker and William Lloyd Garrison, and thus one of the most outspoken critics of Indian-white relations.

Selected Publications of William Apess

Eulogy on King Philip, as Pronounced at the Odeon, in Federal Street, Boston. Boston: By the author, 1836; repr. Boston: By the author, 1837.

The Experiences of Five Christian Indians of the Pequot Tribe; or, An Indian's Looking-Glass for the White Man. Boston: By the author; James B. Dow, Printer, 1833; repr. as *Experience of Five Christian Indians of the Pequot Tribe.* Boston: By the author, 1837.

The Increase of the Kingdom of Christ: A Sermon. New York: By the author; G.F. Bunce, Printer, 1831.

Indian Nullification of the Unconstitutional Laws of Massachusetts Relative to the Marshpee Tribe; or, The Pretended Riot Explained. Boston: Jonathan Howe, 1835; repr. Stanfordville, N.Y.: Earl M. Coleman, Publisher, 1979.

O'Connell, Barry. ed., *On Our Own Ground: The Complete Writings of William Apess, A Pequot.* Amherst: University of Massachusetts Press, 1992.

A Son of the Forest: The Experience of William Apess, a Native of the Forest, Comprising a Notice of the Pequot Tribe of Indians. New York: By the author, 1829.

Revised as *A Son of the Forest: The Experience of William Apess, A Native of the Forest.* New York: By the author; G.F.Bunce, Printer, 1831.

Selected Secondary Sources

Dannenberg, Anne Marie. "'Where, then, shall we place the hero of the wilderness': William Apess's *Eulogy on King Philip* and Doctrines of Racial Destiny," in Helen Jaskoski, ed., *Early Native American Writing: New Critical Essays.* New York: Cambridge University Press, 1996: 66–82.

Donaldson, Laura E. "Son of the Forest, Child of God: William Apess and the Scene of Postcolonial Nativity," in C. Richard King, ed., *Postcolonial America.* Chicago: University of Illinois Press, 2000: 201–22.

Donaldson, Laura. "Making a Joyful Noise: William Apess and the Search for Postcolonial Method(ism)," in Malini Johar Schueller and Edward Watts, eds. *Messy Beginnings: Postcoloniality and Early American Studies.* New Brunswick: Rutgers University Press, 2003: 29–44.

Gaul, Theresa Strouth. "Dialogue and Public Discourse in William Apess's *Indian Nullification.*" *American Transcendental Quarterly* 15, no. 4 (December 2001): 275–94.

Gustafson, Sandra M. "Nations of Israelites: Prophesy and Cultural Autonomy in the Writings of William Apess." *Religion and Literature* 26, no. 1 (Spring 1994): 31–53.

Haynes, Carolyn. "'A Mark for Them All to . . . Hiss at': The Formation of Methodist and Pequot Identity in the Conversion Narrative of William Apess." *Early American Literature* 31, 1 (1996): 25–44.

Konkle, Maureen. "'William Apess, Racial Difference, and Native History," in Konkle, *Writing Indian Nations: Native Intellectuals and the Politics of Historiography, 1827–1863.* Chapel Hill: University of North Carolina Press, 2004: 97–159.

Krupat, Arnold. *The Voice in the Margin: Native American Literature and the Canon.* Berkeley: University of California Press, 1989: 132–201.

_____. *Ethnocriticism: Ethnography, History, Literature.* Berkeley: University of California Press, 1992: 201–31.

McQuaid, Kim. "William Apes, Pequot: An Indian Reformer in the Jackson Era." *New England Quarterly* 50, 4, (December 1977): 605–626.

Moon, Randall. "William Apess and Writing White." *Studies in American Indian Literatures* 5, 4 (Winter 1993): 44–54.

Murray, David. *Forked Tongues: Speech, Writing and Representation in North American Indian Texts.* Bloomington: Indiana University Press, 1991: 49–64.

Nielsen, Donald M. "The Mashpee Indian Revolt of 1833." *New England Quarterly* 58, 3 (September 1985): 400–20.

O'Connell, Barry. "Introduction," in O'Connell, ed., *On Our Own Ground: The Complete Writings of William Apess, A Pequot.* Amherst: University of Massachusetts Press, 1992: xii–lxxvii.

_____. "'Once More Let Us Consider': William Apess in the Writing of New England Native American History," in Colin G. Calloway, ed., *After King Philip's War: Presence and Persistence in Indian New England.* Hanover, N.H.: Dartmouth College/University Press of New England, 1997: 162–77.

Peyer, Bernd C. "William Apess, Pequot-Mashpee Insurrectionist of the Removal

Era," in Peyer, *The Tutor'd Mind: Indian Missionary-Writers in Antebellum America*. Amherst: University of Massachusetts Press, 1997: 117–65.

Ruoff, A. LaVonne Brown. "Three Nineteenth-Century American Indian Auto-biographers," in A. LaVonne Brown Ruoff and Jerry W. Ward, *Redefining American Literary History*. New York: Modern Language Association of America, 1990: 251–69.

Stevens, Scott Manning. "William Apess's Historical Self." *Northwest Review* 35, no. 3 (1997): 67–84.

Tiro, Karim M. "Denominated 'SAVAGE': Methodism, Writing, and Identity in the Works of William Apess, A Pequot." *American Quarterly* 48, 4 (December 1996): 653–79.

Warrior, Robert A. "Eulogy on William Apess: Speculations on His New York Death." *Studies in American Indian Literatures* 16, no. 2 (Spring 2004): 1–13.

Weaver, Jace. *That the People May Live: Native American Literatures and the Native American Community*. New York: Oxford University Press, 1997: 53–59.

Wyss, Hilary E. "Captivity and Conversion: William Apess, Mary Jemison, and Narratives of Racial Identity." *American Indian Quarterly* 23, nos. 3–4 (Summer 1999): 63–82.

_____. *Writing Indians: Literacy, Christianity and Native Community in Early America*. Amherst: University of Massachusetts Press, 2000: 154–67.

NORTHEAST

THE NEW YORK INDIANS

ADDRESS ON THE PRESENT CONDITION AND PROSPECTS OF THE ABORIGINAL INHABITANTS OF NORTH AMERICA

Maris B. Pierce (1838)

The condition and circumstances of the race of people of whom I am by blood *one,* and in the well being of whom I am, by the ties of kindred and the common feelings of humanity, deeply interested, sufficiently apologise, and tell the reason for my seeking this occasion of appearing before this audience, in this city. Not only the eyes and attention of *you,* our neighbors—but also of the councils of this great nation are turned upon us. We are expected to do, or to refuse to do, what the councils of this nation, and many private men are now asking of us—what many favour and advocate—yet also what many discountenance and condemn.

My relation to my kindred people being as you are aware it is, I have thought it not improper—rather that it was highly *proper*—that I should appear before you in my own person and character in behalf of my people and myself, to present some facts, and views, and reasons, which must necessarily have a material bearing upon our decisions and doings at the present juncture of our affairs.

Hitherto our cause has been advocated almost exclusively, though ably and humanely by the friends of human right and human weal, belonging by *nature* to a different, and by *circumstances* and *education,* to a superior race of men. The ability and humanity of its advocates however, does not do away the expediency, nor even the *necessity* of those of us who can, standing forth with our own pen and voices, in behalf of that *same right* and *that same weal* as connected with ourselves, which have been and now are by a powerful and perhaps *fatal* agency almost fatally jeopardized.

It has been said and reiterated so frequently to have obtained the familiarity of household words, that it is *the doom* of the Indian to disappear—to vanish like the morning dew—before the advance of civilization; and melancholy is it to us—those doomed ones—that the history of this country, in respect *to us* and its civilization, has furnished so much ground for the saying, and for giving credence to it.[1]

But *whence* and why are we thus doomed? Why must we be crushed by the arm of civilization, or the requiem of our race be chanted by the waves of the Pacific which is destined to engulph us?

It has been so long and so often said as to have gained general credence, that our *natural constitution* is such as to render us incapable of apprehending and incompetent to practice upon those principles from which result the *characteristic* qualities of Christian civilization, and so by a necessary consequence, under the sanction of acknowledged principles of moral law, we must yield ourselves sacrifices, doomed by the constitution which the Almighty has made for us, to that *other race* of human beings, whom the same Almighty has endowed with a more noble and more worthy constitution.

These are the premises: these the arguments: these the conclusions; and if they are *true and just* and *legitimate,* in the language of the Poet, we must say

> "God of the just—thou gavest the bitter cup,
> We bow to thy behest, and drink it up."[2]

But are they *true* and *just,* and *legitimate!* Do we as a people, lack the capacity of apprehending and appreciating any of the principles which form the basis of Christian civilization? *Do we lack* the competency of practising upon those principles in any or *all their* varieties of application?

A general reference to facts as they are recorded in the history of the former days of our existence, and as they now are transpiring before the eyes of the whole enlightened world give an answer which should ever stifle the question, and redeem us from the stigma.

Before citing particular exemplifications of the truth of this, I will allude to one question which is triumphantly asked by those who adopt the doctrine of the untameable nature of the Indian, viz: Why have not the Indians become civilized and christianized as a consequence of their intercourse with the whites—and of the exertions of the whites to bring about so desirable a result? Who that believes the susceptibilities and passions of human nature to be in the main uniform throughout the rational species, needs an answer to this question from me?[3]

Recur to the page, which records the dealings both in manner and substance, of the early white settlers and of their successors, down even to the present day, with the unlettered and unwary Red man, and then recur to the susceptibilities of your own bosom, and the question is answered.

Say ye, on whom the sun light of civilization and Christianity has constantly shone—into whose lap Fortune has poured her brimful horn, so that you are enjoying the *highest* and *best spiritual* and *temporal* blessings of this world. Say, if some beings from fairy land, or some distant planet, should come to you in such a manner as to cause you to deem them children of *greater light* and *superior wisdom* to yourselves, and you should open to them the hospitality of your dwellings and the *fruits* of your *labor,* and they should, by dint of their *superior wisdom* dazzle and amaze you, so as for what to them were *toys and rattles* they should gain freer admission and fuller welcome, till finally they should claim the *right* to your possessions and of hunting you, like wild beasts, from your long and hitherto undisputed domain, how ready would *you* be to be taught of *them.*—How cordially would you open your *minds* to the conviction that they meant not to deceive you *further* and still more fatally in their proffers of pretended kindness.

How much of the kindliness of friendship for them, and of esteem for their manners and customs would *you feel?* Would not "the milk of human kindness" in your breasts be turned to the gall of hatred towards them?

And have not *we,* the original and undisputed possessors of this country, been treated *worse* than *you* would he, should any supposed case be transformed to reality?

But I will leave the consideration of this point for the present, by saying, what I believe every person who hears me will assent to, that the manner in which the whites have habitually dealt with the Indians, make them *wonder* that their hatred has not burned with tenfold fury against them, rather than that they have not laid aside their own peculiar notions and habits, and adopted those of their civilized neighbors.

Having said thus much as to the question, "Why have not the Indians been civilized and christianized by the intercourse and efforts of the whites?"

I would now call your attention to a brief exemplification of the point I was remarking upon before alluding to the above-mentioned question, viz: "That the Indian is capable of apprehending and appreciating, and is competent to practice on those principles which form the basis of Christian civilization."

I do not know that it has ever been questioned and especially by those who have had the best opportunities to learn by *experience and observation,* that the Indian possesses [*sic*] as perfect a physical constitution as the whites, or any other race of men—especially in the matter of hardy body, swift foot—sharp and true eye, accompanied by a hand that scarcely ever drew the bow-string amiss or raised the tomahawk in vain.

I believe also, that it is not denied that he is susceptible of *hatred*—and equally of friendship—that he even can love and pity, and feel gratitude—that he is prone to adoration of the Great Spirit—that he possesses an imagination, by which he pictures fields of the blessed in a purer and more glorious world than this; that he possesses the faculty of memory and judgment, and such a combination of faculties as enabled him to invent and imitate; that he is susceptible of ambition, emulation, pride, vanity; that he is sensitive to honor and disgrace; and necessarily has the *elements* of a *moral sense* or conscience. All these are granted as entering into his *native spiritual constitution.*

For instances of those *natural endowments,* which by *cultivation,* give to the children of civilization their great names and far-reaching fame, call to mind Philip of Mount Hope, whose consummate talents and skill made him the white man's terror, by his display of those talents and skill for the white man's destruction.[4]

Call to mind Tecumseh, by an undeserved association with whose name, one of the great men of your nation has obtained more of greatness than he ever merited, either for *deeds* or his *character*—Call to mind *Red Jacket,* formerly *your neighbor,* with some of you a friend and a familiar, of the same tribe with whom I have the honor to be a *humble member:* to have been a *friend* and *familiar* with whom none of you feel it a *disgrace.*[5] Call to mind Osceola, the victim of the white man's treachery and cruelty, whom neither his enemy's cunning or arm could conquer on the battle field, and who at last was consumed "in durance vile," by the corroding of his own spirit.[6] "In durance vile," I say, (blot the fact from the records of that *damning baseness,* of that violation of *all laws,* of all humanity, which that page of your nation's history, which contains an account of it must ever be—*blot out the fact,* I say, before you rise up to call an Indian treacherous or cruel.) Call to mind *these* and a thousand others, whom I have not time to mention, and my point is gained.

Here then the fundamental elements of the best estate of human nature are admitted as existing in the natural constitution of the Indian. The question now comes, are these elements susceptible of cultivation and improvement, so as to entitle their possessors, to the rank which civilization and Christianity bestow?

For an instance of active pity of *deep, rational active* pity, and the attendant intellectual qualities, I ask you to call to mind the story—*surpassing*—*romance* of Pocahontas; she who threw herself between a supposed inimical stranger, and the deadly club which had been raised, by the stern edict of her stern father—she begged for the victim's life—she obtained his deliverance from the jaws of death by appealing to the affections which existed in the bosom of her Father, savage as he was, and which affections overcame the fell intent which had caused him to pronounce tho white man's doom. From this time she received the instruction, imbibed the principles and sentiments; adopted the manners and customs of the whites; in her bosom burned *purely and rationally* the flame of love, in accordance with the promptings of which, she offered herself at the Hymenial altar, to take the nuptial ties with a son of Christian England. The offspring of this marriage have been, *with pride* claimed as *sons* and citizens of the noble and venerable State of Virginia.

Ye who love prayer, hover in your imagination around the cot of [David] Brown, and listen to the strong supplications as they arise from tho fervent heart of Catherine [Brown], and then tell me whether "the poor Indian whose untutored mind sees God in clouds and hears him in the wind," is not capable by cultivation, of rationally comprehending the *true God* whose pavillion, though it be the *clouds,* still giveth grace even *to the humble.*[7]

But perhaps I am indulging too much in minuteness. Let me then refer to one more instance which covers the whole ground and sets the point under consideration beyond dispute. The ill-starred Cherokees stand forth in colors of living light, redeeming the Indian character from the foul aspersions that it is not susceptible of civilization and Christianization. In most of the arts which characterise civilized life, this nation in the aggregate, have made rapid and long advances. The arts of peace in all their varieties, on which depend the comforts and enjoyments of the enlightened, have been practised and the results enjoyed by them. The light of revelation has beamed in upon their souls, and caused them to exchange the blind worship of the Great Spirit, for the rational worship and service of the God of the Bible. Schools have been established. An alphabet of the language invented by one of their own men; instruction sought and imparted; and letters cultivated in their own as well as the English language.

Hence many individuals have advanced even to the refinements of civilised life, both in respect to their physical and intellectual condition. A John Ross stands before American people in a character both of intellect and heart which many of the white men in high places may *envy*, yet *never be* able *to attain*. A scholar, a patriot, an honest and honorable man; standing up before the "powers that be," in the eyes of heaven and men, now demanding, now supplicating of those powers a regard for the right of humanity, of justice, of law— is still a scholar, a patriot, an honest and honorable man; though an Indian blood coursing in his veins, and an Indian color giving hue to his complexion, dooms him, and his children and kin to be hunted at the point of the bayonet by those powers, from their home and possessions and country, to the "Terra incognita" beyond the Mississippi.[8]

I now leave this point on which perhaps I need not to have spoken, thus briefly, from the fact that it is granted by all of you as soon as announced, and proceed to make a few remarks confined more exclusively to my own kindred tribe, a part of whom live near this city.

Taking it as clearly true that the Indians are susceptible of cultivation and improvement, even to the degree of physical, intellectual and moral refinement, which confers the title of civilized and christianized. I now proceed to consider whether their condition and feelings are such as to render feasible, the undertaking to bring them up to *that degree*—whether in fact they do not themselves *desire* to come up to it. When I say *they* I mean those who constitute the body and stamina of the people. As to this point, I take it upon myself to say that such an undertaking *is* feasible, and doubly so from the fact that the object of the undertaking is earnestly desired by themselves. I know of no way to set this matter in a clearer light than by presenting you with some facts as to the spirit and the advance of improvements amongst them. And this I crave the liberty of doing by a brief detail of items, prefacing the detail by the remark of a highly respectable individual formerly of Holland, Erie Co., but for some eighteen years a resident of Illinois. After an absence of about fifteen years, he returned two or three years ago, and spent the summer in this region, and several days of the time on the Reservation. He frequently remarked that the Indians during his absence, had improved far more rapidly than their neighbours in the country around them.

In business there is much greater diligence and industry; their teams in respect to oxen, horses, wagons, sleighs, &c. are greater in number and better in quality, than formerly, and in these respects there is a constant improvement. The men labor more, comparatively, and the women less, except in their appropriate sphere, than formerly.

With regard to buildings, they are much more conveniently planned, and of the best materials, both dwelling houses and barns, and new ones constantly going up. Those who have not lands of their own under cultivation, are much more willing to hire out their services to others, either by the year or by shares; this shows that the idea, "to work is thought to be dishonorable" has been done away. There are amongst us, good mowers, and cradlers, and reapers. Blacksmiths, carpenters, shoe-makers and other mechanics, find work enough for their own brethren. There are several wagons in the nation, which are worth more than one hundred dollars in cash: tools of the best quality and of various kinds; manure and other things are sometimes applied, but five years ago, almost or quite universally wasted.

With regard to mode of living, tables, chairs, and bedsteads and cooking apparatus, have generally been purchased of the whites or manufactured in imitation of them, and they are used to a greater or less extent in almost every family. The habit of taking regular meals is gaining ground, and the provision luxurious. The care of the sick; they are more attentive and judicious, and rely less on notions and quackery; they employ skilful [sic] physicians, and use the medicine with less prejudice, and a great deal more confidence.

Other evidences of improvement we have in the increase of industry, and a consequent advance in dress, furniture and all the comforts and conveniences of civilized life. The fields of the Indians have never been kept in so good order, and managed with so much industry, as for the few years past; at public meetings and other large assemblies, the Indians appear comfortably and decently and some of them richly clad. The population is increasing gradually, except when visited with epidemics. The increase of general information is visible; there are many of them, who keep themselves well informed of what is going on in the country; several newspapers have been taken from the cities of Washington, D.C., Philadelphia, New York, and other cities in the Union, and two or three copies of the Genesee Farmer.[9] Some young men have a choice selection of books and libraries. All these improvements are advancing at a rapid rate *except when* they are *distracted with oilier cares* and *anxieties.*

In view of *these* facts, I deem it unnecessary to say any thing farther, as to the question, whether or not the undertaking is feasible to bring the Senecas up to the standard, which shall entitle them to be called civilized and christianized.

The only question which I shall now consider, included in the subject I am treating, is, *how* can this undertaking be carried into operation most advantageously for securing its ultimate object?

Can it be by remaining where we now are located, or by selling our lands and removing to the afore-mentioned "terra incognita?" The right and possession of our lands is undisputed—so with us it is a question appealing directly *to our interest;* and how stands the matter in relation *to that?* Our lands are as fertile and as well situated for agricultural pursuits as any we shall get by a removal. The graves of our fathers and mothers and kin are here, and about them still cling our affections and memories. Here is the theatre on which our tribe has thus far acted its parts in the drama of its existence, and about are it wreathed the associations which ever bind the human affections to the soil, whereon one's nation, and kindred, and self, have arisen and acted. We are here situated in the midst of facilities for physical, intellectual and moral improvement; we are in the midst of the enlightened; we see their ways and their works, and can thus profit by their example. We can avail ourselves of their implements and wares and merchandise, and once having learned the convenience of using them, we shall be led to deem them indispensable; we here are more in the way of instruction from teachers, having greater facilities for getting up and sustaining schools, and as we, in the progress of our improvement, may come to feel the want, and the usefulness of books and prints, so we shall be able readily and cheaply to get whatever we may choose. In this view of facts surely there is no inducement for removing.

But let us look at the other side of the question. In the first place the white man wants our land; in the next place it is said that the offer for it is liberal; in the next place that we shall be better off to remove from the vicinity of the whites and settle in the neighborhood our fellow red men, where the woods flock with game, and the streams abound with fishes. These are the reasons offered and urged in favour of our removal.

Let us consider each of these reasons a little in detail. The fact that the whites want our land imposes no obligation on us to sell it, nor does it hold forth an inducement to do so, unless it leads them to offer a price equal its value to us. We neither know nor feel any debt of gratitude which we owe to them, in consequence of their "loving kindness or tender mercies" towards us, that should cause us to make a sacrifice of our property or our interest, to their wonted avarice and which like the mother of the horse leach, cries give, give, and is never sated.

And is the offer liberal? Of that who but ourselves are to be the final judges? If we do not deem one or two dollars an acre liberal for the land, which will, to the white man's pocket bring fifteen to fifty, I don't know that we can be held heinously criminal for our opinion. It is well known, that those who are anxious to purchase our Reservations, calculate safely on fifteen dollars the acre for the poorest, and by gradation up to fifty and more, for the other qualities. By what mode of calculation or rules of judgement, is one or two dollars a liberal offer to us, when many times that sum would be only fair to the avarice of the land speculator? Since in us is vested a perfect title to the land, I know not why we may not, when we wish, dispose of it at such prices as we may see fit to agree upon.

"But the [Ogden] land company have the right of purchase," it is said— granted: but they have not the right, nor we trust in God, the power, to force us to accept of their offers. And when that company finds that a whistle or a rattle, or one dollar or two, per acre, will not induce us to part with our lands, is it not in the nature of things, that they should offer better and more attractive terms? If they could not make forty-nine dollars on an acre of land, I know no reason why they would fail of trying to make forty-five, or thirty, or ten. So I see no obstacle to our selling when and at such reasonable prices as we may wish, in the *fact* that the land company have the right of purchase: nor do I see any thing extortionate in us, in an unwillingness to part with our soil, on the terms offered—nor even in *the desire*, if our lands are sold, of putting into our *own* pockets a due portion of their value.

But the point of chief importance is, shall we be better off? If our object was to return to the manners and pursuits of life which characterised our ancestors, and we could be put in a *safe, unmolested* and *durable* possession of a wilderness of game, whose streams abound in fish, we might be better off; but though that were our object, I deny that we could possess *such a territory* this side of the shores of the Pacific, with *safety, free of molestation* and in *perpetuity.*

"Westward the Star of Empire takes it way," and whenever that empire is held by the white man, nothing is safe or unmolested or enduring against his avidity for gain.[10] Population is with rapid strides going beyond the Mississippi, and even casting its eye with longing gaze for the woody peaks of the Rocky Mountains—nay even for the surf-beaten shore of the Western Ocean. And in process of time, will not our territory there, be as subject to the wants of the whites, as that which we now occupy is? Shall we not then be as strongly solicited, and by the same arguments, to remove still farther west? But there is one condition of a removal which must certainly render it hazardous in the extreme to us. The proximity of our then situation to that of other and more warlike tribes, will expose us to constant harrassing by them; and not only this, but the character of those worse than Indians, those *white borderers,* who infest, yes *infest,* the western border of the white population, will annoy us more fatally than even the Indians themselves. Surrounded thus by the natives of the soil, and hunted by such a class of whites, who neither "fear God nor regard man," how shall we be better off there than where we now are?[11]

Having said thus much as to our condition after a removal, under the supposition that we wish to return to and continue in the habits of life which prevailed when the country was first taken possession of by the Europeans, I proceed now to say, that we do not wish so to do, and to repeat, that so far from it, we desire to renounce those habits of mind and body, and adopt in their stead, those habits and feelings—those modes of living, and acting and thinking, which result from the cultivation and enlightening of the moral and intellectual faculties of man. And on this point, I need not insult your common sense by endeavoring to show that it is *stupid folly* to suppose that a removal from our present location to the western wilds would improve our condition: What! leave a fertile and somewhat improved soil—a home in the midst of civilization and Christianity, where the very breezes are redolent of improvement and exaltation—where by enduction as it were, we must be pervaded by the spirit of enterprise—where books and preaching, and conversation, and business, and conduct, whose influence we need, are all around us, so that we have but to stretch forth our hands, and open our ears, and turn our eyes to experience in full, their improving and enlightening effects; leave these! and for what? and echo answers *for what?* but methinks I hear the echo followed by the anxious guileful whisper of some government land company agent—for one or two dollars the acre and a western wilderness beyond the white man's reach, where an Eden lies in all its freshness of beauty for you to possess and enjoy. But ours, I reply, is sufficiently an Eden now, if but the emissaries of the arch fiend, not so much in the form of a serpent as of man, can be kept from its borders.

But I will relieve your patience by closing my remarks; it were perhaps needless, perhaps useless, for me to appear before you with these remarks feebly and hastily prepared as they were: but as I intimated on the outset, the crisis which has now arrived in the affairs of our people furnish the apology and reason for my so doing. And now I ask, what feature of our condition is there which should induce us to leave our present location and seek another in the western wilds? Does justice, does humanity, does religion in their relations to us demand it? Does the interest and well being of the whites require it? The plainest dictates of common sense and common honesty, answer *No!* I ask then in behalf of the New-York Indians and myself, that our white brethren will not urge us to do that which justice, humanity, religion not only do not require but condemn. I ask then to let us live on, where our fathers have lived—let us enjoy the advantages which our location affords us: that thus we, who have been converted heathen, may be made meet for that inheritance which the *Father* hath promised to give to his *Son,* our Saviour: so that the deserts and waste places may be made to blossom like the rose, and the inhabitants thereof utter forth the high praises of our God.

Notes

Originally an address delivered on August 28, 1838, at the Baptist Church in Buffalo, New York. It was published as a sixteen-page tract titled *Address on the Present Condition and Prospects of the Aboriginal Inhabitants of North America, with Particular Reference to the Seneca Nation. By M. B. Pierce, A Chief of the Seneca Nation, and a Member of Dartmouth College* (New York: Steele's Press, 1838; repr., Philadelphia: J. Richards, 1839); repr. in Bernd C. Peyer, ed., *The Elders Wrote: An Anthology of Early Prose by North American Indians, 1768–1931* (Berlin: Dietrich Reimer Verlag, 1982), 56–65. The pamphlet, also published in Buffalo, contains an appendix with a sample of an unauthorized contract between a representative of the Ogden Land Company and John Snow, a Seneca leader, followed by a contradicting resolution by the Senate. The second edition has a preface dated January, 1839. Pierce's antiremoval arguments closely resemble previously published editorials and articles by Cherokee writers like David Brown, John Ridge, Elias Boudinot, or John Ross. He was obviously well informed about the peaceful resistance tactics of the Cherokee before their removal in 1839.

1. One of the most widely read treatises on "doomed" Indians at the time was Washington Irving's essay "Traits of Indian Character," which first appeared in *The Analectic Magazine* in 1814 and was reprinted in his *Sketchbook* in 1819.

2. Henry Kirke White (1785–1806), "Sonnet", from his collection titled *Clifton Grove, a Sketch in Verse, with other Poems* (1803), lines 13–14.

3. Although the Enlightenment view of humans as innately equal beings with the same capabilities for "improvement" was not abandoned during the first half of the nineteenth century, the number of those who contended that Indians were incapable of being assimilated into American society because of racial handicaps grew steadily. Empirical "proof" seemed to be provided by the theory of polygenesis, which challenged the notion of a single human species (monogenesis) with the contention that distinct species of humans with inherent abilities and disabilities had evolved separately. Polygenesis received a tremendous boost in the United States during the 1830s with the publication of Charles Caldwell's *Thoughts on the Original Unity of the Human Race* (1830) and Samuel George Morton's *Crania Americana* (1839). Following the wide dissemination of polygenetic literature during the

1830s–1840s, the notion of predetermined racial distinctions became a major topic of public discussion in conjunction with removal and American expansionism. As Reginald Horsman has pointed out, there is sufficient historical evidence that by the 1830s most American people and their political leaders had become convinced that Indians could not be integrated into American society for purely racist reasons. See Reginald Horsman, "Scientific Racism and the American Indian in the Mid-Nineteenth Century," *American Quarterly,* 27 no. 2 (May 1972): 152–69; and Horsman, *Race and Manifest Destiny: The Origins of American Racial Anglo-Saxonism* (Cambridge, Mass.: Harvard University Press, 1981), 189–207.

4. In contrast to earlier Puritan accounts, early nineteenth-century American authors were more predisposed to present Metacom, also known as King Philip (Wampanoag, d. 1676), as a heroic figure. See, for example, Washington Irving's essay "Philip of Pokanoket" in *The Analectic Magazine* (1814), James Wallis Eastburn's and Robert Charles Sand's *Yamoyden, A Tale of the Wars of King Philip: in Six Cantos* (1820), or James Fenimore Cooper's *The Wept of Wish-Ton-Wish* (1829). The most popular image of King Philip was created by actor Edwin Forrest's portrayal of him as a tragic hero in John Augustus Stone's play, *Metamora; or, the Last of the Wampanoags,* which opened at New York on December 15, 1829.

5. This may be a reference to General William Henry Harrison (1773–1841), the so-called Hero of Tippecanoe, whose somewhat inflated reputation as the man who defeated Tecumseh (Shawnee, 1768–1814) would ultimately get him elected president in 1840. Red Jacket (Soogooyawautau, ca. 1758–1830) was a noted Seneca leader and orator who played a central role in the negotiations with the U.S.

6. Osceola (1804–38), the famous Creek resistance leader of the Second Seminole War (1835–42), was apprehended while under a flag of truce in 1837 and subsequently died in prison.

7. Alexander Pope (1688–1744), "A Essay on Man," (1733–34), Epistle I: Of the Nature and State of Man, with Respect to the Universe, lines 99–100.

8. A Seneca delegation met with John Ross in Washington and delivered an address to him on April 7, 1834, suggesting a renewal of friendship and communication between the Cherokee and Seneca nations. Ross gave a positive answer on April 14, calling for unity among Indians and stating that the Cherokees would stand firm against removal. See John Ross, *The Papers of Chief John Ross,* 2 vols., ed. Gary E. Moulton (Norman: University of Oklahoma Press, 1985), I: 284–88.

9. The *Genesee Farmer and Gardener's Journal* (1831–40) was a monthly agricultural and horticultural journal established by Luther Tucker in Rochester, New York.

10. The original citation ("Westward the star of empire makes its way") is from Bishop George Berkeley's *On the Prospect of Planting Arts and Learning in America* (1752). John Quincy Adams cited a slightly modified version ("takes" instead of "makes") in his oration at Plymouth on December 22, 1802, commemorating the landing of the Pilgrims. It was made famous as an epigraph to George Bancroft's *History of the United States, from the Discovery of the American Continent,* first published in Boston in 1834.

11. Luke 18:4.

BIOGRAPHY

Maris Bryant Pierce (Seneca, 1811–74), or Ha-dya-no-doh (Swift Runner), was born on an unrecorded day in "Old Town" on the Allegany Reservation in New York, the son of John Pierce. He attended a local Quaker primary school, probably Tunessa, and was subsequently sent to Fredonia Academy in Pamfret, western New York. From there he transferred to Homer Academy in Courtland County. Pierce then studied at Thedford Academy, Vermont, before enrolling at Dartmouth College in 1836. He attended Dartmouth on a Society of Scotland for Propagation of Christian Knowledge stipend drawn from the funds originally collected in Great Britain by Samson Occom in 1765–68. Pierce, who by then had joined the Presbyterian church, graduated from Dartmouth in August of 1840, the fourth Indian to do so. He then moved to the Buffalo Creek Reservation in New York, where he resumed his duties as a "Young Chief" of the Seneca and also read law in the Buffalo offices of Tillinghast and Smith for the next two years.

Pierce had already been assigned to the responsible position of a "Young Chief" during his sojourn at Dartmouth and was actively involved in the critical events leading up to the signing of the fraudulent removal Treaty of Buffalo Creek in 1838 and the ensuing public debate over its legitimacy. Although among those who signed the treaty on January 15, 1838, Pierce obviously rued his action and immediately joined the majority of Seneca leaders who lobbied against it. On July 4, 1838, he delivered an address on the subject of temperance at Canaan, New York, in which he asserted that many treaties with Indians had been concluded with the aid of distilled spirits. On August 28, 1838, Pierce delivered an antiremoval address at the Baptist Church in Buffalo that was published and widely circulated as *Address on the Present Condition and Prospects of the Aboriginal Inhabitants of North America, with Particular Reference to the Seneca Nation* that same year. Soon after, on September 7, 1838, Pierce and fourteen other Seneca leaders sent a letter to President Martin Van Buren expressing their opposition to the treaty and transmitting a formal council decision against it. In January of 1839, Pierce was one of four Senecas appointed to act as attorneys for the Tonawanda, Allegany, Cattaraugus, and Buffalo Creek reservations in Washington along with Charles R. Gould, a legal counsel hired by the Senecas in December of the previous year. In Washington, on January 24, Pierce and three other Seneca leaders presented a petition to Secretary of War Joel Roberts Poinsett requesting a modification of the treaty. Despite massive protest from the majority of the Seneca leaders and their primary non-Indian allies, the Society of Friends (Quakers), the treaty was ratified by the Senate on March 25, 1840, and proclaimed by Van Buren on April 4.

Pierce continued his oratorical campaign against the treaty, delivering promotional lectures on the manners and customs of the Six Nations Confederacy in New Jersey and Vermont in the spring of 1840. After graduating from

Dartmouth in mid-August, that same year he served the Seneca leaders as translator and secretary, once again accompanying a protest delegation to Washington in that capacity. The efforts of the Seneca leaders and the Society of Friends finally resulted in the writing of a supplemental treaty on May 20, 1842, under which the Senecas retained title to the Allegany and Cattaraugus reservation but had to give up Buffalo Creek and Tonawanda. Pierce, who acted as interpreter during these proceedings, was among the seventy-eight leaders signing this document.

In November of 1843 Pierce married Mary Jane Carroll, the daughter of a British officer. When the Senecas abandoned Buffalo Creek in 1845 in accordance with the supplemental treaty, Pierce and his wife removed to Cattaraugus. Here he continued to serve the Seneca nation as interpreter and secretary. Dissatisfaction over the events between 1838 and 1842 eventually resulted in the so-called Seneca Revolution of 1848 in which the "Old Chiefs" were deposed in favor of an elective system of government. Maris Bryant Pierce apparently supported the "Old Chiefs" in this internal crisis. For the remainder of his life he advocated education among the Senecas and remained a supporter of both Christian and Longhouse factions.

Selected Publications of Maris Bryant Pierce

Address on the Present Condition and Prospects of the Aboriginal Inhabitants of North America, with Particular Reference to the Seneca Nation. By M.B. Pierce, A Chief of the Seneca Nation, and a Member of Dartmouth College. New York: Steele's Press, 1838; repr. Philadelphia: J. Richards, 1839. Reproduced in Bernd C. Peyer, ed., *The Elders Wrote: An Anthology of Early Prose by North American Indians, 1768–1931.* Berlin: Dietrich Reimer Verlag, 1982: 56–65.

Unpublished Writings

Several letters by Pierce are found in the Maris Bryant Pierce Papers, Buffalo and Erie County Historical Society, Buffalo, New York. Pierce also described his experiences at Dartmouth in an unpublished diary titled "Book of Memorandum 1840." The original is housed at the Pennsylvania Museum and Historical Commission, Harrisburg, Pennsylvania. A microfilm copy of the diary is available at the Buffalo and Erie County Historical Society; a photocopy of the diary, along with a few letters, is in the Maris Bryant Pierce Papers, Dartmouth College, Hanover, New Hampshire.

Selected Secondary Sources

Littlefield, Jr., Daniel. "'They Ought to Enjoy the Home of their Fathers': The Treaty of 1838, Seneca Intellectuals, and Literary Genesis," in Helen Jaskoski, ed., *Early Native American Writing: New Critical Essays.* New York: Cambridge University Press, 1996: 83–103.

Society of Friends (Hicksite), Joint Committee on Indian Affairs. *The Case of the*

Seneca Indians in the State of New York. Philadelphia: Merrihew and Thompson, 1840.

Society of Friends (Hicksite). *A Further Illustration of the Case of the Seneca Indians in the State of New York, in a Review of "An Appeal to the Christian Community, &c. By Nathaniel T. Strong, A Chief of the Seneca Tribe."* Philadelphia: Merrihew and Thompson, 1841.

Vernon, H. A. "Marys Bryant Pierce: The Making of a Seneca Leader," in L. G. Moses and Raymond Wilson, eds., *Indian Lives: Essays on Nineteenth and Twentieth Century Native American Leaders.* Albuquerque: University of New Mexico Press, 1985: 19–42.

APPEAL TO THE CHRISTIAN COMMUNITY ON THE CONDITION AND PROSPECTS OF THE NEW YORK INDIANS

Nathan T. Strong (1841)

TO THE CHRISTIAN PUBLIC

Being a Chief of the Seneca Tribe of Indians lately arrived in this city, my attention has been called to a volume composed and widely circulated by the Society of Friends, under the title of "The Case of the Seneca Indians, in the State of New York," the avowed design of which is to defeat the treaty lately concluded between the United States and the New York Indians, and after mature consideration by the president and senate of the United States, constitutionally ratified.[1] The charges contained in this book, the proofs in support of them, and also the proofs in opposition to them, having all been deliberately investigated and passed on by the appropriate tribunals of your country, our people, after years of suspense and anxiety, considered the question of emigration as settled, and they fondly hoped that their rights under the treaty, being secure and inviolable, they might commence the preparations necessary for their removal, and with the kind wishes and encouragement of their white brethren, be permitted to enter on the new path which a kind Providence had opened for their escape from bondage, degradation and misery, with the cheering hope of enjoying in the asylum provided for them by your government, the blessings of freedom and independence. But alas! as at the outset so in the progress, of our journey, we are met by enemies, powerful in numbers and discipline, but more dangerous in artifice and cunning; disguising their attacks under the false banner of friendship and good will, and seeking to withdraw from us the support even of those who are in reality our friends. Thus we see simultaneous movements in different parts of the country, all organized under the same banner, and all urged on by the same influence. These are but the sequels of continued attempts for two years past to control, through the agency of public opinion and prejudice, the constitutional section on the treaty of the president and senate; and (although now binding both on you and us) through popular agitation and excitement to prevent its execution. I will not stop to discuss the propriety of these proceedings, nor their consistency with those principles of peace and order professed by the Society of Friends; but in regard to this their last publication, I must be permitted to say, that its gross abuse, garbled statements and repeated misrepresentations, are in my poor judgement, as incompatible with the law of Christian charity, as with the rules of candor and fair discussion; nor can I in adequate terms express my surprise, that on an appeal like this to an intelligent community upon a question involving the dearest interests of an unfortunate and suffering race of beings, coming from a body of Christian men professing to be the steady friends of that race and the

100

faithful advocates of their cause, no reasoning should be employed to enlighten the public mind on the merits and effects of the treaty as an instrument to them of good or evil; and that its beneficent provisions in their favor, should be noticed only to condemn and censure them, as too liberal and costly on the part of the Government . . .

The subject of emigration is not new to the New York Indians. The advancing settlements of the whites, more than thirty years since, admonished them to the necessity of that measure, and long before the existence of what is called the "Ogden Company," led them, as the result of their own calm deliberations, to resolve on securing a seat among their red brethren on the west.[2] Being encouraged in these views by the then president, their attention was first directed to the acquisition of a tract on the White River of Indians, but that tract being included in a treaty soon afterwards made with the Indian occupants by the government, that attempt of course failed.[3] Subsequently and as early as 1821, it was renewed under the like encouragement, and a purchase was then made from the Menominee and Winnebago tribes by the Six Nations, the St. Regis, Stockbridge, the Munsee tribes, (composing all the Indians in this state) of a tract on the Fox River emptying into Green Bay; which purchase was confirmed by the government and was in the following year greatly enlarged. This acquisition soon proved to be so important, that the Menominees, under the influence of the white inhabitants of the territory of which it then formed part, were induced to deny the validity of the bargain—disputes and bad feeling followed, and before these could be allayed the United States purchased from the Menominees the most valuable part of this tract. The New York tribes remonstrated against this purchase, and the senate after investigating their complaints, in the year 1832 ratified the Menominee treaty, on condition that a tract of 500,000 acres should be set apart for the use of the New York tribes, to be held under the same title by which they held their lands in this state. A portion of the Oneidas and the whole of the Stockbridge and Brotherton Indians removed to, and now reside on that tract—but the arrangement was not satisfactory to others of the New York tribes, who have been since much divided as to the course best for them to pursue, the greater portion of the Christian party among the Seneca tribe and most of the educated and respectable chiefs, being decidedly in favour of emigration . . .[4]

For many years past the condition of the Indians generally, and especially that of the feeble remnants of the once powerful nations residing within the old states of the Union, has excited the sympathy of the benevolent and called forth the talents of the learned, in devising plans by which to rescue them from impending extinction. The subject has by successive presidents been repeatedly urged upon the attention of congress, until at length a well considered system of policy was adopted by the national legislature, having for its object the ultimate civilization of the whole body of Indians within the United States.[5] This system embraces all that seems to be necessary to its final success. In a mild and healthful climate, an extensive territory composed of land easy of cultivation and particularly adapted to the raising of corn, cattle and horses, has been set apart for the exclusive and permanent occupation of the Indians. Sufficient land is to be granted to them in fee, by patent, subject to no pre-emptive right, and by such a tenure as to enable the owners to hold and enjoy in severalty—to transmit to their posterity, and to sell and dispose of among themselves, their respective estates at their own pleasure. Ample protection is guaranteed to them in their new home, and the government is pledged to furnish to them the means of elementary education—to provide for their instruction in agriculture and the mechanical trades, and to confer on them the privileges and powers of self government. These benign provisions together with a just equivalent for the relinquishment of the claims of the New York tribes on the lands at Green Bay, form the basis of the treaty which the Society of Friends, during its negotiation and ever since its conclusion, have been seeking to defeat by every means which wealth and combination, talents and sophistry can furnish . . .

After the question of the removal and the sale of the Seneca lands had been debated for several weeks, the commissioner gave notice that on a certain day he would submit to the council the draft of the treaty, which was presented accordingly with the draft of the conveyance for the Seneca lands; both were read, article by article, to the council and faithfully interpreted in the presence of several persons acquainted with the Indian language; and I here state, of my own knowledge, that both were regularly signed, in general council, by a majority of the Seneca chiefs according to the usage of the Six Nations, each chief signing in his own proper person, except two or three were prevented by sickness from attending and who signed by attorney, as was known to all attending chiefs.

The council was closed by short speeches from the commissioner and superintendent, in which they considered the treaty as a concluded compact, and no dissent was uttered by a single chief on either side.

Up to this period, there was little interference by white men in the deliberations of the council, which were conducted in the usual manner; but when the amended treaty came back, the scene was changed. The opposition had been organized. No particular amendment proposed by the senate was objected to, because as is well known to the authors of the "case" the provisions of the original treaty in reference to the Seneca tribe were left substantially unchanged. The object was to defeat the whole treaty. For this purpose the council was overrun by white men—meetings were called and speeches made in opposition to the treaty. The Senecas were exhorted not to sell the lands of their fathers—were told that the government would never redeem their pledges to them—and if they removed they would be destroyed by the wild Indians of the West. In short every argument, which could be addressed to the fears, the passions and the prejudices of an ignorant and suspicious people were made use of. This was done by a combination composed of 1st, the dram-sellers—2d, the lumberers—3rd, the lessees of mill seats—4th, the holders of hydraulic privileges near Buffalo—5th, the holders of licences to live on Indian lands—6th, the missionaries—and 7th, the Society of Friends.

As to the first five of these various classes of Indian advisers and the motives which actuated them, it is unnecessary to speak. The ground of opposition assigned by the missionaries (except those of Baptist denomination, who abstained from any interference in the matter,) was, that the treaty made no provision for refunding the money expended by the Board of Missions in making their different establishments on our lands; whilst on the part of the Quakers, it was insisted, as is still done, that the New York Indians possessed in their present positions, all requisite advantages and needed no new system of policy for their improvement. Their soft speech and strong professions of disinterested friendship, blended with insidious suggestions considering the sincerity and good faith of the government—the validity of its title to the tract of country appropriated for the new homes of the Indians—the insalubrity of that country and the fearful dangers to which we should be there exposed, could not fail to produce their intended effect on the more timid of our people . . .

In accordance with such a beginning, our once peaceful council ground was soon converted into an arena for the display of the worst passions of our nature. An organized system of intimidation was employed to deter our weaker brethren from signifying their assent to the amended treaty. Some of them were driven by threats of death to the woods and if, as is alleged in the "case," runners were employed to bring them back to the council house, it was because they were deterred by fear from appearing there, and our friends were therefore obliged to follow them to their retreats and rally them to the independent exercise of their rights . . .

I now pass to the consideration of the remaining charge, impeaching the validity of the assents to the amended treaty—viz: the employment of bribery to obtain them . . . Let me ask what is the meaning of the term bribery as applied to the Indians? If a right to personal gratuities be the privilege of chiefs according to the general and well understood usage of Indian communities, then the acceptance of them, being consistent with the official fidelity, involves no violation of duty, and the payment of them is not bribery. Now, according to the unbroken custom which has prevailed among the Senecas since the first sale of their extensive possessions in this state, the chiefs have demanded and received personal allowances. This custom was acted on the at the treaty of 1797, between Robert Morris and that tribe, held by the late distinguished Colonel Jeremiah Wadsworth as commissioner of the United States, and by a highly respectable superintendent of Massachusetts—annuities for life were then granted to all the principle chiefs of that day and secured by the purchase of public government stocks. Corn-planter, Farmer's Brother, Red Jacket and many others were of the number, and to the first of these great men no less than two hundred and fifty dollars per annum was granted for his life that of his wife and those of his eight children, several of whom are still in the enjoyment of it.[6] At the treaty of 1826, the same usage prevailed. Red Jacket, who opposed the treaty and could claim no allowance, was persuaded, as the opposition chiefs now are, to proceed to Washington and on this same charge to contest the validity of the treaty. Then, as now, the usages of our people were

referred to, and there was no interference on the part of the government.[7] At
the council held by the secretary in August, 1839, the fact of personal allowances
to chiefs was referred to by the orator of the opposition party and stigmatized
by the epithet of bribery; on which a leading chief on the other side, rose in his
place and in the face of the assembled tribes, avowed and justified the practice
as one founded on ancient and well-understood usage; and after expressing his
surprise that such a complaint should come from such a quarter, pointed with
scorn to several chiefs on the opposition benches who were then in the receipt
of personal annuities under the treaty of 1826. This usage is not peculiar to any
one tribe; it is common, as I understand, to all, and (as is universally understood) the government of the United States in their Indian negotiations are
compelled to conform to it.[8] Nor is the usage of modern origin. At the earlier
periods of the settlement of this country, presents, as they were often called, were
freely distributed among the chiefs. At this day, and especially among tribes
whose constant intercourse with white men has taught them that money is the
surest means of purchasing both luxuries and comforts—when the increased
value of their lands enhances their official importance and busy white advisers
are ready to stimulate their cupidity, it is not strange that the chiefs should be
disposed to make the most of their official perquisites. The difference in practice between the pre-emptive owners of the present time, and those of the time
of [William] Penn and other colonists is, that what passed under the name
presents is now termed *bribery:* that the chiefs were content then to receive
blankets and cloths, gay calicoes and glittering baubles and trinkets, whereas
now they demand more substantial allowances in money. In principle there is
no difference either as to the giver or receivers of personal gratuities.

With us the chiefs act for the nation in the sale of their land, and if the nation
are satisfied with the price, there is no complaint on account of any further
benefits that the chiefs can secure for themselves . . .

I now turn in the further examination of this angry and most uncandid appeal of the Society of Friends, to the contemplation of the present condition
and prospects of the New York Indians, and to a calm consideration to a means
by which, under the gracious providence of the common Father of all, we, the
most hapless branch of the human family, can be raised to the rank that you,
his more favoured children, have so long enjoyed, and made to participate in
those rich blessings which have been so bountifully bestowed on you . . .

In discussing the theory of civilization we are met at the threshold, by the
fact, that every attempt which has hitherto been made, whether by legislatures
or religionists, to produce a radical and enduring change in manners, habits
and pursuits of Indian communities, has proved utterly abortive.

This fact, whilst showing the inherent difficulties of the problem, points to
the propriety of applying for its solution to the master spirits of the age, and
of ceasing to rely on the crude systems of conceited visionaries and heated fa-
natics, who, content with the use of palliatives, never look to the source of the
disease. Such master spirits have at length approached the subject, and guided
by their lights and the information I have been able to collect in the course of

my education and subsequent associations with some of the better classes of white society, I am fully persuaded, as I think must be every intelligent man who dismissing preconceived opinions will devote the powers of his mind to the subject, that the true cause of the failure of past efforts to improve the conditions of Indians, is the disabilities under which they labor in respect to those rights and privileges of person and property, which are the common inheritance of white men.

The aborigines of this continent, from their first intercourse with the nations of Europe, have been the victims of that most unjust principle of colonization upon which the government of each nation first discovering any particular portion of this vast country, assumed over it an unqualified dominion, both as to soil and inhabitants. Upon this principle, the extensive regions claimed to have been discovered by the British subjects were parceled out into colonies and granted to them or to individuals, in fee simple—a title carrying with it the power of alienation to all other subjects, and leaving to the Indian occupants, a mere right of possession which the holders of the government title (hence called the pre-emptive owners) were alone authorized to purchase . . .

The rights of Great Britain and her colonies which passed by revolution to the states of this union, have since been asserted and exercised by them, in the fullest extent. We Indians thus hold our lands by a title comparatively worthless, and as to personal rights, are placed under restrictions equally severe and humiliating.[9] We are shut out by all political privileges, and in the country of our birth, are regarded as aliens, being not only deprived of the control of our own lands but incapacitated from acquiring and holding any other, even by purchase from white men! Thus oppressed and degraded, we find ourselves surrounded by white settlements, where a comparison between the condition and privileges of the two populations, would alone be sufficient to check aspirings and subdue the energies of every intelligent member of our community, even were he not compelled further to witness the demoralizing effects of this proximity to the more ignorant and more numerous portion of our people. These, constantly associating with the corresponding classes are always ready to contract with individual Indians for the cultivation of their cleared lands on shares, and to purchase from them a vague license to cut and remove the valuable timber still to be found in our forests; and although cheated and over reached in all these transactions, the poor Indian (after a fruitful harvest) is enabled to draw from them the means of a scanty subsistence, with such small supplies of money and credit as suffice to gratify his propensity to idleness and his thirst for ardent spirits; but when, as often happens, the corn crop fails, he is thrown a mendicant on the bounty of his white neighbours for the necessaries of life . . .

If proofs were required as to the practical effects of the disabilities under which we labor, they are to be found in the last 50 years of our history with which many of you must be familiar. Within this period, you have seen that the wide wilderness of the Genesee Country, and the still wider wilderness of the West, have been made "to blossom as the rose." The most needy of your people, planting themselves everywhere among the forests, have been able by their own exertions, to provide a comfortable subsistence for their families, establish schools, erect churches, build up villages and cities and acquire wealth and consideration, whilst the New York Indians, with the "example of a civilized state with all its advantages" continually before them—possessed of better lands, enjoying the benefit of missionaries and teachers and all the aids of active benevolence, have in the great work of civilization, achieved nothing to justify a hope that, whilst deprived of the incentives and rewards which animate the freeman, they can ever be more successful . . .

With these accumulated evidences of the yet deplorable condition of the New York Indians, no man whose eyes are not blinded to the truth, can fail to see the urgent necessity of some more efficient system of measures for its melioration. No man whose heart is not insensible to human misery, can wish to withhold from them its benefits. And yet when under such a system, devised by the collected wisdom, and based on the ample resources of your government, the portals of civilization are thrown open to us, we are met at the threshold, by an organized body of christians professing to be friends, yet acting as enemies. The New York Indians although exposed on all sides to extraneous influences chiefly exerted to subserve private views, have nevertheless succeeded in securing to themselves the advantages of the government system, and the Seneca tribe have at the same time effected a sale of their remaining lands, on terms incomparably more just and liberal than any previous sale. The dearest interests of all demand a speedy consummation of these arrangements; yet the Society of Friends, are still obstinately trying to defeat them . . .

There is yet another instance of inconsistency in their conduct. The public are constantly edified by yearly discourses from this society on the subject of negro slavery, setting forth its sinfulness and urging emancipation as an act of christian obligation. Yet how different is their conduct in regard to the Indian tribes in this state, of whom they profess to be special protectors and who, although free in name, are more effectually shut out from all privileges which render freedom a blessing, than are the negroes! The negro slave it is true, owes obedience to, and labours for the benefit of his master, but he and his children are bountifullly fed and clothed, kindly nursed in sickness and provided for in old age. We are not compelled indeed to labour; but when overtaken by want, visited by sickness or enfeebled by old age, have no right to ask of white men to feed, clothe, nurse or support us. The negro, by a long course of voluntary exertion, may perhaps purchase his freedom—buy lands and dispose of them—and many also (in this State at least) acquire the right of suffrage and other civil rights. To us, all these privileges are forever denied by your laws. Negro slavery can only be abolished by subverting private rights, whilst national policy sustained by public opinion, encourages and facilitates efforts for Indian emancipation. Yet the Friends plead without ceasing, the cause of the negro whilst they labour indefatigably to perpetuate the bondage of the Indian . . .

To conclude—the Society of Friends may succeed in wresting from us the charter of our freedom and leave us in hopeless dependence on the worthless charities of short-sighted enthusiasts, but what, let me ask, will be to us, the consequences of their triumph? I put this inquiry with solemn earnestness, and again use the words of that venerated chief, whose impressive appeal is already before you. "The question is, will the government now do what is promised in the treaty? What will become of us if no new homes are given? Whether it gives them or not, does not affect our arrangement with the pre-emptive purchasers. That stands by itself. The other New York Indians have secured their new homes, and shall we not have them also? If the president rejects our doings what will be our fate? We shall suffer for having listened to his advice. Those who have scorned to adopt his council, will place their feet upon our necks, and grind us into the earth."[10]

N. T. STRONG
New York, 29th January, 1841

Notes

The full title of the twenty-two-page pamphlet is *Appeal to the Christian Community of the Conditions and Prospects of the New York Indians, in Answer to a Book Entitled "The Case of the New York Indians", and Other Publications of the Society of Friends* (Buffalo: Press of Thomas and Co, 1841; New York: E. B. Clayton, 1841). The latter version is excerpted here. Strong incorporated numerous letters and statements by American administrators into the text which have been omitted due to excessive length. Strong argues that the previous dealings with the Seneca were conducted in a correct manner that corresponded with Indian traditions on the one hand and the legacy of William Penn on the other. Like Pierce, he feels that the Senecas are fully capable of "advancement" but adds that this could best be achieved west of the Mississippi. Together with Elias Boudinot's *Letters and Other Papers Relating to Cherokee Affairs* (1838), this is one of the few pro-removal statements to be published by an American Indian.

1. The publication referred to is Society of Friends (Hicksite), Joint Committee on Indian Affairs, *The Case of the Seneca Indians in the State of New York* (Philadelphia: Merrihew and Thompson, 1840). The object of contention is the Treaty with the New York Indians (Buffalo Creek Treaty) concluded January 15, 1838. An "amended treaty" was signed by a minority of chiefs on June 11. In spite of serious doubts about its legitimacy, it was ratified by the Senate on March 25, 1840, and proclaimed by President Martin Van Buren on April 4 of the same year. The Society of Friends refuted Strong's arguments in *A Further Illustration of the Case of the Seneca Indians in the State of New York, in a Review of "An Appeal to the Christian Community, &c. By Nathaniel T. Strong, A Chief of the Seneca Tribe"* (Philadelphia: Merrihew and Thompson, 1841), esp. 6–7, 58–61.

2. The Ogden Land Company was founded in the 1790s by the Ogden brothers: David Aaron, Thomas Ludlow, and Gouverneur.

3. Representatives for the New York Indians traveled to White River, Indiana, early in 1817. This effort was thwarted when the Miamis were forced to sell their lands to the United States in 1818.

4. See Thomas Commuck's "Sketch of the Brothertown Indians," *Wisconsin Historical Collections* 4 (1855): 291–98; repr. in Bernd C. Peyer, ed., *The Elders*

Wrote: An Anthology of Early Prose by North American Indians, 1768–1931 (Berlin: Dietrich Reimer Verlag, 1982), 95–100.

5. The Indian Removal Act of 1830, effective May 28, 1830, authorized the president to set up districts west of the Mississippi, to which Indian title had been transferred, and to exchange such districts for Indian-held lands in the East. It also provided for payment for improvements on the lands to be forfeited, for costs of removal, and a year's subsistence in the West for those who migrated.

6. Under the Treaty of Big Tree in 1797 the Senecas sold most of their territory in New York to Robert Morris (1733–1806), a signer of the Declaration of Independence and financier of the American Revolution with preemptive rights to the lands. The Senecas were subsequently confined to several small reservations. Cornplanter (Koeentwahke), Red Jacket (Soogooyawautau), and Farmer's Brother (Onayawos) signed the treaty and derived personal benefits from it. Col. Jeremiah Wadsworth (1743–1804) was a veteran of the American Revolution and congressman who functioned as U.S. commissioner at the signing of the treaty. The "superintendent" referred to was William Shepard (1737–1817), major-general of the militia and congressman, who confirmed the treaty.

7. Under the treaty of August 1826, the Senecas sold a portion of their remaining reservations to the Ogden Land Company. The treaty was never ratified by the Senate nor proclaimed by the president.

8. Rewarding tribal leaders was a common practice in the treaty-making process since colonial days. Section 9 of the Indian Trade and Intercourse Law of March 2, 1793, authorized the president to give goods and money to the tribes to promote civilization and secure their friendship. See Francis P. Prucha, *American Indian Policy in the Formative Years: The Indian Trade and Intercourse Laws* (Lincoln: University of Nebraska Press, 1970), 47.

9. In *Johnson and Graham's Lessee v. McIntosh*, 1823, Chief Justice John Marshall declared that the federal government owned all "public" lands by virtue of "discovery" and "conquest." This gave the government the preemptive right to purchase Indian land or confiscate it after a war. The Indians remained "the rightful occupants [rather than proprietors] of the soil, with a legal as well as just claim to retain possession of it." Indian title could henceforth neither be bought nor sold without federal authorization.

10. Strong quotes here from a previously excerpted talk by Captain Pollard (Geeodowneh) dated December 26, 1838. Pollard was one of the Seneca leaders who signed the Treaty of Buffalo Creek.

BIOGRAPHY

Nathaniel Thayer Strong (Seneca, 1810–72) was an educated and converted "Young Chief" like Maris Bryant Pierce. Little is known about him, other than that he worked as a U.S. interpreter and assistant to James Stryker, the sub-agent to the New York Indians at Buffalo. He corroborated with Stryker behind the lines to help the Ogden Land Company conclude a favorable treaty securing its previously purchased preemptive rights to Seneca lands. Strong was not only among the Seneca leaders who signed the Treaty of Buffalo Creek in 1838, but also served as its interpreter. In contrast to Pierce, Strong remained steadfast in the belief that removal to Kansas as stipulated by the treaty was the only viable alternative for the Senecas. In response to the public debate revolving around the treaty—specifically the appearance of an anti-removal tract titled *The Case of the Seneca Indians in the State of New York* by the Society of Friends in 1840—Strong wrote a lengthy defense that was published in Buffalo and New York as *Appeal to the Christian Community of the Conditions and Prospects of the New York Indians* in 1841. During the so-called Seneca Revolution of 1848, Strong apparently took the same position as his former ideological adversary Pierce, namely that of favoring the deposed "Old Chiefs."

Selected Publications of Nathaniel Thayer Strong

Appeal to the Christian Community of the Conditions and Prospects of the New York Indians, in Answer to a Book Entitled "The Case of the New York Indians", and Other Publications of the Society of Friends. Buffalo: Press of Thomas and Co., 1841; New York: E. B. Clayton, 1841.

Unpublished Writings

Several manuscripts, including a biography of Red Jacket, are in the Nathaniel T. Strong Papers, Buffalo and Erie County Historical Society, Buffalo, New York.

Selected Secondary Sources

Littlefield, Jr., Daniel. "'They Ought to Enjoy the Home of their Fathers': The Treaty of 1838, Seneca Intellectuals, and Literary Genesis," in Helen Jaskoski, ed., *Early Native American Writing: New Critical Essays.* New York: Cambridge University Press, 1996: 83–103.
Society of Friends (Hicksite). Joint Committee on Indian Affairs. *The Case of the Seneca Indians in the State of New York.* Philadelphia: Merrihew and Thompson, 1840.
Society of Friends (Hicksite). *A Further Illustration of the Case of the Seneca Indians in the State of New York, in a Review of "An Appeal to the Christian Community, &c. By Nathaniel T. Strong, A Chief of the Seneca Tribe."* Philadelphia: Merrihew and Thompson, 1841.

SOUTHEAST AND INDIAN TERRITORY

THE FIVE TRIBES

EXTRACT OF A LETTER FROM CATHERINE BROWN, TO HER BROTHER DAVID

Catherine Brown (1822)

My dear brother,—As Mr. Ross has lately arrived from Brainerd, and will probably return in a few days, I improve this favorable opportunity of writing a few lines to you. Are you still living as a stranger and pilgrim in the earth? Is the Saviour near your heart, and the object of your chief delight and conversation? I trust that you will continually possess and imitate that meek and lowly spirit, which Jesus possessed in the days of his flesh. I should like to converse with you all day. When I consider the distance we are separated, my ever dear brother, I weep. But the Lord is a present help in every time of trouble. I think I never have desired so much to see you, as I have these several days past. Happy should I be could I but see you at this moment, and relate to you our late trials and affliction, which we have received from our kind heavenly Father. I hope you will lean on the Saviour, who is able to give the consolation which you need, and recollect we are in the hands of an infinitely wise and good Being, who will order every thing for his own glory, and the best good of his children. Since we are the children of a glorious and holy God, may we be submissive to all the dispensations of his Providence, not only in prosperity, but also in adversity, and say, The will of the Lord be done.

I can scarcely compose my mind to write; but you will easily imagine our situation at present, and what I would say, if you were now here. You have recently received the account of brother John's affliction with a consumption. And no doubt, you have often thought of him, and hoped to see him again when you return. But the Lord has ordered otherwise. He has taken him to himself. Yes, our beloved brother is no more! He is dead! Distressing news to you, I know, my brother, and to us. Come, then, let us weep together; and while we mourn our absent brother, let us remember Jesus Christ, who, we trust, has sanctified his heart, and brought him to love God in sincerity. O! let us bless God, that we do not weep for him who lived and died without hope. It is now two weeks since he departed this life into eternity. It is indeed the most painful event that ever has taken place in this family. I think I feel for our dear father and mother. They mourn much for him. I do not wonder; for he was their only son who was here, and on whom they depended for every comfort of life, and support in their declining days. Do not forget to pray for them, particularly that the Spirit of God may dwell richly in their hearts, and support them in this short journey of life. They appear more like Christians than before. Father said, brother John was not ours, but the Lord's, and he had a right to take him whenever he pleased. He appears to pray more fervently, and takes a greater delight in attending family duties, morning and evening.[1] But I must hasten to give you a more particular account of our departed brother . . .

Though he suffered great pain, not one word of complaint was heard from him, during the whole of his sickness. He appeared reconciled, to the will of God, and said the Saviour suffered more than he did. He said he was perfectly willing to be in the hands of God, and to be disposed of in such a way as seemed him good. About one week before his death, he tried to talk to the family, but being very weak, was not able to say much.—Though he spoke but few words, it was truly affecting, and I trust will never be forgotten by us. May we remember his words, and imitate his holy walk. He said—It is now more than a year since we began to follow Christ, and what have we done for him since that time? Do we live like Christians? I fear we are too much engaged about worldly things. When the people come to see you, I do not hear you tell them about the Saviour; and ask them their feelings with respect to another world. We are professors of religion, and why do we not show it to others? He added particularly, You should remember to keep the Lord's day. You are too much engaged in the kitchen on the Sabbath day. You should keep the blacks from work, and take them with you to meeting; when you return, keep them still in the house, and not let them play any on this day.[2] He looked earnestly toward me, and asked if the missionaries cooked on the Sabbath? I told him, they generally made preparations on Saturday. He said, that is what you ought to do. He used frequently to ask me to pray with him, and read and explain the Bible, which I did with great pleasure. For three or four days before he died he was deranged. When he had his reason, he appeared very pleasant, would smile, &c. The night before he died, he spoke your name frequently.

Sabbath morning, the day that he died, being told that it was Sabbath, he requested us to sing and pray with him, which we did. Immediately after this he fell into a state of insensibility, in which he continued till about 5 o'clock, when his spirit ascended to his heavenly home. On Monday, P. M. February 4th, we followed his remains to the cold and silent grave, and bid him a long farewell. It was hard to part with him; but a great consolation that we shall soon meet in the kingdom of Christ, never more to part. His Christian life was short; but long enough to prove that Christ's religion was not in vain. I often remember, he was always ready to instruct and guide the dear heathen to the cross of Christ. I remember those affectionate eyes so often bathed in tears for his poor countrymen. But he has gone before us, and will no longer weep for us, and the dear Cherokees in darkness. His lips are silent in the grave. His prayers are not heard on earth. Hen I stop—my heart bleeds. O! may we follow his example, as far as he followed Christ, and live devoted to God; be in constant readiness for our own departure, that we may at last meet our brother around the throne of that blessed Redeemer, who hath brought us from death unto life eternal. I hope you will not think we are unhappy, or that we wish you to return. Father and mother are willing that you should stay as long as you think best. Write to them often. May God bless you, and make you an instrument of great good to your countrymen, is the prayer of your truly affectionate sister, Catherine Brown.

Notes

The letter, dated February 16, 1822, was originally excerpted in *The Religious Remembrancer* 9, no. 37 (May 4, 1822): 146–47. David Brown (ca. 1802–29), or A-with, was the brother of Catherine Brown. He attended the Foreign Mission School along with Elias Boudinot from 1820–23 and then studied at Andover Theological Seminary, where he assisted Rev. Daniel Butrick and John Arch (Atsi). Arch was a fellow Brainerd student, interpreter, and co-founder of the Creek Path Mission. Before his death in 1825 as a result of tuberculosis, Arch and David Brown prepared a Cherokee spelling book. In 1824, while still at Andover, Brown assisted the noted philologist John Pickering to construct a Cherokee orthography in English characters. Together with his father-in-law, George Lowery, David Brown translated the New Testament directly from the Greek into Cherokee in 1825. They also prepared an official compilation of Cherokee Laws for the Cherokee Council. It is said that he assisted Sequoyah on a portion of the Cherokee syllabary. David Brown served as secretary of the Cherokee Council, lectured widely on Cherokee progress, and traveled throughout the Cherokee Nation to report on the current situation for the Secretary of War, Thomas L. McKenney. David Brown contracted tuberculosis and died in 1829. His report, in the form of a letter addressed to the editor of the Family Visitor dated September 2, 1825, was published in two missionary journals. See "The Cherokee Indians," *Niles' Register* 5, no. 7, (October 15, 1825): 105–107; and "Cherokees. Views of a native Indian, as to the present condition of his people," *The Missionary Herald,* 21 no. 11 (November 1825): 354–55. The report is also included in Walter Lowie, et al., eds., *American State Papers, Indian Affairs,* 2 vols. (Washington, D.C.: Gales and Seaton, 1832–1834), 2: 651. Several letters were also published in contemporary missionary journals. John Brown, Jr., was converted by Catherine and her brother David. When he became ill with tuberculosis, his sister Catherine cared for him until his death in 1822, in the process contracting the deadly disease herself. Personal letters such as these were frequently used by missionary societies for propaganda purposes. Nevertheless, Catherine's letter is also exemplary for the ardor with which some Cherokee mission school scholars adopted and promoted Christianity. At the same time, it illustrates the exceptionally high mortality rate at the mission boarding schools as a result of infectious diseases. See also *Memoir of John Arch, A Cherokee Young Man, compiled from Communications of Missionaries in the Cherokee Nation* (2nd ed., Boston: Massachusetts Sabbath School Union, 1832).

1. Catherine's parents converted sometime in early 1820 and were admitted to the church founded at Creek Path in the fall of that year. Her father, John Brown, a part-Cherokee farmer and owner of a ferry and tavern, became one of the signers of the Cherokee Constitution of 1827 and was later elected principal chief of the Old Settlers following the Cherokee removal to present-day Oklahoma in 1839.

2. Many well-to-do Cherokee families held slaves until the conclusion of the Cherokee Reconstruction Treaty in 1866. See Theda Perdue, *Slavery and the Evolution of Cherokee Society, 1540–1866* (Knoxville: University of Tennessee Press, 1979). The question of slavery among the Southeastern Indians was obviously a source of much embarassment for most missionaries residing among them and abolitionists elsewhere who otherwise supported their anti-removal efforts. See Robert T. Lewit, "Indian Missions and Anti-slavery Sentiment: A Conflict of

Evangelical and Humanitarian Ideals," *Mississippi Valley Historical Review* 50, no. 1 (June 1963): 39–55; Linda K. Kerber, "The Abolitionist Perception of the Indian," *Journal of American History* 62, no. 2 (September 1975): 271–95; and William G. McLoughlin, "Indian Slaveholders and Presbyterian Missionaries, 1837–1861," *Church History* 42 (December 1973): 535–51.

BIOGRAPHY

Catherine Brown (Cherokee, ca. 1800–23) was born in Will's Valley, in the northeastern part of present-day Alabama, the daughter of John Brown (Yau-nu-gung-yah-ski), one of the headmen of the Creek Path community, and his second wife Sarah Webber Brown (Tsa-luh). On July 9, 1817, Catherine Brown was among the first female students to be admitted to Brainerd, the model mission school established by Rev. Cyrus Kingsbury of the American Board of Commissioners for Foreign Missions (ABCFM) near present-day Chattanooga, Tennessee, in March 1817. Catherine attended Brainerd intermittently for almost three years, and was baptized there on January 25, 1818. On May 8, 1820, Catherine left Brainerd to accept a teaching position at a new ABCFM mission in the Cherokee settlement of Creek Path in present-day Guntersville, Alabama. Acting upon an official request by John Brown and other Creek Path leaders, Creek Path Mission was established in March of 1820 by Rev. Daniel S. Butrick and John Arch (Atsi), a fellow Brainerd student. Together with Catherine Brown's brother David, Arch had previously assisted Butrick in preparing a Cherokee spelling book. Catherine Brown lived, taught, and studied at Creek Path Mission until the fall of 1821, when she moved to the home of her ailing brother, John Brown, Jr., who had contracted tuberculosis. Catherine cared for her brother until his death on February 2, 1822, then contracted the disease herself. She moved to the home of a physician in Limestone County, Alabama, where she died on July 18, 1823, at the age of twenty-three.

Catherine Brown's total devotion to her family, exemplary religious fervor, and early death led the ABCFM to exalt her life in a number of mission school texts. Several of her letters were printed in contemporary missionary journals, and the ABCFM published her memoirs posthumously in 1824.

Selected Publications of Catherine Brown

Anderson, Rufus B. ed. *Memoirs of Catherine Brown, a Christian Indian of the Cherokee Nation.* Philadelphia: American Sunday School Union, 1824; repr., New York: John P. Haven, 1825.

"Letter to David Brown." February 21, 1821, *The Missionary Herald* 17, no. 8 (August 1821): 258–59.

"Letter to David Brown." August 10, 1821, *The Religious Remembrancer* 9, no. 8 (October 13, 1821): 30–31.

"Letter to David Brown." February 16, 1822, *The Religious Remembrancer* 9, no. 37 (May 4, 1822): 146–47.

Secondary Sources

American Board of Commissioners for Foreign Missions. *First Ten Annual Reports of the American Board of Commissioners for Foreign Missions, with Other Documents of the Board.* Boston: Crocker and Brewster, 1834.

Anonymous. "Biography: Memoir of Catherine Brown, a Christian Indian of the Cherokee Nation." *The Missionary Herald* 21, no. 7 (July 1825): 193–200.

Arch, John. *Memoir of John Arch, A Cherokee Young Man, compiled from Communications of Missionaries in the Cherokee Nation*, 2nd ed. Boston: Massachusetts Sabbath School Union, 1832.

Higginbotham, Mary A. "The Creek Path Mission." *Journal of Cherokee Studies* 1, no. 2 (Fall 1976): 72–86.

Kidwell, Clara Sue. "Brown, Catherine." In *Native American Women: A Biographical Dictionary*, edited by Gretchen M. Bataille. New York: Garland Publishing Co., 1993: 44–45.

Perdue, Theda. "Catherine Brown: Cherokee Convert to Christianity." In *Sifters: Native American Women's Lives*, edited by Theda Perdue. New York: Oxford University Press, 2001: 77–91.

Wright, Alfred, and Cyrus Byington. *Chahta Holisso a tukla, or the Second Chahta Book: Conteining Translations of Portions of the Scriptures, Biographical Notices of Henry Obokiah and Catherine Brown, a Catechism, and Dissertations on Religious Subjects*. Cincinnati, Ohio: Lodge and Fisher, 1827.

INDIAN ADDRESS

John Ridge (1822)

The inconveniencies [*sic*] attached to uncivilized habits and the degraded state of untutored savages cannot be duly estimated, without a particular knowledge of their history and daily avocations. On a former occasion, I unfolded to you the happy effect of missionary labour among them, and the prominent advantages resulting in the transition from a savage to civilized life. Among the remarkable causes of mortality which exist among them, their habits greatly accelerate their final extermination. That "vinum causa malorum magnorum est," all nations are ready to acknowledge; but in greater degree, the powerful and baneful effects of it have been felt by the poor Indians. The laws of honor and morality are great checks to this contagion in civilized countries; but where no barriers, of consequence, to its promulgation exist, these intoxicating liquors reign triumphant.[1] The roving disposition of the aborigines of this country, tends to their extinguishment: (I now speak of Indians in general who are deprived of Missionaries, and who have made no advances in civilization.) As they have no permanent habitations, their continual perigrinations must expose their wives and children to the inclemencies of the weather, to hunger and neglect, which as a matter of course must impair the constitutions of the most healthy, and the feeble fall certain victims to these hardships. Among the numerous speculations of the learned, many erroneous theories have been advanced on the comparative happiness and contentment of the enlightened and savage life.[2] It is said by some that there is more real enjoyment predominant in the savage, than in the civilized man; but I question whether the gentlemen who support this argument would be willing to renounce the privileges of polished society, and voluntarily adopt the manners of savages, and take their abode in the wilderness far from civilized people. Will any one believe that an Indian, with his bow and quiver, who walks solitary in the mountains, exposed to cold and hunger, or to the attacks of wild beasts, trembling at every unusual object, his fancy filled with agitating fears, lest the next step should introduce his foot to the fangs of the direful snake, or entangle it "amidst his circling spires that on the grass float[ed] redundant," actually possesses undisturbed contentment superior to a learned gentleman of this commercial city, who has every possible comfort at home?[3] Can any one convince me, that the degraded Hottentot in Africa, or the wild Arab in the desert of Sahara, whose head is exposed to the piercing rays of a meridian sun, entirely dependant on his camel for safety, enjoys more real contentment of mind than the poorest peasant of England? Will any one compare the confined pleasures of the Hindoo, whose mind is burthened with the shackles of superstition and ignorance, who bows before the car of Juggernaut, or whose wretched ignorance compels him to invoke the river Ganges for his salvation,—Will any one, I say, compare his pleasures, to the noble end well regulated pleasures of a Herschel or a Newton, who

surveys the regions of the universe—views the wisdom of the Deity in forming the lights of heaven with all the planets and attending satellites revolving
in their orbit, irradiating infinite space as they move around their common
centers—and who demonstrate, with mathematical exactness, the rapid flights
of the comet, and its future visits to our Solar system![4]

I have made this contrast, to show the fallacy of such theories, and to give
you a general view of the wretched state of the Heathen, particularly of the
aborigines of this country, who are gradually retiring from the stage of action to
sleep with their fathers. It is to the exertions of the benevolent that their safety
depends, and the hand of charity can only pluck them from final extermination.
The measures adopted for their education and civilization, is the only hope
to save the sons of the forest from oblivion; and I congratulate all the friends
of Indians, that their endeavours have not been in vain, as I have attempted to
show on a former occasion.[5]

The Indians are naturally possessed of firm decisive characters, and their
minds are obviously of no common cast. Their friendships are permanent, and
no one can bestow his confidence with less exposure to violation, than in the
superior heart of an Indian. This thought has often entered my mind, that as
the Cherokees, Choctaws, and all nations within the limits of the United States,
are making great advances in civilization, whether they would be more happy
to continue distinct, independent governments from the United States? Every
thing considered, I think that it will be for the advantage and utmost benefit
to the Indians, to coalesce with the general government.

This has been a subject of considerable disquisition by influential characters
of this Republic; and, as far as I can conjecture, the President of the United
Slates and many respectable gentlemen are favourable to its accomplishment.[6]
Will any one refuse them this privilege, or suspect their loyalty? Let such peruse
the transactions of the late Creek war, when the Cherokees and the Choctaws
distinguished themselves in battle by the side of the hero of the South. Gen.
Jackson bears witness that their intrepidity in the heat of action was equal to
his own troops, whose courage you so much admire. The bravery of their heroic
sons, who sacrificed their lives in defending the rights of the United States, will
not be entirely forgotten.[7] When the subjects of his Catholic Majesty bid defiance to Jackson, and when that hero took Pensacola by storm, he tells us that
the "Choctaws went boldly lo the charge," and speaks in honourable terms of
their courage.[8] It is evident, that the natives in general, are friendly and respect the government of the United States; and that they will all establish their
governments on republican principles, is reasonable to suppose, as agreeable
to their freedom of thought and natural dispositions. It is one of my greatest
desires, to live long enough to see the Cherokees adopted into the United States.
However, this proposition for such an union, must be made by their own sons
in whom they can confide. They have justly adopted such precautionary measures, that if such a proposition should be advanced by a white man, it would
excite their suspicion, and perhaps reject it altogether.

The liberality of the public is now devoted to the support of Indian Children in the missionary schools, who, we trust, will in due time, become ornaments to society and useful to the world. They are now perhaps educating some, whose names will adorn the page of future history, and generations yet unborn delight to contemplate them as statesmen of superior mould, or devoted missionaries of the cross! Who knows, but that some of the little girls at Brainerd and Elliot, will become Harriet Newels![9] Who knows, but that the young Chickasaw, who is supported by the benevolent of South Carolina, will be a future Buchanan, or Henry Martyn, who shall set up the standard of the cross beyond the Rocky Mountains?[10] Who knows, but that some will become distinguished politicians in congress?—The public do not sufficiently appreciate the importance of their charge. They little think, that when they cast their mite into the Lord's treasury, that it is to advance the object of their liberality, to fill the most important offices of his country. They little think, that the youth they support, may display the patriotism of an Alfred, the wisdom of Socrates, or the legislative talents of a Lycurgus![11]

The Indians stand with open arms to receive missionaries, and your missionaries are ready to engage in this great enterprize [sic]. What then is wanting?—Shall the schools be discontinued for want of funds? Shall the ardent expectations of the Indians be frustrated? *Your liberality will not permit it;* and I presume to be confident, that as South Carolina is distinguished for its information and patriotism, that she will be stimulated to be the very first among the benevolent.

Notes

Originally an address delivered in the Circular Church in Charleston on November 15, 1822 and published in the *Religious Remembrancer* 10, no. 18 (December 21, 1822): 70. This is a typical "progressive" statement affirming the Cherokees' advancement in matters of "civilization." Like other Cherokee intellectuals of his day, John Ridge explicitly favored the incorporation of the Cherokee Nation into the United States. See also David Brown's (Cherokee, ca. 1802–29) "The Cherokee Indians," *Nile's Register* 5, no. 7 (October 15, 1825):106–107. A shorter version titled "Cherokees. Views of a native Indian, as to the present condition of his people" appeared in *The Missionary Herald* 21, no. 11, (November 1825): 354–55. The address was also included in Walter Lowie, et al., eds., *American State Papers, Indian Affairs*, 2 vols. (Washington, D.C.: Gales and Seaton, 1832–1834), 2: 651; and Elias Boudinot's *An Address to the Whites Delivered in the First Presbyterian Church, on the 20th of May, 1826, by Elias Boudinot, A Cherokee Indian* (Philadelphia: Printed by William F. Geddes, 1826); repr. in Bernd C. Peyer, ed., *The Elders Wrote: An Anthology of Early Prose by North American Indians, 1768–1931* (Berlin: Dietrich Reimer Verlag, 1982), 34–43; and Paul Lauter, ed., *The Heath Anthology of American Literature* 2 vols. (Lexington, Mass.: D.C. Heath and Company, 1990), I: 1761–69.

1. "Wine is the greatest cause of illness." Since the publication of Benjamin Rush's *Inquiry into the Effects of Ardent Spirits upon the Human Mind and Body* in 1784, alcohol abuse was considered to be a major cause of death in America,

second only to tuberculosis. A main branch of the early nineteenth-century moral reform enterprise in the U.S. was the temperance movement, which organized as the American Temperance Society in Boston in 1826. Temperance was also an important issue in the Cherokee Nation. Educated Cherokees, among them Elias Boudinot, founded the Cherokee Temperance Society in 1829. See Izumi Ishii, "Alcohol and Politics in the Cherokee Nation before Removal," *Ethnohistory* 50, no. 4 (Fall 2003): 671–95.

2. Ridge is referring to the popular western European tradition of primitivism, which asserted that simpler societies were somehow happier and more "civilized" than one's own. This idea was taken up by late nineteenth-century American writers like Hector St. Jean de Crèvecoeur, William Bartram, and Philip Freneau. See Roy Harvey Pearce, *Savagism and Civilization: A Study of the Indian and the American Mind* (Baltimore: The Johns Hopkins University Press, 1965), 135–68.

3. John Milton, *Paradise Lost* (1667–74), Book IX.

4. Friedrich Wilhelm Herschel, or Sir William Herschel (1738–1822) was a noted astronomer who discovered Uranus and the infrared range of sunlight; Sir Isaac Newton (1643–1727), whose primary concern was with physics and celestial mechanics, established the theory of universal gravitation.

5. In 1819 Congress passed a law authorizing an annual sum of $10,000 for a "civilization fund" to be used at the President's discretion to employ "capable persons of good moral character, to instruct [Indians] in the mode of agriculture suited to their situation; and for teaching their children reading, writing, and arithmetic." This fund was maintained until 1882. See Francis P. Prucha, *American Indian Policy in the Formative Years: The Indian Trade and Intercourse Acts, 1790–1834* (1962; repr., Lincoln: University of Nebraska Press, 1970), 213–24. Most of the initiative in Indian education prior to the 1870s, however, came from American religious societies formed after the Revolution, many of whom were particularly successful among the southeastern tribes. See Robert Berkhofer, Jr., *Salvation and the Savage: An Analysis of Protestant Missions and American Indian Response, 1787–1862* (Lexington: University of Kentucky Press, 1965); and Henry W. Bowden, *American Indians and Christian Missions* (Chicago: University of Chicago Press, 1981).

6. The first official pact between the Continental Congress and an Indian nation, the Fort Pitt Treaty of 1778 with the Delawares, invited them to join the confederation as a separate state with the prerogative of sending a representative to Congress. The Treaty of Hopewell with the Cherokees in 1785 anticipated the sending of a Cherokee deputy to Congress. From the acquisition of Louisiana Territory and lasting up until the late 1840s, several proposals of a similar nature were introduced in Congress but never passed into law. See Annie H. Abel, "Proposals for an Indian State, 1778–1878," *Annual Report of the American Historical Association for the Year 1907* (Washington, D.C.: Government Printing Office, 1908), 1: 87–104.

7. Cherokee, Creek, and Choctaw warriors served voluntarily under General Andrew Jackson in the Creek War (Red Stick War) of 1813–14.

8. Choctaw warriors under the command of David Folsom (1791–1847) and Pushmataha (ca. 1764–1824) participated in Jackson's successful campaign against Spanish-held Pensacola in 1814.

9. Brainerd was a successful mission school established by the American Board of Commissioners for Foreign Missions (ABCFM) for Cherokees near Chattanooga,

Tennessee, in 1817. Eliot was a mission school subsequently established by the ABCFM for the Choctaws in Mississippi in 1818. Harriet Atwood Newell (1793–1812) is considered the "first American heroine of missionary enterprise." She accompanied her husband, Samuel Newell, on a mission to India and then to the Isle of France (Mauritius), where she died at a young age. The *Life and Writings of Mrs. Harriet Newell,* first published posthumously in London in 1817, went through numerous editions and was translated into several languages.

10. James Buchanan (1791–1868) served in the House of Representatives and Senate for many years and as President of the United States from 1857 to 1861. Henry Martyn (1781–1812) was a missionary with the East Indian Company and noted translator of Biblical texts.

11. King Alfred the Great (ca. AD 848–899) successfully defended Anglo-Saxon England against Viking attacks and was also a respected scholar. Lycurgus (ca. 800 BC), Spartan political reformer, was immortalized in Plutarch's *Parallel Lives.*

BIOGRAPHY

John Ridge (Cherokee, 1803–39), or Skahtlelohskee, was born at Oothcaloga in present-day Gordon County, Georgia, the son of The Ridge (Major Ridge) and Susanna Wickett Ridge. His father, The Ridge, or Kahmungdaclageh (ca. 1770–1839), a part-Cherokee proprietor of extensive farm operations with slave labor, a ferry, and part-owner of a trading store, was one of the most affluent and influential citizens of the Cherokee Nation. As an active supporter of Protestant missionary activities in the Cherokee Nation, The Ridge made sure that his children received a formal education. John Ridge consequently attended the Moravian Spring Place Mission School in 1810–15; Brainerd Mission School in 1817; an academy at Knoxville, Tennessee, from 1817–18; and the Foreign Mission School at Cornwall, Connecticut, from 1818–21. Because of poor health and a severe hip problem, he was forced to remain at Cornwall until 1822. During this time John Ridge fell in love with Sarah Bird Northrup, the fourteen-year-old daughter of the school's steward, and eventually married her on January 27, 1824, much to the chagrin of the local white population.

Upon his return to the Cherokee Nation, John Ridge settled at Running Waters, near his father's home, and drew a solid income from his law practice, farming operations, and a partnership in a ferry business. Like his father, John Ridge was also actively involved in Cherokee affairs. He served as interpreter during the annual council in 1823, and was elected to the National Committee the following year. On November 5, 1824, John Ridge co-founded the Moral and Literary Society of the Cherokee Nation. He formulated the society's constitution and goals, which were then published that same year in the *Boston Recorder and Telegraph*. In 1825–26 John Ridge functioned as secretary and advisor to the Creek delegation to Washington that sought to amend the illicit removal treaty signed by William McIntosh in 1825. The delegation negotiated an amended treaty on January 24, 1826, and ultimately paid John Ridge $10,000 for his assistance. In 1829 John Ridge was appointed as clerk of the National Council. He was elected to membership of the National Committee from 1830 to 1832, also serving as president of that body. In addition, John Ridge accompanied Cherokee delegations to Washington in 1831, 1832, 1835, and 1836. Until 1832, John Ridge was a firm supporter of Principal Chief John Ross and his anti-removal campaign.

Following a meeting with Andrew Jackson in April of 1832, John Ridge began to have second thoughts about his political stand. During the meeting it became clear that the president, whom Ridge referred to disparagingly as "Chicken Snake," would not shield the Cherokees from further incursions by Georgians. At the same time, influential Americans such as Senator Theodore Frelinghuysen, Associate Justice John McLean, and Secretary of the ABCFM David Greene, all of whom had been outspoken champions of the Cherokee cause, now advised John Ridge to consider negotiating with the federal government because removal seemed inevitable. Acting as president of the National

Committee during the fall council of 1832, John Ridge proposed to send delegates to Washington to discuss the possibility of removal with Jackson. But the Council resolved instead to send a delegation of anti-treaty men with John Ross as their chief counselor. Ross eventually rejected a government offer of three million dollars to remove, much to the annoyance of the pro-treaty faction. When the delegation returned from Washington in the spring of 1833, Elias Boudinot, John Ridge and Major Ridge signed a petition of protest against the course hitherto followed by the Ross administration.

Frustrated by their failure to make any progress at the following fall council, Boudinot, the Ridges and a number of pro-treaty Cherokees enrolled for emigration. On November 27, 1834, they called a meeting at John Ridge's home at Running Waters and officially founded the Treaty (or Ridge) Party. A special committee headed by John Ridge and Boudinot prepared a draft of the Treaty Party's resolutions. The document was signed by fifty-seven Cherokees. Late in 1835, John Ridge joined a delegation of Treaty (Ridge) Party representatives in Washington. On December 29, 1835, a committee that included Major Ridge, Boudinot, and eighteen other Cherokees signed the Treaty of New Echota at Boudinot's home. John Ridge, in Washington at the time, first wrote a letter of protest to the Secretary of War upon hearing of the unauthorized treaty. But once the maverick committee arrived in Washington, he decided to join its ranks and assist in formulating a supplementary treaty with more favorable conditions on March 1, 1836.

The Ridge left the Cherokee Nation in the spring of 1837 to settle in the vicinity of Honey Creek, on the border between Missouri and Arkansas. He was followed in late fall by John Ridge and his family. The Ridges managed to obtain substantial remuneration for their "improvements" in the Cherokee Nation East and were thus in the position to establish themselves comfortably as merchant-farmers and stock raisers in the Cherokee Nation West. Troubles between members of the Treaty (Ridge) Party and National (Ross) Party flared up again when most of the remaining Cherokee were finally forced to move west along the "Trail of Tears" in 1838–39. John Ridge, The Ridge, and Elias Boudinot were killed in different locations by unidentified bands of Cherokees on June 22, 1839. According to a Cherokee law—said to have originally been proposed by The Ridge and put in writing by John Ridge in October, 1829—the unauthorized sale of Cherokee lands was a capital crime.

Selected Publications of John Ridge

Cherokee Cavaliers: Forty Years of Cherokee History as Told in the Correspondence of the Ridge-Watie-Boudinot Family. Edited by Edward E. Dale and Gaston L. Litton. Norman: University of Oklahoma Press, 1939.

"Cherokee Memorial," with William Shorey Coodey and John Martin, *Cherokee Phoenix and Indians' Advocate* (March 24, 1832).

"The Cherokee War Path," ed. by Carolyn T. Foreman, *Chronicles of Oklahoma* 9, 3 (September 1931): 233–263.

"Constitution of the Moral and Literary Society." *Boston Recorder and Telegraph* 10, no. 11, (March 12, 1825): 44, chaps. 3–4.

"For the Cherokee Phoenix." *Cherokee Phoenix and Indians' Advocate* (June 25 and July 2, 1828).

"Indian Speech." *The Religious Remembrancer* 10, no. 18 (December 21, 1822): 70.

"Letter." *Cherokee Phoenix and Indians' Advocate* (March 4, 1829).

"John Ridge on Cherokee Civilization in 1826," ed. by William C. Sturtevant, *Journal of Cherokee Studies* 6, 2, (Fall 1981): 79–91; repr. as "Essay on Cherokee Civilization," in D. McQuade et al., eds., *Harper Anthology of American Literature.* New York: Harper and Row, 1987: 730–37.

"Letter." *Cherokee Phoenix and Indians' Advocate* (April 16, 1831).

"Letter." *Cherokee Phoenix and Indians' Advocate* (May 21, 1831).

"Letter." *Cherokee Phoenix and Indians' Advocate* (July 9, 1831).

"Letter." *The Christian Herald* 10, no. 15 (December 20, 1823): 467–68.

"Letter." *Niles' Register.* 40 (April 9, 1831): 96.

"Letter." *Niles' Register* 40 (June 18, 1831): 286.

"Memorial of the Delegates from the Cherokee Indians," with William Shorey Coodey and Richard Taylor. *Cherokee Phoenix and Indians' Advocate* (March 5, 1831).

"Sequoyah and the Cherokee Alphabet," in Charles Hamilton, ed., *Cry of the Thunderbird: The American Indian's Own Story.* Norman: University of Oklahoma Press, 1972: 241–42. Originally a speech quoted in Peter Jones's *History of the Ojebway Indians: With Especial Reference to Their Conversion to Christianity.* London: A.W. Bennett, 1861: 187–88.

Unpublished Writings

Ridge and Boudinot Family Papers, 1835–1890, Cherokee Nation Papers, 1801–1982, Western History Collections, University of Oklahoma Library; Georgia Department of Archives and History; Manuscript Division, University of Texas; and John Howard Payne Papers, Ayer Collection, Newberry Library. The Ayer Collection includes twenty-two poems written by John Ridge in 1819 and a letter addressed to President Monroe relating his views on the present situation of the Cherokees, dated March 8, 1822.

Selected Secondary Sources

Konkle, Maureen. "The Cherokee Resistance." In Konkle, *Writing Indian Nations: Native Intellectuals and the Politics of Historiography, 1827–1863.* Chapel Hill: University of North Carolina Press, 2004: 42–96.

McKenney, Thomas L., and James Hall. *History of the Indian Tribes of North America, with Biographical Sketches and Anecdotes of the Principal Chiefs* (1838; repr. Edinburgh: John Grant, 1934): 2: 326–32.

Sweet, Timothy. *American Georgics: Economy and Environment in Early American Literature.* Philadelphia: University of Pennsylvania Press, 2002: 122–52.

Wilkins, Thurman. *Cherokee Tragedy: The Story of the Ridge Family and the Decimation of a People.* New York: Macmillan, 1970.

LETTER TO THE EDITOR OF THE *CHEROKEE PHOENIX*

Elias Boudinot (1832)

Sir: I have read in your last paper the remarks which you have been pleased to bestow upon my letter of resignation.[1] I regret that the common courtesy, that of noticing the retirement of a brother editor, which some of the conductors of the papers with which I exchanged seem to have exercised towards me, should have made it necessary for you to direct your attention to that letter. It is hardly entitled to the importance you have given it. I certainly did not think but that it would be "like the fleeting wind, to be heard of no more." As you have, however, bestowed some remarks upon its merits, it may not be improper for me to recur to such parts of it, by way of explanation, as seem to have been misapprehended by you, and to correct the impression which may be created in the mind of the reader by the *import* of your language.

I have no objection to your subjecting any remarks which I may have published while I was honored with the management of the Cherokee Phoenix to your editorial scrutiny, provided such remarks or sentiments are presented to the public *just what they are.* I have nothing to recall from what I have said—I am willing that my words should speak for themselves, and that reprehension should be cast upon them where they *deserve* reprehension.

When we write in a language which we understand but imperfectly, and which is not our mother tongue, we are liable, as I know by experience, to use words or phrases which do not express our meaning. Such, I take it, is the case in the very first sentence of your remarks, where you represent my letter as "setting forth my *indisposition* to sustain the cause of the Cherokees." You did not mean, I presume, what these words would seem to imply; because, in my letter and explanations upon it, as your readers will recollect, I say nothing as to what my "disposition" is to sustain the cause of the Cherokees. In my *letter,* my object was merely to give a few reasons why I thought it necessary to leave my station as editor.—In my *explanations,* I alluded to some of the great, and, in my view, *insurmountable difficulties,* that are in the way of our rights being secured to us. If I had said any thing about my *disposition,* or *inclination,* if you please, I would have said that it was *strong—as strong as ever.*

One who has not read my letter would suppose that there has been an important change of sentiment in my views in regard to the all-engrossing subject among us, from such expressions as the following, which I find in your remarks: "The right of the late Editor to *change* his *opinions,* on questions involving the dearest rights of the Cherokees"—"The *change* of *sentiment* of the Editor, which this letter would seem to indicate, as despairing of the redress of our wrongs," &c. Such change of opinions or sentiments, that is, in regard to the rights of the Cherokees, and the redress of our wrongs, is not, however, implied in my letter. As to the first, you could not have meant that I had undergone such a complete "revolution" as *to deny* the "dearest rights" of the

Cherokees, or that I ever *questioned* them. As to the latter, I do not know whether, in my public capacity, I have ever expressed the opinion that our rights *would certainly be redressed;* I have the impression that I have never, however desirous I have been that such should be the case. I have been careful not to commit myself on this point, and thus create hopes, which, by possibility, to say the least, would exist only to be disappointed and frustrated. To say, then, which I have thought it my duty, in frankness, to say to my countrymen, that I do not believe that our rights will be secured to us, is not in opposition to any previous opinion expressed.

You seem, however, to intimate that I have *favored a treaty* with the Government. Your readers will recollect that I said nothing about a treaty, but urged the importance of considering our situation, and coming to some definite and satisfactory conclusion as to what ought to be done in the *last alternative.* My views as to what ought to be done *may* be somewhat different from those I formerly entertained; but if they are, they are such, in my humble opinion, as are *patriotic,* and I know they are founded upon mature and most serious reflection.

I should consider myself very hardly dealt with if I thought that you really intended to convey the idea that I was now *no more* a patriot. You could not have meant what these words would seem to imply: "As a *breach* in the *patriotic rank* of the Cherokees."—"However valuable the services of this *once* devoted *patriot,* we must bear the *loss.* The *loss* is but a drop from the bucket." There is nothing in my letter of resignation, or in my explanations, which shows a want of patriotic views and motives; my motives certainly were of the most patriotic kind. But it is needless to enlarge. My past acts will speak for themselves, and I am willing to be tried and tested for the future. I will give you a definition of the patriotism by which I profess myself to be actuated.

In one word, I may say that my patriotism consists in the *love of the country* and the *love of the people.* These are intimately connected, yet they are not altogether inseparable. They are inseparable if the people are made the first victim, for in that case the country must go also, and there must be an end of the objects of our patriotism. But if the country is lost, or is likely to be lost to all human appearance, and the people still exist, may I not, with a patriotism true and commendable, make a *question* for the safety of the remaining object of my affection?

In applying the above definition of patriotism to my conduct, I can but say that I have come to the unpleasant and most disagreeable conclusion (whether that conclusion be correct is another question) that our lands, or a large portion of them, are about to be seized and taken from us. Now, as a friend of my people, I cannot say *peace, peace,* when there is no peace. I cannot ease their minds with any expectation of a calm, when the vessel is already tossed to and fro, and threatened to be shattered to pieces by an approaching tempest. If I really believe there is danger, I must act consistently, and give the alarm; tell my countrymen our true, or what I believe to be our true, situation. In the case under consideration, I am induced to believe there is danger, "immediate and appalling," and that it becomes the people of this country to weigh the matter

rightly, act wisely, not rashly, and choose a course that will come nearest ben-
efitting the nation. When we come to the last crisis, (and my opinion is, that
we are that point,) one of three things *must* be chosen. 1. Nature's right of all
nations to resist and fight in the defence of our lands. 2. Submit and peaceably
come under the dominion of the oppressor, and suffer, which we most assuredly must if we make that choice, a *moral death!* 3. Avoid the two first by a
removal. Now the article which has given rise to your remarks merely suggests
the importance of making choice of one of the three evils, (for evils they are,)
in time. In saying this, I do not disguise that I, as one of the nation, have an
opinion on this delicate point, and am willing to express it when occasion requires. But this is not the place and time to express it, for we are merely considering the "merits" of my letter of resignation.

It may be said, to consider the matter now is premature. It may be so. If
it is, the error which I commit is an error of *judgment,* not of the *heart,* and
cannot, of course, be attributed to any want of patriotism. If it is premature to
consider this matter, it must be because there is still hope that our rights will
be "redressed." That hope, I have already said, is "undefined," and rests upon
"contingencies." The contingencies of which I speak do not at all terminate
in the election of a President, although that may not indeed be now, as our
good friend of the N.Y. Spectator seems to suppose, one of the contingencies.
He is better able to judge than I am. But suppose the present incumbent is not
re-elected, and that another individual succeeds him, whose sentiments on the
Indian question are correct, and is disposed to do us justice? I still make it a
question whether our rights can be restored to us, for the new President cannot take his seat until the 4th of March, 1833, and there is, to say the least, a
great danger of the enemy having a complete possession of one-half of our
country before that time.[2] Can the Chief Magistrate then, however disposed
he may be to do right, remove all intruders, to whom the protection of a State
is pledged, and place us *in peace,* upon our former privileges, *under the present circumstances of the country?* But there is still another contingency in
regard to the contemplated change in the administration. Suppose the new
President succeeds in restoring to us our rights? What security have we that
the restoration of our rights will be permanent, and that a President similar to
the present one will not succeed the one who does us justice, and thus the game
will not be played over anew? I can hardly consent to trust the peace and happiness of our people to political changes and party triumphs. Unfortunately for
us, the Indian question has been made a party and sectional question.

Your expression, "the loss is but a drop in the bucket," may be interpreted
in two ways. It may mean that my opinions or exertions as an individual are
nothing compared to the nation, and, of course, the *loss* to them is but of little
moment; or it may mean that I am *detached* from the nation, and that no one
approves of the views I have given in my letter of resignation. If you mean the
first, you are certainly correct, for my opinions or exertions are of little consequence—they are but a "drop from the bucket." If you mean the second, I will
only say that I am not *detached from,* but *attached to,* the nation, and that there

are those connected with the Judicial, Executive, and Legislative departments of our little Government, men of intelligence and patriotism, who cordially approve of the remarks and suggestions contained in the article upon which you have commented.

In alluding to a letter signed by a number of our friends in Congress, addressed to Mr. Ross, and another from one of the Judges of the Supreme Court, I had no other object than to show my readers the views entertained by those gentlemen on the subject, and to strengthen, by such high authority, the opinions I had expressed. I thought those views, coming as they did from such a quarter, were worthy of all attention and respect, and I had every reason to believe that the motives of those who communicated them were of the purest kind.[3]

Respectfully,
E. BOUDINOT.

Notes

The letter, dated October 2, 1832, was originally addressed to Elijah Hicks, brother-in-law and devoted follower of John Ross, who assumed the editorship of the *Cherokee Phoenix* early in September. (The first issue under his name appeared September 8, 1832.) Boudinot wrote the letter in response to derogatory comments Hicks made in the September 29 issue of the *Phoenix* concerning Boudinot's resignation. Hicks refused to publish the response at the time because "the authorities of the nation are opposed to the introduction of controversial matter in the Phoenix." Boudinot then included it in his forty-three-page tract tilted *Letters and Other Papers Relating to Cherokee Affairs; Being in Reply to Sundry Publications Authorized by John Ross. By E. Boudinot, Formerly Editor of the Cherokee Phoenix* (Athens, Ga.: Southern Banner, 1837), 7–10. Boudinot published this tract in response to two anti-removal tracts published earlier by John Ross: *Letter from John Ross, Principal Chief of the Cherokee Nation of Indians, in Answer to Inquiries from a Friend Regarding the Cherokee Affairs with the United States* (n.p.: 1836), excerpted in *Nile's Weekly Register* (October 1, 1836): 90–92; and *Letter from John Ross, Principal Chief of the Cherokee Nation, to a Gentleman of Philadelphia* (n.p.: 1837). See John Ross, *The Papers of Chief John Ross, 1807–1839,* ed. Gary E. Moulton (Norman: University of Oklahoma Press, 1985), 1:444–56, 490–503. Governor Lumpkin of Georgia had approximately four hundred copies of Boudinot's tract reprinted and distributed as propaganda to members of the Senate as *Documents in Relation to the Validity of the Cherokee Treaty of 1835 . . . Letters and Other Papers Relating to Cherokee Affairs: Being a Reply to Sundry Publications Authorized by John Ross* (Washington, D.C.: Blair & Rives, 1838). The letter reproduced here is from the 1837 edition.

1. Boudinot wrote a letter of resignation to John Ross on August 1, 1832. It was printed in the *Cherokee Phoenix* August 11, 1832. Boudinot's letter of resignation, also included in his *Letters and Other Papers Relating to Cherokee Affairs,* is reproduced in Elias Boudinot, *Cherokee Editor: The Writings of Elias Boudinot,* ed. Theda Perdue (Knoxville: University of Tennessee Press, 1983), 163–64; John Ross, *The Papers of Chief John Ross,* 1:247–48.

2. Prior to the Twentieth Amendment to the United States Constitution, presidents were inaugurated on March 4 rather than January 20. Two presidential candidates running against Jackson in 1832 were sympathetic to the Cherokees: Henry Clay, the candidate of the National Republican party; and William Wirt, attorney for the Cherokees and the candidate for the Anti-Masonic party.

3. Once it became clear that President Jackson either would not or could not enforce the Supreme Court's favorable decision in *Worcester v. Georgia* in late February 1832, outspoken champions of the Cherokee cause such as Senator Theodore Frelighuysen, Associate Justice John McLean, and David Greene of the ABCFM advised the Cherokee that further resistance was deemed futile by most of the "friendly" congressmen. For different interpretations of Jackson's role in this key case, see Anton-Hermann Chroust, "Did President Jackson Actually Threaten the Supreme Court with Nonenforcement of Its Injunction Against the State of Georgia?" *American Journal of Legal History* 5, (January 1960): 76–78; Edwin A. Miles, "After John Marshall's Decision: *Worcester v. Georgia* and the Nullification Crisis," *Journal of Southern History* 39, no. 4 (November 1973): 519–44; Francis P. Prucha, "Andrew Jackson's Indian Policy: A Reassessment," *Journal of American History* 56, no. 3 (December 1969): 527–39; and Ronald N. Satz, "Rhetoric Versus Reality: The Indian Policy of Andrew Jackson," in William L. Anderson, ed., *Cherokee Removal: Before and After* (Athens: University of Georgia Press, 1991), 29–54.

RESOLUTIONS OF THE TREATY PARTY

Elias Boudinot and John Ridge (1834)

RESOLUTIONS.

Whereas, a crisis of the utmost importance, in the affairs of the Cherokee people has arrived, requiring from every individual the most serious reflection and the expression of views as to the present condition and future prospects of the Nation; and whereas a portion of the Cherokees have entertained opinions which have been represented as hostile to the true interest and happiness of the people, merely because they have not agreed with the Chiefs and leading men; and as these opinions have not heretofore been properly made known, therefore,

Resolved, That it is our decided opinion, founded upon the melancholy experience of the Cherokees within the last two years, and upon facts which history has furnished us in regard to other Indian nations, that our people cannot exist amidst a white population, subject to laws which they have no hand in making, and which they do not understand; that the suppression of the Cherokee Government, which connected this people in a distinct community, will not only check their progress in improvement and advancement in knowledge, but, by means of numerous influences and temptations which this new state of things has created, will completely destroy every thing like civilization among them, and ultimately reduce them to poverty, misery, and wretchedness.

Resolved, That, considering the progress of the States' authorities in this country, the distribution and settlement of the lands, the organization of counties, the erection of county seats and court houses, and other indications of a determined course on the part of the surrounding States, and considering, on the other hand, the repeated refusal of the President and Congress of the United States to interfere in our behalf, we have come to the conclusion that this nation cannot be reinstated in its present location, and that the question left to us and to every Cherokee, is, whether it is more desirable to remain here, with all the embarrassments with which we must be surrounded, or to seek a country where we *may* enjoy our own laws, and live under our own vine and fig-tree.[1]

Resolved, That in expressing the opinion that this nation cannot be reinstated, we do it from a thorough conviction of its truth; that we never will encourage our confiding people with hopes that can never be realized, and with expectations that will assuredly be disappointed; that however unwelcome and painful the truth may be to them, and however unkindly it may be received from us, we cannot, as *patriots* and well-wishers of the Indian race, shrink from doing our duty in expressing our decided convictions. That we scorn the charge of selfishness and a want of patriotic feelings alleged against us by some of our countrymen, while we can appeal to our consciences and the searcher of all hearts for the rectitude of our motives and intentions.

Resolved, That, although *we love the land* of our fathers, and should leave the place of our nativity with as much regret as any of our citizens, we consider the lot of the *exile* immeasurably more to be preferred than a submission to the laws of the States, and thus becoming witnesses of the ruin and degradation of the Cherokee people.

Resolved, That we are firmly of the opinion, that a large majority of the Cherokee people would prefer to remove, if the true state of their condition was properly made known to them. We believe that if they were told that they had nothing to expect from further efforts to regain their rights as a *distinct community,* and that the only alternatives left to them is either to remain amidst a white population, subject to the white man's laws, or to remove to another country, where they *may* enjoy peace and happiness, they would unhesitatingly prefer the latter.

Resolved, That we were desirous to leave our Chiefs and leading men to seek a country for their people, but as they have thought proper not to do any thing towards the ultimate removal of the nation, we know of none to which the Cherokees can go as asylum but that possessed by our brethren west of the Mississippi; that we are willing to unite with them under a proper guaranty from the United States that the lands shall be secured to us, and that we shall be governed by our own laws and regulations.[2]

Resolved, That we consider the policy pursued by the Red Clay Council, in continuing a useless struggle from year to year, as destructive to the present peace and future happiness of the Cherokees, because it is evident to every observer that while this struggle is going on, their difficulties will be accumulating, until they are ruined in their property and character, and the only remedy that will then be proposed in their case will be, *submission to the laws of the States* by taking reservations.

Resolved, That we consider the fate of our poor brethren, the Creeks, to be a sufficient warning to all those who may finally subject the Cherokees to the laws of the States by giving them reservations.[3]

Resolved, That we will never consent to have our own rights and the rights of our posterity, sold *"prospectively"* to the laws of the States by our Chiefs, in any compact or "compromise" into which they may choose to enter with the Government; that we cannot be satisfied with any thing less than a release from State Legislation; but, while we do not intend to have our own political interests compromised, we shall not oppose those who prefer to remain subject to State laws.

Resolved, That we were disposed to contend for what we considered to be our own rights, as long as there was any hope of relief *to the nation,* but that we never can consent to the waste of our public moneys in instituting and prosecuting suits which will result only to individual advantage.

Resolved, That it is with great surprise and mortification we have noticed the idea attempted to be conveyed to the minds of our people that the *nation* can be relieved by the courts of Georgia; that we regard the appealing to those

Courts, *by the nation,* for redress, as an entire departure from the true policy maintained by the Cherokees in their struggle for national existence.[4]

NOVEMBER, 1834.

Notes

During a meeting at Running Waters on November 27, 1834, Boudinot, John Ridge and other Cherokee dissenters officially founded the Treaty (or Ridge) Party. The ad hoc council named a panel of delegates, including John Ridge and Boudinot, to represent the Treaty Party's cause in Washington. A special committee headed by John Ridge and Boudinot prepared a draft of the Treaty Party's resolutions, which was then signed by fifty-seven Cherokees. Boudinot also included the resolutions in his *Letters and Other Papers Relating to Cherokee Affairs* (1837), 10–13.

1. Georgia's legislature reacted at once to the decision in *Worcester v. Georgia* by passing an act in April 1832 authorizing the survey of Cherokee lands to prepare for distribution to white citizens by a lottery system. This move, and the re-election of Andrew Jackson that same year, was the primary motivation behind the founding of the Treaty Party.

2. Chief Bowles had already led a group of voluntary exiles to Arkansas territory in 1794. In 1808 they were followed by approximately a thousand Chickamaugan Cherokees. In 1817, another two to three thousand Cherokees agreed to give up their lands in exchange for new territory on the Arkansas and White Rivers in a dubious treaty with the United States that had only been signed by a minority of chiefs. In all, approximately five thousand Cherokees had moved west of the Mississippi by 1828, where they became known collectively as the "Arkansas Cherokees," or "Old Settlers."

3. On April 4, 1832, a Creek delegation was coerced into signing a second removal treaty in Washington, eventually forcing more than 20,000 Creeks to make the difficult journey west. Approximately 2,500 Creeks who decided instead to choose allotments under state jurisdiction lost most of their land through fraud. See Mary E. Young, *Redskins, Ruffleshirts and Rednecks: Indian Allotments in Alabama and Mississippi* (Norman: University of Oklahoma Press, 1961).

4. The Treaty Party members believed that if the Cherokees filed a suit in Georgia's courts this would be a tacit admission that they were subject to state law.

BIOGRAPHY

Elias Boudinot (Cherokee, ca. 1804–39), or Gallegina ("The Buck"), was born at Oothcaloga, Cherokee Nation, the oldest son of Oowatie and Susanna Reese. Oothcaloga was founded around 1800 in the northwestern part of Georgia by "progressive" Cherokees like Oowatie, who took the name David Watie, and his elder brother, The Ridge. In 1810, The Ridge convinced David Watie to send "Buck" Watie to the Moravian Spring Place Mission School, where Buck was instructed from 1811 to 1815 and from 1816 to 1818. That same year Rev. Elias Cornelius of the American Board of Commissioners for Foreign Missions (ABCFM) chose Buck Watie, John Ridge, David Brown, and five other promising Cherokee students to attend the Foreign Mission School in Cornwall, Connecticut. On his way to the school, Buck Watie met with the elderly philanthropist Elias Boudinot. Boudinot who bequeathed to Watie his Christian name and made him his beneficiary. Buck Watie, now Elias Boudinot, remained at the Foreign Mission School until the fall of 1822. During this time he joined the First Congregational Church. Late in 1822 he enrolled in the Andover Theological Seminary in Massachusetts, along with David Brown. Boudinot soon had to give up his studies there, however, and return to the Cherokee Nation because of poor health.

During the 1824 fall meeting at New Town (New Echota), the General Council resolved to establish a national academy for Cherokee students and a national museum in which samples of traditional Cherokee material culture were to be kept under the care of Elias Boudinot. Although these plans were only partially realized at a later date, they showed that Boudinot was already actively involved in Cherokee affairs. On November 5, 1824, Boudinot cofounded the Moral and Literary Society of the Cherokee Nation and was appointed to be its corresponding secretary. He also served the General Council as clerk from 1825 to 1827. During a fall session in 1825, the General Council appointed Boudinot to embark upon a fund-raising tour for the establishment of a Cherokee national press and seminary. Boudinot departed in the spring of 1826 and gave promotional speeches in Charleston, New York, Salem, Boston, and Philadelphia. A speech delivered in Philadelphia was published that same year as a promotional tract titled *An Address to the Whites*. Boudinot visited Cornwall long enough to marry Harriet Ruggles Gold, daughter of the agent for the Foreign Mission School, on March 28. The wedding unleashed such a storm of protest within the local Congregationalist community that the Foreign Mission School was forced to shut down in the autumn of 1826. Boudinot and his wife moved to Hightower, Cherokee Nation, where he briefly taught school.

On October 18, 1826, the General Council approved the founding of a national newspaper and the hiring of an editor. Boudinot moved to New Echota in 1827 to assume the functions of an editor and to assist Rev. Samuel Worcester of the ABCFM in translating religious texts into Cherokee using Sequoyah's syllabary. The first issue of the *Cherokee Phoenix* (later *Cherokee Phoenix and Indians' Advocate*) appeared under Boudinot's editorship on February 21, 1828. Boudinot continued to serve as editor of the *Cherokee Phoenix* until his resignation on August 1, 1832. Under his guidance, the Cherokee national newspaper evolved into a formidable anti-removal organ of the Cherokee administration. After Boudinot resigned, the *Cherokee Phoenix* only appeared irregularly until May of 1824.

After a second fund-raising tour of the United States on behalf of the *Cherokee Phoenix* from the fall of 1831 to the summer of 1832, Boudinot began having second thoughts about the feasibility of resisting removal. It became increasingly clear that the Jackson administration would not interfere with Georgia's actions in spite of the Supreme Court's injunction. In the spring of 1833 Elias Boudinot, John Ridge, and Major Ridge signed a petition of protest against the course hitherto followed by the Ross administration. On November 27, 1834, Boudinot co-founded the Treaty (Ridge) Party at John Ridge's home at Running Waters and assisted his cousin in preparing a draft of the party's pro-removal resolutions. Under political pressure, John Ross attempted to reach a compromise with the Treaty (Ridge) Party late in 1835. Ross appointed Boudinot and John Ridge as delegates to Washington, but Boudinot declined the assignment in favor of his brother, Stand Watie (1806–71). On December 29, 1835, Boudinot, The Ridge, and eighteen other Cherokees signed the Treaty of New Echota at Boudinot's home. Although the Treaty of New Echota was never authorized by the Cherokee administration, an amended version was subsequently ratified by Congress in 1836. The Cherokees were given until May 26, 1838, to move west of the Mississippi.

Following the death of his wife in 1836, Boudinot married Delight Sargeant, a teacher at Brainerd, and moved with his family to Park Hill, Cherokee Nation West, in the fall of 1837. Here he resumed his translating work with Rev. Worcester. That same year Boudinot also published *Letters and Other Papers Relating to Cherokee Affairs,* an attempt to legitimize the Treaty (Ridge) Party's minority standpoint. On June 22, 1839, Elias Boudinot met the same violent end as Major Ridge and John Ridge, undoubtedly in retaliation for having signed the Treaty of New Echota five years earlier. Stand Watie managed to thwart plans for his assassination and took up the leadership of the Treaty (Ridge) Party thereafter in a prolonged conflict that would threaten to split the Cherokee Nation West into two independent political entities.

Selected Publications of Elias Boudinot

An Address to the Whites Delivered in the First Presbyterian Church, on the 20th of May, 1826, by Elias Boudinot, A Cherokee Indian. Philadelphia: Printed by William F. Geddes, 1826.

Cherokee Cavaliers: Forty Years of Cherokee History as Told in the Correspondence of the Ridge-Watie-Boudinot Family. Edited by Edward E. Dale and Gaston L. Litton. Norman: University of Oklahoma Press, 1939.

Cherokee Editor: The Writings of Elias Boudinot. Edited by Theda Perdue. Knoxville: University of Tennesee Press, 1983.

Letters and Other Papers Relating to Cherokee Affairs; Being in Reply to Sundry Publications Authorized by John Ross. By E. Boudinot, Formerly Editor of the Cherokee Phoenix. Athens, Ga.: Southern Banner, 1837; repr. as *Documents in Relation to the Validity of the Cherokee Treaty of 1835 . . . Letters and Other Papers Relating to Cherokee Affairs: Being a Reply to Sundry Publications Authorized by John Ross.* Washington, D.C.: Blair and Rives, 1838.

"Letters of the Two Boudinots." Edited by Edward E. Dale, *Chronicles of Oklahoma* 6, no. 3 (September 1928): 328–47.

"Prospectus for Publishing at New Echota, in the Cherokee Nation, a Weekly Newspaper, to be Called the *Cherokee Phoenix.*" Broadside, 1827.

Unpublished Writings

Ridge and Boudinot Family Papers, 1835–1890, Cherokee Nation Papers, 1801–1982, Western History Collections, University of Oklahoma Library.

Selected Secondary Sources

Church, Mary Boudinot. "Elias Boudinot," *The Magazine of History* 17, no. 6 (December 1913): 209–21.

Franks, Kenny. *Stand Watie and the Agony of the Cherokee Nation.* Memphis: Memphis State University Press, 1979.

Gabriel, Ralph Henry. *Elias Boudinot, Cherokee, and His America* Norman: University of Oklahoma Press, 1941.

Konkle, Maureen. "The Cherokee Resistance." In Konkle, *Writing Indian Nations: Native Intellectuals and the Politics of Historiography, 1827–1863.* Chapel Hill: University of North Carolina Press, 2004: 42–96.

Luebke, Barbara F. "Elias Boudinot, Indian Editor: Editorial Columns from the Cherokee Phoenix." *Journalism History* 6, no. 2 (Summer 1979): 48–53.

Perdue, Theda. "Introduction." In *Cherokee Editor: The Writing of Elias Boudinot* ed. The da Perdue. Knoxville: University of Tennessee Press, 1983: 3–38.

Peyer, Bernd. "Elias Boudinot and the Cherokee Betrayal." In Peyer, *The Tutor'd Mind: Indian Missionary-Writers in Antebellum America.* Amherst: University of Massachusetts Press, 1997: 166–223.

Sweet, Timothy. *American Georgics: Economy and Environment in Early American Literature.* Philadelphia: University of Pennsylvania Press, 2002: 122–52.

Weaver, Jace. *That the People May Live: Native American Literatures and the Native American Community.* New York: Oxford University Press, 1997: 69–75.

Wilkins, Thurman. *Cherokee Tragedy: The Story of the Ridge Family and the Decimation of a People.* New York: Macmillan, 1970.

TO THE SENATE AND HOUSE OF REPRESENTATIVES

John Ross et al (1836)

Most respectfully, and most humbly showeth: That your memorialists, the Chiefs, National Committee and Council, and people of the Cherokee Nation in General Council assembled, solicit permission to approach your honorable bodies, under circumstances peculiar in the history of nations; circumstances of distress and anxiety beyond our power to express. We earnestly bespeak your patience, therefore, while we lay before you a brief epitome of our griefs.

It is well known that for a number of years past we have been harassed by a series of vexations, which it is deemed unnecessary to recite in detail, but the evidence of which our delegation will be prepared to furnish. With a view to bringing our troubles to a close, a delegation was appointed on the 23rd of October, 1835, by the General Council of the nation, clothed with full powers to enter into arrangements with the Government of the United States, for the final adjustment of all our existing difficulties. The delegation failing to effect an arrangement with the United States commissioner, then in the nation, proceeded, agreeably to their instructions in that case, to Washington city, for the purpose of negotiating a treaty with the authorities of the United States.

After the departure of the Delegation, a contract was made by the Rev. John F. Schermerhorn, and certain individual Cherokees, purporting to be a "treaty, concluded at New Echota, in the State of Georgia, on the 29th day of December, 1835, by General William Carroll and John F. Schermerhorn, commissioners on the part of the United States, and the chiefs, headmen, and people of the Cherokee tribes of Indians.[1] A spurious Delegation, in violation of a special injunction of the general council of the nation, proceeded to Washington City with this pretended treaty, and by false and fraudulent representations supplanted in the favor of the Government the legal and accredited Delegation of the Cherokee people, and obtained for this instrument, after making important alterations in its provisions, the recognition of the United States Government. And now it is presented to us as a treaty, ratified by the Senate, and approved by the President, and our acquiescence in its requirements demanded, under the sanction of the displeasure of the United States, and the threat of summary compulsion, in case of refusal. It comes to us, not through our legitimate authorities, the known and usual medium of communication between the Government of the United States and our nation, but through the agency of a complication of powers, civil and military.[2]

By the stipulations of this instrument, we are despoiled of our private possessions, the indefeasible property of individuals. We are stripped of every attribute of freedom and eligibility for legal self-defence. Our property may be plundered before our eyes; violence may be committed on our persons; even our lives may be taken away, and there is none to regard our complaints. We are denationalized; we are disfranchised. We are deprived of membership in the human family! We have neither land nor home, nor resting place that can be called our own. And this is effected by the provisions of a compact which assumes the venerated, the sacred appellation of treaty.

We are overwhelmed! Our hearts are sickened, our utterance is paralized, when we reflect on the condition in which we are placed, by the audacious practices of unprincipled men, who have managed their stratagems with so much dexterity as to impose on the Government of the United States, in the face of our earnest, solemn, and reiterated protestations.

The instrument in question is not the act of our Nation; we are not parties to its covenants; it has not received the sanction of our people. The makers of it sustain no office nor appointment in our Nation, under the designation of Chiefs, Head men, or any other title, by which they hold, or could acquire, authority to assume the reins of Government, and to make bargain and sale of our rights, our possessions, and our common country. And we are constrained solemnly to declare, that we cannot but contemplate the enforcement of the stipulations of this instrument on us, against our consent, as an act of injustice and oppression, which, we are well persuaded, can never knowingly be countenanced by the Government and people of the United States; nor can we believe it to be the design of these honorable and highminded individuals, who stand at the head of the Govt., to bind a whole Nation, by the acts of a few unauthorized individuals. And, therefore, we, the parties to be affected by the result, appeal with confidence to the justice, the magnanimity, the compassion, of your honorable bodies against the enforcement, on us, of the provisions of a compact, in the formation of which we have had no agency.

In truth, our cause is your own; it is the cause of liberty and of justice; it is based upon your own principles, which we have learned from yourselves; for we have gloried to count your Washington and your Jefferson our great teachers; we have read their communications to us with veneration; we have practised their precepts with success. And the result is manifest. The wildness of the forest has given place to comfortable dwellings and cultivated fields, stocked with the various domestic animals. Mental culture, industrious habits, and domestic enjoyments, have succeeded the rudeness of the savage state.

We have learned your religion also. We have read your Sacred books. Hundreds of our people have embraced their doctrines, practised the virtues they teach, cherished the hopes they awaken, and rejoiced in the consolations which they afford. To the spirit of your institutions, and your religion, which has been imbibed by our community, is mainly to be ascribed that patient endurance which has characterized the conduct of our people, under the laceration of their keenest woes. For assuredly, we are not ignorant of our condition; we are not insensible to our sufferings. We feel them! we groan under their pressure! And anticipation crowds our breasts with sorrows yet to come. We are, indeed, an afflicted people! Our spirits are subdued! Despair has well nigh seized upon our energies! But we speak to the representatives of a Christian country; the friends of justice; the patrons of the oppressed. And our hopes revive, and our prospects brighten, as we indulge the thought. On your sentence, our fate is suspended; prosperity or desolation depends on your word. To you, therefore, we look! Before your august assembly we present ourselves, in the attitude of deprecation, and of entreaty. On your kindness, on your humanity, on your compassion, on your benevolence, we rest our hopes. To you we address our reiterated prayers. Spare our people! Spare the wreck of our prosperity! Let not our deserted homes become the monuments of our desolation! But we forbear! We suppress the agonies which wring our hearts, when we look at our wives, our children, and our venerable sires! We restrain the forebodings of anguish and distress, of misery and devastation and death, which must be the attendants on the execution of this ruinous compact.

In conclusion, we commend to your confidence and favor, our well-beloved and trust-worthy brethren and fellow-citizens, John Ross, Principal Chief, Richard Taylor, Samuel Gunter, John Benge, George Sanders, Walter S. Adair, Stephen Foreman, and Kalsateehee of Aquo-hee, who are clothed with full powers to adjust all our existing difficulties by treaty arrangements with the United States, by which our destruction may be averted, impediments to the advancement of our people removed, and our existence perpetuated as a living monument, to testify to posterity the honor, the magnanimity, the generosity of the United States. And your memorialists, as in duty bound, will ever pray. Signed by Ross, George Lowrey, Edward Gunter, Lewis Ross, thirty-one members of the National Committee and National Council, and 2,174 others.[3]

Notes

File Copy, National Archives, RG 233, 25th Cong.; Printed Copy, Cong. Serial 315, Senate Doc. 120, 799–802; Printed Copy, Cong. Serial 325, House Doc. 99, 11–13. Drafted at the Red Clay Council Ground, Cherokee Nation, September 28, 1836. Ross included it in his *Letter from John Ross, Principal Chief of the Cherokee Nation, to a Gentleman of Philadelphia* (n.p.: 1837), 22–24. Reproduced in *The Papers of Chief John Ross*, 1: 458–61. Reprinted with permission of the University of Oklahoma Press. This is one of many desperate memorials to Congress attributed to Ross in which the official Cherokee government protested the illegal Treaty of New Echota.

1. Rev. John Schermerhorn (1786–1851) was U. S. Commissioner for Cherokee emigration in 1835–36; William Carroll (1788–1844) was Governor of Tennessee in 1829–35 and Commissioner to the Cherokee in 1836.

2. On December 29, 1835, a committee that included Elias Boudinot and eighteen other Cherokees signed the notorious Treaty of New Echota at Boudinot's home. John Ridge and Boudinot's brother Stand Watie, members of the delegation in Washington at the time, wrote a letter of protest to the Secretary of War upon first hearing of the illicit treaty. Once the maverick committee arrived in Washington with Schermerhorn, however, Ridge and Watie decided to join its ranks and assist in formulating a supplementary treaty on March 1, 1836, comprised of somewhat more favorable conditions. In spite of a storm of protest from the Cherokees and numerous congressmen the treaty was ratified in the Senate by a "majority" of one vote on May 17, 1836. It was then promptly declared law by

President Jackson on May 23. The federal government gave the Cherokees until May 26, 1838 to leave their ancestral homelands permanently and join their relatives west of the Mississippi.

3. Walter Scott Adair (1791–1854) was a former district judge and justice of the Cherokee Supreme Court from 1826–30. John Benge (1796?–1853) served as a delegate to Washington on several occasions between 1836 and 1844. Samuel Gunter (1787?–1838) was member of the National Committee from 1833–35 and 1838. Edward Gunter (1789–1842) was a Methodist minister and member of the Executive Council in 1834. Stephen Foreman (1807–81) studied at Union Theological Seminary, Virginia, and Princeton Theological Seminary, New Jersey, from 1830–33. He served as Presbyterian minister from 1834–38 and as clerk of the National Committee from 1836–38. George Lowrey (1770?–1852) translated Cherokee laws from English into Cherokee with David Brown in 1828 and served as assistant principal chief in 1828 and from 1843–51. Lewis Ross (1792–1870), brother of John Ross, was a member of the Executive Council in 1835 and 1838. Richard Taylor (1788–1853) was agency interpreter and member of the National Committee from 1827–29. See "Biographical Sketches" in *The Papers of Chief John Ross*, 2: 715–39.

BIOGRAPHY

John Ross (Cherokee, 1790–1866) was born at Turkey Town (present-day Alabama) on October 3, the son of Daniel Ross, a Scottish trader, and a part-Cherokee mother. John Ross grew up at his father's home near Lookout Mountain (Tennessee), where he received instruction from private tutors for an unknown number of years and may have attended a mission school near Chickamauga and an academy in Kingston, Tennessee. In 1813 he married Elizabeth Brown Henley (Quatie), said to have been a full-blood Cherokee. John Ross served as an adjutant in the Red Stick War (1813–14), and afterward established a highly profitable warehouse and trading post on the Tennessee River known as Ross's Landing (now Chattanooga, Tennessee). Later he turned to agricultural ventures using slave labor.

John Ross became involved in Cherokee politics in 1811, when he joined the Standing Committee as one of the so-called young chiefs. During an internal crisis in 1808–11, when the Lower Town chiefs wanted to remove to lands in present-day Arkansas and a segment of Upper Town Cherokee favored separation, the "young chiefs" took a firm stand for a unified nation, a more highly centralized form of government, and tribal ownership of land. John Ross also served as a delegate to Washington in 1816 and was elected to the presidency of the National Committee in 1819. His reputation among the Cherokees was enhanced in 1823 when he publicly rejected a bribe offered by William McIntosh, the Creek leader executed by his own people two years later for signing an unauthorized removal treaty. In 1827, John Ross established a new home near New Echota (now Rome, Georgia) in order to be closer to the seat of the Cherokee administration. That year he presided over the Cherokee constitutional convention and is thought to have played a substantial role in its formulation. In October of 1828, John Ross was elected Principal Chief, a position he held until his death in 1846.

John Ross, who converted to Methodism in 1829, believed that it was under the "fostering care" of the United States that the Cherokees had emerged "from the darkness of ignorance and superstition to [their] present degree of advancement in civilized improvement." He thus shared the ideology of selective adaptation propagated by the Ridges and Boudinot. A lasting association between Ross and the conservative majority of the Cherokees emerged as a result of both Ross's resistance of removal and his unremitting efforts to keep the Cherokee Nation unified and sovereign. John Ross was the primary force behind the Cherokee tactic of nonviolent resistance to the Removal Act of 1830, including, for example, the appeals to the Supreme Court that resulted in the fundamental "Cherokee Nation Cases" in 1831–32. From the 1836 congressional ratification of an amended version of the unauthorized Treaty of New Echota, to 1838, John Ross was in Washington almost continually. He lobbied for the abrogation or at least forestallment of the treaty. Ross also wrote numerous letters and petitions to a substantial number of American administrators and philanthropists who sympathized with the Cherokees. When he returned to the Cherokee Nation in the summer of 1828, John Ross took on the thankless task of supervising Cherokee removal in order to make the arduous passage west as bearable as possible. Among the many casualties of the Cherokee Trail of Tears was John Ross's wife, Elizabeth, who died near Little Rock, Arkansas, on February 1, 1839.

In the Cherokee Nation West, John Ross had to contend with serious factional disputes that immediately developed between the resident Western Cherokees ("Old Settlers"), who wished to retain their own form of government; the recently arrived Treaty (Ridge) Party people, who voluntarily placed themselves under the rule of the "Old Settlers"; and the vast majority of "New Emigrants," who wanted to reestablish their constitutional government. In 1839, the "New Emigrants" ratified a new constitution without the approval of the "Old Settlers" and reelected John Ross as Principal Chief. With the assassinations of the Ridges and Boudinot by members of the National (Ross) Party that same year, violence threatened to escalate into civil war. In the winter of 1845–46, the "Old Settlers" and Treaty (Ridge) Party people headed by Stand Watie sent delegates to Washington to attain a political and geographical partition of the Cherokee Nation West. Largely through the efforts of John Ross, a compromise was finally reached with a treaty enacted August 6, 1846, bringing temporary peace and prosperity to the Cherokee Nation West. John Ross married Mary Brian Stapler, a young Quaker from Delaware, and settled down at his new home at Park Hill.

With the outbreak of the American Civil War, the feud among the Cherokees flared up again. Under pressure, John Ross called for an alliance with the Confederacy at a general council held in August of 1861. Shortly thereafter, when Union troops invaded the Cherokee Nation West, Ross fled to Washington and then later Philadelphia, and tried to convince Lincoln that the Cherokee alliance with the Confederacy had been involuntary. After the Civil War, the Southern faction elected Stand Watie—said to have been the last Confederate general to surrender—as Principal Chief and sent delegates to Washington once again to press for the formation of two separate Cherokee states. Although impaired by poor health, John Ross also traveled to the nation's capital to lobby for the preservation of a unified Cherokee Nation. He died there on August 1, 1866. Ross's efforts to keep the Cherokee Nation together ultimately bore fruit under the Cherokee Reconstruction Treaty, signed at Fort Smith on July 19 and proclaimed August 11, 1866.

Selected Publications of John Ross

The Papers of Chief John Ross. Edited by Gary E. Moulton. 2 vols. Norman: University of Oklahoma Press, 1985.

Selected Secondary Sources

Conser, Jr., Walter H. "John Ross and the Cherokee Resistance Campaign, 1833–1838," *Journal of Southern History* 44, no. 2, (May 1978): 191–212.

Eaton, Rachel. *John Ross and the Cherokee Indians.* Menasha, Wisc.: George Banta Publishing Co., 1914. Reprint, Chicago: University of Chicago, 1921.

Konkle, Maureen. *Writing Indian Nations: Native Intellectuals and the Politics of Historiography, 1827–1863.* Chapel Hill, University of North Carolina Press, 2004: 42–96.

Moulton, Gary E. *John Ross, Cherokee Chief.* Athens, Ga.: University of Georgia Press, 1978.

_____. "John Ross." In *American Indian Leaders: Studies in Diversity.* Edited by David R. Edmunds. Lincoln: University of Nebraska Press, 1980: 88–106.

Perdue, Theda. "John Ross and the Cherokees." *Georgia Historical Quarterly* 70, no. 3, (Fall 1986): 456–76.

Sweet, Timothy. *American Georgics: Economy and Environment in Early American Literature.* Philadelphia: University of Pennsylvania Press, 2002: 122–52.

THE CHEROKEES. THEIR HISTORY—PRESENT CONDITION AND FUTURE PROSPECTS

John Rollin Ridge (1849)

The Cherokee people have, more than any other Indians perhaps, engaged the attention of the citizens and government of the United States. So many associations have existed between the whites and them; so many noble and thrilling incidents have filled up their history; so many tragical events have occurred amongst them, and finally, their doom, for the last twelve or thirteen years, has been so unfortunately dark, that philanthropists and statesmen could not but look upon them with the intensest interest. To behold a branch of the aborigines of this continent, quietly seated in their acknowledged territory; having abandoned their savage customs and habits for the condition of civilized life; creating for themselves a simple but a wise form of government, and gathering around them all those circumstances which were favorable to their advancement in human knowledge and human happiness, was indeed a lovely and beautiful vision. But, to see them, while thus prosperous and happy, rudely thrown, by the iron arm of cold State policy, from the proud elevation which they had attained by the work of long and painful years; to see the fire-brands of discord and contention hurled in their midst, to blast and wither their energies, and almost effectually to cancel all the good which they had wrought themselves, was truly a painful contrast, and a heart-rending sight. [Ah, well may the intelligent Cherokee weep over the fallen condition of his tribe, and curse, deeply, and bitterly curse, the hand which placed it there.]

The meagre [sic], but fatal pretensions of Georgia, and the surrounding States to the territory of the Cherokees, on the miserable ground that it lay within their "chartered limits," are well known to every intelligent man. It is unnecessary to recount the events of that unfortunate period. It is a matter of history, that the Cherokees, when their country was so unjustly about to be wrested from them, contended nobly on their behalf, and that a brilliant array of native intellect was called forth from amongst them to defend their natural and guaranteed rights. It is known that the contest was vain. The Treaty of 1835, which removed them to the west of the Mississippi, was literally forced upon them by a dire train of imperious circumstances, and those, who, actuated by a generous devotion to their people, dared to sign that instrument shortly afterwards poured their pure and patriot blood on the altar of Revenge, where they were sacrificed by their own sadly mistaken race.[1]

The stern denial of justice by the Supreme Court of the United States in 1831, produced that deadly difference of opinion, which has reigned amongst the Cherokees ever since that date.[2] They saw that the last hope was crushed. A portion became in favor of removal, the other against it. The Old Settlers were already in possession of the country now occupied by the entire nation, and consequently, after the Treaty of 1835, and the removal of the eastern

Cherokees to the west of the Mississippi, there were three distinct parties existing in that one tribe. These divisions have been extremely fatal. Excitement has reigned for a long continuance of years, conspiracies have been laid and blood has flowed in torrents. It is true that a treaty, made in 1846 between the three Cherokee delegations, representing the three different parties, and the government of the United States, established peace in the nation.[3] But this peace is based upon such terms as render it entirely unsatisfactory to a large portion of all parties. Members of the Ross party who are actuated by bitter animosity towards the Ridge or Treaty Party, are dissatisfied that any quarters should be allowed them, and would fain see the bloodhound system of "Policemen" revived, whose habit it was to hunt down and slay all men, whose sentiments were opposed to the Cherokee government, as it was then administered.[4] Old Settlers are dissatisfied, because their portion of the money due the Cherokees by the Gov. U.S. was rendered so small by the Treaty of 1846; and they also agree with the Treaty Party in their main cause of dissatisfaction, that matters are left by the Treaty of '46, precisely where they were before. John Ross is permitted to remain in the authority which he usurped, and at the head of a government, erected on the ruins of another, the first legitimate government of the Old Settlers. Then there is another portion of the nation, (not inconsiderable by any means) who have framed themselves into a banditti, and attracting to themselves the lawless and corrupt in the nation and on the line, both, white and red, bid defiance to society and law. Some of the banditti have recently been killed, and although their daring wickedness was everywhere acknowledged yet so numerous were the relations and friends of these lawless men, that a high excitement on their account alone arose in the nation, and the lives of prominent individuals were threatened.[5]

Another feature of Cherokee affairs truly deplorable is this: So numerous is the party which supports John Ross, and approves his acts, and so vindictive are their individual feelings towards his opposers, that it is impossible for the laws, either civil or criminal, to be impartially administered. It almost necessarily happens that juries for the trial of any case are composed of Ross men—frequently the lawyers are of the same party, and judges always, for none other can be appointed. What chance then has a Treaty man or an Old Settler who is so obnoxious to the other party, for his life, or his property, tried as he is in a Court of his enemies, where Prejudice and Hatred, instead of Justice, hold the scales?

While things continue as they are, there must ever be a suffering minority, standing isolated from the general mass, marked for destruction, hated and oppressed. And it is the more to be deplored, when we consider that this general mass is ignorant, superstitious, and revengeful, paying blind and stupid obedience to one man, while this suffering minority is patriotic and intelligent, and composed of the best and purest intellects of the nation. It has been said, enlighten this ignorant mass, but it is in vain to try it. For whosoever, with a noble purpose, undertakes this work, must express sentiments of horror and disgust towards John Ross, and the moment he does this, the fatal order is given, and he falls! Such has been the case, as is well known, and such will be the case again. I have drawn up the preceding picture for the purpose of presenting it to the people of the United States. I wish them to reflect on the conditions of Cherokee affairs, only to understand them, and then answer in their own judgments "what ought to be done in our present situation?" It is a question to which they should not be indifferent. For it was the policy of the U.S. Gov., which removed not only them, but the numerous other Indian tribes, west of the Mississippi; and it was owing to the oppressions, practised upon them by the State of Georgia, and those who followed her example, that parties arose amongst them, producing confusion and bloodshed, whose effects are yet fearfully apparent.

It is not my purpose, by any means, to revive old animosities. If the fire-brand has burnt out, I do not wish to rekindle it. But animosities are not dead—the fire-brand is yet burning, and standing on the dangerous ground occupied by the Cherokee nation, I am looking forward to discern a ray of hope; some permanent security in the future for this unhappy people.

I believe that confusion must reign amongst them; one faction must tyrannize over another—a furious banditti must exist, defying law and order, and all the miserable consequences, which flow from such a state of things, must surround and oppress the Cherokee people, until a strong arm is extended over them—I mean the laws of the United States, I would advocate a measure therefore, which looks to the event of making the Cherokee nation an integral part of the United States, having Senators and Representatives in Congress, and possessing all the attributes, first of a territorial government, and then of a sovereign State.

At present, she stands in an uncertain attitude. It has been decided by the Supreme Court of the United States [*Cherokee Nation v. Georgia*], that she is not a foreign State in the sense of the Constitution. Although she pretends to individual sovereignty, yet she is entirely dependent on the General Government. She cannot dispose of her territory, no matter how tempting the offer, to any other power but the United States. Neither her dependence on the General Government nor her individual sovereignty can do her any good. For these reasons I would say, let her rid herself of this useless peculiarity. Let her change this nominal sovereignty for a real one. Let her attach herself to the Union as one of its members, and rise with the fair sisters of the Republic to a position which is truly lofty and rationally independent. Then Cherokee genius could be nobly exerted. Whenever a brilliant fight arose it would not be extinguished in blood but a large sphere would be given and it would shine like a serene star, over the fortunes of a hitherto unhappy race.

I hope that intelligent citizens of the United States will give this subject attention.—It will certainly at some day become a question, and the sooner it is decided, the better it will be both for the Cherokees and the Government of the United States, for it is well known that Cherokee differences have long been a source of extreme annoyance and aggravation to the General Government.

Dec 8, 1848.

Notes

Originally appeared in the Clarksville (Texas) *Northern Standard*, January 20, 1849. Reproduced in David Farmer and Rennard Strickland, eds., *A Trumpet of Our Own: Yellow Bird's Essays on the North American Indian* (San Francisco: Book Club of California, 1981), 49–53. This was one of several articles produced by John Rollin Ridge in which he holds the Ross Party responsible for the violence in the Cherokee Nation West during the 1840s and 1850s. Like his father before him, John Rollin highlights the extraordinary "advances" made by the Cherokees and advocates the annexation of the Cherokee Nation as a state.

1. According to Cherokee law, the illegal sale of Cherokee lands carried the death penalty. Consequently, on June 22, 1839, Boudinot, Major Ridge and John Ridge were killed by unidentified bands of Cherokees at different locations in the Cherokee Nation West.

2. In *Cherokee Nation v. Georgia* (1831), Chief Justice John Marshall concluded that the Court could not rule on Georgia's nullification of Cherokee laws because the Cherokees were not a foreign nation, designating them instead as a "domestic dependent nation." In *Worcester v. Georgia* (1832), Marshall partially reversed the Court's opinion and declared Georgia's actions as null and void, but the decision was never enforced by the executive branch.

3. Following the arrival of the great bulk of the Cherokees in 1839, a conflict of interests arose between the National (Ross) Party on one side and the Old Settlers and Treaty (Ridge) Party on the other. The ensuing feud between the Treaty Party and the Ross Party after the assassination of the Ridges and Boudinot resulted in many casualties on both sides and ultimately threatened the territorial and political cohesion of the Cherokee Nation West itself. The situation became especially critical on June 2, 1846, when a bill was introduced in the House of Representatives calling for a special commission to negotiate the division of the Cherokee Nation. This crisis was temporarily averted on August 14 with the conclusion of the Cherokee Treaty in Washington, D.C., under which the opposing parties agreed to cease hostilities. See William G. McLoughlin, *After the Trail of Tears: The Cherokees' Struggle for Sovereignty, 1839–1880* (Chapel Hill: University of North Carolina Press, 1992), 34–58; Gerard Reed, "Postremoval Factionalism in the Cherokee Nation," in Duane H. King, ed., *The Cherokee Indian Nation: A Troubled History* (Knoxville: University of Tennessee Press, 1979), 148–63; and Morris Wardell, *A Political History of the Cherokee Nation, 1838–1907* (Norman: University of Oklahoma Press, 1963), 3–75.

4. In 1808, the Cherokee National Council created an internal police force called the Lighthorse Guard, appointing The Ridge as its head. John Ross reconstituted this police force after his removal to the Cherokee Nation West in 1839.

5. Several outlaw gangs began to terrorize the Cherokee population under the guise of political motivation in the 1840s. Particularly notorious among these was the so-called Starr Gang. Although the Treaty Party, including John Rollin Ridge, came to regard these desperados as patriotic rebels, the followers of John Ross persecuted them as despicable criminals. The most notorious of these outlaws was Tom Starr, whom John R. Ridge referred to as "a second Rinaldo Rinaldini." Starr probably served as a model for Ridge's depiction of the famous California bandit in his novel, *The Life and Adventures of Joaquín Murieta* (1854). See Grant Foreman, *The Five Civilized Tribes* (1934; repr. Norman: University of Oklahoma Press, 1972), 338–51.

BIOGRAPHY

John Rollin Ridge (Cherokee, 1827–67), or Chees-quat-a-law-ny (Yellow Bird), was born on March 19, 1827, on a farm on the Oostanaula River, Cherokee Nation, the son of John Ridge and Sarah Bird Northrup. He first attended a school in New Echota run by the American Board of Commissioners for Foreign Missions (ABCFM). From 1834 to 1836, he was then privately instructed by Sophia Sawyer, an ABCFM missionary from Massachusetts, in a school that his father built adjacent to his own home. Two years after his father signed the Treaty of New Echota (1835), John Rollin Ridge's family moved to Honey Creek in the Cherokee Nation West (now Missouri). Here he received additional instruction from Sophia Sawyer. On July 22, 1839, the twelve-year-old Ridge witnessed the brutal killing of his father, an event that obviously marked him for the rest of his life. Although there is no evidence that John Ross was directly involved in the assassinations of 1839, Ridge would forever hold him personally accountable for the death of his relatives. After the killing, his mother took refuge with her children in Fayetteville, Arkansas. Here Ridge eventually resumed his studies in a new school established by Sophia Sawyer. In 1841, he transferred to an institution at Mount Comfort run by Episcopalian minister Cephas Washburn. Two years later he enrolled at the Great Barrington Academy in Barrington, Massachusetts. Health problems prevented him from attending an Eastern college as planned, so he returned to Arkansas in 1845. Ridge spent an additional year in a school at Mount Comfort and then began to read law in Fayetteville.

After the signing of the Cherokee Treaty on August 14, 1846, which temporarily ended the feud between the Treaty Party and the Ross faction, Ridge was able to return to the Cherokee Nation West. In 1847 he purchased a farm near his father's former settlement at Honey Creek using money due from the Treaty of New Echota. In May of that year he married Elizabeth Wilson, a white woman from Fayetteville. Ridge also began publishing romantic verses in Arkansas and Texas newspapers. His return to a normal family life in the Cherokee Nation West was brief, however. In the summer of 1849, Ridge killed a fellow Cherokee during a dispute over a horse and subsequently fled to Springfield, Missouri. Soon after he moved to Osage Prairie, Arkansas, where his mother resided. Fearing reprisals for the killing and facing financial difficulties, Ridge and his brother Aeneas decided to join the Argonauts headed for the gold fields of California in the spring of 1850. Ridge gave a vivid description of the tortuous overland journey in a letter to his mother on October 4, 1850. The letter, a unique Cherokee contribution to American overland crossing narratives, was published in the *Fort Smith Herald* the following year.

Having failed to make a strike in California, Ridge turned to writing for a living. He functioned as a contributing editor for Horace Greeley's *Golden Eagle* in San Francisco in 1842, and his poems began to appear regularly in major California periodicals such as the *Golden Era, Hutching's Illustrated California Magazine,* and *The Hesperian (Pacific Monthly).* By 1854, when he rejoined his wife and daughter in Marysville, Ridge had already distinguished himself as an author. That year in San Francisco he published a novel, *The Life and Adventures of Joaquin Murieta.* Better known as Yellow Bird, Ridge became a standing member of a literary group known as the "Golden Era School," which included notable writers like Francis Bret Harte, Mark Twain, Joaquin Miller, and Charles Warren Stoddard.

Ridge eventually established himself as one of California's foremost journalists. In 1855 he worked briefly for the Sacramento *Daily Democratic State Journal.* On January 2, 1856, he became editor of the *Californian American* (later the *Daily Bee* and now *Sacramento Bee*). After leaving the *Daily Bee* in July of 1857, he edited (and sometimes co-owned) the following California newspapers: the Marysville *Daily California Express* (July 1857–August 1858); the Marysville *Daily National Democrat* (August 1858–April 1861); the *San Francisco Evening Journal* (May–July 1861); the *San Francisco National Herald* (July–September 1861); *The Red Bluff Beacon* (June–October 1862); the Weaverville *Trinity National* (1862); and the Grass Valley *The Daily National* (June 1864, until his death in 1867).

Ridge was a staunch Douglas Democrat and propagated the party's doctrine of "popular sovereignty" on the slavery issue. He also identified closely with the "Young America Movement" and its filibustering propaganda. When the Civil War broke out, Ridge became an ardent anti-abolitionist and joined the Union (or Peace) Democrats. After the war, when Reconstruction negotiations between the federal government and the Cherokee began in 1865, Ridge had hopes of returning once again to the Cherokee Nation West. He was invited to join the Southern Cherokee party in Washington, D.C., headed by Stand Watie and Elias Cornelius Boudinot, in an effort to effect the division of the Cherokee Nation West in opposition to the Union Cherokees under John Ross. Together with Boudinot, Ridge published *Comments on the Objections of Certain Cherokee Delegates to the Propositions of the Government to Separate the Hostile Parties of the Cherokee Nation* (1866). The delegation failed to bring about a division, however, and following a falling-out with Boudinot over financial matters, Ridge returned to Grass Valley, California, to edit the *The Daily National.* John Rollin Ridge died on October 5, 1867. A gravestone erected in 1933 by the Native Sons of the Golden West at the Greenwood Cemetery in Grass Valley bears the following inscription: "John Rollin Ridge— California Poet, Author of 'Mount Shasta' and Other Poems."

A selection of Ridge's poetry, written between 1850 and 1862, was published posthumously in 1869 in San Francisco by his wife under the title *Poems. By John R. Ridge.* Several of his poems appeared in major anthologies then and now. His novel created the standard literary formula of the Californian social bandit in American and Hispanic popular culture, and has been reprinted repeatedly since 1955.

Selected Publications of John Rollin Ridge

"The Cherokees. Their History—Present Condition and Future Prospects." *Northern Standard,* January 20, 1849. Reprinted in *A Trumpet of Our Own: Yellow Bird's Essays on the North American Indian.* Edited by David Farmer and Rennard Strickland. San Francisco: Book Club of California, 1981, 49–53.

Dale, Edward E. and Gaston L. Litton, eds. *Cherokee Cavaliers: Forty Years of Cherokee History as Told in the Correspondence of the Ridge-Watie-Boudinot Family.* Norman: University of Oklahoma Press, 1939.

"The Digger Indian." *The Daily Bee,* April 7, 1857.

With Elias C. Boudinot, et al. *Comments on the Objections of Certain Cherokee Delegates to the Propositions of the Government to Separate the Hostile Parties of the Cherokee Nation.* Washington, DC: Intelligencer Publishing House, 1865.

The Life and Adventures of Joaquín Murieta, the Celebrated California Bandit, by Yellow Bird. San Francisco: William B. Cooke and Company, 1854. Reprint, Norman: University of Oklahoma Press, 1955.

"More of the Cherokee Indians." *New York Tribune,* May 28, 1866.

"The North American Indians." *The Hesperian,* 8, no. 1 (March, 1862): 5–18; 8, no. 2 (April, 1862): 51–60; 8, no. 3 (May, 1862): 99–109. Reprinted in Farmer and Strickland, *A Trumpet of Our Own,* 67–103.

"Oppression of Digger Indians." *The Daily Bee,* July 12, 1857. Reprinted in Farmer and Strickland, *A Trumpet of Our Own,* 63–65.

"Overland to California in 1849," "Arkansas Travelers Reach Salt Lake," "Alkali Dust Causes Suffering," "Arkansans Reach Gold Fields," originally published in the *Fort Smith Herald* in 1851. Serialized in *Northwest Arkansas Times* (March 10–14, 1973).

Poems. By John R. Ridge. San Francisco: Henry Payot & Company, 1869.

"Sympathy for Walker." *The Daily Bee,* May 6, 1857.

"A True Sketch of 'Si Bolla,' a Digger Indian." *The Daily Bee,* June 24, 1857. Reprinted in Farmer and Strickland, *A Trumpet of Our Own,* 55–60.

A Trumpet of Our Own: Yellow Bird's Essays on the North American Indian. Edited by David Farmer and Rennard Strickland. San Francisco: Book Club of California, 1981.

Unpublished Writings

Ridge-Boudinot Family Papers, 1835–1890, and Cherokee Papers 1801–1982, Western History Collections, University of Oklahoma Library. John Rollin Ridge Papers, Bancroft Library, University of California, Berkeley, California.

Selected Secondary Sources

Christensen, Peter G. "Minority Interaction in John Rollin Ridge's *The Life and Adventures of Joaquín Murieta.*" *MELUS* 17, no. 2 (Summer 1991–92): 61–72.

Dale, Edward E. "John Rollin Ridge." *Chronicles of Oklahoma,* 4, no. 4 (1926): 312–21.

Debo, Angie. "John Rollin Ridge." *Southwest Review,* 17, no. 1 (Autumn 1931): 59–71.

Ellis, Clyde. "'Our Ill Fated Relative': John Rollin Ridge and the Cherokee People." *Chronicles of Oklahoma* 48, no. 4 (Winter 1990–91): 376–95.

Foreman, Carolyn T. "Edward W. Bushyhead and John Rollin Ridge, Cherokee Editors in California." *Chronicles of Oklahoma* 14, no. 3 (1936): 295–311.

Lowe, John. "Space and Freedom in the Golden Republic: Yellow Bird's *The Life and Adventures of Joaquin Murieta, the Celebrated California Bandit*." *Studies in American Indian Literatures* 4, nos. 2–3 (Summer–Fall 1992): 106–22.

Michaelsen, Scott. *The Limits of Multiculturalism: Interrogating the Origins of American Anthropology*. Minneapolis: University of Minnesota Press, 1999: 139–63.

Mondragón, Maria. "'The [Safe] White Side of the Line': History and Disguise in John Rollin Ridge's *The Life and Adventures of Joaquín Murieta: the Celebrated California Bandit*." *ATQ: The American Transcendental Quarterly*, n. s. 8, no. 3 (September 1994): 173–87.

Owens, Louis. *Other Destinies: Understanding the American Indian Novel*. Norman: University of Oklahoma Press, 1992: 32–40.

Parins, James W. *John Rollin Ridge: His Life & Works*. Lincoln: University of Nebraska Press, 1991.

Powell, Timothy B. "Historical Multiculturalism: Cultural Complexity in the First Native American Novel," in Timothy B. Powell, ed., *Beyond the Binary: Reconstructing Cultural Identity in a Multicultural Context*. New Brunswick, N.J.: Rutgers University Press, 1999: 205–35.

Ranck, M. A. "John Rollin Ridge in California," *Chronicles of Oklahoma* 10, no. 4 (December 1932): 560–69.

Rowe, John Carlos. "Highway Robbery: 'Indian Removal,' the Mexican-American War, and American Identity in *The Life and Adventures of Joaquín Murieta*." *Novel: A Forum on Fiction* 3, no. 2 (Spring 1998): 149–73.

Walker, Cheryl. "John Rollin Ridge and the Law," in Cheryl Walker, *Indian Nation: Native American Literature and Nineteenth-Century Nationalisms*. Durham: Duke University Press, 1997: 111–38.

Weaver, Jace. *That the People May Live: Native American Literatures and the Native American Community*. New York: Oxford University Press, 1997: 75–81.

REMARKS OF ELIAS C. BOUDINOT, OF THE CHEROKEE NATION, IN BEHALF OF THE BILL TO ORGANIZE THE TERRITORY OF OKLAHOMA

Elias C. Boudinot (1874)

Mr. Chairman and Gentlemen of the Committee on Territories:

A few days ago I took my seat in the gallery of the House of Representatives of the Congress of the United States of America, attracted by the discussion of the Indian question in the greatest (if not the most orderly) legislative body in the world. Learned statesmen and eloquent orators were giving their views upon the subject, and discoursing of the wrongs and the rights and the interests of the Indian race. Looking towards the Speaker's desk, I saw, in the position once occupied by a [Henry] Clay, a [Nathaniel] Macon, and a [Nathaniel Prentice] Banks, a distinguished representative of the lately enfranchised African; a colored man, but yesterday a slave, was presiding over the deliberations of the representatives of proud States, and directing the discussion upon the rights and interests of the Indian, the original owner of all their country, and always as free as the birds of his mountains und plains.[1] I observed in this spectacle how perfectly the African enjoyed his new-born rights and privileges; but what a commentary upon the doctrine of equality and civil rights! Everybody seems to be invested with the legacy of equal rights in this "land of the free and home of the brave," except the original owner of the country.

I propose to reply to the elaborate argument made before you by Colonel W.[William] P.[Potter] Ross, on behalf of the Indian delegations, in opposition to the bill to organize the Territory of Oklahoma.[2]

The argument comprises twenty-nine pages of printed pamphlet, the first fifteen pages of which, are devoted to a review of old treaties and lengthy quotations from decisions of the Supreme Court, all for the purpose of proving that the Indian tribes have an absolute fee simple title to the lands they occupy. This display of learning and research does credit to the industry of the speaker, but it has nothing to do with the questions at issue.

Texas is a State, and owns the lands within her limits; but she is nevertheless subject to the political jurisdiction of the United States. There is quite a difference between *property* rights and *political* rights, though Mr. Ross seems incapable of understanding such difference.

It is a little singular, however, that if the Cherokee Nation has an *absolute* title to her lands, these Indian delegates should display so much solicitude to protect it against the machinations of "railroad corporations and land grabbers."

These delegates appeal to you not to "extinguish the Indian title," and place their lands at the mercy of soulless and heartless corporations. Why this piteous appeal, if they have an *absolute title?*

Let us consider the *real* point at issue.

I affirm that the treaties of 1866, with the Choctaws, Chickasaws, Creeks, and Seminoles, expressly authorize the passage by Congress of a territorial bill . . .[3] A great deal has been said about Indian treaties made thirty and a hundred years ago. Mr. Ross was not weary in quoting from their provisions. Why did he ignore the only treaties which had anything to do with the bill before you—the treaties of 1866? They are the *last* that have been made—the last that ever *will* be made. Are *they* entitled to no consideration in the discussion of a territorial government?

I referred you, in my remarks heretofore made, to the articles of the treaties upon which I rely in advocating this legislation.[4] Not a word is offered in reply in the lengthy and labored speech which I am considering.

I am determined that these provisions of the treaties shall *not* be ignored; but that they shall be presented to the consideration of this committee. I challenge these Indian delegates and all their paid attorneys to break the force of the plain, simple, and effective stipulations of the treaties themselves. I rest the whole case, so far as I am concerned, upon the 7th article of the Choctaw and Chickasaw treaty of 1866, the 10th article of the Creek treaty of 1866, and the first paragraph of the 7th article of the Seminole treaty of 1866 . . .[5]

Now, while Mr. Ross was delving in the old treaties so industriously, to prove a proposition which has nothing to do with the bill before you, why is it that he has nothing to say about *these* articles of the last treaties? It is because they are too plain, and utterly crush his statement, that the treaties do not authorize the legislation proposed.

There can be no two constructions placed upon these agreements which I have quoted. It is argued that the consent of the Indians should be first obtained. What more unqualified and *positive* consent can you expect than is already given in the articles of the treaties just read? "These Indians agree to such legislation as Congress and the President may deem necessary." Can you have the consent of the Indians in stronger language? Such legislation must conform to the stipulations of the proviso of these articles; and this bill *does* so conform.

It is expressly declared in the bill that nothing in it shall be construed as affecting in the slightest degree the tribal organizations of the various Indian tribes. They remain intact and undisturbed. Examine the bill and see if this is not strictly true. Then, if the tribal organizations of these Indian tribes which I have mentioned are *not* disturbed, and if, in your opinion, this bill shall be deemed necessary for the better administration of justice in the Indian Territory, is there any escape from the conclusion that the Indians of these tribes have most solemnly consented to the passage of the bill? And can there be a more childish theory than that suggested by Mr. Ross, "*that Congress has no moral or legal right to legislate upon the question without the consent of the Indians?*"

I have thus demonstrated from the treaties that they expressly authorize this legislation, and that the Indians have already consented thereto . . . The only difference, then, between us is, that I think the bill before you is the form of government fixed by the treaties, while Mr. Ross thinks otherwise. It is for you, gentlemen of the committee, to judge which is right.

If the bill before you is *not* such a form of government as is fixed by the treaties, in the name of civilization and progress change it, so that it *will* conform to the treaties. In behalf of thousands of intelligent and industrious inhabitants of the Indian Territory, I will accept with gratitude any form of government which you may decide is fixed by these treaties. Only give us such legislation as will put us more nearly on an equality with all other people, white and black, in this country. If we *must* pay taxes to support your Government, give us representation. If we must be subject to your laws and your courts, establish courts in our Territory, and do not suffer us longer to be dragged into a neighboring State for every offense charged against us . . .

The bill before you simply gives a general civil government to the civilized tribes, without disturbing in the least their tribal organizations; and the 8th article of the Choctaw and Chickasaw treaty of 1866 has been selected as a model for such bill, because it was more complete than any of the provisions of the other treaties.

For myself, I would rejoice in more radical legislation than is contained in this bill. I would hail the sectionizing and division of the lands in severalty, the sale of surplus lands to actual white settlers, and the merging of *Indian* citizenship into *American* citizenship, as the greatest blessings, for my race. But the treaties do not expressly provide for this, and I am content to wait. Only give us what they do provide for, and the rest will come before long . . .[6]

It is charged in the arguments and protests against this bill that it is advocated by persons having only their own selfish interests to enhance. I was content to rest this question simply upon the arguments. You will bear me witness that I accused no one of unworthy motives in opposing this legislation; but I shrink from no examination of *my* motives; and as a prejudice has been sought to be produced against me by impugning them, those indiscreet enough to turn the discussion into that channel must take the consequences. I am interested in a government which will give better protection to life and property in the Indian Territory, which will give us United States courts in the Territory, and a direct representation in Congress, to *just* the extent that every law-abiding individual in the Indian Territory is interested, *and no more.*

What do I gain? What is it possible I *could* gain, more than this, if this bill should become a law? I do not even get my land in severalty. There is no possible advantage which could accrue to me that will not equally apply to every person who desires a good government and wishes to save the resources of the Cherokee Nation from pillage . . .

Whenever it is proposed to give the Indians their lands in severalty, and make them citizens of this great Government, you are met with the stupid and senseless objection, from so-called philanthropists, that the poor Indians would speedily be overrun by unprincipled white men and robbed of all their property; that they would be imposed upon by land-sharks, and exterminated. Indian delegates and Indian agents who are receiving extravagant salaries from the moneys of these poor Indians, echo the nonsense, and appeal to you to save the Indians from such a grievous fate. American manhood and American citizenship, with all their attendant rights and privileges, which were considered the only salvation for the ignorant slave, are looked upon by these unreasoning zealots as *death* to the civilized American Indian . . .

Perhaps there has never been a subject of great importance before this country, concerning which so many wild and impracticable theories have been advanced as upon the Indian question. It has been tinkered and doctored by political quacks until your Indian policy deserves the derision of the intelligent world.

There are persons who, after robbing the Indians of their lands, driving them from their homes, and deliberately violating the most solemn treaties, now assume a virtue which their acts do not sustain.

In 1868 Congress extended the revenue laws over the Indian Territory, in direct and flagrant violation of the Cherokee treaty of 1866. The Supreme Court has decided that the act was an abrogation of provisions of that treaty. So, although the Cherokee treaty expressly stipulated that Indians should *not* be taxed in the Indian Territory, yet, by an act of the grossest bad faith on the part of this Government, they *are* taxed, and have for that purpose been incorporated with a revenue district in Missouri.[7]

Some distinguished Senators and members of Congress who voted to violate that treaty, now hold up their hands in pious horror at the suggestion of organizing a civil government over the Indian Territory, which would give its inhabitants the rights and privileges of a tax-paying people, because they imagine it would be an act of bad faith. If the custodians of the public faith would compare the bill before you with the treaties of 1866 with the civilized tribes, they would see that the civil government proposed in the bill is specially provided for in such treaties. But no! they will not examine the *latest* treaties. They prefer to stand upon the broken fragments of the treaties of 1866, and talk loudly about good faith and the sacred character of Indian treaties made fifty years ago. They meet the proposition to legislate for the better protection of life and property in the Indian Territory with the objection that it is contrary to the treaties, and therefore an act of bad faith.

If this were true, (and I have shown that it is *not* true,) it would come with exceeding bad grace from those who have voted to tax the Indians without their consent, and stand on the record as violators of public faith, and repudiators of the most solemn stipulations of treaties. They claim a virtue which their official acts belie . . .

The Cherokee treaty of 1866 was violated by these very men who talk loudest of good faith. Only a day or two ago they deliberately voted to abrogate a treaty with the Sioux Indians of 1868, and to make it look better on the statute books, they agreed to change the title from the truthful one of a bill "to abrogate and declare void a certain portion of the treaty with the Sioux Indians, concluded April 29, 1868," so that it would read, a bill "to declare the true intent and meaning of a certain portion of the treaty with the Sioux Indians, concluded April 29, 1868." It *sounds* much smoother, I acknowledge. But would it not be more manly to say in plain words that this treaty was made with our wards, and we, as their guardian, decide that it must be abrogated? This is a power you possess, and which you exercised in the Cherokee treaty of 1866; and whether right or wrong, all the gentle words in the English language cannot hide the facts.[8]

A distinguished Senator from an eastern State [Lot Myrick Morrill] asserted, from his place in the Senate, that the true Indian policy is, to remove all the wild Indians from the mountains and plains of the great West into the Indian Territory, there to be "fed," fattened, and "kept quiet" at a cost of $300,000 a year, or, according to his estimate of their numbers, (800,000,) *for one dollar a head.* Another big medicine man of the House of Representatives [John Peter Cleaver Shanks], for several years, chairman of the Committee on Indian Affairs, after long and laborious investigation, is convinced that the true solution of the Indian problem is, to compel the savage Sioux and Apache, by an act of Congress, "to wear civilized clothes."

As an illustration of the gross ignorance of these Indian doctors, I refer you to a bill recently introduced in Congress by this gentleman, the first section of which gravely provides that the Indian shall "hereafter be a competent witness in the United States courts," when any tyro in the law must know that Indians are and always have been competent witnesses in the United States courts. A few weeks ago, in the trial before the United States court of this district, in the case of United States *v.* John W. Wright, nearly one hundred Indians from the Indian Territory appeared here as competent witnesses. Give the Indian the right of a citizen of the United States, to sue in the United States courts, and there would be some sense in the thing.[9]

It is not strange that, gentlemen entertaining such ridiculous notions should consider that the only method to civilize the Indian is to keep him as far as possible from civilization.

The history of Indian civilization demonstrates that the Indian advances and improves just in proportion to his contact *with* civilization, provided that his rights as a man are protected and defended by the laws of the country. In a conversation a few days ago with the late United States Minister to Mexico, Mr. [Thomas Henry] Nelson, I was informed that seven-tenths of the present population of Mexico were of the native Indian race, and the controlling element of that country in all its political and literary relations. [Benito] Juarez was a full-blooded Indian, and one of the most learned and accomplished men of his time. Could the Indians of Mexico have attained their high position under an Indian policy such as has been followed in the United States? The President [Ulysses S. Grant], in several of his messages to Congress, has earnestly recommended the organization of a territorial government over the Indian Territory. He has broader and more statesmanlike views upon the Indian question than those gentlemen who advocate the herding of 300,000 savages in a corral, and feeding them at a cost of one dollar a head, or the legislating them into swallow-tailed coats, white chokers, and other civilized apparel.

You have made the Indian responsible as a citizen, to your laws. You have trampled his treaties under your feet by taxing him for the support of your Government. Do not refuse him that representation and those equal rights before the law which you have given to all other people in this great country.

Notes

Originally published as an eighteen-page tract titled *Remarks of Elias C. Boudinot, of the Cherokee Nation, in Behalf of the Bill to Organize the Territory of Oklahoma, Before the House Committee on Territories, May 13, 1874* (Washington, D.C.: McGill and Witherow, 1874). This is one of several lengthy promotional tracts that E. C. Boudinot penned and published in an effort to promote territorial status for Indian Territory.

1. African Americans were granted citizenship under the Civil Rights Act of 1866, which specifically excluded Indians. It was reinforced with the 14th amendment in 1868 and supplemented with the right to vote under the 15th amendment in 1870. Twenty African Americans served in the House of Representatives during Reconstruction. Nathaniel Macon, Republican from North Carolina, was speaker of the House in 1801–1807; Henry Clay, Republican from Kentucky, was speaker in 1811–14; Nathaniel Prentice Banks, Republican from Massachusetts, was speaker in 1856–57.

2. The reference is to William Potter Ross, *Indian Territory; Remarks in Opposition to the Bill to Organize the Territory of Oklahoma Before the Committee on Territories of the House of Representatives, February 9th, 1874* (Washington, D.C.: Gibson Bros., 1874). It was reproduced as "Speech of W. P. Ross, Principal Chief Cherokee Nation, Before the House Committee on Territories," *Cherokee Advocate* February 21, 1874. William Potter Ross (1820–91), nephew of John Ross, graduated with honors from Princeton in 1842 and became editor of the *Cherokee Advocate* in 1844. He served as principal chief in 1873–75 and opposed congressional plans for the establishment of Oklahoma Territory. He is the author of numerous articles, speeches and memorials to Congress. On W. P. Ross see John Bartlett Meserve, "Chief William Potter Ross," *Chronicles of Oklahoma* 15, no. 1 (March 1937): 21–29; and Mrs. William P. Ross, ed., *The Life and Times of Honorable William P. Ross of the Cherokee Nation* (Fort Smith, Ark.: Weldon and Williams, 1893).

3. The Restoration Treaties of 1866 were concluded with the Seminoles on March 21, the Choctaws and Chickasaws on April 28, the Creeks on June 14, and the Cherokees on July 19. See Charles J. Kappler, comp. and ed., *Indian Affairs, Laws, and Treaties,* 7 vols. (Washington, D.C.: Government Printing Office, 1903–1904), II: 910–15, 918–31, 931–37, 942–50.

4. See *Speech of Elias C. Boudinot, a Cherokee Indian, Delivered before the House Committee on Territories, February 7, 1872, in Behalf of a Territorial Government for the Indian Territory, in Reply to Wm. P. Ross, a Cherokee Delegate, in His Argument Against Any Congressional Action upon the Subject* (Washington, D.C.: McGill & Witherow, 1872); and *Speech of Elias C. Boudinot, of the Cherokee Nation, Delivered before the House Committee on Territories, March 5, 1872, on the Question of a Territorial Government for the Indian Territory, in Reply to*

the Second Argument of the Indian Delegations in Opposition to Such Proposed Government (Washington, D.C.: McGill & Witherow, 1872).

5. The cited articles state that said nations agree that Congress and the president may pass legislation deemed "necessary for the better administration of justice and the protection of the rights of persons and property within the Indian Territory . . ." Such legislation was not to interfere with or annul their governments or customs.

6. On June 28, 1898, the Curtis Act extended allotment to Indian Territory. An act on May 3, 1901, declared all Indians in Indian Territory citizens of the United States.

7. On July 20, 1868, Congress passed "An Act imposing taxes on distilled spirits, and for other purposes," which was applied to Cherokee territory. Boudinot and Stand Watie owned a tobacco factory that was confiscated in 1869 for violating the law, which Boudinot in turn considered to be in violation of article 10 of the Cherokee Reconstruction Treaty of 1866. Boudinot brought the case before the Supreme Court in 1870. In a hallmark decision rendered in December 1870, known as *The Cherokee Tobacco*, the Supreme Court recognized congressional power to modify an Indian treaty and to pass an act in violation of the treaty, "as if the treaty were not an element to be considered." See Robert K. Heimann, "The Cherokee Tobacco Case," *Chronicles of Oklahoma* 41, no. 3 (Fall 1963): 299–322.

8. Several attempts were made to abrogate the Fort Laramie Treaty of 1868 in order to reduce or change the boundaries of the Great Sioux Reservation, especially after gold was discovered in the Black Hills in 1874. On February 28, 1877, Congress finally passed an act in which 7.5 million acres, including the Black Hills, were removed from the reservation.

9. Congress declared Indians to be competent witnesses on March 3, 1847, as part of an amendment to the "Indian Trade and Intercourse Act" of 1834.

BIOGRAPHY

Elias Cornelius Boudinot (Cherokee, 1835–90) was born at New Echota in the eastern Cherokee Nation, the son of Elias Boudinot and Harriet Gold Boudinot. Following his father's assassination in 1839, E. C. Boudinot and his brothers were raised in New England by the Gold family. E. C. Boudinot attended Burr Seminary in Manchester, Vermont, and The Gunnery, a preparatory school in Connecticut.

After teaching school in Danby, Vermont, until 1853, E. C. Boudinot moved to Fayetteville, Arkansas, to study law in the office of A. M. Wilson. He was admitted to the Arkansas bar in 1856. Besides practicing as a lawyer, E. C. Boudinot was also part owner and editor of the Fayettville *Arkansian* and editor of the Little Rock *True Democrat*. In 1860 he served as chair of the Arkansas Democratic State Central Committee. In 1861 he joined Stand Watie's Cherokee confederate forces and rose to the rank of lieutenant colonel. He gave up the commission in 1863, however, to serve as the Cherokee delegate to the Confederate Congress in Richmond. After the war, he headed the Southern Cherokee delegation in Washington and tried without success to have the Cherokee Nation divided into northern and southern sectors. Privately, he and his uncle operated a tobacco factory in the Cherokee Nation West. The factory was seized by federal agents in 1869 for failure to pay federal excise taxes according to a revenue act passed by Congress in 1868. E. C. Boudinot maintained that the factory was exempted from taxation according to Reconstruction Treaty signed with the Cherokees in 1866. The dispute ended up in the Supreme Court, where the seizure was affirmed in *The Cherokee Tobacco* case of 1871, an important decision that initiated a series of legal measures extending federal jurisdiction over Indian domestic affairs.

During the 1870s and 1880s, E. C. Boudinot was busy lobbying in Washington for the incorporation of Indian Territory as an official territory of the United States. In 1871 he co-founded the town of Vinita, Indian Territory, at the junction of the Katy and Atlantic & Pacific railroads. He also turned to professional lecturing, advocating the formation of a "Territory of Oklahoma" in Indian Territory, the private allotment of Indian lands, and the granting of citizenship to all Indians. E. C. Boudinot's radical views brought him into direct conflict with Cherokee nationalists like William Potter Ross (1820–91), editor of the *Cherokee Advocate* and principal chief in 1873–75, and his own elder brother, William Penn Boudinot (1830–98), who also edited the *Advocate* temporarily.

Elias C. Boudinot started his own newspaper, the Muskogee *Indian Progress*, in 1875. When the Creeks forced him to close it down because they disagreed with his political views, he continued to publish the paper in Vinita until the spring of 1876. In 1879, E. C. Boudinot wrote a letter to the editor of the Chicago *Times*, asserting that some fourteen million acres in Indian Territory (Unassigned Lands) had been ceded to the government and were thus open to homestead laws. That same year he expanded this statement in a circular letter to August Albert of Baltimore. The letter contained similar misinformation and was accompanied by a detailed map of Indian Territory and the Unassigned Lands that Boudinot had printed in Washington. E. C. Boudinot's questionable promotional ventures helped to start the Boomer movement, eventually leading to the opening of two million acres in the Unassigned Lands for homestead claims by U.S. citizens on April 22, 1889.

E. C. Boudinot, long a supporter of the Democratic Party, came very close to being nominated Commissioner of Indian Affairs in 1885. When his aspirations to the post were dashed by the newly elected Cleveland administration, he abandoned his highly controversial political career and returned to practice law again at his home in Fort Smith. Elias C. Boudinot died there on September 27, 1890.

Selected Publications of Elias C. Boudinot

Indian Territory: Argument Submitted to the Senate Committee on Territories, January 17, 1879, the Committee Having Under Consideration the Resolutions of D. W. Voorhees, Relating to the Indian Territory. Washington, D.C.: T. McGill, 1879.

Oklahoma: An Argument by E. C. Boudinot, of the Cherokee Nation, Delivered before the House Committee on Territories, February 3, 1876. Washington, D.C.: McGill and Witherow, 1876.

Oklahoma. Argument of Col. E. C. Boudinot before the Committee on Territories, January 29, 1878. The Committee Having under Consideration H. R. Bill No. 1596. Alexandria, Va.: G. H. Ramey & Sons, 1878.

Remarks of Elias C. Boudinot, of the Cherokee Nation, in Behalf of the Bill to Organize the Territory of Oklahoma, Before the House Committee on Territories, May 13, 1874. Washington, D.C.: McGill and Witherow, 1874.

Speech of Col. E. C. Boudinot, of the Cherokee Nation, on the Indian Question, Delivered at Vinita, Cherokee Nation, the Junction of the Atlantic and Pacific and the Missouri, Kansas and Texas Railroads, on Thursday, September 21. Terre-Haute, Ind.: Journal Office Print, 1871.

Speech of Elias C. Boudinot, a Cherokee Indian, Delivered before the House Committee on Territories, February 7, 1872, in Behalf of a Territorial Government for the Indian Territory, in Reply to Wm. P. Ross, a Cherokee Delegate, in His Argument Against Any Congressional Action upon the Subject. Washington, D.C.: McGill & Witherow, 1872.

Speech of Elias C. Boudinot, of the Cherokee Nation, Delivered before the House Committee on Territories, March 5, 1872, on the Question of a Territorial Government for the Indian Territory, in Reply to the Second Argument of the Indian Delegations in Opposition to Such Proposed Government. Washington, D.C.: McGill & Witherow, 1872.

With John Rollin Ridge, et al. *Comments on the Objections of Certain Cherokee Delegates to the Propositions of the Government to Separate the Hostile Parties of the Cherokee Nation.* Washington, D.C.: Intelligencer Publishing House, 1865.

With William Penn Adair. *Reply of the Southern Cherokees to the Memorial of Certain Delegates from the Cherokee Nation, Together with the Message of John Ross, Ex-Chief of the Cherokees, and Proceedings of the Council of the "Loyal Cherokees," Relative to the Alliance with the So-Called Confederate States.* Washington, D.C.: McGill and Witherow, 1866.

Unpublished Writings

Ridge and Boudinot Family Papers, 1835–1890, Cherokee Nation Papers, 1801–1982, Western History Collections, University of Oklahoma Library.

Selected Secondary Sources

Adams, John D. *Elias Cornelius Boudinot.* Chicago: Rand, McNally and Co., 1890.
Colbert, Thomas B. "Visionary or Rogue: The Life and Legacy of Elias Cornelius Boudinot." *Chronicles of Oklahoma* 65, no. 3 (Fall 1987): 268–81.
Colbert, Thomas B. "Elias Cornelius Boudinot, 'The Indian Orator and Lecturer'." *American Indian Quarterly* 13, no. 3 (Summer 1989): 248–59.
Heimann, Robert K. "The Cherokee Tobacco Case." *Chronicles of Oklahoma* 41 (Fall 1963): 299–322.
Parins, James W. *Elias Cornelius Boudinot, a Life on the Cherokee Border.* Lincoln: University of Nebraska Press, 2006.
Wright, Muriel H. "Notes on Colonel Elias C. Boudinot." *Chronicles of Oklahoma* 41, no. 3 (Winter 1963–64): 382–407.

THE INDIAN'S HARD LOT

DeWitt Clinton Duncan (1898)

The Indian now has a hard time of it in Washington. He is looked upon here somewhat as an outlaw—not indeed a criminal, that is not what we mean exactly—but as a man whose rights (if he can be said to have any at all) have no reliable foundation in law, a man who is politically just what he is, and has what he has, merely as a matter of sufferance; a man whose status in the world is only a question of public policy; a thing which may be this today, and that, or something else, tomorrow, just as the popular choice may chance to require at the hand of arbitrary legislation. His condition, from a legal standpoint, is truly anomalous; it seems especially so in a land like this, where we have a right to claim and expect for him a state of things much better than this—where, for instance, the light of civilization is so bright and pervasive; and all the fine humanities suggested by the divine law are thought to bloom and fruit so grandly.

There is something curious in all this; something truly unique.

There is no class, or race, of men now on the earth who, when they come up to the seat of government on errands of business, have to contend with an array of disadvantages so formidable as those which, on such occasions, usually confront the Indian. If it be a citizen of the United States, his power of the ballot invests him with respectability, and introduces him at once to favorable attention; if a foreigner, the backing which he has from his home government throws around his person the charm of safety and shelters his rights under the aegis of law; if a stranger from the islands of ocean, he is received with demonstrations of cordiality, and, when civilization has done parading him as a proud trophy of its own missionary benevolence, he is dismissed and sent back to his wave washed home loaded with gifts and godspeeds.

But how is it with reference to our own continental Indian, the man without a flag behind him; that familiar football of civilization, whose importuning presence at the capital comes up more in the nature of an indictment than a compliment?

There is, and has been for a long time, something of a controversy between him and his Great Father at Washington; and he happens to be in the predicament of one of those unfortunate sons from whom paternal affection has been withdrawn, and yet of whom are expected nevertheless the usual manifestations of filial devotion. Consequently when he comes to Washington to make known his wants and grievances, the justness of his cause is but a secondary matter, and usually insufficient to secure him a suitable hearing. The first question which he has to answer is, "How much are you disposed to concede?" He must needs [sic] bring along with him a basket, or some such thing, stuffed with conciliatory concessions; otherwise he forfeits the pleasure, as well as the advantage, of a cordial reception at the parental mansion.

The government, wisely, or unwisely, early adopted the policy of dealing

163

with the Indians as with men; that is to say, in matters of intercourse, it respected their rights and, in reference to them, generally deferred to their wishes. This practice was certainly fair and honorable; yet, it proved to be the origin of all the most perplexing problems that have been met with in the administration of Indian affairs. During the first years of its existence, the government, in getting along with the Indian tribes, endeavored, in general, to proceed on the theory of amicable agreement; instances of absolute coercion, though not entirely unknown, were rare. Many treaties were made with them very solemn in form, and abounding in guarantees purporting to endure forever. But the arrangements with them attained in this way were not generally in accord with the aggressive spirit of the white population; and however satisfactory they may have seemed to be at first, they soon came to be regarded in every instance, as serious obstructions in the way of legitimate emigration. Popular clamor arose denouncing them as nuisances and demanding their abrogation; and the government never failed to find itself, in due time, confronted with the alternative of either allowing these treaties to be shamefully overriden by the lawless multitude, or to save its honor by securing amicable concessions from the Indians. This practice, from a moral point of view, proved to be correct, in many instances, only in theory; for many of these "amicable" concessions were obtained by the most galling of coercive measures. Indeed, the most of these so called treaties seemed to have been made for the sake rather of guarding the good name of history, than for the benefit of the Indians. Though appearing to be exceeding fair upon the printed page, there were but few of them but what, if tested by the rules of equity in a court of competent jurisdiction, would be annulled on the ground of fraud and duress.

Speaking more particularly in reference to the Cherokees—there was a time in their early history when it was quite an easy matter for them to comply with these periodical demands for concession in a way that was really magnificent— when they were rich and the United States was young and poor. In those early days of thoughtless affluence, ere the malignant beam of fortune had been tipped the other way, they were in the habit of regarding it as but a light thing to bring along now a state, and then a state, and again, and again, a state, and throw them down as love gifts at the feet of the stripling who was soon to fatten upon their liberality, grow mighty and finally arrogate to himself the mastery of his old host and benefactor. In this way, it was, that Virginia, the mother of presidents, was "conceded;" in the same way, too, the Carolinas were "conceded;" and Georgia, the golden, and wild Kentucky, with Alabama, the beautiful land of plenty and rest, were all "conceded."[1] And yet, in return for all these imperial benefactions at the hand of the Cherokees, what have they ever received but a transient smile of ungrateful satisfaction, and a wretched little volume of false promises called treaties?

But the time came at length, in the course of years, when it was deemed by the Cherokees that this extravagant species of liberality had needs to be discontinued. It had been found to be trenching so seriously upon the amplitude of their original domain, that the motives of self-preservation suggested with much emphasis the impracticability of further "concessions;" they could give no more. "Concessions," with them, came to bear the significance of expatriation, impoverishment, starvation, beggary, and despised tramps and strolling from door to door in quest of ill-paid labor and poor bread.

In their new home west of the Mississippi, they had been induced by the flattering promises of the government, to entertain very cheerful hopes of a future eternity of repose; but in this also they were deluded. The old demand for "concession," like a trailing spectre, hung upon their heels, and, at the close of the late war, found out their retreat and set upon them with renewed and quite unexampled ferocity. At the first note of alarm, heralding the breaking out of hostilities, the government hastened to withdraw her troops from the south, leaving her helpless wards, the Cherokees, to shift for themselves in the heart of the Southern Confederacy. At the close of the struggle, Congress professed itself to be seriously offended with them, because they had, in the meantime, failed to keep the Union flag aloft over ground upon which even Mr. Lincoln's armies had deemed it unsafe, at the time, to bivouac for a single night. The result was, they had to "concede" the western half of their country as a penalty for disloyalty. Nor was this the whole of that most unjust and unreasonable punishment. The Cherokees were, at this time, owning a handsome tract of eight hundred thousand acres, lying, like a jewel, snug down in the southeastern corner of the state of Kansas; this was included in the penalty, and had to be "conceded" accordingly.[2] Nor was this the whole of it. It was found that those ancient surveyors who ran the western boundary line of the state of Arkansas and the southern line of Kansas, had made a mistake, fixing the former, in many important places, much too far toward the east, and the latter throughout, some miles too far to the north. Hence it came to pass, apparently as an uncontrived necessity, that, when these two lines were corrected by the modern sticklers for "concession," the Cherokees found that they had again to "concede" many thousand additional acres, to be shared by these two states in proportion to the gravity of the wrong which had been practiced upon them respectively in the old survey. Nor was this all; the penalty was still further enlarged in the following manner.

The Cherokees were required by the government to assent to the construction of as many, at least, as two railroads through their lands, and to "concede" to these corporations, as a mere gratuity, all and whatever of their realty that might be needed for such a purpose. This, however, was but a little matter compared with the magnitude of the injustice by which this measure was subsequently supplemented. Congress, without the knowledge or consent of the Cherokees, and in violation of the most sacred forms of plighted faith, made a conditional free gift to one of these corporations of about eight hundred thousand acres in the very center of the Cherokee home lands.[3] Now, the government had, for valuable consideration, engaged with the Cherokees to keep them in peaceful possession of this, their home tract for all time to come; but instead of observing this promise, she in this way virtually subsidized one of the most powerful agencies on earth to annoy them without ceasing. Accordingly, for the last thirty years this corporation has been tireless in contriving schemes for the bringing about of that specified condition (the extinguishment of the Cherokee title) which, according to the terms of the grant, was to perfect its own title and give it possession of these Cherokee lands; while, during the same long period of tedious years, the harassing apprehension, kept ever alive by the threatened consummation of this great wrong, has never allowed these people the enjoyment of a single hour of undisturbed repose.

But all the "concessions" so far made by the Cherokees, however extensive, were not enough. Accordingly, at a late day, the Dawes commission was authorized to pay them a visit with propositions asking them to "concede" some more. They said, "We have not come to discuss with you the question of your rights, we have come simply to tell you what the government wants of you. It desires you to 'concede' the abolition of your tribal existence, to allot your lands, and become citizens of the United States, and the less fault you can find, and the quicker you can come to terms with our commission, the better, far the better, it will be for you, for if you defer, and prove so unfortunate as to fall into the hands of Congress, you will be sure to be made to feel all the rough treatment due to your folly."[4]

These dishonorable, and yet very fearful, words of prophecy are just now seeming to have been only too true. The Cherokees refused to "concede;" hence they are enjoying at Washington just now the reputation of being a bad set of Indians, the most "unconceding" and impractical tribe on the continent. On this account, while the reconciled countenance of the great Father is dispensing the smiles of summer in every other direction, the Cherokees are left out to shiver alone in the dreary winter of disapprobation. Be assured, the chilliest thing that the Indian has to encounter in the world, is the "cold shoulder" of his great Father at Washington; it is the frostiest thing imaginable.

With these words it has been the mind of the writer to close this article, but just now word comes to him that the senate committee of Indian affairs has finished its review of the Curtis bill and that the results of their labor is now before the senate.[5] In some respects they have improved it, in others, they have most unfortunately degraded it. It is hardly credible, yet it is true as the decalogue, they have admitted a section confirming that fraudulent and most infamous Clifton freedman roll. With unquestionable evidence of its infamy in writing now on file in the office of the Secretary of the Interior, it is hardly thinkable that it can possibly become a law. The section will undoubtedly be stricken out. It is known in all quarters that should that roll be confirmed by legislation, the mouth of a hideous pit of corruption would be closed forever; which might otherwise continue to send up its stench and stink through the annals of all future history.[6]

Let it be conceded that the Cherokees showed themselves to be bad boys in declining to treat with the Dawes commission; let it also be admitted that the great Father has had some good ground for the exercise of parental displeasure, yet there is, in the nature of things, no vanity of ill humor possible that could justify him in treating his helpless children unjustly.

Notes

"The Indian's Hard Lot," *Indian Chieftain* (June 2, 1898); repr. in Daniel F. Little-field, Jr., and James W. Parins, eds., *Native American Writing In the Southeast: An Anthology, 1875–1935* (Jackson: University Press of Mississippi, 1995), 37–42. Reprinted with the kind permission of James Parins and the University Press of Mississippi. Duncan, a staunch supporter of Cherokee territorial integrity, opposes further "concessions" of Cherokee lands and argues against the passage of the Curtis Bill.

1. In exchange for the "civilization program" promoted by the Washington and Jefferson administrations and codified by Congress in a series of "Indian Trade and Intercourse Acts" passed between 1790 and 1834, Indians were expected to give up some of their "excess" lands from time to time. The Cherokees thus found themselves having to negotiate more than twenty land cession agreements with the federal government during the same period. See Grace Woodward, *The Cherokees* (Norman: University of Oklahoma Press, 1963), 131.

2. Under article 16 of the Restoration Treaty, concluded with the Cherokees on July 19, 1866, the Cherokee Nation ceded lands in the western half of Indian Territory known as Oklahoma District for the avowed purpose of resettling "friendly" Indians and freedmen. This area was opened to white settlement in 1889 and then granted territorial status the year after under the Oklahoma Organic Act. Under article 17 of the treaty the Cherokee Nation also ceded lands in Kansas which had been sold to the Cherokees by the United States under the Treaty of New Echota in 1835. See Charles J. Kappler, comp. and ed., *Indian Affairs, Laws, and Treaties,* 5 vols. (Washington, D.C.: Government Printing Office, 1903–1941), 2: 942–50.

3. Under article 11 of the Reconstruction Treaty of 1866 the Cherokees agreed to grant a right-of-way "to any company or corporation which shall be duly authorized by Congress to construct a railroad . . . which may pass through, the Cherokee Nation." Congress passed an act on July 4, 1884, granting a right of way to the Southern Kansas Railway Company without approval of the Cherokees. The Cherokee administration issued a decree against the grant and challenged it in the Supreme Court in *Cherokee Nation v. Southern Kansas Railroad Company* in 1890, but the decree was reversed. See Craig H. Miner, *The Corporation and the Indian: Tribal Sovereignty and Industrial Civilization in Indian Territory, 1865–1907* (Columbia: University of Missouri Press, 1975).

4. On March 3, 1893, an Indian Appropriation Act provided for the appointment of a three-member commission, later known as the Dawes Commission, to negotiate with the Five Tribes for the extinction of their communal land titles toward eventual incorporation of the Indian Territory as a state. Three years later, another Indian Appropriation Act authorized the Dawes Commission to determine who could be enrolled as citizens of the Five Tribes. The Cherokee administration, in keeping with the repeated resolutions of the intertribal councils called by the leaders of the Five Tribes, steadfastly refused to cooperate with the Dawes Commission. Official resistance began to break down, however, after the federal government abolished tribal laws and courts in Indian Territory with the passage of the Curtis Act in 1898.

5. The bill introduced by Congressman Charles Curtis (Kaw, 1860–1936), was enacted as the Curtis Act on June 28, 1898. It prepared the way for the allotment of Cherokee lands, which the Cherokee administration finally agreed to in 1900.

6. The National Council of the Union Cherokees abolished slavery in 1863. Under article 9 of the Reconstruction Treaty of 1866 the Cherokee administration agreed to fulfill this pledge as well as agreeing "that all freedmen . . . as well as free colored persons who were in the country at the commencement of the rebellion, and are now residents therein, or who may return within six months, and their descendants, shall have all the rights of native Cherokees." Following the arrival of the Dawes Commission in 1893, it became apparent that people of African American descent would share in Cherokee allotments. The roll mentioned here was compiled by William Clifton, William Thompson, and Robert H. Kern in 1896–97. It was repudiated by the Cherokees on the grounds that it contained hundreds of names of freedmen with fraudulent claims to Cherokee rights. See Daniel F. Littlefield, Jr., *The Cherokee Freedman: From Emancipation to American Citizenship* (Westport, Conn.: Greenwood Press, 1978).

BIOGRAPHY

DeWitt Clinton Duncan (Cherokee, 1829–1909), or Too-qua-stee, was born near Dahlonega, Cherokee Nation, on February 27, 1829, the son of John Gordon Duncan, a part-Cherokee, and Elizabeth Abercrombie Duncan, a white woman. In 1839 Duncan's family removed to Indian Territory along with the remainder of the Cherokee. DeWitt Duncan attended the Cherokee Male Seminary in Tahlequah before enrolling at Dartmouth College in 1857. He graduated from Dartmouth with honors in 1861, a member of Phi Beta Kappa. Due to the outbreak of the Civil War and its repercussions in Indian Territory, Duncan did not return home after graduation but instead taught school at Lisbon and Littleton, New Hampshire; at Eagle, Wisconsin; at Belvedere, Illinois; and at Clarksville, Iowa. On December 22, 1863, he married Helen Rosencrans. By 1866 Duncan had settled down in Charles City, Iowa, where he practiced law after being admitted to the bar in 1869, held petty political offices, served as mayor for one year, and taught school. After 1880 Duncan commuted between the Cherokee Nation West and Iowa while serving the Cherokees as attorney, teacher of English, Latin and Greek at the Cherokee Male Seminary, and translator of the Cherokee laws. Sometime in the 1890s he took up permanent residence in Vinita, Cherokee Nation West. In the early 1870s Duncan also began to write regularly for Indian Territory newspapers, particularly the Tahlequah *Cherokee Advocate* and, later, the Vinita *Indian Chieftain*. Although he penned several poems and short stories, Duncan was best known for a series of letters that appeared under the pen name Too-qua-stee. The predominant subject of the letters was the federal government's attacks on Cherokee sovereignty following the Reconstruction treaty of 1866. Consequently, Duncan was highly critical of the allotment policies promoted after the formation of the Dawes Commission in 1893 and implemented with the Curtis Act of 1898. DeWitt Clinton Duncan died in Vinita, now Oklahoma, on November 2, 1909, only two years after the dissolution of the Cherokee Nation West with the incorporation of Indian Territory into the state of Oklahoma.

Selected Publications of DeWitt Clinton Duncan

"A Momentous Occasion." *Indian Chieftain*, June 24, 1897. Reprinted in Daniel F. Littlefield, Jr., and James W. Parins, eds., *Native American Writing In the Southeast: An Anthology, 1875–1935*. Jackson: University Press of Mississippi, 1995: 31–37.

"An Open Letter to Hon. Charles Curtis." *Indian Chieftain* February 17, 1898. Reprinted in *Chronicles of Oklahoma* 47, no. 3 (Fall 1969): 289–311.

"Passage of the Curtis Bill." *Daily Chieftain*, June 21, 1900. Reprinted in Littlefield and Parins, *Native American Writing In the Southeast*, 42–45.

"Story of the Cherokees." *Cherokee Advocate*, October 6, 13, 20, 27, 1882. Reproduced in the Digital Library, American Native Press Archives, University of Arkansas at Little Rock.

Selected Secondary Sources

Garrett, Kathleen. "Dartmouth Alumni in the Indian Territory." *Chronicles of Oklahoma* 32, no. 2 (Summer 1954): 123–41.

Foreman, Carolyn Thomas. "Notes on DeWitt Clinton Duncan and a recently Discovered History of the Cherokees." *Chronicles of Oklahoma* 47, no. 3 (Fall 1969): 305–11.

Marable, Mary Hays and Claire Boylan. *Handbook of Oklahoma Writers.* Norman: University of Oklahoma Press, 1939: 55–56.

PASSING OF CREEK LANDS

Charles Gibson (1901)

Chas. Gibson Tells of the Passing of the Last Stomping Ground.

For twenty-five years there has been hatched without number, all leading in one direction, some way to gobble up this, the last resting place, the last home of the red man.

Now that the Creek treaty has been ratified, was it the lick or feather that broke the Creek citizens back?[1]

He is declared a citizen of the United States of America.[2] Does he know what that means, does he know what that is, being a citizen of this great U.S.? How will he know when his rights are being trespassed upon? Who will advocate his cause? Must he not speak for himself? As long as he does not say, I am a citizen of this great government and that the world of men must respect, his nose will be kept to the grind stone. As some old pelican said in olden times, "the watch word of all citizens of the Indian Territory should be 'give me statehood and liberty or give me home rule at least.'"

There are men, white, red and black, who are as able, in the five tribes, to look after the affairs of this country as they have in any little old state. But no, congress has rashly promised us more laws than any little province on the face of the earth. Here among the five tribes we have a slight touch of the Arkansas law; we have some Curtis laws, we have some Creek, Cherokee, Chickasaw, Choctaw and Seminole laws; we have no peace and order. That is what the Indian Territory is accused of at any rate.[3]

What this country would need, right now, is statehood in short order. Get a new broom and foreverlasting sweep these half dozen remnants of disjointed rules and regulations off the face of the Indian Territory.

If the five tribes are U.S. citizens why not they be recognized as such and give them home rule as their rights demand?

All the agreements and treaties go on to say we will endeavor by strict laws to keep all intoxicants out of the Indian Territory. Why have such stuff in a treaty? If there is anything that an Indian likes it is whiskey. And if there is any production that a white man loves to sell it is red whiskey. Whiskey selling to Indians is like hanging for murder—the idea of stopping either is preposterous. As the fellow said, that little thing can't be did, and furthermore, history repeats itself. It is always essential to have whiskey very handy when Indian lands are on the market. It makes an Indian feel rich enough to sell his land. It is whiskey that he wants then—it is not land or money—Mr. Injun is now a great pet. His fur is being rubbed down the right way. He is a bully good fellow now. A cigar and a social drink don't cost him anything. Just now he is gulping down great tubs full of flattery. Why? Well, you know. But say five years from now the place that knew him once will not be apt to recognize him any more because by that time he will have worried down his throat enough red whiskey

171

to overflow his 160 acres of land.[4] Then he will wake up to find himself a be-fuddled Indian pauper.

Thus will end the Indian's interest in this beautiful garden spot of the United States. Chas. Gibson.

P.S.—The writer is Indian but don't drink, hence the scorching and advice is given free of charge.

Notes

Originally in the *Indian Journal* (June 21, 1901). Reproduced in "Selected Works of Charles Gibson," ed. Thomas Murray, Digital Library, American Native Press Archives, University of Arkansas at Little Rock. Reprinted with the kind permission of James Parins. Following allotment and citizenship there was an ongoing public debate over whether Indian Territory should apply for separate statehood or be joined with Oklahoma Territory into a single state. The movement for separate statehood among the Creeks gained momentum after the fall of 1902, when it was promoted by Principal Chief Pleasant Porter at the first of a series of inter-tribal councils of the Five Tribes called together specifically to discuss the issue. The idea of a separate Indian state was finally rendered obsolete with the passage of the Enabling Act of 1906, providing for the admission of Oklahoma Territory and Indian Territory as the single state of Oklahoma. Like Alexander Lawrence Posey, Gibson favored separate statehood for Indian Territory. See also Charles Gibson, "As to Statehood," *Indian Journal* (November 21, 1902); reproduced in "Selected Works of Charles Gibson," ed. Thomas Murray, Digital Library, Native American Press Archives, University of Arkansas at Little Rock.

1. On May 25, 1901, the Creek National Council ratified an allotment agreement with the United States. The agreement also provided for the dissolution of the tribal government by March 4, 1906. The agreement was proclaimed on June 25, 1901.

2. A congressional act passed on May 3, 1901, declared all Indians in Indian Territory citizens of the United States.

3. The establishment of a federal court system with limited jurisdiction in Indian Territory in 1889 extended Arkansas civil and criminal law over the territory. The Curtis Act of 1898 dissolved tribal courts and gave the federal government authority over such matters as land disputes. The tribal laws remained in effect until the passage of the Five Tribes Act in 1906, when Congress denied the legislatures of the Five Tribes the right to meet more than thirty days per year and made their legislative action subject to presidential veto. See Jeffrey Burton, *Indian Territory and the United States, 1866–1906: Courts, Government, and the Movement for Oklahoma Statehood* (Norman: University of Oklahoma Press, 1995).

4. According to the General Allotment Act of 1887, from which the Five Tribes were exempted, each head of a family was to receive 160 acres (based on the provisions of the Homestead Act of 1862). Allotment policy was officially promoted in Indian Territory by the Dawes Commission as of 1893 and initiated under the Curtis Act of 1898.

BIOGRAPHY

Charles Gibson (Creek, 1846–1923) was born in the vicinity of Eufaula, in the southeastern part of the Creek Nation, on March 20, 1846, the son of John C. Gibson, a white farmer from Georgia, and Polly Gibson. Charles Gibson attained his tribal status from his mother, a niece of Chief Opothleyoholo and member of the Creek town of Tuckabatchee. Gibson received a rudimentary education at the Creek common schools and the Methodist Asbury Mission near Eufaula, but was largely self-educated. For twenty years Gibson worked as head clerk and buyer in the Grayson Brothers store at North Fork Town. He then established his own store in the booming town of Eufaula in 1896. In 1901 he married Modeania Aultman, with whom he had one child.

Beginning around 1900, Charles Gibson began to write extensively for Indian Territory newspapers and journals, especially the Eufaula *Indian Journal,* owned and edited by his friend and fellow journalist Alexander Lawrence Posey from early 1902 until the fall of 1903. Although Gibson's countless publications cover a wide range of subjects, he is best remembered for his witty "horse sense" commentaries on Indian Territory affairs, particularly a regular feature column for the *Indian Journal* titled "Gibson's Rifle Shots." With Alexander Posey, he is considered one of the foremost representatives of Indian Territory humor.

Selected Publications of Charles Gibson

"The Passing of the Indian"; "The Indian—His Present"; "The Indian—His Past"; "The Indian—His Future"; "The Way of the Spokogee"; "Wild Cat's Long Swim"; "Why the Lion Eats His Meat Raw." All in Daniel F. Littlefield, Jr., and James W. Parins, eds., *Native American Writing in the Southeast: An Anthology, 1875–1935.* Jackson: University Press of Mississippi, 1995: 111–23.

"Selected Works of Charles Gibson," ed. by Thomas Murray, Digital Library, American Native Press Archives, University of Arkansas at Little Rock (www.anpa.ualr.edu).

Selected Secondary Sources

O'Beirne, H. F. and E. S. O'Beirne. *The Indian Territory: Its Chiefs, Legislators, and Leading Men.* St. Louis: C. B. Woodward Co., 1892: 296–98.

Benedict, John D. *Muskogee and Northeastern Oklahoma.* Chicago: S. J. Clarke Publishing Co., 1922: 1: 499.

Gideon, D. C. *The Indian Territory: Descriptive, Biographical and Genealogical.* New York: Lewis Publishing Co., 1901: 891–92.

FUS FIXICO LETTER

Alexander Lawrence Posey (1905)

"Well, so," Hotgun he say, "Colonel Clarence B. Duglast [Douglas], he was dee-lighted and Chief P. Porter, he was dee-lighted, and Charley Gibson he was dee-lighted, and Alice M. Lobbysome [Robertson] she was dee-lighted too."[1]

And Tookpafka Micco he was look down his old pipe-stem and say, "Well, so what for?"[2]

And Hotgun he go on and say, "Well, so 'cause the Great White Father from Washington was suffered 'em to come unto 'im on the grand stand, while he was showing his teeth and shaking the Big Stick before the multitude up to Muskogee."[3]

Then Tookpafka Micco he spit out in the yard and say, "Well, so what kind of a thing's the Big Stick, anyhow?"[4]

And Hotgun he look wise, like the supreme court, and explain it, "Well so the Big Stick was the symbol of power, like a policeman's billy. In the jungles a Afriky it was called a war-club; and in the islands a the sea, like Australia, it was called a boomer-rang; and among us fullblood Injins we call it a ball-stick; and if it was fall in the hands a the women folks, it was called a rolling-pin, or maybe so, a broom-handle. It was had lots a different names, like breakfast food. Over in Europe a king was had precious stones put in it, to make it more ornamental than useful, and call it a scepter. The brass-knucks was the latest improvement on it. In olden time Samson was had a Big Stick made out of a jaw-bone of a ass, and was made a great hit with it among the Philistines.[5] Same way when the Great White Father was want to show his influence all he had to do was to flourish the Big Stick and everybody was get out from under it."

(Wolf Warrior and Kono Harjo they was grunt and Tookpafka Micco he was pay close attention and spit out in the yard again.)[6]

Then Hotgun he smoke slow and go on and say, "Well, so, like I first start to say, Colonel Clarence B. Duglast he was dee-lighted and Chief P. Porter he was dee-lighted, and Charley Gibson he was dee-lighted and Alice M. Lobbysome she was dee-lighted too. They was all butt in before the reception committee could see if they badges was on straight. They was put the Great White Father on they shoulders and histed 'im upon the grand stand, and he was made a talk to the multitude. He say, 'Well, so I was mighty glad to see you all and hope you was all well. I couldn't complain and I was left Secretary Itscocked [Hitchcock] enjoying good health. (Big cheers and somebody out in the crowd say, Bully for Itscocked!)[7] Look like you all was had a fine country down here. You all ought to had statehood and let Oklahoma show you how to run it. (Colonel Clarence B. Duglast, he pay close attention and listen for some word 'bout 'imself.) I want everybody to had a square deal down here. (Lots more big cheers and everybody smiling but the Snake Injin.)[8] You all was had a fine town here too. You could run flat boats up to it from Ft. Smith, and deliver the goods over lots of railroads, and pump out oil, and develop salt-licks and float bee-courses.[9] But I didn't had time to talk any more, 'cause I couldn't stop here but two minutes and I have been here put near five. So long.'

"Then the special train was kick up a cloud of dust and hide behind it, and the multitude was climb down off the houses and telegraph poles and go tell they neighbors 'bout it. Colonel Clarence B. Duglast he go and tell his friends the President think he was ten cents straight, and Chief P. Porter he go and tell his friends the President say he was the greatest living Injin, and Charley Gibson he go and write a 'Rifle Shot' 'bout giving the President a fan made out a tame turkey feathers instead of eagle plumes, and Alice M. Lobbysome she go and buy the platform the President stood on for a souvenir. Maybe so she was made a bedstead out of it and distribute the sawdust and shavings among the full-bloods to look at."

And Tookpafka Micco he say, "Well, so I might need some kindling next winter and the keepsakes was come in handy."

(Wolf Warrior and Kono Harjo they was give another big grunt.)

Then Hotgun he go on and say, "Well, so the next stop the Great White Father make was out in Oklahoma in a big pasture, where they was lots of cayotes. He was got after one a horseback and crowd it over the prairies till he was get good results and captured it alive. He was had lots of fun with it before he was run it down. The President was a great hunter and was kill big game well as a cayote or jackrabbit. So he was go on to the Rocky Mountains to beard the bear and lion in they den."[10]

And Tookpafka Micco he say, "Well, so this time the Lord better help the grizzly."

Notes

Originally in the *Muskogee Daily Phoenix*, April 16, 1905. Reproduced in Alexander L. Posey, *The Fus Fixico Letters*, edited by Daniel F. Littlefield, Jr., and Carol A. Petty Hunter (Lincoln: University of Nebraska Press, 1994), 202–207. Reprinted with permission of the Gilcrease Museum, Tulsa, Oklahoma. This is one of the rare pieces in which Posey also touches upon a transregional subject by lampooning Theodore Roosevelt's "Big Stick" policy as well as his hunting exploits.

1. Hotgun is based on a historical figure, Mitcka Hiya, a medicine man and prominent leader of the conservative faction of Creeks known as the Snakes. As of the spring of 1903 he replaced Choela, a noted Creek medicine man and legislator, as the principal character in the Fus Fixico letters. Clarence B. Douglas was the editor of the *Muskogee Phoenix*. Pleasant Porter (1840–1907) was Principal Chief of the Creeks from 1899 to 1907. Alice Mary Robertson (1854–1932) was superintendent of public instruction for the Creek Nation from 1900 to 1905 and then served as postmaster at Muskogee from 1905 to 1913.

2. Tookpafka Micco, Hotgun's conversation partner who also began to appear regularly in the Fus Fixico letters after the spring of 1903, was based on a living Creek town leader.

3. On April 5, 1905, President Theodore Roosevelt rushed through Indian Territory on his way to hunt in the Rocky Mountains. His train stopped for only a few

minutes at Muskogee, a disappointing gesture for Indian Territory residents immersed in the vital political issue of single or double statehood. Roosevelt favored the incorporation of Indian Territory and Oklahoma Territory as a single state. In other letters he is referred to as "President Rooster Feather," a play on Theodore Roosevelt's cockiness.

4. Reference to Roosevelt's aggressive foreign policy. One of his favorite adages was, "Speak softly and carry a big stick; you will go far."

5. Judges 15:16.

6. Wolf Warrior, who may be remotely based on Posey's friend and fellow journalist George W. Grayson (1843–1920), and the fictional Kono Harjo made their regular appearance beginning in November 1903, when Posey began publishing his letters in the *Muskogee Evening Times.* They do little more than grunt or spit in response to what Hotgun and Tookpafka Micco are discussing. The Fus Fixico letters evolved from the single persona commentaries by Fus Fixico (Heartless Bird) into a more complex narrative format. While Fus Fixico's role gradually shifted from that of a commentator (persona) to a mere bystander (framing device) who reports conversations between Hotgun and Tookpafka Micco, the exchange between Hotgun and Tookpafka Micco now appeared in standard dialogue form, with minimal setting and character action added.

7. Ethan Allen Hitchcock (1835–1909) was Secretary of the Interior from 1898 to 1907 and actively involved in Indian affairs. Like most Republicans, he favored single statehood. "Secretary Itscocked" is a below the belt reference to Ethan Allen Hitchcock's vacillating policies—i.e., a gun that is cocked but never fires.

8. Under the leadership of Chitto Harjo (1846–1909?), better known to whites as Crazy Snake, a group of conservative Creeks gathered in the fall of 1900 and established their own government within the Muskogee Nation. Their goal was to bring about the recognition and enforcement of the Treaty of 1832, and to reinstall the old tribal regime. Together with other irreconcilable members of the Five Tribes, who had coalesced earlier into an organization known as the Four Mothers Society, the Snake faction made a desperate attempt to block the Dawes Commission's plans to allot lands in severalty. Most stubbornly refused for years to accept allotment, and some even seriously considered removing to Mexico in order to maintain their ancient way of life. See Mel H. Bolster, *Crazy Snake and the Smoked Meat Rebellion* (Boston: Brandon Press, 1976).

9. To float a bee course is to find a colony of wild bees by triangulating their flight course.

10. From Sir Walter Scott's *Lochinvar* (1808), stanza 14. Roosevelt's hunting exploits on this trip were widely reported in the press.

FUS FIXICO LETTER

Alexander Lawrence Posey (1906)

"Well, so," Hotgun he say, "I like to know who done it, anyhow."

An' Tookpafka Micco he smoke 'is ol' hatchet-pipe slow an' say, "Well, so, in olden times, seven cities want to be Homer's birthplace; an', same way, all the politicians claim the credit for statehood an' dispute with one 'nother. Delegate Makefire [McGuire] he say he done it an' couldn't tell a lie 'bout it.[1] He say if the fight he put up for statehood wasn't worth a decent burial in the Statesman's corner o' the capitol buildin' it wasn't worth takin' the Father o' His Country's example in vain. Clarence Duglast [Douglas] he say he done it—with Washington Post interviews written by 'imself—an' he want a outside lot facin' the main aisle in the Poet's Corner; also 'is statue, with a sword buckled on, standin' 'straddle o' lot o' carpetbaggers.[2] An' they was some commissioner court lawyers an' not'ry publics claim the honor, too, but they wasn't entitled to it no more than Crazy Snake."[3]

Then Hotgun he say, "Well, so Delegate Makefire an' Clarence Duglast was imposin' on that razorback the statehood rooters take to congress last winter an' someone ought to report 'em to the humane society.[4]

(Wolf Warrior an' Kono Harjo give big grunt an' spit in the ragweeds an' pay close 'tention.)

Then Hotgun he go on an' say, "Well, so before statehood they was too much sentiment mixed up in the Injin problem. The missionary he tell the Injin he must lay up treasures in Heaven, but didn't show 'im how to keep body an' soul together on earth and lay by for the rainy day; an' the school teacher he learn 'im how to read an' shade 'is letters when he write, but didn't teach 'im how to make two blades o' grass grow out o' one; an' the philantropist remind 'im o' the century o' dishonor instead o' the future individual responsibility; an' the government dish out beef an' annuity to 'im instead of a mule an' a plow.[5] Everything like that make the Injin no count, except give jobs to government clerks."

An' Tookpafka Micco he say, "Well so the ol' order was passed away. Maybe so now the politician tell the Injin how to win salvation in the Democrat party, or Republican party, an' party bosses teach 'im how to put in two votes instead o' one."

Then Hotgun he go on an' say, "Well, so if the Injin know 'is business, he was better off than before. All he had to do was be a Injin an' stay to 'imself like an ol' bull in the winter time. He don't want to be Democrat or Republican. Maybe so 'is hair was long enough for a Populist, but he better not. If he take sides he wont 'mount to nothin' an' couldn't be dog pelter."

An' Tookpafka Micco he say, "Well so I was raised on Democrat sofky an' don't care who find it out, but I don't vote for yellow dogs on 'count o' the color."[6]

(Wolf Warrior an' Kono Harjo grunt an' spit in the ragweeds ag'in an' move further in the shade.)

Then Hotgun he go on an' say, "Well, so we was all one people now an' neighbors, anyhow, regardless o' race or politics or religion. Instead o' Choctaws an' Chickasaws an' Seminoles an' Creeks an' Cherokees an' Boomers an' Osages an' Sequoyahans we was all Oklahomans. Muskogee wasn't in Injin Teritory an Oklahoma City wasn't in the Short Grass Country.[7] You didn't had to slip over the line for the stomach's sake now.[8] You could be at home in Beaver county same as at Hickory Ground. You could say, 'I'm from Oklahoma' an' be proud of it same as if you was from Ol' Dominion."[9]

Notes

Originally in the *Muskogee Daily Phoenix*, June 24, 1906. Reproduced in Alexander L. Posey, *The Fus Fixico Letters*, edited by Daniel F. Littlefield, Jr., and Carol A. Petty Hunter (Lincoln: University of Nebraska Press, 1994), 246–50. Reprinted with permission of the Gilcrease Museum, Tulsa, Oklahoma. The so-called Enabling Act, approved on June 16, 1906, provided for the admission of Oklahoma Territory and Indian Territory as the single state of Oklahoma. Hotgun and Tookpafka Micco discuss Indian prospects in the fledgling state.

1. Bird S. McGuire (1865–1930) was a Republican delegate to Congress for Oklahoma Territory and an avid promoter of single statehood.

2. Clarence Douglas, the editor of the *Muskogee Phoenix*, reported on the statehood bill debates in Washington and gave numerous interviews in which he styled himself as a key figure of the pro-statehood faction.

3. Crazy Snake, or Chitto Harjo (1846–1909?), was the leader of the conservative Snake faction seeking to maintain traditional tribal ways. Although Posey was convinced that the old ways had to be abandoned and often poked fun at the Snakes in his Fus Fixico Letters, Chitto Harjo stood for everything that he admired in what he called the "real Indian." In a lyrical tribute to Chitto Harjo titled "On the Capture and Imprisonment of Crazy Snake, January, 1900," Posey eulogized the conservative Creek leader as a noble relic of the past whose desperate struggle took on heroic proportions. See *The Poems of Alexander Lawrence Posey*, compiled by Minnie H. Posey (Topeka, Kans.: Crane and Company, Printers, 1910), 88. For a fictional treatment of Chitto Harjo see Robert J. Conley, *Crazy Snake* (New York: Pocket Books, 1994).

4. In December of 1905 supporters of single statehood paraded the streets of Washington, D.C., with a razorback hog carrying a placard with "Statehood" printed on it.

5. Reference to Helen Hunt Jackson's *A Century of Dishonor* (1881), an indictment of federal Indian policy and one of the most widely read publications of the Indian reform movement leading to the passage of the General Allotment Act in 1887.

6. Sofky, a traditional Creek food, is composed of corn grits cooked in lye water. A yellow dog is an unswerving Democratic Party loyalist.

7. "Short Grass Country" refers to Oklahoma Territory.

8. The sale of alcohol was prohibited in Indian Territory, but patent medicines with a high alcohol content like Peruna, the favorite of Hotgun and Tookpafka, could

be obtained through drugstores. When Peruna was banned from Indian Territory in December of 1905, the only alternative was to cross the border into Oklahoma Territory.

9. Beaver County is located in the Oklahoma panhandle; Hickory Ground was a Creek town near present-day Henryetta, in eastern Oklahoma, where the Snakes called out their separate government in 1900.

BIOGRAPHY

Alexander Lawrence Posey (Creek, 1873–1908), or Chinnubbie Harjo, was born near Eufaula, Muskogee Nation, on August 3, 1873. His father, Lewis Henderson Posey, was an adopted Creek citizen of Scotch-Irish heritage; his mother, Pohos Harjo (Nancy Phillips), was a Chickasaw-Creek from the Upper Creek tribal town of Tuskegee Canadian and member of the Wind Clan. Creek was Posey's primary language until the age of fourteen, when his father forced him to speak English while at home. Soon thereafter he was sent to a Creek national public school in Eufaula in order to improve upon the rudimentary instruction he had received from a private tutor earlier. In November 1889 Posey enrolled at Bacone Indian University in Muskogee. He left Bacone in the spring of 1894 without graduating.

Following a brief stint as a salesman for a mercantile house at Sasakwa in the Seminole Nation in the winter of 1894, Posey entered Creek politics. In 1895 he was elected to the House of Warriors, the lower chamber of the Creek legislature, as a representative from Tuskegee, his tribal town by virtue of the Creek custom of reckoning descent from the mother's line. Later that same year he received an appointment as superintendent of the Creek Orphan Asylum at Okmulgee, a post he held until his resignation in October 1897. During this time he met and fell in love with Minnie Harris, a young white teacher from Arkansas, whom he married on May 9, 1896. Early in December 1897 Posey was nominated as superintendent of public instruction for the Muskogee Nation for a term that ended in October 1898. Thereafter he took over the position of superintendent of the National High School at Eufaula and the Wetumka National School until the spring of 1901.

Early in 1902 Posey bought the Eufaula *Indian Journal,* a newspaper originally established in Muskogee by William Potter Ross in May of 1876. In June 1902 he also purchased the *Eufaula Gazette* and merged it with the *Journal.* On June 15, 1903, Posey established the *Daily Indian Journal,* the first daily newspaper published by an Indian, which he edited alongside the regular weekly edition. Posey sold the *Indian Journal* in October of 1903 and became co-owner and city editor of the daily *Muskogee Evening Times.* The paper apparently proved to be a poor investment, however, as Posey gave it up again at the end of March, 1904.

In the spring and summer of 1904, Posey worked as interpreter for the Office of Indian Affairs. He was then assigned to the Dawes Commission early in October, first as official interpreter at the Creek National Council at Okmulgee and then as clerk in charge of a Creek enrollment field party. His task was to collect testimony on Creeks who had applied for allotment before the proscribed date of May 25, 1901, but whose names appeared on tribal rolls without the necessary verification for the issuance of allotment certificates. He was apparently so successful in this capacity that the Dawes Commission directed him to travel throughout the Muskogee Nation in search of the remaining "lost"

Creeks, who would be excluded from their due share in the Creek assets after allotment was completed if not found and properly registered. The Creek rolls were finally closed on July 25, 1906. Posey left the Indian service in the spring of the following year.

Posey then found employment with the International Land Company in Muskogee, an enterprise headed by C. M. Bradley, one of the most notorious grafters in Indian Territory. In May 1907 Posey also became a partner in the Posey-Thornton Oil and Gas Company, which specialized in the buying and selling of real estate, dealing in livestock, engaging in mercantile business, prospecting for oil and gas, and mining for coal and other minerals.

In the spring of the following year, Posey and some associates repurchased the *Indian Journal.* He then devoted himself once more to the task of newspaper editing in Eufaula alongside his other business ventures in Muskogee.

Posey was an uncompromising advocate of allotment. Although he respected the conservative and anti-allotment Creek faction known as the Snakes, Posey believed that their admirable way of life was no longer tenable. He enrolled his own family with the Dawes Commission in 1899 and continued to promote its policies in his capacity as a journalist. In addition to allotment, Posey was also deeply concerned with the ongoing public debate over whether Indian Territory should apply for separate statehood or be joined with Oklahoma Territory into a single state. At first Posey found the idea of forming a separate state impractical but then reversed his position by late spring 1903. Posey continued sporadically to support the separate statehood movement throughout his editorship of the *Indian Journal.* He also joined the constitutional convention held in Muskogee on August 21, 1905, for the purpose of creating the "State of Sequoyah." The Enabling Act of 1906, providing for the admission of Oklahoma Territory and Indian Territory as the single state of Oklahoma, finally aborted the single state movement.

On May 27, 1908, Alexander Lawrence Posey drowned as he tried to ford a rain-swollen river while commuting from Muskogee to Eufaula.

Although Posey's "progressive" views and entrepreneurial activities tarnished his reputation among the Creeks then and now, he is still celebrated today as the poet laureate of Indian Territory, an office specifically created for him in the spring of 1903 by the Indian Territory Press Association. Between 1893 and the turn of the twentieth century, Posey produced almost two hundred poems, most of which appeared in the *Indian Journal, Muskogee Daily Phoenix,* and the Muskogee *Twin Territories.* Some of Posey's verse drew attention beyond Indian Territory, reappearing in the St. Louis *Republic,* the *Kansas City Journal,* the *Kansas City Star,* the New York *Evening Sun,* Carlisle's *The Red Man,* and the Women's National Indian Association's *Indian's Friend.* A collection of his poetry was published posthumously by his wife titled *The Poems of Alexander Lawrence Posey* (1910). Although heavily influenced by romantic literary conventions, his particular regional style has nevertheless influenced succeeding generations of Creek poets, notably Joy Harjo and the late Louis (Little Coon) Oliver (1904–91). Oliver, who received the first Alexander Posey Literary

Award given by the Este Mvskoke Arts Council on April 3, 1987, lauded Posey as "the greatest Creek Indian poet known."

Posey's most memorable literary achievement, however, can be found in more than seventy humoristic sketches known collectively as the "Fus Fixico Letters," produced between October 24, 1902, and May 22, 1908, and published primarily in the *Indian Journal, Fort Smith Times, Muskogee Evening Times*, and *Muskogee Daily Phoenix*. In these "letters," a group of fictive and semi-historical full-blood Creek characters quip about various contemporary Indian Territory issues, particularly allotment and single or double statehood. Posey's masterful rendition of the Creek-English dialect and sharp wit make him one of the foremost representatives of an ongoing tradition of Indian Territory humor that culminated with the career of Will Rogers.

Selected Publications of Alexander Lawrence Posey

The Fus Fixico Letters. Edited with an introduction by Daniel F. Littlefield, Jr., and Carola A. Petty. Lincoln: University of Nebraska Press, 1993.
"The Journal of Alexander Lawrence Posey, January 1 to September 4, 1897." *Chronicles of Oklahoma* 45, no. 4 (Winter 1967–68): 393–432.
"Journal of Creek Enrollment Field Party 1905 by Alexander Posey." *Chronicles of Oklahoma* 46, no. 1 (Spring 1968): 2–19.
The Poems of Alexander Lawrence Posey. Compiled by Minnie H. Posey. Topeka, Kans.: Crane and Company, Printers, 1910. A revised edition was prepared by the Okmulgee Cultural Foundation and Five Civilized Tribes Museum. Muskogee, Okla.: Hoffman, 1969.

Unpublished Writings

The primary source of material by and about Posey is the Alexander Lawrence Posey Collection, Thomas Gilcrease Institute of American History and Art, Tulsa, Oklahoma. Some of his writings are also found in the Mrs. Alfred Mitchell Collection, Western History Collections, University of Oklahoma Libraries, Norman, Oklahoma.

Selected Secondary Sources

Barnett, Leona G. "Este Cate Emunkv: Red Man Always." *Chronicles of Oklahoma* 46, no. 1 (Spring 1968): 20–38.
Challacombe, Doris. "Alexander Lawrence Posey." *Chronicles of Oklahoma* 11, no. 4 (December 1933): 1010–18.
Connelley, William Elsey. "Memoir of Alexander Lawrence Posey." In *The Poems of Alexander Lawrence Posey:* 5–65.
Hogan, Linda. "The 19th Century Native American Poets." *Wassaja/The Indian Historian* 13, no. 4 (1980), 24–29.
Kosmider, Alexia M. "Reinventing Trickster: Creek Indian Alex Posey's Nom de Plume, Chinnubbie Harjo." In *Tricksterism in Turn-of-the-Century American*

Literature. Edited by Elizabeth Ammons and Annette White-Parks, Hanover, N.H.: University Press of New England, 1994: 93–105.

_____. "'Hedged in, Shut up and Hidden from the World': Unveiling the Native and the Landscape in Alex Posey's Poetry." *MELUS* 21, no. 1 (Spring 1996): 3–19.

_____. *Tricky Tribal Discourse: The Poetry, Short Stories, and Fus Fixico Letters of Creek Writer Alex Posey.* Moscow, Idaho: University of Idaho Press, 1998.

Littlefield, Jr., Daniel F. "Evolution of Alex Posey's Fus Fixico Persona." *Studies in American Indian Literatures* 4, nos. 2–3 (Summer–Fall 1992): 136–44.

_____. *Alex Posey: Creek Poet, Journalist, & Humorist.* Lincoln: University of Nebraska Press, 1992.

Lowe, John. "Newsprint Masks: The Comic Columns of Finley Peter Dunne, Alexander Posey, and Langston Hughes." In *Beyond the Binary: Reconstructing Cultural Identity in a Multicultural Context,* edited by Timothy B. Powell. New Brunswick, N.J.: Rutgers University Press, 1999: 185–204.

Weaver, Jace. *That the People Might Live: Native American Literatures and Native American Community.* New York: Oxford University Press, 1997: 88–95.

Wiget, Andrew. *Native American Literature.* Boston: Twayne Publishers, 1985: 59–61.

Womack, Craig S. *Red on Red: Native Literary Separatism.* Minneapolis: University of Minnesota Press, 1999: 131–86.

Womack, Craig S. "Alexander Posey's Nature Journals: A Further Argument for Tribally-Specific Aesthetics." *Studies in American Indian Literatures* 12, nos. 2/3 (Summer–Fall 2001): 49–66.

WRITES ON FEEDING DEMOCRATS RAW ORATORY AT JACKSON DINNER

Will Rogers (1928)

Well, all I know is just what I see in the papers, or what I hear as I sit behind the free lunch table and listen to the boys bark for their meals. Did I ever tell you about the time I broke bread with the Democrats in Washington? I passed myself off as a Democrat one night just to get a free meal.

I had watched the Republicans eat, but I never had seen them feed the Democrats, so I crawled in under the tent and watched 'em throw the good old raw Jeffersonian Oratory right into the cages with 'em. They call it a Jackson Day Dinner. I made the mistake of my life. I went there with a speech prepared about Jackson, telling how "He stood like a stone wall," and here it wasn't that Jackson that they were using as an alibi to give the dinner to.[1] It was old "Andy" Jackson.

Well, to tell you the truth, I am not so sweet on old Andy. He is the one that run us Cherokees out of Georgia and North Carolina. I ate the dinner on him, but I didn't enjoy it. I thought I was eating for Stonewall. Old Andy, every time he couldn't find any one to jump on, would come back and pounce onto us Indians. Course he licked the English down in New Orleans, but he didn't do it till the war had been over two weeks, so he really just fought them as an encore. Then he would go to Florida and shoot up the Seminoles.[2] That was before there was a bathing suit in Palm Beach. Then he would have a row with the Government, and they would take his command and his liquor away from him, and he would come back and sick himself onto us Cherokees again.

He was the first one to think up the idea to promise everybody that if they will vote for you, why, you will give them an office when you get in, and the more times they vote for you the bigger the office you will give them.[3] That was the real starting of the Democratic Party. It was called Democratic because you was supposed to get something for your vote. Then the Republicans come along and improved on the Democrats and Jackson's idea by giving them money instead of promises of jobs. In that way you got paid whether your man was elected or not. So naturally that's why more people are Republicans than Democrats. Nobody with any business sense wants to wait till after election to see if they get something. They liked the Republican idea of "Paying as you go."

But old Andy made the White House. He got in before the Republicans got their scheme working. The Indians wanted him in there so he would let us alone for awhile. Andy stayed two terms, and was the first man that didn't "choose" to run again. He had to get back to his regular business, which was shooting at the Indians. They were for a third term for Andy. They sent the Indians to Oklahoma. They had a treaty that said, "You shall have this land as long as grass grows and water flows." It was not only a good rhyme but looked like a good treaty, and it was till they struck oil. Then the Government took it away from us again. They said the treaty only refers to "Water and Grass; it don't say anything about oil."

So the Indians lost another bet. The first one was to Andrew Jackson, and the second was to [John D.] Rockefeller, [Edward L.] Doheny, [Harry F.] Sinclair and Socony.[4] After the Cherokees went back and saw where they used to live in Georgia, North Carolina and Alabama, why, we always felt that Andy had unconsciously done us a favor. For Georgia never was heard of again till Ty Cobb.[5] North Carolina was in a rut till Lucky Strikes and Camels pulled them out, and Alabama laid dormant till Tom Heflin made the first page for them.[6] So we Cherokees can always kinder forgive old Andy for not knowing what he was doing. Got to give old Andy credit, he fought duels when duels was duels, and not just the inconvenience of getting up before sunrise.

Now we got an election coming along and us "Injuns" got an entry in the race. It's Charley Curtis, who was smart enough to live in a Northern State, which is a physical hardship, but a political advantage.[7] Charley has used awful good judgment in the Presidential ambitions. Al Smith and Jim Reed and [Alvin Victor] Donahey and [Albert Cabell] Ritchie all have splendid qualifications and have studied and acquired traits that will help them to the Presidency, but Indian Charley Curtis with one swoop embraced a requirement that will be of more advantage in a Presidential race than all the combined qualifications of the other I mentioned.[8] He is a Republican. Of course that ain't saying much. But it's just that little thing that is lacking in any of these others that will be their principal handicap. So if we get Charley in there we will see what he does for the Indians. I hope he don't send us back.

I thought at the time of the dinner that the Democrats were going mighty far back to find some hero that they could worship. But I happened to be in Cuba when President Coolidge delivered his speech to the Latins, and the Republicans had to go even further back than the Democrats did for Jackson.[9] He went back to Columbus. I had never known or even heard Columbus's political faith discussed before. But he must have been a Republican, the way Cal was boosting for him. So you see neither party hasn't got much when they have to reach back that far to find some one to boost.

The dinner started at 7 o'clock on Thursday and run till 3 a.m. on Friday the 13th. We didn't eat that long. We only eat as long as they brought it. They run out of food about 8 p.m. From then on you had to subsist on "Prohibition, with or without a license," and "Party Harmony." Jim Reed closed the show with "Corruption" at exactly 3 A.M. the next morning and held 'em in their seats. You know the Democrats can just naturally stand more oratory than any other race.

But it was all mighty fine. The Democrat is just naturally a better orator than the Republican. The Democrats have the best side. They are always attacking and the Republicans have to defend. The Democrats always have things to attack, for the Republicans furnish them plenty, and on the other hand the Republicans haven't got much to defend. Their only defense is, "We are in; try to get us out." So if you ever get a chance don't miss one of these Jackson Day Dinners; they only hold 'em on election years. They save up four years stuff to tell about the Republicans and it's sure worth the money.

Notes

Originally published as "Feeding the Democrats Some Raw Oratory," *Tulsa Daily World*, February 5, 1928: Section 5, page 2; repr., James M. Smallwood and Steven K. Gragert, eds., *Will Rogers' Weekly Articles* (Stillwater, Okla.: Oklahoma State University Press, 1981), 3: 128–30. Reprinted with the kind assistance of Steven K. Gragert and permission of the Will Rogers Memorial Museums, Claremore, Oklahoma. Will Rogers obviously shares the Cherokee antipathy for Andrew Jackson, who played a major role in the Cherokee removal.

1. Thomas Jonathan Jackson (1824–63), or "Stonewall" Jackson, was a Confederate officer known for gallantry. He received the appellation "Stonewall" during the Battle of Bull Run (the First Manassas) on July 21, 1861.

2. The Battle of New Orleans was fought on January 8, 1815, just over two weeks after peace had been concluded with the signing of the Treaty of Ghent on December 24, 1814. Andrew Jackson led a successful campaign against the Florida Seminoles in 1818, which also opened the way for the United States' acquisition of Florida.

3. Under Jackson's administration federal posts were granted on the basis of political affiliation, or what became known as the "spoils system."

4. American oil magnates: John D. Rockefeller, Sr. (1839–1937) founded Standard Oil; Edward L. Doheny (1856–1935) discovered oil in the Los Angeles area; Harry F. Sinclair (1876–1951) founded Consolidated Sinclair Oil Corporation. Socony was the trade name for the Standard Oil Company of New York.

5. Tyrus Raymond Cobb was a star baseball player for the Detroit Tigers and the Philadelphia Athletics.

6. James Thomas Heflin (1869–1951) was a Democrat and served as Senator from Alabama from 1920 to 1931.

7. Charles Curtis (Kaw, 1860–1936) was a part-Kaw Republican Senator from Kansas in 1907–13 and 1915–29. He was elected Vice President under Hoover in 1928. As chairman of the Committee on Indian Affairs he drafted "An Act for the Protection of People in Indian Territory and for Other Purposes" in 1898, institutionalized as the Curtis Act in 1902. This act brought allotment policies to the Five Tribes, which had been exempted from the General Allotment Act of 1887. Curtis was an active member of the Society of American Indians and a promoter of Indian citizenship. See William E. Unrau, *Mixed Bloods and Tribal Dissolution: Charles Curtis and the Quest for Indian Identity* (Lawrence: University of Kansas Press, 1989).

8. Alfred Emanuel Smith (1873–1944), or "The Happy Warrior," was Democratic governor of New York from 1919 to 1921 and 1923 to 1929; James A. Reed (1861–1944) was Democratic Senator for Missouri from 1911–29; Alvin Victor Donahey (1873–1946) was Democratic governor of Ohio from 1923 to 1929; Albert Cabell Ritchie (1876–1936) was Democratic governor of Maryland from

1920 to 1935. All were candidates for the Democratic presidential nomination in 1928.

9. The Latin American countries were so embittered over U.S. imperial policies that they assembled for their triennial conference in Havana in 1928. Coolidge personally attended the conference and delivered an appeasing speech.

STORY OF A MISSPENT BOYHOOD

Will Rogers (1929)

Well all I know is just what I read in the papers. Course football is getting all the play now and it beehooves us old Alumni's to get out with the cash and do our bit for old (I forgot the name).

I don't mean spend the money now. I mean get ready to spend it for later on when you see whether they need ends, or backs, or tackles. But get out now and go all over the country and see all the Prep school games you can and when a promising head arises why get on the job. Every time a good tackle is made go to the boy and explain to him the advantages of a free education under a splendid coach at old "Bohunk College."

I was just a thinking what I would have to do if I was to start out to help out my old schools. "Drumgoul" was a little one-room log cabin four miles east of Chelsea, Indian Territory, (where I am right now writing this article).[1] It was all Indian kids went there and I being part cherokee (had enough white in me to make my honesty questionable).

Now that school is not now in existance. Why? Why because the old Alumni let the football material fall down.

There must have been about thirty of us in that room that had rode horseback and walked miles to get there, and by the way it was a Co-Ed Institution. About half of 'em was Coo Coo Eds. We graduated when we could print our full name and unumerate to the teacher, or Principle, or Faculty, (Well whenever we could name to her) the nationality of the last Democratic President.

But as I say the school went out of business. We wasent able to get games with was profitable. It seems that other schools grabbed off all the other good dates, and got the breaks in the newspapers. We couldent seem to ever be accused of proffessionalism. I could see the finish even as far back as when I was there along in 1887. I could tell then that the old Grads wasent getting us the material that we should have to complete for the big gate receipts. We could tell it there in the school.

Why I can remember when the Coach couldent get enough out of us 15 Boys out to make a team. We got to running Horse races instead. Why there was just lots of days I dident go out for Skull practice at all. I had a little chestnut mare that was beating everything that any of them could ride to school and I was losing interest in what we was really there for. I was kinder forgetting that we was there to put the old school on a Paying basis by seeing how many times we could get through that Goal with that old pigskin.

I got to thinking well Horseracing is the big game, that's where the money is, that's what the crowds pay to see. But as years went along it showed that I was a Lad of mighty poor foresight. Little did I dream that it was football that was to be the real McCoy. Course we had no way of hardly telling it then, for we was paid practically nothing at all. In fact we had what I would call a Real

188

Simon Pure Amateur Team. Course we got our side line, (Schooling) free. The Cherokee Nation, (we then had our own Government, and the name Oklahoma was as foreign to us as a Tooth Paste). Well the Cherokee Nation paid the Teacher, and I guess Rockefeller paid the Football Coach.

But anyhow there was mighty few of us what was there under any kind of a guarantee. Course I will admit one of the Alumni got me to go there. He had spent three weeks there and couldent get along with the Teacher and he wanted to do what he could for the old School so he procured me. I looked like a promising End. I could run pretty fast. In fact my nickname was and is to this day among some of the old timers "Rabbit." I could never figure out if that referred to my speed or my heart.[2] But I, like a fool, dident make him put up anything, or guarantee me any privileges while at school.

Mind you, you wouldent believe it, but we dident even have a Stadium. Think of that in this day and time! Thousands and Thousands of acres surrounded us with not a thing on it but Cows and not a concrete seat for a spectator to sit on. Well you see as I look back on it now, a school like that dident have any license to exist. It had to perish. It just staid with books, such as Ray's Arithmatic, and McGuffy 1st, 2nd, (and two pupils in the 3rd) Readers.[3] We had even a Geography around there but we just used it for the pictures of the cattle grazing in the Argentine and the wolves attacking the sleighs in Rusia. Well you see they just couldent see what was the future in Colleges. They just wore out the old books instead of wearing out some footballs. We was a printing our ABC's when we ought to have been marking down "Tackles Back" and "Lateral Passes." We had Indian Boys that could knock a Squirrel out of a Tree with a rock. But do you think the Regents knew enough to get a Pop Warner and teach 'em how to hide a Ball under their Jerseys?[4] No. They just had the old fashioned idea that the place must be made self-sustaining by learning alone, and you see where their ignorance got them. Now the weeds is higher than the School house was, and that's what is happening in a few places in this country. We got those same "Drumgoul" ideas. Course not many but a few. They won't switch and get to the new ideas that it's open field running that gets your old College somewhere and not a pack of spectacled Orators, or a mess of Civil Engineers. It's better to turn out one good Coach then Ten College Presidents. His name will be in the papers every day and it will always be referred to where he come from. But with the College Presidents, why as far as publicity is concerned they just as well might have matriculated in Hong Kong. So don't let your school be another Drumgoul.

Notes

From the original manuscript held by the Will Rogers Memorial, Claremore, Oklahoma; published as "A Misspent Boyhood," *Tulsa Daily World*, September 29, 1929: Section 5, page 1; repr., James M. Smallwood and Steven K. Gragert, eds., *Will Rogers' Weekly Articles* (Stillwater, Okla.: Oklahoma State University Press, 1981), 4: 67–69. Reprinted with the kind assistance of Steven K. Gragert and permission of the Will Rogers Memorial Museums, Claremore, Oklahoma. Off-reservation manual labor boarding schools for Indians, especially Carlisle Indian Industrial School, were best known for their formidable football records. One of the criticisms directed at this type of institution (and Indian education in general) was that more attention was being paid to Indian sportsmanship than scholarship.

1. Drumgoole (proper spelling) Academy was located near Chelsea, Cherokee Nation West. Rogers was sent to this school in 1887.

2. The rabbit is also an important trickster figure in Cherokee oral tradition. Both foolish and wise, he is often defeated at his own game by those he tries to deceive, thereby teaching his listeners a meaningful lesson in a roundabout way.

3. Joseph Ray (1805–55) published a series of arithmetic and algebra textbooks (Ray's Mathematical Series) that were among the most popular and widely used American mathematics textbooks of the nineteenth century. William Holmes McGuffey (1800–73) was a noted educator whose series of four sequential *McGuffy Readers* were the standard textbooks used in American schools until well into the twentieth century.

4. Glenn Scobey "Pop" Warner (1871–1954) was a legendary football coach who invented various standard football tactics ("Warner System"), including the "Hidden Ball Play," as well as equipment. Also known as a lawyer, painter, and poet, "Pop" Warner coached at Carlisle Indian Industrial School from 1899 to 1903 and 1907 to 1914.

BIOGRAPHY

William Penn Adair Rogers (Cherokee, 1879–1935) was born on November 4 near present-day Oologah, Oklahoma. His father, Clement Vann Rogers, was a wealthy part-Cherokee rancher who had fought under Confederate General Stand Watie in the Civil War and later served in the Cherokee Senate for many years; his mother, Mary America Schrimsher, also a part-Cherokee and member of the Paint Clan, died when Will Rogers was ten. Obviously a reluctant student, Will Rogers was in and out of the following Indian Territory schools between the ages of seven and eighteen: Drumgoole School near Chelsea, the Cherokee National Male Seminary in Tahlequah, Harrell International Institute in Muskogee, and Willie Halsell College in Vinita. He also attended Scarritt Collegiate Insititute in Neosho and Kemper School in Boonville, both in Missouri. Will Rogers's relationship with his stern father was strained, and in 1898 Will ran away from Kemper to become a cowboy on a Texas ranch.

Upon his return to Indian Territory in 1899, Will Rogers won his first roping contest in Claremont, a skill which he would perfect to become one of the world's best trick ropers. He managed the family ranch until 1902, when he embarked for Argentina with plans of purchasing a ranch there with money from a herd of cattle that his father had provided three years earlier. Financial problems, lack of Spanish-language skills, and discomfort with local living and working conditions in Argentina prompted him to join a cattle boat headed for South Africa. There Rogers broke horses for the British army and then joined Texas Jack's Wild West Show in 1903 under the stage name "Cherokee Kid." From South Africa he traveled to Australia to join the Wirth Brothers Circus. Following his return to Oologah in 1904, Will Rogers joined Colonel Zack Mulhall's Rough Rider Congress as a trick roper. On June 12, 1905, Will Rogers introduced his horse-and-lariat act to the world of vaudeville at Keith's Union Square Theatre in New York. The following year he performed at various establishments in Europe, including the Wintergarten Theatre in Berlin and the Palace in London. Over time he supplemented his trick roping repertoire with humorous social and political commentaries in the mask of the shrewd illiterate, creating a style of humor that would soon endear him throughout America as the "Cowboy Philosopher." On November 25, 1908, Rogers married Betty Blake from Rogers, Arkansas, with whom he had four children.

In 1915 he joined Florenz Ziegfeld's *Midnight Frolics* and then appeared regularly in the *Ziegfeld Follies* the year after. Confronted with the necessity of producing new material daily, Rogers followed his wife's suggestion to use newspapers as a source of material. This led to his famous opening line, "All I know is what I read in the papers."

By the eve of World War I, the "Cowboy Philosopher" had become an established entertainer and began to expand his career into writing and film acting. In 1918 he appeared in his first motion picture, *Laughing Bill Hyde,* but

191

his early film-acting career was not very successful. In 1919 he published two books on the most topical themes of the day: *The Cowboy Philosopher on the Peace Conference* and *The Cowboy Philosopher on Prohibition*. Beginning on December 30, 1922, Rogers began writing a column for the McNaught Newspaper Syndicate. Two years later he published *The Illiterate Digest,* which featured several of his syndicated newspaper articles. In 1926 he traveled to Europe as a correspondent for *The Saturday Evening Post,* as well as a self-proclaimed ambassador for President Coolidge. That same year he collected the articles he wrote for the *Post* in a book titled *Letters of a Self-Made Diplomat to His President*. In 1926 Will Rogers also wired to the *New York Times* the first of what would become known popularly as the "Daily Telegrams." A series of short comments on current events, they were syndicated along with his weekly columns and continued to appear until his death. In 1927 he produced *There's Not a Bathing Suit in Russia,* also based on his travels for the *Post* in the previous year. In 1929 he published *Ether and Me,* a book that contains personal rather than political commentary.

Because Will Rogers's forte was dialogue, it is not surprising that his motion picture career did not take off until after he made his first talking movie in 1929. Among his more popular films were *A Connecticut Yankee* (1931) and *State Fair* (1933).

Rogers debuted on radio in 1922. In the spring of 1930 he began a regular radio program titled *The Gulf Headliners,* which turned out to be his most celebrated medium and cemented his reputation as the champion of the underdog. Will Rogers's career was cut short when he died in a plane crash near Point Barrow, Alaska, on August 15, 1935. At the time he was considered to be the most popular man in America.

Will Rogers's status as a national icon and the broad scope of his subject matter have dwarfed the relevance of his Cherokee background, which he nevertheless publicly acknowledged on numerous occasions. Among his most cited lines, "My ancestors didn't come over on the Mayflower, but they met the boat." His particular style of writing—bizarre spellings, random capitalizations, idiosyncratic punctuation, frequent inclusion of Americanisms, irregular use of the past tense of verbs, penchant for puns—also has its roots in the same vibrant Indian Territory tradition of journalistic humor that shaped the earlier careers of Alexander Posey and Charles Gibson.

Selected Publications of Will Rogers

The Cowboy Philosopher on the Peace Conference. New York: Harper and Brothers, 1919.

The Cowboy Philosopher on Prohibition. New York: Harper and Brothers, 1919.

Ether and Me. New York and London: G. P. Putnam's Sons, 1929.

The Illiterate Digest. New York: Albert and Charles Boni, 1924.

Letters of a Self-Made Diplomat to His President. New York: Albert and Charles Boni, 1926.

The Papers of Will Rogers. Edited by Arthur Frank Wertheim and Barbara Blair. 3 vols. Norman: University of Oklahoma Press, 1996–2001.

The Papers of Will Rogers. Edited by Steven K. Gragert and M. Jane Johansson. Vol. 4. Norman: University of Oklahoma Press, 2005.

Radio Broadcasts of Will Rogers. Edited by Steven K. Gragert. Stillwater: Oklahoma State University, 1983.

Will Roger's Daily Telegrams. Edited by James M. Smallwood and Steven K. Gragert. 4 vols. Stillwater: Oklahoma State University, 1978–79.

Will Rogers' Weekly Articles. Edited by James M. Smallwood and Steven K. Gragert. 6 vols. Stillwater: Oklahoma State University Press, 1980–82.

There's Not a Bathing Suit in Russia. New York: Albert and Charles Boni, 1927.

Selected Secondary Sources

Alworth, Paul. *Will Rogers.* Boston: Twayne, 1974.

Brown, William R. *Imagemaker: Will Rogers and the American Dream* Columbia: University of Missouri Press, 1970.

Day, Donald. *Will Rogers: A Biography.* New York: David McKay Co., Inc., 1962.

Gibson, Arrell M., editor. "Will Rogers: A Centennial Tribute." Special edition of *Chronicles of Oklahoma* 57, no. 3 (Fall 1979).

Ketchum, Richard. *Will Rogers, His Life and Times.* New York: American Heritage, 1973.

Rogers, Betty. *Will Rogers: His Wife's Story.* Indianapolis: Bobbs-Merrill, 1941. Reprinted Norman: University of Oklahoma Press, 1979.

Yagoda, Ben. *Will Rogers: A Biography.* New York: Alfred A. Knopf, 1993.

GREAT LAKES

THE THREE FIRES

AN ACCOUNT OF THE CHIPPEWA INDIANS, WHO HAVE BEEN TRAVELLING AMONG THE WHITES, IN THE UNITED STATES, ENGLAND, IRELAND, SCOTLAND, FRANCE AND BELGIUM

George Henry (1848)

I will not ask the reader for pardon. The short notice of me on another page will induce him to excuse me for using improperly the English language.[1]

We left the shores of lake Huron in the year 1843, visited Detroit city, Cleaveland [sic], Buffalo city, Utica, Albany, New York city and other towns. Left New York city on the first day of March for England with the ship called Victoria; landed in England, called Portsmouth, on the 26th of the same month. While on the sea our middle mast got blown away. The waves were like mountains; we did not get sea-sick, only got little hurt sometimes when thrown out of our berths. Sometime got a good ducking with salt water by the waves, pouring into our cabin. The flour and corn barrels got loose and knocked against one another and spilt all that was inside of them. The rats had great feasting. Every night after they had their bellies full were very mischievous; they helped the waves in tormenting us, by biting us on our toes and noses. The sea in the night was like the blaze of fire.

We landed at Portsmouth on the 26th of the same month. Portsmouth is a great place for ships. We went to see Lord Nelson's war ship [*HMS Victory*] and saw the place where he fell when he was killed.[2] The officers living in this sea-house were very kind to us. The great sea-war chief took us into the navy yard where they are making many war ships. Another war chief invited us and showed us all his warriors under him in the barracks.

From Portsmouth we went to London, and we remained a long time in this wonderful city; performed every day in the Egyptian Hall, in Piccadilly.[3] This city is about ten miles broad, but some parts of it is about twenty miles long. Like musketoes in America in the summer season, so are the people in this city, in their numbers and biting one another to get a living. Many very rich, and many very poor; about 900 berths [sic] and about 1100 deaths every week in this city alone. There are many stone and iron bridges over the river Thames. The steamboats in this river are not so handsome as those in America. The St. Paul's church and the Council House are very large buildings indeed. Most of the houses are rather dark in color on account of too much smoke.

Many ladies and gentlemen ride about in carriages. The carriages, servants and horses are covered with gold and silver. Hundreds of them walk about in the parks, the servants leading little dogs behind them to air them. The English women cannot walk alone; they must always be assisted by the men. They make their husbands carry their babies for them when walking.

Mr. Harris took us into the Queen's [Victoria] house [Windsor Castle]. She is a small woman but handsome. There are many handsomer women than she is. Prince Albert is a handsome and well built man.[4] Her house is large, quiet country inside of it. We got tired before we went through all the rooms in it. Great many warriors with their swords and guns stands outside watching for the enemy. We have been told that she has three or four other houses in other places as large. The one we saw they say is too small for her, and they are building a much larger one on one side of it.

When she goes out she has a great many warriors before and behind, guarding her; most of them seven feet tall. Their coats and caps are of steel; long white horse-hair waves on their heads. They wear long boots, long gloves, and white buckskin breeches. Their swords, guns, and everything about them are kept very clean and bright. Their horses are all black, and much silver and gold about them. They do not shave the upper part of their mouths, but let the beards grow long, and this makes them look fierce and savage like our American dogs when carrying black squirrels in their mouths.

The nobility and ministers and the Society of Friends [Quakers] invited us most every day to take tea with them. Sometimes we were about two hours in eating; the plates, knives, forks, spoons and everything we used in eating were of gold and silver. The servant's heads were white powdered [wigs]; they gave us many handsome presents, and caused us to see many things that others have never seen. We went to hear Lord John Russell and Sir R.[obert] Peel talk in the council; went also in the lower house and saw and heard the speakers in it.[5] We were kindly invited to dine with Daniel O'Connell.[6] He was very kind to us. We went through the tunnel under the bed of the river Thames. The ships were sailing over us while walking below.

Our war-chief shot a buck in the Park, through the heart, and fell down dead three hundred yards, before four thousand ladies and gentlemen. This was done to amuse them. Travelling on the Great Western Railway, the Engine knocked down several rooks or crows while flying over the railway. We saw three men out of the Zoological Gardens going up to the country of stars. They had something very large in the shape of a bladder over their heads; they called it a balloon. One man said to us, "You see now that we Englishmen can go and see upper world with our bodies." Lord [Benjamin] Bloomfield invited us to see the big guns at Woolwich; three of us got inside of one of them.[7]

They say that there are eighty thousand common wives [prostitutes] in the City of London. They say that they are allowed to walk in the streets every night for the safety of the married women. The English officers invited us to eat with them in the barracks in our native costume. When the tea got ready, the ladies were brought to the table like sick women; it took us about two hours in eating. The ladies were very talkative while eating; like ravens when feasting on venison. Indeed, they have a proverb which says, "Thieves and robbers eat and drink a little, and make no noise when they eat." They are very handsome; their waists, hands and feet are very small; their necks are rather longer than those of our women. They carry their heads on one side of the shoulder; they hold the knife and fork with the two forefingers and the thumb of each hand;

the two last ones are of no use to them, only sticking out like our fish-spears, while eating.

The English officers are fine, noble, and dignified looking fellows. The voice of them when coming out of the mouth, sounds like the voice of a bull-frog. The only fault we saw of them, are their too many unnecessary ceremonies while eating, such as, allow me Sir, or Mrs. to put this into your plate. If you please Sir, thank you, you are very kind Sir, or Mrs. can I have the pleasure of helping you?

Many of the Englishmen have very big stomachs, caused by drinking too much ale and porter. Those who drink wine and brandy, their noses look like ripe strawberries.

When we got ready to leave, one of the officers said to us, our ladies would be glad to shake hands with you, and we shook hands with them. Then they were talking amongst themselves; then another officer said to us, "Friends, our ladies think that you do not pay enough respects to them, they desire you to kiss them; then we kissed them according to our custom on both cheeks. "Why! they have kissed us on our cheeks; what a curious way of kissing this is." Then another officer said to us, "Gentlemen, our pretty squaws are not yet satisfied; they want to be kissed on their mouths." Then we kissed them on their mouths; then there was great shout amongst the English war-chiefs. Say-say-gon, our war-chief, then said in our language to the ladies: "That is all you are good for; as for wives, you are good for nothing." The ladies wanted me to tell them what the war-chief said to them. I then told them that he said he was wishing the officers would invite him very often, that he might again kiss the handsome ladies. Then they said, "Did he? then we will tell our men to invite you again, for we like to be kissed very often; tell him so." They put gold rings on our fingers and gold pins on our breasts, and when we had thanked them for their kindness, we got in our carriage and went to our apartments.

The great war chief with the big nose, Duke of Wellington, invited us, and he was very kind to us in his house. He and his son gave us handsome presents.[8]

Sir Augustus d'Este, cousin to the Queen, son of the Duke of Sussex, invited us very often to take tea with him. He is a great friend to the Indians; he introduced us to many of his friends. This great man is an invalid, and not able to walk alone.[9]

The Archbishop of Canterbury Cathedral [William Hawley] was very kind to us; he showed us everything in the Cathedral, curious and wonderful works of the ancient Britons. He said that this building is thirteen hundred years old. This is the most curious, the largest, and beautiful one we have seen. The top of its steeple our arrows could not reach.

We went to see Dover; we went through the subterraneous roads in the Rocks.

We went to France; stayed five months in Paris with [George] Catlin's Indian Curiosities. Shook hands with Louis Phillippe [sic] and all his family in the Park, called St. Cloud; gave them little war dance, shooting with bows and arrows at a target, ball play; also rowed our birch bark canoe in the artificial lake, amongst swans and geese. There were about four thousand French ladies and gentlemen with them. We dined with him in the afternoon in his Palace. He said many things concerning his having been in America when he was a young man.[10] He gave us twelve gold and silver medals; he showed us all the rooms in his house.

The French ladies are handsome, very gay in their dresses, both men and women. Many of the gentlemen never shave their faces; this makes them look as if they had no mouths. Others wear beards only on the upper part of their mouths, which makes them look as if they had black squirrel's tails sticking on each side of their mouths.

Monsieur [Charles] Lafontaine, the great mesmeriser, invited us to see him perform.[11] He gave us a needle to stick those he made sleep, and we pulled the needle through their eye-brows, and between the big thumb and finger, and they knew nothing about it. He caused the young lady to put her arms around our necks, and kissed us, saying at the same time, "My dear." We left some of the paint on her cheeks that was on our faces.

Another French gentleman made moulds of plaster paris from our heads; some of our young men got frightened. Louis Phillippe ordered Mons. J.[ean] Gudin to paint our likenesses on a large sheet of canvass, and when it was done, he took it to his Palace.[12]

The country in France is like our prairies; the fields are not divided with hedges and stone walls.

The common wives are very numerous in Paris; some of them are called "industrious fleas."

Mrs. [Clara] Catlin and one of their youngest children died in Paris. She was a very kind lady, of Albany.[13]

From Paris we went to Brussells. The king [Leopold I] of this country was very kind to us.[14] The Belgians are like the French. Here poor Aunimuckwuhum and Mishimaung died with the small pox; and after we visited other towns on the borders of Germany, we returned to London again; and here our much respected war-chief, Say-say-gon, died with the same dreadful disease that the others had died with. These three men would not allow the white doctors to vaccinate them. They said that we were very foolish to place ourselves in the care of the whites;—ourselves were saved by this simple remedy, through the kindness of our friends the Quakers.[15]

While in Ipswich we visited Thomas Clarkson Esq. He was very glad to see us, though he was very ill; his kind daughter gave us a good dinner and handsome presents. This great and good man died soon after we left him.[16]

At Norwich, J.[oseph] J.[ohn] Gurney, Esq. the great man of the Quakers, invited us to his house called Earlham. He and his wife, of Philadelphia, also his son, gave us rich presents. This great man died while we were in Scotland; his horse fell down with him.[17]

While we were in Norwich, we saw one man killed; he was killed for killing a woman at Yarmouth for a little money. Many thousand people got together where the man was to be killed, before a large stone house, on a high hill, long time before the appointed hour arrived. Then they brought the man out they wanted to kill; they made him to stand on a platform with a strong cord around his neck, and when the teacher of wisdom and Christian religion had prayed for him, they pulled down his white cap over his face, and also fastened one end of the cord that was round his neck on a beam over his head. Then another man slipped down the platform he was standing on; he dropped down a little, and was hanging in the air with the cord that was round his neck, his hands tied together behind his back. Then he began to kick and twist about for life, and one of the murderers ran down and caught hold of his legs and pulled him down, and very soon killed him. They said that he was not fit to live on earth, but they believed that he is gone to the happy country in the other world, where he will be out of mischief forever.

We went through Sheffield, Manchester, and many other towns between them,—saw many good people and wonderful things.

From Liverpool to Dublin city, we went to see Father [Theobald] Mathew.[18] We performed in the Rotunda, also in the Zoological Gardens; each evening had three thousand people to see us; went to south and back again to north, Belfast and Londonderry. The Irish are very kind-hearted people. The country people make fire of turf; many of them are very poor; the British government is over them.

We crossed to Scotland and landed at the place called Adrosson; we went to see R.[obert] Burns's cottage, small, with straw roof. We went to see [William] Wallace's Oak Tree near Paisely; went to Glasgow and Edinburgh.[19] Edinburgh is large of the Scotch people; the new town is very handsome, but the old town is rather filthy. All the dirt is thrown in the streets before people get up, and carts rake it away, but still the smell of it is most offensive all day. One of the chiefs told us that a Scotchman some years ago, who was born in the city, was away from it for some years, and returning to it he said, "There is nothing like home;" and when he began to smell the streets, he said, "Ah! sweet auld Edinburgh, I smell thee now." The Scotch chiefs showed us the Crown of Scotland in the Castle, also the Palace. We went to see about seventy young men, who are to be medicine men. They had thirty dead bodies, and they were skinning and cutting them same as we do with venison.

The Scotch people are very religious and industrious, very kind-hearted to strangers. They keep Sunday very strictly. A great many are teetotalers; their country is mountainous. The old men and women are very fond of snuff; they carry it in rams horns; they put one spoonful of it in each nostril at a time; this causes their words to sound nasal, something like pig grunting.

At Glasgow, two of my children died, another in Edinburgh; buried them in the burying ground of our friends the Quakers; and after we visited other towns at the North and South, we went to England again; my wife died at Newark. The vicar of that church was very kind to us, in allowing us to bury her remains near the church.

Riding through a town in our native costume, we saw a monkey performing in the street upon a music box, about fifty young men looking at him. He was dressed like a man. When the young men saw us, they began to make fun of us, and made use of very insulting language, making a very great noise;—at the same time when the monkey saw us he forgot his performances, and while we were looking at him, he took off his red cap and made a bow to us. A gentleman standing by, said to the audience, "Look at the monkey take off his cap and make a bow in saluting those strangers; which of the two the strangers will think are most civilized, you or the monkey? You ought to be ashamed of yourselves. You may consider yourselves better and wiser than those strangers, but you are very much mistaken. Your treatment to them tells them that you are not, and you are so foolish and ignorant, you know nothing about it. I have been travelling five years amongst these people in their own country, and I never, not once, was insulted, but I was always kindly treated and respected by every one of them. Their little children have far better manners than you. Young men, the monkey pays you well for all the pennies you have given him; he is worthy to become your teacher." We then threw some money to the monkey, and he jumped down from his platform and picked up the money and jumped up again, and put the money into his master's mouth, and he made another bow to us as we were going away; at the same time heard one of the young men saying to his friends, "See the teacher making another bow to the Indians." "Yes," said another, "this is to teach you, for you are the very one that was making fun and blackguarding the Indians."

We visited New Castle upon Tyne, Hull, Leeds, York, Birmingham, and many other Towns; visited Shakspeare's [sic] house and his grave at Stratford on Avon. We visited Lord Byron's house. Col. [Thomas] Wildman was very kind to us; went to Nottingham and to London again.[20]

We left London on the 23d of April, 1848, with the ship called Yorktown, of New York. Capt. Seba was very kind to us all the way. Sixteen children of the Germans died on the way; also an English lady. Ourselves did not get sea sick. The waves were like mountains; saw seven whales and many porpoises; landed in New York city on the 4th of June, and we were very thankful to the Great Spirit for bringing us back again to America.

On the voyage Capt. Seba was very careful that there was no smoking with pipes and cigars inside the ship, drinking firewater; quarrelling and fighting he prohibited, but when the sea had been very rough for two or three days, the English and the Germans had little fighting, because there was no room for all their teapots in the cooking place; but no one got much hurt, only a few faces got little cut and scratched, and afterwards received four or five blows of rope by the powerful chief mate on their backs.

He allowed the religious minister to preach in the cabin every Sunday. Every few days we had the inside of the ship cleaned; outside, every day, that there might be no sickness among us. He was like a father to us; all the sailors loved him and were very obedient to him.

When the sun could be seen he would look at it with a little glass, curiously constructed with brass [sextant]; and by this he could tell us where and how far we were from England and America. Sometimes he would get one of his men to sink a piece of lead with a long cord, some tallow on the bottom of it, and when it was hoisted up, there was sand on the tallow, and he, by looking at it and seeing its color, he knew exactly where we were, he received much wisdom by looking at the sun and the sand.

He also had something in a glass tube look like melted lead [barometer], by which, in looking at it, he could always tell when the storm was coming, and had the ship ready for it. He is very good as well as a great man.

In Ipswich we dined with our friends the Quakers, about sixty in number; their names are Alexanders and Ransoms. After we had eaten many good things and all the plates taken away, a small round but high cheese was put on the table, and one of the oldest Friends said to us, "Now, friends, this is our English cheese; the poor of our people cannot afford to eat this. We never think that our dinner is finished until we have ate some of it; will thou have little of it; I said yes. Will thou have little of it, &c., until every one of us had it before us, and we ate much of it, because it was from our friends. When our eating was over, a doctor, whose name is F. W. Johnson, placed on the table, what he calls microscope; it had three brass legs and a small glass to it, and when he had put a very small bit of the cheese we had to eat on a clean plate, he made us look at it through the little glass that was on the three legged brass, and we saw hundreds of worms moving in it. This made all our fiends laugh, and we tried to laugh too, but we were very much frightened at the same time knowing that we must have swallowed thousands of them. When our friends saw that we were frightened, the medicine man dropped one drop of rain water in a clear glass, and he made us look at it again through the little glass, and we saw hundreds of living creatures swimming in it; some like beasts, some like snakes, some like fish, some had horns and some had no horns, some with legs and some had no legs; some had wheels on each side of their bodies, and with these they were moving about like steamboats, hooking, chasing, fighting, killing and eating one another. Then one of our oldest friends said to us, "Now, friends, you must not think that this is the first time you have been eating worms. We swallow thousands of them every day either with food or water. They are floating in the air, and we inhale them, when we draw breath; thousands of them are also floating in our veins. The Great Spirit, who made us and all other beings is wonderful in power and wisdom. We sincerely hope that you will at all times love him, and obey what he tells you in your hearts." We waited two or three days for the worms to bite. Sometimes we would be looking for them, thinking that they might have grown larger while they were in our bodies, but we did not feel their bites nor saw any of them. We have oftentimes been thinking since, that our friends must be something like bears, who loves to eat living worms or maggots.

Since the 4th of June we have visited many towns between New York and Boston: went to see Plymouth Rock, where our forefathers first saw the white men; saw the stone first touched by white man's foot; went in the Pilgrim Hall. The Americans have been very kind to us in all places; they are not so fleshy as the English, but very persevering in all their ways. They pay more respect to their females than the English, and they like to see things belong to others without leave. The working classes of the English call their rich men "Big Bugs," but the Yankee call them, "Top Notches." They put their feet upon tables, chairs, and chimney pieces when smoking their cigars or reading newspapers. They are not so much slaves to their civilization as the English; they like to be comfortable, something like ourselves, placing one leg upon the other knee, while basking ourselves in the sun. A real comfort is better than an artificial one to the human nature.

The Mayors of all the cities and towns of this country are very kind in allowing us to make use of their Town Halls and Court Houses.

Notes

Taken from the sixteen-page tract titled *An Account of the Chippewa Indians, Who Have Been Travelling in the United States, England, Ireland, Scotland, France, and Belgium; with Very Interesting Incidents in Relation to the General Characteristics of the English, Irish, Scotch, French, and Americans, with Regard to Their Hospitality, Peculiarities, etc.* (Boston: By the Author, 1848). A letter Maungwudaus wrote to Peter Jones on October 19, 1845, describing the dance troupe's visit to France is very similar in content and style. Peter Jones included the letter (erroneously dated 1854) in his *History of the Ojebway Indians: With Especial Reference to Their Conversion to Christianity* (London: A.W. Bennett, 1861), 219–20. It is reproduced in Carolyn Foreman, *Indians Abroad, 1493–1938* (Norman: University of Oklahoma Press, 1944), 194–95; Penny Petrone, ed., *First People, First Voices* (Toronto: University of Toronto Press, 1983), 94–95; and Donald B. Smith, *Sacred Feathers: The Reverend Peter Jones (Kahkewaquonaby) & the Mississauga Indians* (Lincoln: University of Nebraska Press, 1987), 201–202. Together with George Copway's *Running Sketches of Men and Places* (1851), George Henry's earlier account is a unique Indian contribution to antebellum American travel literature, a popular genre of the day. One of its main purposes, other than entertaining readers with glowing accounts of famous individuals and historical sites in the Old World, was to demonstrate by comparison the moral, political, and physical superiority of the New World and its inhabitants. Apocryphal accounts attributed to real or imagined Indian travelers, or "rational savages" who cast a critical eye on European customs, were first published in sixteenth-century France and then reappeared more frequently in eighteenth-century French literature. They made their debut in England in the early issues of the *The Spectator* and then became a fairly common character in English letters thereafter. See the fictive accounts of the Iroquois sachem "King Sa Ga Tean Qua Rash Tow" written by Addison in *The Spectator* 1, 50 (April 27, 1711); and 1, 56 (May 4, 1711); repr. in Donald F. Bond, *The Spectator* (Oxford: Clarendon Press, 1965), 211–21, 236–40. See Anthony Pagden, "The Savage Critic: Some European Images of the Primitive," *The Yearbook of English Studies* 13 (1983): 32–45.

1. A brief biographical statement by Superintendent of Indian Affairs William Heating is included along with a testimony by George Catlin dated April 20, 1848, on pages 11–12. Maungwudaus also appended five hymns "translated and composed by [him]" on pages 14–16.

2. Lord Horatio Nelson (1758–1805) was killed in the Battle of Trafalgar on October 21, 1805.

3. Egyptian Hall was a famous museum in Piccadilly, London, built by William Bullock in 1812 and demolished in 1905.

4. Prince Consort Albert (1819–61) married Queen Victoria in 1840.

5. Lord John Russel (1792–1878), noted Whig reformer, was Prime Minister from 1846–52; Sir Robert Peel (1788–1850) was Prime Minister from 1841–46.

6. Daniel O'Connell (1775–1847) was elected Lord Mayor of Dublin in 1841. He promoted the repeal of the union act and the establishment of an Irish parliament.

7. Lord Benjamin Bloomfield (1768–1846) was an artillery officer and diplomat. The dockyard at Woolwich, built during the reign of Henry VIII, is the site of the Museum of Royal Artillery.

8. Arthur Wellesley Duke of Wellington (1769–1852) was Cabinet Minister without a Portfolio under Sir Robert Peel.

9. Sir August d'Este (1794–1848) suffered from multiple sclerosis. He kept a diary in which he meticulously detailed the progress of his illness.

10. Louis Philippe (1773–1850) was King of France from 1830–48. During the French Revolution and the reign of Napoleon Bonaparte he traveled widely, including to the United States, spending four years in Philadelphia.

11. Charles Lafontaine (1803–80) was a famous traveling mesmerist.

12. Jean-Antoine Théodore Gudin (1802–80) was a leading French painter who specialized in marine subjects. Louis Philippe commissioned him to paint scenes from the history of the French Navy.

13. Clara Bartlett Gregory (1807–45) married George Catlin in 1828. She died of pneumonia in Paris on July 28, 1845. Their son, George, Jr., died of typhoid the following year.

14. Leopold I (1790–1865) became the first King of Belgium in 1831.

15. Seven members of the dance troupe fell ill and died while in Europe, including George Henry's own wife Hannah Henry and three of their newborn children.

16. Thomas Clarkson (1760–1846) was a dedicated abolitionist and vice president of the Anti-Slavery Society, founded in 1823.

17. Joseph John Gurney (1788–1847) was a noted Quaker reformer involved in prison reform, abolitionism, and the ending of the death sentence. He is the author of several books on religion and morality.

18. Father Theobald Mathew (1790–1856) was an Irish-Catholic temperance reformer.

19. William Wallace's Oak Tree near Paisley was said to have hidden Wallace and three hundred of his followers from an English patrol. Souvenir hunters gradually decimated the great tree until it fell over in 1856.

20. Colonel Thomas Wildman, a schoolfellow and friend of Lord Byron's, bought Newstead Abby from the bankrupt poet in 1817 and had it restored.

BIOGRAPHY

George Henry (Mississauga Ojibwe, ca. 1811–88), or Maungwudaus (Great Hero), was probably born along Forty Mile Creek in Upper Canada, the son of Chief Mesquacosy and Tuhbenahneequay (Sarah Henry), the daughter of Chief Wahbanosay. On his mother's side he was the half-brother of the noted Mississauga Ojibwe missionary Peter Jones (1802–56). George Henry was converted by Methodist Episcopalian ministers around 1824 and attended a mission school at the Credit River Mission (present-day Mississauga) in the late 1820s. During the 1830s he served at various missions, including at Munceytown (north of Brantford, Ontario), where he taught school in the winter of 1835, and at Sarnia (Ontario). George Henry was elected in 1837 as the third chief of the Credit River Band. In the late 1830s he moved to Walpole Island, where he functioned as a Native preacher. In 1840 he officiated as the government interpreter at the St. Clair Mission (near Port Sarnia on the Thames River). That same year Henry resigned from the Canadian Methodist Conference, perhaps in connection with the split that occurred with the British Wesleyans.

In the summer of 1844, Henry organized a dance troupe consisting of his own family and several non-Christian Walpole Island Ojibwe in order to tour England. While in England, Henry, now known as Maungwudaus, and his troupe were entertained by numerous notable personalities. At some point he decided to join the Roman Catholic Church, much to the chagrin of his pronounced antipapal half brother Peter Jones, who stated in his *History of the Ojibway Indians* (1861) that he "never discovered any real difference between the Roman Catholic Indian and the pagan, except the wearing of crosses." In the fall of 1845, artist George Catlin moved his famous "Indian Gallery" from England to France, and sponsored the dance troupe's subsequent tours through France and Belgium until 1846. The dance troupe moved back to England on their own and finally embarked for the United States on April 23, 1848. Seven members of the dance troupe—including George Henry's wife, Uh-wus-sig-gee-zhig-goo-kway (Hannah Henry) and three of their children—had died of small pox or some other infectious disease during their sojourn in Europe.

George Henry's dance troupe arrived in New York on June 4 and continued to perform in the United States and Canada. During a visit to Gull Corners, Michigan, in 1850–51, Henry met and married Taundoqua, an Ojibwe with French ancestry. By the spring of 1851, Henry had given up Roman Catholicism. His dance troupe performed in the St. Lawrence Hall in Toronto at about this time. In 1854 George Henry finally settled at the New Credit River Reserve in the southwestern corner of the Grand River Reserve, a Mississauga community established by Peter Jones on lands donated by the Six Nations in 1847.

Henry recorded his experiences in Europe in a pamphlet titled *Remarks Concerning the Ojibway Indians, by One of Themselves Called Maungwudaus, Who Has Been Travelling in England, France, Belgium, Ireland, and Scotland,* first published in Leeds, England, in 1847 and reprinted in Boston the following year. Said to have been over six feet tall, George Henry must have made a striking appearance. He was portrayed by notable artists such as George Catlin, Jean-Antoine Gudin, and Paul Kane.

Publications of George Henry

Remarks Concerning the Ojibway Indians, by One of Themselves Called Maungwudaus, Who Has Been Travelling in England, France, Belgium, Ireland, and Scotland (Leeds, England: C.A. Wilson, 1847); repr. as *An Account of the Chippewa Indians, Who Have Been Travelling in the United States, England, Ireland, Scotland, France, and Belgium; with Very Interesting Incidents in Relation to the General Characteristics of the English, Irish, Scotch, French, and Americans, with Regard to Their Hospitality, Peculiarities, etc.* (Boston: By the Author, 1848); repr. as *An Account of the North American Indians, Written for Maungwudaus, a Chief of the Ojibway Indians Who Has Been Travelling in England, France, Belgium, Ireland, and Scotland* (Leicester, England: T. Cook, 1848). The Boston edition is reproduced in Bernd C. Peyer, ed., *The Elders Wrote: An Anthology of Early Prose by North American Indians, 1768–1931* (Berlin: Dietrich Reimer Verlag, 1982), 66–74; and in Penny Petrone, ed., *First People, First Voices* (Toronto: University of Toronto Press, 1983), 87–94.

Secondary Sources

Catlin, George. *Notes of Eight Years' Travels and Residence in Europe, With His North American Indian Collection. With anecdotes and incidents of the travels and adventures of three different parties of American Indians whom he introduced to the Courts of England, France, and Belgium.* 2 vols. London: by the author, 1848.

Konkle, Maureen. "Traditionary History in Ojibwe Writing." In Maureen Konkle, *Writing Indian Nations: Native Intellectuals and the Politics of Historiography, 1827–1863.* Chapel Hill: University of North Carolina Press, 2004: 160–223.

Little, Frank. "Early Recollections of the Indians." *Michigan Pioneer and Historical Collections* 27 (1896): 335–37.

Mulvey, Christopher. "Among the Sag-A-Noshes: Ojibwa and Iowa Indians with George Catlin in Europe, 1843–1848." In *Indians in Europe: An Interdisciplinary Collection of Essays.* Edited by Christian F. Feest. Aachen: Rader Verlag, 1987: 253–75.

Smith, Donald B. "Maungwudaus Goes Abroad." *The Beaver Magazine* 307, no. 2 (Autumn 1976): 4–9.

_____. *Sacred Feathers: The Reverend Peter Jones (Kahkewaquonaby) & the Mississauga Indians.* Lincoln: University of Nebraska Press, 1987.

THE AMERICAN INDIANS

George Copway (1848)

The history of a nation is always interesting. The more obscure the means of tracing it, the more of interest attaches to it, as it slowly discloses itself to the eye of research.

The past of American history is to every meditative man full of silent instruction. The struggle between the two races, the European and the American, has been in steady progress since their first intercourse with each other. The pale-face has bequeathed his history's bloody page to his children after him. The Indians, on the other hand, have related the story of their wrongs to their children in the lodge, and have invariably taught them to look upon a pale-face as a hard brother.

The account of their hatred to each other in years long past, is, no doubt, without foundation. Its relation has, however, had the evil tendency of embittering one against the other, has kept them at variance, and prevented them from learning of each other those noble qualities which *all* will acknowledge each possessed.

What a change! The progress of aggression has gone on with its resistless force westward with emigration, from the time the first colony was planted on the Atlantic's shores. Wave after wave has rolled on, till now there appears no limit to the sea of population. The North resounds with the woodman's axe; the South opens its valleys to make room for the millions that are swarming from the Old World to the New.

The rivers that once wound their silent and undisturbed course beneath the shades of the forest, are made to leave their natural ways, and, bending to the arbitrary will of man, follow the path he marks out for them. Man labors, and gazes in astonishment at the mighty work his hands perform—he gazes at the complicated machinery he has set in motion. The Indian is out of sight—he sends no horror to the pale-face by his shrill war-whoop, nor pity by the wail of his death-song.

Steam thunders along over hills and vales that once were peaceful—on, on, to the mighty West.

The groans of the Indian are occasionally heard by the intoxicated and avaricious throng in the way of complaint; he has waited for justice, while those who have wronged him, like the wild horses of his prairie, neigh over his misfortunes.

The eagle of liberty stretches her wings north and south. The tide of emigration will soon reach the base of the Rocky Mountains and rise to the summit. Enterprise follows in its train; yet when blessings are lavishly bestowed on the palefaces, as the consequence of attainments in knowledge, the red-man has been denied the least of those which the American government guarantees to its humblest subject.

These thoughts have arisen in my mind previous to calling the attention of the Members of this Congress to a plan for the effectual consolidation of the western tribes, with a view to their temporal and spiritual improvement.

Before stating the plan, which I have already laid before the American people, as the only means which can be used to save the Indians from extinction, I shall, in as brief a manner as possible, give a few reasons why they have not materially improved, and why their numbers have been greatly lessening.

1. *Why has not the Indian improved when coming in contact with civilization?* To give a statement of all the disadvantages he has had to encounter would not be in accordance with my present object; I will mention a few. In their intercourse with the frontier settlers they meet the worst classes of pale-faces. They soon adopt their foolish ways and their vices, and their minds being thus poisoned and pre-occupied, the morality and education which the better classes would teach them are forestalled. This will not be wondered at when it is generally known that the frontier settlements are made up of wild, adventurous spirits, willing to raise themselves by the downfall of the Indian race. These are traders, spirit-sellers, horse-thieves, counterfeiters, and scape-gallowses, who neither fear God nor regard man. When the Indians come in contact with such men, as representatives of the American people, what else could be expected from them? They scarcely believe that any good can come out of such a Nazareth as they think the United States to be; and all are aware that man is more prone to learn from others their vices than their virtues. It is not strange, that, seeing as he does the gross immorality of the white men whom he meets, and the struggle between the pale-face for wrong and the red-man for right, which begins when they first meet, and ends not until one dies, that he refuses to follow in the footsteps of the white man.

"What!" said an Indian to me once, in the North-west, when I was endeavoring to convince him of the necessity of schooling his children, "shall my children be taught to lie, steal, kill, and quarrel, as the white man does? No, no," he continued, shaking his head. Having never been in the midst of refined and civilized society, he knew not of its blessings. He judged from what he saw around him, and with such examples, he decided rightly.

There has been one class of adventurers who have moved westward, whose fathers were murdered by the Indians. These having an implacable hatred against the poor Indian, do all they can to enrage one race against the other, and if possible involve the two in war, that they may engage in their favorite work of depredation.

2. *Their love of adventurous life.* The suddenness with which a band of white men has ever intruded upon them, has prevented them from gradually acquiring the arts of civilized life; and leaving local employment, they have hunted for a living, and thus perpetuated that independent, roaming disposition, which was their early education. Their fathers having been Nimrods, in a literal sense, they followed in their steps.[1] Not that I would have you suppose that there is no such thing as teaching the American Indian the peaceful arts of agriculture, for he has already proved himself teachable.

3. *The perpetual agitation of mind which they experience in the annoyance*

they receive from mischievous men, and the fear of being removed westward by the American government. None but an Indian can, perhaps, rightly judge of the deleterious influence which the repeated removals of the Indians has wrought, since they began in the days of Jefferson, in 1804, and have been continued by succeeding administrations, until the last. Here let me say to Members of Congress, Mature a pacific policy, for the mutual good of the red man and the white man. Let each love the other with the same spirit that animated the bosom of William Penn, and we shall yet have many sunny days—days when the white man and the red man shall join hands, and together, as brothers, go up yet higher on the mount of noble greatness. Fear has prevented the Indian from making any very great advancement in agricultural science. Having seen the removal of many tribes, he is conscious of the fact, that the government may, and doubtless will, want more land, and they be obliged to sell at whatever price government may see fit to give, and thus all improvements they may have made become valueless to them.

The missionaries, in many instances, have done nobly in subduing the wild and warring disposition of many of the Indians, but these lessons have all been lost by the removal of the Indian west. And if he say aught, he is represented by the agent in an antagonistic attitude toward his government, and the Indians become the sufferers.

4. *The want of schools of the character that are required for the education of the Indians.* You will, no doubt, tell me that the Indians have been taught the advantages of education—that some have even attended, not only the common school, but schools of a higher order and colleges, and have returned again to the forest, have put on the blanket and roamed the woods. This has not always been the case. I might name a great many, who, to my knowledge, have done well, and are doing well for themselves and for their people.

I have never heard of any inquiry having been made by any society or government, as to what is the best mode of education for Indian youth. My opinion may differ from that of more aged and experienced men, yet after much observation and inquiry, I am convinced that the three most requisite things for an Indian youth to be taught, are a good mechanical trade, a sound code of morality, and a high-toned literature.

The reason of their returning back again, was the absence of a good moral training, and their not having learned any trade with which to be employed on their leaving the schools. Having no employment and no income, they found themselves in possession of all the qualities of a gentleman, without the requisite funds to support themselves.

Their training in moral culture had not been attended to, because some of those men who had been their instructors knew Christianity by theory only, not by a practical knowledge of the pleasing and persuasive influence of the Bible.

The Indian ought not to be allowed to stand still in the way of improvement; for if he does not advance, he will surely recede, and lose the knowledge he may already have attained. Let him taste the pleasures of education, and he will, if proper care be taken at the commencement, drink deep of the living spring.

5. *The great quantity of land which they have reserved to themselves for the purpose of hunting.* This wide field, filled with a variety of game, perpetuates their natural propensities to live by the use of the bow or gun, instead of the hoe or plow; to roam the fields instead of having a local habitation. When they have land that they can call their own, and limited, so that the scarcity of game will oblige them to till the soil for a subsistence, then they will improve, and the sooner this state of affairs is brought about, the better.

Some of my Indian brethren may wonder that I should offer this as one of my reasons, and my white brethren may think that I would limit the Indian to rather narrow quarters. If any argument I now bring forward will not bear investigation, why, throw it out. I but write what in my humble judgment is an impartial view of the subject, and state plans which I think best adapted to advance the interests of all, and which should be adopted in order to elevate the condition of the Indians of America.

6. *The mode generally adopted for the introduction of Christianity among the Indians.* This mode has not, I think, been one that would induce them to speedily relinquish their habits of life. I am aware that I here tread on delicate ground. There is zeal enough among the missionaries who labor among them to move the world, if there were any *system* of operation. There is piety enough to enkindle and fan to a blaze the fine devotional feelings of the Indians, if there were one uniform course taken by all those who go to teach them.

The *doctrines* which have been preached in this civilized country may be necessary for the purpose of stimulating various denominations to zealous labor, but in our country they have had a tendency to retard the progress of the gospel. The strenuous efforts that have been made to introduce doctrinal views, and forms of worship, have perplexed and prejudiced the mind of the Indian against Christianity.

It is true that every man who has been among the Indians as a missionary to them has not been as judicious as he should have been. The idea that *anything* will do for the Indian, has also been a mistaken one.

We want men of *liberal education* as well as of devoted piety. It is not requisite that a missionary carry with him the discipline of churches, but it *is* requisite that he carry with him consistency, in order to meet with success among the Indian tribes.

When they preach love to God and to all men, and act otherwise toward ministers of differing denominations, it creates doubts in the mind of the watchful Indian as to the truth of the word he hears. Let the men advocating the sacred cause of God go on together, let them labor side by side for the good of the Indian, and he will soon see that they intend his good. The Indian is not willfully blind to his own interests.

I have tried to convince the different missionaries that it is better to teach the Indians in English, rather than in their own language, as some have done and are now doing. A great amount of *time* and *money* have been expended in the translation of the Bible into various languages, and afterward the Indian has been taught to read; when he might have been taught English in much less amount of time and with less expenditure of money. Besides this, the few books that have been translated into our language are the *only books* which they *can* read, and in this are perpetuated his views, ideas and feelings; whereas, had he been taught English, he would have been introduced into a wide field of literature; for so *very* limited would be the literature of his own language, that he could have no scope for his powers; consequently, the sooner he learned the almost universal English and forgot the Indian, the better. If the same policy is pursued that has been, the whole of the world's history must be translated into Indian, and the Indian be taught to read it before he can know the story of the past.

There are other reasons that might be given, why the condition of the Indian has not improved, did space allow. I proceed to give the reasons for the gradual diminution of their numbers since their first intercourse with the whites, three hundred and fifty-six years ago.

1. *Diseases introduced by Europeans.* They had no knowledge of the *small-pox*, measles, and *other* epidemics of civilization's growth. The small-pox destroyed the Mandans, a tribe once occupying the shores of the upper waters of the Missouri, in '37 and '38. Entire families perished. American history relates many a distressing fact in relation to that ill-fated tribe. Foreign disease has preyed on the vitals of the Indian, and he knew not what remedies to use to arrest its progress, however skillful he might have been in curing the infirmities which were found with him. He knew no cure for the new diseases that ravaged among them.[2]

2. *Wars among themselves since the introduction of firearms among them.* The weapons they used, previous to their meeting the whites, were not as destructive as the rifle. With the gun they have been as expert as they were with the bow and arrow. Champlain, in the year 1609, supplied the Algonquin tribes of the north with weapons of war for them to subdue the Six Nations, and the Dutch supplied the Six Nations in the now State of New York. The Spaniards of the South, and others, might be cited. They received these weapons of war from civilized nations, guaranteeing to them the free use of them.

3. *The wars among the white people of this country.* During these wars the Indian has been called to show his fearless nature; and for obeying, and showing himself true to the code of a warrior, as he understood it, he has been called a *savage* by the very men who needed his aid and received it. In the midst of these contests the Indians have been put in the front ranks, in the most dangerous positions, and have consequently been the greatest losers.

4. *The introduction of spirituous liquors.* This has been another, and perhaps greater than all other evils combined. The *fire-water* has done a most disastrous work, and the glad shout of the Indian boy has been hushed as he bended over the remains of his father, whose premature death has been brought on by its use.[3] The Indian has not sufficient moral fortitude to withstand its evil seductiveness. Disease, war, and famine have preyed upon individual life, but alcoholic drinks have cut off from the list of nations many whose records are inscribed on the face of the mountain.

Peace and happiness entwined around the firesides of the Indian once—

union, harmony, and a common brotherhood cemented them to each other. But as soon as these vile drinks were introduced among them dissipation commenced, and the ruin and downfall of a noble race went on. Every year lessened its numbers. The trader found this to be one of the easiest means of securing him rich gains. Wave after wave of destruction invaded the wigwam of the Indian, while the angel of death hovered over his lodge-fires with its insatiable thirst for victims.

In mockery of his wrongs, the eye of the distant observer has looked on the destruction of the Indian, and when he saw him urged to desperate deeds, the white man would calmly say, "Ah, the Indian will be an Indian still."

You say he loves it so well that it is impossible to keep it from him. There was a time when the cool water from the mountain tops was all that allayed his thirst. He loved that, because the Great Spirit sent it to him.

Traders carry the fire-water into the western country by hundreds of barrels, and it has become a common saying among the Indians, "If you see a white man, you will see a jug of rum."

The tide of avaricious thirst for gold rolls on, and the trader resorts to those means to satisfy it, that bring upon the Indian poverty, misery, and death. One reason why the gospel has not been more readily received is, because the Indians have not been allowed to remain in a condition to hear and understand it.

The fears I entertain that the Indians will never have a permanent hold upon any part of their lands are from the following reasons.

1. *Their position before the press of emigration.* Their rights will be trampled upon by new settlers, and this, with other annoyances they may receive, will unsettle their minds, and consequently they will remove step by step to escape such annoyance.

The present belief of the Indians is, that they will never again be removed, and that the land they now have is to be their own forever. But American enterprise will require railroads to be built, canals to be opened, military roads to be laid out through that western country, and this land will be demanded.[4] The Indians will soon see that their permanency will be destroyed, and they will cease to improve the soil; since such labor would not be for their own benefit, but for the benefit of the white men who are crowding upon them.

The superior quality of the land for agricultural purposes, will also be an inducement for the emigrant to use all possible endeavors to obtain it.

2. *The quantity of the land* always has and always will retard the progress of their civilization. The game on those lands being abundant, will induce them to neglect the improvement of the soil, which otherwise they would attend to. What do we want land for, when the quantity we possess is a preventive to our improving any particular portion of it?

3. *Necessity will oblige them to sell.* They have ever reasoned thus: Our fathers sold their lands to the government and lived on the proceeds of the sale, and soon the government will want to buy this land, and our children will live on their annuities as we now do on ours; so they will fare as well as we have. In this way they become improvident.

4. *The scarcity of food when the game has gone.* This will produce trouble between the Indians and the white people of the West. However desirous the government may be to maintain peace with the Indians, it will itself occasion the trouble it so much fears.

The game is being killed more and more every year. It is computed by recent travelers, that one hundred thousand buffaloes are killed by trappers for their tongues and hides, which are sold to traders up the Missouri. Game of all kinds is fast disappearing from this side of the mountains. When, by force of circumstance, the Indian is forced to live on the cattle of the frontier settlers, as soon as the first bullock is killed, the cry will be heard, "The Indians are coming! To arms! to arms!" and the soldiery of the United States must be sent to destroy them. The boom of a thousand cannon, the rattle of the drum, and the trumpet's blast, will be heard all over the western prairies; the fearful knell that tells of the downfall of a once noble race.

Desperation will drive the Indian to die at the cannon's mouth, rather than "*remove*" beyond the Rocky Mountains.

Should this time come, (God grant it never may) the paleface must not be surprised should he hear the battle cry resound from peak to peak, and see them descending upon the frontiers, to avenge their wrongs and regain their once happy possessions.[5]

5. *Their isolated condition.* This will be perpetuated as long as the American government addresses them as distinct tribes. It should, instead of this, treat them as one nation. Not till they amalgamate, will they lose the hostile feelings they now have for each other.

Having, in as few words as possible, given the causes which, in my opinion, have prevented them from improving, have decreased their numbers, and the foundation of my fears that they are yet in a critical situation, I will state the plan I have drawn up, and which I have been laying before the American people during the past year. I have had the honor of addressing legislative bodies from South Carolina to Massachusetts, as also the people of various cities and towns.

My object is to induce the general government to locate the Indians in a collective body, where, after they are secured in their lands, they may make such improvements as shall serve to attach them to their homes.

This will be more applicable to the Indians of the Northwest than to those of the Southwest; for I would not be understood as thinking or legislating for the civilized portion, who are by far the most enlightened of the American Indians.[6]

The questions naturally arise, When and how can this be accomplished? Is it practicable?

I feel that I am inadequate to perform the task of showing plainly the *place* where they ought to be settled, as well as the *manner* in which it is to be brought about. Different individuals will have different opinions on these points.

The location which I have chosen for their home, is the unsettled land, known as the Northwest Territory, between the territories of Nebraska and Minnesota, on the eastern banks of the Missouri river. The great Sioux river being the eastern boundary, from its head waters draw a line westward until it meets the Missouri river; thence down the Missouri to the place of beginning. This would form an Indian territory large enough for all the scattered tribes of Michigan Wisconsin, Iowa, &c.[7]

The reasons why I have named this as the most suitable location for them are the following:

I would not be understood as dictating as to the country, where they are to form a nucleus of settlements. It is the idea with some that in the upper waters of the Mississippi river, would likely be the place. But my own ideas differ much from this. Because the upper waters of the Mississippi are going to be the greatest source of lumber trade, and the races coming in contact with one another must cause trouble along the river.

They will go away from the course of emigration which goes up the Missouri and thence westward. They would be two hundred and fifty miles north of this trail. The climate is best for them. Either north or south would not do. In the first, they would suffer from cold; in the last, from sickness.

The distance of this territory westward would cause their removal to be gradual, and by the time the whites should reach there, the Indians would be so far improved as to be enabled to live as neighbors, and could compete with the whites in point of intelligence, and mechanical and agricultural skill.

The last, but not the least question which arises, is this.

Is it practicable? I think it is.

1. Their interests being in the hands of the United States government, the government would have an influence for good in reference to their annuities. By an annual distribution of these, they would become attached to the place of concentration.

2. All the treaties, having for their end the removal of the Indians, may be made with an understanding, that they are never to be moved again, should they go. This would be one of the greatest inducements that could be presented to them, and they would soon go. They are not stubborn beings. Convince them it is for their good, and you will speedily attain your object.

3. The Indians are a social race. They would rather live in large bodies than in small ones, particularly when they are partially civilized. The oftener they see one another, the more rapidly would their jealousies cease to exist. Their children, growing up together, would acquire a mutual attachment and a mutual regard for each other's welfare.

4. The language of the northwest tribes is peculiarly adapted for such a state of society; they would soon understand each other, the Ojibwa language being the great family language of all the Algonquin tribes west. This is one of the best appeals I made to them when I visited them. Tradition says we were all one people once, and now to be re-united will be a great social blessing. Wars must then cease.

5. By giving encouragement to those who would go there to settle, there would be no difficulty in getting them there, for the educated portion of them would be the first to go and lay the foundation for a settlement. And such are those whom I would have go, for they do so from good motives.

6. Should they not be induced to go in collective bodies? A proclamation from the President of the United States, calling upon all the northwest tribes to till the ground, as they must soon have recourse to farming for a living, would induce them individually to go without the chiefs, and they would, as soon as they entered the new territory, frame laws founded on republicanism. The hereditary chiefship must cease to exist, before they can make any rapid advancement; for when you allow the meritorious only to rule, there will be found a great many who will study hard to improve in general information, and fit themselves for statesmen and divines.

Having stated the reasons why I deem my scheme practicable, I will, in conclusion, allude to the advantages that would accrue, not only to the United States, but to the Indians.

To the American Government. This system would simplify the Indian department. They would not have so much perplexity in adjusting difficulties. The outlay in Indian agencies would be lessened. Establish a court of justice in the Indian territory, and no trouble would be had with them, as the difficulties would be legally settled.[8]

The expense of fortifying the western country from the encroachments of the Indians would be dispensed with, and even now they are not actually required. But if the government *must* build forts, and establish military posts, let there be one, in the center of the new Indian territory, to give efficiency to the laws of the Indian government, to protect the peace and persons in that country.

Go in the spirit of the illustrious William Penn, that noble personification of Christianity, and you will have no trouble with the Indians this side of the Rocky Mountains.

The outlay for transporting the Indians would cease to be a burden. I believe the Indians would now go of their own accord, did they know that the land could be thus occupied by them. The buying of the land from the Indians over and over would not then have to be done.

The peaceful and friendly relations that must then exist would be one of the strongest bonds of union in time of peace, and cause them to be neutral in time of war.

The advantages to the Indians. By having *permanent* homes they would soon enjoy the fruit of their labor. Poverty would be unknown, plenty would reign, and cheerfulness aid them in their work.

Seminaries of learning would be permanently located; every stone you laid for the foundation of a school would tell. The repeated removals of the Indians have retarded the progress of moral and physical training among them, and caused many good men to become discouraged in their alms, giving for their improvement. It has not been so much the fault of the Indian as it has been the error of judgment in the distribution of these means.

The appropriation by the United States, for the education of the Indians, of $10,000, would then be a benefit to those for whom it is intended.[9] Let the government endow a college in the central part of the Indian country, and it would have an influence for good to the end of time.

But say you, How will you reconcile the different denominations of Christians who may go there to teach?

Having no predilection to *division* and discord, I would not have one dollar of the money which the generosity of the government should give, go toward perpetuating discordant elements. No! I want to make the great family of the Indians ONE, should I live long enough—*one* in interest, *one* in feeling, *one* while they live, and *one* in a better world after death.

Emulation among themselves would spring up; and each would labor for the other's good, a spirit of rivalry would soon be seen were a premium to be given to those who should raise the largest amount of agricultural produce.

The result of all this would be a rapid increase of intelligence among the Indians, and steps would soon be taken to have a representation in Congress.

Education must commence, in order to proceed. Begin, then, to educate the Indians, and the result will exceed your utmost expectations.

It is hoped that, without making any special plea for the red men, that sense of justice which dwells in the heart of every *true American* will lead the members of Congress to give the above reasons a passing consideration.

Notes

Originally in the *American Whig Review* 9 (June 1849): 631–38. Reproduced in Bernd C. Peyer, ed., *The Elders Wrote: An Anthology of Early Literature Written by North American Indians, 1768–1934* (Berlin: Dietrich Reimer Verlag, 1982), 75–86. Following the acquisition of Louisiana Territory and until the late 1840s, several proposals of this nature were introduced in Congress but never passed. Some of the most vociferous advocates of removal, such as the Reverends Jedediah Morse and Isaac McCoy, had also propagated the notion of a separate Indian state. An almost identical plan was forwarded by Secretary of War John Bell in 1841. Canadian Ojibwes had formulated similar plans for a permanent Indian territory at a council meeting in 1845 where Copway functioned as vice president. Nevertheless, Copway's fantastic plan—referred to by Francis Parkman as a "flash in the pan"—received the support of some weighty individuals. At the end of his lengthier pamphlet titled *Organization of a New Indian Territory*, Copway included twelve letters recommending his project. His supporters included Benjamin F. Butler and George Briggs, governors of Massachusetts; Alexander Ramsey, governor of Minnesota, senator and secretary of war; Charles Manly, governor of North Carolina; Edward Everett, former governor of Massachusetts and president of Harvard University; Ephraim G. Squier, chargé d'affaires to Central America and archaeologist; Kenneth Rayner, congressman; William F. Havemayer, mayor of New York; John P. Bigelow, editor of the New York *Evening Post;* Professor Benjamin Silliman, noted Yale scientist; and Asa Whitney, railroad promoter. See Annie H. Abel, "Proposals for an Indian State, 1778–1878," *Annual Report of the American Historical Association for the Year 1907* (Washington, D.C.: Government Printing Office, 1908), I: 87–104; George A. Schulz, *An Indian Canaan; Isaac McCoy and the Vision of an Indian State* (Norman: University of Oklahoma Press, 1972). For more recent treatises on a sovereign Indian state, see Ward Churchill, *Struggle for the Land: Indigenous Resistance to Genocide, Ecocide and Expropriation in*

Contemporary North America (Monroe, Md.: Common Courage Press, 1993), 423–31; and Vine Deloria, Jr., *Behind the Trail of Broken Treaties* (New York: Dell Publishing Co., 1974), 161–86.

1. Nimrod is a descendant of Ham represented in Genesis as a mighty hunter.

2. In 1837–38 a great epidemic of smallpox swept through the northern plains. The Mandans were particularly affected, with only about 130 surviving. The survivors later followed the Hidatsas to Fort Berthold, where a reservation was finally established for them. On the devastating effect of epidemics see Alfred W. Crosby, Jr., "Virgin Soil Epidemics as a Factor in the Aboriginal Depopulation in America," *William and Mary Quarterly* 33 (April 1976): 289–99.

3. Copway's own father, John Copway, succumbed to alcohol.

4. As a result of the California gold rush in 1848, a transcontinental route tying the historic Santa Fe Trail to the Oregon/California Trail, also known as the Cherokee Trail, was opened in 1849, allowing hundreds of thousands to move across Indian lands. In 1862 Congress chartered a transcontinental railroad, pledging to extinguish Indian title to lands as soon as possible.

5. More than two dozen Indian resistance wars occurred throughout the West between the 1850s and 1880s.

6. The reference here is to the so-called Five Civilized Tribes in Indian Territory.

7. Coincidentally or not, this would have placed Copway's "New Indian Territory" in the midst of Dakota (Eastern Sioux) hunting territory—the foremost enemies of the Ojibwas since the 1730s. See William Whipple Warren (Ojibwa, 1825–53), "History of the Ojibways, Based Upon Traditions and Oral Statements," Collections of the Minnesota Historical Society 5 (1885): 21–394; repr. as *History of the Ojibway Nations* (Minneapolis: Ross and Haines, 1920; repr. St. Paul: Minnesota Historical Society, 1984).

8. In 1883 Secretary of the Interior Henry M. Teller approved the establishment of a system of Courts of Indian Offenses on reservations with Indian police serving as judges.

9. Congress passed an act in 1819 authorizing an annual sum of $10,000 for a "civilization fund" to be used at the president's discretion to promote civilization by employing "capable persons of good moral character, to instruct them in the mode of agriculture suited to their situation; and for teaching their children reading, writing, and arithmetic." The fund was maintained until 1882. See Francis P. Prucha, *American Indian Policy in the Formative Years: The Indian Trade and Intercourse Acts, 1790–1834* (1962; repr., Lincoln: University of Nebraska Press, 1970), 213–24.

BIOGRAPHY

George Copway (Mississauga Ojibwe, 1818–69), or Kah-ge-ga-gah-bow (Firm Standing), was born in the fall of 1819 near the mouth of the Trent River (Ontario), the son of John Copway. According to his autobiography, the only source on his early life, Copway was brought up in a traditional way until his conversion to Methodism in the 1820s, when a group of Christian Indian missionaries under the leadership of Peter Jones visited Rice Lake. Copway attended a Methodist mission school at Rice Lake from about 1830 to 1834, and was then recruited by the American Methodist Episcopal Church, along with his cousin John Johnson (Enmegabowh) and two other Ojibwe converts to assist in its missionary work. Copway and Johnson served at La Pointe, on Madelaine Island, from 1835 to 1836. There Copway helped Rev. Sherman Hall of the American Board of Commissioners for Foreign Missions to translate the Gospel of St. Luke and the Acts of the Apostles into Ojibwe. In the winter of 1836–37, Copway, Johnson, and another Ojibwe convert named Peter Marksman established a Methodist mission at Lac Court Oreille (Ottawa Lake) in Wisconsin. In the fall of 1837 the Illinois Conference of the Methodist Church sent Copway, Johnson, and Marksman to the Ebenezer Methodist Church Manual Labor School in Jacksonville, Illinois.

Copway returned to Canada following his graduation in late 1839. At Peter Jones's house he met Elizabeth Howell, daughter of an immigrant farmer from Yorkshire. They married on June 1, 1840. The couple departed Canada immediately to join the American Upper Mississippi Mission in present-day Wisconsin and Minnesota. On August 30, 1841, Copway was ordained as deacon at the Rock River Conference convention at Plattsburg, Wisconsin. Dissatisfied with his treatment at the Upper Mississippi Mission, Copway responded to Peter Jones's invitation to assist him in missionary activities in Canada. Copway left the United States to teach school temporarily at the Credit River Mission. In connection with the Upper Canadian Methodists, Copway subsequently served as an itinerant preacher among the Saugeen and Rice Lake Ojibwes until 1845. In early 1846 the Saugeen and Rice Lake bands brought charges of embezzlement against Copway. He was expelled by the Canadian Conference of the Wesleyan Methodist Church.

Copway then returned to the United States, where he soon embarked upon a fairly successful career as public speaker and author. In 1847 Copway published his autobiography, *The Life, History, and Travels of Kah-ge-ga-gah-bowh,* which went through seven editions by the close of 1848 and circulated in the United States and England. Copway's striking appearance and oratorical skills also gained the attention of eastern literary giants such as Henry Wadsworth Longfellow and Francis Parkman. In an 1849 article published in the *American Whig Review,* Copway outlined an ambitious plan for the creation of a Northwestern Indian Territory. He subsequently submitted the plan to the 31st Congress of the United States in a pamphlet titled *Organization of A New Indian*

Territory (1850). Although this scheme was hardly practicable, it did receive temporary support from numerous influential politicians and philanthropists. In 1850 Copway published *The Traditional History and Characteristic Sketches of the Ojibway Nation* in London. Although not as popular as his autobiography, it was reprinted in the United States in 1851 and ultimately became his most frequently cited work. In 1850 Copway also produced an epic poem under his name tilted *The Ojibway Conquest,* the authorship of which has been convincingly disputed. Judging from Copway's poorly written letters, it is probable that he was assisted in his literary work by his wife, an accomplished writer.

In the summer of 1850 Copway received an impromptu invitation by Elihu Burritt, founder of the League of Universal Brotherhood, to represent the "Christian Indians of America" at the Third World Peace Congress in Frankfurt on the Main, Germany. On July 10, 1850, Copway departed from Boston to begin a long journey that would take him through parts of England, Scotland, France, Belgium, and Germany. At the third sitting of Third World Peace Congress on August 24, Copway was accorded the honor of introducing the fifth resolution of the Congress acknowledging the principle of nonintervention and the sole right of every state to regulate its own affairs. He subsequently delivered a lengthy speech eulogizing the virtues of universal peace and ended it by presenting the president of the Congress with a catlinite peace pipe.

On August 29, Copway returned to England. He delivered dozens of speeches on temperance and other Indian-related topics until finally setting sail for America from Liverpool on December 7. Shortly after his return to New York, Copway published a lengthy and largely plagiarized account of his travels titled *Running Sketches of Men and Places* (1851). From July 10 to October 4, 1851, Copway also produced thirteen issues of his own newspaper, *Copway's American Indian,* in New York City.

Copway's European tour was the apex of his comet-like career, which began to fade rapidly after his return to the United States. He continued to lecture, but eventually was forced to seek other means of making a living, at times on the fringes of legality. Early in 1852 he became a member of the New York chapter of the Order of United Americans and sought to enlist the support of the radical nationalist American Party for his Northwestern Indian Territory project. This came to naught, however, following the collapse of the nativistic movement after 1856. In 1852 he also drew the ire of the Senecas for disinterring the remains of Red Jacket without their permission, supposedly to prevent desecration by white pilferers. Copway also tried a variety of other scurrilous schemes, including the collection of bounties for each Canadian Indian he could convince to volunteer for the Union army in 1864 and the selling of homemade medicine in Detroit as "Dr. Copway" in 1867. Bankrupt, snubbed by former literary "friends," stricken by the death of three of his four children in 1849–50, and separated from his wife permanently sometime after 1861, Copway's final days were obviously wrought with severe personal difficulties. In the summer of 1868 he appeared alone at the Lake of Two Mountains (Oka) Reserve near

Montreal. Just before his death on January 17, 1869, Copway converted to Roman Catholicism and changed his name to Joseph Antoine.

Publications of George Copway

"The American Indians." *American Whig Review* 9 (June 1849): 631–38. Reprinted in *The Elders Wrote: An Anthology of Early Literature Written by North American Indians, 1768–1934,* edited by Bernd C. Peyer. Berlin: Dietrich Reimer Verlag, 1982: 75–86.

"The End of the Trail." *The Saturday Evening Post* 248, no. 5 (July–August 1976): 25.

The Life, History, and Travels of Kah-ge-ga-gah-bowh (George Copway), a Convert to the Christian Faith, and a Missionary to His People for Twelve years; With a Sketch of the Present State of the Ojebwa Nation, in Regard to Christianity and Their Future Prospects. Albany: Weed and Parsons, 1847. Reprinted as *Recollections of a Forest Life: or, the Life and Travels of Kah-ge-ga-gah-bowh, or, George Copway, Chief of the Ojibway Nation.* London: C. Gilpin, 1851. Reprinted as *The Life, Letters and Speeches of George Copway (Kahgegagahbowh),* edited by A. LaVonne Brown Ruoff and Donald B. Smith. Lincoln: University of Nebraska Press, 1997.

Organization of a New Indian Territory, East of the Missouri River. Arguments and Reasons Submitted to the Honorable the Members of the Senate and House of Representatives of the 31st Congress of the United States: By the Indian Chief Kah-ge-ga-gah-bowh, or Geo. Copway. New York: S. W. Benedict, 1850.

Running Sketches of Men and Places, in England, France, Germany, Belgium, and Scotland. New York: J. C. Riker, 1851.

The Traditional History and Characteristic Sketches of the Ojibway Nation. London: C. Gilpin, 1850. Reprinted New York: AMS Press, 1978.

Unpublished Writings

Letters by Conway are found in the Miscellaneous Manuscripts Collection, Box 57, George Conway materials, Library of Congress; Grace Lee Mute Papers, Minnesota Historical Society; and Pennsylvania Historical Society.

Selected Secondary Sources

Bellin, Joshua David. *The Demon of the Continent: Indians and the Shaping of American Literature.* Philadelphia: University Pennsylvania Press, 2000: 187–99.

Eid, Leroy V. "The Ojibwa-Iroquois War: The War the Five Nations Did Not Win." *Ethnohistory* 26, no. 4 (Fall 1979): 297–324.

Knobel, Dale T. "Know-Nothings and Indians: Strange Bedfellows?" *Western Historical Quarterly* 15 (April 1984): 175–98.

Konkle, Maureen. "Traditionary History in Ojibwe Writing." In Maureen Konkle, *Writing Indian Nations: Native Intellectuals and the Politics of Historiography, 1827–1863.* Chapel Hill: University of North Carolina Press, 2004: 160–223.

MacLeod, D. Peter. "The Anishinabeg Point of View: The History of the Great

Lakes Region to 1800 in Nineteenth-Century Mississauga, Odawa, and Ojibwa Historiography." *Canadian Historical Review* 73, no. 2 (June 1992): 194–210.

Michaelsen, Scott. *The Limits of Multiculturalism: Interrogating the Origins of American Anthropology.* Minneapolis: University of Minnesota Press, 1999: 107–38.

Moyne, Ernest J. "Longfellow and Kah-ga-ga-gah-bowh." In *Henry W. Longfellow Reconsidered: A Symposium,* edited by J. Chelsey Mathews. Hartford: Transcendental Books, 1970: 48–52.

Peyer, Bernd C. "George Copway, Canadian Ojibwa Methodist and Romantic Cosmopolite." In Peyer, *The Tutor'd Mind: Indian Missionary-Writers in Antebellum America.* Amherst: University of Massachusetts Press, 1997: 224–77.

_____. "A Nineteenth-Century Ojibwa Conquers Germany." In *Germans and Indians: Encounters, Fantasies, and Projections,* edited by Colin G. Calloway, Gerd Gmunden, and Susanne Zantop. Lincoln: University of Nebraska Press, 2002: 141–64.

Smith, Donald B. "Kahgegagahbowh." *Dictionary of Canadian Biography (DCB).* Toronto: University of Toronto Press, 1976: 419–21.

_____. *Sacred Feathers: The Reverend Peter Jones (Kahkewaquonaby) & the Mississauga Indians.* Lincoln: University of Nebraska Press, 1987.

_____. "The Life of George Copway or Kah-ge-ga-gah-bowh (1818–1869)—and a review of his writings." *Journal of Canadian Studies* 23, no. 3 (Autumn 1988): 5–38.

_____. "Kahgegagahbowh: Canada's First Literary Celebrity in the United States," In *The Life, Letters and Speeches of George Copway (Kahgegagahbowh)* edited by A. LaVonne Brown Ruoff and Donald R. Smith. Lincoln: University of Nebraska Press, 1997: 1–21.

Ruoff, A. LaVonne Brown. "George Copway: Nineteenth-Century American Autobiographer." *Auto/Biography* 2, no. 1 (1987): 6–17.

_____. "The Literary and Methodist Contexts of George Copway's *Life, Letters and Speeches.*" In Copway, *The Life* (1997): 23–60.

Sweet, Timothy. "Pastoral Landscape with Indians: George Copway and the Political Unconscious of the American Pastoral." *Prospects* 18 (1993): 1–27.

Vizenor, Gerald. "Three Anishinaabeg Writers." In Gerald Vizenor, *The People Named the Chippewa.* Minneapolis: University of Minnesota Press, 1984: 56–74.

THE DEATH OF CHIEF I. H. TUTTLE

John Johnson (1874)

White Earth Reservation, Minn., *January 13, 1874.*
Rev. and Dear Sir : Permit me to have a little talk with you in the way of writing. I am not going to talk about our humble work at this time. The news that I am going to tell you about is a very sad news to us, and to me very particularly. It is the death of that noble Christian Chief, *Nabunashkong*, called Isaac H. Tuttle, who expired on the second of this month.

Four years ago, I believe, his portrait with his war costume was given in Home and Abroad.[1] When his death was announced, it was a sad and a gloomy day to my people—like the children of Israel when they mourned over the death of their leader, Moses.

I have lost dear little ones, too; but I must say that I never before was so much afflicted as in the loss of my beloved brother in CHRIST. I was and am like a child, saying, like Elisha of old, "My father, my father," and asking God to give us the double portion of his noble spirit.[2] Tuttle was indeed our hope, our leader, and our comfort, in the days of our trials. The one who was able to guide us has fallen, and I am disheartened, and it seems to us that we never can be comforted.

The only comfort and the only rest we must find in the words of Him Who never fails to comfort His poor Servants. "Go on, go on with your work, and I will be with you."

Permit me to say one or two words about him before he was brought to the knowledge of JESUS Whom he so dearly loved.

Hole-in-the-Day was a head Chief of the Chippewa Nation, and was considered one of the bravest war chiefs of his people.[3] To choose him a warrior, he must select one of the best and bravest of warriors. He selected Tuttle, and he ranked next to himself, and, in the course of few years, by his daring exploits and successful warfare, he was made a Chief over fifty warriors, or one hundred and sixty souls.

After he was appointed as a Chief, he felt more interest and sought more for the good of his people, and gradually gained the confidence of his people. His counsels and advice at all times were considered of much importance. On one occasion, when *Hole-in-the-Day*, the head Chief, proposed to have nothing to do with the Missionary, but to go on with their heathen religion, he objected to it strongly, and said, "No, no; let the Missionaries come among us, and let them teach and do their duty. Let us try them with unprejudiced minds. If we find anything to the disadvantage of our people, then it will be time to say to the Missionaries that we do not want their Services amongst us." When the Chiefs, warriors, and head men heard this, they gave their general assent. Though individually caring but very little about the Missionaries, he said this for the good of his people generally.

In the Summer of 1861, I invited him to have a little talk about his people and their condition generally. I ask him, "*Nabunashkong,* tell me plainly, and tell me as a friend, what is your hope for your people? You know as a Nation we are fast sinking. Your country and your hiding places tell you, soon or later you will in one day be swept away from the face of the earth. And besides, a strong pressure is now upon our people. This great Continent will be peopled by a higher class of Nation—far stronger and more powerful than our chiefs and warriors were. And this great and mighty movement of the Palefaces has already taken place, and has gone forward like some great tidal wave, sweeping through to our beloved land and country. Now, *Nabunashkong,* tell me plainly, what is your future hope for our people?"

For a few moments, he said not a word. I know he was in deep study to find an answer.

"My friend," he said, "I never thought of these things and never cared to trouble myself about them. The most I thought of was how to take scalps and to follow the war-paths. But, my friend, these things, and the questions you have asked me, are questions of great importance and questions to think of all the time."

Again I ask him, "*Nabunashkong,* only one question more. Can you say that you love and pity your people, that you seek their interest and welfare? If so, what provision are you preparing for them?"

"Yes, my friend, I love and pity my poor people. I seek their interest. I have made no provision for them but this war-club and the scalping knife. I have defended them day and night. Why? Because I love them. My fathers have conquered much land and country. My fathers have driven the enemy away from this country I now occupy, and sealed their lives for this country I now enjoy, and I will follow the brave steps of my fathers and will seal my blood for my country and people."

"But, my friend," I said, "there is a far better and more efficient way to defend your people, without your war-club and scalping knife. It is to have Missionary to tell you about the GREAT SPIRIT, to teach you how to worship Him, and, when you die, go to *ish pe ming.*"

"Yes," he said, "my fathers have taught me, that, when a Red man dies, he goes direct to the great Hunting Ground, beyond the setting sun, which the Great Spirit had prepared for them. Some time ago," he continued, "a Grand Medicine man became a Christian. He died, and started to go to heaven. He reached at the gate near where the Great Spirit was. The Great Spirit told him that no praying Red men are allowed to go to heaven. He started to come down, and started to go to the great Hunting Ground. He reached there. Some one met him at the gate and told him that he had been a praying man, that he could not come to the beautiful Ground. He started back, and came to life, and told the wonderful stories of what he saw and heard, and warned all the Indians throughout the whole country never to become praying men and women. And for this, as well as the instructions received of my fathers, I hope I shall never turn to a praying man. But, at the same time, I shall not prevent Missionary from entering into our country, and if my people want to become Christians, I shall not prevent them, nor discourage them; but as to myself, I hope I shall never be one. I am too much of a man to stoop down so low like a woman; and besides, to cut my long hair locks would be a disgrace to myself and to my standing."

I must hasten to be brief. Six years ago [1868], when he started for this unknown country, he came to see me and ask my advice on the subject. I told him, "Arise and go; and that was the best thing his people can do." The day was named when his Band and others should start, and bid goodbye to their beloved land and country.[4] *Hole-in-the-Day* and a few of his warriors got ready to stop the movement, and made war dances before Chief Tuttle, and threatened that the first man whoever moved one step toward the new country was a dead man. The day arrived when all should move. Tuttle had put on all his war costume, with feathers waving on his head, and led the moving caravan—four hundred in number. *Hole-in-the-Day,* with his warriors, had already posted on the road where Tuttle should pass. Tuttle, when he saw them, walked with firm steps before them, and passed unmolested. And when this was over, his people almost kissed him, and said, "Our leader! Our leader!" and his people loved him more and more.

I must hasten. I overtook them at their first encampment, and told Tuttle that it was uncertain whether I should follow them: previous to this I had made up my mind, that I would not take a step towards White Earth while *Hole-in-the-Day* was a living man, for I know he was a man of blood and that he never would give a peace to Tuttle and his people until he carry out his wicked project against them. Tuttle grasped my hand, and that occasion I never shall forget.

About four months after Tuttle started, *Hole-in-the-Day* was assassinated by his own people, and in about two weeks I was ready to bid my last farewell to the land and country I loved so well, and started to follow the steps of Tuttle. I started with my own caravan which consist of three ox-teams, and with all my war implements always ready for any case of emergency. When the Chiefs heard I had started for White Earth, Chiefs Tuttle, Wright, Washburn, Twing, and a few of their warriors, started to meet me. As we were trudging along peacefully on the beautiful prairie, between what is now called Palmer and Otter Tail City [Minnesota]—this was then a wild country, Otter Tail was only inhabited by a few halt-breeds—as I said, as we were walking on peacefully, all at once we saw half a dozen horses in full gallop, men on the horses, feathers waving on their heads, making towards us. Sure I said, as the Mainites would say, "*goner!*" My hairs all stood straight up, and shook like the leaves, for my wife and children. We thought they were Sioux. Imagine how we felt. The warwhoop, and how to wield my implements of war of flesh, I have not learned. As they approached near and nearer, we saw them, they are our friends! Chief Tuttle took and grasped both of my hands, and said he was as glad as man can be to see me.

This was late in the Fall of 1869. To hold my public Services, there was no place to be found. Chief Tuttle first offered his house to use for that purpose.

All who desired to come to our Services were not able to find room in the house. For three years we have held our Services from house to house, and in the Summer had them in the open air, or under the shade of the beautiful trees.

I must here omit his own words, what he said, about his faith, his hope, and his Grand Medicine, and go on to give you a little of his experience, preparation, and his hard struggles, when he gave himself up to the GREAT SPIRIT.

On one occasion, when we were alone together, I told him plainly his duty, to stand among his brethren, and to come at once and openly renounce his heathenism; that this was the only hope and salvation of his people.

"Yes," he said, "I am fully aware of that. I am preparing for it. I do not want to go into it, half-hearted, and unprepared for the great battle. When I wanted to follow the war-path, I have never gone unprepared. I studied and imagined the hard battle before me—if I turn back from the enemy while the battle is going on, my warriors will laugh at me and say that I was no brave, nor to be trusted. From what I have understood from you, and what little I have learned, the ways of the GREAT SPIRIT are far greater warfare to be engaged in than those hard battles I have won. Hence, due preparation is important. The battle to be fought is not only one day, or one year, but all the days of my life." Yesterday, he said, was the most hard struggle he ever experienced—it was about cutting his long hair locks. Well may he feel proud of them, for the only chief and warrior who had the longest hair braided down to his shoulders.

So, the following Friday, he called on me again. His mind was troubled; that I could see plainly. I lost no opportunity, but pointed to him the SAVIOUR Who came to die for him. He went home. Early, Saturday, he came in again with scissors in his hand. "Your last advice about GOD'S love," he said, "has troubled me much. If the GREAT SPIRIT has so big a love for poor Indian, surely Indian ought and must give back big love to the GREAT SPIRIT. Now, dear brother," he said, "to be true to return my big love to the GREAT SPIRIT, I brought this scissors, to have you cut my hair locks which I shall throw away for ever."

I took him away from the house, and this he requested: when it was all over, he took wild, and threw his head in every direction, to see if any one coming to see him. I smiled, and pitied him greatly. "Friend," he ask, "what made you smile?" I said: "You look precisely like the baboon I saw at Barnum's Museum in New York, some years ago." "O friend," he said, "do not discourage me. My experience during the past night has been great. I am in earnest. I want to count every step as I go along. GOD being my helper, I will be a Christian all the days of my life."

On Saturday the news spread like the wind that the great war Chief had cut his hair locks, and was to receive Baptism the following Sunday. Early, before the hour of prayers, half-breeds, wild men and women, and Christian Indians, have already arrived, to see *Nabunashkong* receive Baptism. Before his baptism took place, he ask permission to say a few words to his brethren. I gave him the permission, and will only say in few words what he said to his brethren.

"Brothers!" he said, throwing his hand over his head, "You all know my past life; how I have led you to the war-path; how I have loved and defended you, day and night, in time of danger. Today I have made up my mind fully to worship GOD all the days of my life. I rise before you all to lead you to the battle in the cause of GOD. I ask you all to follow and join me as you have done heretofore. My fellow-chiefs and warriors, come! Come with your whole hearts! Let us all worship the only true GOD—GOD Who so loved us as to give us His dear SON. I hope," he said, "I shall always make it my point to lead you on to the great cause of the GREAT SPIRIT."

He came forward to receive the Baptism. "Isaac H. Tuttle," (in Ojibway) "Dost thou renounce the devil and all his works, the vain pomp and glory of the world, etc.?" In a very loud voice, "I renounce them all." "Dost thou believe all the Articles of the Christian Faith, etc.?" "I do." And to all the questions he spoke out the answers loud and distinctly.

The Service was over. Now comes the struggle. As he walked homeward, he met a Grand Medicine man, who told him how foolish he was to cut his hair locks, and become a Christian man; and how his people would look upon him, and he would lose his influence among his people; and the best thing he could do was to retract his new religion.[5]

Tuttle said to his friend, "Do you see, yonder, those rocks that lie on the hill? Go to them direct, and ask them to give me permission to retract my new religious faith. If they cannot, I shall be more firm and unmoveable to the great work I have engaged in."

He went along towards home, and found his wife alone in the house. He threw himself on the bed. His wife took notice of him that he was restless, that his mind was agitated greatly. Now and then he looked out through the window to see any one coming to see him and laugh at him. He sat down on a chair, holding his head down. At this time she ask her husband, "*Nabunashkong,* do you feel unwell?" (She understood what troubled her husband.) He said not a word. She went near him and said: "*Nabunashkong,* does this little thing—cutting your hair locks trouble you? O, no. Look back at the war-paths and the hard battles you came through. Surely the battle field you entered for GOD and for the good of your people ought certainly to make you more brave and firmer for the cause of the GREAT SPIRIT." "Yes, *Nevuobeek,*" as he arose from his chair, "Yes; I will be more brave for GOD and for His cause "—and wept like a child, and by GOD'S grace overcame his trials.

Early Monday morning, he came over to our house and told us all about his trials, and how the devil came to him to discourage and try him to give up his profession. He laughs at it heartily, and said, that poor, frail woman of his, how she encouraged him.

To tell you of his work, his teachings, advice and counsels, would require a few pages of paper. But I must close by telling you of his sickness and happy death.

In the early part of last Summer he lost a son, fourteen years old. As the child was breathing his last, "My son," he said, "all is right with you. Go on; go on. Very soon I shall follow you. Tell your little sisters who have gone before us, to look for me, and wait for me." About two months after, another son, eighteen years old, was taken sick—a most promising young man, who was then preparing for Missionary work. During the sickness of the young man, I visited him frequently. On one occasion, on the near approach of death, I ask him, "My son, how do you feel as you are tending towards the grave?" Pointing to the picture of our SAVIOUR, near him, he said: "You see that picture of JESUS is very near me. JESUS is nearer me. I am all ready to go and join my little brother and sisters who have gone before me. Only I feel pity for my poor father. I know he will cry for me." Tuttle said, "No, my son, I will not cry; for JESUS bids you come." The young man died in the Christian big faith of the Palefaces. Here is one Indian witness more for the love of JESUS in his heart.

In the latter part of last November, Tuttle was taken sick with cough, which he contracted through the exposure in hunting.

He was very soon unable to come to Church. I had advised him not to come any more. I had on three occasions held public Services in his house at his request, and visited him on many occasions. In the middle of December he sent for me. I ask him: "Do you know that you will soon leave us?" "I know it well, and it is the will of JESUS. I desire nothing else but resign myself to the will of my heavenly FATHER." I said: "Tuttle, I come here to administer to you the LORD'S SUPPER." "O, that is what I wanted to ask you, yesterday. Will you please put it off till the morrow," he said, "and invite my fellow chiefs and others? I want to say a few words to them all." I did so according to his request. So, the following day, nearly all the chiefs, men and women, came in to participate in their last Communion with their dying Chief. After the Holy Communion, he said: "My brothers, hear a dying request from your unworthy brother. I must soon leave. It is the will of our heavenly FATHER. My advice to you all is, be true, be firm, and be earnest to your calling, and, as long as you are true to our FATHER, fear nothing. Attend to your family prayers, and be punctual to your public Services. Never stay from Public Worship, unless you are sick; and, above all, love GOD with your hearts. I am going home to the GREAT SPIRIT, and there I shall be waiting for you all. Love our poor Missionary. Assist him to talk to our poor brethren. Again I say to you all, be true to the GREAT SPIRIT. He will bless you and your children. Farewell, farewell to you all."

As he was near dying, he called me again to see him. After short prayers, I turn towards him and ask him: "My friend, how do you feel to-day?" "My brother," he said, "I am sinking. My time is short. Very soon I must leave you to be with my blessed SAVIOUR. Go on, dear brother, go on with your work. GOD bless you! I love JESUS, and JESUS loves me, and is very precious to my soul. My time is short. I have finished my course. GOD be praised that ever He turned my poor heart to love Him. I love to go home. GOD'S will be done!" He said again: "No pain and no death can separate me from the love of JESUS."

These were his last words to my hearing. I was then taken sick suddenly, and for nearly two weeks was unable to get about. At his last hours I was not present.

Here, then, is another big Indian witness for the love of JESUS. Poor Tuttle! For many years he was expecting to go to that beautiful Hunting Ground: he worked, fought, and lived for it. But of late, or before he died (strange to say, and contrary to the thought of many Christian Palefaces), he said, "I love JESUS, and JESUS loves me." His humble house was a house of prayer. He loved to speak about the GREAT SPIRIT, and the love of the SAVIOUR. I am lonely, lonely. I feel sick at heart. I miss him greatly. I feel homeless like. O, let my last end be like his!

I know, my dear brother, that you will be able to understand the above, as you feel a deep interest for your Red brothers, more particularly for those who have turned their hearts to the GREAT SPIRIT. Tell the Palefaces, then, who have their doubts of an Indian becoming truly Christian, that Indian can love JESUS with all his heart and can be happy as well as any of your Palefaces who love JESUS.

J. J. ENMEGAHBOWH.

Notes

The full title of the original is *The Church and the Indians: Letter from the Rev. J. J. Enmegahbowh: the Death of Chief I. H. Tuttle* (New York: Office of the Indian Commission, Protestant Episcopal Church, 1874?). It is probably addressed to Episcopal Bishop Henry Benjamin Whipple (1822–1901), forerunner of the Indian reform movement, with whom Enmegahbowh maintained regular contact following his removal to the White Earth Reservation in 1868. Indian missionaries since the days of Occom kept a careful record of their success in the field. These records, usually included as part of a missionary journal, can be said to represent a Christian Indian version of traditional warrior (or coup) tales in which an individual's accomplishments in battle were publicly celebrated.

1. *The Missionary Herald at Home and Abroad* (1806–1951) was an organ of the American Board of Commissioners for Foreign Missions.

2. Kings 2:12.

3. The reference is to Hole-in-the-Day II (Ojibwe, 1828?–1868), principal leader of the Southwestern Ojibwes after the death of Hole-in-the-Day the elder in 1847. He at first favored the work of missionaries and adaptation of white agricultural practices, but after the disastrous results of the 1855 treaty for the Southwestern Ojibwes, he eventually adopted a confrontational stance against the United States. Hole-in-the-Day opposed the removal of his people to White Earth, and was assassinated on June 27, 1868. See Charles A. Eastman, *Indian Heroes and Great Chieftains* (1918; repr. Lincoln: University of Nebraska Press, 1991), 225–41; Mark Diedrich, *The Chiefs Hole-in-the-Day of the Mississippi Chippewa* (Minneapolis: Coyote Books, 1986).

4. In a treaty concluded on March 19, 1867, and proclaimed on April 18, the Southwestern Ojibwes gave up their remaining lands in Minnesota in exchange for reservations better suited to agricultural purposes than those granted in a previous treaty. These included an area around White Earth Lake, which became known

as the White Earth Reservation. Ojibwe emigrants left Gull Lake on June 4, 1868, and arrived at White Earth on June 14.

5. The Medicine Lodge Society, or Midewiwin, was an important curative society among the Algonquian tribes of the western Great Lakes and eastern prairie regions of North America.

BIOGRAPHY

John Johnson (Mississauga Ojibwe, 1808?–1902), or Enmegahbowh (One Who Stands Before His People), was born into a Rice Lake Mississauga Ojibwe community near Peterborough (Ontario). Some sources maintain that he was an adopted Odawa, others that he was the son of a Mississauga Ojibwe chief. According to his own account, Johnson was taken to Sault St. Marie in 1832 by a Methodist missionary and subsequently taught school at L'Anse on Keweenaw Peninsula for two years. In 1834 he was recruited for further missionary work by the American Methodist Episcopal Church along with his cousin George Copway and two other Ojibwe converts. Johnson and Copway served at La Pointe, on Madelaine Island, from 1835 to 1836. In the winter of 1836–37 Johnson, Copway, and Peter Marksman accompanied Methodist Superintendent Alfred Brunson on a mission among the Dakotas (Eastern Sioux) at Kaposia in Minnesota, and subsequently established another mission at Lac Court Oreille in Wisconsin. In the fall of 1837 the Illinois Conference of the Methodist Church sent Johnson, Copway, and Marksman to the Ebenezer Methodist Church Manual Labor School in Jacksonville, Illinois. In 1839, Rev. B. T. Kavenaugh employed Johnson and Marksman as assistants for missionary work in the Upper Mississippi region. Between 1840 and 1845 Johnson served at Methodist missions at Rabbit River, Whitefish Lake, Fond du Lac, and Sandy Lake. On July 4, 1841, he married Charlotte, or Biwabikogiziokwe (Iron Sky Woman), a relative of the Ojibwe band leader Hole-in-the-Day (the elder). They had eleven children, one of whom, George Johnson, also became an Episcopal minister. Around 1845 Johnson left the Sandy Lake Mission to live with his wife's people near Rabbit River. In 1849 he followed the band, now under the leadership of Hole-in-the-Day the younger, to Gull Lake.

At some point Johnson broke off relations with the Methodists, either because they had ceased their missionary activities in the Upper Mississippi region by 1849 or because he was expelled following a violent confrontation with the resident trader at Fond du Lac that same year. In 1851 Johnson began to communicate regularly with Episcopalians. At the instigation of Hole-in-the-Day, Johnson requested a missionary for Gull Lake. Rev. James Lloyd Beck arrived at Gull Lake the following year and with Johnson founded St. Columba Mission. The threat of an Indian uprising in 1857 drove the Episcopalian missionaries away temporarily, but Johnson remained at Gull Lake with partial assistance from the Church of England in Canada. In 1859 Johnson was ordained as an Episcopalian deacon by Bishop Jackson Kemper. That same year Henry Benjamin Whipple was consecrated as Bishop of Minnesota. Following a visit to Gull Lake, Whipple established a lifelong association with Johnson. In 1862 Johnson abandoned Saint Columba to seek asylum at Fort Ripley and the Crow Wing agency. He received death threats from Hole-in-the-Day, who formed a secret alliance with Little Crow, the legendary Mdewakanton leader of the Minnesota Sioux Uprising. It is said that Johnson warned the soldiers at Fort

Ripley of an intended attack by Hole-in-the-Day, further incurring the Ojibwe leader's enmity.

In 1863 Johnson accompanied an Ojibwe delegation to Washington, D.C., as interpreter. Here he was apparently given an enthusiastic reception, meeting with notables like President Andrew Johnson and Jenny Lind. In 1867 Bishop Whipple ordained Johnson as a full priest in the cathedral at Faribault. Following the assassination of Hole-in-the-Day on June 27, 1868, Johnson was finally able to rejoin his congregation at White Earth, a reservation established by the Treaty of 1867.

In 1869 Johnson was instrumental in the conclusion of a peace agreement between leaders of the Southwestern Ojibwes and the Dakotas ending a century-old hostility. Johnson was also active in a circle of Episcopalians that included noted Indian reformers such as Bishop Whipple and William Welsh, who influenced and cooperated with President Ulysses S. Grant's execution of the "Peace Policy" following his inauguration in 1869. Rev. J. J. Enmegahbowh remained at White Earth until his death on June 12, 1902. On August 3, 2003, he was placed on the Episcopal Church's commemorative calendar, or Lesser Feasts and Fasts, to mark the day of his death.

Selected Publications of John Johnson

The Church and the Indians: Letter from the Rev. J. J. Enmegahbowh: the Death of Chief I. H. Tuttle. New York: Office of the Indian Commission, Protestant Episcopal Church, ca. 1874.

En-me-gah-bowh's Story: An Account of the Disturbances of the Chippewa Indians at Gull Lake in 1857, and Their Removal in 1868. Minneapolis: Women's Auxiliary, St. Barnabas Hospital, 1904; reprinted, Brainerd, Minn.: St. Paul's Parish, 1985.

"The Story of Enmegabowh's Life." In Henry Benjamin Whipple, *Lights and Shadows of a Long Episcopate.* New York: Macmillan, 1902: 497–510.

"The Voice of the Red Man to the White." *The Spirit of Missions* 35 (April 1870).

Unpublished Sources

Correspondence with and from John Johnson is found in the Henry B. Whipple Papers, 1833–1934, Minnesota Historical Society, St. Paul; and Lucie Leigh Bowie Collection, 1795–1959, Maryland Historical Society, Baltimore.

Selected Secondary Sources

Meyer, Melissa L. *The White Earth Tragedy: Ethnicity and Dispossession at a Minnesota Anishinaabe Reservation, 1889–1920.* Lincoln: University of Nebraska Press, 1994.

Zanger, Martin N. "Straight Tongues, Heathen Wards: Bishop Whipple and the Episcopal Mission to the Chippewas." In *Churchmen and the Western Indians: 1820–1920,* edited by Clyde A. Milner II and Floyd A. O' Neil. Norman: University of Oklahoma Press, 1985: 177–214.

THE RED MAN'S REBUKE

Simon Pokagon (1893)

> Shall not one line lament our forest race,
> For you struck out from wild creation's face?
> Freedom—the selfsame freedom you adore,
> Bade us defend our violated shore.

In behalf of my people, the American Indians, I hereby declare to you, the pale-faced race that has usurped our lands and homes, that we have no spirit to celebrate with you the great Columbian Fair now being held in this Chicago city, the wonder of the world.

No; sooner would we hold high joy day over the graves of our departed fathers, than to celebrate our own funeral, the discovery of America. And while you who are strangers, and you who live here, bring the offerings of the handiwork of your own lands and in admiration, rejoice over the beauty and grandeur of this young republic, and you say, "Behold the wonders wrought by our children in this foreign land," do not forget that this success has been at the sacrifice of *our* homes and a once happy race.

Where these great Columbian show-buildings stretch skyward and where stands this "Queen City of the West" *once* stood the Red Man's Wigwam; here met their old men, young men and maidens; here blazed their council fires. But now the eagle's eye can find no trace of them. Here was the center of their wide-spread hunting grounds, stretching far eastward, and to the great salt Gulf southward, and to the lofty Rocky Mountain chain westward. All about and beyond the Great Lakes northward roamed vast herds of buffalo that no man could number, while moose, deer and elk were found from ocean; pigeons, ducks, and geese in near bow-shot moved in great clouds through the air, while fish swarmed our streams, lakes and seas close to shore. All were provided by the Great Spirit for our use; we destroyed none except for food and dress; had plenty and were contented and happy.

But alas! the pale faces came by chance to our shores, many times very needy and hungry. We nursed and fed them,—fed the ravens that were soon to pluck out our eyes and the eyes of our children; for no sooner had the news reached the Old World that a new continent had been found, peopled with another race of men, than locust-like, they swarmed on all our coasts: and, like the carrion crows in spring, that in circles wheel and clamor long and loud, and will not cease until they find and feast upon the dead, so these strangers from the East long circuits made, and turkey-like, they gobbled in our ears, "Give us gold, give us gold." "Where find you gold, where find you gold?"

We gave for promises and "gewgaws" all the gold we had, and showed them where to dig for more. To repay us they robbed our homes of fathers, mothers, sons and daughters; some were forced across the sea for slaves in Spain while

multitudes were dragged into the mines to dig for gold and held in slavery there
until all who escaped not, died under the lash of the cruel taskmaster. It finally
passed into their history that, "the red man of the West, unlike the black man
of the East, will die before he'll be a slave."[1] Our hearts were crushed by such
base ingratitude; and, as the United States has now decreed, "No Chinaman
shall land upon our shores," so we then felt that no such barbarians as they,
should land on ours.[2]

In those days that tried our father's souls, tradition says: "A crippled grey-
haired sire told his tribe that in the visions of the night he was lifted high above
the earth, and in great wonder beheld a great spiderweb spread out over the
land from Atlantic Ocean toward the setting sun. Its network was made of rods
of iron; along its lines, in all directions rushed monstrous spiders, greater in
strength and larger far than any beast of earth, clad in brass and iron, dragging
after them long rows of wigwams with families therein, outstripping in their
course the flights of birds that fled before them. Hissing from their nostrils
came forth fire and smoke, striking terror to both fowl and beast. The red men
hid themselves in fear, or fled away, while the white men trained these mon-
sters for the war path, as warriors for battle.

The old man who saw the vision claimed it meant that the Indian race would
surely pass away before the pale-faced strangers. He died a martyr to his belief. Centuries have passed since that time, and we now behold in the vision,
as in a mirror, the present network of railroads, and the monstrous engines with
their fire, smoke and hissing steam, with cars attached, as they go sweeping
through the land.

The cyclone of civilization rolled westward; the forests of untold centuries
were swept away; streams dried up; lakes fell back from their ancient bounds
and all our fathers once loved to gaze upon was destroyed, defaced or marred,
except the sun, moon and starry skies above, which the Great Spirit in his wisdom, hung beyond their reach.

Still on the storm cloud rolled while before its lightning and thunder the
beasts of the field and the fowls of the air withered like grass before the flame—
were shot for love of power to kill alone, and left, to spoil upon the plains. Their
bleaching bones now, scattered far and near, in shame declared the wanton
cruelty of the pale-faced men. The storm, unsatisfied on land, swept our lakes
and streams while before its clouds of hooks, nets, and glistening spears the
fish vanished from our shores like the morning dew before the rising sun. Thus
our inheritance was cut off, and we were driven and scattered as sheep before
the wolves.

Nor was this all. They brought among us fatal diseases our fathers knew not
of; our medicine men tried in vain to check the deadly plague; but they themselves died, and our people fell as fall the leaves before the autumn's blast. To
be just, we must acknowledge there were some good men with these strangers
who gave their lives for ours, and in great kindness taught us the revealed will
of the Great Spirit through his Son Jesus, the mediator between God and man.
But while we were being taught to love the Lord our God with all our heart,

mind and strength, and our neighbors as ourselves, and our children were taught to lisp, "Our Father who art in heaven, hallowed be thy name," bad men of the same race, whom we thought of the same belief, shocked our faith in the revealed will of the Father, and as they came among us with bitter oaths upon their lips, something we had never heard before, and cups of "fire-water" in their hands, something we had never seen before, they pressed the sparkling glasses to our lips and said, "Drink, and you will be happy." We drank thereof, we and our children, but alas! like the serpent that charms to kill, the drink-habit coiled about the heart-strings of its victims, shocking unto death, friend-ship, love, honor, manhood—all that makes men good and noble; crushing out all ambition, and leaving naught but a culprit vagabond in the place of a man.

Now as we have been taught that our first parents ate of the forbidden fruit and fell, so we as fully believe that this fire-water is the hard cider of the white man's devil, made from the fruit of that tree that brought death into the world, and all our woes. The arrow, the scalping knife, the tomahawk used on the warpath were *merciful* compared with it; *they* were used in our defense, but the accursed drink came like a serpent in the form of a dove. Many of our people partook of it without mistrust, as children pluck the flowers and clutch a scorpion in their grasp; only when they feel the sting, they let the flowers fall. But Nature's children had no such power; for when the viper's fangs they felt, they only hugged the reptile the more closely to their breasts, while friends be-fore them stood pleading with prayers and tears that they would let the deadly serpent drop. But all in vain. Although they promised so to do, yet with laugh-ing grin and steps uncertain like the fool, they still more frequently guzzled down this hellish drug. Finally, conscience ceased to give alarm, and, led by deep despair to life's last brink, and goaded by demons on every side, they cursed themselves, they cursed their friends, they cursed their beggar babes and wives, they cursed their God, and died.

You say that we are treacherous, vindictive and cruel; in answer to the charge, we declare to all the world, with our hands uplifted before high Heaven that before the white man came among us, we were kind, outspoken, and for-giving. Our real character has been misunderstood because we have resented the breaking of treaties made with the United States, as we honestly under-stood them. The few of our children who are permitted to attend your schools, in great pride tell us that they read in your own histories, how William Penn, a Quaker and a good man, made treaties with nineteen tribes of Indians, and that neither he nor they ever broke them; and further, that during seventy years, while Pennsylvania was controlled by the Quakers, not a drop of blood was shed nor a war-whoop sounded by our people. Your own historians, and our traditions, show that for nearly two hundred years different Eastern powers were striving for the mastery in the new world, and that our people were per-suaded by the different factions to take the war-path, being generally led by white men who had been discharged from prisons for crimes committed in the Old World . . .[3]

It is clear that for years after the discovery of this country, we stood before the coming strangers as a block of marble before the sculptor, ready to be shaped into a statue of grace and beauty; but in their greed for gold, the block was hacked to pieces and destroyed. Child-like we trusted in them with all our hearts; and as the young nestling while yet blind swallows each morsel given by the parent bird, so we drank in all they said. They showed us the compass that guided them across the trackless deep and as its needle swung to and fro, only resting to the north, we looked upon it as a thing of life from the eternal world. We could not understand the lightning and thunder of their guns, be-lieving they were weapons of the Gods; nor could we fathom their wisdom in knowing and telling us the exact time in which the sun or moon should be darkened; hence we looked upon them as divine; we revered them—yes, we trusted in them as infants trust in the arms of their mothers.

But again and again was our confidence betrayed, until we were compelled to know that greed for gold was all the balance-wheel they had. The remnant of the beasts are now wild and keep beyond the arrow's reach, the fowls fly high in the air, the fish hide themselves in deep waters. We have been driven from the homes of our childhood and from the burial places of our kindred and friends, and scattered far westward into desert places where multitudes have died from home-sickness, cold and hunger, and are suffering and dying for want of food and blankets.

As the hunted deer, when night comes on, weary and tired, lies down to rest, mourning for companions of the morning herd, all scattered, dead and gone, so we through many weary years have tried to find some place to safely rest. But all in vain! Our throbbing hearts unceasingly say, "The hounds are howl-ing on our tracks." Our sad history has been told by weeping parents to their children from generation to generation; and as the fear of the fox in the duck-ling is hatched, so the wrongs we have suffered are transmitted to our children and they look upon the white man with distrust as soon as they are born. Hence our worst acts of cruelty should be viewed by all the world with Christian char-ity as being but the echo of bad treatment dealt out to us.

Therefore we pray our critics everywhere to be not like the thoughtless boy who condemns the toiling bees wherever found as vindictive and cruel because in robbing their homes he once received the poisoned darts that nature gave for their defense. Our strongest defense against the onward marching hordes, we fully realize, is as useless as the struggles of a lamb borne high in the air, pierced to its heart, in the talons of an eagle.

We never shall be happy here any more; we gaze into the faces of our little ones, for smiles of infancy to please, and into the faces of our young men and maidens, for joys of youth to cheer advancing age, but alas! instead of smiles of joy, we find but looks of sadness there. Then we fully realize in the anguish of our souls that their young and tender hearts, in keenest sympathy with ours, have drank in the sorrows we have felt, and their sad faces reflect it back to us again.

No rainbow of promise spans the dark cloud of our afflictions; no cheering hopes are painted on our midnight sky. We only stand with folded arms and watch and wait to see the future deal with us no better than the past. No cheer of sympathy is given us; but in answer to our complaints we are told that the triumphal march of the eastern race westward is by the unalterable decree of nature termed by them "the survival of the fittest."[4] And so we stand as upon the seashore, chained hand and foot, while the incoming tide of the great ocean of civilization rises slowly but surely to overwhelm us.

But a few more generations and the last child of the forest will have passed into the world beyond, into that kingdom where Tche-ban-gou-booz, the Great Spirit, dwelleth, who loveth justice and mercy, and hateth evil; who has declared that the "fittest" in his kingdom, shall be those alone that hear and aid his children when they cry, those that love him and keep his commandments. In that kingdom many of our people in faith believe he will summon the pale-faced spirits to take position on his left and the red spirits upon his right, and that he will say, "Sons and daughters of the forest, your prayers for deliverance from the iron heel of oppression through centuries past are recorded in this book now open before me, made from the bark of white birch, a tree under which for generations past you have mourned and wept. On its pages silently has been recorded your sad history. It has touched my heart with pity, and I will have compassion."

Then, turning to the left, he will say, "Sons and daughters of the East, all hear and give heed unto my words. While on earth I did great and marvelous things for you—I gave you my only Son, who declared unto you my will, and as you had freely received, to so freely give, and declare the gospel unto all people. A few of you have kept the faith; and through opposition and great tribulation have labored hard and honestly for the redemption of mankind regardless of race or color. To all such I now give divine power to fly on lightning wings throughout my universe. Now therefore listen; and when the great drum beats, let all try their powers to fly. Only those can rise who acted well their part on earth to redeem and save the fallen."

The drum will be sounded, and that innumerable multitude will appear like some vast sea of wounded birds struggling to rise. We shall behold it and shall hear their fluttering as the rumbling of an earthquake, and to our surprise shall see but a scattering few in triumph rise, and hear their songs re-echo through the vault of heaven as they sing, "Glory to the highest who hath redeemed and saved us."

Then the Great Spirit will speak with a voice of thunder to the remaining shame-faced multitude: "Hear ye: it is through great mercy that you have been permitted to enter these happy hunting grounds. Therefore I charge you in the presence of these red men that you are guilty of having tyrannized over them in many and strange ways. I find you guilty of having made wanton wholesale butchery of their game and fish, I find you guilty of using tobacco, a poisonous weed made only to kill parasites on plants and lice on man and beast. You found it with the red men. who used it only in smoking the pipe of peace, to confirm their contracts in place of a seal. But you multiplied its use, not only in smoking but in chewing, snuffing, thus forming unhealthy, filthy habits, and by cigarettes, the abomination of abominations, taught little children to hunger and thirst after the father and mother of palsy and cancers.

"I find you guilty of tagging after the pay agents sent out by the great chief of the United States, among the Indians, to pay off their birth-right claims to home, and liberty and native lands, and then sneaking about their agencies by deceit and trickery, cheating and robbing them of their money and goods, thus leaving them poor and naked. I also find you guilty of following the trail of Christian missionaries into the wilderness among the natives, and when they had set up my altars, and the great work of redemption had just begun, and some in faith believed, you then and there stuck out your sign, Sample Rooms. You then dealt to the sons of the forest a most damnable drug, fitly termed on earth by Christian women, 'a beverage of hell', which destroyed both body and soul, taking therefor all their money and blankets, and scrupling not to take in pawn the Bibles given them by my servants.

"Therefore, know ye, this much—Neither shall you with gatling gun or otherwise disturb or break up their prayer meetings in camp any more. Neither shall you practice with weapons of lightning and thunder any more. Neither shall you use tobacco in any shape, way or manner. Neither shall you touch, taste, handle, make, buy or sell anything that can intoxicate any more. And, know ye, ye cannot buy out the law or skulk by justice here; and if any attempt is made on your part to break these commandments, I shall forthwith grant these red men of America great power, and delegate them to cast you out of Paradise, and hurl you headlong through its outer gates into the endless abyss beneath—far beyond, where darkness meets with light, there to dwell, and thus shut out from my presence and the presence of angels and the light of heaven, forever and ever."

> Is not the Red Man's wigwam home
> As dear to him as costly dome?
> Is not his lov'd one's smile as bright
> As the dear one's of th'man that's white?

Notes

The Red Man's Greeting (Hartford, Mich.: C. H. Engle, Publisher, 1893). It originally appeared under the title *The Red Man's Rebuke*. Why Pokagon changed the title is unknown. I have used the edition found in the Chicago Historical Society. In the preface to this sixteen-page booklet, Pokagon explains why he chose to produce some of his work on birch bark instead of regular paper: "My object in publishing the 'Red Man's Greeting' on the bark of the white birch tree is out of loyalty to my own people, and gratitude to the Great Spirit, who in his wisdom provided for our use for untold generations this most remarkable tree with manifold bark used by us instead of paper, being of greater value to us as it could not be injured by sun or water." Slightly different versions are reproduced in Cecilia B. Buechner, "The Pokagons," *Indiana Historical Society Publications* 10, no. 5 (1933): 331–37; Frederick E. Hoxie, ed., *Talking Back to Civilization: Indian Voices from the Progressive Era* (Boston: Bedford/St. Martin's, 2001), 31–35; Cheryl Walker, *Indian Nation: Native American Literature and Nineteenth-Century Nationalisms* (Durham, N.C.: Duke University Press, 1997), 211–20. Though similar to William Apess's "An Indian's Looking-Glass for the White Man" and *Eulogy on King Philip* in its indictment of Indian-white relations, Pokagon tends to lapse into the hackneyed lamentations of popular American "vanishing Indian" poetry and prose produced between the 1780s and 1850s.

1. This argument was first used by Fray Bartolomé de las Casas in an effort to curb Spanish enslavement of Indians. He has consequently been held partly responsible for the ensuing African slave trade.

2. Reference to the 1882 Chinese Exclusion Act, which was extended in 1892 for another ten years.

3. Here Pokagon cites from Peter Martyr d'Anghiera's "Opera, Legatio, Babylonica, Oceanidecas, Paemata, Epigrammata" (Seville, 1511); and Columbus's widely published letter of 1493.

4. Social Darwinism, which became popular in the United States during the final decades of the nineteenth century, linked the stages of cultural evolution with physical and mental development and postulated that "savages" could not live with civilized human beings because their inferior intellectual capacity made them incapable of comprehending the complex associations of civilization. See Brian Dippie, *The Vanishing American: White Attitudes and U.S. Indian Policy* (Middleton, Conn.: Wesleyan University Press, 1982), 81–94; Reginald Horsman, *Race and Manifest Destiny: The Origins of American Racial Anglo-Saxonism* (Cambridge: Harvard University Press, 1981), 139–207.

BIOGRAPHY

Simon Pokagon (Potawatomi, 1830–99) was born in the Pokagon Village near the present border of Michigan and Indiana, the youngest son of Leopold and Kitesse Pokagon. Leopold Pokagon (ca. 1776–1841) was a village headman and spokesman for several Catholic Potawatomi communities of southwestern Michigan from whom the Pokagon band of Catholic Potawatomi derived its general name after the 1830s. Because Simon Pokagon's father died when the boy was eleven years old, it is likely that his mother, converted by Father Frederick Rézé (Reese) in 1830 along with Leopold, was largely responsible for his Catholic upbringing. According to his own account, Simon Pokagon was monolingual until the age of twelve. His mother then supposedly sent him to Notre Dame Academy, where he claimed to have studied for four or five years. Pokagon also maintained that he attended Oberlin Collegiate Institute (Ohio) for one year and Twinsburg Institute (Ohio) for another two years. However, there are no records of his attendance at either the University of Notre Dame or Oberlin College. Instead, he may have attended the mission school at Silver Creek staffed by Holy Cross sisters from Saint Mary's Academy (now a college), which was affiliated with Notre Dame until its takeover by the Diocese of Detroit in 1852. Pokagon may also have attended Twinsburg Institute, a school that offered free tuition, board, and lodging to a few Indians at that time.

From the scanty information available on his life, it appears that Pokagon actively promoted the interests of the Catholic Potawatomi community in Michigan until the early 1880s, particularly in their drawn-out claims against the United States after 1862. Pokagon was elected chair of the newly created Business Committee of the Potawatomi of Michigan and Indiana in 1869. In this official capacity he advocated the hiring of private lawyers to initiate litigation to revise the unsatisfactory congressional joint resolution on July 28, 1866, in which the Michigan bands of Potawatomi were to receive the sum of $39,000 under the condition that it be accepted as final compensation for all claims against the United States and at the dispensation of further annuities. Following Pokagon's advice, the Catholic Potawatomis enlisted the services of an attorney and then lobbied Congress for an enabling act to permit them to bring their case before the Court of Claims. Pokagon eventually faced accusations of having sold discounted notes on the expected proceeds from the claims case without the permission of the General Council. He was consequently ousted as chair of the Business Committee in 1882. In the two decades that followed, Pokagon continued to lobby without the official sanction of the Business Committee under the self-designated title of "Chief of the Pokagon Band of Pottawatomie Indians." He turned directly to prominent American businessmen in southwestern Michigan for assistance, some of whom wrote letters to the commissioner of Indian affairs on his behalf. He even hired a private attorney to represent his own claims. In 1892, while the issue of Potawatomi back annuities was still under discussion in the Court of Claims, Pokagon agitated for a substantial share of the expected award. On April 17, 1893, the Supreme Court affirmed the court's 1890 decision to grant the Pokagon band a final remuneration of $104,626, plus the interest that would accrue on that sum until the date of payment. In 1894, with the help of friends and relatives, Pokagon formed a rump Business Committee of his own in order to more effectively promote his private interests in the matter. His claims to leadership and special monetary compensation were both officially rejected, however, by a general council of Catholic Potawatomis on October 22, 1895. In spite of this rebuff, Simon was still given full credit in the local press when the award was finally distributed among the Pokagons at the close of 1896.

Regardless of how pretentious Simon Pokagon's claims to leadership may actually have been after his removal from office in 1882, his subsequent involvement in the affairs of the Michigan Potawatomis should not be underestimated. It seems very likely that, along with the lobbying activities of the attorneys, his at times selfishly motivated promotional tactics did serve to generate the publicity needed for the political realization of the Pokagons' claims against the United States. On September 21, 1994, President Clinton signed a bill officially recognizing the Pokagon Band of Potowatomi Indians, who trace their ancestry to Leopold and Simon Pokagon.

Simon Pokagon's ingenuity in finding new methods to demand redress from the dominant society occasionally achieved trickster-like proportions. In 1897, in what has become known as the "Sand Bar Claim," Simon made the fantastic assertion that almost all of Chicago's reclaimed lakefront was situated on submerged property never ceded by the Potawatomis. This real-estate chimera was finally taken before the Federal District Court in 1914 by a law firm supposedly acting on behalf of the Business Committee, where it was summarily dismissed.

Simon Pokagon made his debut as an Indian celebrity at the 1893 World Columbian Exposition. Undoubtedly aware of the ongoing discussions about race-related controversies revolving around the fair, including the barring of African Americans from active participation, Pokagon joined reformers such as Richard Henry Pratt in criticizing a retrogressive representation of Indians as primitive savages in the extensive ethnological exhibits prepared by the Bureau of Indian Affairs and the Bureau of American Ethnology. As a form of protest, he wrote a somewhat doleful résumé of Indian-white relations titled *The Red Man's Rebuke* (later changed to *The Red Man's Greeting*), which he had printed up on manifold native birch bark and then sold to visitors at the American Indian village situated on the Midway. He also proposed that a congress of progressive Indians be held on the fairgrounds, foreshadowing the formation of the Society of American Indians eighteen years later. Simon was invited as a special guest of honor for the celebration of "Chicago Day" on October 9. He rang the replica "Liberty Bell" and then delivered an address on the "Indian problem." Later that evening, he changed into a full Plains Indian costume to take up a prominent place reserved for him on a historical float.

Pokagon's dramatic appearances at the World Columbian Exposition enabled him to launch a modest career as a public speaker and author. Between 1892 and his death from pneumonia on January 28, 1899, about a dozen magazine articles, five birch-bark booklets, and two hymns appeared under his name. *Queen of the Woods,* a part-autobiographical Victorian temperance novel, was published posthumously in 1899. Judging from the unpolished composition of his letters (no manuscripts have been recovered so far), it is probable that his publications were heavily edited.

Selected Publications of Simon Pokagon

Algonquin Legends of Paw Paw Lake. Hartford, Mich.: C. H. Engle, n.d.
Algonquin Legends of South Haven. Hartford, Mich.: C. H. Engle, 1900.
"The Future of the Red Man." *Forum* 23 (July 1897): 698–708. Excerpted as "An Indian on the Future of His Race." In *The American Monthly Review of Reviews* 16, no. 3 (September 1897): 334–35. Reprinted in *The Elders Wrote: An Anthology of Early Prose by North American Indians, 1768–1931,* edited by Bernd C. Peyer. Berlin: Dietrich Reimer Verlag, 1982: 115–25.
"A Grateful Friend." *Indian's Friend* 10 (June 1898): 8.
"Indian Native Skills." *The Chautauquan* 26 (February 1898): 540–42.
"An Indian on the Problems of His Race." *The Review of Reviews* 12 (July–December 1895): 694–695. Reprinted in part in *The Word Carrier* 24, nos. 11–12 (November–December 1895): 1.
"Indian Superstitions and Legends." *The Forum* 25 (July 1898): 618–19. Reprinted in *Native American Folklore in Nineteenth-Century Periodicals,* edited by William M. Clements. Athens: Ohio University Press, 1986: 237–52.
"An Indian's Observations on the Mating of Geese." *The Arena* 16 (July 1896): 245–48.
"An Indian's Plea." *The Red Man* 15, no. 2 (October/November 1898): 5, 8.
Lord's Prayer in Algonquin Language. Hartford, Mich.: C. H. Engle, n.d.
"The Massacre of Fort Dearborn at Chicago." *Harper's New Monthly Magazine* 98, no. 586 (March 1899): 649–56.
O-gî-mäw-kwì Mit-i-gwä-kî (Queen of the Woods). Also Brief Sketch of the Algaic Language. Hartford, Mich.: C.H. Engle, 1899. Reprinted Berrien Springs, Mich.: Hardscrabble, 1972.
"Our Indian Women." *The Chautauquan* 22 (March 1896): 732–34.
Pottawatamie Book of Genesis. Legend of the Creation of Man. Hartford, Mich.: C. H. Engle, 1901. Reprinted in Charles S. Winslow, *Indians of the Chicago Region.* Chicago: 1946: 4–8.
"The Pottawatomies in the War of 1812." *The Arena* 26 (July 1901): 48–55.
The Red Man's Rebuke. Hartford, Mich.: C. H. Engle, Publisher, 1893. Reprinted in Cecilia B. Buechner, "The Pokagons." *Indiana Historical Society Publications* 10, no. 5 (1933): 331–37; and Cheryl Walker, *Indian Nation: Native American Literature and Nineteenth-Century Nationalisms* (Durban: Duke University Press, 1997), 211–220.
"Simon Pokagon on Naming the Indians." *The American Monthly Review of Reviews* 16, no. 3 (September 1897): 320–21.
"Wild Pigeons of North America." *The Chautauquan* 22 (November 1895): 202–206.

Unpublished Writings

A number of Simon Pokagon's letters are found in the Leon J. Cole Papers, Wisconsin State Historical Society, Madison; and the Simon Pokagon Collection, Chicago Historical Society.

Selected Secondary Sources

Buechner, Cecilia B. "The Pokagons." *Indiana Historical Society Publications* 10, no. 5 (1933): 281–340.

Clifton, James A. *The Pokagons, 1683–1983: Catholic Potawatomi Indians of the St. Joseph River Valley.* Lenham, Md.: University Press of America, 1984.

———. "Simon Pokagon's Sandbar: Potawatomi Claims to Chicago's Lakefront." *Michigan History* 71, no. 5 (September–October 1987): 12–17.

Cumming, John. "Pokagon's Birch Bark Books." *American Book Collector* 18, no. 8 (1968): 14–17.

Dickason, David H. "Chief Simon Pokagon: 'The Indian Longfellow'." *Indiana Magazine of History* 57, no. 2 (1961): 127–40.

Engle, C. H. "A Brief Sketch of Chief Simon Pokagon's Life." In Pokagon, *Queen of the Woods,* 5–33.

Flower, B. O. "An Interesting Representative of a Vanishing Race." *The Arena* 16, no. 2 (July 1896): 240–50.

Hochbruck, Wolfgang. "Between Victorian Tract and Native American Novel: Simon Pokagon's *O-GÎ-MÄW-KWE MIT-I-GWÄ-KÎ* (1899)." In *Victorian Brand/Indian Brand: The White Shadow on the Native Image,* edited by Naila Clerici. Torino: Il Segnalibro, 1993: 13–29.

Larson, Charles A. *American Indian Fiction.* Albuquerque, N. Mex.: University of New Mexico Press, 1978: 37–46

Ruoff, A. LaVonne Brown. "Simon Pokagon." In *Dictionary of Native American Literature,* edited by Andrew Wiget. New York: Garland Publishing, Inc., 1994: 277–79.

THE INDIAN PROBLEM;
FROM THE INDIAN'S STANDPOINT

Andrew J. Blackbird (1900)

Many white people think that what are called savage nations do not know any thing of their former history, but we all have records and traditions of events in very ancient times.

Perhaps every white inhabitant of this peninsula of Michigan has the idea that the Ottawa and Chippewa tribes of Indians were the first occupants of this country, because they were the ones who ceded this land to the United States. But according to our knowledge of this subject, there were six different tribes of Indians who resided in this peninsula before any one of the Ottawas or Chippewas ever set foot on Michigan soil, and each speaking a different language; which shows that they must evidently have originally sprung from different nations. Where are these people gone? Alas: they are extinct; vanished away into nothingness. No trace of their history exists, except in the allusions to them in our legends.

Our traditions say that the Ottawas formerly lived on the Canada side of the Great Lakes, but they made war against the tribes in Michigan, particularly against the Mash-ko-desh [Mascouten] tribe and the U-ron [Huron] tribe and took possession of the country. Part of them settled along the Detroit River, but most of them located around the Straits of Mackinac and southwardly, where they were quite numerous, and were a warlike people. One of their principal settlements was a continuous village, fifteen or sixteen miles in length, situated where now is the western border of Emmet Co. on the shore of Lake Michigan.[1]

All this region was formerly named "L'Arbre Croche" [now Harbor Springs], in the French language, as the French were the first white people who came here. This name is the translation of the Ottawa name, Waw-gaw-na-ki-sy, which means "Crooked top of the tree." But now this last race of Indians is nearly vanished away, from one cause and another. Their existence as a tribe was extinguished by a treaty with the United States, in the year 1855.[2] Then they were attached to this government, just as you see them now and never again will they have their own government as in former times. But with no suitable education, they can only, in a poor manner imitate their white neighbors in agricultural and other civilized ways.

The reports of the Commissioner of Indian Affairs, of Indian Agents, of some of the Government School Officials, and Missionaries, usually create a great sensation, saying that the Indians are all improving and advancing toward civilization. Christianity, and industry, and that their numbers are increasing instead of decreasing. This official yearly report of "improvement," is well illustrated by one of our race, Dr. Carlos Monte Zuma [sic], in the story of the sick person who died although his physician daily reported him "improving."

244

Said a friend: "He died of improvement."[3] Therefore it is high time that the red flag or some other danger signal be hung upon the present Indian policy, or the Indians will all die with "improvements."

But I have heard white people say that the Indians might just as well die, for nothing can be done with them, as they will always be wild and savage and cruel. They might as well all die or be killed, every one of them, from the face of the earth, for a dead Indian is better than a live Indian. These frightful statements are heard all over the United States and every Caucasian child and every Indian child that is able to understand, knows this dreadful feeling toward us. These statements are translated and republished in foreign countries, so every foreigner coming to America comes with a prejudice and a persecuting spirit toward the aborigines of America. Therefore there is no peace nor shelter for the Indians, from injustice. They are exposed to hate, to be shot at, and to be robbed in every way and manner, of their little possessions of lands which the government has allotted to them in treaties. They are cheated by the crooked works of the law.

Every white man knows that the Indians stand very helpless before the law of the country. Their oaths and evidence are scarcely regarded in the courts of justice, while the white man's oath is accepted. When a case is between an ignorant Indian and a white man it would be a terrible disgrace if the Indian should beat the white man in the court of justice.

Frauds, by aid of law, are continually perpetrated against Indians. I will give an illustration which occurred in Emmet county. An Indian widow living in Harbor Springs owned 7 acres of land in the center of Bay View, which is near the city of Petoskey. It was a very desirable location for building summer cottages for renting to people who come here by thousands to enjoy our summer climate. A white man, whom she thought her friend, told her he would arrange for her to sell it, as it was worth a good sum of money. So she signed what he told her was a power of attorney with two ignorant Indians as witnesses. But the paper was a warrantee deed and was recorded at once.

The next day the man sold it for $700 and left this town, and the poor widow never received one cent. This man had a beautiful residence on the Island of Mackinac, was living in luxury, and was very popular and influential among the people of the Island. Very soon after this he died suddenly, as though the hand of God struck him. Then the Indian woman with her children went to Mackinac and told his widow that her husband had owed her for the seven acres of land, she was told that the administrators would have to see about it, and that was the end of it. After waiting for years and years the Indian woman also passed away into the spirit land. There she probably saw the respected speculator, perhaps in the lake of fire, if that religious teaching is faithful and true.

In another case a widow was persuaded to sign a paper which was so ingeniously constructed that no one could understand the true import, unless in the habit of doing business by sharp practices. At her signature she received just one dollar. By this means she lost one of the best lots in Harbor Springs, with the house in which she lived, from which she was forcibly ejected by the sheriff of the county, and also half of her farm of 80 acres was taken from her.

These two cases are given simply as illustrations. There are too many to be told in this lecture, here in this part of the country, and in all places wherever Indians live. These poor people evidently had been taken advantage of, on account of their ignorance and timidity and inability to protect their rights as American citizens. I am of the opinion that before another generation shall pass away, there will be no land any where in the state of Michigan for the Ottawa and Chippewa that would be big enough to spread their blanket on which to sit. What will become of them then? They will be nothing but the scum of the earth; and slaves for other people to maintain, simply for their living.

I, Andrew J. Blackbird, meaning Mac-ka-te-pi-nas-sy in my native tongue, son of the Ottawa chief, have lived among the Ottawa and Chippewa tribes nearly 90 years, yet in all these years I have not witnessed one case of cruelty to have been consumated among them. All the cruelties that I ever heard related happened many, many years ago in their warfare; killing their enemies indiscriminately and scalping them; and every warrior keeping an account of the scalps he had taken from his enemies. So after he was dead the record of his bravery and courage was marked on a square timber and set up at the head of his grave. And he was honored as a brave man.

All the tortures I ever heard related could not be compared with the cruelties that I have heard occurred during the rebellion in the United States, at Fort Pillow and in the prisons and later, burning negroes.[4] All of this is done in the midst of civilization and Christianity. So who can boast of humanity toward our fellow creatures, when they are even more cruel than the savages on the plains of Dakota?

We Indians, although rude and dark, yet love to tread upon this broad land, where our forefathers' bones are now bleaching, although they were once the lords of the country. We are aware that our skins are dark, but our lives are just as precious and sweet to us as to any Caucasian race coming to this country. We have reason to believe that we have our senses and reason because we know when we are unhappy and when we are rejoicing. We feel love for our friends and pity for those who are suffering, even for strangers.

Years ago, before I knew anything about English A, B, C, I was walking along the shore of Lake Michigan, between Harbor Springs and Grand Traverse Bay, and I came across a white family, a man and wife and little child, sitting by a camp fire with no shelter and nothing about them but an old English blanket; what clothes they had were very poor. My heart throbbed with sorrow and sympathy for these poor people, but I had nothing to give them. I asked them as well as I knew how if they had anything to eat. The man said no, only one little fish caught in the shallow water. At these words I went to their little skiff; there was nothing in the boat but the old net, and no other equipment such as long ropes with which he might set his net out in deep water and catch fish fit to eat, such as white fish and mackinac [sic] trout, for Lake Michigan was full of such fish in those days, but they stayed mostly in the deep water.

Good heavens: thought I, these poor people are going to perish on this des-
olate shore. There was a small Indian settlement some distance away on the
shore where I thought of stopping. I told them to get in the boat and I would
go with them and bring them where they could find some relief. After much
coaxing we started. It was a very pleasant afternoon in the summer of 1844.
There was not a breath of wind on the lake; it was like a sea of glass. I rowed
very hard to come to the settlement before dark. We reached it just before sun-
down. Every one came to meet us and were very much surprised to see me
traveling with these poor people in this little boat. After I told them of their
starving condition, the Indian women cried out with sorrow and compassion;
they took this white child, who was almost naked, on their laps and wept and
kissed him, the same as they would their own. They did not have to wait long
before they were supplied with plenty of food such as Indians had; not anything very fine, but such as broiled white fish, potatoes, corn soup, well sea-
soned with wild meats, wild fruit, and maple sugar. I saw the Indian women go
to their wigwams and bring things to this poor white family. They took the child
and tore off its tattered rags and dressed it with nice, new clean little garments
from head to foot, so that it looked quite respectable. Also they contributed
enough blankets to keep them warm, even if they had to lie out in the coldest
night under the canopy of Heaven. I jumped high for joy to see the suffering
people so well cared for and provided for.

I tell you this little story, not as praiseworthy on my part, but simply to show
that the Indian in his wild state has just as kind and sympathetic a heart as any
civilized and christianized people in the world, even much more, in many respects. But, the Indian of today is not the Indian of the past. For their simplicity and dignity of character has been changed by abuse, poisoned by vice,
particularly by the introduction of the demon of alcohol, which is slowly and
surely wiping them off the face of the earth.

The Apache Indian [sic], Dr. Carlos Monte Zuma, says: "the Indians have
been cut off from the advantages of barbarism, and thus far have not profited
by civilization. This makes Indians of the present day more degraded than their
forefathers ever were."5

My Apache Indian brother gives a sad picture of our people, which I believe
to be correct and true, judging from my own personal knowledge. The greatest harm is done to us by the white man's poison of intoxicating liquor. In this
once quiet village, new saloons are added and keep on coming till they out-
number your denominational churches. In the former Indian reservation,
where is now the city of Cheboygan, there are about 40 whiskey shops and vile
places, but only 9 churches. This deadly poison is dealt out every day, even Sunday; so often, there is more drunkenness on the Sabbath than on week days.

It seems there is one saloon in our village which is most resorted to by the
Indian population. Now remember, these Indians are all professing to be Christians in the Roman Catholic denomination. There are three priests at the head,
beside other holy men and women.

Once as I was passing along in our main street I saw a great crowd of drunken

Indians in this particular saloon, mixed up with white men, cursing, swearing, and making terrible racket. Some Indians were standing at the door and I stopped and said to them: "What is the matter with our people always flocking to this saloon? Why not go to others as well as this one?" One of the fellows standing there, whom I knew to be a very strong Romanist, said to me: "Do you not know the man who keeps this whisky shop belongs to our religion?" I turned quickly to go, saying to myself: "Good Lord deliver us." The poor Indian who made this remark, four years ago, September 22, 1896, was stabbed to the heart, at his own door by a white man. What for? Simply in a mania of drunkenness. Was the white man punished for this murder? No. His white brothers of course let him off on his own evidence. When these poor people think they have sins enough, they go and confess to their priest and invariably receive absolution and forgiveness of sin. Then next would be the sacrament at the altar; this sacrament is in the form of a thin wafer, which every member of this denomination is made to believe is very God, Christ's flesh and blood, which the priest shoves into their mouths. A little while after, these persons will be seen standing at the bar drinking the intoxicating poison.

I feel very sad when I see my brother, white or Indian, fighting and staggering along the walk, till perhaps he falls down in the mud of the street. An officer of the village comes, who may be half drunk himself, and seizes him, uttering dreadful oaths which will make your very hair stand up like a porcupine's last quill, and drags his fellow drunkard to another place of improvement, established by white people, called the jail. There he is locked up till he has paid money for the benefit of the treasury of the town and for the benefit of those who keep the jail. It is a perfect shame on civilization and Christianity.

I have studied this Indian subject for years, in connection with Bible history. I have faced your christianized and unchristianized Indians in their own homes. After much study of this subject I come to this conclusion: that in order to civilize and christianize them, (and not only Indians, but every nation on the earth), long continued education is what is required, even a classical education, such as white people have. Five year's schooling is no more education for the Indian than for the white; it is only a whitewash education and it is dangerous. After teaching the children how to cipher a little, some geography, some grammar, and manual training, for 5 years in a boarding school, they say these children have graduated and they must be let loose, or sent adrift to go to their heathen parents. In a few years they become worse heathens than their parents, very much disposed to dissipation and degradation.

If these children were taken over the bridge, by giving them proper surroundings for living, they would soon find out that man is to live by the Lord's own appointed way, which is by the sweat of the brow.

Most certainly the government of the United States has been very liberal in establishing the so-called Industrial Schools for Indian children. It must take very much money to maintain these institutions, considering the cost of buildings, land upon which they stand, and other expenses, besides the salaries of the white managers and teachers.

If the Indian children who are now in these institutions should be distributed among the public institutions of this country, it is my humble opinion, the expense would be less and the benefits would be much greater. I do not mean the denominational, mission schools, but the common public schools and colleges where white children go.

I brought up this subject as long ago as 1855, in the Council of Detroit, before the Honorable Commissioner of Indian Affairs [George W. Manypenny], who was sent there to hold the Council with Michigan Indians. I advocated and urged common school education for our children, because there was at that time some more money set apart or appropriated for the education of our children, thousands of dollars a year, for ten years.[6] But what I said was of no use. All was disposed of as before. That is, our educational fund was given into the hands of missionaries who had already conducted mission stations for years among the Ottawas and Chippewas of Michigan. They were paid all this money, quarterly by the United States Government, for educating Indian children. Although we had tried this system already 20 years, at that time there was not one of our youth able to spell the simplest word in the English language. After spending enormous sums of money, (over $100,000), what good had it done?

Not any. It was just as though we never went to school at all.

What then constituted our education?

In reply, I would say, year after year we were catechised in our own language in the Romish doctrine of religion; which made us much more superstitious than ever before. These missionaries made very flattering reports yearly to the Government, saying they were teaching the children to read and write and to learn arithmetic and geography and grammar; and at the same time naming such teachers as "D. En-i-wes-kee," "Michael Ki-nee-ce," "Paul Kaw-go-no-ah," and others, all of whom were some of our own people. We knew them and we knew that they were not able nor qualified to teach such branches as they were represented as teaching; because they did not understand anything in the English language. They could only write their own Indian names probably. The reports said the children were taught to sew and to trim with porcupine quills. That was most absurd, for this kind of little art, trimming with porcupine quills, belongs exclusively to Indian people from unknown ages. If the missionaries knew anything of making this kind of ornaments, they learned from the Indians.

Therefore, it is plain that these reports were misrepresentations made by men who pretended to teach the Christian religion. By these reports the United States Government was also deceived, just the same as we were with regard to the disposition of our educational funds, during 20 years time, using this money contrary to the intention of the treaty stipulations. All this educational fund was only used to establish Romanism amongst the Ottawas and Chippewas of Michigan. Should any one doubt as to the veracity of these statements, I refer them to the Government reports of the Indian Bureau for 1851, and particularly to report No. 6, and pages 46, 57, and 58, by C. Bishop, P. P. S., of Detroit, and they will be convinced that this is the truth.

Therefore, in the Council of Detroit, which was concluded July 31, 1855, of which I was a member as chief of L'Arbre Croche, I urged that this new appropriation for our children's education should remain in the hands of the Government, to be used more for general education of Indian children; that is, to take the small children, the smaller the better, and distribute them in small lots, among public institutions of the United States to let them be educated among English speaking people; to sit down side by side with white children in their study of knowledge and science; to give them equal chances, equal privileges, every thing the same as white children; to come in contact, face to face, with all the phases of civilized life and become good citizens of this country. My conviction arose from the facts I have already told you. The objection has been made to this plan that it would be cruel to take children from their parents and homes in this way, but it is every where done by white people and is not considered cruel. My system would be that each child should have a friend, or kind guardian, to advise and give encouragement in the many difficulties that would naturally be presented to the child. Small difficulties to the children always appear to them like mountains, insurmountable; therefore, the children are sometimes greatly discouraged, if they have no friend to lead them.

The cure of ignorance must come by direct association with refined, intelligent, well-cultivated people, in order to be taken out of natural barbarism into true civilization. Perhaps some people have the idea that professing Christianity is the only necessary means of bringing about the true civilization of the aborigines of America. From my own personal observation, this is not the fact, because there are too many denominational religions, and it constantly makes these poor, ignorant people uncertain and disputing among themselves on account of denominational matters. They are not educated enough to understand that the mystery of the Kingdom of God is a spiritual and a new life. To illustrate this: one young Indian said he joined the Catholic religion for the sake of a new coat, and many converts are made to other sects in this way. Therefore, I am not an advocate of any particular denomination for them, but to help them and to encourage them as much as possible to feel that it is their special privilege to study, all the days of their lives, the sacred Bible which contains true wisdom; and to give obedience to the commandment of God and the religion of Jesus Christ, which is to love one another. "Whatsoever ye would that men should do to you, do ye even so to them, for this is the end of the law."[7]

When Indians are educated, help them and encourage them as much as possible, by placing them where they can exercise their ability according to the means and strength of their knowledge. After one generation has passed away, eventually all the old ones will be entirely gone, and consequently a new generation, who will be civilized, intelligent and cultivated, will represent the old race of America, once the home of their forefathers. In this way the difficulty of bringing the Indians into civilization will be done away with, as they will know how to live and work.

This plan has been my war-song, ever since 1855, but my days are being numbered and soon I will be no more among the living. But I pray to God that somebody may step in my footsteps and continue to sing the same, until every inhabitant, including the Government of the United States, would deign to listen to this war-song, and understand why there is so much difficulty in bringing the natives into the light of civilization. Perhaps some kind-hearted people may say that it would be very cruel to take these children away from their parents, for they would mourn for their children. But why cannot this be done among Indians as it is often done among white people?

But, again it may be objected, these Indian people are subjects, or wards of the government; therefore, they should be handled very carefully, and gradually and slowly brought into the light of civilization. There is an old story which goes this way: A saint, who found it necessary to cut the tail off his dog, was unwilling to give pain to the animal, therefore he concluded to take it off gradually and slowly, by cutting off a little at a time until it was the right length. I do not believe in this principle. But I say, cut at once the right length. It will be much better than cutting by slow degrees.[8]

There are many things yet to be said on this Indian problem, but I fear you may be tired of listening to this subject.

Notes

Obviously one of Blackbird's lectures, this selection was originally published as a twenty-two-page tract titled *The Indian Problem, from the Indian's Standpoint* (Philadelphia: National Indian Association, 1900). It closes with a separate doleful indictment of Indian-white relations titled "The Indian's Lament," followed by a list of the names of the chiefs who signed the treaty of 1855. The "Lament," which is very similar to Simon Pokagon's "The Red Man's Rebuke," was included earlier in his *History of the Ottawa and Chippewa Indians of Michigan* (Ypsilanti, MI: Ypsilanti Job Publishing House, 1887), 100–102. Reproduced in Bernd C. Peyer, ed., *The Elders Wrote: An Anthology of Early Prose by North American Indians, 1768–1931* (Berlin: Dietrich Reimer Verlag, 1982), 126–34. Blackbird's advocacy of public school education as the solution to the "Indian Problem" was in line with contemporary reform trends. During the final decade of the nineteenth century, off-reservation manual-labor schools such as Carlisle had become increasingly unpopular among reformers primarily because of the high costs involved. As one alternative, the federal government began in 1891 to offer public schools a $10 per capita payment for each Indian pupil enrolled. In his annual report for 1900 Secretary of Interior Ethan Allen Hitchcock suggested that a public school education for Indians only made sense in areas where coeducation with white students was practicable. On April 16, 1934, the government enacted the Johnson-O'Malley (JOM), a basic federal aid program specifically designed to provide funds to local off-reservation communities and other Indian-owned, tax exempt land areas where Indian tribal life was largely broken up and Indians were mixed with the general population. By 1928 the number of Indian students enrolled in public schools was substantially higher than in federal schools. See Margaret Connell Szasz, *Education and the American Indian: The Road to Self-Determination Since 1928* (2nd ed.; Albuquerque: University of New Mexico Press, 1977), 89–105.

1. In the course of the Iroquois Wars (1641–1701), the Odawas were dispersed westward from their ancestral lands in present-day Ontario. They eventually came into conflict with the Dakotas (Eastern Sioux) and retreated back to Michilimackinac (Michigan) around 1673, where they in turn clashed with the Mascoutens. The Hurons (Wendats), on the other hand, actually sought refuge among the Odawas after the Iroquois destroyed Huronia (near Lake Simcoe, Ontario) in 1649. See Helen H. Tanner, ed., *Atlas of Great Lakes Indian History* (Norman: University of Oklahoma Press, 1987), 29–35.

2. Article 5 of the Treaty with the Ottawas and Chippewas concluded in Detroit on July 31, 1855, dissolved the tribal governments of the Michigan communities. See Charles J. Kappler, comp. and ed., *Indian Affairs, Laws, and Treaties*, 7 vols. (Washington, D.C.: Government Printing Office, 1903–1904), 2: 725–31.

3. Carlos Montezuma used this illustrative anecdote on numerous occasions. He also liked to attribute his own success to public school education. Blackbird obviously had access to some of Carlos Montezuma's early publications such as "From an Apache Camp to a Chicago Medical School: The Story of Carlos Montezuma's Life as Told by Himself," *Red Man* 8 (July–August 1888): 3; or *The Indian of Tomorrow: An Address by Dr. Carlos Montezuma and The Indian of Yesterday: The Early Life of Dr. Carlos Montezuma Written by Himself* (Chicago: Published for the National Women's Christian Temperance Union, 1888). Blackbird's title also calls to mind Montezuma's "The Indian Problem from the Indian's Point of View," *Red Man* 15 (February, 1898): 1–2 and *The Indian Problem from an Indian's Standpoint* (Chicago: Chicago Indian Association, 1898). This was originally an address delivered by Montezuma at the Fortnightly Club of Chicago on February 10, 1898.

4. Following the Battle of Fort Pillow on April 12, 1864, Confederate troops were accused of perpetrating a massacre on the 292 African American infantrymen there, only sixty-two of whom survived. The battle subsequently became a rallying cry for Union troops. By the last two decades of the nineteenth century, lynching became an institutionalized method among southern whites to intimidate African Americans and maintain white supremacy.

5. Although he preferred to refer to himself as a "full-blooded Apache," Montezuma was actually a Mohave-Apache, or Yavapai.

6. Article 2 of the Treaty of 1855, which Blackbird signed as a witness, provided the sum of $80,000 in ten equal installments for educational purposes.

7. Matthew 7:12.

8. Montezuma related the same story in *Let My People Go* (Chicago: Hawthorne Press, 1915).

BIOGRAPHY

Andrew Jackson Blackbird (Odawa, ca. 1810–1900), or Mack-e-te-be-nessy, was born in the L'Arbre Croche area (now Harbor Springs, Michigan), the youngest of ten children of an Odawa council speaker also named Blackbird. At the age of fourteen Andrew Blackbird moved to Wisconsin, where he resided among white farmers for some time before becoming the assistant government blacksmith at Grand Traverse, an Ojibwe-Odawa community to the south of L'Arbre Croche. In 1845 Blackbird enrolled at Twinsburg Institute in Ohio, where he studied for four years without graduating. He then returned to L'Arbre Croche and devoted himself to the promotion of public school education and citizenship for his people. Blackbird participated as a witness in the treaty concluded at Detroit between the United States and the Odawa and Ojibwe communities of the Michigan area on July 31, 1855. Under this treaty their tribal organizations were dissolved in exchange for annuities, individual allotments, and citizenship. Sometime after 1855 Blackbird renounced Catholicism and became a Protestant, serving as interpreter at the newly established Protestant mission at L'Arbre Croche. On the recommendation of Lewis Cass, first governor of Michigan and Secretary of War under Andrew Jackson, Blackbird attended Yipsilanti State Normal School (now Eastern Michigan University) for two years, again failing to graduate. He then returned to L'Arbre Croche, now known as Little Traverse, where he married a white woman of English descent. He served in a variety of government functions, such as interpreter at the Mackinac Agency, auxiliary prosecutor of Civil War veterans' claims, and postmaster of Little Traverse. When Little Traverse was incorporated as the city of Harbor Springs in 1880, Blackbird lost his position as postmaster and turned to lecturing and writing on Indian subjects for a living. In 1887 he published *History of the Ottawa and Chippewa Indians of Michigan,* which was revised and reprinted in 1897, and a polemic pamphlet titled *The Indian Problem, from the Indian's Standpoint* in 1900. The post office in which Blackbird served as postmaster for eleven years now houses the Andrew J. Blackbird Museum.

Selected Publications of Andrew Jackson Blackbird

History of the Ottawa and Chippewa Indians of Michigan. Ypsilanti, Mich.: Ypsilanti Job Publishing House, 1887; revised as *Complete Both Early and Late History of the Ottawa and Chippewa Indians, of Michigan, a Grammar of Their Language, Personal and Family History of Author.* Harbor Springs, Mich.: Babcock & Darling, 1897. Reprinted, Petoskey, Mich.: Little Traverse Historical Society, 1977.

The Indian Problem, from the Indian's Standpoint. Philadelphia: National Indian Association, 1900.

Selected Secondary Sources

Feest, Christian F. "Andrew J. Blackbird and Ottawa History." *Yumtzilob* 8, no. 2 (1996): 114–23.

Jaskoski, Helen. "'A Terrible Sickness Among Them': Smallpox and Stories of the Frontier." In *Early Native American Writing: New Critical Essays,* edited by Helen Jaskoski. New York: Cambridge University Press, 1996: 136–57.

MacLeod, D. Peter. "The Anishinabeg Point of View: The History of the Great Lakes Region to 1800 in Nineteenth-Century Mississauga, Odawa, and Ojibwa Historiography." *Canadian Historical Review* 73, no. 2 (1992): 194–210.

TRANSREGIONAL VOICES

THE SOCIETY OF AMERICAN INDIANS

REPORT BY COLONEL PARKER ON INDIAN AFFAIRS

Ely S. Parker (1867)

Headquarters Armies of the United States,

Washington, D.C., January 24, 1867.

General: In compliance with your request, I have the honor to submit the following-proposed plan for the establishment of a permanent and perpetual peace, and settling all matters of differences between the United States and the various Indian tribes.

I am, very respectfully, your obedient servant,

E. S. PARKER, *Colonel and aide-de-camp.*

General U. S. Grant,

Commanding armies of the United States.

First. The retransfer of the Indian bureau from the Interior Department back to the War Department, or military branch of the government, where it originally belonged, until within the last few years.[1]

The condition and disposition of all the Indians west of the Mississippi river, as developed in consequence of the great and rapid influx of immigration by reason of the discovery of the precious metals throughout the entire west, renders it of the utmost importance that military supervision should be extended over the Indians. Treaties have been made with a very large number of the tribes, and generally reservations have been provided as homes for them.[2] Agents appointed from civil life have generally been provided to protect their lives and property, and to attend to the prompt and faithful observance of treaty stipulations. But as the hardy pioneer and adventurous miner advanced into the inhospitable regions occupied by the Indians, in search of the precious metals, they found no rights possessed by the Indians that they were bound to respect. The faith of treaties solemnly entered into were totally disregarded, and Indian territory wantonly violated. If any tribe remonstrated against the violation of their natural and treaty rights, members of the tribe were inhumanly shot down and the whole treated as mere dogs. Retaliation generally followed, and bloody Indian wars have been the consequence, costing many lives and much treasure.

In all troubles arising in this manner the civil agents have been totally powerless to avert the consequences, and, when too late, the military have been called in to protect the whites and punish the Indians, when if, in the beginning, the military had the supervision of the Indians, their rights, would not have been improperly molested, or if disturbed in their quietude by any lawless whites, a prompt and summary check to any further aggressions could have been given. In cases where the government promises the Indians the peaceable and quiet possession of a reservation, and precious metals are discovered or found to exist upon it, the military alone can give the Indians the needed

257

protection and keep the adventurous miner from encroaching upon the Indians until the government has come to some understanding with them. In such cases the civil agent is absolutely powerless.

Most of Indian treaties contain stipulations for the payment annually to Indians of annuities, either in money or goods, or both, and agents are appointed to make these payments whenever government furnishes them the means. I know of no reason why officers of the army could not make all these payments as well as civilians. The expense of agencies would be saved, and, I think, the Indians would be more honestly dealt by. An officer's honor and interest is at stake, and impels him to discharge his duty honestly and faithfully, while civil agents have none of those incentives, the ruling passion with them being generally to avoid all trouble and responsibility, and to make as much money as possible out of their offices.

In the retransfer of this bureau I would provide for the complete abolishment of the system of Indian traders, which, in my opinion, is a great evil to Indian communities. I would make government the purchaser of all articles usually brought in by Indians, giving them a. fair equivalent for the same in money or goods at cost prices. In this way it would be an easy matter to regulate the sale or issue of arms and ammunition to Indians, a question which of late has agitated the minds of the civil and military authorities. If the entry of large numbers of Indians to any military post is objectionable, it can easily be arranged that only limited numbers shall be admitted daily.

By an act approved March 10, 1802, it was made the duty of military agents "to purchase, receive, and forward to their proper destination all military stores and other articles for the troops in their respective departments, and all goods and annuities for the Indians, which they may be directed to purchase, or which shall be ordered into their care by the Department of War." In the retransfer of the Indian bureau, this act, so far as it relates to the Indians, could be revived, as well as the act of June 30, 1834, which authorizes "the President to require any military officer of the United States to execute the duties of Indian agent."

With reference to the discontinuance of the present Indian trading system, the arguments set forth in President Jefferson's confidential message, dated January 18, 1803, seem more cogent now than at that time. He says: "The Indian tribes residing within the limits of the United States have, for a considerable time, been growing more and more uneasy at the constant diminution of the territory they occupy, although effected by their own voluntary sales; and the policy has long been gaining strength with them of refusing absolutely still further sales on any conditions; insomuch that at this time it hazards their friendship and excites dangerous jealousies and perturbations in their minds to make any overture for the purchase of the smallest portions of their land. A very few tribes only are not yet obstinately in these dispositions. In order peaceably to counteract this policy of theirs, and to provide an extension of territory which the rapid increase of our numbers will call for, two measures are deemed expedient: First, to encourage them to abandon hunting, to apply to the raising stock, to agriculture, and domestic manufactures, and thereby prove to themselves that less land and labor will maintain them in this better than in their former mode of living. The extensive forests necessary in the hunting life will then become useless, and they will see the advantage in exchanging them for the means of improving their farms and of increasing their domestic comforts. Secondly, to multiply trading houses among them, and place within their reach those things which will contribute more to their domestic comfort than the possession of extensive but uncultivated wilds. Experience and reflection will develop to them the wisdom of exchanging what they can spare and we want for what we can spare and they want. In leading them thus to agriculture, to manufactures, and civilization, in bringing together their and our settlements, and in preparing them ultimately to participate in the benefits of our government, I trust and believe we are acting for their greatest good. At these trading-houses we have pursued the principles of the act of Congress which directs that the commerce shall be carried on liberally, and requires only that the capital stock shall not be diminished. We consequently undersell private traders, foreign and domestic; drive them from the competition, and thus, with the good will of the Indians, rid ourselves of a description of men who are constantly endeavoring to excite in the Indian mind suspicions, fears, and irritations towards us. A letter now enclosed, shows the effect of our competition on the operations of the traders, while the Indians, perceiving the advantage of purchasing from us, are soliciting generally our establishment of trading-houses among them."[3]

The Indian department has increased to such magnitude since this was written that every argument advanced has a tenfold more force than at that date. And had the policy then advocated been adopted and steadily pursued to this day, there is no doubt that great good would have resulted, bloody wars been averted, and many valuable lives saved. It is believed that a return now to the wise and humane measures advocated by the fathers of the republic would still result beneficially to the government and the Indian races. Some definite and permanent policy should be adopted, and circumstances made to bend to its establishment.

In 1793 General Washington, then President, remarks in a special message in Congress, that "next to a vigorous execution of justice on the violators of peace, the establishment of commerce with the Indian nations, on behalf of the United States, is most likely to conciliate their attachment. But it ought to be conducted without fraud, without extortion, with constant and plentiful supplies; with a ready market for the commodities of the Indians, and a stated price for what they give in payment and receive in exchange. Individuals will not pursue such a traffic unless they be allured by the hope of profit; but it will be enough for the United States to be reimbursed only."

It is greatly to be regretted that this beneficent and humane policy had not been adhered to, for it is a fact not to be denied, that at this day Indian trading licenses are very much sought after, and when once obtained, although it may be for a limited period, the lucky possessor is considered as having already made his fortune. The eagerness also with which Indian agencies are sought after, and large fortunes made by the agents in a few years, notwithstanding the inadequate salary given, is presumptive evidence of frauds against the Indians and the government.

Many other reasons might be suggested why the Indian department should altogether be under military control, but a familiar knowledge of the practical workings of the present system would seem to be the most convincing proofs of the propriety of the measure. It is pretty generally advocated by those most familiar with our Indian relations, and so far as I know, the Indians themselves desire it. Civil officers are not usually respected by the tribes, but they fear and regard the military, and will submit to their counsels, advice, and dictation, when they would not listen to a civil agent.

Second. The next measure I would suggest is the passage by Congress of a plan of territorial government for the Indians, as was submitted last winter, or a similar one.[4] When once passed, it should remain upon the statute books as the permanent and settled policy of the government. The boundaries of the Indian territory or territories should be well defined by metes and bounds, and should remain inviolate from settlement by any except Indians and government employees.

The subject of the improvement and civilization of the Indians, and the maintenance of peaceful relations with them, has engaged the serious consideration of every administration since the birth of the American republic; and, if I recollect aright, President Jefferson was the first to inaugurate the policy of the removal of the Indians from the States to the country west of the Mississippi; and President Monroe, in furtherance of this policy, recommended that the Indians be concentrated, as far as was practicable, and civil governments established for them, with schools for every branch of instruction in literature and the arts of civilized life.[5] The plan of removal was adopted as the policy of the government, and, by treaty stipulations, affirmed by Congress; lands were set apart for tribes removing into the western wilds, and the faith of a great nation pledged that the homes selected by the Indians would be and remain their homes forever, unmolested by the hand of the grasping and avaricious white man; and, in some cases, the government promised that the Indian homes and lands should never be incorporated within the limits of any new State that might be organized. How the pledges so solemnly given and the promises made were kept, the history of the western country can tell. It is presumed that humanity dictated the original policy of the removal and concentration of the Indians in the west to save them from threatened extinction. But to-day, by reason of the immense augmentation of the American population, and the extension of their settlements throughout the entire west, covering both slopes of the Rocky mountains, the Indian races are more seriously threatened with a speedy extermination than ever before in the history of the country.[6] And, however much such a deplorable result might be wished for by some, it seems to me that the honor of a Christian nation and every sentiment of humanity dictate that no pains he spared to avert such an appalling calamity befalling a portion of the human race. The establishment of all the Indians upon any one territory is perhaps impracticable, but numbers of them can, without doubt, be consolidated in separate districts of country, and the same system of government made to apply to each. By the concentration of tribes, although in several and separate districts, government can more readily control them and more economically press and carry out plans for their improvement and civilization, and a better field be offered for philanthropic aid and Christian instruction. Some system of this kind has, at different periods in the history of our government, been put forward, but never successfully put into execution.[7] A renewal of the attempt, with proper aids, it seems to me cannot fail of success.

Third. The passage by Congress of an act authorizing the appointment of an inspection board, or commission, to hold office during good behavior, or until the necessity for their services is terminated by the completion of the retransfer of the Indian bureau to the War Department. It shall be the duty of this board to examine the accounts of the several agencies, see that every cent due the Indians is paid to them promptly as may be promised in treaties, and that proper and suitable goods and implements of agriculture are delivered to them, when such articles are due; to make semi-annual reports, with such suggestions as, in their judgment, might seem necessary to the perfect establishment of a permanent and friendly feeling between the people of the United States and the Indians.

This commission could undoubtedly be dispensed with in a few years, but, the results of their labors might be very important and beneficial, not only in supervising and promptly checking the delinquencies of incompetent and dishonest agents, but it would be a most convincing proof to the Indians' mind that the government was disposed to deal honestly and fairly by them. Such a commission might, indeed, be rendered wholly unnecessary if Congress would consent to the next and fourth proposition which I submit in this plan.

Fourth. The passage of an act authorizing the appointment of a permanent Indian commission, to be a mixed commission, composed of such white men as possessed in a large degree the confidence of their country, and a number of the most reputable educated Indians, selected from different tribes. The entire commission might be composed of ten members, and, if deemed advisable, might be divided so that five could operate north and five south of a given line, but both to be governed by the same general instructions, and impressing upon the Indians the same line of governmental policy. It shall be made their duty to visit all the Indian tribes within the limits of the United States, whether, to do this, it requires three, five, or ten years. They shall hold talks with them, setting forth the great benefits that would result to them from a permanent peace with the whites, from their abandonment of their nomadic mode of life, and adopting agricultural and pastoral pursuits, and the habits and modes of civilized communities. Under the directions of the President the commission shall explain to the various tribes the advantages of their consolidation upon some common territory, over which Congress shall have extended the aegis of good, wise, and wholesome laws for their protection and perpetuation.

It would be wise to convince the Indians of the great power and number of the whites; that, they cover the whole land, to the north, south, east, and west of them. I believe they could easily understand that although this country was once wholly inhabited by Indians, the tribes, and many of them once powerful, who occupied the countries now constituting the States east of the Mississippi, have, one by one, been exterminated in their abortive attempts to stem the western march of civilization.[8]

They could probably be made to comprehend that the waves of population and civilization are upon every side of them; that it is too strong for them to re-sist; and that, unless they fall in with the current of destiny as it rolls and surges around them, they must succumb and be annihilated by its overwhelming force. In consequence of the gradual extinction of the Indian races, and the failure of almost every plan heretofore attempted for the amelioration of their condition, and the prolongation of their national existence, and also because they will not abandon their savage tastes and propensities, it has of late years become somewhat common, not only for the press, but in the speeches of men of intelligence, and some occupying high and responsible positions, to advo-cate the policy of their immediate and absolute extermination. Such a propo-sition, so revolting to every sense of humanity and Christianity, it seems to me, could not for one moment be entertained by any enlightened nation. On the contrary, the honor of the national character and the dictates of a sound policy, guided by the principles of religion and philanthropy, would urge the adoption of a system to avert the extinction of a people, however unenlightened they may be. The American government can never adopt the policy of a total ex-termination of the Indian race within her limits, numbering, perhaps, less than four hundred thousand, without a cost of untold treasure and lives of her people, besides, exposing herself to the abhorrence and censure of the entire civilized world.

The commission shall assure the tribes that the white man does not want the Indian exterminated from the face of the earth, but will live with him as good neighbors, in peace and quiet. The value of maintaining friendly and brotherly relations among themselves is to be urged upon the tribes, and its continual discussion to be made one of the permanent duties of the commission. They are also to urge constantly the propriety, necessity, and benefit to result from their concentration in certain districts of the country, there to live peaceably as members of the same family, as brothers and friends having the same inter-ests and the same destiny. I am free to admit that the most difficult task for the commission would be to obtain the consent of the Indians to consolidate, by removing into certain defined districts. But by constantly keeping the subject before them, and by yearly visitations, the wisdom and humanity of the policy would gradually develop in the Indian mind, and one by one the tribes would come into the measure, and the whole policy be adopted. There would be very many prejudices to combat and overcome. As members of the great human family, they know and feel that they are endowed with certain rights. They possess fair intellectual faculties. They entertain the most ardent love for the largest liberty and independence. Originally their greatest desire was to be left undisturbed by the overflowing white population that was quietly but surely pressing to overwhelm them, and they have been powerless to divert or stem the current of events. They saw their hunting grounds and fisheries disappear before them. They have been reduced to limits too narrow for the hunter state, and naturally many of them at times have sought by violence the redress of what they conceived to be great and heinous wrongs against their natural rights. Though ignorant, in the common acceptation of the term, they are a proud people, and quickly resent the least suspicion of dictation in the government of their actions, come from what quarter it may. Most of the tribes are eminently subject to the influence and control of interested, unprincipled, and crafty individuals, who, to retain their influence and power, would oppose the idea of a consolidation of the tribes, because now they are something, while under the new order of things they might be nothing. They will pander to the prejudices of their people by preaching the sanctimoniousness of their separate creation, nationality, and customs, and claim that as their Creator made them, so they must ever remain. They flatter the pride of the Indian mind. Their reasoning is specious, but yet it is all sophistry.

To combat and overcome such influences the commission would have much labor to perform. It may be imagined that a serious obstacle would be presented to the removal of the Indians from their homes on account of the love they bear for the graves of their ancestors. This, indeed, would be the least and last objection that would be raised by any tribe. Much is said in the books about the reverence paid by Indians to the dead, and their antipathy to deserting their ancestral graves. Whatever may have been the customs for the dead in ages gone by, and whatever pilgrimages may have been made to the graves of their loved and distinguished dead, none of any consequence exists at the present day. They leave their dead without any painful regrets or the shedding of tears. And how could it be otherwise with a people who have such indefinite and vague ideas of a future state of existence, and to my mind it is unnatural to assume or suppose that the wild and untutored Indian can have more attachment for his home, or love for the graves of his ancestors, than the civilized and enlightened Christian.[9]

The appointment of a number of reputable educated Indians upon this commission is suggested because they are familiar with the best modes of communicating with the tribes, whether friendly or unfriendly; they are familiar with the peculiarities of the Indian mind, and know how to make the desired impression upon it, and it would add greatly to the confidence of the tribes in the earnestness, sincerity, and humanity of the government.

The commission shall be required to invite and hear all complaints from the Indians, transmit them verbatim to Washington, and communicate to the Indians the answers thereto. If the complaints be against any agent or citizen of the United States, such agent or citizen shall be furnished with a correct copy of the complaint, an answer thereto obtained, when all the papers in the case shall be sent to Washington, a prompt decision given upon the same, and returned to the commission for promulgation to the parties interested. In my opinion nothing could occur that would tend more strongly to advance the happiness of the Indians, and attach them firmly to the United States government, than the realization of the benefits of an impartial dispensation of justice among themselves and between them and the whites. It has been lately suggested that Indian agents be vested with magisterial powers to administer and dispense justice among the Indians, and between Indians and the whites. Such a plan does not seem to me practicable, because the agent would be absolutely powerless to enforce his judgments, not only against the Indians, but against the whites. If, however, the Indian business is retransferred to the military branch of the government, officers acting as Indian agents could act efficiently as magisterial officers, because they could always have troops to enforce their decrees, and such a measure I should deem very desirable, and I think would result in the greatest good in checking mischief, by summarily punishing lawlessness and crime, whether committed by whites or Indians.

Most of the tribes would have to be visited several times by the commission before the Indian mind would come to a conclusion upon the matters and things that might from time to time be submitted to them, and the government and people of the United States would be compelled to exercise the Christian virtue of patience, until the aboriginal mind was fully prepared and ripened to adopt the plans of the government, when general councils of tribes could be called and a permanent union or confederation of peace formed among themselves and the United States, and they be made to settle down upon lands within certain defined and permanent limits and bounds, where ample aid and protection could be easily and economically afforded them.

No suggestions have been made regarding the disposition of lands at present held or occupied by the tribes, or their annuities, or the amount and kind of aid they ought to receive when concentrated within defined districts, it being deemed premature to discuss such questions now, as circumstances and future legislation will probably better determine them.

This project, at first blush, may seem to be devised on too extensive a scale, and involving too much expense for an experiment. I cannot so regard it. On the contrary, I believe it to be more economical than any other plan that could be suggested. A whole army of Indian agents, traders, contractors, jobbers, and hangers-on would be dispensed with, and from them would come the strongest opposition to the adoption of this plan, as it would effectually close to them the corrupt sources of their wealth.

In 1865 the Secretary of the Interior estimated the cost to the government of maintaining each regiment of troops operating against the Indians on the frontier at two millions of dollars per annum, and that only a few hundred Indians had been killed. By a recent publication in the newspapers (but whether true or not I cannot say) it was stated that the cost of operations against the Indians during the past year was thirty millions of dollars; that a certain number only of Indians had been killed, each life costing the government sixty thousand dollars. Though the cost of carrying on a war is now pretty will understood in this country, the expense of an Indian war extending along a frontier of thousands of miles cannot be safely estimated.[10] The expense of the Florida Indian war, against a few Indians, who long refused to leave a country hardly inhabitable by civilized man, it is known, cost millions of treasure, and many valuables lives.[11]

The expense of this entire plan for establishing peace, saving lives, making every route of travel across the continent entirely safe, civilizing and perpetuating the Indian race, and developing immense tracts of country now held by hostile bands of Indians, would be but a mere tithe to the amount now annually paid by the government for these purposes. There are plenty of troops already in the Indian country, and after the commission has commenced its labors hostilities would very soon cease. Yet the military would have to be maintained in the country until the labors of the commission were fairly and fully developed, and, if successful, the troops could be moved into or contiguous to the Indian districts, to protect them from frauds and impositions, to maintain them in their just and legal rights, and to act as the magisterial agents of the government. The benefits to result from even a partial success of this plan would, to my mind, justify the government in attempting it, especially as it seems so much more economical than the prosecution of the present Indian policy.

E. S. PARKER.

Notes

"Letter from the Secretary of War, addressed to Mr. Schenck, chairman of the Committee on Military Affairs, transmitting a report by Colonel Parker on Indian affairs," House of Representatives, 39th Cong., 2nd sess., Misc. Doc. No. 37 (Washington, D.C.: Government Printing Office, 1867). This early report by Parker outlined some of the major axioms of what became known as Grant's Peace (or Quaker) Policy, 1867–82.

1. In order to cope with the ever-growing task of managing Indian-white relations, Secretary of War John C. Calhoun established a special unit within the War Department in 1824, the Bureau of Indian Affairs (BIA), later expanded as the Office of Indian Affairs (OIA) in 1832 and finally transferred to the new Department of Interior in 1849. There was a strong movement among American administrators between 1867 and 1879 to relocate the OIA in the War Department. As late as 1890, about half of the agencies were still headed by army officers in spite of earlier federal prohibitions. See Theodor W. Taylor, *The Bureau of Indian Affairs* (Boulder, Colo.: Westview Press, 1984). On the efforts to return the OIA to the War Department see Henry E. Fritz, *The Movement for Indian Assimilation, 1860–1890* (Philadelphia: University of Pennsylvania Press, 1963), 120–34; Loring B. Priest, *Uncle Sam's Stepchildren: The Reformation of the United States Indian Policy, 1865–1887* (New Brunswick, N.J.: Rutgers University Press, 1942), 15–27; and Francis Paul Prucha, *American Indian Policy in Crisis: Christian Reformers and the Indian, 1865–1900* (Norman: University of Oklahoma Press, 1976), 72–102.

2. Recommendations to settle Indians on reservations were first made public in Commissioner of Indian Affairs William Medill's annual report for 1848, and then

officially promoted with the passage of an Indian appropriation act in 1851, which also enlarged the Indian Office. Reservations and annuities were negotiated in a series of treaties concluded with California Indians during the early 1850s, but these failed ratification in the Senate. Nevertheless, by 1860 Indian reservations had been established in California, Oregon, and Texas, as well as in the territories of Washington, New Mexico, Nebraska, and Kansas. After the Civil War the policy was extended to the Southwest and the Great Plains. See George Harwood Phillips, *Indians and Indian Agents: The Origins of the Reservation System in California, 1849–1852* (Norman: University of Oklahoma Press, 1997); Robert A. Trennert, Jr., *Alternative to Extinction: Federal Policy and the Beginnings of the Reservation System, 1846–1851* (Philadelphia: Temple University Press, 1975); Robert M. Utley, *The Indian Frontier of the American West, 1846–1890* (Albuquerque: University of New Mexico Press, 1984), 31–63.

3. Uncontrolled trade, especially involving the sale of alcohol, was regarded as one of the main sources of frontier violence by early American administrators. Accordingly, Congress passed the first of several Indian Trade and Intercourse Laws in 1790 and created the federal factory system in 1796. The latter, abolished in 1822, sought to place all trade under the direct control of the government. See Francis P. Prucha, *American Indian Policy in the Formative Years: The Indian Trade and Intercourse Acts, 1790–1834* (1962; repr., Lincoln: University of Nebraska Press, 1970).

4. The idea of forming a separate Indian state or territory was not new. Several proposals to that effect had been brought before Congress since the Louisiana Purchase of 1803, the latest being the Harlan Bill of 1865. Similar notions had already been expressed in writing by Elias Boudinot, John Ridge, and George Copway; see contributions in this anthology. "Indian Territory" is a misleading term in this context as it never attained official territorial status. With the passage of the Enabling Act of 1906 it was finally joined with Oklahoma Territory to form the state of Oklahoma. See Annie H. Abel, "Proposals for an Indian State, 1778–1878," *Annual Report of the American Historical Association for the Year 1907* (Washington, D.C.: Government Printing Office, 1908), I: 87–104.

5. The policy of removal was given brief consideration by John Adams and then taken up again by Thomas Jefferson following the Louisiana Purchase of 1803. Lobbying for total removal began to take effect during the Madison administration (1808–1812), was officially endorsed by James Monroe in a special report to Congress in 1825, and pushed halfheartedly by John Quincy Adams before it was finally written into law under the presidency of Andrew Jackson on May 28, 1830. See Annie H. Abel, *The History of Events Resulting in Indian Consolidation West of the Mississippi* (1908; repr., New York: AMS Press, 1972); Bernard W. Sheehan, *Seeds of Extinction: Jeffersonian Philanthropy and the American Indian* (New York: W. W. Norton and Co., 1974).

6. By the 1840s nearly five million settlers had crossed the Appalachian watershed into Indian lands, a dozen new states were added to the original thirteen, and one of the greatest real estate transactions in American history was consummated. See Michael P. Rogin, *Fathers and Children: Andrew Jackson and the Subjugation of the American Indian* (New York: Alfred A. Knopf, 1975).

7. Between the 1840s and 1870s there was a strong movement among administrators to consolidate all Indian tribes in two to five large reservations, primarily in Indian Territory. Though officially abandoned after 1879, it still found a few

advocates as late as 1885. See Brian Dippie, *The Vanishing American: White Attitudes and U.S. Indian Policy* (Middleton, Conn.: Wesleyan University Press, 1982), 149–54; Priest, *Uncle Sam's Stepchildren*, 3–14; Prucha, *American Indian Policy in Crisis*, 104, 113–19.

8. Congress established a Board of Indian Commissioners on April 10, 1869. The president was to nominate nine to ten voluntary philanthropists (not including Indians as Parker recommended) who were to exercise joint control with the secretary of the interior in disbursing Indian appropriations. They were also expected to investigate and make recommendations regarding all aspects of Indian affairs. In its first report for that year, the Board urged the concentration of Indians on small reservations, division of tribal lands in severalty, discouragement of tribal relations, abandoning of annuities, abolition of the treaty system, establishment of schools to teach Indian children English, nomination of teachers and establishment of missions by religious bodies, and automatic citizenship for the Five Civilized Tribes. This widely ranging list of proposals would serve as a guideline for federal Indian policy until the 1920s. In 1874 the original board members resigned because the secretary of interior rejected their suggestion to establish an independent Indian Department. Nevertheless, the board resumed its duties under new appointees and continued its operations until it was finally terminated in 1933. See Henry E. Fritz, "The Board of Indian Commissioner of Indian Affairs and Ethnocentric Reform, 1878–1893," in Jane F. Smith and Robert M. Kvasnicka, eds., *Indian-White Relations: A Persistent Paradox* (Washington, D.C.: Howard University Press, 1976), 57–78

9. Parker's views on this particular subject have proven to be misguided. Continued Indian concern for the burial grounds of ancestors finally led to the passage of the Native American Graves Protection and Repatriation Act on November 16, 1990. This law protects Native grave sites and stipulates that museums, universities, and agencies must make inventories of human remains and associated funerary objects in cooperation with tribal governments and Indian religious leaders. Tribes are to have access to these and may request repatriation.

10. On March 3, 1865, Congress created a Joint Special Committee to investigate Indian affairs. It submitted a report on January 26, 1867, estimating that it would cost thirty million dollars and require an army of ten thousand men to be in the field for several years to subdue the Plains Indians. The ongoing Sioux War (Red Cloud's War, 1866–68) over the Bozeman Trail and the recent annihilation of a cavalry detachment under Captain William J. Fetterman on December 21, 1866, had led the committee to conclude that it was cheaper on the long run to feed and "civilize" the Plains Indians than to fight them. See William T. Hagan, "United States Indian Policies, 1860–1900," in Wilcomb E. Washburn, ed., *Handbook of North American Indians*, vol. 4, *History of Indian-White Relations* (Washington, D.C.: Smithsonian Institution, 1988), 51–65; David A. Nichols, *Lincoln and the Indians: Civil War and Politics* (Columbia: University of Missouri Press, 1978), 76–118.

11. The Second Seminole War (1835–42) was one of the costliest campaigns against Indians for the United States.

LETTER TO HARRIET MAXWELL CONVERSE

Ely S. Parker (n.d.)

. . . To you though I will confess, and you must not abuse or betray my confidence, that I have little or no faith in the American Christian civilization methods of treating the Indians of this country. It has not been honest, pure or sincere. Black deception, damnable frauds and persistent oppression has been its characteristics, and its religion today is, that the only good Indian is a dead one. Guns stand, loaded to the muzzle, ready to prove this lie. Another creed under which the Indian is daily sinking deeper into the quagmire of oppression is that "might makes right," and on it is based the fallacy transferred or transposed from the Negro to the Indian "that the Indian has no rights which the white man is bound to respect." The matter of Indian civilization is assuming the character of Joseph's coat—of many colors—the most conspicuous and prominent just now, being the compulsory allotment of lands and enforced citizenship, nolens volens. All other methods of dispossessing the Indian of every vested and hereditary right having failed, compulsion must now be resorted to, a sure, certain death to the poor Indians. Misguided Indian philanthropists tell us that absorption of the aboriginal race into the great body politic is their only hope of salvation. I see nothing in the experiment but an accelerated motor for the absorption of the Indian race back into the bosom of Mother Earth. The only salvation for the Indians, and the only solution of the great Indian problem is to give them secular and industrial schools in abundance. There is land enough on this portion God's footstool called America for the Indian and the white man to live upon without jostling and exemplifying the Kilkenny cat game.[1] The Indian wishes to be left alone in his wigwam. His good life is bound up and interwoven with his land, his women and his children . . . The Indians, as a body, are deadly opposed to the scheme, for they see in it too plainly the certain and speedy dissolution of their tribal and national organizations. It is very evident to my mind that all schemes, to apparently serve the Indians, are only plausible pleas put out to hoodwink the civilized world that every thing possible has been done to save this race from total annihilation, and to wipe out the stain on the American name for its treatment of the aboriginal population . . . But I am writing an uncalled for thesis on Indian rights and wrongs, an almost inexhaustible theme, so I drop it since no good can result to continue it—Education [should] be made first above all. Other good things will follow.

Notes

Ely Samuel Parker to Harriet Maxwell Converse, n.d., in Ely Samuel Parker Papers, Edward E. Ayer Collection, MS 673, Newberry Library, Chicago. Excerpted with permission of the Newberry Library. Parker met poet and magazine reporter

Harriett Maxwell Converse (1836–1903) in 1881 and developed a close friendship with her. With Parker as informant and advisor, Converse wrote extensively about the Six Nations and became involved in their behalf in a campaign to obtain citizenship and remunerations from the Ogden Land Company. Converse was adopted into the Snipe Clan and made a "chief" of the Six Nations in 1891. Parker and Converse maintained a regular correspondence for fourteen years, often addressing each other as "Snipe" and "Wolf" with reference to their clan membership. Most of this correspondence is found in the Henry E. Huntington Library and Art Gallery. Converse obviously reawakened Parker's interest in Indian affairs and caused him to reconsider his past views. Arthur C. Parker edited Converse's collection of essays in *Myths and Legends of the New York State Iroquois* (Albany: University of the State of New York, 1908). See William H. Armstrong, *Warrior in Two Camps: Ely S. Parker, Union General and Seneca Chief* (Syracuse, N.Y.: Syracuse University Press, 1978), 174–78.

1. A limerick involving a pair of proverbial cats in Kilkenny, Ireland, which fought until only their tails were left.

BIOGRAPHY

Ely Samuel Parker (Seneca, 1828–95), or Ha-sa-no-an-da (Leading Name), was born at Indian Falls on the Seneca Tonawanda Reservation in western New York, the son of William Parker (Jo-no-es-sto-wa), a Baptist deacon and chief of the Tonawanda Senecas, and Elizabeth Parker (Ga-ont-gwut-twus), a descendant of Handsome Lake. Ely Parker was instructed at a local Baptist mission school until 1843 and then attended Yates Academy in Orleans County for two years before transferring to Cayuga Academy in Aurora, where he studied until the spring of 1846. Subsequently he read law at the law office of Angel and Rice in Ellicottville, but abandoned that vocation after being refused admission to the New York bar because he was not a citizen. Parker then took a course in civil engineering at Rensselaer Polytechnic Institute and held positions in that field with the New York State Canal Board, the Chesapeake and Abermarle Ship Canal in Virginia and North Carolina, and the U.S. Department of Treasury.

While still in school Parker began to gain political expertise by accompanying tribal delegations to Albany, New York, and Washington, D.C., as an interpreter and adviser in the dispute over the Ogden Land Company's preemptive rights to Seneca lands. In 1852 he was nominated as one of the fifty sachems of the Iroquois Confederacy and given the name Do-ne-ho-ga-wa (Open Door). His people's immediate concern was to retain the Tonawanda Reservation rather than having to move to Kansas according to the supplemental treaty signed on May 20, 1842, under which the Senecas had retained title to the Allegany and Cattaraugus reservations at the cost of giving up Buffalo Creek and Tonawanda. Parker and his fellow delegates managed to reverse this compact by 1857, when the government allowed them to buy back most of the Tonawanda Reservation with funds granted them for relinquishment of their claims in Kansas.

After some initial difficulties on account of his race, Parker obtained a commission in the army as captain of the engineers in the summer of 1863. On September 18 he was appointed as General Ulysses S. Grant's staff officer. On August 30, 1864, he was promoted to the rank of lieutenant-colonel as Grant's military secretary. Parker witnessed General Lee's surrender at Appomattox on April 9, 1865, and transcribed the official copies of the terms of capitulation. Parker continued serving as Grant's secretary after the Civil War, finally resigning from the army on April 26, 1869, with the rank of brigadier-general. Two years earlier, on December 25, Parker married Minnie Orton Sackett, the adopted daughter of a Union general killed in action in 1864.

Parker gained additional experience in Indian affairs while still serving in the army. In 1865 he conferred with representatives of Confederate Indian tribes in Indian Territory and cosigned punitive treaties with them the year after. In

1867 he helped investigate the causes of the so-called Fetterman massacre and toured several Indian reservations in the Upper Missouri region. Parker was also instrumental in the completion of the final report of the general peace commission that had been sent to the western tribes in 1867–68. In an 1867 report on Indian affairs addressed to Ulysses S. Grant, Secretary of War at the time, Parker presented a four-point plan proposing to retransfer the Bureau of Indian Affairs to the War Department (the BIA had been transferred to the Department of Interior in 1849), to abolish private trade with Indians, to consolidate tribes in a number of districts under a territorial government, and to create a permanent commission to monitor Indian affairs. Congress did establish a Board of Indian Commissioners on April 10, 1869, which functioned until 1933.

When Grant assumed the presidency in 1869, he appointed Parker as the first Indian Commissioner of Indian Affairs on April 13. Even though Parker had fought hard to save the Tonawanda Reservation and was familiar enough with Iroquois traditions to become Lewis H. Morgan's primary informant— Morgan dedicated his famous *League of the Ho-de-no-sau-nee, or Iroquois* to Parker, and some scholars believe that he should have been credited as coauthor—he was still a firm believer in the policy of selective adaptation. He even sanctioned the use of force against "hostile" tribes, a harsh policy that led to the massacre of a group of Piegan Blackfeet men, women, and children in Montana on January 23, 1870. In his first annual report as commissioner in 1869, Parker also recommended that the treaty-making process be terminated at once. Congress later followed this recommendation in an attachment to the Indian Appropriations Act of 1871. Parker evidently changed his mind about returning the Office of Indian Affairs to the War Department while he served as commissioner, as he fully approved a plan to appoint missionaries as Indian agents in his annual report for 1870. He also spoke strongly in favor of promoting citizenship and allotments. Considering that Grant had very little experience in Indian matters prior to the Civil War, it stands to reason that Parker exerted substantial influence on the strategy known as Grant's Peace Policy, which sought the collaboration of religious bodies in the administration of Indian reservations.

Parker held the post of Commissioner of Indian Affairs until 1871, when charges of defrauding the government were made against him by Episcopal reformer William Welsh. A special investigative committee of the House of Representatives acquitted Parker, but his judgment in handling monetary matters was called into question. On the committee's recommendation a law was subsequently passed by Congress limiting the authority of the commissioner. Disappointed, Parker resigned as commissioner on July 24 and retired to Fairfield, Connecticut, where he tried his hand as a private businessman. Bad investments ultimately forced him to accept a minor clerical position with the New York City Police Department, a post he held for nineteen years. Ely S. Parker died in Fairfield in the fall of 1895.

Selected Publications of Ely Samuel Parker

Ely S. Parker to Board Members, May 26, 1869. In *First Annual Report of the Board of Indian Commissioners.* Washington, D.C.: Government Printing Office, 1869: 3–4.

"Iroquois Confederacy of the Five Nations (Iroquois)." *The Heath Anthology of American Literature,* 2 vols., 2nd ed., edited by Paul Lauter. Lexington, Mass.: Heath and Company, 1994: 1: 59–62.

"Report of the Commissioner of Indian Affairs, made to the Secretary of Interior, for the Year 1869." *House Executive Document,* No. 1, 41st Cong., 2nd sess., serial 1414. Washington, D.C.: Government Printing Office, 1870: 3–42.

"Report of the Commissioner of Indian Affairs, made to the Secretary of Interior, for the Year 1870." *House Executive Document,* No. 1, 41st Cong., 3d sess., serial 1449. Washington, D.C.: Government Printing Office, 1871: 467–75.

"Report of Hon. E. S. Parker, Commissioner of Indian affairs, to the Hon. Secretary of the Interior, on the Communication of William Welsh, Esq., relative to the Management of Indian Affairs." Washington, D.C.: Joseph C. Pearson, Printer, 1971.

"Writings of General Parker." *Proceedings of the Buffalo Historical Society* 8 (1905): 520–36.

Unpublished Writings

Manuscript works are found in the Ely Parker Papers and Arthur C. Parker Papers, Buffalo and Erie County Historical Society, Buffalo, New York. Additional manuscripts, including a diary, are housed at the American Philosophical Society Library, Philadelphia.

Selected Secondary Sources

Armstrong, William H. *Warrior in Two Camps: Ely S. Parker, Union General and Seneca Chief.* Syracuse, N.Y.: Syracuse University Press, 1978.
_____. "Parker, Ely S (Do-ne-ho-ga-wa)." In *Encyclopedia of North American Indians,* edited by Frederick E. Hoxie. Boston: Houghton Mifflin Company, 1996: 466–68.
Chipman, Norton Parker. *Investigation into Indian Affairs, before the Committee on Appropriations of the House of Representatives.* Washington, D.C.: Powell, Ginck and Co., 1871.
Deloria, Philip J. *Playing Indian.* New Haven: Yale University Press, 1998: 71–94.
Keller, Jr., Robert H. *American Protestantism and United States Indian Policy, 1869–82.* Lincoln: University of Nebraska Press, 1983: 81–85.
Konkle, Maureen. *Writing Indian Nations: Native Intellectuals and the Politics of Historiography, 1827–1863.* Chapel Hill: University of North Carolina Press, 2004: 256–65.
Michaelsen, Scott. "Ely S. Parker and AmerIndian Voices in Ethnography." *American Literary History* 8, no. 4 (Winter 1996): 221–52. Reprinted and expanded in Scott Michaelsen, *The Limits of Multiculturalism: Interrogating the Origins of American Anthropology.* Minneapolis: University of Minnesota Press, 1999: 84–106.

Parker, Arthur C. *The Life of General Ely S. Parker: Last Grand Sachem of the Iroquois and General Grant's Military Secretary.* Buffalo, N.Y.: Buffalo Historical Society, 1919. Reprinted New York: AMS Press, 1985.

Tooker, Elisabeth. "Ely S. Parker." In *American Indian Intellectuals, 1976 Proceedings of the American Ethnological Society,* edited by Margot Liberty. St. Paul: West Publishing Co., 1978: 15–30.

Waltmann, Henry G. "Ely Samuel Parker 1869–71." In *The Commissioners of Indian Affairs, 1824–1977,* edited by Robert M. Kvasnicka and Herman J. Viola. Lincoln: University of Nebraska Press, 1979: 123–31.

LETTER TO MAJOR HENRY DOUGLAS

Sarah Winnemucca (1870)

Sir,—I learn from the commanding officer of this place that you desire full information in regard to the Indians around this place, with a view if possible, of bettering their condition by sending them on the Truckee River Reservation [section of the Pyramid Lake Reservation]. All the Indians from here to Carson City belong to the Pah Utes tribe. My father whose name is Winnemucca, is head chief of the whole tribe, but he is now getting too old and has not energy enough to command, nor to impress on their minds the necessity of their being sent on the reservation, in fact I think he is entirely opposed to it. He, myself, and the most of the Humboldt and Queen's [Quinn] River Indians were on the Truckee Reservation at one time, but if we had stayed there it would have been only to starve. I think that if they had received what they were entitled to from the agents they would never have left there. So far as their knowledge of agriculture extends they are quite ignorant as they never had an opportunity of learning; but I think if proper pains were taken that they would willingly make the effort to maintain themselves by their own labor, if they could be made to believe that the products were to be their own, and for their own use and comfort. It is needless for me to enter into details as to how we were treated on the reservation while there. It is enough to say that we were confined to the reserve and had to live on what fish we could catch in the river. If this is the kind of civilization awaiting us on the reserve, God grant that we may never be compelled to go on one, as it is more preferable to live in the mountains and drag out an existence there in pure native manner.

So far as living is concerned, the Indians at all the military posts get enough to eat, and considerable cast-off clothing; but how long is this to continue? What is the object of the Government in regard to the Indians? Is it enough that we are at peace? Remove all the Indians from the military posts, and place them on reservations, such as the Truckee and Walker river (as they were conducted), and it will require a greater military force stationed round to keep them in the limits than it now does to keep them in subjection.

On the other hand if the Indians have any guarantee that they can secure a permanent home on their own native soil, and that our white neighbors can be kept from encroaching on our rights, after having a reasonable share of ground allotted to us as our own, and giving us the required advantage of learning etc., I warrant that the savage as he is called to-day will be a law-abiding member of the community fifteen or twenty years hence.

Sir, if at any future time you should require information regarding the Indians here, I will be happy to furnish the same if I can. Yours, respectfully,

Sarah Winnemucca
Pah-Ute Interpreter
Camp McDermit, Nevada

Notes

Sarah Winnemucca to Major Henry Douglas, April 4, 1870, National Archives, United States Office of Indian Affairs, Nevada Superintendency, Letters Received, 1861–80, Record Group 75, M234, Roll 539. I have used the hand-written transcript of the letter in the special collections of the Bancroft Library, University of California at Berkeley (BANC MSS P-G 37: 1). The letter was excerpted in *Harper's Weekly* (May 7, 1870): 291; and reprinted in Helen Hunt Jackson, *A Century of Dishonor: A Sketch of the United States Government's Dealings with Some of the North American Tribes* (New York: Harper, 1881), Appendix VII, 395–96. It has also been reproduced in George F. Brimlow, "The Life of Sarah Winnemucca: The Formative Years," *Oregon Historical Quarterly* 53 (June 1952): 103–134, 126–27; Jack D. Forbes, *Nevada Indians Speak* (Reno: University of Nevada Press, 1967), 96–97; and George Martin Kober, *Reminiscences of George Martin Kober* (Menasha, Wisc.: George Banta Publishing Co. for The Kober Foundation of Georgetown University, 1930), 258–59. In the fall of 1869, the Indian superintendency to Nevada was assigned to a Civil War veteran, Major Henry Douglas, whose goal was to remove squatters from the Pyramid Lake Reservation and to induce the Paiutes to move there so they could be taught farming. When he requested information from the commanding officer at Fort McDermit, Colonel McElroy, concerning the Paiute living there, McElroy turned to Winnemucca for a qualified response. Sarah regarded allotment as the only viable measure to secure a permanent Indian land base. Her widely distributed letters to that effect undoubtedly inspired members of the reform movement such as Senator Henry Dawes and Helen Hunt Jackson. Winnemucca probably composed this communiqué with the editorial assistance of Fanny Corbusier, wife of the army surgeon stationed at Fort McDermit from 1869 to 1871. Fanny Corbusier maintained that Winnemucca "had a little education acquired in a convent, and occasionally wrote letters in behalf of her people, whose welfare she had at heart, many of which I corrected, revised and sent to the newspapers to be published." See William T. Corbusier, *Verde to San Carlos: Recollections of a Famous Army Surgeon and His Observant Family on the Western Frontier,* 1869–1886 (Tucson, Ariz.: Dale Street King, Publisher, 1968), 94.

LETTER TO COMMISSIONER ELY S. PARKER

Sarah Winnemucca (1870)

I have the honor to respectfully submit the following statement to you for your information and for such action as you may deem necessary. Having learned that it is contemplated by the military authorities to abandon Camp McDermit, Nevada and to remove the troops therefrom, I would respectfully represent that such action will have a deplorable effect not only upon the Indians but upon the white settlers in this Quins [sic] River valley. At the present time these Indians are comparatively well behaved, orderly and quiet, knowing that there are troops here to punish them if they commit any acts of violence, they are quite well satisfied with the treatment they receive and the way in which they are governed, and are kindly disposed toward the authorities and whites, generally, and will doubtless continue so as long as there is a sufficient number of troops stationed amongst them to keep them in awe. They have been accustomed to receive their supplies regularly, and have been allowed free access to all parts of the valley for the purposes of hunting and fishing, and they do not want any change made *now* in their mode of life against their will, and will not go upon a reservation unless by force. But if the post be abandoned and the small force are now stationed here be removed as contemplated, and if it be attempted to force them on to a reservation, their limits restricted and their supplies curtailed by *dishonest officials,* they will become utterly demoralized, and commence a series of depredations which will be very difficult to check [and] the white settlers will have to flee—if happily they escape with their lives, leaving their homes and stock behind subject to fire and theft but in the end the Indians will be the greater sufferers, although at the time they cannot be brought to consider it so. Whereas by keeping a sufficient force stationed here, all difficulty and trouble and perhaps unnecessary loss of life will be saved. It will be not only criminal in the authorities to remove the troops now, but it will be far more expensive to the government to restore order and quiet after the Indians have once broken out, and it does not require much provocation to make them do so. I know more about the feeling and prejudices of these Indians than any other person connected with them, therefore I hope this petition will be received with favor. Sir I am the daughter of the Chief of the Piutes. I am living at Camp McDermit and have been in this employ of the U.S. government for nearly three years as interpreter and guide. I have the honor to be, Sir, your

most obedient servant
Sarah Winnemucca
Camp McDermit Nev.

PS please answer this short Epistle if you consider me worthy and I promise you that my next letters will be more lengthy. Direct to Camp McDermit Nev.

Sarah Winnemucca
August 9th 1870

Notes

Sarah Winnemucca to Commissioner Ely S. Parker, August 9, 1870; National Archives, United States Office of Indian Affairs, Nevada Superintendency, Letters Received, 1861–80, Record Group 75, M234, Roll 539. Reproduced in Jack D. Forbes, *Nevada Indians Speak* (Reno: University of Nevada Press, 1967), 97–99. Sarah shared Ely S. Parker's view that the management of Indian affairs should be entrusted to the military. That she should have had more confidence in the administrative capabilities of military personnel is not surprising, given her own negative experiences with Indian agents and the particularly negative record of civilian dealings with Great Basin Indians. Even though the cavalry had committed its own share of depredations among them, including the 1865 Mud Lake massacre in which several of Sarah's relatives were killed, nonpartisan federal authority was only really present in the Great Basin wherever United States military personnel was stationed. Otherwise, law and order was entirely in the hands of local power groups who usually acted out of purely opportunistic interests. See Jack D. Forbes, *Native Americans of California and Nevada* (Healdsburg, Calif.: Naturegraph Publishers, 1969), 59–66.

PETITION TO CONGRESS

Sarah Winnemucca (1883)

Whereas, the tribe of Piute Indians that formerly occupied the greater part of Nevada, and now diminished by its sufferings and wrongs to one-third of its original number, has always kept its promise of peace and friendliness to the whites since they first entered their country, and has of late been deprived of the Malheur Reservation decreed to them by President Grant:—

I, Sarah Winnemucca Hopkins, grand-daughter of Captain Truckee, who promised friendship for his tribe to General Freemont, whom he guided into California, and served through the Mexican war,—together with the under-signed friends who sympathize in the cause of my people,—do petition the Honorable Congress of the United States to restore to them said Malheur Reservation, which is well watered and timbered, and large enough to afford homes and support for them all, where they can enjoy lands in severally without losing their tribal relations, so essential to their happiness and good character, and where their citizenship, implied in this distribution of land, will defend them from the encroachments of the white settlers, so detrimental to their interests and their virtues. And especially do we petition for the return of that portion of the tribe arbitrarily removed from the Malheur Reservation, after the Bannock war, to the Yakima [sic] Reservation on Columbia River, in which removal families were ruthlessly separated, and have never ceased to pine for husbands, wives, and children, which restoration was pledged to them by the Secretary of the Interior [Carl Schurz] in 1880, but has not been fulfilled.

Notes

Included at the end of Sarah Winnemucca Hopkins, *Life Among the Paiutes: Their Wrongs and Claims* (Boston: Cuppler, Upham & Co., 1883), 247. Reproduced in Katherine Gehm, *Sarah Winnemucca: Most Extraordinary Woman of the Northern Paiutes* (Phoenix, Ariz.: O'Sullivan Woodside and Co., 1975), 181. Following the close of the Bannock War in September of 1878, the peaceful bands of Northern Paiutes were informed by military authorities that they were to be interned at the Yakama Reservation in Washington together with the hostile faction rather than being allowed to return to the Malheur Reservation in Oregon as they had been promised. In spite of their pleadings, on January 6, 1879, they and the other Paiute prisoners of war were forced to set off on a 350-mile trek to Yakama in the dead of winter without proper supplies or clothing. On this small-scale repetition of the infamous Cherokee Trail of Tears, the Paiutes lost several people along the way before finally arriving at Yakama on January 31. Due largely to the lobbying activities of Sarah, her brother Natchez, and her father Old Winnemucca in Washington, D.C., in January of 1880, Secretary of Interior Carl Schurz provided them with a letter authorizing all of the Paiutes at Yakama who wished to leave the reservation and rejoin their relatives at Malheur to do so without expense to the government and providing that they should be allotted lands in severalty once there to cultivate for their own benefit. The agent at Yakama, Captain Henry Wagner, did not comply with Schurz's directive. Although Sarah failed in this endeavor, most of the Paiutes eventually managed to leave Yakama without her assistance after 1882 and relocate at Camp McDermit, Pyramid Lake, or Duck Valley reservations in Nevada. Others went on to Fort Bidwell in California or to the Warm Spring and Umatilla reservations in Oregon (Malheur was closed in 1882). In this petition Sarah specifically links allotment with the maintenance of "tribal relations," obviously a strategy of selective adaptation rather than total assimilation. See "Sarah Winnemucca: The Cindarella Princess," in Katherine C. Turner, *Red Men Calling on the Great White Father* (Norman: University of Oklahoma Press, 1951), 159–81.

BIOGRAPHY

Sarah Winnemucca (Northern Paiute, ca. 1844–91), or Thocmetony (Shell Flower), was born in the vicinity of the Sink of the Humbolt River in present-day western Nevada, the daughter of Poito (Deep Eyes, later named Old Winnemucca), a headman from the region north of Pyramid Lake, and Tuboitonie. Her maternal grandfather, known as Captain Truckee, served as a guide to the Stevens-Townsend-Murphy expedition to California in 1844 and joined John Charles Frémont's "California Battalion of Volunteers" in the Bear Flag Rebellion of 1846. Around 1850 Truckee decided to take his daughter Tuboitonie and her five children with him to the vicinity of Stockton, California, along with a group of about thirty other Paiutes. Sarah Winnemucca and her brothers accompanied Truckee on several additional trips to California. She probably did household chores for a number of white families, acquiring both a working knowledge of English and her Christian name. Truckee also maintained friendly relations with the Mormons who settled in Nevada in 1855. He arranged for Sarah Winnemucca and her sister Elma to live and work at Mormon Station (later Genoa) in the household of Major William M. Ormsby, an adventurer and entrepreneur from Kentucky. Just before his death in the summer of 1860, Truckee requested a white friend to take Sarah and Elma to California to be enrolled at the Academy of Notre Dame in San Jose run by the Sisters of Mercy. In her autobiography Winnemucca claims to have spent three weeks at the elitist school before protests from white parents forced her and Elma to abandon their studies and return to the Great Basin. In interviews conducted in 1873 and 1879, however, Winnemucca declared that she had received a total of three years of schooling in San Jose. In all probability, she was an autodidact who received occasional instruction from the white families she worked for intermittently from 1857 to 1866.

Sarah made her first public appearance in the fall of 1864, when she and part of her family performed a series of tableaux vivants on stages in various cities in California and Nevada in order to raise money for their people. The Winnemuccas' brief excursion into show business proved to be a financial disaster, however. Whatever royalties they may have garnered for their efforts ended up in their agent's pockets just before he left them stranded somewhere in California.

In 1867 Winnemucca became more directly involved in tribal affairs when the commanding officer at Camp McDermit in Oregon enlisted her and her brother Natchez as scouts and interpreters in an effort to locate wandering bands of Northern Paiutes and convince them to come in to the military post rather than risk confrontation with American troops. Sarah continued to serve periodically as interpreter for the army at Camp McDermit and Fort Harney in Oregon until 1875, occasionally turning to domestic labor for additional income. In the spring of 1875 she obtained a post as teacher and interpreter at Malheur Indian Reservation in Oregon, but had to give it up at the close of

1876 because of strained relations with the new Indian agent. Following the outbreak of the Bannock War in Idaho in 1848, Winnemucca functioned once again as interpreter and scout under General Oliver Otis Howard. Her remarkable exploits during this campaign were reported in national newspapers such as the *New York Times* and *Chicago Times*. After the war she worked temporarily as a teacher at Vancouver Barracks and Yakama Reservation in Washington, where her father's band had been forcibly interned.

Throughout this time Winnemucca tried to enlist both public and official support for a permanent land base for her people and to have them placed under military administration. In 1879 she began lecturing regularly on the plight of the Northern Paiutes in various cities in California and Nevada. Early in 1880 she accompanied a delegation of Northern Paiute to Washington, D. C., in a futile effort to obtain their people's release from the Yakama Reservation. In 1883 Winnemucca went East again on an extensive lecture tour, making numerous public appearances in major cities. She spoke in the homes of Ralph Waldo Emerson and Senator Henry L. Dawes. Winnemucca also established a close friendship with Elizabeth Palmer Peabody, a noted pioneer in kindergarten education, and her sister, Mary Mann. With their assistance Winnemucca published her autobiography *Life Among the Paiutes* in 1883. On at least six occasions between December 1883, and April 1884, Sarah presented petitions to Congress for a permanent land grant for the Northern Paiutes, first at Malheur and then at Camp McDermit. One of her petitions was presented to Congress in its first session in the spring of 1884. She was called before the Senate Subcommittee on Indian Affairs to present her case to Senator Dawes on April 22. Winnemucca's immediate diplomatic efforts to have her people permanently settled failed because the various Northern Paiute bands in Washington, Oregon, and Nevada had conflicting interests. Finally, without her doing, the bands in Oregon were granted a reservation at Camp McDermit in 1899, which was allotted in severalty only three years later.

Among her supporters Winnemucca was fondly referred to as the "Paiute Princess," but her open criticism of Indian agents, advocation of military administration of Indian affairs, and rather unconventional lifestyle for the times (she married at least three times and apparently had various liaisons) also made her subject to much slander in the press and incurred the resentment of influential Indian reformers such as Herbert Welch and Thomas A. Bland. Nor was her role as intermediary ever entirely free from controversy among the Northern Paiutes. Disappointed, Winnemucca turned away from politics and devoted the remaining years of her life to the education of Indian children. With the assistance of Elizabeth Peabody and Marry Mann, she established the Peabody Indian School at Lovelock, Nevada, in 1885. This unique Indian-controlled bilingual educational institution in the Far West remained in operation until 1888, when a lack of funds forced Winnemucca to close it down. With her own health impaired, Winnemucca went to live with her sister Elma at Harney's Lake, Idaho, where she died on October 17, 1891.

Other than her still widely read autobiography, Sarah Winnemucca published an ethnographic article titled "The Pah-Utes" in *The Californian* in 1882, as well as numerous open letters in various California and Nevada newspapers. In 1994 the Sarah Winnemucca Elementary School in Reno was named in her honor. That same year she was inducted into the National Women's Hall of Fame in Seneca Falls, New York, along with Susette La Flesche.

Selected Publications of Sarah Winnemucca

Life Among the Paiutes: Their Wrongs and Claims. Boston: Cuppler, Upham & Co., 1883. New York: G. P. Putnam's Sons, 1883. Reprinted Bishop, Calif.: Chalfant Press, 1969. Reprinted Reno: University of Nevada Press, 1994.
"The Pah-Utes." *The Californian, A Western Monthly Magazine* 6 (September 1882): 252–56. Reprinted in *The Elders Wrote: An Anthology of Early Prose by North American Indians, 1768–1931,* edited by Bernd C. Peyer. Berlin: Dietrich Reimer Verlag, 1982: 108–114.

Selected Secondary Sources

Anderson, Eric Gary. *American Indian Literature and the Southwest: Context and Dispositions.* Austin: University of Texas Press, 1999: 112–32.
Brimlow, George F. "The Life of Sarah Winnemucca: The Formative Years." *Oregon Historical Quarterly* 53 (June 1952): 103–134.
Brumble III, H. David. *American Indian Autobiography.* Berkeley: University of California Press, 1988: 60–71.
Bryant, Shelle C. Wilson and Patrick W. Bryant, "Sarah Winnemucca Hopkins (1844–1891)." In *Nineteenth-century American Women Writers: A Bio-Bibliographical Critical Sourcebook,* edited by Denise D. Knight. Westport, Conn.: Greenwood Press, 1997: 241–46.
Canfield, Gae Whitney. *Sarah Winnemucca of the Northern Paiutes.* Norman: University of Oklahoma Press, 1983.
Fowler, Catherine S. "Sarah Winnemucca, Northern Paiute, 1844–1891." In *American Indian Intellectuals, 1976 Proceedings of the American Ethnological Society,* edited by Margot Liberty. St. Paul: West Publishing Co., 1978: 33–42.
Gehm, Katherine. *Sarah Winnemucca: Most Extraordinary Woman of the Northern Paiutes.* Phoenix, Ariz.: O'Sullivan Woodside and Co., 1975.
Georgi-Findlay, Brigitte. "The Frontiers of Native American Women's Writing: Sarah Winnemucca's *Life Among the Paiutes.*" In *New Voices in Native American Literary Criticism,* edited by Arnold Krupat. Washington, D.C.: Smithsonian Institution Press, 1993: 222–52.
Gridley, Marion. "Sarah Winnemucca: Army Scout." In Marion Gridley, *American Indian Women.* New York: Hawthorn Books, 1974: 54–60.
Howard, O. O. *Famous Indian Chiefs I Have Known.* New York: The Century Co., 1912: 222–37.
Inter-Tribal Council of Nevada. *Life Stories of Our Native People: Shoshone—Paiute—Washo.* Reno: Inter-Tribal Council of Nevada, 1974: 41–45.
Karttunen, Frances. *Between Worlds: Interpreters, Guides, and Survivors.* New Brunswick, N.J.: Rutgers University Press, 1994: 45–73.
Lape, Noreen Groover. "'I would rather be with my people but not to live with

them as they live': Cultural Liminality and Double Consciousness in Sarah Win-
nemucca Hopkins's *Life Among the Paiutes: Their Wrongs and Claims.*" *American Indian Quarterly* 22, no. 3 (Summer 1998): 259–79.

Lukens, Margo. "Her 'Wrongs and Claims': Sarah Winnemucca's Strategic Narratives of Abuse." *Wicazo Sa Review* 13, no. 1 (Spring 1998): 93–108.

McClure, Andrew S. "Sarah Winnemucca: [Post] Indian Princess and Voice of the Paiutes." *MELUS* 24, no. 2 (Summer 1999): 29–51.

Peabody, Elizabeth P. *Sarah Winnemucca's Practical Solution of the Indian Problem.* Cambridge, Mass.: John Wilcox and Son, 1886.

———. *The Paiutes: Second Report of the Model School of Sarah Winnemucca.* Cambridge, Mass.: John Wilcox and Son, 1887.

Ruoff, A. LaVonne Brown. "Early Native American Women Authors: Jane Johnson Schoolcraft, Sarah Winnemucca, S. Alice Callahan, E. Pauline Johnson, and Zitkala-Sa." In *Nineteenth-Century American Women Writers: A Critical Reader,* edited by Karen L. Kilcup. London: Blackwell, 1998: 80–111.

Sale, Maggie Montesinos. "Reconceptualizing America." *Legacy: A Journal of American Women Writers* 15, no. 1 (1998): 29–34.

Sands, Kathleen Mullen. "Indian Women's Personal Narrative: Voices Past and Present." In *American Women's Autobiography: Fea(s)ts of Memory,* edited by Margo Culley. Madison: University of Nebraska Press, 1992: 268–94.

Senier, Siobhan. *Voices of American Indian Assimilation and Resistance: Helen Hunt Jackson, Sarah Winnemucca, and Victoria Howard.* Norman: University of Oklahoma Press, 2001: 73–120.

Stewart, Patricia. "Sarah Winnemucca." *Nevada Historical Society Quarterly* 14, no. 4 (Winter 1971): 23–38.

Turner, Katherine C. *Red Men Calling on the Great White Father.* Norman: University of Oklahoma Press, 1951: 159–81.

Walker, Cheryl. "Sarah Winnemucca's Mediations: Gender, Race, and Nation." In Cheryl Walker, *Indian Nation: Native American Literature and Nineteenth-Century Nationalisms.* Durham: Duke University Press, 1997: 139–63.

Zanjani, Sally. *Sarah Winnemucca.* Lincoln: University of Nebraska Press, 2001.

THE INDIAN QUESTION

Susette La Flesche (1880)

The solution of the Indian Problem, as it is called, is citizenship. Like all great questions which have agitated the world, the solution is simple: so simple that men cannot understand it. They look for something complicated, something wonderful, as the answer to a question which has puzzled the wisest heads for a hundred years. The question, I believe, is, "What shall be done with the Indian?" One part of the American people try to solve it by crying, "Exterminate him." The answer to such people is, that he has a Creator who will avenge his extermination. The other part cry, "Civilize him." Forthwith they go to work, tell him that his laud shall be his as long as the "grass grows and the waters run." Then they say to him, "You must not pass beyond this line without the permission of this agent whom we place over you," thus effectually preventing him from seeing or moving in any civilization except his own. Then again they say to him, "You must trade only with this man whom we appoint," thus effectually preventing his engaging in commerce or trade should he so desire. Then to crown the whole, they say, "Above all, you must do just as we say or we won't feed you." After thus putting a premium on idleness they close the whole by saying, "We have adopted this policy in order to civilize you, and you must become civilized." As the process of civilization is rather slow, it having taken the Anglo-Saxon race about a thousand years or so to become what they are now, and as the Indian, being a man, objects decidedly to being placed in a nursery subject to the bidding of a man who may be his inferior in moral character or intelligence, he is termed rebellious or sullen, and troops are oftentimes sent for to bring him into subjection. Again, somebody wants his land, or can make money by moving him, a pretext is found, and as he, being a man and not a child or thing, objects decidedly to giving up what he looks on as his own, he is termed rebellious, sullen and incapable of civilization.

When the Indian, being a man and not a child or thing, or merely an animal, as some of the world's civilizers have termed him, fights for his property, liberty and life, they call him a savage. When the first settlers in this country fought for their property, liberty and lives, they were called heroes. When the Indian in fighting this great nation wins a battle it is called a massacre: when this great nation in fighting the Indian wins it is called a victory.

After the Indian is prevented from earning his own living and from taking care of himself by this system of nursing and feeding—although I have heard it reported at different times within the last few years that whole tribes have been found in a state of starvation—he is reported to be incapable of taking care of himself, and would starve if the government let him alone. It seems to me that it was because Standing Bear was trying to take care of himself that this powerful government sent out its armed forces to carry him back to a land from which he had fled because the terror of death was on him in that land. It sounds like some strange story to think of this powerful government sending out its armed forces against a miserable little band composed of eight men, twenty-two women and children, all of them half starved, and half of them sick with the malarial diseases caught in that strange climate.[1]

Why did the government do this? Because the Indian is a child, thing or ward, and must be taken care of and fed; moreover, he left that strange land without permission from his father, master or guardian, whichever you will. But the government feeds them. Was the government feeding them when it took from them their land and carried them to a strange, unbroken country, reeking with malaria, there to live in canvas tents and likely to starve because their great father, guardian or master failed to issue them rations for three months? This is not a solitary instance, but has happened again and again, and will happen again and again until this system is done away with. It is either extermination or citizenship for the Indian. This system has been tried for nearly a hundred years, and has only worked ruin on the Indian. It has resulted only in the shedding of blood and mutual hatred between the two nations. It has resulted in the expenditure of vast sums of money: but all the money is nothing to the loss of a single human life. Set aside the idea that the Indian is a child and must be taken care of, make him understand that he is to take care of himself as all other men do, give him a title to his lands, throw over him the protection of the law, make him amenable to it, and the Indian *will* take care of himself. Then there will be no more wars to settle the Indian problem, for there will be no problem to settle.

Notes

Originally in *The Christian Union* 40, no. 10 (March 10, 1880): 222–23. Susette La Flesche proclaims one of the primary goals of the reform movement and platform of Society of American Indians: Indian self-sufficiency through citizenship.

1. Of the many widely publicized events that disclosed the shortcomings of the reservation system, it was the so-called Ponca case of 1879 that became the cause celebre of the Indian reform movement. Henry Tibbles took up the Poncas' cause and organized a promotional campaign that included a six-months speaking tour for Standing Bear in the Midwest and East. Tibbles was assisted by Susette La Flesche, who was in turn chaperoned by her half-brother Francis La Flesche. Following the landmark decision in *Standing Bear et al. v. Crook* (1879), in which the federal court concluded that "an Indian is a 'person' within the meaning of the laws of the United States, and has, therefore, the right to sue out a writ of habeas corpus in federal court," the Poncas were eventually given the choice of remaining in Indian Territory under improved conditions or returning to their homelands in Nebraska. See Francis P. Prucha, *American Indian Policy in Crisis: Christian Reformers and the Indian, 1865–1900* (Norman: University of Oklahoma Press, 1976), 113–23.

BIOGRAPHY

Susette La Flesche (Omaha, 1854–1903), or Inshta Theamba (Bright Eyes), was born on the Omaha Reservation in Nebraska, one of five children of Joseph La Flesche (Insta Maza, or Iron Eye), a tribal leader of Franco-Ponca ancestry, and Mary Gale (Hinnuagsnun, or the One Woman), the part-Omaha daughter of a U.S. Army physician. Joseph La Flesche also had three children with his second, additional wife, Ta-in-ne (Elizabeth Esau). Although not an Omaha by birth, Joseph La Flesche rose to a leadership position in 1853 following the death of his adoptive father, Big Elk, a principal chief. Joseph La Flesche was a party to the Treaty of 1854, under which the Omahas ceded most of their lands in eastern Nebraska, retaining only a fraction for a reservation on the western bank of the Missouri River. As a member of the progressive "Young Men's Party," Joseph La Flesche was an early supporter of mission schools among the Omaha and saw to it that his eight children received a good education. Three eventually rose to national prominence: Francis La Flesche (1857–1932) established himself as a professional ethnologist with the Bureau of American Ethnology; Susan La Flesche Picotte (1865–1915) graduated from the Woman's Medical College in Philadelphia as the first American Indian woman doctor of medicine; and Susette La Flesche became widely known as a public speaker and author.

Susette La Flesche attended the Presbyterian Mission School at the Omaha Agency headquarters in Thurston County from about 1860 to 1869, when the school was forced to shut down after the federal government cut off its funds. Three years later she enrolled at the Elizabeth Institute for Young Ladies in Elizabeth, New Jersey, where she graduated with honors in 1875. After some initial difficulties she managed to secure a teaching position at the Omaha Agency School from 1877 through 1879.

The turning point in her life came about in April of 1879, when she was called upon to testify in the trial of Ponca chief Standing Bear. The Poncas, closely related neighbors of the Omahas, were removed involuntarily to Indian Territory in 1877. Numerous deaths among them due to the unaccustomed climate, diseases, and inadequate supplies finally motivated Standing Bear and about thirty Poncas to make their way back to Nebraska without official permission. Here the group was eventually arrested and interned at Fort Omaha until arrangements could be made for their return to Indian Territory. Thomas H. Tibbles (1838–1928), a preacher and newspaper editor, publicized the Poncas' cause and motivated Omaha lawyers to sue for a writ of *habeas corpus* in order to prevent their renewed removal. In a landmark decision in *Standing Bear et al. v. Crook* (1879), the federal judge declared that Indians were "persons" within the meaning of the law and thus could not be incarcerated without a just cause. Following the trial a committee of church men from Omaha requested that Susette La Flesche and her father make an investigative visit to the Ponca reservation and report their findings. In October of 1879, Susette began a lecture tour of eastern cities in order to bring public attention to the plight of the Poncas. Together with her half-brother Francis, Standing Bear, and Tibbles, she spent about six months speaking to audiences in Chicago, Pittsburgh, Boston, New York, and Washington. Now widely known as "Bright Eyes," her emotional presentations in Indian costume kindled the concern for Indian affairs among influential New Englanders such as Senator Henry L. Dawes, author Helen Hunt Jackson, and archaeologist Alice Fletcher. They joined with other concerned philanthropists and founded the Boston Indian Citizenship Committee and the Indian Treaty Keeping and the Protective Association (later Women's National Indian Association) in Philadelphia in 1879, initiating the organized Indian reform movement that culminated in the General Allotment Act of 1887. In March and December of 1880 Susette La Flesche also testified before the Senate committee concerning the Poncas' removal. The Poncas were eventually given the choice of remaining in Indian Territory under improved conditions or returning to their homelands in Nebraska.

On July 23, 1881, Susette La Flesche married Tibbles and lived with him on the Omaha Reservation between lecture tours and positions as newspaper editor and reporter. Following the allotment of land in severalty on the Omaha Reservation in 1884, Susette and her husband became involved in the heated debate over the leasing of unallotted tribal land and self-government for the tribe. The Tibbles opposed all plans for leasing and self-government and instead advocated immediate citizenship for the Omahas, placing them in direct conflict with other members of the La Flesche family, notably Susette's sister Rosalie La Flesche Farley (1861–1900) and her husband. The issue was permanently settled in 1887 when the Omahas were made citizens and came under the jurisdiction of the State of Nebraska.

That same year Susette and her husband toured England and Scotland, lecturing extensively on Indian affairs. Besides Indian reform, the Tibbles also became outspoken advocates of the Bimetallic League and the Populist Party. In the winter of 1890–91 Susette, her husband, and her sister Marguerite La Flesche Picotte Diddock (1862–1945) witnessed the Wounded Knee Massacre as reporters for the *Omaha World Herald*. In the mid-1890s, Susette worked in Washington, D.C., as a correspondent for the *American Nonconformist*, a Populist newspaper in Indianapolis. From 1894 until 1900 Susette and her husband lived in Lincoln, Nebraska, where she assisted him in editing *The Independent*, another Populist newspaper. Ill health drove Susette back to the Omaha Reservation, where she died on May 26, 1903.

Other than newspaper articles, Susette La Flesche published a few stories for the juvenile audience in *St. Nicholas* and *Wide Awake*. She also collaborated in the publication of and provided the illustrations for Fanny Reed's *Oo-ma-ha Ta-wa-tha: Omaha City* (1898), and wrote the prefaces to Tibble's *Ploughed Under* (1880) and *The Ponca Chiefs* (1881). In 1994 she was inducted into the National Women's Hall of Fame along with Sarah Winnemucca.

Selected Publications of Susette La Flesche

"The Indian Question." *The Christian Union* 40, no. 10 (March 10, 1880): 222–23.
"An Indian Woman's Letter." *Southern Workman* 8 (April 1879): 44.
"Nedawi." *St. Nicholas* 8 (January 1881): 225–30.
"The Newspaper Writings of Susette La Flesche." Edited by Amanda L. Paige. Digital Library, American Native Press Archives, University of Arkansas at Little Rock.
"Omaha Legends and Tent Stories." *Wide Awake* 17 (June 1883): 21–25.

Unpublished Writings

Papers of La Flesche, 1859–1933, Nebraska State Historical Society, Lincoln, Nebraska.

Selected Secondary Sources

Boughter, Judith A. *Betraying the Omaha Nation, 1790–1916.* Norman: University of Oklahoma Press, 1998.

Clark, Jerry E. and Martha Ellen Webb. "Susette and Susan La Flesche: Reformer and Missionary." In *Being and Becoming Indian: Biographical Studies of North American Frontiers,* edited by James A. Clifton. Chicago: The Dorsey Press, 1989: 137–59.

Crary, Margaret. *S. La Flesche: Voice of the Omaha Indians.* New York: Hawthorn Books, 1973.

Green, Norma Kidd. "Four Sisters: Daughters of Joseph La Flesche." *Nebraska History* 45 (1964): 165–76.

_____. *Iron Eye's Family: The Children of Joseph La Flesche.* Lincoln, Nebraska: Johnsen Publishing, 1969.

Parins, James W. "La Flesche Tibbles, Susette." In *Native American Women: A Biographical Dictionary,* edited by Gretchen M. Bataille. New York: Garland Publishing Co., 1993: 150–52.

Wilson, Dorothy Clarke. *Bright Eyes: The Story of Susette La Flesche, An Omaha Indian.* New York: McGraw-Hill, 1974.

AN INDIAN ALLOTMENT

Francis La Flesche (1900)

In the spring of 1883 I was detailed by the Commissioner of Indian Affairs [Hiram Price] to assist, by way of interpreting and doing clerical work, in the task of making allotments to the Omaha Indians, the tribe to which I belong.

The special agent who was appointed to make the division of the land [Alice C. Fletcher] undertook the work more from an earnest desire to scatter the Indians on the choicest parts of their reservation than to earn the meager compensation offered her by the Government, because it was through her efforts that the law authorizing the allotment was enacted by Congress.[1]

With this purpose in mind, the allotting agent, upon her arrival on the reservation, drove over the land to ascertain where the best portions lay. She saw that the lands best suited for agriculture and the most conveniently located as to market lay along the valley of the Logan and its slopes. So there she pitched her tent and called for the Indians to come and make their selections.

One morning, as we were driving from corner to corner, running the lines of the quarter sections, we came to a man standing on a section mound. As we halted at his side, he looked up at the allotting agent and said: "This is my land," making a sweeping motion with his outstretched arm. The surveyor gave the description of the land, and the agent entered the numbers in her block book. This done, she held out her right hand to him, and as he grasped it she said:

"I congratulate you upon making such a beautiful selection. I want you to build a nice house, a barn and granaries upon it and to cultivate the land. And I wish you every success."

With his hand still grasping that of the special agent, the Indian replied:

"We have had agents here to manage our affairs, but none of them have ever offered us advice such as you have just given me. My people are not prone to follow the advice of women, but I shall strive to follow yours."

It is the story of this man to which I desire to direct attention, because it has much to do with the success of Indian allotments.

One day a solitary tent appeared on the land thus selected, a woman moved in and about it in her daily domestic toil, while day after day a man following a team of horses and a plow around and around from morning till night until a large portion of the quarter section turned into a great dark field, in striking contrast to the grassy hills. In the course of a year the tent disappeared and a neat little house stood in its place. Soon a barn and then a granary appeared. The man had striven to make good his word given to the special agent, and had succeeded.

While he was thus improving his land the man would call together the other Indians who had taken up lands near to his, and try to persuade them to come out there to live. Two returned students from Hampton, with the aid of some friends in the East, built houses on their lands out there, and the man felt greatly

289

encouraged. A few others followed, and this little colony worked happily together until there came a time when they learned that Congress had passed a law which gave them the privilege of leasing their rich lands. Then, one by one, including the returned Hampton students, these people left their lands to the use of white men and returned to the poorest part of the reservation, some to live on the forty-acre lots of their children, and others to crowd upon their relations.

The first man, greatly to his disappointment, was left to struggle alone. He was not discouraged, however, but pushed on, and he now lives like a white man among white men. He has his little house, his barn, his well-filled granaries, a number of fine cattle and splendid horses, while those Indians who leased their lands and left him have scarcely anything to show for the rent received by them.

One day this man said to his Indian neighbors before their departure: "Let us build a little church and ask a white preacher to come and teach us. I am not a member of the church as some of you are, but I want to know something about the white man's religion. We are getting along nicely, and we can each afford to contribute something toward the little house. Let it be on my land or on some one of yours, as you may choose."

He had almost persuaded them when the leasing privilege spoiled his plan. His friends of his own race having abandoned him, he turned to his white neighbors for sympathy, and they responded with a will.

If I did not know that the two men had never met, I might suspect that Major Pratt, of Carlisle, had been whispering to him on matters of Indian education, for I found that this man had been putting into effect the Major's very ideas about mingling white men and red men together. The man went to his white neighbors and said to them:

"You want to educate your children, and I want to educate my little grandson, but we can do nothing unless we have a school. If you will build a school house I will let you have the use of one acre of my land; then we will have a school. I don't want to send my boy to the Government school; children do not learn very fast there. I want my boy to grow up with your children; he will then learn faster."

The white men built the school house and employed a teacher, and this Indian and his white friends have to-day a good school.

Last summer when I was visiting my home this man came to see me. Said he:

"I wish to send a message by you to the white people, to any of them who might wish to help us. The leasing business is ruining the Omahas in every way. It is producing idleness among them, and idleness brings out the worst that is in man. It has proved to be injurious rather than a help. Nearly all of the land is leased, and most of the Indians have scarcely a thing to show for the rent they receive. Many of them loaf about the towns, and some of them come to my house in a shameful state of intoxication and expect hospitality of me. When they should be at work upon their farms, they go in large bodies to visit other tribes, spending their rent money in railroad fare. Labor is the only thing that will maintain the dignity of man and command respect from every one. So long as the system of indiscriminate leasing exists, work among the people will be almost an impossible thing. Cannot the friends of the Indians relieve us of this curse in some way?"

I have delivered my message.

Washington. D. C.

Notes

Originally in *The Independent* 52, no. 8 (November 8, 1900): 2686–688. Reproduced in *Proceedings of the Eighteenth Annual Meeting of the Lake Mohonk Conference of the Friends of the Indian 1900* (Lake Mohonk, N.Y.: The Lake Mohonk Conference, 1901), 76–78; and Bernd C. Peyer, ed., *The Elders Wrote: An Anthology of Early Prose by North American Indians, 1768–1931* (Berlin: Dietrich Reimer Verlag, 1982), 135–37. Francis La Flesche, who candidly endorses allotment in this article, eventually came to have second thoughts about the benefits of this policy. See "Address by Mr. Francis La Flesche: Protection of Indian Lands," *Proceedings of the Thirty-Third Annual Meeting of the Lake Mohonk Conference of the Friends of the Indian and Other Dependent Peoples 1915* (Lake Mohonk, N.Y.: The Lake Mohonk Conference, 1915), 70–72.

1. Alice Cunningham Fletcher (1838–1923), noted anthropologist and collaborator with Francis La Flesche, was an ardent advocate of allotment. It was due in large part to her efforts in Washington, D.C., that the Omaha Allotment Act was passed August 7, 1882, later serving as a model for the General Allotment Act of 1887. In 1883–84 she served as a special agent of the Bureau of Indian Affairs to oversee the distribution of allotments at the Omaha agency, with Francis La Flesche as her interpreter. Fletcher also fulfilled this function among the Winnebagos in 1887–89 and the Nez Perce in 1889–93. Like Francis La Flesche, Fletcher became more critical of certain effects of allotment after 1900, particularly problems involving the increasing practice of leasing of private allotments to whites rather than farming them. See Joan Mark, *A Stranger in Her Native Land: Alice Fletcher and the American Indians* (Lincoln: University of Nebraska Press, 1988).

BIOGRAPHY

Francis La Flesche (Omaha, 1857–1932) was born on the Omaha Reservation near present-day Macy in northeastern Nebraska, the son of Joseph La Flesche and his second wife, Ta-in-ne. He was thus the half-brother of Susette La Flesche, although such a distinction between siblings would not be made under Omaha social norms. Like Susette, Francis La Flesche attended the Presbyterian Mission School on the Omaha Reservation from about 1865 until it closed in 1869. In 1877 he was apparently briefly married to a woman named Alice Mitchell. Francis La Flesche's interest in ethnology was probably sparked in 1878, when he acted as interpreter and informant for James Owen Dorsey. In this capacity he contributed substantially to Dorsey's subsequent publications: *Omaha Sociology* (1884) and *The Cegiha Language* (1890). In 1879 Francis La Flesche accompanied his sister Susette and journalist Henry Tibbles on their promotional campaign for Standing Bear's Poncas in the Midwest and East. During this tour Francis La Flesche met Alice Cunningham Fletcher, with whom he would form a close personal and professional relationship. In 1881 Francis La Flesche served as interpreter for the Senate Committee on Indian Affairs. That same year Secretary of Interior Samuel J. Kirkwood appointed him clerk for the Bureau of Indian Affairs, a position he occupied until 1910.

In 1882 Francis La Flesche collaborated with Alice Fletcher to obtain Omaha and Sioux artifacts for Harvard's Peabody Museum. When Fletcher, who lobbied intensively in Washington for the passage of the Omaha Allotment Act in 1882, was appointed as special agent of the Bureau of Indian Affairs to make allotments to the Omahas in 1883, Francis La Flesche was detailed to go along as her interpreter and informant. Their activities brought them into conflict with Susette La Flesche and Henry Tibbles, now married, who advocated citizenship and legal rights for the Omahas rather than total assimilation. Subsequent disputes among the Omahas over leasing, in which members of the La Flesche family were also embroiled, eventually forced Francis La Flesche to have second thoughts about the policy of allotment. At the thirty-third annual meeting of the Lake Mohonk Conference of Friends of the Indian in 1915, for instance, La Flesche called upon those in control of Indian affairs to protect the remaining Indian land base.

In 1891 Alice Fletcher informally adopted Francis La Flesche as her son and lived with him at her home in Washington until her death in 1923. She taught him methods of ethnographic research. He, in turn, assisted her in the completion of a volume titled *A Study of Omaha Indian Music*, published by the Peabody Museum in 1893. Francis La Flesche also studied law at National University Law School, earning an L. L. B. degree in 1892 and an L. L. M the following year. Around 1895, German anthropologist Edouard Seler contracted him to collect Omaha objects for the Berlin Museum. In 1900 La Flesche published *The Middle Five,* an autobiographical account of his experiences at the

Presbyterian Mission School. The book was reprinted in 1906 and 1909. Between 1900 and 1901 he wrote a collection of short stories for a juvenile audience titled *Ke-ma-ha,* but failed to find a publisher. (With two exceptions these were not published until 1995.) Disappointed, Francis La Flesche gave up creative writing and resumed his ethnographic work on the Omahas.

In 1906 La Flesche married Rosa Bourassa, of Ojibwe descent, only to divorce her two years later. In 1910 he transferred from the Bureau of Indian Affairs to the Bureau of American Ethnology, where he served as an ethnological investigator until his retirement on December 26, 1929. His collaboration with Alice Fletcher culminated in the publication of *The Omaha Tribe* as the twenty-seventh annual report of the Bureau of American Ethnology in 1911. The following year La Flesche became an active member of the recently formed Society of American Indians. In contrast to the radical faction of the SAI led by Carlos Montezuma, La Flesche believed that reservations should be preserved. He proposed that future SAI meetings be conducted there in cooperation with rank-and-file Indians. Along with Thomas L. Sloan and John Milton Oskison, he eventually joined the contingent supporting the peyote religion and testified in favor of its use at the hearings on Representative Carl M. Hayden's anti-peyote bill before the House Subcommittee on Indian Affairs in 1918.

Following the publication of *The Omaha Tribe* in 1911, Francis La Flesche dedicated himself to the study of the Osages, a people closely related to the Omahas. His opus, comprising some 1600 pages under the general title *The Osage Tribe,* was published as the 36th, 39th, 43rd, and 45th Annual Reports of the Bureau of American Ethnology between 1922 and 1930. It embodies one of the most thorough ethnographic accounts ever dedicated to a single tribe and secured La Flesche widespread recognition as a scholar. He also produced an incomplete *Dictionary of the Osage Language,* published by the Bureau of American Ethnology in 1932. Francis La Flesche was a member of the American Anthropological Association, nominated as the president of the Anthropological Society in Washington in 1922–23, and awarded the honorary degree of Doctor of Letters by the University of Nebraska in 1926. After retiring from the Bureau of American Ethnology in 1829, Francis La Flesche moved back to Nebraska to live with his brother Carey at the Omaha community near Macy, Nebraska. He died there on September 5, 1932.

Selected Publications of Francis La Flesche

"Address by Mr. Francis La Flesche: Protection of Indian Lands." *Proceedings of the Thirty-Third Annual Meeting of the Lake Mohonk Conference of the Friends of the Indian and Other Dependent Peoples, 1915.* Lake Mohonk, N.Y.: The Lake Mohonk Conference, 1915:70–72.

A Dictionary of the Osage Language. Bulletin of the Bureau of American Ethnology, No. 109. Washington, D.C.: Government Printing Office, 1932.

"An Indian Allotment." *The Independent* 52, no. 8 (November 8, 1900): 2686–688. Reprinted in *Proceedings of the Eighteenth Annual Meeting of the Lake Mohonk*

Conference of the Friends of the Indian 1900. Lake Mohonk, N.Y.: The Lake Mohonk Conference, 1901:76–78.

Ke-ma-ha: The Omaha Stories of Francis La Flesche. Edited by James W. Parins and Daniel F. Littlefield. Lincoln: University of Nebraska Press, 1995.

The Middle Five: Indian Schoolboys of the Omaha Tribe. Boston: Small, Mayard and Co., 1900. Reprinted Lincoln: University of Nebraska Press, 1978.

The Omaha Tribe, Twenty-Seventh Annual Report of the Bureau of American Ethnology, 1905–1906. With Alice C. Fletcher. Washington, D.C.: Government Printing Office, 1911.

The Osage and the Invisible World: From the Works of Francis La Flesche. Edited by Garrick A. Bailey. Norman: University of Oklahoma Press, 1995.

The Osage Tribe: Rite of the Chiefs; Sayings of the Ancient Men. New York: Johnson Reprint Corporation, 1970.

The Osage Tribe: The Rite of Vigil, Thirty-Ninth Annual Report of the Bureau of American Ethnology, 1917–1918. Washington, D.C.: Government Printing Office, 1925: 31–630.

The Osage Tribe: Rite of Wa-xo-be, Forty-Fifth Annual Report of the Bureau of American Ethnology, 1927–1928. Washington, D.C.: Government Printing Office, 1930: 523–833.

The Osage Tribe, Thirty-Sixth Annual Report of the Bureau of American Ethnology, 1914–1915. Washington, D.C.: Government Printing Office, 1922: 37–604.

The Osage Tribe: Two Versions of the Child-Naming Rite, Forty-Third Annual Report of the Bureau of American Ethnology, 1925–1926, Washington, D.C.: Government Printing Office, 1928: 23–164.

"Who Was that Medicine Man?" *Journal of American Folklore* 18 (October 1905): 269–75.

Unpublished Writings

The Papers of Alice Cunningham Fletcher and Francis La Flesche, National Anthropological Archives, Smithsonian Institution, Washington, D.C. This collection totaling thirty-three boxes includes the Francis La Flesche Papers (boxes 14–17) and Papers Relating to the Anthropological Research of Alice Fletcher and Francis La Flesche (Boxes 18–33).

Selected Secondary Sources

Alexander, Hartley Burr. "Francis La Flesche." *American Anthropologist* 35 (1933): 328–31.

Boughter, Judith A. *Betraying the Omaha Nation, 1790–1916.* Norman: University of Oklahoma Press, 1998.

Barnes, R. H. "A Legacy of Misperception and Invention: The Omaha Indians in Anthropology." In *The Invented Indian: Cultural Fictions & Government Policies,* edited by James A. Clifford. New Brunswick, N.J.: Transaction Publishers, 1994: 211–26.

Coleman, Michael C. "The Mission Education of Francis La Flesche: An American Indian Response to the Presbyterian Boarding School in the 1860s." *American Studies in Scandinavia* 18 (1986): 67–82.

Green, Norma Kidd. *Iron Eye's Family: The Children of Joseph La Flesche*. Lincoln, Neb.: Johnsen Publishing, 1969.

Liberty, Margot. "Francis La Flesche: The Osage Odyssey." In *American Indian Intellectuals, 1976 Proceedings of the American Ethnological Society*, edited by Margot Liberty. St. Paul: West Publishing Co., 1978: 44–59.

_____. "Native American Informants: The Contribution of Francis La Flesche." In *American Anthropology: The Early Years*, edited by John V. Murra. St. Paul: West Publishing Co., 1978: 99–110.

Mark, Joan. "Francis La Flesche: The American Indian as Anthropologist." *ISIS*, 73, no. 269 (1982): 497–510.

_____. *A Stranger in Her Native Land: Alice Fletcher and the American Indians*. Lincoln: University of Nebraska Press, 1988.

Parins, James W. and Daniel F. Littlefield. "Introduction." In *Ke-ma-ha: The Omaha Stories of Francis La Flesche*. Lincoln: University of Nebraska Press, 1995: vii–xli.

Ramsey, Jarold. "Francis La Flesche's 'The Song of Flying Crow' and the Limits of Ethnography." In *American Indian Persistence and Resurgence*, edited by Karl Kroeber. Durham and London: Duke University Press, 1994: 181–97.

Smith, Sherry Lynn. "Francis La Flesche and the World of Letters." *American Indian Quarterly* 25, no. 4 (Fall 2001): 579–603.

WHY I AM A PAGAN

Gertrude Bonnin (1902)

When the spirit swells my breast I love to roam leisurely among the green hills; or sometimes, sitting on the brink of the murmuring Missouri, I marvel at the great blue overhead. With half-closed eyes I watch the huge cloud shadows in their noiseless play upon the high bluffs opposite me, while into my ear ripple the sweet, soft cadences of the river's song. Folded hands lie in my lap, for the time forgot. My heart and I lie small upon the earth like a grain of throbbing sand. Drifting clouds and tinkling waters, together with the warmth of a genial summer day, bespeak with eloquence the loving Mystery round about us. During the idle while I sat upon the sunny river brink, I grew somewhat, though my response be not so clearly manifest as in the green grass fringing the edge of the high bluff back of me.

At length retracing the uncertain footpath scaling the precipitous embankment, I seek the level lands where grow the wild prairie flowers. And they, the lovely little folk, soothe my soul with their perfumed breath.

Their quaint round faces of varied hue convince the heart which leaps with glad surprise that they, too, are living symbols of omnipotent thought. With a child's eager eye I drink in the myriad star shapes wrought in luxuriant color upon the green. Beautiful is the spiritual essence they embody.

I leave them nodding in the breeze, but take along with me their impress upon my heart. I pause to rest me upon a rock embedded on the side of a foothill facing the low river bottom. Here the Stone-Boy, of whom the American aborigine tells, frolics about, shooting his baby arrows and shouting aloud with glee at the tiny shafts of lightning that flash from the flying arrow-beaks. What an ideal warrior he became, baffling the siege of the pests of all the land till he triumphed over their united attack.[1] And here he lay,—Inyan our great-great-grandfather, older than the hill he rested on, older than the race of men who love to tell of his wonderful career.[2]

Interwoven with the thread of this Indian legend of the rock, I fain would trace a subtle knowledge of the native folk which enabled them to recognize a kinship to any and all parts of this vast universe. By the leading of an ancient trail I move toward the Indian village.

With the strong, happy sense that both great and small are so surely enfolded in His magnitude that, without a miss, each has his allotted individual ground of opportunities, I am buoyant with good nature.

Yellow Breast, swaying upon the slender stem of a wild sunflower, warbles a sweet assurance of this as I pass near by. Breaking off the clear crystal song, he turns his wee head from side to side eyeing me wisely as slowly I plod with moccasined feet. Then again he yields himself to his song of joy. Flit, flit hither and yon, he fills the summer sky with his swift, sweet melody. And truly does it seem his vigorous freedom lies more in his little spirit than in his wing.

With these thoughts I reach the log cabin whither I am strongly drawn by the tie of a child to an aged mother. Out bounds my four-footed friend to meet me, frisking about my path with unmistakable delight. Chan is a black shaggy dog, "a thoroughbred little mongrel" of whom I am very fond. Chan seems to understand many words in Sioux, and will go to her mat even when I whisper the word, though generally I think she is guided by the tone of the voice. Often she tries to imitate the sliding inflection and long-drawn-out voice to the amusement of our guests, but her articulation is quite beyond my ear. In both my hands I hold her shaggy head and gaze into her large brown eyes. At once the dilated pupils contract into tiny black dots, as if the roguish spirit within would evade my questioning.

Finally resuming the chair at my desk I feel in keen sympathy with my fellow-creatures, for I seem to see clearly again that all are akin. The racial lines, which once were bitterly real, now serve nothing more than marking out a living mosaic of human beings. And even here men of the same color are like the ivory keys of one instrument where each resembles all the rest, yet varies from them in pitch and quality of voice. And those creatures who are for a time mere echoes of another's note are not unlike the fable of the thin sick man whose distorted shadow, dressed like a real creature, came to the old master to make him follow as a shadow. Thus with a compassion for all echoes in human guise, I greet the solemn-faced "native preacher" whom I find awaiting me. I listen with respect for God's creature, though he mouth most strangely the jangling phrases of a bigoted creed.

As our tribe is one large family, where every person is related to all the others, he addressed me:—

"Cousin, I came from the morning church service to talk with you."

"Yes?" I said interrogatively, as he paused for some word from me.

Shifting uneasily about in the straight-backed chair he sat upon, he began: "Every holy day (Sunday) I look about our little God's house, and not seeing you there, I am disappointed. This is why I come today. Cousin, as I watch you from afar, I see no unbecoming behavior and hear only good reports of you, which all the more burns me with the wish that you were a church member. Cousin, I was taught long years ago by kind missionaries to read the holy book. These godly men taught me also the folly of our old beliefs.

"There is one God who gives reward or punishment to the race of dead men. In the upper region the Christian dead are gathered in unceasing song and prayer. In the deep pit below, the sinful ones dance in torturing flames.

"Think upon these things, my cousin, and choose now to avoid the after-doom of hell fire!" Then followed a long silence in which he clasped tighter and unclasped again his interlocked fingers.

Like instantaneous lightning flashes came pictures of my own mother's making, for she, too, is now a follower of the new superstition.

"Knocking out the chinking of our log cabin, some evil hand thrust in a burning taper of braided dry grass, but failed of his intent, for the fire died out and the half-burned brand fell inward to the floor.[3] Directly above it, on a shelf, lay the holy book. This is what we found after our return from a several days' visit. Surely some great power is hid in the sacred book!"

Brushing away from my eyes many like pictures, I offered midday meal to the converted Indian sitting wordless and with downcast face. No sooner had he risen from the table with "Cousin, I have relished it," than the church bell rang.

Thither he hurried forth with his afternoon sermon. I watched him as he hastened along, his eyes bent fast upon the dusty road till he disappeared at the end of a quarter of a mile.

The little incident recalled to mind the copy of a missionary paper brought to my notice a few days ago, in which a "Christian" pugilist commented upon a recent article of mine, grossly perverting the spirit of my pen.[4] Still I would not forget that the pale-faced missionary and the hoodooed aborigine are both God's creatures, though small indeed their own conceptions of Infinite Love. A wee child toddling in a wonder world, I prefer to their dogma my excursions into the natural gardens where the voice of the Great Spirit is heard in the twittering of birds, the rippling of mighty waters, and the sweet breathing of flowers. If this is Paganism, then at present, at least, I am a Pagan.[5]

Notes

Originally in the *Atlantic Monthly* 90 (December 1902): 801–803. Reproduced in slightly altered form as "Great Spirit" in Zitkala-Ša, *American Indian Stories* (Washington, D.C.: Hayworth Press, 1921), 101–107. This is Bonnin's most widely read essay. It introduces the concept of universal kinship as a fundamental distinction between Indian and Christian thought. The idea of a kinship-based connection between Indians and the land and other living creatures was expanded on by noted Sioux authors such as Charles Eastman, Luther Standing Bear, Ella Deloria, and Vine Deloria, Jr. It has since evolved into the very fiber of contemporary American Indian ideology. See Charles A. Eastman, *The Soul of the Indian: An Interpretation* (Boston: Houghton Mifflin company, 1911; repr., Lincoln: University of Nebraska Press, 1980); Vine Deloria, Jr., *God Is Red: A Native View of Religion* (New York: Dell Publishing Company, Inc., 1973; repr. Golden, Colorado: Fulcrum Publishing, 2003).

1. Stone Boy (Inyanhoksila) is a culture hero whose extraordinary feats are celebrated in many Sioux oral narratives. See "The Four Brothers or Inyanhoksila (Stone Boy)" in Marie L. McLaughlin, *Myths and Legends of the Sioux* (Bismarck, N.D.: Bismarck Tribune Co., 1910).

2. According to Sioux belief, Inyan (Rock) is the primal power and grandfather of all things, as well as the creator of Maka (Earth). Stone Boy, who materializes from a pebble, is closely connected to Inyan. See Julian Rice, *Before the Great Spirit: The Great Many Faces of Sioux Spirituality* (Albuquerque: University of New Mexico Press, 1998); James R. Walker, *Lakota Belief and Ritual*, edited by Raymond J. DeMallie and Elaine A. Jahner (Lincoln: University of Nebraska Press, 1980).

3. The taper of braided grass is probably "sweet grass" (*Hierochloe odorata*), commonly used as a purifying incense in traditional Sioux ceremonies.

4. Bonnin's autobiographical sketches, published in the *Atlantic Monthly* in 1900, and her story titled "The Soft-Hearted Sioux," published in *Harper's Monthly* in 1901, elicited a negative response from some readers. In a letter to Carlos Montezuma dated March 5, 1901, she wrote that at Carlisle her story was pronounced "trash" and herself as "worse than a pagan." An anonymous reviewer for the Santee Normal School's *The Word Carrier* condemned her story as "morally bad" and chastised her for being "utterly unthankful for all that has been done for her by the pale faces, which in her case is considerable." In another letter to Carlos Montezuma dated May 1, 1902, announcing the impending publication of "Why I Am a Pagan," Bonnin predicted that "Carlisle will rear upon its haunches at sight of the little sky rocket!" See "Zitkala Sa in the Atlantic Monthly," *The Word Carrier* 29, no. 4 (April 1900): 14; "The Soft Hearted Sioux," *The Word Carrier* 30, nos. 2–3 (February–March 1901): 5; *The Red Man* 16, no. 13 (September 14, 1900). The letters are in the Carlos Montezuma Papers, State Historical Society of Wisconsin, Division of Archives and Manuscripts, Madison, Wisconsin.

5. In the version reproduced in *American Indian Stories* this last sentence is excised and the following paragraph added: "Here, in a fleeting quiet, I am awakened by the fluttering robe of the Great Spirit. To my innermost consciousness, the phenomenal universe is a royal mantle, vibrating with His divine breath. Caught in its flowing fringes are the spangles and oscillating brilliants of sun, moon, and stars."

AMERICA, HOME OF THE RED MAN

Gertrude Bonnin (1919)

To keep the home fires burning, the Society of American Indians held its annual conference this fall at Pierre, South Dakota.[1] While en route to the West, the Secretary was accosted by a traveler whose eyes fairly gleamed under the little service pin she wore. At length curiosity spoke. The only preliminary introduction was a clearing of the throat. "You have a relative in the war?" asked the voice. "Yes, indeed," was the quick reply. "I have many cousins and nephews, somewhere in France. This star I am wearing is for my husband, a member of the great Sioux Nation, who is a volunteer in Uncle Sam's Army." A light spread over the countenance of the pale-faced stranger. "Oh! Yes! You are an Indian! Well, I knew when I first saw you that you must be a foreigner."[2]

The amazing speech dropped like a sudden curtain behind which the speaker faded instantly from vision. In figures of fire, I saw, with the mind's eye, ten thousand Indian soldiers swaying to and fro on European battle-fields—finally mingling their precious blood with the blood of all other peoples of the earth, that democracy might live. Three-fourths of these Indian soldiers were volunteers and there were those also who did not claim exemption, so eager were they to defend their country and its democratic ideals. The Red Man of America loves democracy and hates mutilated treaties.

Twelve million dollars had been subscribed by the American Indians to the Liberty Loans. Generous donations they made to war funds of the Red Cross, Y. M. C. A. and other organizations.

I beheld rapidly shifting pictures of individual sacrifices of Indians both young and old.

An old grandmother, whom someone dubbed a "Utah squaw" now appeared wonderously glorified. Her furrowed face was aglow with radiance. Her bent form, clad in pitiful rags, changed in a twinkle of an eye to strength and grace. Her spirit shining through earth's misfortunes, revealed an angel in disguise. She donated five hundred dollars to the Red Cross and had left only thirteen dollars. "Thirteen dollars left? That is enough for me," the toothless old grandmother lisped in her own native tongue. It was her mite in this cause of world democracy.

Beside her stood an Indian brave in the Army uniform. Earlier he went overseas for active service at the front. A treasured file of his letters filled the air like white-winged pigeons, telling a story stranger than fiction.

He was a machine gunner. It was his duty to stand by his gun till he should drop. One day he fell, but the wound was not fatal. After his recovery he served as an infantryman. A Hun shrapnel found him again. His time, apparently, had not yet come to die. He recovered. Undaunted, he was glad when he was reassigned to the Remount Station. "I have nothing to do now," his letters read, "only to break army horses for riding."[3] True, he was an expert horseman but with a crippled knee, no telling what moment he might ignominiously break his own neck. This thought never occurred to him. Later a message came again from France. "I am no longer in the Remount. I have been assigned to garden work. I am digging spuds to help with the war."

And now I saw little French orphans, babes with soft buckskin moccasins on their tiny feet. Moccasins, that Indian women of America had made for them, with so much loving sympathy for an anguished humanity.

Time and distance were eliminated by the fast succession of pictures crowding before me. The dome of our nation's Capitol appeared. A great senator of Indian blood introduced upon the floor of the United States Senate a resolution that all Indian funds in the United States Treasury be available to our government, if need be, for the prosecution of the war.[4] From coast to coast throughout our broad land not a single voice of the Red Man was raised to protest again it.

America! Home of the Red Man! How dearly the Indian loves you! America! Home of Democracy, when shall the Red Man be emancipated? When shall the Red Man be deemed worthy of full citizenship if not now?

A slight motion of the strange pale-face standing before me attracted my notice. I scanned him closely, to see what part of the dream he was. I wondered if a part of any dream could be cognizant of the rest of the actors, dream fellows, beheld by the dreamer or seer of visions. A pity he could not have seen the pictures that held me spellbound a moment ago. Alas, I did not have the courage to try to put them into words. When at last I spoke, the luster of his eye grew less bright. He was fast losing interest. From the questions with which I plied him, he probably guessed I was a traveling book agent.

Did you ever read a geography? The Red Man is one of the four primary races into which the human family has been divided by scientists.[5] America is the home of the Red Man. Have you read the June *Designer,* 1918, about Indian children in Red Cross work? Have you read the April *National Geographic Magazine*, 1918, in which the Secretary of the Interior, Hon. Franklin K. Lane, has contributed an article entitled, "What is it to be an American?" In the third paragraph of this article we are told "There has been nothing of paternalism in our government."[6] I would like to ask "How does this apply to the Red Men in our midst?"

Slowly shaking his head, the stranger withdrew cautiously, lest he be snared into subscribing for one or all of these publications.

Notes

Originally in the *American Indian Magazine* 6, no. 4 (Winter 1919): 165–67. It first appeared in the *Home Mission Monthly,* published in New York by the Women's Board of Home Missions of the Presbyterian Church in the United States. Reproduced in Zitkala-Ša, *American Indian Stories, Legends, and Other Writings,* edited by Cathy N. Davidson and Ada Norris (New York: Penguin Classics, 2003), 193–95. More than ten thousand American Indians served in World War I. Active members of the SAI pointed to the Indian war effort to bolster their arguments in favor of citizenship. Shortly after this article appeared, on November 6, 1919, a Congressional Act granted U.S. citizenship to all Indian veterans of World War I if so desired. All American Indians were made citizens under the Indian Citizenship Act of 1924. See Thomas A. Britten, *American Indians in World War I: At Home and at War* (Albuquerque: University of New Mexico Press, 1997).

1. The eighth SAI conference (actually the seventh as the prospective meeting in Oklahoma in 1917 was cancelled) took place in Pierre, South Dakota, on September 25–28, 1918.

2. In *Elk v. Wilkins* (1884), the Supreme Court rejected a citizenship claim by an Indian who had voluntarily moved from the reservation and renounced his tribal affiliation. The Court declared that "Indians born within the territorial limits of the United States, members of, and owing immediate allegiance to, one of the Indiana tribes, (an alien though dependent power,) although in a geographical sense born in the United States, are no more 'born in the United States and subject to the jurisdiction thereof,' within the meaning of the first section of the fourteenth amendment, than the children of subjects of any foreign government born within the domain of that government, or the children born within the United States, of ambassadors or other public ministers of foreign nations."

3. In 1908 Congress authorized the Remount Service, a special unit that was to procure and train horses for military purposes. It was inactivated in 1948.

4. Probably a reference to Charles Curtis (1860–1936), part-Kaw Republican Senator from Kansas (1907–13, 1915–29), Vice President of the United States (1929–33), and active member of the SAI.

5. Swedish naturalist Carolus Linnaeus (1707–78) differentiated four varieties of the *homo diurnus* (a subdivision of the *homo sapiens*): American, European, Asiatic, and African.

6. Franklin Knight Lane (1864–1921) was a Canadian-American lawyer and politician. He served as Secretary of Interior from 1913 to 1920. Lane is best known for his involvement in establishing the National Park Service.

BIOGRAPHY

Gertrude Simmons Bonnin (Yankton Sioux, 1876–1938), or Zitkala-Ša (Red Bird), was born at the Yankton Agency in South Dakota on February 22, the daughter of Ellen Simmons, or Tate'Iyohiwin (Reaches for the Wind), and her third husband, a white trader by the name of Felken who abandoned his pregnant wife. Gertrude attended the Presbyterian agency school from 1882 to 1884 and then enrolled at White's Indiana Manual Labor School, a Quaker educational institution in Wabash, Indiana, in February of 1884. She returned to the Yankton Agency in February of 1887 to live with her mother, and studied briefly at the Santee Normal Training School at the Dakota Mission in Nebraska from the fall of 1888 to the summer of 1890. In February of 1891 she resumed her studies at White's Indiana Manual Labor School, receiving her diploma in June of 1895. She then attended Earlham College in Richmond, Indiana, from September of 1895 until June of 1897, when ill health and financial difficulties forced her to discontinue her studies.

In the summer of 1897 Gertrude Simmons obtained a teaching position at Carlisle Indian Industrial School in Carlisle, Pennsylvania. She resigned after eighteen months after her relations with Richard Henry Pratt became increasingly strained. Among other things, she disagreed with his emphasis on agricultural training for Indians and believed that all schools should be located on reservations so that the elders would not feel abandoned. Gertrude Simmons departed for Boston in 1899 with plans to study the violin at the New England Conservatory of Music. In 1900 she accompanied the Carlisle band throughout the United States and to Paris as a solo violinist. At this time she also began to devote herself seriously to writing, taking the pen name Zitkala-Ša. She published three autobiographical sketches and several short stories in the *Atlantic Magazine, Harper's Monthly,* and *Everybody's Magazine* between 1900 and 1902. These were reproduced collectively in 1921 under the title *American Indian Stories.* Her critical appraisal of the boarding school system and vivid portrayal of Indian deracination stood in marked contrast to the more idealistic writings of most of her contemporaries.

Gertrude Simmons returned to the Yankton Agency in the summer of 1901 to take care of her ailing mother and to gather material for her collection of traditional Sioux tales, published as *Old Indian Legends* that same year. Earlier that year, Gertrude Simmons was engaged to Carlos Montezuma, whom she had probably met while he functioned as caretaker of the Carlisle band in 1900, but she broke off the relationship by August when he refused to give up his private medical practice in Chicago and relocate to the Yankton Agency along with her.

In the spring of 1902 Gertrude Simmons worked as an issue clerk at the Standing Rock Agency in North Dakota. Here she met and married Raymond Talefease Bonnin, a Yankton Sioux, and accompanied him to the Uintah Ouraye Ute Agency in Duchesne, Utah, where he had a BIA appointment as clerk. In

Duchesne she taught at a local school from March 1905 to November 1906, and collaborated with composer William Hanson to produce an opera titled *The Sun Dance*, which premiered in Vernal, Utah, in 1913. The New York Light Opera Guild performed *The Sun Dance* posthumously as the American opera of the year in 1937.

Although she had discussed the feasibility of establishing an Indian organization with Montezuma as early as 1901, Gertrude Simmons, now Gertrude Bonnin, did not officially join the Society of American Indians (SAI) until late in 1914, when she was registered as a member of the advisory board. The following year, she organized an SAI-sponsored community center project for the Ute at Fort Duchesne in Utah. At the sixth annual conference of the SAI in Cedar Rapids, Iowa, on September 26–30, 1916, she was elected secretary of the organization and subsequently moved with her family to Washington, D.C., to carry out her duties. From 1918 to 1919 she also edited and wrote several editorials and articles for the *The American Indian Magazine*.

As an SAI representative Bonnin emphasized Indian war efforts, promoted citizenship and the abolition of the BIA, and mounted an aggressive campaign against Indian use of peyote. She and Charles A. Eastman testified at the hearings on Representative Carl M. Hayden's anti-peyote bill before the House Subcommittee on Indian Affairs in 1918. She took a particularly antagonistic stand in her oral and written testimonies at the hearings, claiming that peyote excited "the baser passions" and accused practitioners of the peyote religion of drinking and defrauding other Indians.

When Thomas L. Sloan (1863–1932), an Omaha attorney and defender of the Indian use of peyote, displaced Charles Eastman as president of the SAI in 1919, Gertrude Bonnin turned down an appointment as secretary-treasurer and terminated her relationship with the disintegrating organization. In 1920 she was increasingly involved in the Yankton claims hearings on tribal rolls and allotments, and became a staunch advocate of preserving the Indian land base. In 1921 Bonnin helped to establish the Indian Welfare Committee under the auspices of the General Federation of Women's Clubs (GFWC). In 1923 she traveled to Oklahoma as an investigator for the Indian Rights Association and the GFWC, where she witnessed rampant corruption in connection with white guardianship over Indian properties and oil leases. Together with Charles N. Fabens and Mathew K. Sniffen, she published in 1924 a scathing report titled *Oklahoma's Poor Rich Indians: An Orgy of Graft and Exploitation of the Five Civilized Tribes—Legalized Robbery*. Bonnin also functioned temporarily as a member of the National Advisory Board of the American Indian Defense Association (AIDA), founded by John Collier and others in 1923. In 1926 she and her husband established the National Council of American Indians (NCAI), a new all-Indian political association that she headed as president until her death in 1938. Its slogan was "Help Indians Help Themselves in Protecting Their Rights and Properties." The NCAI shared an office with AIDA from 1927 to 1932, and Gertrude Bonnin initially lent her full support to the new reform policies promoted by Collier, which led to the passage of the Indian Reorganization Act (IRA, or Wheeler-Howard Act) in 1934. However, she and her husband eventually advocated the formation of an independent rather than IRA-affiliated tribal government at Yankton. Gertrude Simmons Bonnin died in Washington, D.C., in January of 1938, and was buried in Arlington Cemetery.

Selected Publications of Gertrude Simmons Bonnin

"America's Indian Problem." *Edict* 2, no. 11 (December 1921): 1–2, 10.

American Indian Stories. Washington, D.C.: Hayworth Press, 1921. Reprinted Lincoln: University of Nebraska Press, 2003.

American Indian Stories, Legends, and Other Writings, Edited by Cathy N. Davidson and Ada Norris. New York: Penguin Classics, 2003.

"The Black Hills Council." *The American Indian Magazine* 7 (Spring 1919): 5–7.

"The California Indians of Today." *California Indian Herald* 1 (July 1923): 10.

Dreams and Thunder: Stories, Poems, and the Sun Dance Opera. By Zitkala-Ša. Edited by P. Jane Hafen. Lincoln: University of Nebraska Press, 2001.

The Flight of Red Bird: The Life of Zitkala-Ša. Re-created by Doreen Rappaport. New York: Dial Books, 1997. Reprint New York: Puffin Books, 1999.

"Hope in the Returned Indian Soldier." *The American Indian Magazine* 7 (Summer 1919): 61–62.

"Impressions of an Indian Childhood." *Atlantic Monthly* 85 (January 1900): 381–86.

"The Indian Dance: A Protest Against Its Abolition." *Boston Transcript,* January 25, 1902: 24. Reprinted as "A Plea for the Indian Dance." *Word Carrier of Santee Normal Training School* 31 (January–February 1902): 2. Reprinted as "A Protest Against the Abolition of the Indian Dance." *Red Man and Helper* 3 (August 22, 1902): 1, 4.

"Indian Gifts to Civilized Man." *Indian Sentinel* 1 (July 1918): 13–14. Reprinted *The American Indian Magazine* 6, no. 3 (July–September 1918): 115–16.

"Letter to the Chiefs and Headmen of the Tribes." *The American Indian Magazine* 6, no. 4 (Winter 1919): 196–97. The 1918 issue appeared late.

"Lost Treaties of the California Indians." *California Indian Herald* 1 (April 1923): 7.

"An Indian Teacher Among Indians." *Atlantic Monthly* 85 (March 1900): 381–86.

Oklahoma's Poor Rich Indians: An Orgy of Graft and Exploitation of the Five Civilized Tribes—Legalized Robbery, with Charles N. Fabens and Matthew K. Sniffen. Publication of the Indian Rights Association, 2nd Series, no. 127. Philadelphia: Indian Rights Association, 1924.

Old Indian Legends. Boston: Ginn and Co., 1901. Reprinted Lincoln: University of Nebraska Press, 1985.

"The School Days of an Indian Girl." *Atlantic Monthly* 85 (February 1900): 185–93.

United States House of Representatives. *Hearings on House Resolution 2614,* 2 Parts. Washington, D.C.: Government printing Office, 1918: 1: 123–35.

"Why I Am a Pagan." *Atlantic Monthly* 90 (December 1902): 801–803.

"A Year's Experience in Community Service Work Among the Ute Tribe of Indians." *The American Indian Magazine* 4, no. 4 (October/December 1916): 307–310.

"The Ute Grazing Land." *The American Indian Magazine* 7 (Spring 1919): 8–9.

Unpublished Writings

The Gertrude Simmons and Raymond T. Bonnin Papers, University Archives, Brigham Young University, Provo, Utah; Carlos Montezuma Papers, Microfilm, Reels 1, 3, 4, State Historical Society of Wisconsin, Division of Archives and Manuscripts, Madison, Wisconsin; Richard Henry Pratt Papers, Incoming Letters, Group No. S1174, Series 1, Box 2, Folder 35, Beinecke Rare Book and Manuscript Library, Yale University, New Haven, Connecticut; Indian Rights Association Papers, 1868–1968, Microfilm, Reels 36, 40, 91, 125, Historical Society of Pennsylvania, Philadelphia, Pennsylvania, Microfilming Corporation of America.

Selected Secondary Sources

Batker, Carol. "'Overcoming All Obstacles': The Assimilation Debate in Native American Women's Journalism of the Dawes Era." In *Early Native American Writing: New Critical Essays*, edited by Helen Jaskoski. New York: Cambridge University Press, 1996: 190–203.
Bell, Betty Louise. "'If This Is Paganism . . .': Zitkala-Ša and the Devil's Language." In *Native American Religious Identity: Unforgotten Gods*, edited by Jace Weaver. Maryknoll, N.Y.: Orbis Books, 1998: 61–68.
Bernardin, Susan. "The Lessons of a Sentimental Education: Zitkala-Ša's Autobiographical Narratives." *Western American Literature* 32, no. 3 (1997): 212–38.
Carpenter, Cari. "Gertrude Bonnin's Investigation of Native American Identity." *Wicazo Sa Review* 21, no. 1 (Spring 2005): 139–49.
Carpenter, Ron. "Zitkala-Ša and Bicultural Subjectivity." *Studies in American Indian Literatures* 16, no. 3 (Fall 2004): 1–28.
Cutler, Martha J. "Zitkala-Ša's Autobiographical Writings: The Problems of a Canonical Search for Language and Identity." *MELUS* 19, no. 1 (Spring 1994): 31–44.
Dominguez, Susan R. "Zitkala-Ša (Gertrude Simmons Bonnin), 1876–1938: (Re)discovering The Sun Dance." *American Music Research Center Journal* 5 (1995): 83–96.
Enoch, Jessica. "Resisting the Script of Indian Education: Zitkala-Ša and the Carlisle Indian School." *College English* 65, no. 2 (November 2002): 117–41.
Fisher, Dexter. "Zitkala-Ša: The Evolution of a Writer." *American Indian Quarterly* 5, no. 3 (August 1979): 229–38.
Hafen, P. Jane. "Zitkala Ša: Sentimentality and Sovereignty." *Wicazo Sa Review* 12, no. 2 (Fall 1997): 31–41.
———. "Gertrude Simmons Bonnin: For the Indian Cause." In *Sifters: Native American Women's Lives*, edited by Theda Perdue. New York: Oxford University Press, 2001: 127–40.
Heflin, Ruth J. *"I Remain Alive": The Sioux Literary Renaissance*. Syracuse, N.Y.: Syracuse University Press, 2000: 105–37.
Johnson, David L. and Raymond Wilson. "Gertrude Simmons Bonnin, 1876–1938: 'Americanize the First Americans'." *American Indian Quarterly* 12, no. 1 (Winter 1988): 27–40.
Okker, Patricia. "Native American Literatures and the Cannon: The Case of

Zitkala-Ša." In *American Realism and the Canon*, edited by Tom Quick and Gary Scharnhorst. Newark: University of Delaware Press, 1994: 87–101.

Smith, Jeanne. "'A Second Tongue': The Trickster's Voice in the Works of Zitkala-Ša." In *Tricksterism in Turn-of-the-Century American Literature: A Multicultural Perspective*, edited by Elizabeth Ammons and Annette White-Parks. Hanover: University Press of New England, 1994: 46–60.

Spack, Ruth. "Re-visioning Sioux Women: Zitkala-Ša's Revolutionary American Indian Stories." *Legacy* 14, no. 1 (1997): 25–42.

———. "Dis/engagement: Zitkala-Ša's Letters to Carlos Montezuma" *MELUS*, 26, no. 1 (Spring 2001): 172–204.

Susag, Dorothea M. "Zitkala-Ša (Gertrude Bonnin) A Power(full) Literary Voice." *Studies in American Indian Literatures* 5, no. 4 (Winter 1993): 3–24.

Totten, Gary. "Zitkala-Ša and the Problem of Regionalism: Nations, Narratives, and Critical Traditions." *American Indian Quarterly* 29, nos. 1–2 (Winter–Spring 2005): 84–123.

Warrior, Robert Allen. *Tribal Secrets: Recovering American Indian Intellectual Traditions.* Minneapolis: University of Minnesota Press, 1995: 9–10, 19–20.

Welch, Deborah. "Zitkala-Ša: An American Indian Leader, 1876–1938." Ph.D. Dissertation, University of Wyoming, 1985.

Willard, William. "Zitkala-Ša: A Woman Who Would Be Heard!" *Wicazo Sa Review* 1, no. 1 (Spring 1985): 11–16.

———. "The First Amendment, Anglo-Conformity, and American Indian Religious Freedom." *Wicazo Sa Review* 7, no. 1 (Spring 1991): 25–41.

INDUSTRIAL ORGANIZATION FOR THE INDIAN

Laura Cornelius Kellogg (1912)

Whether he is a citizen or not, or whether he has lands or not, whether his trust funds continue or not, whether he is educated or ignorant, one thing remains unchanged with the Indian: he has to have bread and butter, he has to have a covering on his back, he has to live.

Of all the phases of our national problem, none other seems so immediately important to me as our industrial status. It at once decides whether we shall become degraded toward pauperism or whether we may secure to ourselves permanent independence. Whatever our political or social status may be, we are and always will be tried and judged on our ability individually to maintain ourselves, indeed our very integrity depends upon it. I repeat what I have said elsewhere, that this country does not set aside the Indian because he is brown or because be wears beads around his neck. It is more often a question of soap and water, a lack of fitness to turn a good furrow in a field, or to labor by the sweat of his brow for what he eats. Now I am not saying that he shall be as clean as the man with a porcelain bath tub in his house, when the Indian has to haul water in a cup or an olla from a mile away. No! What I do say is: the bath tub and the pipes must move to the Indian, and that he must make them move to him in a system. Not only this, but he must produce adequate supplies out of his own environment. He must labor—and he must labor to the best advantage for himself and not to the exploiter.

It is upon this conviction that I shall proceed in this paper. The good things of life must move to the Indian by a system. Instead of wasting what he already has, and looking for himself in the outside world, he must make his own world *at home.* This point of view is the result of some years of close economic study of the industrial conditions not only in this country but those of Europe, and a study, too, of the Indian himself.

Realizing that he was turning his face toward Caucasian institutions as his ultimate good, I have looked into them critically, with his advantage uppermost in my mind, and I have become convinced that he cannot copy *everything* the white man does with advantage. Certainly is it a mistake in some important phases of his industrial life to follow him exactly as he is to-day.

This imitation is on the part of the Indian an indication of our own weakness and inability to present a better program than his own. I do believe much of this is born of our growing disbelief in ourselves due to our having been misrepresented so long, and in deferring everything to the white man's opinions of us.

Under the heading "Industrial Organization for the Indian," then, I wish at once to suggest that the way out for the Indian, of his present situation, is along the lines of organization for himself and by himself—organization of these things which shall control his livelihood and which shall be based on a special consideration for his needs. In the present space allotted to me for this subject I can but briefly pass over a great many phases I should like to dwell upon at length, leaving out much of the detail.

Before I proceed further I wish to be understood as to my attitude toward the "Pratt Ideal."[1] I am wholly in accord with its idea of equal opportunity for the Indian, its belief in the ability of the Indian and the need of a proper environment for demonstration. And I am just as strong against Paternalism and Wardship and Reservations as a regime as any self-respecting Indian or educator can be. But I do not agree with certain failures on its part to calculate upon the possibilities of the Indian on the reservation, neither do I believe we can overlook the influence of human ties. A good majority of the Carlisle students, who have been taught to leave the reservation to establish themselves outside, come back to it even after they have learned trades. From unbiased observation this seems to point to the fact that the Indian's ties are very strong. He is naturally clannish, he does not seek to mix with the paleface either in interest or blood, down deep in his heart he feels superior to the ordinary white man,—and the real Indian is. A proof of that is that after he has been surrounded by whites on every reservation for several hundred years, he has not amalgamated enough to have changed the face of his racial problems. What I do not see is the necessity of crowding him to become a white man, when opportunity is all he needs. I do not wish to be understood to mean, when I speak of the Carlisle students going back to the reservation, that he is a failure. Far from it. I have been careful to observe certain localities upon this point, and I have found that Carlisle has no more failures than high schools in the outside communities, and in some instances less, in proportion to the population, than the outside.

A second factor, aside from the ties of home, is his interests in the way of allotments and inheritances on the reservation. The Indian naturally comes back to these if it is no more than to look at them.

This being the case, there seems the need of a complement to the Pratt Ideal. It is this I propose to meet. Instead of forsaking what we already have in holdings, to go away to the white world of industry to be there too often wage-earners for life (I am taking into account the majority rule), instead of being fixtures in an industrial world, which is itself still largely problematic for the white man, I maintain that the line of least resistance to the greatest possible good under our present circumstances is to citizenize the possibilities and to reorganize the opportunities of the Indian *at home;* to organize the Indians' holdings into a system of economic advantages; to convert his large wastes into industrial centers which he can take care of to modernize his affairs and to assure him at least a comfortable maintenance if he will work. I believe in struggle and in competition in whatsoever vocation he shall prefer. I believe in struggle and in competition with the outside world. I am one who knows at first hand what the knocks in it are. I am a product of almost every institution of the outside except the insane asylum and Tammany Hall.[2] Struggle is the making of men, but I do not believe in thrusting the weak, without due preparation,

into the intense and unfavorable industrial strife of a foreign world. Awhile ago
I said that I did not believe in copying everything the white man did, if we could
improve upon it. I want to explain what I mean by that.

Some of the gravest problems in this country to-day are to be found in the
industrial world of the white man. With all his acumen, with all his advantages,
with all his training, the great masses of labor (who make the things he wears
and the things he eats, and who serve the money despots) are by no means
rewarded for their toil or taken care of when they need care, much less have
they the leisure or the means or the energy for higher education. Why?

The social conscience in this country is not generally enlightened, and it is
far from being ethical. Those that are enlightened are in a very small minority,
and they have their difficulties in effectively bringing about legislation to the
protection and betterment of labor, because public sentiment has to be educated first before it will move to anything, and it isn't so easy to educate it in a
land where politics would control. There is something in the social order that
is responsible for this. The development of intense individualism and the age of
unprecedented prosperity no doubt are largely responsible for the selfishness
of the American people.

Look about you into the working world outside and see that first of all there
is no uniform and happy adjustment between labor and capital in this country.
For while the conditions of labor differ between the country and the city, between different localities between cities themselves, they all come under one
grand general wage system and modern capitalism. The wage system is a
product of the nineteenth century and has not yet triumphed altogether above
slavery and serfdom (the two conditions it aims to escape) for the reason that
it is dependent upon capital, and capital in this land is suffering from acute
despotism.

In order to save the cost of production, and to supply the growing demand
of civilization (and in this it is evolutionary), capital has taken the work originally done on a small scale and put it into big machines; hence the factory system. The factory system is then at once responsible for some of the biggest
problems for the Caucasian mind. Here are some of the evils to which it has
given birth: child labor, employed in place of adult employment, with light-
running machinery, because it is cheaper; industrial accidents, due to large
machines without protective appliances, because protection is an item of expense to the employer and the laborer himself is still too ignorant to demand
protection before he takes the work that at any moment may take his limb and
life; factory regulation and unemployment; unsanitary conditions and long
hours—though the last two have been improved by legislation in the past few
years, they are by no means above reproach today, Unemployment is the result of the invention of labor-saving machines and the unsettled condition
created by differences between labor and capital.

The fact that capital is such a terrific power in the hands of the civilized but
unenlightened is producing a class struggle in this democratic country of ours
where they shout, "equal opportunity for all men," and then thieve it. The wage

earner to-day is a wage earner always. Once he gets into it he cannot get out of it . . . .

Take particularly the wage earner in the city where the most of the population of the country is congested. Even a casual look at the labor market there is enough to show that the conditions of the white man's toil are far from being happy or equitable, indeed, they are tragic; look at the wan faces of the ill-nourished multitude closely packed, like a lot of cattle, in a foul car hurrying to their work in the city. Follow a hollow-chested bent old man at forty-five years into the close [sic] shop where the wind never made a clean sweep, where the sun never had a chance to creep in through the high walls of the neighboring buildings; listen to the story of the boy to earn and save enough to buy his mother a home,—he never did. Watch him go out of the dingy shop at six o'clock, a bent and sick old man, he would like one day off to-morrow, but he would lose his place and his means of support. He is still dependent upon to-morrow's toil for to-morrow's bread. Follow him into the old and dismal quarter of the city where rent is cheap and where the noises never cease. Follow him up the rickety old steps into the rented rooms, damp, sickly smelling dark rooms, whose windows closely face another wall, stay and hear him ask for a good sirloin, and see him get a red sausage and a dill pickle; hear him cough and remember that he helps to make the clothes you buy in the shops. No, I cannot see that everything the white man does is to be copied. The tragedy of young hopes and healths crushed out by the heavy heel of money despotism in the industrial world is not an unusual thing in this country. The average man in the white labor markets lives a miserable existence to-day that he may live another miserable day to-morrow, and so on till disease or accident take pity upon him. I do not look with optimism upon these conditions, not for any race of people under the sun . . . .

I have given the sweatshop as only one of the evils of the white industrial world.[3] Skilled labor has better conditions, of course, but outside of the agricultural pursuits skilled labor, too, is confined to indoor life.

The Indian does not realize that under proper sanitation he is a superior man to any other class in this country, physically. The fact that he is an outdoor man is perhaps the chief reason why he has sustained himself and survived conditions of housing which is killing the white man, only he doesn't acknowledge it. His tendency to the great white plague is not so inherent as it is a matter of environment. With proper conditions thrown about him, which means returning to the observance of his original laws of health, the Indian would eradicate this tendency toward tuberculosis. The great white plague thrives in the indoor shop. Several years ago I had the pleasure of breaking the record in the investigation of the causes of tuberculosis in the city of Milwaukee. In this particular investigation we found that the average working family numbered five members, and the heads of families were earning nine dollars a week. When the rent and the fuel were taken out it left ninety-four cents for each one to live on per week. As a consequence the laboring population was dying from tuberculosis. These people represented not only the sweat shop but the general conditions of city employment. The white man laborer cannot earn enough to feed him properly, and, as for the sanitation of his house, the Indian tepee isn't a circumstance to the cheap tenement house. I have never forgotten the smells of the closed parlors with their heavy draperies and the dismalness of drawn shades. The tenement house of the city has since become a dread to me, and I fear some Indians who have an undue worship of Paleface ways will likewise follow closed windows and drawn shades. I may be departing a little when I dwell upon this beyond a passing mention, but when I have looked over the white man's conditions of living, with the idea of putting the Indian into it I have seen things that we do too often pass over without due consideration.

Wherever there is intelligence in the land, there is a return to the Indian's habit of living out of doors. And when you stop to think that out of twenty-four hours each one of us is taking 25,000 breaths it is easy to see that one of the reasons why we have been particularly free from the white man's foul diseases before he contaminated us is because we drew in health 25,000 times instead of poisons. An indoor race cannot have the reddest of blood.

It is a matter of statistics that as soon as a people hive had long experience with tenement life and city employment they return to the country. Now then my plea is that we avoid the things that are killing off the majority of the laboring population in the country among the whites.

It has been agreed by all thinkers that the ideal life is the small community life, which combines the advantages of concentration with the health of the uncongested freedom. Before I go into the details of the organization I here propose let me sum up the reasons why the Indian should seek to organize something different and better for himself than already exists.

1. He has lands, a valuable asset in the business world. He does not need to buy sites for the construction of industrial centers.

2. He has funds which could be called out for organization expense—enough of it to cover the whole Indian population with organization.

3. Certain ideas of his own way of living: namely, the devotion to simplicity and outdoor life, and he ought to insist upon their being reinstated.

4. The conditions of labor in the outside world are inferior to the conditions which he can establish for himself.

The organization which I believe to be most effective for our uses is called the Garden City. In this country it has triumphed in the experiment on Long Island. In Europe it has triumphed generally wherever it has been tried and it has been tried extensively—the most modern examples being found in England and Germany and France.[4] The kind I propose for the Indian I prefer to call the Industrial Village, for the simple reason that it has been suggested to me that the name Garden City sounds too much like an Utopian idea, or a soft notion of philanthropy. This thing I propose is a hard-headed, practical scheme which is not dependent upon charity to carry it out.

In distinction from the experiment in New York, the industrial village is not a relief from the congestion of population, but it is a planned concentration of population.

The tendency in the cities to move back to the small community life is a sign of progress, and quite logical. Here are some of the chief reasons for it:

1. The social nature of man is more satisfied in a village than on isolated farms, and the isolation of city life where families side by side do not need to know each other.

2. The advantages of systematized life can be readily and more economically secured.

Sewage, lighting, and water-works can be had by a group of people of moderate means when the same people individually cannot have them at all.

3. The enforcement of regulations for the public good can be more effectively carried out. This includes not only the purely ethical institutions, but sanitation and education and amusements.

4. Facilities of transportation can be more easily secured.

5. The successful carrying out of commerce in modern times requires concentration of population. There is greater economy of manufacture and running business in the organized community. In this it is a practical school for wholesome citizenship and it develops municipal efficiency.

With the installment of the industrial village, there must be instituted at the same time the industry which shall be the source of revenue for the villagers. This industry among our Indians need not be the same for the different localities. We have among ourselves the consideration of the different stages of anthropologic culture to consider. There are four stages in the development to conventional civilization of any primitive people; first, the hunting and fishing stage; second, the pastoral or the keeping and tending of flocks; third, the agricultural; fourth, the horticultural stage. All these stages the Indians of the United States had at the time of the advent of the Caucasian.

Some of them fished and hunted only, some of them herded the buffalo, some of them planted maize enough to trade or make it a tribute to their conquerors among themselves. The Cherokee actually knew and practised the art of raising orchards and even of grafting. There is nothing more densely ignorant than the white man on these various stages of the American Indian's development, as is evident in the Indian policy. The Navajo is in the height of the second stage. The Nez Perce and the Oneida are in the height of the third stage. I might enumerate at length. It would be nothing short of folly to impose upon the Navajo a change of industry. The thing to do for him is to place his industry on a modern business scale and to go one step beyond—eliminate the middle man's interference with him. Instead of the white trader getting the 60 per cent of the profits as he does in the white man's world of commerce, let the Navajo so organize that he can sell his wares to the consumer direct and get 90 per cent of the profits.

In Oneida, Wisconsin, where soon every individual Indian will become a full-fledged citizen, the organization of the village we hope to make along lines which combine the foreign Garden City with the Mormon idea of communistic cooperation.

The point of improvement on the foreign Garden City plan is a triumph over the white man's institutions of to-day the world over. The foreign and the American city both are corporate institutions, capitalized by money. Every member of the corporation holds so many shares of stock, which represent tangible assets. The man then who enters into the corporation must be represented by some form of money. If he have not this, he either cannot become a member of the organization or else he must go in debt for it. Now there is nothing under the sun that is more unproductive than gold itself. Money is merely a medium of exchange for the products of the earth. That saying that "it takes an ounce of gold to get an ounce of gold out of the mine" illustrates my meaning. Money represents an exchange of values, and when you trace these values to their sources they are *soil* and *labor*. In other words, *the wealth of a country is in her soil and her men*. Gold lies dormant in the earth till man comes along and handles it, and the only thing that never fails to produce is the soil. Herein is the failure of the modern systems of business to become at once equitable, in the fact that money represents the worth of a man. Now what did the Mormon do? How did he go into the desert with his destitute colony and establish economic freedom to every individual man the way it has never been done in the history of the white man in Western civilization? How did he keep from starving in the desert where there was neither water, markets, nor money? Some one among that Colony had the right inspiration about organization. Some one reckoned out this defect in relying upon capital for everything. He had men and he had the soil. What did he do?[5]

He saw that he needed water on the sand to make things grow. The Colorado river must be tapped. How was it possible to do it? Labor must do it, and it did. The Mormon practised irrigation twenty years before the rest of the country did. He did it without money because he capitalized labor. Men were worth just exactly what they will always be worth when the estimate is right: men were worth just what they could do for the community. They brought that water from the Colorado by the labor of their own hands, and whether they were educated or ignorant. How were they paid? Each man was paid in shares of stock in the cooperative store and he received the best the community had for a living.

As soon as they established the water system, they put the seed in the ground, and they divided their labor so that no one man had more than twenty acres to look after. They placed every man at the oversight of a competent man who knew land values and the secrets of cultivation. They took no risks. Wherever their colonies went, they sent with them the expert who oversaw to the quality of industry, and to the economy of energy and space; their traveling missionaries were men more bent upon learning the local conditions, the proper methods, the secret of successes, the market requirements, the development and advancement of every locality, than upon converts. They took no risks.

And note how they understood the meaning of economy. They had to build a reservoir, for example. They did it with their own hands and thus avoided the rake-off to the contractor, the banker, the bonding company, and the promoter. They had 90 per cent of their value at home, and when they established their cooperative stores this is the way they did it: They sent their wool, their hides, their grain, their mutton and their beef to the market and traded them in goods. They paid for the hauling of these in shares of Community stock. Now being one Community, every one was in the family. If a hard, lean year came along, he had credit given on his shares of stock,—this being appropriable for payment.

At Woodruff, Arizona, 150 people used less than 600 acres making a distribution of 20 acres for adult labor per capita. The reduction of space to intensive use of the soil did away with too broad a distribution of one man's energy. This resulted in a greater success from 20 acres than outside individual farmers made on three and four hundred acres. At St. Joe, Arizona, there are two farms not larger than 20 acres that have amassed a fortune of $50.000 each for their owners, showing that men in the Mormon Commune may prosper individually according to their ability, which is the great note in the New Socialism. When men are equal in their opportunities they receive the maximum of economic advantage.

Where Socialism fails to triumph in this country is because under the present form of corporate rights, the individual has as many votes as he has shares of stock. A man, therefore, who has 51 per cent of all the stock decides and rules. And he may outdistance the small share holder who may be a superior man to the organization.

There are two remedies I would suggest for this:

1. Apply the Rochdale system of "one man, one vote," regardless of the number of shares of stock, or,

2. Provide against 51 per cent control in the hands of any one individual.[6]

The foreign American and European idea of the division of dividends to the share holder is a communistic idea of capital and not of men. The Mormon idea is a communistic idea of men. In his institution every man draws his proportion performed. Each man in it shall own lands, but the work and the advantages are communistic. The Mormons to-day are the richest people per capita in the world. There is one precaution they took among other things. And that is they fortified themselves against the lazy man. If he could not perform a fixed minimum of labor he had to get out of the Community. The Community might take his property at its own price.

The principle of intensive cultivation as carried out by the Mormons has been carried out in other countries to a remarkable extent. Denmark, for example, is one-fourth the size of the State of Wisconsin, yet she supplies all Europe with butter and eggs.

The American scientific agriculturist is realizing that space is not necessary with soil for returns. The great note in Western civilization to-day is toward practical science.

Awhile back I said that we had four stages of anthropologic culture to consider in our organization. Let me reiterate in conclusion that no one industry can be uniformly installed on the Reservations if we would intelligently handle every locality and group. Expert service must be secured to look over Indian territory, to judge for what the locality is best adapted, and to find the market. The town-site for the Industrial Village should be chosen after determining these. In short, I believe that were the Industrial Village organized with the Mormon idea of capitalization, combined with the European and American idea of the market, that we would secure the maximum advantage. That we must calculate to meet and to use modern business methods goes without saying, but the great distinction I wish to impress upon your minds is that to reach a state of economic equity we must follow the Mormon idea of making men the capital of the community.

In these pages I have not berated white institutions because they are white, but because all economists have agreed already that they are neither as economic nor as equitable as they hope to be. Let us take the natural advantages the race already has in its possessions and make for ourselves Gardens and teach the white man that we believe the greatest economy in the world is to be just to all men. It is my belief that the old saying, "Be good and you will be happy" is fast coming to mean "Be happy and you will be good." Man is only a creature of circumstance after all.

Notes

Originally a speech delivered at the first annual convention of the Society of American Indians in Columbus, Ohio, on October 13, 1911. Published in *Report of the Executive Council on the Proceedings of the First Annual Conference of the Society of American Indians* (Washington, D.C., 1912), 43–55. Laura Cornelius's presentation on reservation based industrial villages was so out of line with SAI ideology that the chairman of the meeting, Charles E. Dagenett, precluded the usual panel discussions following each speaker's talk on account of its excessive length.

1. Richard Henry Pratt (1840–1924) was the founder of Carlisle Indian Industrial School. His educational policy entailed no less than total Indian assimilation to American ways. See Richard Henry Pratt, *Battlefield and Classroom: Four Decades with the American Indian, 1867–1904,* ed. Robert M. Utley (New Haven: Yale University Press, 1964).

2. "Boss Tweed" and New York City's Tammany Hall represented one of the most notorious cases of political corruption in U.S. history. It was an organization that tied members of the Democratic Party to the Society of St. Tammany, a patriotic fraternal organization started in 1789 and supposedly named after the legendary Delaware leader Temmenund. The corruption in the New York City administration was finally curbed under the Roosevelt administration in 1934.

3. One of the main concerns of Progressive Era social workers was labor reform. Although anti-sweatshop activity had been going on previously (i.e., Florence Kelly in Chicago during the 1890s), widespread public notice of the problem in the United States was sparked by Upton Sinclair's novel *The Jungle* (1907) and the tragic "Triangle Shirtwaist Fire" in Manhattan on March 25, 1911, which resulted in the death of over 140 garment workers. The Fair Labor Standards Act of 1938 finally helped to curb some of the evils of the sweatshop industry in the United States.

4. Alexander Turney Stewart (1803–78), wealthy American merchant, built the planned workers' community of Garden City in Long Island in 1869. Following the

publication of Ebenazer Howard's (1850–1928) book *Garden Cities of To-morrow* (1898), the Garden City Association was founded in England in 1899 with a goal of improving the terrible living conditions in the congested cities. The first Garden City experiment was established at Letchworth in 1903, followed by Welwyn Garden City in 1919. Garden City communities also cropped up in France, Germany, and Russia.

5. Mormons (Church of Jesus Christ of Latter-Day Saints) led by Brigham Young established the "Free State of Deseret," now Salt Lake City, in Utah in 1847, where they instituted a cooperative system (United Order) based on the visions of its founder Joseph Smith. Their "communistic" system was long regarded as anti-American and unconstitutional.

6. In 1844 English artisans founded the Rochdale Equitable Pioneer's Society, the prototype of all modern cooperative societies. Among its principles were democratic control ("one member, one vote"), limited returns on capital, distribution of surplus to members according to work done, cash trading only, providing for the education of its members, and political and religious neutrality.

BIOGRAPHY

Laura Miriam Cornelius Kellog (Oneida, 1880–ca. 1949) was born on the Oneida Reservation near Green Bay, Wisconsin, the daughter of Adam Poe Cornelius and Celicia Bread Cornelius. She was a descendant of Daniel Bread and Skenandore, two New York Oneida chiefs who followed the eccentric Anglo-Mohawk Episcopal missionary Eleazer Williams (1788–1858) to Wisconsin in 1822. During the 1890s Laura Cornelius attended Grafton Hall, an Episcopal boarding school for girls located at Fond du Lac, Wisconsin. Following her graduation in 1898 she spent about two years traveling in Europe and then studied sporadically at Barnard College, Cornell University, the New York School of Philanthropy (later Columbia University School of Social Work), Stanford University, and the University of Wisconsin without ever receiving a degree from any of these institutions. It was probably at Columbia, where the first class in social work was offered in 1898, that she became acquainted with the principles of social work and community service that would shape her ideas about Indian policy reform.

On April 3–4, 1911, Laura Cornelius cofounded the American Indian Association (later Society of American Indians). As a secretary of the Temporary Executive Committee she helped to organize the first meeting of the Society of American Indians in Columbus, Ohio, on October 12 of that same year, at which time she was elected vice president of education. Cornelius was extremely critical of federal Indian policy. She advocated the incorporation of the remaining Indian land base into independent industrial villages modeled after traditional Indian settlements and earlier cooperative projects such as the Rochdale Equitable Pioneer's Society, the Garden City municipal experiment, and the Mormon system of United Order. Years later she would expand her concept of reservation based industrial villages, which she designated as the "Lolomi Program of Self-Government," in a book titled *Our Democracy and the American Indian* (1920). Cornelius's views, obviously influenced in part by the contemporary labor movement, differed markedly from most of the other members of the Society of American Indians. She was particularly antagonistic toward Arthur C. Parker, who was elected as secretary-treasurer of the Society of American Indians in 1912. Following her marriage to Orrin Joseph Kellogg, a non-Indian attorney from Minnesota, on April 22, 1912, she gradually distanced herself from the Society of American Indians. Together with other disgruntled members such as the Catholic Ojibwe editor Gustave H. Beaulieu (1852–1917), she founded the Grand Council of American Indians in Washington, D.C., in 1913, a rival national Indian organization that was practically defunct by 1917.

In the period between 1913 and 1927, Laura Cornelius Kellogg and her husband dedicated themselves to organizing a major Iroquois land-claims suit. In order to obtain funds for their legal efforts they made delusive promises to donors and collected money from impoverished Indians in the United States and Canada, tactics that would forever tarnish Laura Cornelius reputation among the Oneidas as well as fellow Indian reformers. Although never convicted of fraud, the questionable collection methods employed by the Kelloggs led to their arrests in Oklahoma in 1913 and Montreal in 1925. Finally, in 1927, the United States District Court dismissed the Kelloggs' land-claims suit in *Deere v. St. Lawrence River Power Company,* claiming lack of jurisdiction over the dispute (reversed by the Supreme Court in *Oneida Nation v. County of Oneida* in 1974). Laura Cornelius Kellogg, whose political views were in many ways ahead of her time, died in obscurity in New York City sometime in the late 1940s. Other than several articles on Indian affairs and *Our Democracy,* she is credited as the author of numerous short stories and plays.

Selected Publications of Laura Cornelius Kellogg

"Building the Indian Home." *Indian's Friend* 13 (May 1901): 2, 11–12.
"Industrial Organization for the Indian." *Report of the Executive Council on the Proceedings of the First Annual Conference of the Society of American Indians.* Washington, D.C., 1912: 43–55.
Our Democracy and the American Indian. Kansas City, Mo.: Burton Publishing, 1920.
"Some Facts and Figures on Indian Education." *The Quarterly Journal of the Society of American Indians* 1, no. 1 (January–April 1913): 36–46.

Selected Secondary Sources

Batker, Carol. "'Overcoming All Obstacles': The Assimilation Debate in Native American Women's Journalism of the Dawes Era." In *Early Native American Writing: New Critical Essays,* edited by Helen Jaskoski. New York: Cambridge University Press, 1996: 190–203.
Hauptman, Laurence M. "Designing Woman: Minnie Kellogg, Iroquois Leader." In *Indian Lives: Essays on Nineteenth and Twentieth Century Native American Leaders,* edited by L. G. Moses and Raymond Wilson. Albuquerque: University of New Mexico Press, 1985: 159–88.
McLester, Thelma Cornelius. "Oneida Women Leaders." In *The Oneida Indian Experience: Two Perspectives,* edited by Jack Campisi and Laurence M. Hauptman. Syracuse, N.Y.: Syracuse University Press, 1988: 108–25 (esp. 109–11).

NATIVE INDIAN ART

Angel De Cora Dietz (1912)

I have been asked often just what is meant by Native Indian Art. I hardly think this audience will put up such a question, but on the other hand there might be diversified views on the subject, and since I have been invited to speak on the subject, I will give you my interpretation of Native Indian Art by right of practical experience with the art.

To begin at the very foundation of the subject, art in all its forms, is the expression of man's best impulses; from the joy of the heart man sings or writes a poem, when the inspiration comes through his visual sense, he makes a pictorial record of it in form, line or color.

There is no people without art. The early history of every race has come down to us through the medium of graphic, plastic and textile arts, and if we wish to attain a scientific knowledge of art we must begin at the foundation and study the nature of the art of primitive peoples.

Up to the present time the art of the American Indian has appealed to just two classes of professional men, the scientist and the artist. The Indian in his natural state was a source of inspiration to the artist. Painter, poet and sculptor have immortalized him on canvas, in marble and in verse. They have realized that he was akin to the arts, but it was the general effect of the Indian in buckskin and feathers that the artist took for art, never dreaming there was a cause for effect. (I came across a newspaper cartoon some time ago that illustrated well this point. The picture was an old, so-called "blanket" Indian and an old eagle standing before two coins, one with the head of an Indian with a feather bonnet and on the other coin was the eagle, the national emblem. The old Indian apparently addressing the old eagle says, "Nature and Art— that's us.")

The Indian is an artist and on the details of his garments he lavished his utmost skill. The Indian artist's first aim was to picture his thoughts, and he drew them on the material at hand. His skin garments, utensils and nearly all his personal possessions bore record of his thought. At first no attempts were made at realism, the simple forms and figures had practical significance, but gradually, through the process of evolution, the pictorial arrangements tended to cultivate his decorative sense and thereby started his art on the more aesthetic plane.

Aesthetics in art is the study or practice of art for art's sake, for the sensuous pleasure of form, line and color. As to what is pleasing, that each person must decide for himself.

All art is founded on the primitive efforts of people's needs in their daily life—each nation shows individual taste, always developed by environment. This makes Egyptian and Greek art distinctive, and neither can be or has been adopted by any other people, although their classical designs are often adapted to the uses of other countries, yet none claim them as their own original work. The Greeks and Italians have reached the highest order of art, and will always stand as models for the whole world. Every town and hamlet testifies to the grave love of the beautiful developed in their ordinary daily life.

But to the American people the European art is not the only art. They copy every nationality. They adopt the simplest forms of peasant dress, adopt the form of ordinary home-spun material to the richest fabric. Tourists from the East buy every vestige of Indian handiwork that they can see at the stations of the Southwest. They use these varied articles for decoration in houses in close contact with curios from Japan and China. Some use belts and chains with impunity which may be more or less appropriate.[1]

How much they can learn if they properly consider the true significance of these designs that they are the correct form for which they are used upon articles in use by Indians.

The designs, if thoughtfully considered, form the nucleus of Native Indian Art which can be exploited and adapted to as many and varied uses as any of the designs brought from foreign countries.

To-day the oak leaf and acorn adorn the coronation robes of the British Sovereign. The thistle of Scotland and shamrock of Ireland are also incorporated in many designs. The Swastika of the Southwestern Indians is closely allied to the designs of antiquity. Other designs are equally valuable and have their artistic merits.

The Indians are gifted in original ideas of ornamentation as can be seen on their personal decorations. To train and develop this decorative instinct of the Indian to modern methods and apply it on up-to-date house furnishings is the nature and intent of the Native Indian Art Department as now carried on at the United States Indian School at Carlisle, Pennsylvania. The Indian's training for keen observation makes him an apt pupil in the pictorial art as those of you who have taught in Indian schools can readily verify.

Some years ago I attended a National Educational Association convention. I spent some time looking over the Indian school exhibit. The art work was the same as is prescribed for public schools, the usual spray of flower or budding twig done in "wash" after the manner of Japanese brush work, and some stilted forms of geometric figures apparently made under the strict directions of a teacher.[2] The only trace of Indian about the exhibition was some of the names denoting clannish nomenclature.

As I stood there studying the accurately copied work of the Indian scholars, it occurred to me that the American Indians had two art systems, the sign language and a decorative art, the two mediums of communication which were almost universal with the whole Indian race. There were the tribal differences, but the two systems were well founded and well established. The fact is not so well known that the hand manual of the deaf mutes was the outcome of the Indian's sign language.[3] However, this little blessing of the Indian to the human race does not eclipse his glorious record as preserved by the War Department.

Further contemplation and study convinced me that the Indian's art was a well-established system of designing and if the young school Indian was permitted to practice it in the class room it would make as interesting an exhibition as the one I saw at that National Education Association convention, and moreover it might be further cultivated by the educated Indians and adapted to modern methods.

The nature of Indian art is formed on a purely conventional and geometric basis, and our endeavors at the Carlisle Indian School have been to treat it as a conventional system of designing.

From the best specimens of bead work designs, we study the symbolic figures, first of the Sioux, as they represent a certain style of Indian designing peculiar to the tribes of the middle west or those whose habitat was the prairie. The Indian pictured the broader aspects of nature, such as sky, clouds, hills, lakes, rivers, trees and rocks in symbolic figures of geometrical shapes, so the general character of the country had much to do with each tribal scheme of symbolisms.

The study of the fundamental figures was followed by the combined figures, made up of two or more of the elements of design, then the still more complex figures made by repeated use of two or more of the elements of design. Under this analytic system we have studied the various tribal styles, the Arapahoe system which represents the tribes of the mountainous regions, and the Winnebago which treats of the forest and lake country; the Navajo presents still another style showing the character of desert country. The Zuni, Pueblo and Hopi offer a much more developed system of decorative designing which lends itself wonderfully to interior wall decoration. After much drilling in this geometric system of designing, the unit system was introduced. By this development all the page ornamentations of the Carlisle school magazine, the Red Man, were made by the pupils. We have made stencil designs for the friezes and draperies, designs for rugs, embroideries, applique, wood carving, tiles and metal work. We not only have produced the designs, but they have been applied whenever we had the material at hand. Rugs, draperies, sofa cushion covers and smaller articles were designed and made by the girls of the Art Department and the boys of the Art Department under Mr. [William Lone Star] Dietz, who is also a trained artist, have done all the pen and ink decorations for the Red Man, such as the page borders, initial letters and other page ornaments. In the metal work Indian designs were wrought in silver jewelry, copper and brass trays in all the novelty shapes.

The Indian designs modified and applied to interior house decoration are especially in harmony with the so-called "mission" style, the geometric designs lend themselves well to the simple and straight lines of mission furniture.

One of the best art schools in the country thought it worth while to have Indian students in their midst who would impart some of their native ideas of designing to their pupils, in return for which the Indian pupil would receive the full technical training of the institution. Some of the students were sent from our preparatory training to the Pennsylvania School of Industrial Art in Philadelphia, but lack of means prevented some from completing the course.

There has been much expression of sentiment from various sources over the efforts made by the art pupils of the school to apply Indian designs on modern house furnishings, and the purpose of this talk is to show how the school-trained Indian, with little technical training, has made use of this geometric system of designing.

By careful study and close application many hundred designs have been evolved. Many of these designs have been thrown upon the market of the country and each one has brought its financial reward, but more than that, from these small and unassuming ventures, we have drawn the attention of artists and manufacturers to the fact that the Indian of North America possessed a distinctive art which promises to be of great value in a country which heretofore has been obliged to draw its models from the countries of the eastern hemisphere. Its continued development shows that much more can be expected as time and opportunity offer new occasions for its application. Its scope grows wider each year and the future has much in store.

My experience at Carlisle shows me that in addition to the creative ability in designing, it is no effort for the school Indian to acquire the technique of any art handiwork, but in all probability none of these excellent designers will ever find their way to any art school for a finished training, but should one care to look into their future homes, however modest they might be, one will find there a sense of harmony peculiar to the American Indian. These young people have shown resourceful minds in application of their native designs to modern furnishings. Indian designs could be used very effectively in brick and slate works, in parquet and mosaic floors, oilcloths, carved wood furniture, tiles, stencil designs for friezes and draperies, designs for rugs, embroideries, applique, metal work, enameled jewelry and page decorations.

Manufacturers are now employing Indian designs in deteriorated forms. If this system of decoration was better understood by the designers, how much more popular their products would be in the general market.

An Indian with the technical training of a good art school would readily find employment with establishments that employ designers.

The Indian in his native dress is a thing of the past, but his art that is inborn shall endure. He may shed his outer skin, but his markings lie below that and should show up only the brighter.

As all peoples have treasured the history of their wanderings in some form, so has the American Indian had his pictograph and symbolic records, and with the progress of time he has evolved it into a system of designing, drawing his inspiration from the whole breadth of his native land. His art like himself is indigenous to the soil of his country, where, with the survival of his latent abilities, he bravely offers the best productions of his mind and hand which shall be a permanent record of the race.

Notes

Originally in *Report of the Executive Council on the Proceedings of the First Annual Conference of the Society of American Indians* (Washington, D.C., 1912), 82–87.

Reproduced in *Southern Workman* 36 (October 1907): 527–28; and *The Indian Historian* 3, no. 1 (Winter, 1970): 27–29. One of several recorded talks De Cora gave on American Indian art, this talk was delivered at the first annual convention of the Society of American Indians in Columbus, Ohio, on October 13, 1911. It made a particularly favorable impression on Charles Eastman, who shared De Cora's enthusiasm for Indian design. See Charles A. Eastman, "My People: The Indian's Contribution to the Art of America," *The Craftsman* 27, no. 2 (November 1914): 179–86.

1. With the rise of regular railroad tourism to the American West at the turn of the twentieth century the commerce in Indian-made goods like blankets, baskets, or pottery reached major proportions. A veritable collecting craze broke out at this time fanned by the blossoming American Arts and Crafts Movement (Craft Revival) and its major organ, *The Craftsman*, which regularly dedicated space to articles about "authentic" Indian material culture. Among other things, it promoted so-called Indian corners (a corner of a room filled with Indian objects), which became particularly popular among contemporary American home owners. It did not take long for Indian reformers to sense that this was a golden opportunity to increase Indian self-sufficiency and thereby speed up the process of integration. Promotion of Indian arts and crafts eventually became an official aspect of federal Indian policy during the New Deal era. See T. C. McLuhan and William E. Kappler, *Dream Tracks: The Railroad and the American* Indian (New York: Abrams, 1985); Robert Fay Schrader, *The Indian Arts & Crafts Board: An Aspect of New Deal Indian Policy* (Albuquerque: University of New Mexico Press, 1983).

2. A "wash" is a sweep or splash especially of color made by or as if by a long stroke of a brush.

3. American Indian sign languages, though highly sophisticated, apparently had no direct influence on the major deaf-mute sign languages developed by Europeans and Americans.

BIOGRAPHY

Angel DeCora Dietz (Winnebago, 1871–1919), or Hinook-Mahiwi-Kilinaka (Fleecy Cloud Floating Into Place), was born at the Winnebago Agency in Dakota County (now Thurston), Nebraska, on May 3, the daughter of David Tall DeCora, a Winnebago of French ancestry. Her mother was a member of the influential LaMere family; Angel was thus first cousin to Winnebago author Oliver LaMere. In 1883 Angel DeCora was sent to Hampton Normal and Agricultural School, a special institution for freedmen in Hampton, Virginia, that also took on Indian students after 1878. She returned to the Winnebago Agency in the summer of 1887 and then resumed her studies at Hampton in the winter of 1888.

Following her graduation from Hampton in 1891, Angel DeCora briefly attended a private school in Northampton, Massachusetts, and then transferred to Smith College in 1892 to study art under the direction of landscape painter Dwight T. Tryon. She graduated from Smith College in 1896 and went to Philadelphia to study illustration at Drexel Institute under Howard Pyle. In 1899 Angel DeCora continued her art studies at the Cowles Art School in Boston under Joseph DeCamp. That same year she published two short stories in *Harper's New Monthly Magazine,* "The Sick Child" and "Grey Wolf's Daughter," both of which she also illustrated. Between 1899 and 1902 she maintained a private studio in Boston while at the same time taking courses with Frank Benson and Edmund C. Tarbell at the Boston Museum of Fine Arts School. From 1902 until 1906 she maintained a private studio in New York City. During this period Angel DeCora worked on an Indian exhibit at the 1904 Louisiana Purchase Exhibition in St. Louis, Missouri, and did the illustrations for Francis La Flesche's *The Middle Five* (1900) and Mary Catherine Judd's *Wigwam Stories* (1906). In 1907 she provided the illustrations for Gertrude Bonnin's *Old Indian Legends* and Natalie Curtis's *The Indian's Book.*

In February of 1906 Commissioner of Indian Affairs Francis E. Leupp, following the advice of Indian music collector Natalie Curtis, appointed Angel DeCora as instructor of Indian arts at the Carlisle Indian Industrial School in Carlisle, Pennsylvania. As head of the Leupp Art Studio at Carlisle from 1906 to 1915, she developed an intensive art program for Indian students, encouraging them to apply various traditional tribal designs to marketable modern art media such as book plates, textiles, and wallpaper. She also promoted the combination of Indian artistic elements with the techniques of Middle Eastern and Asian artisans. Although Angel DeCora's program basically adhered to the economics-oriented guidelines set by reformers such as Leupp, who had come to see Indian arts and crafts as an effective means of "industrializing" their charges and thereby speeding up the process of adaptation, she nevertheless proceeded from the premise that Indian artistic traditions could make a marked contribution to American art. Accordingly, she promoted art instruction to

Indians at the annual meeting of the International Congress of Americanists in Quebec in 1906, the National Educational Association convention in Los Angeles in 1907, and the twenty-sixth annual meeting of the Lake Mohonk Conference of the Friends of the Indian in 1908. She also spoke on the subject at the first convention of the Society of American Indians in 1911, having become an active member of the organization that same year. Earlier, in 1907, she arranged an exhibit based on her students' work at the Jamestown Tercentennial Exposition.

In July of 1908 Angel DeCora married William Lone Star Dietz, a part Oglala Sioux and part German artist whom she had instructed at Carlisle. Angel and William Dietz cooperated on several artistic projects, such as providing the illustrations for *Yellow Star,* a book published by Charles Eastman's wife Elaine Goodale Eastman in 1911. When William Dietz received an offer to coach football at Washington State University in 1915, Angel gave up her position at Carlisle to join him at Pullman. Three years later Angel DeCora Dietz divorced her husband and returned to New York. During the summer of 1918 she taught arts and crafts at Camp Oahe, a summer camp for girls run by Charles and Elaine Eastman at Granite Lake (near Keene), New Hampshire. In the fall of that year she worked as an illustrator of Devonian fauna for the New York State Museum. During the winter of 1918–19 Angel DeCora Dietz contracted pneumonia and moved to a former college friend's home in Northampton, Massachusetts, where she died on February 6, 1919. In her will she bequeathed $3,000 to the Society of American Indians.

Selected Publications of Angel DeCora Dietz

"Angel De Cora: An Autobiography." *The Red Man* 3, no. 7 (March 1911): 279–85.

"Encourage Indian Art." *Congrès International des Américanistes, XV Session Tenue à Québec en 1906,* 2 vols. (Québec: Dussault & Proulx, Imprimeurs, 1907), 2: 205–209.

"Gray Wolf's Daughter." *Harper's New Monthly Magazine* 99, no. 594 (November 1899): 860–62.

"The Native Indian Art." *The Indian School Journal* 7 (September 1907): 45.

"Native Indian Art." *Journal of Proceedings and Addresses of the Forty-Fifth Annual Meeting of the National Association of Education Held at Los Angeles, California July 8–12, 1907* (Winona, Minn.: National Education Association, 1907), 1005–1007.

"Native Indian Art." *Proceedings of the Twenty-Sixth Annual Meeting of the Lake Mohonk Conference of the Friends of the Indian and Other Dependent Peoples, 1908* (Lake Mohonk, N.Y.: The Lake Mohonk Conference, 1908), 16–18.

"Native Indian Art." *Report of the Executive Council on the Proceedings of the First Annual Conference of the Society of American Indians* (Washington, D.C., 1912), 82–87.

"The Sick Child." *Harper's New Monthly Magazine* 98, no. 585 (February, 1899): 446–48.

Selected Secondary Sources

Bonnin, Gertrude. "Gift of Our Angel De Cora Dietz." *The American Indian Magazine* 7, no. 2 (Summer 1919): 62.

Curtis, Natalie. "An American Indian Artist." *Outlook: An Illustrated Weekly Journal of Current Events* 124, no. 2 (January 14, 1920): 64–66.

Eastman, Elaine Goodale. "In Memoriam: Angel De Cora Dietz." *The American Indian Magazine* 7, no. 1 (Spring 1919): 51–52.

Folsom, Cora M. "Angel DeCora-Dietz." *The Southern Workman* (March 1919): 104–105.

Gere, Anne Ruggles. "An Art of Survivance: Angel DeCora at Carlisle," *American Indian Quarterly* 28, nos. 3–4 (2004): 649–84.

Hutchinson, Elizabeth W. "Indigeneity and Sovereignty: The Work of Two Early Twentieth-Century Native American Art Critics." *Third Text: Critical Perspectives on Contemporary Art and Culture* 52 (Summer 2000): 21–29.

McAnulty, Sarah. "Angel DeCora: American Indian Artist and Educator." *Nebraska History* 57, no. 2 (Summer 1976): 143–99.

Martin, E. L. "The Story of Two Real Indian Artists." *The Red Man* 5 (February 1913): 231–41.

THE TEACHING OF ETHNOLOGY
IN INDIAN SCHOOLS

J. N. B. Hewitt (1913)

Should the ethnology of the American Indian be taught in the schools provided for the American Indian student? The writer believes that anthropology, or at least, the elements of American Indian ethnology should be taught in such schools and institutions. It has been his business for more than twenty years to collect and record information regarding the ethnology of the American Indian from the members of many American Indian tribes in North America, and it has been his experience, as it has been that of other investigators, that only a very few persons in every tribe knew what the characteristic culture of his tribe was and is.

It is equally true that many and complex causes have conspired to bring about this unfortunate condition. But it must not be overlooked that a similar condition confronts many of the peoples of the Old World who have settled in this country. It is but necessary in connection with this to point to the numerous societies formed to preserve the culture and history of these peoples. We have Irish, French, Italian, Swedish, Norwegian, and numerous other organizations formed to perpetuate the traditions and culture of the several people forming these bodies.

This question is one of no little importance to every American Indian who has the welfare, the upbuilding and the conservation of the American Indian race, at heart. The well-attested fact that not one American Indian in 5,000 knows what his own tribe, not to say the American Indian race, has done in the past as expressed in terms of human culture, makes this question one that should receive the intelligent and sympathetic attention of this Society of American Indians, at this Conference.

There is no proof that the mental and the physical capacity of the American Indian race, as expressed in terms of past achievement and present ideals of accomplishment, is inferior to that of any other race of mankind. And the great body of brilliant facts to support this statement should be made the common heritage and property of every American Indian through judicious and effective instruction in schools which are devoted to his or her education.

In most cases, economic and historical causes and hereditary tendencies, interacting with changing and often hostile environment, are largely responsible for the apparent diversity of capacity in races of men.

As past achievements of the American Indian race the ancient civilizations of Peru and of Central America, and of Mexico in a lower degree, may be cited, and they will compare favorably with those ancient civilizations which once flourished in the valleys of the Euphrates and the Nile. In the cases cited from American soil there had been formed and developed highly complex social organizations, reflecting and expressing a high stage of political achievement;

there were also division of labor and ecclesiastical institutions of ritualistic worship and religious expression; great architectural works were projected and completed, and massive monolithic and other monuments were sculptured and erected, requiring the co-operation of large bodies of men for great periods of time; animals and plants were domesticated to supply the growing needs of the people; and the art of writing was invented; and judging from the highly conventional character of the symbols employed in this writing, it is safe to infer that they antedate the hieroglyphs of Egypt in their origin.

To understand and to explain the political relation of the American Indian tribes, one with another, was fifty years ago a vast unknown field of research; but to-day much work has been done, if not completely, at least measurably well; and to discover and portray in terms of human culture and enlightenment the deep meaning and significance of what in mental work, historical strivings and spiritual ideals, unites the historical tribes of the American Indian, one with another, is a task which demands accomplishment. It can not be done well, however, by men who are ashamed of the past failings of the American Indian, regardless of his noble and worthy achievements, and who then erroneously impute to the American Indian, accomplishments which he had still to acquire when transatlantic culture blighted the purely native activities.

And a new and still nobler and more important work awaits us: to demonstrate that there is a higher and more significant bond; the relationship of created things, one with another, and their inseverable kinship and relation with that Sovereign Power and Intelligence, whom some men reverence as God, and whom other men call the Unknowable, the Unseen, but whom Philosophy regards as the Totality of all things. And the American Indian race should be found in the advance in this important labor.

Among the objects mentioned in "the Statement of Purpose" of this Society of American Indians are, "to promote the advancement of the American Indian in enlightenment," to conserve the history of the American Indian race, without distortion from ignorance, misconception, or misinterpretation, and to promote by all honorable means the social, ethical, political, and economic welfare and betterment of not only its members but also that of their other brothers of the American Indian race, by conserving and developing what is congruous to their attainment, and eliminating what is not. It is true that before this great work can be done intelligently and effectively the past history and the culture of that people must be known.

Before we may claim that we know a people, a tribe, or a race of human beings, we must know the dominant facts and principles concerning its institutions or social organization, its language—phonetics, grammar, and lexicon, its literature its beliefs, opinions and philosophies, the source of its rituals, ceremonies, customs, and religion. Briefly, we should know comprehensively the entire range and content of its mental activities. It is to be regretted that for no tribe of native people of the American continent has this work been thoroughly done, although much excellent research has been accomplished. To solve a problem of this nature satisfactorily, requires a large amount of intensive and sympathetic study, absorbing years of patient investigation and exhaustive interpretation.

Nevertheless, in some cases, it is now possible to gain from multifarious publications a satisfactory comparative view of the cultures of large groups of tribes and peoples of the American continent, notwithstanding the fact that there are yet many great problems still awaiting solution. But the work of collation and sifting is too great for the average student to undertake and so he is apt to reach subjective conclusions from a lack of sufficient data.

It is possible, however, to collect and to arrange the characteristic facts of American Indian culture in such form and extent as to give the student of human culture in general a broad and intensive view of the peculiar character of the culture and achievements of the American Indian race. Such a summary, it seems to the writer, would lead to the appreciation and the esteem of the character of the American Indian and to a wholesome race pride; and it would comfort, too, those who may now from a want of such knowledge, regard at too high an estimate the culture of the white race. The truth is, the culture of the white race is not the sole product of the so-called white race. A glance through the pages of ancient and modern history will confirm this statement.

A study of the past culture of the American Indian and its survivals to-day is needful in order to enable us to gauge and define the inherited tendencies of the American Indian of to-day.

A fundamental fallacy lurks in the plausible contention that like results, in equally successful and ethical citizens, must result from placing the children of a community in the same excellent environment of training and education— briefly, that in large measure, differences and defects of character and endowment are mainly due to differences of environment. But, such assertions do not prove to be true or correct. The same environment does not produce the same results, for there are marked differences in the outputs. Uniformity in products does not result from the best training and education; as in the best, so in the worst environment, uniformity in results is ever lacking.

The writer believes that inherited traits and tendencies and inherent capacities of persons for acquiring knowledge and for making use of it, and for observing rules of propriety and rectitude, are more important factors in affecting the kind and degree of results than the agencies to which such persons may be subjected.

It is true that a good environment has its advantages, but the inherited capacity or ability to take advantage of these opportunities to make profitable use of the favorable environment, are by far the most dominating factors in the grade and kind of success attained. In large measure, these cannot be imparted by training and education.

On account of these differences in inherited traits or tendencies, abilities or capacities, great differences appear everywhere in all conditions of society. *While great attention is bestowed on improving the environment, none is given to the improvement of the inherited man—the more important factor of the two.*

A convenient, if not natural division of mentality, is into three important parts: that of learning, that of reasoning, and that of executing. In each of these departments, men, and races too, differ in their capacities. Some persons learn better than others; some men learn and reason better than others; and, lastly, some men learn, reason, and execute better than others. The competent man excels in the three departments—he learns (or imitates), reasons (or creates), and executes better than his fellows, in a profitable, practical way. These abilities are inherent, and they cannot be imparted by the schools or by the environment.

The necessity for teaching the ethnology of the American Indian in schools devoted to the education and training of American Indians has been made more urgent and impressive by the institution of this Society of American Indians. Before the Society can intelligently undertake to carry out the enormous task outlined in its statement of purpose, its membership and its officers must know accurately and succinctly the main and the peculiar cultural attainments of the various tribes and stocks of American Indians throughout the entire western hemisphere.

Modern research holds it of supreme importance to trace the course of human evolution through the development of opinions and beliefs, through the development of institutions, or social organization, through the development of language—phonetics, grammar, and the lexicon, and through the development of the arts of welfare and pleasure.

One of the most instructive and highly interesting chapters in the science of mind, or psychology, is to learn the means and the methods by which opinions grow, and new knowledge acquired. Psychology does not search the past to obtain valid opinions; it makes this quest, however, to discover stages of evolution and development in beliefs and opinions, and it is for this reason that the science of opinions, folklore and mythology, is of so much worth and interest to the student of humanity.

In the study of the myths and philosophies of the American Indian enough has been already learned to cause us to be struck with amazement at finding that the American Indian has preserved a form or system of thought which was already ancient when Assyrian and Babylonian scribes were making their first records in cuneiform characters and when swart Egyptian priests recorded their wisdom in weird hieroglyphs,—or at least 8,000 years earlier in human history than our own time.

These considerations, and many more which lack of time forbids the mention, make it seem needful that the facts which have given rise to them should be taught to the youth of the American Indian in such schools as are devoted to their education and training.

So it is the belief of the writer that it is incumbent on this Society through a Committee, or otherwise, to produce or have produced a suitable textbook of American Indian ethnology, not prolix or controversial, but summary and comparative in character, which should fearlessly embody the fads of American Indian culture and achievement in the past, without distortion or unfounded self-adulation. There is nothing in the past of the American Indian race for which we need apologize to any other race. Before we undertake to do so, let us first know at first hand the salient facts of American Indian culture in their extension and in their intention.

A live race of human beings should not merely absorb the wisdom and culture placed before it, but it should digest what it absorbs, and should therefore grow to a higher and broader life in all departments of thought and mentation, in its entire psychic expression.

Notes

Originally an oration delivered at the second conference of the SAI held at Columbus, Ohio, on October 2–7, 1912. Published in *The Quarterly Journal of the Society of American Indians* 1, no. 1 (April 15, 1913): 30–35. Representing a new generation of professional Indian anthropologists such as Francis La Flesche, Arthur C. Parker, and William Jones, Hewitt stresses the importance of accurate knowledge about Indian cultures as a prerequisite for effective Indian adaptation to modernity. Italics in the original.

BIOGRAPHY

John Napoleon Brinton Hewitt (Tuscarora, 1859–1937) was born on December 16 on the Tuscarora Indian Reservation in western New York, the eldest son of Dr. David Brainard Hewitt, an adopted Tuscarora of Scottish and English descent, and Harriet Brinton, a part-Tuscarora of Oneida, French, and English descent. John Hewitt entered a district school in Niagra County in 1860, when he began to learn the Tuscarora language from his classmates. After 1865 he attended Wilson Union Academy and Lockport Union Academy in New York until his health forced him to give up his studies and return to the Tuscarora Reservation. Between 1876 and 1879 he worked as a farmer and a newspaper correspondent, and then operated a private night school for Tuscarora men from 1877 to 1879. In 1880 he met Erminnie A. Smith, an ethnologist with the Bureau of Ethnology (later Bureau of American Ethnology) conducting research on the Iroquois languages and oral traditions. John Hewitt served as her assistant until 1884. Following his employment with the Jersey City Railway Companies in 1884–85 and the Adams Express Company in New York City in 1885–86, he became an ethnologist with the Bureau of American Ethnology in the summer of 1886. Hewitt retained this position until his death fifty-one years later. Hewitt was a member of the Ingram Memorial Congregational Church until 1925, when he decided to join the All Souls Unitarian Church. He was married twice to non-Indian women: the first, whose name is unknown, died in 1918; the second, Carrie Louise Hurlbut, whom he married in 1925, survived him.

At the Bureau of American Ethnology, Hewitt continued his work on Indian languages (especially Iroquoian and Algonquian linguistic stocks) and oral traditions. Other than several articles on the Iroquois for the *American Anthropologist,* he contributed substantially to the Bureau of American Ethnology's two-volume *Handbook of American Indians North of Mexico* (1907–10). Hewitt's most significant work includes the transcription and accompanying translation of Iroquois languages, still largely unpublished, and interpretations of Iroquois oral traditions such as "Iroquois Cosmology" and "Seneca Fiction, Legends, and Myths." Each work appeared in the *Annual Reports of the Bureau of American Ethnology.* On February 28, 1914, the Cayuga County Historical Society conferred on him the "Cornplanter Medal for Iroquois Research." Hewitt was a member of the Anthropological Society of Washington (serving as treasurer 1912–26 and president 1932–34). He was also a cofounder of the American Anthropological Association. In 1911 he became an active member of the Society of American Indians, stressing the organization's commitment to the preservation of accurate knowledge about Indian traditions. John Hewitt died in Washington, D.C., on October 14, 1937.

Selected Publications of John Hewitt

A Constitutional League of Peace in the Stone Age of America. The League of the Iroquois and Its Constitution. Smithsonian Institution, Annual Report, 1918. Washington, DC: Government Printing Office, 1920.

"Era of the Formation of the Historic League of the Iroquois." American Anthropologist 7 (1894): 61–67.

"The Indian's History, His Ideas, His Religion, His Mythology, and His Social Organization." The Red Man 5, no. 3 (1912).

"The Iroquoian Concept of the Soul." Journal of American Folklore (1895): 107–166.

Iroquois Cosmology; First Part. United States Bureau of American Ethnology, Twenty-first Annual Report, 1899–1900. Washington, D.C.: Government Printing Office, 1903.

The Name Cherokee and Its Derivation. New York: G. P. Putnam's Sons, 1900.

Orenda and the Definition of Religion. New York: G. P. Putnam's Sons, 1902.

Polysynthesis in the Languages of the American Indians. Washington, D.C.: Judd and Detweiler, 1893.

Seneca Fiction, Legends, and Myth. With Jeremiah Curtin. United States Bureau of American Ethnology, Thirty-second Annual Report, 1910–1911. Washington, D.C.: Government Printing Office, 1918.

"The Teaching of Ethnology in Indian Schools." The Quarterly Journal of the Society of American Indians 1, no. 1 (April 15, 1913): 30–35. Reprinted in Indian Leader (May 30, 1913).

Unpublished Writings

John Napoleon Brinton Hewitt Papers, Smithsonian Institution, Washington, D.C. (Over 12,000 pages of material).

Selected Secondary Sources

Baldwin, Marie L. B. "John N. B. Hewitt, Ethnologist." The Quarterly Journal of the Society of American Indians 2, no. 2, (April–June 1914): 146–51.

Dockstader, Frederick. "John N. B. Hewitt." Great North American Indians: Profiles in Life and Leadership. New York: Van Nostrand Reinhold Co., 1977: 107–108.

Houghton, Louise Seymour. Our Debt to the Red Man: The French-Indians in the Development of the United States. Boston: The Stratford Company, 1918: 181–83.

Swanton, John R. "John Napoleon Brinton Hewitt." American Anthropologist 40 (1938): 286–90.

Tooker, Elizabeth. "Hewitt, J. N. B.: Tuscarora Ethnologist and Linguist." In Encyclopedia of North American Indians, edited by Frederick E. Hoxie. Boston: Houghton Mifflin Co., 1996: 24.

THE INDIAN RESERVATION SYSTEM

Carlos Montezuma (1913)

The very name "Reservation" contradicts the purpose for which it was instituted. Reservation is from *reserve*. Reserve in this connection is to set apart, and to set apart means to separate from; and to separate from means to deprive the separated from all relations to that from which it is to be kept. Therefore, the purpose being to civilize the Indians, the way to do it is to keep him disconnected from civilization. And this is what the reservation, even if not so designed, has been so highly successful in accomplishing.

In one respect, we have always been and are ready to give credit where credit is due, and we must therefore acknowledge that the thing which the reservation, though not so designed, was yet certain to accomplish, has been thoroughly wrought out.

The Indian has most certainly been reserved, and is still reserved. He is still to be civilized, because he has been reserved from civilization. And after all these years we are thankful at least that those who are and have been most interested (for personal reasons), in this reservation of the Indian, have come to see, to some extent, what a contradiction the whole system is in itself. That they now see, is not so strange, as the fact that they have been so long in getting their eyes opened.

As we have said before, the reservation, in its very name, and the system necessarily embraced in the meaning of the word, carried with it, at the day of its adoption, its own prognosis of the fate of the Indian who should be so unfortunate as to be included within its limits. There are a few—not all belonging to the Indian race, either—who have for years known that the outlook for the Indian was "dark," indeed, and these few had this foresight simply because, knowing the seed, they knew what fruit would spring therefrom. In other words, it is the old, old story over again. No figs from thorns, nor wheat from tares. You reap what you sow, and can expect nothing else.

The reservation system has been a monument to the want of knowledge of human nature on the part of those who have been instrumental in perpetuating it. The failure to recognize the brotherhood of man in the Indian, that he was a multiple being however ignorant he might be, and not more unified in his natural endowments and faculties than other men subject to similar conditions and environments, has been his greatest handicap. And it has been, and it is, this reverse idea of the Indian that has given rise to so much impracticable specializing on the subject of the American Indian's relation to the rest of the people.

In this respect the supporters of the Reservation System and the Bureau behind it, have been traveling in one direction, while they started the Indian at an angle of about ninety degrees along another road. And now, after so many years, they wonder why they are so far apart.

335

In conclusion, we will add that whether the Indian reservation system is inherently wrong, in principle, is no longer an open question, but, that it is so, is an established fact; and its practical workings, therefore, necessarily a failure in respect of what ought to be accomplished toward bringing the Indians into civilized life.

Notes

Originally in *The Quarterly Journal of the Society of American Indians* 1, no. 4 (October–December 1913): 359–60. The abolishment of the reservation system and the Bureau of Indian Affairs was the central demand of the "radical" faction of the Society of American Indians headed by Montezuma.

LET MY PEOPLE GO

Carlos Montezuma (1916)

The iron hand of the Indian Bureau has us in charge. The slimy clutches of horrid greed and selfish interests are gripping the Indian's property. Little by little the Indian's land and everything else is fading into a dim and unknown realm.

The Indian's prognosis is bad—unfavorable, no hope. The foreboding pro-dromic [sic] signs are visible here and there now—and when all the Indian's money in the United States Treasury is disposed of—when the Indian's prop-erty is all taken from him—when the Indians have nothing in this wide, wide world—when the Indians will have no rights, no place to lay their heads—and when the Indians will be permitted to exist only on the outskirts of the towns—when they must go to the garbage boxes in alleys, to keep them from starving—when the Indians will be driven into the streets, and finally the streets will be no place for them—then what will the Indian Bureau do for them? Nothing, but drop them. The Indian Department will go out of business.

In other words, when the Indians will need the most help in this world, that philanthropic department of the government that we call the Indian Bureau, will cease to exist; bankrupt with liabilities—billions and billions—no assets, O Lord, my God, what a fate has the Indian Bureau for my people.

If we depend upon the employees of the Indian Bureau for our life, liberty and pursuit of happiness, we wait a long while. They are too busy looking af-ter the machinery of Indian Affairs; they have no time to look ahead; they have no time to feel the pulse of the Indian; they have no time to think of outside matters; they have no time to adjust matters. "Well, what time have they?" you may ask. All of their time is devoted to the pleasure and will of their master at Washington, that we call the Indian Bureau. Blindly they think they are help-ing and uplifting, when in reality they are a hindrance, a draw-back and a block-ade on the road that would lead the Indian to freedom, that he may find his true place in the realms of mortal beings.

The reservation Indians are prisoners; they cannot do anything for them-selves. We are on the outside, and it is the outsiders that must work to free the Indians from Bureauism. There is no fear of the general public. They are our friends. When they find out that we are not free, they will free us. We have a running chance with the public, but no chance with the Indian Bureau.

The abolishment of the Indian Bureau will not only benefit the Indians, but the country will derive more money annually from the Indians than the govern-ment has appropriated to them. Why? Because by doing away with the Indian Bureau, you stop making paupers and useless beings, and start the making of producers and workers.

Does this seem like a dream to you? Is your position a foreign attitude? From aloft, do you look down? Have you gone so far as to forget your race?

337

Have you quenched the spirit of our fathers? As their children, dare we stay back, hide ourselves and be dumb at this hour, when we see our race abused, misused and driven to its doom? If this be not so, then let whatever loyalty and racial pride be in you awaken and manifest itself in this greatest movement of "Let My People Go!"

The highest duty and greatest object of the Society of American Indians, is to have a bill introduced in our next Congress to have the Indian Bureau abolished and to let the Indians go. We cannot be disinterested in this matter, we cannot be jealous or hate one another, we cannot quibble or be personal in this matter. There must be no suspicion.

We must act as one. Our hearts must throb with love—our souls must reach to God to guide us—and our bodies and souls must be used to gain our people's freedom.

In behalf of our people, with the spirit of Moses, I ask this—The United States of America—"Let My People Go."

Notes

Originally in *The American Indian Magazine* 4, no. 1 (January–March 1916): 32–33. This is an abridged version of an address delivered earlier at the SAI conference at Lawrence, Kansas, on September 30, 1915, and published as a fifteen-page tract titled *Let My People Go* (Chicago: Hawthorn Press, 1915). The text was read during the first session of the Sixty-Fourth Congress in 1916 and included in *Congressional Record*, 64th Cong., 1st sess., vol. 53, no. 123 (Friday, May 12, 1916): 8888–91. Later editions of Montezuma's newsletter *Wassaja* depicted him on the front page holding up this pamphlet in one hand and pointing to the Statue of Liberty with the other. The text is exemplary of Montezuma's "fiery" prose.

TRUTH IS COMING TO LIGHT

Carlos Montezuma (1918)

The greatest obstacle to Indian legislation in the interest of the Indians is the Indian Office. How WASSAJA has cried out again and again that would be the case. No one likes to die. Just so, the Indian Bureau does not want to go out of existence. It has been as poisonous as a rattle snake to the Indians, and it will die hard like a rattle snake. Its life is fed by sucking the blood from incompetent Indians, which it has manufactured from the most competent human beings on the face of the earth, and now, the Indian Office is assorting the Indians—separating the chaff from the seed. Just hear their pious voices: "This is a perfect one, this is a rotten one; this one is an exception, this one we must leave for evolution; this one is competent, this one is incompetent; put that one over there and this Indian over here. That Indian is no good and this one is; this one is a goat and that one is a lamb; this one you can let loose outside of the fence of the Indian Reservation, that one over there must be kept in, he is not a fit creature to associate with our children." If this is not autocracy, what is autocracy?

No one can do any good to another until they place themself [sic] in the same category as the other fellow. Making exceptions for the other fellow and not placing yourself in with him, you are doing wrong. A law for each nationality in America would be very much un-American; then, why should this be done with the Indian race?

What will the cunning Indian Office spring up next in order to use the Indians? Who are its helpers? The Society of American Indians, the Indian Rights Association, the Indian Friends and the Missionaries.[1] It is too bad to pounce upon these splendid organizations. But WASSAJA would not be true to his race if he did not. They are the very people from which the Indians expected the most help, but they are mum and stiffened with pride. Did you ever hear them say one word against the Indian Office? Did you ever hear them say anything about FREEDOM for the Indians? Did you ever hear them say that an Indian was a man? Did you ever hear of them sticking to the Indian through thick and thin against the Indian Office? They cannot make the Indians believe they are working for their interest when they are eating, sleeping and enjoying each other's company. It may be policy, but the Indians do not know what policy is. They have only one face to show. You are either a friend or a foe.

Oh, this *incompetent Indian,* set aside by three human judges that are getting $10 a day. It makes an Indian's heart boil to think of such damnable blasphemy.

It is the most devilish way of helping the Indian Office to live and to continue the manufacturing of incompetent Indians.

Indians, what are we anyway? Are we freaks? Have we no souls? Are we possessed with venomous fans? Is there no living with us until the Indian Office makes us fit subjects? Must we live muzzled and dominated by the hellishness of human government? Are we so low that we cannot thrive within human justice? It is all wrong. God does not show us all the way through life's journey. God's decree is hew out your own destiny. The best educators are those who teach without making any exceptions of their pupils. They put no limits to the possibilities of each student. WASSAJA contends that in order to place the Indian on a just basis as a man, the country must first make him a free man, and then give him his citizenship. But to give him citizenship with conditions attached to it, is not citizenship that is enjoyed by true American citizens. That is a false freedom!

Every bill that comes before Congress has not one ring of freedom for the Indians, nor has it one word of abolishing the Indian Office. It is full of "approvals of the Secretary of the Interior, Indian Office or Superintendent"—NEVER "with consent of the Indian tribe." All the power seems to centralize in the Washington Office and the Indians have not a single voice in their own affairs.

Indians, wake up! If you have money in the treasury, you have a voice in the matter; if you have land, you have a voice in the matter; if you are not free, you have a voice in the matter; if you have a string tied to your citizenship, you have a voice in the matter. You are a man and as such you are entitled to the rights of a man. NOW IS THE TIME TO EXERT YOUR RIGHTS. No one can do it for you. You must do it yourself. You have been asleep long enough. Stir yourself to your manhood and look after your own interest. The future is just as bright for you as for any man in the world.

Notes

Originally in *Wassaja* 2, no. 12 (March 1918): 1–2. Montezuma mounted a relentless campaign of criticism against the Society of American Indians for its "gradual" stand until the more "radical" faction under the leadership of Gertrude Bonnin and Charles Alexander Eastman gained control of the organization temporarily in 1919.

1. The Indian Rights Association, founded in Philadelphia in 1882, was one of the major Indian reform organizations that promoted public and administrative concern for Indian affairs through an extensive network of publications, public talks, meetings, and lobbyist activities. It remained in operation until 1994. Beginning in 1883 and lasting until 1917, self-styled "Friends of the Indian" met every fall at a private resort on Lake Mohonk, New York, to discuss the future course of Indian policy. See William T. Hagan, *The Indian Rights Association: The Herbert Welsh Years, 1882–1904* (Tucson: University of Arizona Press, 1985).

BIOGRAPHY

Carlos Montezuma (Yavapai ca. 1866–1923), or Wassaja (Signaling), was born into a Pinal-Apache (Yavapai) community, the son of Coluyevah and Thilgeyah. In 1871 Wassaja was captured by Pima raiders and subsequently sold by them to Carlos Gentile, an Italian-American photographer, for thirty dollars. Gentile named him Carlos Montezuma and took him back East where, with the support of other benefactors like Baptist minister William Steadman of Urbana, Illinois, he provided for his charge's education in public schools in Chicago, Galesburg, and Brooklyn from 1873 to 1878. After two additional years of prep school in Urbana, Montezuma enrolled at the University of Illinois, receiving a degree in chemistry in 1884. With the aid of a part-time job and a partial scholarship, he finally managed to earn a degree in medicine from the Chicago Medical College in 1889.

Carlos Montezuma then accepted a position in the Indian Service as agency physician, working at the Fort Stevenson Industrial School, North Dakota, in 1889–90; the Western Shoshone Agency, Nevada, in 1890–93; and the Colville Agency, Washington, in 1893–94. From 1894 to 1896 Montezuma served as resident physician at Carlisle Indian Industrial School in Pennsylvania, during which time he became a devoted follower of Richard Henry Pratt's radical brand of Indian reform. Montezuma left the Indian Service in 1896 and returned to Chicago, where he succeeded in making a comfortable living as a private physician. In the spring of 1901 he was engaged to Gertrude Bonnin, but the relationship broke up when she moved to the Yankton Agency soon after. In 1913 Montezuma married Marie Keller, a young Romanian-American woman.

Carlos Montezuma was one of the six original founders of the Society of American Indians. However, he vehemently opposed the election of employees of the Bureau of Indian Affairs—such as cofounder Charles E. Dagenett, a supervisor of employment with the Indian Office—as officers of the society. Montezuma resigned from the Executive Board and refused to attend the first national convention of the society in Columbus, Ohio, in October of 1911. He did attend the second convention in Columbus in 1912 but remained conspicuously absent from the 1913 convention in Denver. Although Montezuma renewed his membership in 1914 and regularly attended the conventions thereafter, he relentlessly attacked the society's officers, especially Arthur C. Parker, for advocating a gradual course of adaptation rather than immediate abolishment of the Bureau of Indian Affairs and the reservation system. In 1915 the "fiery Apache," as he was frequently described, published one of his most vociferous critiques of Indian policy in a polemic tract titled *Let My People Go,* which served as a guideline for the "abolitionist" faction of the Society of American Indians and was read into the record of the first session of the Sixty-Fourth Congress in 1916.

Dissatisfied with the moderate tenor of *The Quarterly Journal of the Society of American Indians* under the editorship of Parker, Montezuma also made his radical views public through his own four-page monthly newsletter, the *Wassaja: Freedom's Signal for the Indians,* published in Chicago from April of 1916 until November of 1922. In 1918, when fellow "abolitionist" Charles A. Eastman was elected president and Gertrude Bonnin assumed the editorship of the *Quarterly,* Montezuma ceased criticism of the organization and from then on gave it his full support. In the spring of 1919 he also joined Eastman and Rev. Philip B. Gordon, a Catholic Ojibwa priest who shared Montezuma's radical standpoint, on a tour to endorse Indian citizenship and the abolition of the Bureau of Indian Affairs, throughout various Indian communities in Wisconsin. Montezuma promoted the increasingly moribund society's activities in his newsletter and attended several of its meetings, including the penultimate one held in Kansas City on October 17–20, 1922, even though he was already deathly ill with tuberculosis at the time. In the final issue of *Wassaja* he countered "rumors spread that the Society was dead," accusing the Bureau of Indian Affairs and certain career-oriented Indians of having encumbered its work. He called for an "executive force composed of fighting individuals" to make the society more powerful and stressed the need to revive its journal. "Members of the Society of American Indians," he pleaded, "if the world be against us, let us not be dismayed, let us not be discouraged, let us look up and ahead, and fight on for freedom and citizenship of our people."

Around 1888 Montezuma began to correspond regularly with surviving Yavapai relatives in Arizona in an effort to retrace his own ancestry. In 1903 the Yavapais living on the San Carlos Reservation were accorded their own reservation at Fort McDowell, but already by 1906 plans for a dam on the Verde River threatened to cause their eviction. In the last two decades of his life Montezuma immersed himself in what proved to be a successful campaign to prevent the eviction of the Yavapais from the Fort McDowell Reservation, earning him the permanent respect of that community. In addition he was instrumental in securing Pima and Maricopa water rights in Arizona. For some time thereafter the older, traditionalist members of the Pima community were referred to as the "Montezumas." When his illness became critical at the close of 1922, the foremost Indian critic of the reservation system, who had sworn on numerous occasions that he would "not go back there," left Chicago to spend his remaining days in a simple brush shelter in the land of his ancestors. Carlos Montezuma died at Fort McDowell on January 31, 1923.

Selected Publications of Carlos Montezuma

"Carter's Bill." *Wassaja,* 2, no. 11 (February 1918): 1.
"Conference of S.A.I. at Kansas City, Mo." *Wassaja* 8, no. 20 (October 1922): 1–2.
"Conference of the Society of American Indians." *Wassaja* 7, no. 9 (September 1921): 4.
"From an Apache Camp to a Chicago Medical School: The Story of Carlos Montezuma's Life as Told by Himself." *Red Man* 8 (July–August 1888): 3
"The Hayden Bill." *Wassaja* 2, no. 9 (December 1917): 1.

"The Indian Bureau—The Slaughter House of the Indian People." *Wassaja* 8, no. 21 (November 1922): 2–4.

"An Indian Commissioner of Indian Affairs." *Wassaja* 5, no. 11 (February 1921): 2.

The Indian of Tomorrow: An Address by Dr. Carlos Montezuma and The Indian of Yesterday: The Early Life of Dr. Carlos Montezuma Written by Himself (Chicago: Published for the National Women's Christian Temperance Union, 1888).

The Indian Problem from an Indian's Standpoint. Chicago: Chicago Indian Association, 1898.

"The Indian Problem from the Indian's Point of View." *The Red Man* 14 (February 1898): 1–2.

"The Indian Reservation System." *The Quarterly Journal of the Society of American Indians* 1, no. 4 (October–December 1913): 359–60.

Let My People Go. Chicago: Hawthorn Press, 1915. Included in *Congressional Record,* 64th Cong., 1st sess., vol. 53, no. 123 (Friday, May 12, 1916): 8888–891.

"Let My People Go." *The Quarterly Journal of the Society of American Indians* 4, no. 1 (January–March 1916): 32–33.

"Light on the Indian Situation." *The Quarterly Journal of the Society of American Indians* 1, no. 1 (January–April 1913): 50–55.

"The Next Conference of the S.A.I." *Wassaja* 2, no. 1 (April 1917): 2.

"The Reservation is Fatal to the Development of Good Citizenship." *The Quarterly Journal of the Society of American Indians* 2, no. 1 (January–March 1914): 69–74.

"The S.A.I. Is Not Dead." *Wassaja* 7, no. 10 (October 1921): 1–2.

"The Society of American Indians Conference at St. Louis." *Wassaja* 5, no. 8 (November 1920): 3–4.

"What Indians Must Do." *The Quarterly Journal of the Society of American Indians* 2, no. 4 (October–December 1914): 294–99.

"What Is the Society of American Indians Now?" *Wassaja* 3, no. 7 (October 1918): 3.

Unpublished Writings

Carlos Montezuma Papers, State Historical Society of Wisconsin, Division of Archives and Manuscripts, Madison, Wisconsin (also on Microfilm); Carlos Montezuma Papers, Edward E. Ayer Collection, Newberry Library, Chicago, Illinois; Carlos Montezuma File, Chicago Historical Society; The Papers of Carlos Montezuma, M.D., edited by John W. Larner, Microfilm, Scholarly Resources, Inc., Wilmington, Delaware.

Selected Secondary Sources

Iverson, Peter. "Carlos Montezuma." In *American Indian Leaders: Studies in Diversity,* edited by R. David Edmunds. Lincoln: University of Nebraska Press, 1980: 206–20.

_____. "Carlos Montezuma and the Fort McDowell Yavapai Community." *The Journal of Arizona History* 22 (Winter 1981): 415–28.

_____. *Carlos Montezuma and the Changing World of American Indians.* Albuquerque: University of New Mexico Press, 1982.

_____. "Montezuma, Carlos (Wassaja)." In *Encyclopedia of North American Indians,* edited by Frederick E. Hoxie. Boston: Houghton Mifflin Company, 1996: 394–96.

_____. "Montezuma, Carlos." In *American National Biography,* edited by John A. Garraty and Mark C. Carnes. Vol. 15. New York: Oxford University Press, 1999: 697–99.

Littlefield, Daniel F. Jr., and James W. Parins, "Wassaja: Freedom's Signal for the Indians." In *American Indian and Alaska Native Newspapers and Periodicals, 1826–1924,* edited by Daniel F. Littlefield and James W. Parins. Westport, Conn.: Greenwood Press, 1984: 382–85.

Shaw, Anna Moore. *A Pima Past.* Tucson: University of Arizona Press, 1974: 238–48.

McDonnell, Janet. "Carlos Montezuma's Crusade Against the Indian Bureau." *The Journal of Arizona History* 22 (Winter 1981): 429–44.

Spack, Ruth. "Dis/engagement: Zitkala-Sa's Letters to Carlos Montezuma." *MELUS* 26, no. 1 (Spring 2001): 172–204.

Speroff, Leon. *Carlos Montezuma: A Yavapai American Hero—The Life and Times of an American Indian, 1866–1923.* Portland, Ore.: Arnica Publishing Inc., 2003.

THE FUNCTION OF THE
SOCIETY OF AMERICAN INDIANS

Sherman Coolidge (1914)

The aim and scope of the new race movement as embodied in the Society of American Indians is the revival of the natural pride of origin, the pride of race. If people become dispirited, progress is impossible. It is easily within our memory when public opinion viewed the Indian as lacking in capacity for advancement. To the white man he was a degraded savage, blood-thirsty, treacherous, and brutal. The superior white alien accepted as truth the teaching that by Divine Will and manifest destiny the aborigine must be exterminated and driven from the earth; "it is the logic of migration, the law of human movement." So this imperious white man decreed: "The Indian must go!" The necessity of driving the Indian away from the spot he called his home and of marching him out at the point of the bayonet were both sad and needless blunders in a land where there is room for all. The white man misunderstood the Indian and the Indian misunderstood the white man. A war and extermination policy was started by the whites and the "irrepressible conflict continued for three centuries. The white invaders introduced a new mode of life, and the native type was to be supplanted by civilization. It was thought that the Indian, for his salvation, must be pressed into the white man's preconceived mold. As a matter of fact, most Indians do not want to become white men. From the first contract between the two races the Indian was considered inferior, and not at all a fellow man of like passions, infirmities, and aspirations; different only in mental texture, hereditary influences, and environment." And therein is the deep-seated disease germ of the whole Indian problem. The reservation system has fostered and accentuated the terrible ills resulting from the misconceptions of the white race concerning the red brother, and consequently the Indian has so deteriorated we can hardly realize him as the same proud monarch of fifty years ago.

To use Dr. [Charles A.] Eastman's words: "The North American Indian was the highest type of pagan and uncivilized man. He possessed not only a superb physique but a remarkable mind. But the Indian no longer exists as a natural and free man. Those remnants which now dwell upon the reservations present only a sort of tableau, a fictitious copy of the past."[1]

On the anniversary of the discovery of America, in the year 1911 a conference was opened at the Ohio State University to organize the Society of American Indians, whose primary function is the revitalizing and cherishing of race pride. Once this task is accomplished the rest will follow. The organization furnishes an annual conference to which delegates of every tribe may come with equal rights. Representatives now do come from the east and the west, from the north and the south. Here, they meet face to face in national council with common language and for a common purpose; here, each Indian can see that he is not alone in the fight against the peril of being utterly crushed; here, the members gather for mutual encouragement, interchange of views and for consultation upon the live issues of the peculiar problem thrust upon them. The best asset the Indians can have is a united body of altruistic men and women of the race, and the Society of American Indians is composed of just such people, anxious to serve and who have lost no time in applying themselves to vital problems and grasping the essential features of the Indian question. The permanent program as outlined by the first organizers is found in the following statement of objects:

First. To promote and co-operate with all efforts looking to the advancement of the Indian in enlightenment which leave him free as a man to develop according to the natural laws of social evolution.

Second. To provide through our open conferences the means for a free discussion on all subjects bearing on the welfare of the race.

Third. To present in a just light the true history of the race, to preserve its records and emulate its distinguishing virtues.

Fourth. To promote citizenship and to obtain the rights thereof.

Fifth. To establish a legal department to investigate Indian problems and to suggest and to obtain remedies.

Sixth. To exercise the right to oppose any movement that may be detrimental to the race.

Seventh. To direct its energies exclusively to general principles and universal interests, and not allow itself to be used for any personal or private interest.[2]

The existence of the Society of American Indians means that the hour has struck when the best educated and most cultured of the race should come together to voice the common demands, to interpret correctly the Indians [sic] heart, and to contribute in a more united way their influence and exertion with the rest of the citizens of the United States in all lines of progress and reform, for the welfare of the Indian race in particular, and all humanity in general. Obviously this noble movement is a tremendous undertaking, but it was ushered in amid general good wishes of church and state. It is at once a bold and a most praiseworthy step. The Society is managed solely for and by the Indians, and no one without Indian blood can be an active member, yet the white friends of the cause are welcomed most cordially as associate members. The membership at present is more than a thousand, over five hundred from the best of each race. A hearty co-operation with each other will produce splendid results; and, while conscious that he must do his full share in bringing order out of chaos, the red brother does not forget to remind his white brother that the nation which created the problem must assist in its solution and that the motto shall be: "The honor of the race and the good of the country shall always be paramount."

We were overjoyed by the fact that we could assemble so many civilized and educated men and women of vision from our scattered tribes who were in dead earnest and who were willing to pay the price of hardship and self-sacrifice as pioneers of the movement. We were not without our foe who said: "Don't listen to those blind dreamers!" "Don't lend yourselves to their false dreams!" "Their hopes are over-rosy." But some of our dreams have already been realized far beyond our expectations. Our suggestions, proposals, and advice have been received with kindly consideration everywhere. We aided in liberating two hundred and sixty Apaches who had been held in bondage as prisoners of war for twenty-six years, and persuaded Congress to appropriate $300,000 for land and homes for them.[3] We helped the Cayugas in getting $247,000 due them from the State of New York. The murderer of Desota Tiger is in irons, thanks to some of our active and associate members and to Hon. Cato Sells, Commissioner of Indian Affairs. Desota Tiger belonged to the Everglade Seminoles of Florida and was a respected member of his tribe. An Indian woman out west tried to get her money through the Indian agent and was put off time and again by some excuse or another for a year or two, and finally wrote to our Society for its service and received her money in three weeks. The fate of a $50,000 item in the last Indian appropriation bill was uncertain; it was for the education of about two thousand Papago children; but the bill passed, including the $50,000 item for the Papagos, and with our assistance. Then, too, the Society is advocating the passage of the Carter Code bill and the Stephens amended bill, both of which look to the solution of the Indian problem.[4] Nor is this all.

The foregoing statement of things achieved is only a glimpse of what we have done and what we desire to do in co-operating with the government. We must work in harmony in order that we may succeed in performing our mutual supreme duty. The Government has charge of $900,000,000 worth of property for the three hundred thousand Indians under its care; $100,000,000 worth of timber land, but will this timber be turned into lumber for the use of Indians, or will it be turned over to some corporation? Again, the Government holds $60,000,000 in cash for our national wards. What shall be done with it? These subjects are of vital interest to the Indian. Besides all this there are millions annually appropriated by Congress for our civilization and education. The Society of American Indians asks: "Are we getting a proportionate good out of this vast expenditure? Is it doing full justice to the tax-payers?"

The Madison meeting was the Fourth Annual Conference of the organization, and it re-affirmed the platform of the Third Annual Conference which took place at Denver, Colo [in 1913].

The Madison Conference placed the financial situation of the Society in a better light. Up to this time the Society was kept in motion apparently by a few who supplied more than their share of energy and much of the sinews of war; our treasury was forever in sore need of funds. We lived a from hand to mouth existence, and our financial inability was almost the death of us. We thought of Uncle Sam with our $60,000,000 in cash, but by our principles we could not ask for one cent of it for the good cause; and by our principles we must not deviate an inch from the trail we are following and must ever look to the "Goddess of Liberty" to play the role of fairy godmother. It is a comfort to know that we are free to go forth and create Indian public opinion among the white people and the Indians. The past is beyond recall. But the present offers opportunities for redeeming the past and for redress. We are writing and making a new history and we can avoid the errors of our forefathers and plan a new day for the Indian American. Let us so shape our policy for his education that it will cease to be decultural, but become constructive; and blame him not if he refuses to become an imitation white man; if he bows not the knee to commercialism, or fails to admit that the white man is the ultimate model of the best citizenship or of noblest manhood.

Notes

Originally in *The Quarterly Journal of the Society of American Indians* 2, no. 1 (January–March 1914): 186–90. Reproduced in Bernd C. Peyer, ed., *The Elders Wrote: An Anthology of Early Prose by North American Indians, 1768–1931* (Berlin: Dietrich Reimer Verlag, 1982), 159–62. Coolidge's article provides a good synopsis of the ideology of the Society of American Indians.

1. Charles A. Eastman, "Preface," *Indian Boyhood* (New York: McClure, Phillips and Co., 1902).

2. This is an expanded version of the six-point platform adopted by the Temporary Executive Committee of the American Indian Association in Columbus, Ohio, on April 3–4, 1911. On October 16, 1911, forty three active members attending a segregated business session during the first annual convention of the organization in Columbus, Ohio, changed the name to the Society of American Indians and further specified its political objects. See "American Indian Association: Purpose," April 4, 1911, in the microfilm edition of *The Papers of the Society of American Indians*, 10 Reels, John W. Larner, Jr., ed., (Wilmington, Del.: Scholarly Sources Inc., 1987), Reel 2, Frame 02 0593. See also *Constitution and Laws of the Society of American Indians* (Washington, D.C.: SAI, 1912), Reel 9, Frames 09 1382 to 09 1391. The minutes of the October 16 business session are found in *Report of the Executive Council on the Proceedings of the First Annual Conference of the Society of American Indians* (Washington, D.C., 1912), 156–62.

3. See John Milton Oskison's "The New Indian Leadership" in this anthology, esp. note 5.

4. A bill recommending the creation of an Indian Code Commission to codify the laws relating to Indians was introduced as House Bill 18334 on January 19, 1912 by Congressman Charles D. Carter (Chickasaw, 1869–1929), an active member of the SAI from Oklahoma. As of the Denver conference in 1913, the SAI also strongly supported the amended Stephens Bill, which would open the U.S. Court of Claims to all tribes and bands in the United States.

BIOGRAPHY

Sherman Coolidge (Arapaho, 1862–1932), Runs-on-Top, was born in the vicinity of Goose Creek in present-day Wyoming, the son of Banasda (Big Heart) and Ba-ahonce (Turtle Woman). In the spring of 1870 Runs-on-Top and his younger brother were taken captive during a Shoshone and Bannock raid and then turned over to American troops. At Camp Brown, Wyoming, the young Arapaho captives were supervised by military families, who bestowed the name of Sherman on Runs-on-Top in honor of William Tecumseh Sherman. Late in 1870, Sherman was officially adopted by Captain Charles A. Coolidge and his wife, a childless couple who encouraged their foster son's education and adoption of American ways. Around 1871 Sherman Coolidge was baptized by Rev. Southgate, an Episcopal bishop, and then enrolled at the Shattuck Military School in Faribault, Minnesota. In 1876 he accompanied his foster father in campaigns against the Sioux, an experience that motivated him to become a missionary among the western tribes. He subsequently attended Seabury Divinity School near Chicago, graduating with a Bachelor of Divinity in 1884. That same year Sherman Coolidge was ordained a deacon in the Episcopal Church by Henry B. Whipple.

Shortly after his ordination Sherman Coolidge moved to the Wind River Reservation in Wyoming to assume his first church assignment. Here he was reunited with his mother, eventually persuading her to convert to Christianity, and helped to ease the tension between the resident Shoshones and Arapahos, who were traditional enemies. From 1887 until 1889 Sherman Coolidge continued his theological studies at Hobart College in Geneva, New York. He was then ordained as an Episcopal priest and returned to his missionary work at the Wind River Agency. In October of 1902 he married Grace Weatherbee, the daughter of an affluent New York family who was also interested in church work and with whom he raised two daughters along with a number of adopted Indian children. Together with his wife, Sherman Coolidge continued to minister to the Wind River Shoshone and Arapaho until sometime after World War I, when the couple transferred to Colorado Springs, Colorado, to serve in the churches of that state. Grace Coolidge wrote numerous articles about her experiences at Wind River in *Collier's Weekly* and the *Outlook,* and also published a book on the same subject in 1917 titled *Teepee Neighbors.* In 1911 Sherman Coolidge became an active member of the Society of American Indians, serving as president until Arthur C. Parker took over the position in 1916. Like Parker, Sherman Coolidge was a "gradualist" who believed that the immediate abolishment of reservations and the Bureau of Indian Affairs as propagated by the "radicals" would be detrimental to Indians. Sherman Coolidge died at Colorado Springs on January 24, 1932.

Selected Publications of Sherman Coolidge

"Address by Rev. S. Coolidge." *The American Indian Magazine* 7, no. 3 (Fall 1919): 157–59.
"The American Indian—His Duty to His Race and to His Country, the United States of America." *The Quarterly Journal of the Society of American Indians* 1, no. 2 (April–June 1913): 20–24.
"The American Indian of Today." *The Quarterly Journal of the Society of American Indians* 2, no. 1 (January–March 1914): 33–35.
"The Function of the Society of American Indians." *The Quarterly Journal of the Society of American Indians* 2, no. 1 (January–March 1914): 186–90. Reprinted in *The Elders Wrote: An Anthology of Early Prose by North American Indians, 1768–1931,* edited by Bernd C. Peyer. Berlin: Dietrich Reimer Verlag, 1982: 159–62.
"Indian as Soldier." *Review of Reviews* 7 (June 1893): 597.
"The Prophet of Light." *Southern Workman* 19 (July 1890): 82.

Selected Secondary Sources

Cornell, George L. "Coolidge, Sherman." In *Encyclopedia of North American Indians,* edited by Frederick E. Hoxie. Boston: Houghton Mifflin Co., 1996: 133–34.
Houghton, Louise Seymour. *Our Debt to the Red Man.* Boston: Stratford, 1918: 154–55.
Parker, Arthur C. "Sherman Coolidge: A Study in the Complexities of an Indian's Legal Status." *The Quarterly Journal of the Society of American Indians* 3, no. 3 (July–September 1915): 220–23.
Coolidge, Grace Weatherbee. *Teepee Neighbors.* Boston: The Four Seas Co., 1917. Reprinted Norman: University of Oklahoma Press, 1984.

THE LEGAL STATUS OF THE AMERICAN INDIAN

Arthur C. Parker (1914)

In all stages of civilized society the great bulwarks safeguarding its integrity are interdependent. Thus, the social economic, intellectual, and religious conditions of a people depend very largely upon their legal condition, and vice versa.

In our attempt to civilize and assimilate the Indian we have neglected to afford him one of the most vital rights of mankind, that of a definite legal status. This has never been determined, and the Indian has been variously called a "domestic subject" and "a perpetual inhabitant with diminutive rights."[1] The Indian as neither citizen, alien nor foreigner has occupied and now occupies a precarious position in our national life. We legislate for him and then tell him his fate is in his own hands. In the same breath we also tell him three other things, "that he cannot sell his own land, or use his own money held by the Government, and that he is not subject to taxation as other able-bodied men are."[2] We rely upon religion and education, coupled with industry, to accomplish the sought-for ends with the Indian, but until there is provided a definition of the Indians' legal status in their various groups and bands, human beings will continue to go to waste, and religion, education and industry will suffer for lack of appreciation. These civilizing forces will fall as seed upon ground only fertile in spots. Shining examples of religious and educational training will continue to be the exception rather than the usual.

Definite legal status in an organized community has an important psychological value. It is for want of this subtle psychological asset that the Indian suffers most greviously [sic]. It is the root of most of his material evils. Witness the change that has come upon the red man of the plains in the last fifty years. The old initiative and independence have been crushed out of the masses, and in spirit "the poor Indian" is low indeed. Whatever Sitting Bull as a man may have been, he expressed a great thought when he exclaimed to General Miles: "God Almighty made me; God Almighty did not make me an agency Indian, and I'll fight and die before any white man can make me an agency Indian." He expressed his horror of surrendering a known status for one he could not know. In his native state each Indian knew what his status was. It was a part of his intellectual life to know it. He felt himself a man and a master. In his present state, wherein he is ruled over and thought for, he feels himself the insignificant non-represented minor and ward that he is. Not knowing what his rights are or what will come next, he becomes chronically despondent, careless, and often degenerate. Out of an undefined status and the resultant uncertainty springs the host of evils deplored by the church, the school, and the Federal departments. These evils are treated with much solicitude by the moral and social forces of the country, but no one seems to recognize a deeper lying cause. Congress, urged by many petitions, steps in and legislates upon the symptoms of the disorder, failing likewise to see a cause beyond.

In my various writings I have frequently used the term, "the legal status of the Indian," but I find that this term is not well understood by some quite familiar with legal expressions. One newspaper editor misquotes and even mildly scores me for "urging the legal status of the Indian," thinking I mean immediate citizenship. For the sake of clearness let me present my definition:

The rights and duties, the privileges and restraints that an inhabitant of an organized community may enjoy or be obligated to by the laws of the country, and that he with the citizen body and the courts clearly knows, constitute his legal status.

There is confusion and anarchy if there be no definition of what those rights and obligations are. There is demoralization and misery where there is incomplete or obscure definition, for then the very foundation of society is insecure. The feeling of insecurity as a conscious or subconscious factor means the coming of all evils. The reservation Indian has his heart strangled by the fears that beset him. He does not know what will happen next. He knows that something is being done to him and perhaps for him, but having little or no part in its initiation his interest may be only a morbid one. He cannot help matters one way or the other. This produces a paralysis of every virile mental force. It is appallingly true that the majority of reservation Indians do not even know what their rights are or where or how to turn in case of difficulty. A well-educated Indian woman in pleading for her tribe three years ago said: "My people don't know when they are citizens and when they are not. They send word to the Department, 'We want thus and so,' and the Department sends word back, 'You are citizens of the United States; we cannot do that for you.' Then they send for something else, and word comes back, 'You are wards of the Government; we cannot grant you that.' Now in what position do we stand?" Out of this uncertainty a feeling of helplessness and hopelessness arises and with it all too often ambition dies. The people then only improvidently drift through existence, greedily grasping at every chance claim or snatching at every pittance meeted [sic] out. The sense of thrift and attainment is thus destroyed. Religion and education cannot be appreciated by a desponding people. *Civilization conveying its religion and education must be consistent in the acts it performs and provide for a legal status for its wards, or hopelessness will continue and faith languish. Let me then say to the conscientious friends of the Indian that a determination of the Indians' legal status is by far the most important matter affecting the welfare of the red race in the United States to-day.* This fact is plainly pointed out in Professor McKenzie's book, "The Indian," a work that I urge every student of Indian affairs to study with care. It is by far the most lucid analysis of Indian matters now in print, yet I venture that this modest author has not placed his thesis in the hands of more than a dozen members of this conference.[3]

Reservation Indians are broadly divisible into two grades, the pure *ward* and the allotted *citizen-ward*. The allotted Indian having his limited patent to a parcel of land is theoretically a "taxed Indian." The chances are, however, that he pays no taxes and has but a hazy notion of what true citizenship means. A further review of the classes of Indians reveals the non-taxed ward, the taxed allottee, the non-citizen Indian, and the citizen Indian. Out of this classification, though natural and legal exigencies, all sorts of combinations arise to make definite status a difficult thing to determine. The result is confusion and endless litigation, to the congestion of the Indian Office and the delight of the claim lawyer. Another view of the inequality of status is shown by a survey of the Indians in the various States. Indians of like capacity and situation, as has already been pointed out by Professor McKenzie, in Oklahoma are citizens, in New York non-citizens. Allottees in Nebraska are citizens, in Wyoming non-citizens. The allotted Indian may or not be a citizen according to the state in which he dwells, notwithstanding Federal control over all. In the State of Wisconsin, citizen Indians are wards of the Nation; in Maine, of the State; in New York, Indians are wards of both State and Nation. In North Carolina, 7,000 Indians are citizens of the State and not of the Nation. But whatever the Government may intend by citizenship to the Indian, the Indian allottee usually finds the name a mere fiction, and that although a citizen of the United States he has a Federal agent ruling his destiny. In many cases this is most humiliating, as I might illustrate by examples.

A consideration of these facts reveals the significant conclusion that no series of definite grades has ever been established that in a uniform way will lift the Indian from a state of pure wardship to complete citizenship. The lack of a definite series of steps has led to much miserable confusion and prevented any true freedom. In realization of these facts the Denver platform of the Society of American Indians states: "Of all the needs of the Indian, one stands out as primary and fundamental. As long as the Indian has no definite or assured status in the Nation, so long as the Indian does not know who and what he is and what his privileges and duties are, there can be no hope of substantial progress for our race. With one voice we declare our first and chief request is that Congress shall provide the means for a careful and wise definition of Indian status through the prompt passage of the Carter code bill." This paragraph affords an idea of what the Indians themselves, through their leaders and their friends, think of the matter. The Carter code bill here mentioned is one introduced by the Society of American Indians in 1912, its operative passage being as follows: "That the President of the United States be, and he hereby is, directed to appoint a Commission of three men qualified by legal and sociological training, as well as by acquaintance with Indian affairs and needs, to study the laws governing and the circumstances affecting the various tribes and groups and classes of Indians and to report [in a given period] a codified law determining the status of the Indians of the United States in accordance with existing legislation and the future best interests of these natives."

It is my belief that the report of such a commission would be most illuminating. The draft of a codified law that it would submit, once passed by Congress, would provide the means for bringing the Indian up definitely, step by step, until he entered the status of complete citizenship. It would work to determine the status of the various groups in such a manner that every Indian might know, and every citizen might know, what the rights of and duties of every Indian were, without resorting to litigation about it or appealing to the Interior Department. Citizenship would be the goal ahead. There would be nothing behind to look back toward. This would then be a spur to endeavor and the road to citizenship would be definite and secure.

In passing, it may be said that if a revised code and the requirements of the bill could be met by a private commission, or one such as suggested by Senator [Joseph Taylor] Robinson or Professor [Warren C.] Moorehead, the boon would be most welcome.[4] It would seem, however, that a special commission of well equipped, highly paid men, appointed by the President, would have the greater weight with Congress. We only ask, however, that the thing be done.

Professor McKenzie, in the *Journal of Race Development,* points out the need of the principles for which we have argued and presents a table suggesting a plan for dividing the Indians into grades.[5] He suggests, for the purpose of outlining his plan, that the Indians who are wards be classed as, first, tribal wards holding communal land, and, second, allotted wards holding land in severalty and having allotted trust funds. Over the communal Indian ward there would be governmental control of land and trust funds through agency administration. The allotted ward would have Federal supervision of land contracts and trust-fund expenditures. The second class of grades would be the citizen-ward and the full-citizen Indian. The citizen-ward would hold his land in fee, have control of his own funds and have a legal standing in the courts. The Government would have a review of his contracts prior to signature, or within three months thereafter. The citizen Indian would have all privileges and disabilities of the rank. This plan, which is not at all revolutionary, is used only as a suggestion for arranging the series of grades, without arguing the adoption of it without further consideration. A commission once appointed might hit upon some other happy plan of similar nature as a working basis for a better grasp of the situation.

In the working out of the plan as suggested, every Indian of every grade would know exactly what his legal status was, what his rights, duties, responsibilities, and restrictions were. He would know how he might relieve himself of his restrictions and disadvantages and step upward to a higher grade, and finally into the status as a contributing, sustaining, positive element of the country in which he lived. The courts, the Federal Indian Bureau, and the citizens of the country would have full knowledge of what a classified Indian was and how to deal with him. The feeling of certain status, of legal security, the knowledge of a definite goal ahead, would afford the culture forcing incentive most necessary to bring the Indian into our national life as a healthful efficient factor.

This plan provides for a new epoch in Indian affairs. Once the legal status is determined and a series of grades established, there will be a more rapid transition from lower to higher stages. Justice will then become a more common matter and civilizing agencies profit by the happier minds of the people. The path to freedom and self-government will be paved and we shall mark the passing of "ward" and "subject," and ultimately give to the Indian now possessing "diminutive rights" every right that the Nation vouchsafes to its sovereign people.

Notes

Originally a paper read at the Lake Mohonk Conference on October 16, 1914, and published in the *Proceedings of the Thirty-Second Annual Meeting of the Lake Mohonk Conference of the Friends of the Indian and Other Dependent Peoples, 1914* (Lake Mohonk, N.Y.: The Lake Mohonk Conference, 1914), 77–82; repr. in *The Quarterly Journal of the Society of American Indians* 2, no. 1 (January–March 1914): 212–18. Establishing a concrete legal status for Indians was one of the main concerns of the Society of American Indians. At the first annual convention in 1911 the organization's officers recommended the creation of an Indian Code Commission to codify the laws relating to Indians. A bill to this effect was introduced as House Bill 18334 on January 19, 1912, by Congressman Charles D. Carter (Chickasaw, 1869–1929), an active member of the SAI from Oklahoma, and it was continually supported by the organization thereafter.

1. Parker lists Attorney General Edward E. Cushman, *U. S. v. Bridleman* (7 Fed., 894), and *Gibbons v. Odgen* (1924) as sources for his citations in the original.

2. Fayette A. McKenzie, *The Indian in Relation to the White Population of the United States* (Columbus, Ohio: Fayette McKenzie, 1908), 30.

3. Fayette Avery McKenzie (b. 1872), sociologist at Ohio State University and later president of Fisk University, was instrumental in the development of the Society of American Indians and its ideology. It was at his invitation that the six original founders of the American Indian Association (then changed to Society of American Indians) met at Columbus, Ohio, in April of 1911. McKenzie's interpretation of the Indian's social status and notions of a new "Indian leadership" had a marked influence on Parker's own ideas. See Hazel Hertzberg, *The Search for an American Indian Identity: Modern Pan-Indian Movements* (Syracuse: Syracuse University Press, 1971), 31–58.

4. Julius Taylor Robinson (1872–1937), Democratic senator from Arkansas, was head of a special commission to investigate conditions at Carlisle Indian Industrial School in 1914. Warren King Moorehead (1866–1939), noted anthropologist and archaeologist, was a member of the Board of Indian Commissioners and later joined the Committee of One Hundred. He is the author of *The American Indian in the United States* (Andover, Mass.: The Andover Press, 1914).

5. "The American Indian of Today and Tomorrow," *Journal of Race Development* 3, no. 2 (1913); repr., *Quarterly Journal of the Society of American Indians* 1, no. 4 (1913), 383–400. Cited by Parker in the original.

THE CIVILIZING POWER OF LANGUAGE

Arthur C. Parker (1916)

Among the features of any civilization quickly borrowed by a cultivated people in contact with it is *language*. The American Indian in all his stocks and tribes in the United States has borrowed the English language. It is not only now his inter-tribal language but to a large extent his daily language. With the clothing of thought in English comes a new mental vision and a new grasp of the world. Can it be that so learned authority as Dr. [Joseph P.] Widney will say that the learning of English, or any language, is simply impossible to the Indian, because the speech has not been evolved by the native mind?[1] Then witness eloquent English, chaste in its elegance, employed by Indian writers and orators. No Roman orator ever spoke with such vigor, no senator of our Congress ever clothed his speech with greater beauty than the orators and writers of the Red race who spoke or wrote in English. Where shall we find an orator with an easier, freer way of thought than Dr. Peter Wilson, the Cayuga, who put even Webster in the background when speaking from the same platform?[2] Marius Pierce [sic], a Seneca, and a Dartmouth graduate, in the early days of the last century, was likewise a master of English diction. Today in the writings of Zit-Kal-Sa [sic] we find a strange and fascinating phrasing, that if it were "translated from the Russian," would be famous. The voice and speech of Sherman Coolidge when roused by the fire of righteous conviction is no less wonderful. Secretary of the Interior [Franklin K.] Lane was willing to say that he had never heard the equal of Coolidge, in his Denver Publicity Association address in 1913, save once, and that was by an Indian chief who had made an appeal to him in behalf of his people.

No one will fail to note the brilliant writings of Ohiyesha [sic], Dr. Charles Eastman, and credit him with a command of a tongue foreign to him and his parents at his birth. Then there is the minor host, whose language we read every now and then in legislative and Congressional appeals.

When we extend our search beyond the realm of the pure blood we find that the blood of the Red race gives something to the flow of the man or woman who is of both Red and White ancestry.

Early Indian territory produced many orators, writers and poets whose works possess real merit. We have only to mention John Ross, Allen Wright, Peter Pitchlynn and Alexander Posey.[3] Today the state of Oklahoma has many Indians who command power and respect by reason of their grasp of English. One visit to Tahlequah, Muskogee, or to the legislative chamber in Oklahoma City proves this. Here the fire of Indian oratory frequently rings out.

The American Indian mind "borrowing" an alien tongue uses it with all the power that civilization has given it. That tongue of a "civilized" people compels a thought expression and weave consistent with civilized ideals. Used to its fullest extent it brings the native mind a hold on the literature, rhetoric, history and science of the race that evolved the language. But woven in the understanding and in the thought fabric of the Indian is a thread and often warp all his own, lending an embellishment that is distinctive.

Language is the outward expression of the thought life of a culture, and may not long be used without a change in the mental life. Savagery, brutality, barbarism, civilization, education and reason are but ways of thinking. If by a language we can make a man or race think correctly by unloosing through that language the knowledge of truth, then that man and that race can achieve anything the language leads men toward. Shall it be said the Red race as a race is unable to think dearly in the channels grooved by the tongues of civilization?

That the Red race through its best representatives will live and become active forces in civilization is demonstrated by the very eloquence and logic of the leaders of that race. In every race the incapable are preyed upon and die. They die because they do not think logically, vigorously and constructively and not because they possess the blood of any certain racial stock.

Notes

Originally published as "Editor's Viewpoint: The Civilizing Power of Language," *The Quarterly Journal of the Society of American Indians* 4, no. 2 (April–June 1916): 126–28. In this editorial Parker cites the confluence of oral traditions and literacy as an example of successful Indian selective adaptation.

1. Dr. Joseph P. Widney, president of the University of Southern California, maintained that there was a "racial and radical difference in bloods" in his widely read racialist treatise *Race Life of the Aryan Peoples*, 2 vols. (New York: Funk and Wagnalls Co., 1907).

2. Peter Wilson, or Waowawanoonk (They Hear His Voice), was a Cayuga chief and noted orator whose speech "On the Empire State" before the New York Historical Society on May 4, 1847, was widely disseminated.

3. Allen Wright (Choctaw, 1826–85), graduate of Union Theological Seminary and an ordained Presbyterian minister, served as a member of the Choctaw National Council, national treasurer, superintendent of schools, and Principal Chief from 1866 to 1870. In 1872 he translated the Choctaw laws from English into Choctaw. In 1885 he was editor and translator for the Atoka *Indian Champion.* Peter Perkins Pitchlynn (Choctaw, 1806–81), graduate of the University of Tennessee, served as Principal Chief from 1864 to 1866 and continually lobbied for Choctaw claims in Washington, D.C., thereafter. He is the author of numerous articles in Indian Territory newspapers as well as political pamphlets. See David W. Baird, *Peter Pitchlynn: Chief of the Choctaws* (Norman: University of Oklahoma Press, 1972).

BIOGRAPHY

Arthur Caswell Parker (Seneca, 1881–1955), or Gawaso Waneh (Big Snow Snake), was born on the Cattaraugus Seneca Indian Reservation in western New York on April 5, the son of Frederick Ely Parker, a non-enrolled part-Seneca, and Geneva Griswold, a Congregationalist school teacher of Scots-English ancestry. His maternal grandfather was Nicholas H. Parker, an influential Seneca leader. Even though a member of a respectable Christian Seneca family (Ely S. Parker was his great-uncle), Arthur Parker had to be officially adopted into the tribe by one of his uncles because of the matrilineal social structure of the Senecas. Arthur Parker's family moved to a suburb of New York City in 1891, where he graduated from public high school in 1897. He attended Centenary Collegiate Institute for a few months and then enrolled at Dickinson Seminary in Williamsport, Pennsylvania, in 1893 to prepare for the ministry. Parker gave up his studies at this institution in the summer of 1903 to become Mark R. Harrington's field assistant in an archaeological survey at Cattaraugus directed by Frederick W. Putnam of the Peabody Museum at Harvard. At the same time he worked briefly as a reporter for the *New York Sun*. In April 1904 he married the Abnaki Beatrice Tahamont.

After a brief term as ethnologist of the State Library in 1904–1905, Parker secured a position as ethnologist for the New York State Museum. He passed a Civil Service examination in 1905 and served as the permanent archaeologist of this institution until 1924. Parker then assumed the directorship of the Rochester Museum in New York, a post he held until retirement in 1946. Although he was not an academically trained anthropologist, Arthur Parker emerged as one of the foremost authorities on Iroquois culture and history, publishing several seminal monographs and countless articles. His most important work in this field is the trilogy *Iroquois Uses of Maize and Other Food Plants* (1910), *The Code of Handsome Lake, the Seneca Prophet* (1913), and *The Constitution of the Five Nations* (1915), all published by the New York State Museum. Furthermore, Parker was a distinguished museologist, one of the first in the field to make regular use of life-size dioramas to illustrate Indian ways of life to museum visitors. In 1935 he published *A Manual for History Museums*, which became a central reference book for the profession. For his academic work Parker was awarded an honorary M.S. from the University of Rochester in 1922, an honorary doctorate in science from Union College in 1940, and a Doctorate of Humane Laws from Keuka College in 1945.

Parker joined the Society of American Indians during the second meeting of the Temporary Executive Committee in the summer of 1911. He soon became its chief intellectual motor, serving as secretary-treasurer (later national secretary) from 1912 to 1915 and as president from 1916 to 1918. In addition, he edited *The Quarterly Journal of the Society of American Indians* (later *The American Indian Magazine*) from 1913 to 1918. Parker believed in the basic tenets of the Indian reform movement, including the eventual termination of the Bureau of Indian Affairs but ultimately concluded that the immediate dismantling of the Indian Service and the reservation system would wreak havoc among Indians. Consequently, in his editorials for the *Quarterly Journal* and elsewhere he tended to advocate a more gradual course under which the federal government was to fulfill prior obligations and improve its services to Indians, particularly in the field of education, until they were in a position to take care of themselves. Parker's moderate course was under constant fire from the radical faction of the Society of American Indians, particularly Carlos Montezuma. Disillusioned, Parker gradually distanced himself from the organization after 1917.

Even though Parker became more concerned with his work as director of the Rochester Museum and his Masonic connections than with national Indian politics after his resignation from the Society of American Indians, he did not turn his back on the organization altogether. On December 12–13, 1923, he joined several active and retired members of the Society of American Indians, including Henry Roe Cloud, Sherman Coolidge, Charles Eastman, J. N. B. Hewitt, and Thomas Sloan, to form the Advisory Council on Indian Affairs, which came to be known as the "Committee of One Hundred." The proposals made by this committee, with Arthur Parker as chairman, foreshadowed in some ways the critical investigation conducted by the Brookings Institute of Government Research in 1928, better known as the Meriam Report, which in turn ushered in the era of the "Indian New Deal." In 1939 John Collier appointed Arthur Parker, D'Arcy McNickle (Cree-Flathead, 1904–77), Ruth Muskrat Bronson (Cherokee, 1897–1982), Archie Phinney (Nez Perce, 1903–49), and other noted Indian scholars as delegates to a Canadian conference on North American Indians that was jointly sponsored by the University of Toronto and Yale University. More significantly, Parker's political expertise was acknowledged in November 1944 when he was elected (along with McNickle and Phinney) as one of the eight councilmen of the executive committee of the National Congress of American Indians, the organization that has effectively carried on the work of the Society of American Indians until the present. Arthur Parker's subsequent involvement with this organization was only marginal, however. Ideologically, "the head heart and Soul of our endeavor to save our race," as Gertrude Bonnin once titled Parker, drifted more and more toward the dubious "science" of eugenics.

Besides his invaluable preservationist work in archaeology and museology, Arthur Parker also promoted contemporary Indian arts and crafts as a means to generate reservation income. Among other activities of that nature, he designed and organized the Seneca Arts and Crafts Project under which the work of about one hundred artists from the Tonawanda and Cattaraugus reservations was financed with grant money from the Works Progress Administration from 1935 to 1941. He thus helped to bring about a revival of traditional Iroquois arts and crafts in New York. A few of the artists involved in this project eventually initiated the modern "Iroquois School of Art."

Other than his anthropological writings, Arthur Parker produced several collections of Seneca oral stories, a biography of Ely S. Parker, a Boy Scout manual, a juvenile novel, and a pamphlet on American Indian masonry. In 1936 Arthur Parker was awarded a medal "for the most distinguished achievement by an American Indian" from the Indian Council Fire (formerly Grand Council Fire), a mixed Indian and white fraternal organization founded in Chicago in 1923. Arthur Parker died on January 1, 1955.

Selected Publications of Arthur Caswell Parker

American Indian Freemasonry. Albany, N.Y.: Buffalo Consistory, 1919.

"Are Your Officers Traitors?" *The Quarterly Journal of the Society of American Indians* 4, no. 1 (January–March 1916): 15–18.

"Certain Important Elements of the Indian Problem." *The Quarterly Journal of the Society of American Indians* 3, no. 1 (January–March 1915): 24–38.

The Code of Handsome Lake, the Seneca Prophet. New York State Museum Bulletin 163. Albany: University of the State of New York, 1913.

The Constitution of the Five Nations or The Iroquois Book of the Great Law. New York State Museum Bulletin 184. Albany: University of the State of New York, 1916.

"The Editor's Viewpoint: The Civilizing Power of Language." *The Quarterly Journal of the Society of American Indians* 4, no. 2 (April–June 1916): 126–28.

"The Editors Viewpoint: The Functions of the Society of American Indians." *The Quarterly Journal of the Society of American Indians* 4, no. 1 (January–March 1916): 8–14.

"The Indian, the Country and the Government: A Plea for an Efficient Indian Service." *The Quarterly Journal of the Society of American Indians* 4, no. 1 (January–March 1916): 38–49.

The Indian How Book. New York: George H. Doran, 1927. Reprinted New York: Dover, 1975.

Iroquois Uses of Maize and Other Food Plants. New York State Museum Bulletin 144. Albany: University of the State of New York, 1910.

"The Legal Status of the American Indian." *The Quarterly Journal of the Society of American Indians* 2, no. 1 (January–March 1914): 212–18.

The Life of General Ely S. Parker: Last Grand Sachem of the Iroquois and General Grant's Military Secretary. Buffalo, NY: Buffalo Historical Society, 1919. Reprinted N.Y.: AMS Press, 1985.

"Making a White Man Out of an Indian Not a Good Plan." *The American Indian Magazine* 5, no. 1 (January–March 1917): 85–87.

"The Perils of the Peyote Poison." *The American Indian Magazine* 5, no. 1 (January–March 1917): 12–13.

"Philosophy of Indian Education." *Report of the Executive Council on the Proceedings of the First Annual Conference of the Society of American Indians.* Washington, D.C., 1912. Reprinted in *The Indian Historian* 3, no. 2 (Spring 1970): 63–64; and *The Indian Historian* 3, no. 3 (Summer 1970): 42–45.

"Problems of Race Assimilation in America, with Special Reference to the American Indian." *The American Indian Magazine* 4 (October–December 1916): 285–304.

"The Red Man's Love of Mother Earth." *The American Indian Magazine* 5, no. 1 (January–March 1917): 14–16.

Red Streak of the Iroquois. Chicago: Children's Book Press, 1950.

Rumbling Wings and Other Indian Tales. New York: Doubleday, Doran and Co., 1928.

Skunny Wundy and Other Indian Tales. New York: George H. Doran Co., 1926. Reprinted Syracuse, N.Y.: Syracuse University Press, 1994.

"The Social Elements of the Indian Problem." *American Journal of Sociology* 22 (September 1916): 252–67. Reprinted in *The Elders Wrote: An Anthology of Early Prose by North American Indians, 1768–1931,* edited by Bernd C. Peyer. Berlin: Dietrich Reimer Verlag, 1982: 169–82.

Unpublished Writings

Arthur C. Parker Papers, 1915–1953, New York State Library, Albany, New York (Microfilm).

Selected Secondary Sources

Campisi, Jack. "Parker, Arthur C." In *Encyclopedia of North American Indians,* edited by Frederick E. Hoxie. Boston: Houghton Mifflin Company, 1996: 464–66.

Fenton, William N., ed. *Parker on the Iroquois.* Syracuse: Syracuse University Press, 1968.

Hauptman, Lawrence M. "The Iroquois School of Art: Arthur C. Parker and the Seneca Arts Project, 1935–1941." *New York History* 60 (July 1979): 253–312.

_____. *The Iroquois and the New Deal.* Syracuse: Syracuse University Press, 1981: 136–63.

Hertzberg, Hazel W. "Arthur C. Parker, Seneca, 1881–1955." In *American Indian Intellectuals, 1976 Proceedings of the American Ethnological Society,* edited by Margot Liberty. St. Paul: West Publishing Co., 1978: 129–38.

_____. "Nationality, Anthropology, and Pan-Indiansim in the Life of Arthur C. Parker." *Proceedings of the American Philosophical Society* 123, 1 (1979): 47–72.

Porter, Joy. *To Be Indian: The Life of Iroquois-Seneca Arthur C. Parker.* Norman: University of Oklahoma Press, 2001.

Thomas, W. Stephen. "Arthur Caswell Parker: 1881–1955." *Rochester History* 17, no. 2 (1955): 1–30.

JUSTICE FOR THE SIOUX

Charles A. Eastman (1919)

"There is no use talking, Kola, the Black Hills claim is like a cork in the water," said a member of the Sioux Council the other day. "The Indian Bureau tries to push it under, but it bobs up every time." It is a fact that the Sioux have been trying for some twenty years to get this matter before Congress and the Court of Claims, but it appears that the Indian Bureau is the judge as to whether they shall have a fair hearing and final settlement of their claim, or not.[1] The day that our Government got the Indians' consent to reservation life, that day the Bureau assumed paternal supervision of their affairs. Then and there we lost our freedom, our personal rights, and the privileges which had been ours for untold ages.

The Indian supposed he had provided for himself, in addition to his birth-right, the protection of United States law. It seems this is not the case. After negotiating treaties as an equal, he was strangely born again a child,—incompetent, irresponsible, and unable to think for himself. Inconsistently enough, whenever the Government is in trouble, he is called upon to come to its defense!

It is unfortunate for the Indian, and it is truly embarrassing for a government, by, for and of the people, to have gotten into such a mix-up as this Indian question. There are several highly Christian and philanthropic (?) explanations of the situation which have been produced with considerable plausibility, notwithstanding the Indian has paid dearly for every service rendered in his behalf. These explanations are no longer held by the well informed. They perceive clearly that he is in reality bound by mere technicalities, or by department rulings passed upon him over his treaty rights and without his knowledge or consent. At best, the arbitrary regulations made for his and his neighbors' protection on reservations when he was wild, are now used to impede his progress, to prevent him from getting justice, and to defraud him of his holdings as an Indian.

One of these chains which binds poor Lo so tightly today is the law passed for his protection from unscrupulous lawyers entering the reservation and fleecing him during the early stages of his apprenticeship to civilization. Today the Indian Bureau refuses to recognize any lawyer whom the Indians may employ, either collectively or singly. It matters not how good the cause, how intelligent the tribe or the individual Indian, or how high the reputation of their chosen counsel.

Again, no Indian band nor any part of it can meet to discuss their own business, unless the Secretary of the Interior through the Commissioner of Indian Affairs gives his permission. These were perhaps necessary expedients fifty years ago, but common-sense finds them out of place among most Indians for at least the past twenty-five years.

Under such regulations as these, and many more equally burdensome, the Indian Bureau has perpetrated a kind of czarism in these United States. This fact must now be faced squarely. Everybody has evaded the responsibility. The people truthfully say: "We have paid the bill. We want to be fair to the Indian." Congress says: "We have generously appropriated large sums every year to carry out our agreements with him." The Indian says: "We have not received in accordance with the agreement; in fact, we do not know what becomes of our money." Who is to blame?

Congressman [Charles D.] Carter of Oklahoma, in a recent letter, gives in effect the reply of Congress, namely: "We pass laws and appropriate moneys for the Indians *on the recommendation of the Indian Bureau.*" Thus, we are inclined to hold the Bureau mainly responsible for all the ills of our Indian civilization.

The Sioux, for example, are trying to bring their Black Hills claim before an impartial tribunal. They wish to be represented by well-known and reputable attorneys, but the Bureau has persistently interfered. The whole matter appears very illogical to some of us who have looked into it. In the first place, this claim is against the United States government therefore a government official cannot properly represent the Indian. How can he receive justice if the government is to select both lawyers?

The Sioux have been patiently waiting for the Secretary to say what is only right: "Go ahead; select your own lawyer!" Why should they be forced to employ a man selected by the Bureau? They are not even permitted to meet for a free discussion of the matter, as the Commissioner has insisted upon appointing a time and place for the meeting, and through his agents naming the delegates. It is claimed by the Indians that delegates of their choosing are unfairly treated by officials, but of course such claims will not be admitted.

I have said to the Sioux, when asked for my advice in the matter, that all the people in the United States have the right to speak in open meeting, political, social or religious, and that there is no law against it. By treaty right, also, they may hold councils and discuss any subject, excepting only war talk against the government. The world is just awake to such abuses of authority as this.

The Black Hills claim is the outcome of a lease given by 246 chiefs, with permission to prospect for gold for certain considerations. On the strength of this lease, the Hills and the region roundabout were taken from the Sioux. This is called the "Black Hills agreement" [Manypenny Agreement] of 1877.

The [Fort Laramie] treaty of 1868 with the same Sioux provides for them a definitely described territory, of which the Black Hills and Big Horn country were the most valuable part. It is stipulated that no part of this territory shall ever be ceded without the signature of three-fourths of the adult males of the Indians concerned. It is further declared, that no white man shall enter it without consent of the Indians, unless on government business.[2]

In 1872–76 the whites poured into the Black Hills. This was the cause of the Indian troubles of that period. Afterward a commission was sent to treat for the coveted region. Our people refused to sell. The government offered to move them into Indian Territory. They refused. A lease was finally agreed to by the said chiefs. The Black Hills are held to this day on the grounds of that lease.

This is, in brief, the history of the case. It is time we should have justice shown us. Our boys fought shoulder to shoulder with your boys. Fellow-countrymen, will you look into our cause? We ask nothing unreasonable—only the freedom and the privileges for which your boy and mine have fought.[3]

Notes

Originally in *The American Indian Magazine* 7, no. 2 (Summer 1919): 79–81. Under the editorship of Gertrude Bonnin, the 1919 editions of the Society of American Indians' journal focused on Sioux affairs. Eastman uses the Black Hills case to illustrate patronage of Indians by the state.

1. In 1874 a military expedition under General Armstrong Custer confirmed the discovery of gold in the Black Hills. Ruthless intruders subsequently led to a war between the Sioux and the United States in 1876–77, resulting in the famous Battle of Little Bighorn and the ultimate defeat of the Sioux. In 1877 a Congressional Act ratified the so-called Manypenny Agreement, under which the Black Hills were taken from the Sioux. The "agreement" also extingished all Sioux rights outside of the Great Sioux Reservation established by the Treaty of Fort Laramie in 1868. The Great Sioux Agreement of 1889 broke up the Great Sioux Reservation. Through the Sioux Act of the following year, six smaller reservations were established: Pine Ridge, Rosebud, Lower Brulé, Crow Creek, Cheyenne River, and Standing Rock. In 1915 the Sioux decided to present claims to the Black Hills in the U. S. Court of Claims. The Sioux Jurisdictional Act authorized the Court of Claims to adjudicate the case, which finally dismissed it in 1942. Lawyer Ralph Case refiled the Black Hills claim in the Indian Claims Commission (ICC) in 1950. After first rejecting the Black Hills claim in 1954, the ICC decided in 1974 to award $17.5 million plus interest for the Black Hills, pending determination of government offsets. In 1980 the Supreme Court affirmed the Court of Claims ruling in the Black Hills case and awarded the Sioux $106 million. So far the Sioux have rejected any monetary compensation for the Black Hills. See Edward Lazarus, *Black Hills White Justice: The Sioux Nation Versus the United States 1775 to the Present* (New York: Harper Collins Publishers, 1991).

2. Articles 2, 12, and 16 of the Fort Laramie Treaty signed on April 29, 1868. See Charles J. Kappler, comp. and ed., *Indian Affairs, Laws, and Treaties*, 7 vols. (Washington, D.C.: Government Printing Office, 1903–1904), II: 998–1007.

3. Charles Eastman's only son, Ohiyesa II, served in World War I along with approximately ten thousand American Indians. An act passed November 6, 1919, declared all Indian veterans could be citizens if they so desired. See Thomas A. Britten, *American Indians in World War I: At Home and at War* (Albuquerque: University of New Mexico Press, 1997).

THE INDIAN'S PLEA FOR FREEDOM

Charles A. Eastman (1919)

I believe this to be an opportune moment for the "little peoples" of the earth to plead for a better observance of their individuality and rights by the more powerful and ruling nations. For we must admit that every race, however untutored, has its ideals, its standards of right and wrong, which are sometimes nearer the Christ principle than the common standards of civilization.

Certainly under the leadership of Woodrow Wilson, we of the United States have an opportunity splendid and far reaching, which may never come again. If the coming Peace Congress will deliberate unselfishly in the interests of humanity, if we can eliminate purely national bias and suspicion, then the world's after-council must establish a new international relationship. And this new order must begin at home. The old rule, the old ambitions for world domination by discovery and conquest must forever pass.

The world is tired, sick, and exhausted by a war which has brought home to us the realization that our boasted progress is after all mainly industrial and commercial—a powerful force, to be sure, but being so unspiritual, not likely to be lasting or stable. On the other hand, being so powerful it might have been expected to be destructive and therefore cruel. The intellectual development connected with it has been largely heartless and soulless. The education of the child has subordinated his higher instincts to the necessities of business. Christ has been preached in vain, since his most unmistakable and unequivocal declarations are directly opposed to our excess of material development, social injustice and the accumulation of wealth.

Now we have come to a point when we may at least hope that this tremendous machine will be used toward a better readjustment of human relationships. An Indian must admire our President for the stand he has taken. It seems we are in a position to pilot the bark of humanity into a safe harbor, if this high stand can be sustained by the allies.

When the vexed Irish question and other knotty problems come up at the peace table, we may be reminded that we too, here in America, have our race troubles.[1] How can our nation pose as the champion of the "little peoples" until it has been fair to its own? "We, too, demand our freedom!" cry those modern Greeks, the North American Indians. Their request is not hard to grant, since it involves no separate government or territory.[2] All we ask is full citizenship. Why not? We offered our services and our money in this war, and more in proportion to our number and means than any other race or class of the population. Yet there are people who insist on keeping us the "wards of the Government," apparently for no other reason than to use our money and our property for their own benefit.

I am proud to say that the Indian has exemplified the American spirit; it is his contribution to mankind. That spirit of America which can not be measured in miles or estimated in dollars, the spirit born of free American soil, air, and sun, every tree, hill and stream proclaims and sings it. Here men of every oppressed race came to find it, enjoyed and proclaimed it to the world.

The first white men who came here met a friendly reception and found a most beautiful and unspoiled home. Most of them came in search of treasure for themselves or their kings. A few came in an entirely different spirit. They sought religious and political self-determination. They found it, and in their contact with the simple Indian tribes, whom they counted godless and heathen, they unconsciously and in spite of themselves absorbed enough of the Indians' culture to modify their own. The friendship, toleration, dignity and sincerity characteristic of the American Indians have never been violated by them, and is their bequest to the nation.

It is not generally known that practically all the basic principles of the original articles of confederation of the Thirteen States were borrowed, either unconsciously or knowingly, from the league of the Six Nations and the Sioux confederacy. You may ask, how came the American eagle to reach its symbolic power? I say to you, it was a reverenced symbol for untold centuries with the American Indians. Its feathers were worn by worthy men for worthy deeds. They could not be bought nor sold.[3]

Now every treaty with the Indians in recent times has included provision for the education of their children, and it was understood that in due time the affairs of their people should be turned over to them, and that as fast as they became able to comply with the usual requirements, they should be admitted to citizenship. In fact, the Constitution expressly excludes "Indians not taxed," therefore, as they are not foreigners, when one pays his taxes, he is a citizen.[4] Yet there has been so much confusing legislation on this matter, that I do not believe there is a learned judge in these United States who can tell an Indian's exact status without a great deal of study, and even then he may be in doubt.

The Indian Bureau, instead of being the servant of the people and of the Indians in accordance with treaty stipulations, has grown into a petty autocracy. The whole system reminds me of the story of Two-Face in the Sioux legend. He stole a child to feed on his tender substance, sucking his blood while still living, and if any one protested, or aroused by the baby's screams, attempted a rescue, he would pat it tenderly and pretend to caress it. This fine intention of the people to develop the Indian into useful citizens has given rise to an institution which is doing them positive injury.

It is not the fault of the people in a way; not perhaps the fault of any particular administration that a soldier returning from the Marne or Chateau Thierry should still find his money and land held by the Indian Bureau. When he asks for freedom, they answer him: "Can you propose anything better than the present system?" He replies: "Is there anything better today than American citizenship?"[5]

Who is there that has faith in the power of self-development and human initiative, that would deny this opportunity to the Indian? It is true that a few will misuse their freedom; some will fall and recover themselves; most will gain direct and useful experience. It is not fair to destroy the manhood of a race by a system which must make them more inactive, dependent and beggarly with each succeeding generation.

There are no more "wild Indians." The majority have had contact with civilization for at least forty years. They have had two generations or more of schooling. Many are nominal citizens and actual tax-payers yet have no real freedom of action. As for shiftlessness and improvidence, that is best produced by Bureau management. A single Act of Congress might and should wipe out the system, saving millions of worse than wasted dollars annually, to say nothing of a people's self-respect.

In view of all that the world has just suffered in the name of justice and a fair deal for all, we appeal to all fair-minded Americans; Is it not our due that we should call this fair land ours with you in full brotherhood? Have we not defended bravely its liberties and may we not share them? We do not ask for territorial grant or separate government. We ask only to enjoy with Europe's sons the full privileges of American citizenship.

Notes

Originally in *The American Indian Magazine* 6, no. 4 (Winter 1919): 162–65. The Paris Peace Conference, which opened January 18, 1919, negotiated treaties of peace between the World War I Allied and Associated Powers and their enemies. On February 14, President Woodrow Wilson submitted the Draft Covenant for the formation of the League of Nations (1920–40). Eastman and other Indian intellectuals believed that Woodrow Wilson's efforts at the Paris Peace Conference on behalf of the "self-determination" of smaller European nations should also include Indians at home, specifically with reference to the granting of American citizenship. See also Gertrude Bonnin, "America, Home of the Red Man" (1919) in this anthology.

1. The "vexed Irish question" refers to the dispute at the Paris Peace Conference over whether or not the "Irish Free State," declared following the Easter Rising in 1916 and represented here by Sinn Fein, should be recognized as an independent state.

2. One of the issues before the Paris Peace Conference was the conflicting territorial claims of Greece and Turkey, especially with reference to Cyprus.

3. See also Charles A. Eastman, "The American Eagle an Indian Symbol," *American Indian Magazine* 7, no. 2 (Summer 1919): 89–92.

4. The Apportionment Clause of the Constitution (Article 1, Section 2, later replaced by 14th Amendment, par. 2) states: "Representatives and direct Taxes shall be apportioned among the several States according to their respective numbers, counting the whole number of persons in each State, excluding Indians not taxed."

5. U.S. troops participated in the second Battle of the Marne and the fighting in the Chateau-Thiery and Bellau Woods in the summer of 1918.

BIOGRAPHY

Charles Alexander Eastman (Mdewakanton-Wahpeton Sioux, 1858–1939), or Ohiyesa (The Winner), was born on September 19, near Redwood Falls, Minnesota, the son of Ite Wakanhdi Ota (Many Lightnings) and Wakantan-kanwin (Sacred Woman). His mother, a part-Mdewakanton Sioux also known as Mary Nancy Eastman, was the daughter of Captain Seth Eastman, the noted frontier artist. Eastman's mother died a few months after his birth and he was consequently named Hakadah (Pitiful Last). Following the imprisonment of his father in Davenport, Iowa, for participating in the Minnesota Sioux Uprising of 1862, Hakadah was raised by his paternal grandmother and uncle in what would become southeastern Manitoba. Here he was eventually renamed Ohiyesa (The Winner) in commemoration of a Wahpeton victory at a stickball game.

During his incarceration, Many Lightnings became a Presbyterian and adopted his wife's Christian family name. In 1868 Jacob Eastman voluntarily left the Santee Reservation in Nebraska in order to take up a homestead along the Big Sioux River in South Dakota, in what became known as Flandreau Colony. In 1872 he brought his youngest son back from Canada and enrolled him at the River Bend Church mission school at Flandreau. Charles Alexander Eastman, as Ohiyesa was known from then on, attended Santee Normal Training School, a bilingual boarding school run by the American Board of Commissioners for Foreign Missions in Nebraska, from 1874 to 1876, and Beloit Preparatory School in Wisconsin from 1876 to 1879. He continued his studies at Knox College in Galesburg, Illinois, before returning to South Dakota in 1881, where he briefly clerked at his brother-in-law's store at Flandreau and taught a term at the First Presbyterian Church mission school. In 1882 Eastman spent a year and a half at Kimball Union Academy in Meriden, New Hampshire, and then entered Dartmouth College as one of the last Indian students to profit from a Scotch endowment based on Samson Occom's collections for Moor's Indian Charity School in the 1760s. Following his graduation from Dartmouth in 1887 Eastman studied medicine at the Boston University School of Medicine, successfully completing the requirements for a medical degree in 1890.

Late in 1890 Eastman was granted an assignment as government physician at the Pine Ridge Agency in South Dakota. Here he witnessed the circumstances leading to the annihilation of Big Foot's band of Minniconjou Sioux at Wounded Knee on December 29. He also met Elaine Goodale (1863–1953), an educator and Indian rights activist from Massachusetts, who was then serving as Supervisor of Education for the Sioux. They married in New York on June 18, 1891. After a dispute with the Indian agent at Pine Ridge, Eastman resigned his position on January 26, 1893, and moved with his wife to St. Paul, Minnesota, planning to practice medicine independently. Although he passed the state medical board examination, this venture turned out to be a financial disaster. Toward the close of 1893, Eastman began to record his reminiscences of his childhood days in Canada. These were serialized in *St. Nicholas*, a popular magazine for a juvenile audience.

From June 1, 1894, until April 1, 1898, Eastman functioned as Indian secretary of the International Committee of the YMCA. In November of 1896 Eastman also signed a ten-year contract as tribal representative in the Santee Sioux Claims Case involving the recovery of annuities canceled by Congress in 1863. Eastman and his legal partner were unable to secure any payments in the time allotted to them but continued to push the case in Washington without tribal authorization. When the U. S. Court of Claims finally granted the Santees close to $390,000 in 1922, Eastman believed that he still had the right to one-half of the attorney fees. The Santee tribal council disputed his claim, however, and he was never able to collect the sum.

In November of 1899 Eastman accepted a position as outing agent at Carlisle Indian Industrial School in Pennsylvania. In the three months they spent at Carlisle, Eastman and his wife developed a close friendship with Richard Henry Pratt, sharing wholeheartedly his radical pedagogical philosophy of total immersion.

In the fall of 1900 Eastman was offered the position of government physician at the Crow Creek Agency in South Dakota. Once again, a personal confrontation with the local Indian agent led to his resignation on March 12, 1903. Eastman then accepted Commissioner of Indian Affairs William A. Jones's offer of a long-term position to revise the names on the Sioux allotment rolls. The "Name Giver," as Eastman came to be known among the Sioux, worked on the Sioux rolls from March 1903 until December 1909, revising the names of more than 25,000 individuals, or practically the entire Sioux Nation. Like Alexander Posey, who was pursuing a similar goal as clerk in charge of the Creek enrollment field party in 1904–1906, Eastman sincerely believed that he was promoting beneficial reformist policies among his people as well as securing their property rights.

While at Crow Creek, Eastman published *Indian Boyhood* (1902), an autobiography based on his earlier sketches for the *St. Nicholas*. In the summer of 1903 he purchased a home in Amherst, Massachusetts, bringing him back into direct contact with eastern philanthropist and literary circles. As he completed the Sioux rolls he also produced two volumes of short fiction, *Red Hunters and the Animal People* (1904) and *Old Indian Days* (1907); a collection of traditional Sioux narratives co-authored by his wife titled *Wigwam Evenings* (1909); and numerous articles and stories for major American magazines such as *Chautauquan, Harper's Monthly Magazine, Ladies' Home Journal, Sunset, Metropolitan, Outlook, Out West,* and *Current Literature.* Eastman's growing popularity as an author—he was invited to the celebration of Mark Twain's seventieth birthday in New York City on December 5, 1905—also led to profitable engagements as a lecturer on Indian issues. James Burton Pond, a major lecture manager who brought notable authors such as Henry Ward Beecher, Conan Doyle, Bill Nye, and Mark Twain to the stage, contracted Eastman for the

American lecture platform shortly after the publication of his first autobiography. Following Pond's untimely death in 1903, Elaine Eastman assumed the task of managing her husband's public appearances and editing his writing while taking care of their six children.

In the summer of 1910 Eastman received a temporary commission from the University of Pennsylvania Museum to collect artifacts among the Ojibwes living in northern Minnesota and Ontario. Eastman found a new sense of identity and spiritual renewal during this eventful journey "back to the woods," manifested in his subsequent writings. It motivated him to produce a sensitive treatise on Indian spirituality titled *The Soul of the Indian* (1911).

Eastman also became increasingly involved with the blossoming American back-to-nature movement. He was an active member of the Boy Scouts of America following its incorporation in 1910 and produced several articles on Indian woodcraft for *Boy's Life, Boy's World,* and *St. Nicholas,* reissued collectively as *Indian Scout Talks* (1914). Eastman's views directly influenced naturalist writer Ernest Thompson Seton. Responding to another out-of-doors trend that swept through America in the first two decades of the twentieth century, the Eastman family opened a summer camp for girls at Granite Lake in New Hampshire, on July 15, 1915. The following year they expanded the lucrative operation to include boys as well, renaming the complex as Camp Oahe for girls and Camp Ohiyesa for boys.

A highlight in Charles Eastman's career as spokesman came in 1911, when he represented the North American Indian at the First Universal Races Congress held in London on July 26–29. In addition he published a treatise on contemporary Indian affairs titled *The Indian To-day* (1915) and a more critical sequel to his autobiography, *From the Deep Woods to Civilization* (1916). His last major publication was a collection of biographical essays titled *Indian Heroes and Great Chieftains* (1918).

Eastman was a founding member of the American Indian Association (later Society of American Indians), and served as corresponding secretary and treasurer of the Temporary Executive Committee. He attended the first annual conference of the SAI in Columbus, Ohio, on October 12–16, but left before the active members business session was closed. Eastman felt that the organization did not adequately represent the interests of the Indian communities and, like Carlos Montezuma, disagreed with the moderate course of its elected officers. It was not until 1918, when Gertrude Bonnin displaced Arthur Parker as the organizational motor of the Society of American Indians, that Eastman became active again. At the seventh annual convention at Pierre, South Dakota, on September 25–28, 1918, Eastman was elected as president of the organization in absentia and accepted the position. Earlier, in February and March 1918, both Bonnin and Eastman had testified against the use of peyote at the hearings on Representative Carl M. Hayden's anti-peyote bill before the House Subcommittee on Indian Affairs. However, Eastman was replaced as president by Thomas L. Sloan at the eighth annual conference in Minneapolis on October 2–4, 1919, and broke off all relations with the organization immediately thereafter. Eastman did participate in the meeting of the Advisory Council on Indian Affairs (or Committee of One Hundred) in Washington on December 12–13, 1923, along with other members of the Society of American Indians.

On August 28, 1923, Eastman received an appointment as Indian inspector for the BIA, a post he held until his resignation in March 1925. His last assignment as inspector was to settle the ongoing dispute about the date of death and burial place of Sacagawea (various spellings). Eastman submitted his report to the commissioner of Indian affairs on March 2, 1925, in which he concluded on the basis of oral traditions that Sacajawea died on April 9, 1884, at Fort Washakie, Wyoming.

On January 21, 1928, Eastman embarked on a second tour to England as a representative of the Brooks-Bryce Foundation, a philanthropist institution promoting better relations between English-speaking people in Great Britain and the United States. Although Eastman claimed he was working on a biography of Sacagawea, a novel on Pontiac, and numerous other manuscripts on Sioux history and oral traditions, he did not publish anything substantial after his separation from Elaine in 1921. There can be little doubt that Elaine Eastman, herself a successful and prolific writer, was actually the co author of all his publications.

In 1928 Eastman purchased some land along the north shore of Lake Huron in Ontario, Canada, and spent most of the remainder of his life in a plain log cabin. On January 7, 1939, Charles Eastman died in a Detroit hospital as a result of pneumonia.

During the celebration of American Indian Day at the Century of Progress exposition at the Chicago World's Fair on September 22, 1933, the Indian Council Fire honored Eastman with its first medal "for the most distinguished achievement by an American Indian." It was a fitting tribute to the most widely read Indian author of the Progressive Era.

Selected Publications of Charles Alexander Eastman

"The American Eagle an Indian Symbol." *The American Indian Magazine* 7, no. 2 (Summer 1919): 89–92.

"A Canoe Trip among the Northern Ojibwas." *The Red Man* 3 (February 1911): 235–44.

"First Impressions of Civilization." *Harper's Monthly Magazine* 108 (March 1904): 587–92. Reprinted in *The Elders Wrote: An Anthology of Early Prose by North American Indians, 1768–1931*, edited by Bernd C. Peyer. Berlin: Dietrich Reimer Verlag, 1982: 142–51.

From the Deep Woods to Civilization: Chapters in the Autobiography of an Indian. Boston: Little, Brown, and Co., 1916. Reprinted Lincoln: University of Nebraska Press, 1977.

"The Indian and the Moral Code." *The Outlook* 97 (January 7, 1911): 30–34.

"The Indian as a Citizen." *Lippincott's* 95 (January 1915): 70–76.

Indian Boyhood. New York: McClure, Phillips and Co., 1902. Reprinted Lincoln: University of Nebraska Press, 1991.

"The Indian's Gift to the Nation." *The Quarterly Journal of the Society of American Indians* 3, no. 1 (January–March 1915): 17–23.

"Indian Handicrafts." *The Craftsman* 8 (August 1905): 658–62.

"The Indian's Health Problem." *Popular Science Monthly* 86 (January, 1915): 49–54. Reprinted *The American Indian Magazine* 4, no. 2 (April–June 1916): 139–45.

Indian Heroes and Great Chieftains. Boston: Little, Brown, and Company, 1918. Reprinted Lincoln: University of Nebraska Press, 1991.

"The Indian's Plea for Freedom." *The American Indian Magazine* 6, no. 4 (Winter 1919): 162–65.

Indian Scout Talks; A Guide for Boy Scouts and Campfire Girls. Boston: Little, Brown and Company, 1914. Reprinted as *Indian Scout Craft and Lore*, New York: Dover, 1974.

The Indian To-day; The Past and Future of the First American. Garden City, N.Y.: Doubleday, Page and Company, 1915. Reprinted New York: AMS, 1975.

"Investigation and Location of the Final Burial Place of Sacajewea." Washington, D.C.: Government Printing Office, 1928.

"Justice for the Sioux." *The American Indian Magazine* 7, no. 2 (Summer 1919): 79–81.

"My People: The Indian's Contribution to the Art of America." *The Craftsman* 27, no. 2 (November 1914): 179–86. Reprinted *The Red Man* (December 1914): 133–40.

"The North American Indian." In *Papers on Inter-Racial Problems Communicated to the First Universal Races Congress Held at the University of London July 26–29, 1911*, edited by Gustav Spiller. London: P. S. King and Son, 1911: 367–76.

Old Indian Days. New York: McClure Company, 1907. Reprinted Rapic City, S.Dak.: Fenwyn, 1970.

"Opening Address." *The American Indian Magazine* 7, no. 3 (Fall 1919): 145–52.

"Recollections of the Wild Life." *St. Nicholas: An Illustrated Magazine for Young Folks* 21 (December 1893–May, 1984): 129–31, 226–28, 306–308, 437–40, 513–15, 607–611.

Red Hunters and the Animal People. New York: Harper and Brothers, 1904. Reprinted New York: AMS, 1976.

"Re-Naming the Indians." *Indian School Journal* 6 (July 1906): 31–32.

"Report By Charles A. Eastman." *Annals of Wyoming* 13, no. 3 (July 1941): 187–94.

"Report to the Commissioner of Indian Affairs March 2, 1925, relative to the final burial place of Sacajewea." Washington, D.C.: Bureau of Indian Affairs, 1925.

"A Review of the Indian Citizenship Bills." *The American Indian Magazine* 6, no. 4 (Winter 1919): 181–83.

"The Sioux Mythology." *Popular Science Monthly* 46 (November 1894): 88–91. Reprinted in *The International Folklore Congress of the World Columbian Exposition, Chicago, July 1893*, Vol. 1, edited by Helen Wheeler Bassett and Frederick Starr. Chicago: Charles H. Sergel Company, 1898: 221–26 (a slightly altered version. Reprinted in *Native American Folklore in Nineteenth-Century Periodicals*, edited by William M. Clements. Athens: Ohio University Press, 1986: 211–16.

"The Sioux of Yesterday and Today." *The American Indian Magazine* 5, no. 4 (October–December 1917): 233–39.

The Soul of the Indian: An Interpretation. Boston: Houghton Mifflin company, 1911. Reprinted Lincoln: University of Nebraska Press, 1980.

"Testimony of Charles A. Eastman, Sixty-Fourth Congress, First Session." *Hearings Before a Subcommittee of the Committee on Indian Affairs, United States House of Representatives, August 15, 1916.* Washington, D.C.: Government Printing Office, 1916: 4–10.
Wigwam Evenings; Sioux Tales Retold by Charles A. Eastman (Ohiyesa) and Elaine Goodale Eastman. Boston: Little, Brown and Company, 1909. Reprinted Lincoln: University of Nebraska Press, 1990.

Unpublished Sources

Charles A. Eastman Folder, Baker Library, Dartmouth College, Hanover; Charles A. Eastman Materials, Young Men's Christian Association Historical Library, New York, New York; Charles A. Eastman Folder, Jones Public Library, Amherst, Massachusetts; H. M. Hitchcock Papers, Ayer Collection, The Newberry Library, Chicago, Illinois.

Selected Secondary Sources

Bess, Jennifer. "'Kill the Indian and Save the Man': Charles Eastman Surveys His Past." *Wicazo Sa Review* 15, no. 1 (Spring 2000): 7–28.
Brumble III, H. David. *American Indian Autobiography.* Los Angeles: University of California Press, 1988: 147–64.
Carlson, David J. "'Indian for a While': Charles Eastman's Indian Boyhood and the Discourse of Allotment." *American Indian Quarterly* 25, no. 4 (2001): 604–625.
Copeland, Marion W. *Charles Alexander Eastman (Ohiyesa).* Boise State University Western Writers Series 33. Caldwell: Caxton Printers, 1978.
Deloria, Philip J. *Playing Indian.* New Haven: Yale University Press, 1998: 95–127.
Gill, Sam D. *Mother Earth: An American Story.* Chicago: University of Chicago Press, 1987: 130–36.
Graber, Kay, ed., *Sister to the Sioux: The Memoirs of Elaine Goodale Eastman, 1885–91.* Lincoln: University of Nebraska Press, 1978.
Heflin, Ruth J. *"I Remain Alive": The Sioux Literary Renaissance.* Syracuse, N.Y.: Syracuse University Press, 2000: 41–77.
Littlefield, Jr., Daniel F. and Lonnie E. Underhill. "Renaming the American Indian." *American Studies* 12 (Fall 1971): 33–45.
Lopenzina, Drew. "'Good Indian': Charles Eastman and the Warrior as Civil Servant." *American Indian Quarterly* 27, no. 3 (2003): 727–757.
Miller, David Reed. "Charles Alexander Eastman, The 'Winner': From Deep Woods to Civilization." In *American Indian Intellectuals, 1976 Proceedings of the American Ethnological Society,* edited by Margot Liberty. St. Paul: West Publishing Co., 1978: 61–73.
Peterson, Eric. "An Indian, An American: Ethnicity, Assimilation and Balance in Charles Eastman's *From the Deep Woods to Civilization.*" *Studies in American Indian Literatures* 4, nos. 2–3 (Summer–Fall 1992): 145–60. Reprinted in *Early Native American Writing: New Critical Essays,* edited by Helen Jaskoski. New York: Cambridge University Press, 1996: 173–89.
Stensland, Anna Lee. "Charles Alexander Eastman Sioux Storyteller and Historian." *American Indian Quarterly* 3, no. 3 (1977): 199–208.

Warrior, Robert Allen. "Reading American Indian Intellectual Traditions." *World Literature Today* 66, no. 2 (1992): 236–40. Reworked in Robert Allen Warrior, *Tribal Secrets: Recovering American Indian Intellectual Traditions.* Minneapolis: University of Minnesota Press, 1995: 5–11, 14.

Wilson, Raymond. "The Writings of Ohiyesa—Charles Alexander Eastman, M. D., Santee Sioux." *South Dakota History* 6 (1975–76): 55–73.

_____. "Dr. Charles Alexander Eastman's Report on the Economic Conditions of the Osage Indians in Oklahoma, 1924." *Chronicles of Oklahoma* 55, no. 3 (Fall 1977): 343–45.

_____. "Forty Years to Judgment: The Santee Sioux Claims Case." *Minnesota History* 47 (Fall 1981): 284–91.

_____. *Ohiyesa: Charles Alexander Eastman, Santee Sioux.* Urbana: University of Illinois Press, 1983.

THE NEW INDIAN LEADERSHIP

John M. Oskison (1917)

They don't even call it a council any more! Today when you go to talk with the Indians, and listen to what they have to say, you simply attend a "meeting." First, the old man who bears the now purely honorary title of chief walks solemnly over to speak a few words to some Indian under forty who wears a black suit, more carefully brushed perhaps than those worn by the others. Standing aside, the chief takes off his hat; all the men crowded around the brush arbor uncover; the women, bareheaded and seated on the ground just outside the arbor, quiet the children; and there follows an impressive pause before the man in the neat, black suit, with eyes closed and face upturned, begins to speak.

"We pray to our Father in Heaven—" The man's English is halting; you realize that you are listening to an alien whose tongue fumbles the language. Yet you are able to sense, in that brief, stiff prayer, a giving up and a reaching forward—the old Indians giving up their ceremonial pipes and their right to speak the first word, and the younger people, equipped with the white man's language and instructed in his ways, reaching forward timidly and awkwardly for the leadership.

The manner of that opening prayer will show you how poorly equipped as yet these younger men are to take the place of the old men as counsellors. Only because the old men know that new leadership must come do they give way. As the meeting goes on, you see the change dramatized.

The old men speak—first of all, one whose face is much wrinkled, whose eyes have retreated to vague slits through which now and then flashes an apparition of command, whose voice is first a mumble and rises later to a quiet eloquence. Your alert, unsmiling interpreter (who was graduated from Carlisle only last year, and who has left his tailor shop for the day to help you out) catches your inquiring eye and leaves his place beside the old man to come and whisper:

"His name is Maricopa Sam." It is an ill-fitting name, lacking proper dignity—you would have preferred to hear the old man's Indian name.

After a minute of talk, the old man turns his face ever so slightly toward the interpreter. That youth, with arms straight down at his sides, his face mask-like, speaks:

"He says he is glad to see you here today; he is glad to shake your hand; he says all of us are glad to see you here today; we are glad to have you see with your own eyes how we are living."

Again the old man takes up the tale, and more than once you catch from those slits of eyes among the wrinkles a disturbing flash. Then the interpreter:

"He says he can remember when the first white man came into this valley. He can remember the words that first white man spoke. He says that first white man spoke different from the way they speak today. In that day, the white man said all he wanted was a place to rest for a while; the white man said he would go on, after he was rested on toward the West, where many other white men had gone ahead. But he did not go on. That time was more than fifty years ago; he says he was a young man then, about as old as I am now."

You had noticed the old man's slight gesture toward the young interpreter, and had wondered what it meant.

For half an hour, the old man goes on, telling over what he has told many times. At the end, he says earnestly:

"We are not satisfied with the way things are going here; we hope you can find a way to help us. For me, it does not matter any more—I am an old man, and I will soon pass away. But for these young people it does matter! I am speaking today for these young people who must go on living with the white men." He steps back.

Even through the colorless rendering of the young interpreter, the old man's words get you by the throat, and you wonder at a power of self-control which permits of quiet talk of the day when he shall have "passed over the border," leaving a great weight of trouble for his people behind.

Other old men speak, in the same strain, but less eloquently and less hopefully.

Toward the end of the day (for there is vast leisureliness, as well as dignity, in the proceedings), the young men are heard; and what a contrast they make with the old fellows!

First among the young men to speak is a "black-coat," who has been persuaded by missionaries to come forward and assert himself in tribal affairs. Looking straight at you, he talks for a little while in halting English; as he pauses, you hear mutterings among the old people who understand no English—those of the twenty-five per cent who know no language but their own—and then, facing away from you, the young "black-coat" speaks to his people. He tells them that he is speaking in favor of immediate allotment of the tribal land; he says that they ought to know their boundaries, so that they can begin at once to build the better houses they all ought to build.

Young "black-coat" is friendly with the Superintendent of the reservation—the same arguments he puts blunderingly before you have been made to you already by the man at the Agency. Some of the Superintendent's very phrases you hear repeated; and in the talk of the young "black-coat" is reflected that white man's impatience of the "conservatism" of the old men.

That night, before they sleep, some of the young men go to the Agency to report to the Superintendent what has been said. Next day, that official sends a summary to the Indian Office at Washington, with a recommendation that he be given authority to forbid any more meetings of the sort.

He is an honest, vigorous, and conscientious official, this Superintendent. He believes that meetings at which the old men talk over their grievances and recall their old life only serve to delay the carrying out of the Government's wise policy. He thinks of you, who have gone to listen to the talk of the old men, as a meddler. He is frank to tell you that you can't understand the situation on that reservation, and that every bit of encouragement the old people receive makes his own job more difficult.

On every reservation—there are one hundred and sixty-one of them, large and small, in the United States, embracing a total area of over 55,000,000 acres—the Superintendent is supreme. To the Indians, he is the voice of Washington—one who must be obeyed. Through him, meetings of the old people are frowned upon and their traditional spiritual practices discouraged; Indian dances are forbidden; long hair must be cut short; allotment of tribal land to individual Indians is pushed; tribal land is traded to whites for water rights in irrigating ditches; Indian money is used for building irrigating systems, bridges, and roads. It is the Superintendent on the reservation who determines what the ninety million whites want done with the 300,000 Indians.

In every move this conscientious Superintendent makes, he calls upon the younger people of the reservation for support. He gives them arguments and sends them out to do missionary service among the old people. His young men of the Indian Police are more than keepers of order; they are the eyes, and ears, and (so far as they can be used with discretion) the tongue of the Superintendent.[1]

After the Civil War, the Government turned with vigor to the settlement of Indian troubles. As a solution, the reservation was chosen; from all corners of the Western country the Government troops rounded up the Indians and segregated them on tracts of land widely scattered over twenty-five Western and Middle Western States and Territories.[2]

That policy amounted to imprisonment; and as soon as it was settled upon, the old Indian was doomed. More than thirty years of imprisonment have served to destroy his power and influence.

For ten years or more after the Indians were imprisoned in idleness on the reservations, the Government was content merely to feed them and keep them peaceable. Then it was thought desirable to get the children into schools to learn the white's man [sic] language and ways. Agents were sent to the reservations to induce the old men and women, who sat idle and hopeless and discontented, to send their children and grandchildren away to the schools. It is wonderful, but true, that these old people consented.

Then the school-trained young men and women—Carlisle school alone has graduated over six hundred, and sent back nearly four thousand eight hundred—returned to find in the eyes of the old people a question: What are you going to do to help our people? Fifteen years ago, a man in the Indian service held a council with the Northern Yankton Sioux and the Assiniboines at Fort Peck; and at that council the old men called upon three young men who had been to Carlisle to speak about the white man's way. One old chief said:

"When I was a young chief, all the young men kept silent, and the old men talked in council; and that was right, for the old men knew what was best, and we did what the old men said. But I have lived to see a time when another thing must be done. We old men must be silent, and we must hear the young men speak. For we must all go the white man's way.

"There is no other way now. The buffalo are gone. There is no game. And the old men could not go East—they could not go to school. But our children have gone East, and they know the white man's way. A light comes from the East, and our young men have seen it. We old men must listen to them. We must keep silent and go as the young men tell us—in the white man's way."

That old man was right—leadership in the white man's way was needed, for there were vast estates to administer. Today, after the process of allotment has gone on for twenty years, the Indians own land and property worth nearly a billion dollars.

After the young people began to come back to the reservations from the schools, the Government faced a new problem: How to cure the evils of the reservation system? Drink, disease, and idleness were destroying the Indians faster than the bullets of the soldiers ever destroyed them. It became the new policy of the Government to break up the reservation system. Congress passed an Allotment Act; schools were multiplied on the reservations (there are 114 boarding schools and 223 day schools now); farmers and work-teachers were sent to the Indians; the health of the Indians became a matter of concern; and the fight to keep liquor away from them was pushed with energy.

Quickly the Indians responded. Today, less than 50 per cent are illiterate, and fewer than twenty-five per cent are unable to speak English. Some 200,000 of them are living in permanent homes on their own land; nearly as many are subject to taxation; and 8,700 of them are employed in Government service. Of the ten millions a year spent for the support of the Bureau of Indian Affairs, four million goes to educate the Indian children.

Truly, a new spirit entered the Indian service when it was decided that the reservations must be broken up; and under the new order the Indians themselves were asked to cooperate. But—and this was the tragedy of the change—the old Indians were not asked. It was assumed that they would not be in sympathy with the new programme, and that, even if they were, they could not help effectively in carrying it out. They had been neglected, debauched and broken by the Government—and when the Government got ready to do some of the things these old men had been urging for years, it wasn't thought worth while to ask them to help.

Well, it really wasn't—that was the bitter truth! Self-confidence, the power to command, were gone from most of the old men—the Government had killed it, deliberately. It was a mockery that the chiefs among them were allowed to keep their nominal titles.

What real power, understanding and influence has been wasted! I have before me some notes made among the Blackfeet Indians of Montana fifteen years ago by Dr. [Merrill E.] Gates, secretary of the Board of Indian Commissioners.[3] Among the notes is a description of the meeting of the "court of Indian offenses," where, on that reservation, minor troubles arising among the

Indians were threshed out and adjusted by three old men. The case of a man who had quarreled with his wife was before the court, and Dr. Gates wrote:

"Judge 'Shorty' White-Grass presided. The two associate justices were Little Plume (a son of Chief White Calf) and Wolf Tail. Let me give you some notion of the presiding justice: He has an immense head with strongly marked features; his chest is deep and he has a voice which would easily fill the chamber of our House of Representatives at its noisiest; he has broad, powerful shoulders, and long arms—sitting, he seems a man of more than six feet, though he measures only four feet, eight. His still-black hair is worn long. He is fond of carrying a green parrot on his left arm (many of the Indians think the parrot whispers wisdom into the old man's ear!) He is a great medicine man among his people, and with old chief White Calf, Lone Plume, Mad Wolf, and other 'conversatives,' he spends his Sundays worshipping [sic] and praying to the beaver god."

Behind a table in one of the buildings of the Agency sat those three old men hearing evidence, arbitrating disputes with success (as in the case which Dr. Gates heard), dealing out just punishments, and maintaining the dignity which properly belongs to a court. Yet as they sat there, helping to keep their people in the right path, all three of those old men knew that a word from the white men in charge of the reservation could nullify every act of theirs, could reverse every decision they made.

Now, what about this new generation—the Carlisle-trained, the literate, the "mixed-bloods"? Few of them are yet proved as leaders—and, after all, they are the creations of yesterday. But one need not become pessimistic about the new Indian leadership.

Some of them think straight and talk effectively; they see with clear vision what lies ahead of their people, and they work intelligently to shape the future. In their speech is an acid quality which makes you sit up and grit your teeth— just as the eloquent old fellows wrung your heart with their simple language, their poetry, their moving stories of wrongs patiently endured.

There was an old Apache chief name[d] Victorio, who went on the warpath in 1880 to fight for the homes of his band. With Victorio and his family when that warfare began was a baby boy—carried strapped to a board on his mother's back. He was Natalish, grandson of Victorio. Before his people stopped fighting for the right to live on land they believed had been given them for their own, he was big enough to go a little way out on the battlefield with his uncle (both father and grandfather were killed in the years of warfare) and learn something about how to fight in the old Apache way.

That boy became one of the famous band of prisoner Apaches which was held in Florida and Alabama from 1886 to 1894, and then sent out to Fort Sill, Oklahoma. From the military prison in Florida, Natalish was sent to school at Carlisle; he studied civil engineering; he has held a place in the Bureau of Highways of New York City; and he is now in the employment of the Government making a family census of the Arizona Apaches.

Within the last two years, that young man has demonstrated the possibilities of the new leadership. He and Henry Roe-Cloud, very largely organized and directed the fight made on behalf of that band of prisoner Apaches to be given allotments of land in Oklahoma, where they might soonest become self-supporting and qualified to stand side by side with the whites as citizens of the State. When you understand that the fight had to be made against the influence in Congress of most of the Oklahoma delegation, backed by thousands of scheming whites who had set out to get the Apaches removed from the State, as well as by the War Department, which wanted for an artillery practice ground the land the prisoner Apaches in Oklahoma occupied you will appreciate the fact that Natalish and his friends were able to force a compromise upon the Government. According to this compromise agreement, instead of the whole band of two hundred seventy prisoner Apaches being removed to the unfertile and mountainous reservation of the Mescalero Apaches in New Mexico, most of them were given the choice of going or staying in Oklahoma.

Natalish and Roe-Cloud wanted them to stay in Oklahoma. They went among them and urged them to resist removal; and it was largely due to their persuasion that seventy-eight (mostly the younger and better educated) decided to remain in Oklahoma.[4]

Such fights to carry out obviously wise policies among the Indians are still ahead—and the need for strong leadership in the tribes is great. Take the case of the Arizona Navahos and Papagos:

We think of the Navahos as a peace-loving and pastoral people, yet for four years (from 1863 to 1867) they were herded at Fort Sumner, New Mexico, as prisoners. A third of their number died in that time, and there were fewer than 8,000 of them when they were sent back to their old land.[5]

After four years of confinement and idleness, they were sent back to the desert and the mountains—and a sheep apiece was given them by the Government. An old Navaho who now owns 1,500 sheep has told about that issue:

"They gave one sheep to me and one sheep to my wife, and they gave a sheep to my little boy." He stopped for a little while, and laughed. "So, we started out and drove our sheep across the desert—three of us, and three sheep. From Fort Defiance way out here beyond the borders of our reservation we drove our three sheep; and that is all the Government has done for us."

Now, the Navahos were used to the desert and the mountains, and when they were sent back there they prospered. From fewer than 8,000 they have increased to more than 30,000—they are now the largest pure-blood tribe in the country. Their reservation embraces over 12 million acres of mountain and desert land; and it is fully stocked with cattle, sheep and horses.

Also, outside the boundaries of the reservation, between 5,000 and 9,000 Navahos are occupying public land. Many of these outside Navahos have been given allotments of public land, but several thousands (no one is sure of the figures) are not yet assured of their title or right to go on occupying Government land outside the reservation; and there is a stiff fight ahead before they will get that assurance. Strong opposition has been aroused by the cattlemen and sheepmen of Arizona—these white men want the unalloted Navahos driven back on the reservation, though they know that the reservation is not adequate to support their herds and flocks.

In Southern Arizona, 6,000 Papago Indians are supporting themselves on public land outside any reservation, and they are up against practically the same problem.

There is work in Arizona for strong Indian leaders of the new generation; and at a score of other points acute problems are demanding the best cooperative effort of the Government and the educated young men and women of the tribes.

Notes

Originally in *The American Indian Magazine* 5, no. 2 (April–June 1917): 93–100. Oskison believed that younger generations of educated Indians should be given more responsibility in Indian affairs and work together with the elders who in turn should not be excluded from the process of adaptation. His views foreshadow in part the philosophy of the National Indian Youth Council founded in Gallup, New Mexico, in 1961 by young college-educated Indians who also sought to mend the gap between the generations by reestablishing connections with reservation elders.

1. In 1878 Congress first provided funds for the creation of an Indian Police. In 1883 Courts of Indian Offenses were established, with Indian police as judges. These measures were not only taken to maintain order on the reservation, but also as agents of acculturation as they displaced traditional policing institutions such as the warrior societies and took judicial power away from tribal leaders. See William T. Hagan, *Indian Police and Judges: Experiments in Acculturation and Controls* (New Haven: Yale University Press, 1966).

2. See Ely S. Parker, "Report by Colonel Parker on Indian Affairs" (1867), note 3, in this anthology.

3. Merrill Edwards Gates (1848–1922), former president of Rutgers University and Amherst College, served as chair and then secretary of the Board of Indian Commissioners from 1899 to 1912. One of the most influential "Friends of the Indian," he was an outspoken advocate of total detribalization. Oskison quotes the same passages in "In Governing the Indian, Use the Indian," *American Indian Magazine* 5, no. 1 (January–March 1917): 36–41.

4. Following his surrender in 1886, Geronimo and approximately five hundred Apaches were sent to military prison at Fort Pickens in Pensacola, Florida. In 1887 they were removed to Mount Vernon Barracks in Alabama, where about one-fourth of this group died of tuberculosis and other diseases. Finally, in 1894, the prisoners were moved to the Kiowa-Comanche Reservation adjoining Fort Still in Indian Territory. Their status as prisoners of war terminated in 1913 and plans were made for their removal to the Mescalero Reservation in New Mexico. Oskison describes their situation in "An Apache Problem," *The Quarterly Journal of the Society of American Indians* 1, no. 1 (January–April 1913): 25–29.

5. Volunteer troops under Kit Carson rounded up the Navajos in 1863–64 and escorted them to the internment center at Bosque Redondo, New Mexico, on what became known as the "Long March." Many suffered from starvation and diseases until they were finally allowed to return to their homeland west of the Rio Grande in 1868. See Lynn Robinson Bailey, *Long Walk: A History of the Navajo Wars, 1846–1868* (Tucson, Ariz.: Westernlore Press, 1981).

BIOGRAPHY

John Milton Oskison (Cherokee, 1874–1947) was born near Tahlequah, Cherokee Nation West, on September 21, the son of John Oskison, an English immigrant, and Rachel Connor Crittenden, a part-Cherokee. From a tender age he and his two brothers helped work on their father's farm, experiencing first hand the hardships and adventures of a settler's life in Indian Territory at the end of the nineteenth century. Oskison attended Willie Halsell College along with his lifelong friend Will Rogers. After graduating in 1894 he went on to study at Stanford University, receiving his Bachelor of Arts degree in 1898. At Stanford, which now holds an annual John Milton Oskison Writing Competition in his honor, he began publishing articles and short stories on a regular basis. In 1899, while he was doing graduate work in English at Harvard, Oskison won a writing contest sponsored by *Century Magazine* with one of his short stories. This motivated him to try his luck as a professional writer. He published at least twenty short stories between 1897 and 1925, some of them in mass-circulating American magazines such as *Century, Frank Leslie's Monthly, McClure's,* and *Collier's.* In addition, he wrote numerous articles on contemporary Indian affairs. In 1903 Oskison married Florence Ballard Day, niece of the notorious entrepreneur Jay Gould. Between 1906 and 1912 he was editor for the Ossining (New York) *The Citizen,* exchange editor and editorial writer for the New York *Evening Post,* associate editor (later finance editor) for *Collier's Weekly,* and special writer on financial topics for a syndicate of Eastern newspapers. He also joined the Temporary Executive Committee of the American Indian Association in 1911 and played an active role in the Society of American Indians thereafter.

During World War I Oskison enlisted in the army and was eventually sent to France as lieutenant in the American Expeditionary Force. In 1920 he divorced Florence Day in Paris and that same year married Hildegard Hawthorne, descendant of the great American author and a prolific novelist in her own right. Oskison, who spent most of his time after the war in New York and Paris, apparently stopped writing short fiction altogether by 1925 and focused on writing regional novels depicting life in Indian Territory prior to its incorporation into the state of Oklahoma in 1907. Between 1925 and 1935 he published four novels: *Wild Harvest* (1925), *Black Jack Davy* (1926), *A Texas Titan* (1929), and *Brothers Three* (1935). *Wild Harvest* and *Black Jack Davy* represent a sequential saga of the American frontier experience in Indian Territory. *A Texas Titan* is a historical novel that focuses in part on Sam Houston's life among the Cherokees. *Brothers Three* is a semi-autobiographical novel about a ranching family trying to hold on to their land on the eve of the Great Depression. In 1938 Oskison published *Tecumseh and His Times,* a biographical tribute to the great Shawnee leader. John Milton Oskison died in Tulsa, Oklahoma, on February 25, 1947. He left behind two unpublished manuscripts: "The Singing Bird," a novel in which a white missionary develops a close friendship with the legendary Sequoyah; and an incomplete autobiography titled "A Tale of the Old I.T."

Selected Publications of John Milton Oskison

"Acquiring a Standard of Value." *The Quarterly Journal of the Society of American Indians* 2, no. 1 (January–March 1914): 47–50.

"An Apache Problem." *The Quarterly Journal of the Society of American Indians* 1, no. 1 (January–April 1913): 25–29.

Black Jack Davy. New York: D. Appleton and Co., 1926.

Brothers Three. New York: Macmillan, 1935.

"In Governing the Indian, Use the Indian." *The American Indian Magazine* 5, no. 1 (January–March 1917): 36–41.

"The New Indian Leadership." *The American Indian Magazine* 5, no. 2 (April–June 1917): 93–100.

"The Outlook for the Indian." *Southern Workman* 32, no. 6 (June 1903): 270–73.

Tecumseh and His Times: The Story of a Great Indian. New York: G. P. Putnam's Sons, 1938.

A Texas Titan: The Story of Sam Houston. New York: Doubleday, Doran and Co., 1929.

"Why Am I an American?" *World's Work* 29 (December 1914): 209–213.

Wild Harvest: A Novel of Transition Days in Oklahoma. New York: D. Appleton and Co., 1925.

Unpublished Writings

John Milton Oskison Papers, Western History Collections, University of Oklahoma Library, Norman, Oklahoma.

Selected Secondary Sources

Colonnese, Tom and Louis Owens. *American Indian Novelists: An Annotated Critical Bibliography.* New York: Garland Publishing, Inc., 1985: 64–73.

Larson, Charles A. *American Indian Fiction.* Albuquerque: University of New Mexico Press, 1976: 46–55.

Littlefield, Jr., Daniel F. and James W. Parins. "Short Fiction Writers of the Indian Territory." *American Studies* 23, no. 1 (Spring 1980–82): 23–38.

Marable, Mary Hays and Claire Boylan. *Handbook of Oklahoma Writers.* Norman: University of Oklahoma Press, 1939: 28–30.

Ronnov, Gretchen. "John Milton Oskison, Cherokee Journalist: A Singer of the Semiotics of Power." *Native Press Research Journal* 4 (Spring 1987): 1–14.

_____. "John Milton Oskison." In *Dictionary of Native American Literature*, edited by Andrew Wiget. New York: Garland Publishing, Inc., 1994: 271–75.

_____. "Oskison, John Milton." In *Encyclopedia of North American Indians*, edited by Frederick E. Hoxie. Boston: Houghton Mifflin Company, 1996: 452–53.

Strickland, Arney L. "John Milton Oskison: A Writer of the Transitional Period of the Oklahoma Indian Territory." *Southwestern American Literature* 2, no. 3 (1972): 125–34.

THE FUTURE OF THE RED MEN IN AMERICA

Henry Roe Cloud (1924)

What part have the children of the Red Man in the America that is to be? In our body politic are those whose ancestry dates back to the dim past—whose ancient civilization on this Western hemisphere compares well with that of European nations. Shall not these contributions of race antiquity, distinctive arts and handicrafts, music and folklore, so colorful with nature, exquisitely beautiful, and a pride to any nation, help to make America what she should be?

The task of conserving what is distinctive in aboriginal American life is one which should engage the interest of every thinking citizen. The America of tomorrow will not have this inheritance of the first American if the boys and girls of this race are not adequately educated and trained in those qualities of character which stand the test of life's vigorous demands.

Compare, if you will, the ancient life and training of the Indian with that of today. The old-time Indian lived in reed wigwams, bark huts or tepees. The furnishings of this home were very scant, and its food supply uncertain. The boy and girl in this primitive home were taught early to be *thankful* for everything—the scarcity of food, clothing, weapons and all other creature-comforts naturally created an attitude of appreciation and thankfulness for every favor conferred, however insignificant in itself.

The conditions of life then demanded energy and resourcefulness. A buffalo hunt would be staged for the young hunter. All skilled hunters would withdraw, repair to some advantageous point, and watch the initiate kill his first buffalo. This was followed by public recognition, praise and honor.

From earliest infancy the Indian child was given Spartan-like training. He was given a piece of bass-wood stick, one point of which was charred for his own dedication to the fast and the search after the knowledge of the gods. He could not eat until the stick was entirely consumed. Repeated experiences of this sort taught the young Indian concentration of thought, hardihood, self-control and a belief in something supernatural.

Absolute obedience was required by rigorous punishments. By an elaborate system of taboo, reverence for Deity, respect for the aged and an insatiable ambition to know the mysteries were inculcated. The training, though primitive and uncouth, produced sound, lusty and majestic Indians like Massasoit, Cornstalk and Red Jacket.[1]

The secret of the success of this early primitive training school is to be found chiefly in the very environment which surrounded the Indian. The greatest incentive to activity is the enforced struggle for existence. There is a constant tax on the resources of mind, body and soul, and in the exercise of these for self-preservation there results a development and growth in those qualities such as fortitude, faithfulness, patience, perseverance, hopefulness and skill in primitive

384

arts. It is not claimed here that environment alone is responsible for the results achieved.

The wise old Indians rooted their educational system in the need of the masses—they created interest in work, they played upon the sense of pride and honor, hope of reward, inspiring ideals, such as a high seat in the world to come, and were uncompromising in their punishment of failure in duty. By invoking the aid of the Great Spirit they recognized the limitations of man, and his need for divine help.

Next to the practice of adapting their education to the needs of the people, they made provisions for the training of leaders, both by descent and by an elaborate system of ceremonial training. A leader had to excel in mentality and in feats of valor.

But a great transition period awaited this child of the original America. By the discovery of America and the rapid influx of a foreign civilization, the aborigines have had to change their mode of life entirely. No race has been required to make such haste in acquiring civilized standards of living as the Indian. Coming out of the school of hard experience, where the environment itself exacted every resource and capacity, the young Indian today finds himself in homes that know no necessity for the struggle for existence. Honors and rewards for efforts expended have been swept away with the old order of things. In return for the injustice done to him, a benevolent government has undertaken to feed him, clothe him, supply homes, hospitals, reservations and schools. Moreover, the Government has supplied agencies to look after all the business of the Indian, such as leasing and selling his lands, inheritances, employment, farming, care of the sick, etc. Nothing but praise and gratitude is due the government that undertakes to carry on such gigantic task. The motive actuating it is one of justice and altruism, and eminently American and democratic.

Everyone conversant with the facts, however, realizes that the effect of giving everything free to the Indian has been a political and economic error. Accordingly, the Government itself is eliminating the wards as fast as it can, through competency commissions, closing the free Federal school for those tribes adjudged able to avail themselves of the public schools of the country. This applies also to those of less than one-half Indian blood, as well as those full-bloods who are capable of paying for their schooling. It is confidently expected that in a decade or two most of the Indian population will begin life again upon a basis of self-support by the struggle for self-preservation. Anything done for the race then will meet with quick response and due appreciation. "The full soul loatheth a honey-comb; but to the hungry soul every bitter thing is sweet."[2] Pride and self-respect will be built up in the race by the very fact of doing for themselves in those things which the Government has done for them in the past. They will have a new regard and a re-birth of respect for law and order, because as tax-paying citizens, they will be supporting that Government by law themselves.

There is grave concern in these days for the future America, because of the prevalence of ideas which are subversive of sound, good government. The right to property and the rewards of individual initiative are being denied. The sanctity of the home, the need of the public school for democracy and the right to existence of the Church are openly questioned.

The following facts must always be kept in view in all efforts for the Indian race. The economic changes necessarily carry with them the decadence of Indian religions. This in turn means the loss of a people's inspirations, conceptions of spiritual truths and certain fundamental hopes. The old home training of the young has passed away forever. There is now very little home training of the young. Children are early taken away to government institutions where organized religious teaching is forbidden owing to the difference in sects and doctrines. The Government can impart knowledge but cannot give religious instruction. Owing to this fact outside religious agencies are brought in, each in their turn, to influence Indian children as best they may. To make up this lack of definite religious training, organization such as the Y. M. C. A. and W. Y. M. C. A., have tried to inspire the Indian students with religious ideals.

In the last year religious work directors have been placed in a few of the larger government schools with the hope of giving more definite religious instruction to government Indian students. There are approximately 312,381 Indians within the confines of the United States. Of this number there are about 83,633 eligible for school. Of all these all but 20,869 are in school, either mission or government. The mission schools, maintained by the Roman Catholic and Protestant Churches, enroll about 4,637. The Federal government assumes the elementary education of the rest.

The emphatic attention of the Church is required for the strengthening of all its missionary programs and church life on every reservation to the end that Christian homes may be multiplied and that the Indian child, like his white playmate may learn at his mother's knee to revere and love the Father who made him, and that he may learn something of his own obligation to his fellow man.

While the Indian youth needs knowledge in this trying transition period, he needs far more those qualities of character shown by men of faith. The disintegrating and demoralizing effect of this sudden economic change and a purely secular education must be met by a thorough-going character-building educational program. A broad-minded educational program will foster those unique contributions which the Indian alone can make to the future America.

Notes

Originally in *The Missionary Review of the World* 47 (July 1924): 529–32. Indian missionaries since the days of Occom sought to fill the post-contact spiritual vacuum among Indians with a mixture of traditional and Christian ideals. Henry Roe Cloud's goal was to establish a special institution for Indians combining regular instruction with an inter-denominational Christian curriculum. In this way, Cloud sought to counteract the loss of influence of religious bodies in the field of Indian education after the federal government began to phase out the mission contract schools in 1897.

1. Massasoit (Metacom), or King Philip (d. 1676), was a Wampanoag leader who united various northeastern tribes in a war against the New England colonists in 1675–76. Cornstalk (ca. 1720–77) was a famous Shawnee leader who fought on the French side during the French and Indian War in 1754–63 and participated in Pontiac's Rebellion in 1763. Red Jacket, or Soogooyawautau (ca. 1758–1830), was a noted Seneca leader and orator.

2. Proverbs 27:7.

BIOGRAPHY

Henry Roe Cloud (Winnebago, 1884?–1950), or Wa-Na-Xi-Lay (War Chief), was born on the Winnebago Reservation in Nebraska on December 28, the son of Na-Xi-Lay-Hunk-Kay and a woman named "Hard-To-See." At the age of about seven, Wa-Na-Xi-Lay was sent to the Genoa Industrial School for Indian Youth in Nebraska. Two years later he returned to the Winnebago Reservation and attended the local government school, where he was baptized as Henry Clarence Cloud. Around the same time both of his parents died and he was assigned a guardian named John Nunn. Henry Cloud was enrolled at the Santee Normal Training School on the nearby Santee Reservation around 1898 and later transferred to Mount Hermon School in Northfield, Massachusetts, in the fall of 1902. In 1906 Henry Cloud entered Yale University, where he graduated with Bachelor of Arts degree in psychology and philosophy in 1910. As a freshman at Yale, Henry Cloud met Walter and Mary Roe, missionaries with the Dutch Reformed Church with whom he formed a lifelong association. During summer vacations Henry Cloud assisted the couple in their missionary efforts among the Southern Cheyennes and Arapahos in Oklahoma, and eventually took "Roe" as his middle name as a sign of respect and affection for them. At the same time he became an active member of the Society of American Indians, affiliating himself with the more moderate faction headed by Arthur Parker and Sherman Coolidge. Although a devout Christian and a firm believer in adaptation to American ways, he defended Native traditions and advocated Indian self-determination, particularly in matters of education.

Following his graduation from Yale, Cloud spent a year at Oberlin Seminary College in Ohio and then attended Auburn Theological Seminary in New York State, where he received a Bachelor of Divinity degree in 1913 and was ordained as a Presbyterian minister that same year. While doing seminary work at Auburn, Cloud also undertook graduate studies at Yale, earning a master's degree in anthropology in 1912. Cloud resumed his theological studies later in life and was granted a doctorate of divinity at Emporia College in Kansas in 1932.

After his ordination Cloud dedicated himself to fulfill Henry Roe's plans for an interdenominational Christian preparatory school for Indians in the West. In the fall of 1915 he established Roe Indian Institute (renamed American Indian Institute in 1920) in Wichita, Kansas. For sixteen years he acted as the institution's president, principal, and chief fund-raiser. He also edited the institution's journal, the *Indian Outlook*, from 1923 to 1932. From 1914 to 1915 Cloud served on the Survey Commission on Indian Education, which conducted a critical study of the Indian school system. On June 12, 1916, he married Elizabeth Bender, daughter of the famous Minnesota Ojibwe pitcher Charles Alfred "Chief" Bender, inducted into the Baseball Hall of Fame in 1953.

On December 12–13, 1923, Cloud participated in the meeting of the Advisory Council on Indian Affairs (or Committee of One Hundred) in Washington, along with other members of the Society of American Indians. Four years later Lewis M. Meriam chose Cloud to be one of the principal investigators for the survey of the Indian situation conducted by the Brookings Institute for Government Research. He assisted in the publication of its influential findings titled *The Problem of Indian Administration* (better known as the "Meriam Report") in 1928. From 1931 to 1933 Cloud served as a field representative at large for the Bureau of Indian Affairs with duties relating to education, health, and land issues. In 1933 Commissioner of Indian Affairs John Collier appointed Cloud superintendent of Haskell Institute in Lawrence, Kansas. At this time he also assisted Collier in developing and later implementing the policies that were institutionalized with the Indian Reorganization Act (Wheeler-Howard Act) of 1934. In recognition of his work in the field of Indian education, the Indian Council Fire awarded him its third medal "for the most distinguished achievement by an American Indian" in 1935. Henry Roe Cloud acted as supervisor of Indian education at the Bureau of Indian Affairs from 1936 to 1947. He also served as superintendent of the Umatilla Agency near Pendleton, Oregon, until 1948, when he was reassigned to the Portland-area office of the Bureau of Indian Affairs as regional representative for the Grande Ronde and Siletz Indian Agencies. Henry Roe Cloud died in Siletz on February 9, 1950.

Selected Publications of Henry Roe Cloud

"Education of the American Indian." *Proceedings of the Twenty-Eighth Annual Meeting of the Lake Mohonk Conference of the Friends of the Indian and Other Dependent Peoples, 1910.* Lake Mohonk, N.Y.: The Lake Mohonk Conference, 1910: 82–87.

"Education of the American Indian." *The Quarterly Journal of the Society of American Indians* 2, no. 3 (July–September 1914): 203–209. Reprinted in *Southern Workman* 44 (January 1915): 12–16.

"From Wigwam to Pulpit: A Red Man's Own story of His Progress from Darkness to Light." *The Missionary Review of the World,* 38 (May 1915): 329–39.

"The Future of the Red Men in America." *The Missionary Review of the World* 47 (July 1924): 529–532.

"The Indian of To-Day." *Southern Workman* 39 (December 1910): 688–90.

"The Indian's Relation to the Community." *Proceedings of the Twenty-Eighth Annual Meeting of the Lake Mohonk Conference of the Friends of the Indian and Other Dependent Peoples, 1910.* Lake Mohonk, N.Y.: The Lake Mohonk Conference, 1910: 14–16.

"Some Social and Economic Aspects of the Reservation." *Southern Workman* 42 (February 1913): 72–77. Reprinted in *The Quarterly Journal of the Society of American Indians* 1, no. 2 (April–June 1913): 149–158.

Unpublished Writings

Henry Roe Cloud Papers, Sterling Memorial Library's Manuscripts and Archives, Yale University.

Selected Secondary Sources

Crum, Steven J. "Henry Roe Cloud, a Winnebago Indian Reformer: His Quest for American Indian Higher Education." *Kansas History* 2, no. 3 (Autumn 1988): 171–84.

Dockstader, Frederick J. *Great North American Indians: Profiles in Life and Leadership.* New York: Van Nostrand Reinhold Co., 1977: 51–52.

Gridley, Marion E., ed. *Indians of Today.* Chicago: Millar Publishing, 1947: 24.

Parker, Arthur C. "History Making News: The Roe-Cloud High School for Indians." *The Quarterly Journal of the Society of American Indians* 3, no. 2 (April–June 1915): 137–39.

Tetzloff, Jason. "Cloud, Henry Roe." In *Encyclopedia of North American Indians*, edited by Frederick E. Hoxie. Boston: Houghton Mifflin Co., 1996: 125–27.

THE TRAGEDY OF THE SIOUX

Luther Standing Bear (1931)

Sixteen years ago I left reservation life and my native people—the Oglala Sioux—because I was no longer willing to endure existence under the control of an overseer.[1]

For about the same number of years I had tried to live a peaceful and happy life; tried to adapt myself and make readjustments to fit the white man's mode of existence. But I was unsuccessful. I developed into a chronic disturber. I was a bad Indian, and the agent and I never got on. I remained a hostile, even a savage, if you please. And I still am. I am incurable.

I was born during the troublous days of the [18]60's, the exact year is not known, when the Sioux were succumbing to the trickery of the whites and the undermining of their own tribal morale. My first years were spent living just as my forefathers had lived—roaming the green, rolling hills of what are now the States of South Dakota and Nebraska. I well remember the first white habitation I ever saw. It was a dugout in Northern Nebraska, whither we had gone on a buffalo hunt. Prior to that time there was not a fence, a field nor even a log-cabin to break the natural beauty of the land. That too, was the first time I ever saw dead buffalo lying around on the plain.[2]

After the death of Crazy Horse in 1877 abrupt changes came for the Sioux. As long as this great leader lived there was a Sioux nation, but his passing meant its death knell. There was no other leader with his power to uphold the integrity of the people. Up to the time of his death some of them were still pursuing their life of freedom, but after that tragic and disrupting incident quick and drastic changes came for the Oglalas. Two years afterward I saw the agency buildings erected at Rosebud. Reservation life then became an actuality for me.[3]

In 1879 I was sent, with some eighty other boys and girls, to Carlisle Indian [Industrial] School in Pennsylvania, to be made over into the likeness of the conqueror. I went dressed in the traditional apparel of the Plains tribes—moccasins, breechclout, leggins and blanket. My hair was long. I left my people trying to settle down and put the ancestral life back of them—the older with resignation or with bitter, resentful memories; the young with wonderment and bewilderment. When, some three or four years later, I returned, things were different. I heard the old men talking of the last buffalo hunt and everyone was learning to eat "spotted buffalo." Instead of the council of chiefs to guide us the White Grandfather (in Washington) sent his emissaries; then came the agent and the white soldiery. The white soldier has always stayed close to us; he is there today.

But it was upon the Indian police, perhaps, that we looked with most disdain.[4] With them was injected into our lives the idea of physical force—something not known in our intertribal life. The Indian police compelled a conduct contrary to all our ancestral notions of lawful and manly action. In organized Sioux society there was no punishment—no jailing, no whipping, no denying of food, no taking away of personal liberty. But there was a very effective system of ostracization: the wrongdoer was ignored and Sioux society was peculiarly free from crime. A few weeks ago, as I left the reservation for my return to the city, one of my relatives expressed his concern for my safety on the journey, and especially after I reached the city. He asked me if I had a weapon and I said no. He thought that I should be prepared to protect myself against the robbers and thieves that infest the city!

Always, in the tribal days, the young deferred to the old, and were so trained from babyhood. It was the old who held the wisdom of the tribe—they were the teachers and instructors.

But under the agency system, oftentimes the policeman was a young fellow who was sent out, by order of the agent, to handcuff and bring in an old man. This happened in the instance of one of my brothers. I felt dishonored and asked him to quit the force, which he did.

There was still another influence that came, almost as soon as the agency buildings were established, and took a place in routing the old life—the church. These things were very foreign, very upsetting, to minds and bodies that had, out of centuries of struggle, achieved a harmony with their surroundings. The Indian fitted the broad plains and loved them just as did the buffalo; and those great grassy spaces, even today, are fit only for the raising of the four-footed beast.

The country at large little knew what these sudden changes meant to my people—both as individuals and as a nation. It simply felt safe in the thought that a "warlike" race had been quelled and quieted; that it had been led into ways of peace and progress; that the "savages" were being kindly treated and their well-being carefully considered by a beneficent government.

There is not and never has been a human attitude taken toward the Indian; no acknowledgement [sic] of his virtues; no friendly acceptance of his native abilities. He has been made to feel his segregation. Since the Indian wars ended the white man has so busied himself wresting riches from the land that its people have been forgotten. Forgotten save for a few friends and humanitarians whose sensitive souls are uneasy and irritated as long as the voices of the oppressed are audible.

II

A few weeks ago I went back to my people for the first time in sixteen years. In the intervening time I have lived constantly in the society of white men, ostensibly one of them, but in spirit and sympathy still living with my people, working for them, listening to their entreaties, and trying to help them with their problems. So, almost as soon as I sat in camp on the reservation, many old friends, hearing of my return, came to see me. They greeted me with tears of gladness in their eyes, but with discontent and dejection in their hearts.

I found the destruction of my people continuing; I found conditions worse than when I left them years ago. I knew, of course, that the Sioux were in desperate straits last Winter—that they suffered from cold and insufficient food, so my first inquiry was about food. An old-time friend pointed to a house from which he had just come. He said, "See that meat drying on the line? That is horse meat, I have just had a meal of it."

Everywhere we went horse meat was drying in the sun. We came to one place—a log cabin near Medicine Root creek—and there was the usual line of it hung up to dry. A fine young colt had just been killed. My friends came out from the house, trying to be happy to see me. The older people were stalwart, the strength and vigor of their forefathers still apparent. But the young— they showed weakness coming on. Their cheeks were hollowed and their lower jaws drooped down—the inevitable sign of hunger. What will my friends do this Winter when the snows drift high?

Further on we stopped to see more friends. Three men leaned against the car as they talked. An older one looked thin and weak. A member of the party inquired if he were ill. He replied that he was not ill but that he did not get enough meat to eat. A Sioux, especially an old Sioux, must have meat. They have been raised on meat and their bodies cannot now be denied.

Another day we knocked at the door of a dirt-floored log cabin where a woman lay sick. We asked her if she would not like to go to the nice new hospital just completed at Pine Ridge. She said that nothing could induce her to go there, for she had heard that the patients were not given enough to eat. We asked what she desired to eat and she said a fresh raw kidney would please her. The ladies of our party lost no time in getting the raw kidney, a delicacy with the old Sioux.

Nancy Red Cloud told us that she was in an agency office one cold wintry day when an old Indian whose money was on deposit there came in. He told the agent that he would like to have some money, for he had been without food for several days and was hungry. The agent put him off, saying he would see about it. The old Indian, Big Head by name, while sitting in a chair, waiting, toppled over dead, Nancy catching him in her arms. The death was pronounced heart failure by the agency doctor. Nevertheless, so much talk was caused by the agent's treatment of Big Head that he resigned. I went to see my old-time friend, Chief Black Horn. He said, "Conditions last year were very bad. The rations allowed were insufficient. The amount which was supposed to last two weeks was actually enough for just one day. If an old person sells a piece of ground the money is placed in the hands of the agent and rations are at once stopped. When the money has been exhausted, rations are again resumed." I asked Black Horn why more land was not cultivated by the Indian farmers and his reply was: "The white farmer can beat us farming because he has tractors. We can't farm extensively, so we raise small gardens. If our land is not leased to the white man it lies idle." Then I inquired about the cattle situation. He corroborated what I had heard from others: "There was a time when all the

Indians had plenty of cattle, but after the white man was allowed to bring his stock in on our reserve there was much confusion. We would like to raise cattle but it's useless to try in the present condition of things."

Food! Meat! Everyone wanting meat! Yet the Sioux live in the finest cattle country in the land. The white farmers scattered liberally all through their reservation have fine-looking cattle, as well as pigs, chickens, turkeys and horses. But not the Indian; he is poverty-stricken!

The truth is that the Sioux has been disinherited; there is no reservation. The fence that once surrounded it, defining its territory, has been torn down. White cattlemen have been allowed to bring their cattle on Sioux grazing ground on the promise to pay twenty-five cents a head for pasturage. But it was not long after the white man's cattle came that the Indian's cattle began to disappear, and the white man's herds began to increase. The Indian's herds have now ceased to exist. My party and I tried to purchase a steer for the feast which we gave for our Indian friends. But no Indian owned one, so we made our purchase from a white man.

We talked of a solution to the cattle question. The country is manifestly a cattle country. The Sioux are not farmers. They can raise cattle and if given a chance will become independent. The logical procedure is to give back their reservation to them. Remove the white man entirely. Fence the reservation if necessary. Stock the land with cattle and let the Sioux do the rest.

III

The old Indians today are pictures of lost hope. Many of them travel daily to the agency office and sit there. Day in and day out—sit and wait. The office is where they draw, now and then, a pittance in tribal money. Last year the amount was $7.50 a head for the sick, disabled and all. The agent told us that it came at a most needed time, but what is $7.50 in purchasing power at a trader's store, where prices are two and three times as high as they are off the reservation?

Most of the old people wear canvas moccasins and almost without exception they need dental treatment. In fact, the most noticeable thing about the Sioux people in general is their dire need of dentistry. Spiritual deterioration is in an advanced stage also. Incentive is gone. Old and young are meek to the point of docility, obeying every command of the agent. They settle no questions for themselves; their overseer decides everything. The system has crushed them; they are nonentities.

For years the Oglala council had been meeting, attended by most of the old men, until recently. Some time ago a meeting had been arranged, and some of the members traveled a distance of fifty miles to attend, when word came from the agent through an Indian policeman forbidding the meeting to take place and ordering the visiting members to return home. During my sojourn at the reservation word came from the agent again, saying that the Oglala council could meet once more. Last Fourth of July the people of several districts wished to get together for a big celebration, but were commanded to hold only district celebrations. This dictatorial order was still causing much comment when I left.

If an Indian wants to leave the reservation he must get permission. Even free-born American citizens—the people who assist in making the laws of the land and pay taxes to keep petty officials in office—are under surveillance once they walk on the ground of this government prison. My party and I were summoned by the agent to make statements concerning the reasons for our presence in the reservation. Not deigning to answer his inquiries over the telephone, we called in person at his office at Pine Ridge and answered the following questions:

What are your names?

What are you doing while on the reservation and what were your purposes in coming? [Here the agent remarked that we had been seen writing in a book.]

Who heads the party?

Who finances the party?

Who owns the car in which you travel?

What is the license number?

Chief [Charles] Turning Hawk is one of the fine old councilors—as splendid a character as one meets in any society, and in spirit of the old school. He is tall, has clear-cut features, and wears his poverty with the same quiet grace as he wears his tribal garments. He showed me a document in embellished writing which was sent to him after the World War:

The United States of America

E Pluribus Unum

To All To Whom These Presents Shall Come, Greetings:

The thanks of the Nation are extended through the President, Commander-in-chief of the Army and Navy of the United States, to the people of

THE DAKOTA OF THE PINE RIDGE RESERVATION

for their unswerving loyalty and patriotism, the splendid service rendered, the willing sacrifice made, and the bravery of their sons in the military and naval service of the United States when the nation was in peril during the World War of 1917–1918.

I asked Turning Hawk if the powers of the medicine men were as strong as ever. He said they could no longer perform their wonders; that the presence of the white people and the rule of the agent had destroyed the faith of the Indians. There had been a time when everyone ate or no one ate; when a man's word was never broken; when there was plenty, for no man killed except for food.

It is this loss of faith that has left a void in Indian life—a void that civilization cannot fill. The old life was attuned to nature's rhythm—bound in mystical ties to the sun, moon and stars; to the waving grasses, flowing streams and whispering winds. It is not a question (as so many white writers like to state it) of the white man "bringing the Indian up to his plane of thought and action." It is rather a case where the white man had better grasp some of the Indian's spiritual strength. I protest against calling my people savages. How can the Indian, sharing all the virtues of the white man, be justly called a savage? The white race today is but half civilized and unable to order his life into ways of peace and righteousness.

IV

Against the young there are many complaints. The government school is changing everything and the young are losing their tribal ideals and manners. One old lady said: "With all the education of the young they do not read or study the treaties in order to help us. We sometimes ask them, but they pay no attention to us." There is undoubted need for the young Indians to help the old ones, who cannot speak English and are bewildered by the routine of an office and legal phrases.

Here is an instance: Mrs. Big Boy brought to me a paper regarding her widow's allotment of $500. Not understanding the correct procedure, she had been holding the paper since early in 1929. She asked me to go to the agent for her and see if it granted her the allotment. I did so and in fifteen minutes the matter was straightened out in favor of Mrs. Big Boy.

Here is an instance which shows how the white farmer is favored: About a year ago I received a letter from one of my friends saying that a white man had taken his horse and would not return it. My friend appealed to the agent but after months of waiting nothing had been done. I at once wrote to the agent asking for an investigation of the matter but my appeal also was ignored. I was on the point of writing to the Bureau of Indian Affairs at Washington when I suddenly arranged to go to the reservation. I had been there but a few days when my friend came to me saying that his horse had mysteriously reappeared and was in his corral. I have reason to believe that my presence had something to do with the matter.

The government school—the segregated school—is a curse and a blight. The mission school is credited by both parents and pupils with being far better than the government school, for all its fine buildings and equipment. But all cannot get into the mission schools. Applications for admittance far exceed the capacity. After graduation from the government school most girls find their life's work in city kitchens and most boys who do not drift back to the reservation lose their identity in a shop.

There are great possibilities in the young Indians. They are capable of becoming doctors, lawyers, engineers, architects and road-builders on the reservations. Then too, they should be trained in the history and arts of their people; it is they who should perpetuate the native dances, songs, music, poetry, languages and legends, as well as the native arts and crafts. Music and dancing are talents peculiar to the Indian—no other people on this continent sing and dance for the same reasons that he does, or in the same way.

With this sort of training the young Indian would be better able to cope with the discrimination he now encounters. In my motion-picture work I have come

in contact with much of this discrimination. Always a white actor is given pref-
erence and no Indian girl is given a chance to lead, even in an Indian picture;
and I want to say that I know of instances in which no Indian girl could exhibit
more stupidity than the white girl who was being coached and actually shoved
into a star part in a picture. This discrimination is not based on looks either.
The Indian girl, and especially the mixed blood, is sometimes very handsome.

Both sexes of the young are addicts to drunkenness and cigarettes and their
language has become profane. These things fill the old Indian with shame.
Black Horn said that vices were destroying the young. Self-mastery—which
the old Indian knew so well—is weakened and the young have not the strength
to deny themselves. When Black Horn was asked if the training of the white
man could be offset he answered: "No, they have been taken too far away. Their
faith is gone. We are powerless to save them."

But they can be saved. If the public conscience can be brought into action
against the slavery of the American Indian it can be wiped out of existence.
When the enormous sum of $20,000,000 has been supplied by the taxpayers of
this land to uphold an evil system it is manifestly their business to look into it.

When I was handed my papers of citizenship in the Washington office, the
commissioner, Belt I think it was, said as he extended his hand: "Here, Standing Bear, are your papers. You are now a citizen and a free man. The cloud from
over your head is gone."[5] I walked out of the office feeling an exaltation I shall
never be able to describe—feeling once more the sweet freedom of my youth.

But the clouds are not yet gone from over the heads of my people—they are
not free. And as long as they are in bondage I shall never cease to be a hostile
savage, if you please.

Notes

Originally in *American Mercury* 24, no. 95 (November 1931): 273–78; repr., Bernd
C. Peyer, ed., *The Elders Wrote: An Anthology of Early Prose by North American
Indians, 1768–1931* (Berlin: Dietrich Reimer Verlag, 1982), 183–90. Reproduced
with permission from the Legion for Survival of Freedom. In this article Standing
Bear vividly describes the shortcomings of the reservation system.

1. Luther Standing Bear was actually a Sicangu (or Brulé) Sioux.

2. By the early 1880s the American bison had been hunted to the point of near-
extinction. Although the federal government never officially condoned this wanton commercial slaughter, many administrators were well aware that the depletion
of the herds was also an effective instrument to enforce the federal government's
reservation policy. Just how important the buffalo was and still is for the self-
understanding of the Sioux is made evident by the founding of the Intertribal Bison
Cooperative (ITBC) in 1990, a nonprofit multitribal organization that is committed to reestablishing buffalo herds on Indian lands in a manner that promotes cultural enhancement, spiritual revitalization, ecological restoration, and economic
development.

3. Crazy Horse (Oglala Sioux, ca. 1849–77), or Tashunka Witko, was killed under
nebulous circumstances at Fort Robinson, Nebraska, on September 5, 1877. Most

Sioux still believe that it was a politically motivated assassination related to the incursions on Sioux lands and sovereignty. That same year a Congressional Act ratified the so-called Manypenny Agreement, taking the Black Hills and extinguishing all Sioux rights outside of Great Sioux Reservation. The Great Sioux Agreement of 1889 broke up the Great Sioux Reservation, and the Sioux Act of 1890 established six reservations: Pine Ridge, Rosebud, Lower Brulé, Crow Creek, Cheyenne River, and Standing Rock.

4. On May 27, 1878, Congress sanctioned the maintenance of an Indian police force on reservations, which practically subverted traditional law enforcement institutions such as the warrior societies. See William T. Hagan, *Indian Police and Judges: Experiments in Acculturation and Controls* (New Haven:Yale University Press, 1966).

5. I have not been able to trace this "commissioner." The commissioner of Indian affairs at the time Standing Bear probably applied for citizenship was Robert Grosvenor Valentine (1909–12).

BIOGRAPHY

Luther Standing Bear (Sicangu Sioux, 1868?–1939), or Ota Kte (Plenty Kill), was born on an uncertain date in the mid-1860s in present-day South Dakota. According to his autobiography he was born in 1868 as an Oglala Sioux, but records indicate that he may have been a few years older and that his father was actually a part-Sicangu (Brulé) leader of the Wears Salt Band. Standing Bear's family moved to the Rosebud Reservation following its establishment in 1868, where he grew up during the disruptive early stages of Western Sioux reservation life. He was among the first students to be enrolled at Carlisle Indian Industrial School in 1879, remaining there for a little over three years. Here he learned the obsolete trade of a tinsmith and became a member of the Episcopal Church. In a letter addressed to Carlos Montezuma in 1911, Richard Henry Pratt confided that "there were no better boys in their time at Carlisle than Luther Standing Bear . . ."

Following his return from Carlisle in 1884, Standing Bear married Nellie De Cory and lived at or in the vicinity of the Rosebud and Pine Ridge reservations, variously employed as clerk, teacher, rancher, and missionary. In 1902 he joined Buffalo Bill's Wild West Show on its eleven-month tour of England, much to the chagrin of Pratt, who believed that his former star pupil had "lost his character." Standing Bear joined the Wild West Show again in 1903, but a train accident left him severely injured and thwarted his plans. According to his own account he was selected as a Sicangu chief when his father died in 1905, but he spent most of his time off the reservation. Between 1907 and 1911 Standing Bear and his second wife May Splicer, a part-Mohawk from Syracuse, lived in Sioux City, Iowa, where he worked for a wholesale dry goods company, and subsequently moved to Walthill, Nebraska. With the assistance of Thomas L. Sloan, noted Omaha attorney and cofounder of the Society of American Indians, Standing Bear did apply for private allotments at Pine Ridge in the hopes that this would make him an American citizen and consequently less dependent upon Indian agents.

In 1912, having successfully applied for citizenship in Washington, D.C., Standing Bear abandoned reservation life altogether to become an Indian actor with the Thomas Ince Studio in Hollywood. He appeared in numerous silent films and grade-B Westerns, including *Ramona* (1912), *Bolshevism on Trial* (1919), *White Oak* (1921), *Conquering Horde* (1931), *Texas Pioneers* (1932), *Murder in the Private Car* (1933), *Cyclone of the Saddle* (1935), *Circle of Death* (1935), *Fighting Pioneers* (1935), and *Miracle Rider* (1935). He also began lecturing on Indian affairs and instructing Boy Scouts and Girl Scouts. Unlike his younger brother Henry Standing Bear (1874–1953), one of the six founding members of the Society of American Indians, Luther Standing Bear apparently had nothing to do with this organization. He did, however, serve a two-year term as president of the American Indian Progressive Association, a California-based organization promoting Indian citizenship and active

participation in civic activities. He also served as president of the Indian Actors' Association, which sought to promote the hiring of Indians to play Indian
roles in Hollywood.

Standing Bear turned to writing relatively late in his life. With the assistance
of his niece Waste Win (Good Woman) he published four books between 1928
and 1934 that are still widely read today: *My People the Sioux* (1928), *My Indian Boyhood* (1931), *Land of the Spotted Eagle* (1933), and *Stories of the
Sioux* (1934). In the last two chapters of *Land of the Spotted Eagle,* his most
important work and written with the editorial assistance of Melvin R. Gilmore,
then curator for ethnology at the University of Michigan, Standing Bear rang
in the beginning of a new era in American Indian thought and literature by advocating a clean sweep of misguided "progressive" ideology, especially in matters of education. As an alternative to segregated government schools such as
Carlisle, which he considered to be "a curse and a blight" for Indians, Standing Bear proposed what amounts to a modern concept of community-oriented
bilingual-bicultural education, geared toward filling in the cultural gap that
separated young from old. Luther Standing Bear died in California on February 20, 1939, while working on Cecile B. DeMille's film *Union Pacific.*

Selected Publications of Luther Standing Bear

Land of the Spotted Eagle. Boston: Houghton-Mifflin, 1933. Reprinted rpt., Lin-
    coln: University of Nebraska Press, 1978.
My Indian Boyhood. Boston: Houghton-Mifflin, 1931. Reprinted Lincoln: Univer-
    sity of Nebraska Press, 1988.
My People the Sioux. Boston: Houghton-Mifflin, 1928. Reprinted Lincoln: Uni-
    versity of Nebraska Press, 1975.
Stories of the Sioux. Boston: Houghton Mifflin, 1934. Reprinted Lincoln: Univer-
    sity of Nebraska Press, 1988.
"The Tragedy of the Sioux." *American Mercury* 24, no. 95 (November 1931):
    273–78. Reprinted in *The Elders Wrote: An Anthology of Early Prose by North
    American Indians, 1768–1931,* edited by Bernd C. Peyer. Berlin: Dietrich
    Reimer Verlag, 1982: 183–90.

Selected Secondary Sources

Coleman, Michael C. *American Indian Children at School, 1850–1930.* Jackson:
    University Press of Mississippi, 1993.
Ellis, Richard N. "Luther Standing Bear." In *Indian Lives: Essays on Nineteenth
    and Twentieth Century Native American Leaders,* edited by L. G. Moses and
    Raymond Wilson. Albuquerque: University of New Mexico Press, 1985: 139–58.
Goode, Richard C. "Standing Bear, Luther." In *American National Biography,*
    Vol. 20, edited by John A. Garraty and Mark C. Carnes. New York: Oxford Uni-
    versity Press, 1999: 535–36.
Hale, Frederick. "Acceptance and Rejection of Assimilation in the Works of
    Luther Standing Bear." *Studies in American Indian Literatures* 5, no. 4 (Winter
    1993): 25–41

Heflin, Ruth J. *"I Remain Alive": The Sioux Literary Renaissance.* Syracuse, N.Y.: Syracuse University Press, 2000: 79–103.

Markowitz, Harvey. "Standing Bear, Luther." In *Encyclopedia of North American Indians,* edited by Frederick E. Hoxie. Boston: Houghton Mifflin Company, 1996: 607–608.

Schöler, Bo. "Images and Counter-images: Ohiyesa, Standing Bear and American Literature." *American Indian Culture and Research Journal* 5, no. 2 (1981): 37–62.

Price, Catherine. *The Oglala People, 1841–1879: A Political History.* Lincoln: University of Nebraska Press, 1996.

Trachtenberg, Alan. *Shades of Hiawatha: Staging Indians, Making Americans, 1880–1930.* New York: Hill and Wang, 2004: 278–310.